Formation and Variation of Contracts

FORMATION AND VARIATION OF CONTRACTS

SECOND EDITION

By

JOHN CARTWRIGHT BCL, MA

Professor of the Law of Contract, University of Oxford
Tutor in Law, Christ Church, Oxford
Solicitor

SWEET & MAXWELL

THOMSON REUTERS

First Edition 2014

978-0-414-06746-2

Published in 2018 by Thomson Reuters, trading as Sweet & Maxwell.
Thomson Reuters is registered in England & Wales Company No.1679046.
Registered Office and address for service:
5 Canada Square, Canary Wharf, London E14 5AQ.

For further information on our products and services, visit
http://www.sweetandmaxwell.co.uk

Computerset by Sweet & Maxwell.

Printed and bound by CPI Group (UK) Ltd,
Croydon, CR0 4YY.

No natural forests were destroyed to make this product:
only farmed timber was used and replanted.

A CIP catalogue record for this book is available from the British Library.

Crown copyright material is reproduced with the permission of the
Controller of HMSO and the Queen's Printer for Scotland.

Thomson Reuters, the Thomson Reuters Logo and Sweet & Maxwell ® are
trademarks of Thomson Reuters.

PREFACE

This new edition is designed to bring the book up to date. Since the last edition, there have been decisions in the Supreme Court, the Court of Appeal and the High Court dealing with a range of matters such as the enforceability of a duty to negotiate (or renegotiate), or to agree, in good faith or using "best endeavours"; certainty of terms; "subject to contract" clauses; contractual intention; finding a contract through offer and acceptance; the interpretation of contracts and implied terms; the enforceability of "no oral modification" clauses; and the applicability of the decision in *Williams v Roffey Bros & Nicholls (Contractors) Ltd*, and of the doctrine of promissory estoppel, to agreements to reduce or remit the balance of a debt.

More significant, though, is the development that has not taken place. The Supreme Court in *MWB Business Exchange Centres Ltd v Rock Advertising Ltd* missed the opportunity to give guidance on the difficulties presented by the decision in *Williams v Roffey* in relation to "practical benefit" as consideration; as well as on the apparent conflict between *Williams v Roffey* and *Foakes v Beer* in relation to part-payment of a debt—or, indeed, in relation to the use of promissory estoppel as a substitute for consideration in the discharge of a debt. The Supreme Court felt able to say only that the decision in *Williams v Roffey*, in relation to *Foakes v Beer*, is a "difficult" issue which is "probably ripe for re-examination"—and that such a re-examination can be done only if a case can be found to raise the issue by way of ratio before an enlarged panel of the Court. It goes without saying that this will happen only if the parties to such a case are interested in incurring the costs of an appeal to the Supreme Court to discover the answer. Perhaps the Law Commission can be activated to consider these issues, some of which remain unresolved since the (unimplemented) recommendation of the Law Revision Committee's Sixth Interim Report in 1937.

I am grateful to Sweet & Maxwell for encouraging me to produce this new edition. As always, I must acknowledge the friendly assistance I have received at every stage from their team in its planning and execution, including the work that they have done in making changes to the formatting which were necessary to enable the book to be published in electronic format as well as on paper. I am also grateful to the publishers for undertaking the compilation of the tables and the index.

John Cartwright
Christ Church
Oxford

ABBREVIATIONS

Books Referred to in the Text

All books are published in the UK unless otherwise indicated

Andrews	N. Andrews, *Contract Rules: Decoding English Law* (Intersentia, 2016)
Anson	J. Beatson, A. Burrows and J. Cartwright, *Anson's Law of Contract*, 30th edn (Oxford University Press, 2016)
Bar (von) and Clive	C. von Bar and E. Clive, *Principles, Definitions and Model Rules of European Private Law, Draft Common Frame of Reference (DCFR)* (Munich: Sellier, 2009)
Burrows (Remedies)	A. Burrows, *Remedies for Torts and Breach of Contract*, 3rd edn (Oxford University Press, 2004)
Burrows (Restatement)	A. Burrows, *A Restatement of the English Law of Contract* (Oxford University Press, 2016)
Burrows, Finn & Todd	J. Finn, S. Todd and M. Barber, *Law of Contract in New Zealand*, 6th edn (Wellington: LexisNexis NZ, 2018)
Cartwright (Misrepresentation)	J. Cartwright, *Misrepresentation, Mistake and Non-Disclosure*, 4th edn (Sweet & Maxwell, 2016)
Cheshire and Burn	E.H. Burn and J. Cartwright, *Cheshire and Burn's Modern Law of Real Property*, 18th edn (Oxford University Press, 2011)
Cheshire, Fifoot and Furmston	M. Furmston, *Cheshire, Fifoot and Furmston's Law of Contract*, 17th edn (Oxford University Press, 2017)
Chitty	H. Beale (ed.), *Chitty on Contracts*, 32nd edn (Sweet & Maxwell Ltd, 2015) with supplements
Cooke	E. Cooke, *The Modern Law of Estoppel* (Oxford University Press, 2000)
Corbin	A.L. Corbin, *Corbin on Contracts* (St. Paul, Minnesota: West, 1950 onwards); revised edn by J.M. Perillo (St. Paul, Minnesota: West, 1993 onwards)
Emmet	J. Farrand and A. Clarke, *Emmet and Farrand on Title* (Sweet & Maxwell Ltd, looseleaf)
Farnsworth	E.A. Farnsworth, *Farnsworth on Contracts*, 3rd edn (New York: Aspen, 2003) with cumulative supplement
Fridman	G.H.L. Fridman, *The Law of Contract in Canada*, 6th edn (Toronto: Carswell, 2011)
Furmston	M. Furmston (ed.), *The Law of Contract* (Butterworths Common Law Series), 6th edn (LexisNexis Butterworths, 2017)
Furmston and Tolhurst	M. Furmston and G.J. Tolhurst, with E. Mik, *Contract Formation: Law and Practice*, 2nd edn (Oxford

University Press, 2016)

Goff & Jones	C. Mitchell, P. Mitchell and S. Watterson, *Goff & Jones: The Law of Unjust Enrichment*, 9th edn (Sweet & Maxwell Ltd, 2016)
Gore-Browne	A. Alcock (gen. ed.), *Gore-Browne on Companies*, 45th edn (Jordan Publishing Ltd, 2004 onwards), looseleaf
Halsbury	*Halsbury's Laws of England*, 4th edn (Butterworths, 1973–2008); 5th edn (LexisNexis, 2008–)
Hanbury and Martin	J. Glister and J. Lee, *Hanbury and Martin: Modern Equity*, 20th edn (Sweet & Maxwell, 2015)
Jones and Goodhart	G. Jones and W. Goodhart, *Specific Performance*, 2nd edn (Butterworths, 1996)
Lando and Beale	O. Lando and H. Beale, *Principles of European Contract Law Parts I and II* (The Hague: Kluwer Law International, 2000)
Lewison	K. Lewison, *The Interpretation of Contracts*, 6th edn (Sweet & Maxwell Ltd, 2015) with supplements
Megarry and Wade	C. Harpum, S. Bridge and M. Dixon (eds), *Megarry & Wade, The Law of Real Property*, 8th edn (Sweet & Maxwell, 2012)
Phang and Goh	A.B.L. Phang and Y. Goh, *Contract Law in Singapore* (Alphen aan den Rijn: Wolters Kluwer, 2012)
Phipson	H.M. Malek (ed.), *Phipson on Evidence*, 19th edn (Sweet & Maxwell Ltd, 2017)
Restatement of Contracts (2d)	*Restatement (Second) of Contracts* (St Paul, Minnesota: American Law Institute, 1981)
Seddon and Bigwood	N.C. Seddon and R.A. Bigwood, *Cheshire and Fifoot: Law of Contract*, 11th Australian Edition (Chatswood NSW: LexisNexis Australia, 2017)
Sinnadurai	V. Sinnadurai, *Law of Contract*, 4th edn (Petaling Jaya: LexisNexis, 2011)
Snell	J. McGhee (ed.), *Snell's Equity*, 33nd edn (Sweet & Maxwell, 2015)
Spencer Bower (Estoppel)	P. Feltham, T. Leech, P. Crampin and J. Winfield, Spencer Bower: *Reliance-Based Estoppel*, 5th edn (Bloomsbury, 2017)
Treitel	E. Peel (ed.), Treitel: *The Law of Contract*, 14th edn (Sweet & Maxwell, 2015)
Waddams	S.M. Waddams, *Law of Contracts*, 7th edn (Toronto: Canada Law Book, 2017)
Wilken and Ghaly	S. Wilken and K. Ghaly, *The Law of Waiver, Variation, and Estoppel*, 3rd edn (Oxford University Press, 2012)
Winfield & Jolowicz	W.E. Peel and J. Goudkamp, *Winfield & Jolowicz on Tort*, 19th edn (Sweet & Maxwell, 2014)

Other Selected Abbreviations

BGB	Bürgerliches Gesetzbuch (German Civil Code)
CA	Companies Act
CCA	Consumer Credit Act
c.civ.	Code civil (French Civil Code)
CJEU	Court of Justice of the European Union
CP	Consultation Paper
C.Pl.	Court of Common Pleas
CPR	Civil Procedure Rules
DC	Divisional Court
DCFR	Draft Common Frame of Reference (see Bar (von) and Clive, above)
Ex.Ch.	Exchequer Chamber
FCA	Federal Court of Australia
HCA	High Court of Australia
HL	House of Lords
HL(Sc)	House of Lords (Scottish Appeal)
IH	Inner House, Court of Session
LPA	Law of Property Act
LP(MP)A	Law of Property (Miscellaneous Provisions) Act
LRA	Land Registration Act
NICA	Northern Ireland Court of Appeal
NIRC	National Industrial Relations Court
NYCA	New York Court of Appeals
NZCA	New Zealand Court of Appeal
NZHC	New Zealand High Court
OED	Oxford English Dictionary
OH	Outer House, Court of Session
PC	Privy Council
PECL	Principles of European Contract Law (see Lando and Beale, above)
PICC	UNIDROIT Principles of International Commercial Contracts (2016 edition)
QB	Queen's Bench Division
SCC	Supreme Court of Canada
SC or Sup. Ct.	Supreme Court
SGCA	Singapore Court of Appeal
SGHC	Singapore High Court

UCC	Uniform Commercial Code [United States]
WP	Working Paper

TABLE OF CONTENTS

PART II CONTRACT FORMALITIES

TABLE OF CASES

TABLE OF STATUTES

TABLE OF STATUTORY INSTRUMENTS

TABLE OF EUROPEAN LEGISLATION

TABLE OF FOREIGN LEGISLATION

CHAPTER 1

INTRODUCTION

I.   SCOPE OF THIS BOOK: FORMATION AND VARIATION

Formation of the contract   This book is concerned with the rules governing the   **1-01**
formation of contracts in English law. It focuses on the positive elements of the
formation of contracts—the mechanisms by which parties, through their negotiations or other mutual dealings by which they come to their agreement, can satisfy
the requirements set by the law for the creation of binding obligations. It does not
seek to address defects in a contract, such as the rules relating to misrepresentation,[1] duress or undue influence[2] exercised by one of the parties against the other
during the formation of the contract; or rules governing the substantive validity of
the terms of the contract in relation to such things as illegality and public policy.[3]
Mistakes made by the parties, even though they can prevent the parties reaching a
sufficient agreement to form the contract, are also generally left to other specialist
works[4] except in so far as they can be analysed as essentially cases of formation.

Variation of the contract   The book is also concerned with the legal require-   **1-02**
ments for the variation of an existing contract by the parties.[5] The rules governing
the variation of a contract belong with the rules governing the initial formation
because the starting point is the same: the variation must itself satisfy the same rules
as are set for the formation of a contract, at least if the variation is to have the same
binding force as the initial contract so as to modify it or supersede it.[6] However, we
need to consider variations of an existing contract separately since some of the

---

1   See Cartwright (Misrepresentation), Pt I.
2   See N. Enonchong, *Duress, Undue Influence and Unconscionable Dealings*, 2nd edn (Sweet &
    Maxwell, 2012).
3   See R.A. Buckley, *Illegality and Public Policy*, 4th edn (Sweet & Maxwell, 2017).
4   See Cartwright (Misrepresentation), Pt II.
5   i.e. the variation of a contract by the agreement of the parties, subsequent to its formation. We are
    not concerned with the validity or application of variation clauses within contracts, such as clauses
    conferring on a party the power to vary the terms of the contact unilaterally: cf. S. Whittaker, "Vari-
    ation and Termination of Consumer Contracts" in L. Gullifer and S. Vogenauer (eds), *English and
    European Perspectives on Contract and Commercial Law* (Hart Publishing, 2014), p.199. Nor are
    we concerned with the discharge of a contract otherwise than by the subsequent agreement of the
    parties, such as by frustration or by reason of breach by one party.
6   See para.9-02; also paras 2-35 (negotiations for a variation), 5-40 and 6-20 (formalities for a varia-
    tion); cf. para7-22 (deeds). A variation of contractual obligations may have a more limited effect
    through other doctrines such as promissory estoppel: see Ch.10.

formation rules apply differently in the case of variations[7]; and there is even a question whether the law should set the same strict requirements for the variation of a contract as it does for the initial formation, given that the parties have already satisfied the requirements for the creation of their contract.[8]

II. KEY QUESTIONS AND PERSPECTIVES

1-03   **Viewing the contract from different angles: contract as agreement; contract as promise; contract as bargain**   A contract can be viewed from different angles. It is an *agreement* between the parties to which the law gives force.[9] But when the contract is enforced, it is the defendant's *promise* that is in question: the breach of contract is the failure to fulfil a contractual obligation—the failure to keep one's promise. So the agreement which forms the contract is agreement on each party's obligations, or promises. The contract can then be seen as[10]:

> "a promise or a set of promises for the breach of which the law gives a remedy, or the performance of which the law in some way recognizes as a duty."

Furthermore, the model of contract adopted in English law is not simply an agreement which contains a promise, but an agreement in which the promise by one party has been given in return for—in exchange for—some other promise or performance by the other party: the contract is an exchange, a *bargain*. These different, but mutually consistent,[11] ways of characterising the contract point to different questions that have to be asked in determining whether a contract has been formed.

1-04   **The agreement**   The first question is whether the parties have formed their agreement in the way, and with the content and characteristics, that the law requires in order to find a valid contract. This is the subject of Part I of the book, which looks at both the negotiations in which the parties may engage in order to come to the agreement[12] and the tests applied by the courts in order to determine what constitutes a sufficient agreement.[13] However, every legal system must draw a line between those promises or agreements which should be given legally binding force, and those which should be left outside the protection of the law and regulated simply by moral pressure or social sanctions. The remaining Parts of the book

---

[7]   See paras 9-16 (consideration, as applied in *Williams v Roffey Bros & Nicholls (Contractors) Ltd* [1991] 1 Q.B. 1, CA); 10-39 (promissory estoppel in the modification of existing obligations, but not creating new obligations: *Combe v Combe* [1951] 2 K.B. 215, CA).

[8]   See para.9-24.

[9]   Treitel, para.1-001.

[10]   Restatement of Contracts (2d), §1; Anson, pp.1–2, prefers this approach. Comment *a* on §1 says "The word 'contract' is often used with meanings different from that given here. It is sometimes used as a synonym for 'agreement' or 'bargain.'" It should be noted that a promise can be binding without an agreement where it is given force by being made in a deed: see para.1-05.

[11]   cf. Chitty, paras 1-014 to 1-016, discussing the difficulties in each of the two "competing definitions" of contract as promise, or as agreement.

[12]   See Ch.2, discussing the legal significance of the negotiations, and the difficulties which can arise where one party suffers loss by reason of the fact that the negotiations are broken off before the parties reach the stage of concluding the contract.

[13]   See Ch.3, discussing the (objective) notion of "agreement", the minimum content required for a contractual agreement (including the requirement of certainty), and the mechanics of coming to the agreement through (normally) the acceptance by one party of an offer made by the other.

explore different techniques that can be used in order to make an agreement, or a promise, legally binding in English law.

Formality   One such technique is formality. Although a requirement of formality is the exception within the law of contract, there are particular types of contract for which the law prescribes a formality, either as a supplementary condition for the formation of the contract, or as an evidential requirement which must be satisfied to allow the contract to be enforced. The reasons for using formality, as well as the rationale for the particular formality requirements set by English law and the consequences of failing to follow the requirements, are discussed in Part II.[14] Special mention must be made, however, of the deed, which operates rather differently as a formality within the law of contract.[15] Although a contract may be informal—and, indeed, most contracts are entered into without formality—the parties may choose to use a deed to formalise their agreement since it carries certain advantages.[16] Most significant for our context, however, is the fact that a deed can be used to give effect to a promise that might otherwise not be binding at all as a contract: a unilateral, gratuitous promise. An undertaking in a deed has binding force by virtue of the formality, and therefore can be binding without having to satisfy the other requirements for the formation of a contract: it need not be accepted (to form an agreement) nor need anything be given in return (by way of consideration).[17]

1-05

Consideration   The general rule, however, is not that a promise is binding on the promisor because it has been expressed in some defined form, but because the claimant (the promisee) has promised, done or forborne to do something in return, at the promisor's request—the doctrine of consideration, which is discussed in Part III.[18] It is this doctrine that gives the English contract the general character of an exchange, or bargain, between the parties. This does not mean that the bargain has to be objectively fair or balanced: the court does not investigate the respective values of the parties' exchange, but only requires that there be some form of exchange that is capable of monetary valuation.[19] Defects in the bargaining process are dealt with by other doctrines such as misrepresentation, duress and undue influence,[20] which render the contract voidable at the instance of the party who has been misled or pressurised into the contract; and there are overriding controls of public policy in relation to the content of the parties' bargain.[21] But the doctrine of consideration sets a fundamental condition for the formation of the contract: without there being an exchange within the meaning of the doctrine, there is simply no contract.

1-06

---

[14] See Chs 4 (the function of formality requirements in general, and their use in contract law in particular), 5 (formality required as a condition for the formation of the contract) and 6 (evidential formality requirements).

[15] See Ch.7. The deed is also used as a formal instrument in property law, and is a formal requirement for the creation and transfer of legal estates and interests in land: see para.7-03.

[16] See paras 7-17 to 7-20.

[17] See paras 7-02, 7-18.

[18] The general rules of consideration are discussed in Ch.8; and their particular application in the context of a contractual variation of a contract, is discussed in Ch.9.

[19] See para.8-25.

[20] See para.1-01 fnn.1, 2.

[21] See para.1–01 fn.3.

The essential characteristic of a contract as bargain is set by the common law,[22] but its application is designed to fit with other underlying principles of the English law of contract; in particular, the freedom of the parties to define their own contract, and the limited role of the court to intervene in the contract. The courts will therefore check that the contract conforms to the model set by the law, but they do not see it as their role to police the content of the contract. That said, we shall see that doubts have been expressed about whether the doctrine of consideration is the best way of achieving this, or whether a test which focuses more openly on the parties' intentions to be bound might be preferable; and whether the search for the parties' intentions might even lie behind some of the courts' more difficult decisions in recent years on the doctrine of consideration.[23] The doctrine of consideration is, however, one of the fundamental building blocks of English contract law, and although the courts have sometimes pushed its limits, they have not sought to change its essential characteristics nor, therefore, the essential characteristics of an informal contract in English law as based on some form of agreed exchange between the parties.[24]

1-07   **Promissory estoppel**   Apart from the case where the promisor embodies his promise in a deed, in principle English law accepts only the doctrine of consideration as being sufficient to give rise to a binding promissory obligation. In the case of a modification of an existing contract, however, the courts have also allowed some scope of operation to the doctrine of promissory estoppel, under which a contracting party may hold the other party to his representation that he would not insist on the performance of the contract strictly according to its terms, where the representee has altered his position in reliance on the representor fulfilling his representation. This doctrine, which is discussed in Part IV, has not been extended in English law to allow a new obligation to be created by simple reliance on a promise, but is limited to the role of a "shield", or defence, where the representor seeks to assert the strict contract contrary to his own representation.[25] In certain other common law jurisdictions, however, promissory estoppel has been developed to allow the promisee who has reasonably relied on a promise to use the doctrine as a "sword", to bring an action to enforce the promise.[26] In essence, this provides a third independent justification for the legal enforceability of promises: the promisee's reasonable reliance, in addition to consideration and the formality of a deed. It is significantly different as a basis of promissory liability, since it focuses principally on the reason for enforcement from the promisee's perspective (his reli-

---

[22]   As with so much of the general English law of contract, the rules have been devised by the courts, with relatively little intervention from statute except to solve particular problems, or to provide special rules for particular types of contract or of parties. For the purposes of this book, it should be noted that there is no statute defining a contract in English law (and therefore when statutes refer to contracts, the common law definition is assumed); nor is there any general statutory regulation of the elements required for the formation of a contract, although we shall see special statutory rules for certain types of contract, or to protect certain parties (in particular, special rules of formality, discussed in Pt II).

[23]   See, paras 8-40 to 8-42.

[24]   The statement of Lord Sumption JSC in *Rock Advertising Ltd v MWB Business Exchange Centres Ltd* [2018] UKSC 24; [2018] 2 W.L.R. 1603 at [18] that the decision in *Foakes v Beer* (1884) 9 App. Cas. 605 "is probably ripe for review" (cf. para.9-22) does not cast doubt on the need for consideration in the formation of a contract.

[25]   See paras 10-38 to 10-39, 10-45.

[26]   See paras 10-47 (US), 10-48 (Australia).

ance) rather than on an exchange between the parties (the benefit to the promisor and the detriment to the promisee by the promisee providing what the promisor asked for: consideration) or the promisor's formally expressed intention (a deed). The fact that other common law jurisdictions have taken the step of allowing this additional basis of promissory liability illustrates that it is compatible with a common law view of contracts. However, although there would be advantages in its development, the English courts have so far been reluctant to take this step which, in any event, would have to be taken by the Supreme Court or by legislation.[27]

Comparative solutions   This book discusses the English law of formation of a   **1-08** contract: agreement, formalities, consideration and the extent to which the English courts recognise the doctrine of promissory estoppel. However, from time to time mention is made of the approaches of other legal systems, and it is important to be clear from the outset about the significance of such material.

It has already been noted above that there is some difference of approach amongst the different common law legal systems in relation to the scope of the doctrine of promissory estoppel.[28] We shall see that, partly in response to the different approach to that doctrine,[29] but also more generally, there are differences between common law systems in the approach to consideration, both in relation to the formation of a contract, and in its requirement for the variation of a contract. Some reference is therefore made to other common law systems, although the focus remains the English common law.

Civil law legal systems, however, take fundamentally different approaches to most of the topics discussed in this book. The reluctance of English law to impose liability on parties negotiating a contract can be contrasted with a broader view in the civil law tradition that during the negotiations the parties are already in a relationship regulated by the law, imposing on each party a general duty to take the other's interests into account.[30] Even if other systems use similar language of "agreement" as the basis of a contract, and their cases reveal similar common fact patterns in the formation of contracts, the underlying legal approaches may be different.[31] But the most significant difference is in the reason for the law's recognition of an agreement or a promise as binding. The doctrine of consideration is a peculiarity of the common law. There is no requirement in civil law systems that the promisee promise, do or forbear to do something in return for the promise if he is to have the right to enforce it. Instead, some modern civil law systems use doctrines of "cause", others just focus on the intention of the promisor to be bound to his promise.[32] But in either case the focus is on the promisor and the reason why he should be bound to his promise. The role of the promisor's intention to be bound to his promise is not ignored, or irrelevant, in English law[33]; but it is not the test of

---

27   See, paras 10-49 to 10-51.
28   See para.1-07 fn.25.
29   See para.10-47 fn.371.
30   See para.2-13.
31   e.g. if the core notion of is a *subjective* agreement, the significance of offer and acceptance is in establishing that subjective agreement, and the parties' silence may more easily constitute a valid acceptance; see paras 3-03, 3-38.
32   See para.8-04.
33   See para.3-09.

enforceability. The English approach is to require the promisee to earn the right of enforcement of the promise by doing what the promisor asked of him.[34]

The different approaches taken by civil law systems are mentioned briefly from time to time in the book, to point to the different ways in which legal systems can deal with the topics which are discussed in detail from the point of view of English law. However, such matters are touched on only lightly in this book since its purpose is to give a detailed analysis of the present state of English law on the formation of contracts.

---

[34] See para.8-08. The doctrine of promissory estoppel, also unknown in the civil law systems, focuses even more on the reasons for the promisee to have the right to enforce the promise: see para.1-07. Civil law systems also use formalities in relation to certain contracts; see para.4-03 fnn.14,15, para.4-07.

PART I THE AGREEMENT

CHAPTER 2

PRE-CONTRACTUAL NEGOTIATIONS[1]

I.   THE PRACTICAL SIGNIFICANCE OF PRE-CONTRACTUAL NEGOTIATIONS

On-the-spot contracts and negotiated contracts   Very many contracts are not **2-01** "negotiated" at all: indeed, the vast majority of everyday contracts entered into by consumers are not the result of a process of negotiation. This is not simply because the consumer is given no freedom to negotiate and is expected to sign up to the standard terms proposed by the seller or supplier of goods or services,[2] but because the nature of the contract and the process by which it is formed do not lend it to negotiation. In theory, the purchaser of goods in a supermarket may face a negotiation at the check-out[3]; but the reality is that in on-the-spot transactions there is simply no space for negotiations. The context in which negotiations have a practical significance is where the parties are discussing a possible future contract for which the terms need to be settled.[4]

Negotiations of varying complexity   The length and complexity of the negotia- **2-02** tions will vary with the nature and complexity of the proposed contract. As we shall see in the following sections of this chapter, the legal questions which arise in relation to pre-contractual negotiations include what significance the law attributes to the negotiations which precede the contract, and in what circumstances, and on what basis, obligations can arise between the parties even before the contract has been formed. In the case of negotiations for a complex contract, the length of the negotia-

---

[1]   Furmston and Tolhurst, Chs 7-11, 13–14; J. Cartwright, *Contract Law: An Introduction to the English Law of Contract for the Civil Lawyer*, 3rd edn (Hart Publishing, 2016), Ch.4; Andrews, arts 6–12.

[2]   The fairness of terms in such standard-form contracts is typically regulated by consumer protection legislation: Chitty, Ch.38.

[3]   *Pharmaceutical Society of Great Britain v Boots Cash Chemists (Southern) Ltd* [1952] 2 Q.B. 795, CA; see para.3-29.

[4]   OED Online, March 2018, "negotiate, v.": "1.a. To communicate or confer (*with* another or others) for the purpose of arranging some matter by mutual agreement; to discuss a matter with a view to some compromise or settlement".

tions may present practical difficulties which require some form of legal solution. For example, the scale of the project may be so significant for one of the parties that the time and effort involved in the negotiations will prevent it taking on other work, and therefore it requires some reassurance from the other party that the time spent in seeking to negotiate the contract is worthwhile. Or although the final details of the contract may not yet be settled, one of the parties may need to make substantial preparations in order to be ready to perform in accordance with the terms of the contract once it is agreed, and so to avoid a delay in the progress and final completion of the project. Or the overall project may have some initial stages in which both parties will be required to perform, and therefore it makes sense for them both to begin that early performance in the hope that the final contract will be settled by the time the initial stages are complete. As we shall see, it will generally be advisable for parties in such a situation to make express provision for the pre-contractual stage, although English law places certain barriers in the way of making even express provision for some of the obligations that commercial parties may wish to impose on each other during the negotiations.[5] When the parties have not made express provision, however, the question is whether the law will imply, or impose, obligations on the parties during the negotiations: obligations in relation to the conduct that is expected of them during the negotiations, and in consequence remedies that one party may have against the other arising during the negotiations where those pre-contractual obligations are not observed. This issue is most significant where the final contract is never in fact concluded, either because the negotiations fail—and one of the parties seeks to hold the other liable for the costs incurred during the failed negotiations, or even for the lost potential profits of the hoped-for contract—or because the performance of the planned contract proceeds to completion without a final concluded set of terms being agreed. But even where the contract is in due course concluded as planned, other questions may also arise both about the regulation of the negotiations during the pre-contractual phase, and about what impact there may be on the contract itself where one party claims that there was some irregularity during the negotiations.

II.   THE LEGAL STATUS OF NEGOTIATIONS IN ENGLISH LAW; NO GENERAL DUTIES BETWEEN NEGOTIATING PARTIES

2-03   **The purpose of the negotiations**   The negotiations for a contract are the discussions which the parties hope will lead to a future contract.[6] By definition, therefore, they are not regulated by the contract which is not yet in existence and may never come into existence.[7] During the negotiations, however, there is in a sense already a relationship between the parties, but it is a relationship which may ebb and flow: the prospects of the hoped-for contract may increase, or decrease, or may be abruptly dashed; and may then be resurrected or abandoned. Legal systems take different views about the legal status that should be attributed to this process of negotiation: are the parties entitled to take into account only their own interests, generally free from liability during the pre-contractual negotiations? Or does the

---

[5]   Especially the difficulty of imposing a duty to negotiate in good faith: see para.2-06.
[6]   See para.2-01 fn.4.
[7]   Once it comes into existence, however, the contract may make provision for what has happened during the negotiations, and therefore (but only in that sense) it retrospectively regulates the negotiating period: *Trollope & Colls Ltd v Atomic Power Constructions Ltd* [1963] 1 W.L.R. 333.

fact that they are engaging in the process of negotiation with a view to the formation of a contract already give rise to some legally-protected relationship which imposes on the parties some duties towards each other?

An adversarial relationship? The view generally taken in English law is that the relationship between negotiating parties is essentially adversarial. This was put most strongly by Lord Ackner in *Walford v Miles*[8]: **2-04**

> "the concept of a duty to carry on negotiations in good faith is inherently repugnant to the adversarial position of the parties when involved in negotiations. Each party to the negotiations is entitled to pursue his (or her) own interest, so long as he avoids making misrepresentations. To advance that interest he must be entitled, if he thinks it appropriate, to threaten to withdraw from further negotiations or to withdraw in fact, in the hope that the opposite party may seek to reopen the negotiations by offering him improved terms. ... In my judgment, while negotiations are in existence either party is entitled to withdraw from those negotiations, at any time and for any reason. There can be thus no obligation to continue to negotiate until there is a 'proper reason' to withdraw."

This statement was made in the particular context of a claim that the parties could agree to continue negotiations (a "lock-in" agreement) which was held by the House of Lords to be no more than an agreement to agree, and therefore incapable of constituting a legally enforceable contract[9]; and it was also held that it would not save such an agreement to imply the standard of *good faith* into the duty to negotiate.[10] The rejection of such a clause was based in part on its uncertain content,[11] but also on the proposition that the negotiations are inherently adversarial and therefore a duty to negotiate in good faith cannot be implied.[12]

A duty to negotiate is uncertain The courts have rejected the notion of a legally enforceable duty to negotiate on the basis that such a duty is not of sufficiently certain content. This is a substantive objection to such an obligation and therefore constitutes a rejection not only of an implied duty to negotiate but also of an express duty to negotiate. Where the parties have agreed to enter into a contract, but have not yet agreed (expressly or impliedly) on all the terms necessary to form the contract, the agreement is not enforceable because the courts have no mechanism to determine the missing terms if the parties have not provided an objectively certain mechanism for the gap to be filled.[13] Similarly, a duty to negotiate is too uncertain **2-05**

---

[8] [1992] 2 A.C. 128, HL, at 138.
[9] See para.2-05.
[10] See further para.2-06.
[11] See para.2-05.
[12] It has been said that this reasoning leads also to the conclusion that the parties cannot even *expressly* contract to negotiate in good faith; cf., however, see para.2-06.
[13] *May and Butcher Ltd v R.* [1934] 2 K.B. 17, HL (prices "shall be agreed upon from time to time"); cf. *Foley v Classique Coaches Ltd* [1934] 2 K.B. 1, CA (implied term that petrol should be sold at "reasonable price"); *Sudbrook Trading Estate Ltd v Eggleton* [1983] 1 A.C. 444, HL (option to purchase at price to be agreed by parties' valuers construed as agreement to sell at fair and reasonable price, which court could determine if the non-essential valuation machinery set by the agreement failed to operate). If the parties provide that one of the parties or a third party shall complete the contract (e.g. by fixing the price), or if objective criteria are provided by the parties which the court can apply (e.g. a "reasonable price") then there may be a valid contract where the third party in fact makes the necessary determination to complete the contract, or as long as the court has objective criteria to determine the matter. But where the third party declines to act, or cannot act, and the

because the courts cannot determine whether the duty has been breached, and cannot therefore supply any remedy for breach. Lord Denning said[14]:

"If the law does not recognise a contract to enter into a contract (when there is a fundamental term yet to be agreed) it seems to me it cannot recognise a contract to negotiate. The reason is because it is too uncertain to have any binding force. No court could estimate the damages because no one can tell whether the negotiations would be successful or would fall through: or if successful, what the result would be. It seems to me that a contract to negotiate, like a contract to enter into a contract, is not a contract known to the law."

2-06   **Duty to use "reasonable endeavours" or "best endeavours" to negotiate, or to negotiate "in good faith"**   It might be thought sufficient for the parties to be under a more specific duty in relation to the standard of conduct required of them during the negotiations, such as to use "reasonable endeavours" or "best endeavours" (or reasonable or best "efforts") to come to an agreement, or to act "in good faith" in seeking to agree. Such a formulation would focus the duty on the parties' conduct during the negotiations, rather than on the failure to agree on their outcome, and therefore identify the breach of duty by reference to the parties' conduct.[15] The law certainly recognises duties to use "best" or "reasonable" or "all reasonable" endeavours, and can give such duties sufficient meaning to render them enforceable[16]; and by undertaking a duty to use "best endeavours" to achieve a the duty to subordinate his own commercial interests to those of the other contracting party.[17] However, if the object which the "endeavours" are to be used to achieve is uncertain, imposing the standard of best endeavours or reasonable endeavours does not render the duty certain[18]; and so[19]

---

court has no objective criteria, there is no complete contract. Moreover, an agreement to refer to arbitration the parties' disagreement over the outstanding term is not sufficient to save the contract where there is nothing in the arbitration clause to enable a contract to be made which in fact the original bargain has left quite open: *May and Butcher v R.* at 21. For further discussion of the requirement of contractual certainty, see paras 3-14 to 3-18.

[14]   *Courtney & Fairbairn Ltd v Tolaini Brothers (Hotels) Ltd* [1975] 1 W.L.R. 297, CA, at 301, discussed (together with other cases which have followed it) and approved in *Walford v Miles*, see para.2-04 fn.8, at 136-138; see also *National Transport Co-operative Society Ltd v Attorney General of Jamaica* [2009] UKPC 48 at [60]. cf. *Corson v Rhuddlan BC* (1990) 59 P. & C.R. 185, CA, at 198 (Staughton LJ, obiter: obligation on parties to negotiate with view to fair rent, where contract set upper limit of the rent and the tenant was willing to pay that upper limit, could give rise to obligation on landlord to agree that figure).

[15]   If such a duty were accepted, however, there would still be a question about the remedy for breach: what has the claimant lost by reason of the fact that the defendant is in breach of a negotiating duty where the contract is then not concluded: the "loss of a chance" of the hoped-for contract? The expenses incurred during the negotiations? This question also arises in relation to breach of a lock-out agreement, which the law does recognise: see para.2-22.

[16]   For the difficulties involved in interpreting such clauses, see Lewison, para.16.07.

[17]   *Jet2.com Ltd v Blackpool Airport Ltd* [2012] EWCA Civ 417; (2012) 142 Con. L.R. 1 at [32].

[18]   *IBM United Kingdom Ltd v Rockware Glass Ltd* [1980] F.S.R. 335, CA, at 348.

[19]   *Little v Courage* (1994) 70 P. & C.R. 469, CA, at 476 (Millett LJ). See also *Phillips Petroleum Co (UK) Ltd v Enron (Europe) Ltd* [1997] C.L.C. 329 (disagreement in CA about whether contractual obligation to use reasonable endeavours to agree commissioning date was, in context, sufficiently certain: the majority held that it was not); *Teekay Tankers Ltd v STX Offshore and Shipbuilding Co Ltd* [2017] EWHC 253 (Comm); [2017] 1 Lloyd's Rep. 387 at [203]–[209] (best efforts to reach agreement was no more than aspirational).

"an undertaking to use one's best endeavours to agree … is no different from an undertaking to agree, to try to agree, or to negotiate with a view to reaching agreement; all are equally uncertain and incapable of giving rise to an enforceable legal obligation."

It has been held that, similarly, it renders the duty "to negotiate" no more certain if one adds the words "in good faith".[20]

In *Walford v Miles* Lord Ackner added a further objection to the recognition of a duty to negotiate in good faith[21]:

"How can a court be expected to decide whether, *subjectively*, a proper reason existed for the termination of negotiations? The answer suggested depends upon whether the negotiations have been determined 'in good faith.' However the concept of a duty to carry on negotiations in good faith is inherently repugnant to the adversarial[22] position of the parties when involved in negotiations. Each party to the negotiations is entitled to pursue his (or her) own interest, so long as he avoids making misrepresentations. … [H]ow is a vendor ever to know that he is entitled to withdraw from further negotiations? How is the court to police such an 'agreement?' A duty to negotiate in good faith is as unworkable in practice as it is inherently inconsistent with the position of a negotiating party. It is here that the uncertainty lies."

This statement appears to assume that the inherently "adversarial" nature of contractual negotiations necessarily renders the parties' decision whether to continue or break off negotiations "subjective": that is, there is no objective standard—in the absence of misrepresentations made by one party to the other—by which the court could determine whether the parties' conduct during negotiations has fallen below the standard of "good faith" required of them. On this account, good faith becomes in itself a subjective, non-justiciable standard. This is questionable: it is not self-evident that the court could not, on a case-by-case basis, determine appropriate standards of conduct between parties negotiating a contract.[23]

---

20 *Walford v Miles*, see para.2-04 fn.8, at 138.
21 *Walford v Miles*, see para.2-04 fn.8, at 138.
22 [The report says "adverserial".]
23 This, in substance, is what continental jurisdictions have done: see para.2-13. "Good faith" may then be seen as defining an objective standard of behaviour: cf. the standard of "good faith and fair dealing" in PECL, art.1:201 and Comment E, and DCFR art.I.–1:103 and Comment A. In Australia there appears to be a gradual recognition of good faith as an ascertainable standard of commercial conduct: Seddon and Bigwood, para.6.15; see also L.E. Trakman and K. Sharma, "The Binding Force of Agreements to Negotiate in Good Faith" [2014] C.L.J. 598, esp. pp.610–617. In Canada, the Supreme Court has recognised good faith as an organising principle of contract law: *Bhasin v Hrynew* (2014) 379 D.L.R. (4th) 385; [2014] 3 S.C.R. 494; the full significance of this is not yet clear, but it opens up the possibility of remedies for breach of (at least) express duties to negotiate in good faith: Waddams, para.46. In those limited cases where English law does impose duties of good faith in the formation of a contract (e.g. in partnership contracts) the duties translate into objective standards, in particular of disclosure: Cartwright (Misrepresentation), para.17-26; and the courts are able to give meaning to express or implied obligations to *perform* a contract in good faith (e.g. *Compass Group UK and Ireland Ltd v Mid Essex Hospital Services NHS Trust* [2013] EWCA Civ 20;, [2013] B.L.R. 265 (express obligation to act in good faith subject to interpretation, but "care must be taken not to construe a general and potentially open-ended obligation such as an obligation to 'co-operate' or 'to act in good faith' as covering the same ground as other, more specific, provisions, lest it cut across those more specific provisions and any limitations in them": Beatson LJ at [154]); *Yam Seng Pte Ltd v International Trade Corp Ltd* [2013] EWHC 111 (QB); [2013] 1 C.L.C. 662 at [134]–[142] (duty of good faith in performance, implied on facts of case, and sensitive to context, but including duties of honesty and other generally accepted standards of commercial dealing and "fidelity to the bargain" (Leggatt J)). This is a quite separate question from

It appears rather to reflect the view, stated clearly by Lord Ackner,[24] that the parties ought to be free to behave in a self-interested way; their conduct should not be regulated. However, at present the courts have taken this to mean that even if the parties *expressly* agree to negotiate in good faith—which one might interpret as the parties' agreeing to waive this self-interest—the clause will not be enforced.[25] There are signs that the courts are reluctant to take such a strong view in the face of a genuinely agreed, commercial undertaking to negotiate in good faith,[26] but it will take a decision of the Supreme Court to review the current approach which is based on the decision of the House of Lords in *Walford v Miles*.[27] However, if the parties not only agree to negotiate in good faith, or to use their "best" or "reasonable" endeavours to settle the terms on which to enter into the contract, but also provide a suitable mechanism for settling the outstanding contract terms if their negotia-

---

whether the law requires a *subjective* standard of "good faith" or honesty in other contexts, such as to determine whether person acquiring property did so in good faith and without notice of third-party property rights so as to take free of such rights: cf. Sale of Goods Act 1979 ss.23, 24, 25, 61(3); Bills of Exchange Act 1882 ss.29, 90. A similar distinction between subjective and objective good faith is also drawn in DCFR, Vol.1, p.72 (definition of "good faith" contrasted with "good faith and fair dealing").

24 *Walford v Miles*, see para.2-04 fn.8, at 138: "he must be entitled, if he thinks it appropriate, to threaten to withdraw from further negotiations or to withdraw in fact, in the hope that the opposite party may seek to reopen the negotiations by offering him improved terms".

25 *Walford v Miles*, see para.2-04 fn.8, has been followed in, e.g. *Multiplex Constructions (UK) Ltd v Cleveland Bridge UK Ltd* [2006] EWHC 1341 (TCC); (2006) 107 Con. L.R. 1 at [634]–[639]; *National Westminster Bank Plc v Rabobank Nederland* [2007] EWHC 1056 (Comm) at [366]; *Bezant v Rausing* [2007] EWHC 1118 (QB) at [60]; *National Transport Co-operative Society Ltd v Attorney General of Jamaica* [2009] UKPC 48 at [61]; *Barbudev v Eurocom Cable Management Bulgaria EOOD* [2012] EWCA Civ 548; [2012] 2 All E.R. (Comm) 963 at [46]; *Shaker v Vistajet Group Holdings SA* [2012] EWHC 1329 (Comm); [2012] 2 Lloyd's Rep. 93 at [7]; *Sax v Tchernoy* [2014] EWHC 795 (Comm) at [67].

26 *Petromec Inc v Petroleo Brasileiro SA* [2005] EWCA Civ 891; [2006] 1 Lloyd's Rep. 121 at [121] (Longmore LJ: "It would be a strong thing to declare unenforceable a clause into which the parties have deliberately and expressly entered"; on the facts the clause was enforceable, and *Walford v Miles* was distinguished); followed in *Secretary of State for Defence v Turner Estate Solutions Ltd* [2015] EWHC 1150 (TCC); [2015] B.L.R. 448 at [104]. cf. *Jet2.com Ltd v Blackpool Airport Ltd* [2012] EWCA Civ 417; (2012) 142 Con. L.R. 1 at [65] (Longmore LJ: "An agreement to use best endeavours to reach an agreement may be unenforceable as an agreement to agree as effectively held in *Little v Courage Ltd* (1995) 70 P & CR 469, but even in such a case the matter may not be completely beyond argument since a best endeavours obligation might at least be held to import an agreement to negotiate in good faith, as to which see *Petromec Inc v Petroleo Brasileiro SA* at [115]–[121]. No doubt, damages for breach of such an obligation could be problematical"). See also J. Steyn, "Contract Law; Fulfilling the Reasonable Expectations of Honest Men" (1997) 113 L.Q.R. 433, 438–439, noting that European jurisdictions, the PICC and the UCC accept duties of good faith. In *Wah v Grant Thornton International Ltd* [2012] EWHC 3198 (Ch); [2013] 1 Lloyd's Rep. 11 at [55], [58] Hildyard J thought that the courts are more ready to give effect to commitments to negotiate in good faith on issues of *costing or price*, construing them as in effect stipulations for a reasonable or fair price, and being willing to imply criteria or machinery to determine the issue. For cases involving the agreement to negotiate the variation of an existing contract, see para.2-36.

27 *Petromec Inc v Petroleo Brasileiro SA* [2005] EWCA Civ 891; [2006] 1 Lloyd's Rep. 121 at [120]–[121]. The statement by Leggatt J in *Knatchbull-Hugessen v SISU Capital Ltd* [2014] EWHC 1194 (QB) at [23], that "[n]otwithstanding the decision of the House of Lords in *Walford v Miles*, it is also now generally accepted that … a contract may impose an obligation on one or both parties to conduct negotiations in good faith, see eg *Petromec Inc v Petroleo Brasileiro SA*" goes too far in failing to identify the ways in which the courts have not ignored but only distinguished *Walford* (e.g. by finding that the clause, properly construed, allows the court to determine the contents of the agreement objectively); cf. *Rosalina Investments Ltd v New Balance Athletic Shoes (UK) Ltd* [2018] EWHC 1014 (QB) at [50]; Chitty, para.1-047.

tions break down, the clause may be saved. Such a mechanism may involve determination by a third party, such as an arbitrator or even mediation or some other form of dispute resolution,[28] or by setting a standard, such as a "reasonable" price, or other objective criteria which a court can apply to decide the case.[29]

It has been said that the courts are more willing to accept as valid an undertaking to use reasonable (or best) endeavours to enter into an agreement *with a third party*, since the court can give such an undertaking sensible content, and whether the party who gave the undertaking has endeavoured to make such an agreement is a question of fact which a court can decide.[30]

---

[28] *Cable & Wireless Plc v IBM United Kingdom Ltd* [2002] EWHC 2059 (Comm); [2002] C.L.C. 1319 at 1326–1327 (Colman J: provision that parties shall "attempt in good faith to resolve" disputes through negotiation, failing which through an alternative dispute resolution (ADR) procedure as recommended to the parties by the Centre for Dispute Resolution: resort to CEDR and participation in its recommended procedure were engagements of sufficient certainty: "this may seem a somewhat slender basis for distinguishing this type of reference from a mere promise to negotiate. However, the English courts should nowadays not be astute to accentuate uncertainty (and therefore unenforceability) in the field of dispute resolution references", given the policy in favour of ADR in the CPR); *Holloway v Chancery Mead Ltd* [2007] EWHC 2495 (TCC); [2008] 1 All E.R. (Comm) 653 at [81] (Ramsey J: ADR clause must meet at least three requirements: the process must be sufficiently certain in that there should not be the need for an agreement at any stage before matters can proceed; the administrative processes for selecting a party to resolve the dispute and to pay that person should also be defined; the process or at least a model of the process should be set out so that the detail of the process is sufficiently certain); following *Aiton Australia Pty Ltd v Transfield Pty Ltd* [1999] NSWSC 996; (1999) 153 F.L.R. 236, Sup. Ct. N.S.W. (Einstein J: obligation to negotiate in good faith could be sufficiently certain to give rise to a binding obligation if expressed: (1) to undertake to subject oneself to a process of negotiation or mediation (which must be sufficiently precisely defined by the agreement to be certain and hence enforceable); (2) to undertake in subjecting oneself to that process to have an open mind in the sense of (a) a willingness to consider such options for the resolution of the dispute as may be propounded by the opposing party or by the mediator as appropriate; (b) a willingness to give consideration to putting forward options for the resolution of the dispute); *Wah v Grant Thornton International Ltd*, see para.2-06 fn.26, at [60] (Hildyard J: to be sufficiently certain, amicable settlement provision requires "without the need for further agreement: (a) a sufficiently certain and unequivocal commitment to commence a process; (b) from which may be discerned what steps each party is required to take to put the process in place; and which is (c) sufficiently clearly defined to enable the court to determine objectively (i) what under that process is the minimum required of the parties to the dispute in terms of their participation in it and (ii) when or how the process will be exhausted or properly terminable without breach"). See also *Mamidoil-Jetoil Greek Petroleum Co. SA v Okta Crude Oil Refinery AD* [2001] EWCA Civ 406; [2001] 2 Lloyd's Rep. 76 at [69]. In *Emirates Trading Agency LLC v Prime Mineral Exports Pte Ltd* [2014] EWHC 2104 (Comm); [2015] 1 W.L.R. 1145, Teare J held at [63] that there was no authority binding him to hold that clause was unenforceable which required the parties to seek to resolve a dispute by friendly discussions in good faith and within a limited period of time before the dispute could be referred to arbitration.

[29] *Queensland Electricity Generating Board v New Hope Collieries Pty Ltd* [1989] 1 Lloyd's Rep. 205, PC, at 210 (price to be renegotiated after five years of 15-year supply contract: implied obligation to make reasonable endeavours to agree, and failing agreement to procure appointment of arbitrator, who would be guided by the implicit standard that the price was to be fair and reasonable); *Petromec Inc v Petroleo Brasileiro SA*, see para.2-06 fn.26, at [117]–[118] (agreement to negotiate in good faith the reasonable costs incurred by one party); *Tramtrack Croydon Ltd v London Bus Services Ltd* [2007] EWHC 107 (Comm) at [90]–[91] ("parties shall in good faith agree (acting reasonably)" sums payable, coupled with expert determination clause: the court could decide, in case of dispute, at least what parties and the expert, acting *reasonably* were bound to take into account and ignore); *Redd Factors Ltd v Bombardier Transportation UK Ltd* [2014] EWHC 3138 (QB) at [28] (parties "shall in good faith agree a variation order" but also provided cost price plus 5% handling fee as basis of agreement).

[30] *Astor Management AG v Atalaya Mining Plc* [2017] EWHC 425 (Comm); [2017] Bus. L.R. 1634 at [67] (Leggatt J), disagreeing at [64] with certain observations made in *Dany Lions Ltd v Bristol*

2-07　　**Risk allocation in the negotiations**　　Whatever regime a legal system accepts for the pre-contractual phase—whether a very restrictive approach, as in England, under which the parties are in principle free to act in a self-interested way, or a wider approach which imposes broader general duties on the parties who are negotiating a contract[31]—the system is taking a basic stance on the risk allocation of the negotiations. The more restrictive the approach, the more each party is held to bear its own risk of the failure of the negotiations, in the sense that its own energy, time and cost incurred during the negotiations will be rewarded only if the negotiations are successful.[32] One way of examining the pre-contractual phase is therefore to consider what mechanisms are available within the legal system to allow one party to shift to the other the risks associated with the contract not being concluded.

2-08　　**Negotiations "subject to contract"**　　Although the starting point in English law is that the parties are not subject to general duties in their negotiations, and therefore each party in principle bears the risk of the failure of the negotiations,[33] one or both parties may reinforce this risk allocation during the course of the negotiations, typically by expressing their participation in the negotiations as "subject to contract"— i.e. making clear that there is no intention to give rise to legally enforceable duties before the conclusion of the negotiations in a fully concluded contract.[34] "In short, a 'subject to contract' agreement is no agreement at all".[35] The formulation "subject to contract" has traditionally been used particularly in relation to negotiations for contracts for the sale of land,[36] but it can apply to negotiations for any contract. Moreover, a "subject to contract" provision may not only negative pre-contractual

---

　　　Cars Ltd [2014] EWHC 817 (QB); [2014] 2 All E.R. (Comm) 403 at [37].
[31]　cf. para.2-13.
[32]　*William Lacey (Hounslow) Ltd v Davis* [1957] 1 W.L.R. 932 at 934.
[33]　See paras 2-04 to 2-07.
[34]　"Subject to contract" is a well-established and commonly-used stand-alone phrase, but any words may be used to similar effect although the actual words may then define the scope of the condition in relation to the particular negotiations: see e.g. *RTS Flexible Systems Ltd v Molkerei Alois Müller GmbH & Co KG* [2010] UKSC 14; [2010] 1 W.L.R. 753 (clause in draft written contract that the contract would "not become effective until each party has executed a counterpart and exchanged it with the other"); *Brookes v Atlantic Marine & Aviation LLP* unreported 28 February 2018, QBD Mercantile Court (email footer made clear that no contract would be binding without signature). It is also possible for the parties *impliedly* to agree that their negotiations will not result in a binding contract until a formal written document is prepared: *Winn v Bull* (1877) 7 Ch. D. 29 at 32; *Whitehead Mann Ltd v Cheverny Consulting Ltd* [2006] EWCA Civ 1303; [2007] 1 All E.R. (Comm) 124 at [45] (Morritt C: "where ... solicitors are involved on both sides, formal written agreements are to be produced and arrangements made for their execution the normal inference will be that the parties are not bound unless and until both of them sign the agreement"). However, it is possible for the parties to conclude a binding contract even though they agree that a formal document is to be executed subsequently: *Air Studios (Lyndhurst) Ltd v Lombard North Central Plc* [2012] EWHC 3162 (QB); [2013] 1 Lloyd's Rep. 63 at [5]; *Pagnan SpA v Feed Products Ltd* [1987] 2 Lloyd's Rep. 601, CA, at 619.
[35]　*Generator Developments Ltd v Lidl UK GmbH* [2018] EWCA Civ 396 at [79] (Lewison LJ). See also *RG Carter Building Ltd v Kier Business Services Ltd* [2018] EWHC 729 (TCC) at [32] (Pepperall QC: "it is open to the parties to agree that, to use an expression much used in connection with the current Brexit negotiations, nothing is agreed until everything is agreed": limitation period under Limitation Act 1980 s.10 for claim for contribution under the Civil Liability (Contribution) Act 1978 does not run as long as negotiations for settlement of contribution are subject to contract).
[36]　Law Com. No.65, "Subject to Contract" Agreements (1975). See e.g. Cheshire and Burn, pp.955–957; Megarry and Wade, paras 15-010 to 15-011.

contractual liability,[37] but also have the effect of negativing a possible cause of action in unjust enrichment,[38] or an equitable right, such as a constructive trust, which would contradict the parties' expressed intention.[39] In *Regalian Properties Plc v London Docklands Development Corp*[40] Rattee J rejected the argument that the law should be extended to permit a claim for compensation or restitution for work done in anticipation of the contract:

"where, however much the parties expect a contract between them to materialise, both enter negotiations expressly (whether by use of the words 'subject to contract' or otherwise) on terms that each party is free to withdraw from the negotiations at any time. Each party to such negotiations must be taken to know (as in my judgment Regalian did in the present case) that pending the conclusion of a binding contract any cost incurred by him in preparation for the intended contract will be incurred at his own risk, in the sense that he will have no recompense for those costs if no contract results. In other words I accept in substance the submission made by Mr Naughton for L.D.D.C., to the effect that, by deliberate use of the words 'subject to contract' with the admitted intention that they should have their usual effect, L.D.D.C. and Regalian each accepted that in the event of no contract being entered into any resultant loss should lie where it fell."

The parties who expressed the negotiations to be "subject to contract" may later withdraw or waive that condition, and if such withdrawal or waiver is not express it may be inferred from the circumstances of the case, although the court will not lightly so hold.[41] However, it may be easier to find a waiver of the condition where

---

[37] For the requirement of an intention to create legal relations in the formation of a contract, see para.3-09.

[38] See para.2-26. cf. *Galliard Homes Ltd v J Jarvis & Sons Plc* [2000] C.L.C. 411, CA, at 423 ("subject to contract" condition coupled with express provision allowing for reimbursement of pre-contract expenditure if contract not concluded explained both doing of the works and the payment therefor, even in the absence of any, or any other, contract).

[39] *Generator Developments Ltd v Lidl UK GmbH*, see para.2-08 fn.35, at [81] (constructive trust; "*Pallant v Morgan* equity").

[40] [1995] 1 W.L.R. 212 at 231.

[41] *RTS Flexible Systems Ltd v Molkerei Alois Müller GmbH & Co KG*, see para.2-08 fn.34, at [56]; see also at [86]–[87] (applying the test of whether a "reasonable honest businessman" in the position of each of the parties would have inferred that the other had intended to waive the "subject to contract" condition, following the approach of Steyn LJ in *G Percy Trentham Ltd v Archital Luxfer Ltd* [1993] 1 Lloyd's Rep. 25, CA, at 27). See also *Barclays Wealth Trustees (Jersey) Ltd v Erimus Housing Ltd* [2014] EWCA Civ 303; [2014] 2 P. & C.R. 23 at [23] (payment of rent during period when party holds over at the end of the term of a lease does not give rise to presumption of periodic tenancy where parties negotiating new lease: "In these circumstances, as in any other subject to contract negotiations, the obvious and almost overwhelming inference will be that the parties did not intend to enter into any intermediate contractual arrangement inconsistent with remaining parties to ongoing negotiations": Patten LJ, applying *Javad v Aqil* [1991] 1 W.L.R. 1007, CA). It may be possible for a party to be estopped from relying on a "subject to contract" condition, e.g. through the doctrine of proprietary estoppel in the case of negotiations for a contract for the sale of land, but this will be rare: *Attorney General of Hong Kong v Humphreys Estate (Queen's Gardens) Ltd* [1987] A.C. 114, PC, at 127–128, distinguishing *Salvation Army Trustee Co Ltd v West Yorkshire Metropolitan CC* (1980) 41 P. & C.R. 179 (where the parties had gone beyond a mere hope that the negotiations would result in a legal relationship and one party had expressly or impliedly represented that the relationship would be entered into). For other cases where such a claim has failed, see *James v Evans* [2000] 3 E.G.L.R. 1, CA; *Edwin Shirley Productions Ltd v Workspace Management Ltd* [2001] 2 E.G.L.R. 16 at [50]; *Secretary of State for Transport v Christos* [2003] EWCA Civ 1073, [2004] 1 P. & C.R. 17 at [41]–[44]; see also *Cobbe v Yeoman's Row Management Ltd* [2008] UKHL 55, [2008] 1 W.L.R. 1752 at [25]. Where "subject to contract" negotiations are intended to be embodied in a court order which, if made, would give rise to an obligation to enter into the terms negotiated "subject to

the parties have performed the very obligations which had been agreed "subject to contract".[42]

2-09   **Finding a legal source for duties in the pre-contractual stage**   In any legal system the search for duties to be imposed on the parties negotiating a contract is necessarily limited by the system's structure of duties in private law. It would be possible to create a special and specific duty governing the negotiations for a contract to sit alongside other sources of obligations,[43] but in the absence of such a special duty the analysis must rest on the established sources of obligations: contract, tort and unjust enrichment. In English law, we must also consider equitable doctrines such as the duty to protect confidential information, as well as the possible role of the doctrine of promissory estoppel. Potential sources of liability during the negotiations are discussed in more detail below.[44] Here we first consider some of the limitations set by English law on the possibility of finding duties on the negotiating parties in the pre-contractual stage.

2-10   **No general duty of disclosure between negotiating parties**   We have already seen that the English courts characterise the relationship between negotiating parties as adversarial,[45] and reject any general positive duty to negotiate in good faith.[46] It is therefore not surprising that there is no general positive duty to disclose information to the other party during negotiations. Even a legal system which recognises a duty to negotiate in good faith may be cautious in imposing duties of disclosure: it would be contrary to the very nature of negotiations to require each party as a matter of course to disclose all information which is relevant to the other's bargaining position.[47] However, whilst many legal systems will define general circumstances where one negotiating party does become subject to a duty to disclose information,[48] the English courts have been notably reluctant to impose du-

---

contract", submission to the Court of a draft order is not sufficient to expunge the "subject to contract" condition: *Taylor v Burton* [2015] EWCA Civ 142.

[42]   *Rugby Group Ltd v Proforce Recruit Ltd* [2005] EWHC 70 (QB), [2005] All E.R. (D) 22 (Feb) at [16] (reversed on different grounds [2006] EWCA Civ 69).

[43]   See para.2-13.

[44]   See paras 2-14 to 2-30.

[45]   See para.2-04.

[46]   See para.2-06.

[47]   cf. *Martel Building Ltd v Canada* (2000) 193 D.L.R. (4th) 1, SCC, at [67]: "It would defeat the essence of negotiation and hobble the marketplace to extend a duty of care to the conduct of negotiations, and to label a party's failure to disclose its bottom line, its motives or its final position as negligent. Such a conclusion would of necessity force the disclosure of privately acquired information and the dissipation of any competitive advantage derived from it, all of which is incompatible with the activity of negotiating and bargaining". For economic arguments, see e.g. A.T. Kronman, "Mistake, Disclosure, Information, and the Law of Contracts" (1978) 7 J.L.S. 1; R.A. Posner, *Economic Analysis of Law*, 9th edn (New York: Aspen, 2014), para.4.7; B. Rudden, "Le juste et l'inefficace pour un non-devoir de renseignement" (1985) R.T.D.Civ. 91.

[48]   e.g. in French law, general principles for a duty of disclosure were developed by academic writers and by case law during the second half of the 20th century: see J. Ghestin, G. Loiseau and Y.-M. Serinet, *Traité de droit civil: La formation du contrat*, Vol.1, 4th edn (Paris: L.G.D.J., 2013), para.1515; P. Giliker, "Regulating Contracting Behaviour: The Duty to Disclose in English and French Law" (2005) 13 *European Review of Private Law* 621; H. Kötz, *European Contract Law*, 2nd edn (trans. G. Mertens and T. Weir, Oxford University Press, 2017), pp.175–180; and a reform of the French Civil Code in 2016 introduced into the text a general principle that "The party who knows information which is of decisive importance for the consent of the other, must inform him of it where, legitimately, the latter does not know the information or relies on the contracting party":

ties of disclosure.[49] Although there are specific situations in which the law imposes duties to disclose particular information, or imposes disclosure duties on parties in particular circumstances,[50] the starting point is a strong rejection of any general duty of disclosure, based on similar ideas to those on which the courts base their rejection of general duties to negotiate in good faith: the individual, adversarial positions of the parties in which they are generally entitled to act in their own self-interest. An indication of this can be seen in a judgment of Blackburn J.[51]:

> "even if the vendor was aware that the purchaser thought that the article possessed that quality, and would not have entered into the contract unless he had so thought, still the purchaser is bound, unless the vendor was guilty of some fraud or deceit upon him, and that a mere abstinence from disabusing the purchaser of that impression is not fraud or deceit; for, whatever may be the case in a court of morals, there is no legal obligation on the vendor to inform the purchaser that he is under a mistake, not induced by the act of the vendor."

Breaking off negotiations is not a tort   We shall see below that there are certain circumstances in which one party may commit a tort against the other during the negotiations and thereby be liable to pay damages for loss caused.[52] However, English law does not have a general principle of tortious liability, but a series of separate torts, designed to protect particular interests in particular circumstances. Pre-contractual negotiations are not as such a protected interest within the law of tort: there is no general duty not to cause loss by breaking off negotiations, because there is no tort where the breaking-off of negotiations will in itself constitute the tortious wrong. Even the deliberate breaking-off of negotiations, in the knowledge that the other party will suffer loss, is not tortious. And although the courts have held that parties negotiating a contract can owe each other a duty of care within the tort of negligence, the scope of the duty is limited to the case where one party provides information—imposing therefore liability in certain circumstances for negligent misrepresentation[53] —and has not been extended to a more general duty of care to respect the other party's interest during the negotiations.[54]

2-11

---

art.1112–1 c.civ, discussed by C. Aubert de Vincelles, "Validity of Contract: Dol, Erreur and Obligation d'Information" in J. Cartwright and S. Whittaker (eds), *The Code Napoléon Rewritten: French Contract Law after the 2016 Reforms* (Hart Publishing, 2017), pp.80–91.

[49] Cartwright (Misrepresentation), Ch.16.

[50] Cartwright (Misrepresentation), Ch.17. See also paras 2-17, 2-18 of this chapter. The most significant exception in practice is in consumer contracts, where traders have broad statutory duties to provide information to consumers before a contract is concluded: Cartwright (Misrepresentation), para.17-59.

[51] *Smith v Hughes* (1871) L.R. 6 Q.B. 597 at 607. See also Cockburn CJ at 604: "The case put of the purchase of an estate, in which there is a mine under the surface, but the fact is unknown to the seller, is one in which a man of tender conscience or high honour would be unwilling to take advantage of the ignorance of the seller; but there can be no doubt that the contract for the sale of the estate would be binding".

[52] See paras 2-14 to 2-18.

[53] *Esso Petroleum Co Ltd v Mardon* [1976] Q.B. 801, CA; see para.2-16.

[54] For explicit refusal to extend the tort of negligence to other aspects of pre-contractual negotiations in other common law jurisdictions, see *Martel Building Ltd v Canada*, see para.2-10 fn.47, at [32]–[72] (conduct of commercial negotiations generally, disclosure of information and consideration of tenders); *Onyx Group Ltd v Auckland City Council* (2003) 11 T.C.L.R. 40 at [52]–[64], NZHC (consideration of tenders). See also P. Giliker, "A Role for Tort in Pre-Contractual Negotiations? An Examination of English, French and Canadian Law" (2003) 52 I.C.L.Q. 969.

2-12 **No general liability based on estoppel** The doctrine of promissory estoppel has been developed in certain other common law jurisdictions in such a way as to allow one negotiating party to have a claim against the other on the basis of his reliance on the latter's representation that he would complete the contract, or on some other specific promise or representation made during the negotiations, even though no contract has been concluded.[55] However, the courts in England have not yet taken such a step. The decision of the Court of Appeal in *Combe v Combe*[56] is still binding to the effect that promissory estoppel cannot be used as a "sword" to create new obligations, and therefore until this is changed by a decision of the Supreme Court[57] promissory estoppel[58] cannot be used to complete failed negotiations or to impose liability in damages for losses caused by the breaking-off of negotiations. We shall see the scope of operation of promissory estoppel within English law, and the potential for its further development, in Chapter 10.

2-13 **Different approaches in other systems of contract law** As we have seen, English law rejects any general duty between negotiating parties, and therefore has no general category of pre-contractual liability. In this, it is followed by many other common law legal systems,[59] even if in some jurisdictions the scope for the imposition of certain specific liabilities may be wider and therefore in practice there may be more scope for certain forms of pre-contractual liability.[60] However, it is well established that the approach taken to the pre-contractual phase by continental civil law legal systems, and other legal systems around the world which draw their inspiration from continental Europe, is generally very different.[61] The source of pre-contractual liability varies from one system to another: some place it within the law of tort, others have developed a separate category of pre-contractual liability alongside contract and tort, often referred to as *culpa in contrahendo*.[62] But civil law systems, whilst starting from the position that the parties are in principle free to decide whether to enter into a contract and therefore merely entering into negotiations does not create a duty not to break them off, generally recognise that during the negotiations the parties are in a relationship which gives rise to duties to take the other party's interests into account, commonly described as a duty to negotiate

---

[55]   In Australia, see e.g. *Waltons Stores (Interstate) Ltd v Maher* (1988) 164 C.L.R. 387, HCA, see para.10-48; in America, see e.g. *Hoffman v Red Owl Stores Inc* (1965) 133 N.W.2d 267, Sup. Ct. Wisconsin, and Restatement of Contract (2d) para.90(1), see para.10-47.

[56]   [1951] 2 K.B. 215, CA.

[57]   *Baird Textile Holdings Ltd v Marks & Spencer Plc* [2001] EWCA Civ 274; [2002] 1 All E.R. (Comm) 737 at [39], [55], [91].

[58]   For a case where the doctrine of *proprietary* estoppel had the effect of completing a contract for the sale *of land*, see *Yaxley v Gotts* [2000] Ch. 162, CA; but cf. *Cobbe v Yeoman's Row Management Ltd* [2008] UKHL 55; [2008] 1 W.L.R. 1752; see para.5-28.

[59]   e.g. Burrows, Finn & Todd, para.2.2.6 (New Zealand).

[60]   e.g. through the doctrine of promissory estoppel in US and Australian law: see para.2-12 fn.55. In Canada, the Supreme Court has recognised good faith as an organising principle of contract law: *Bhasin v Hrynew*, see para.2-06 fn.23.

[61]   See generally J. Cartwright and M. Hesselink, *Precontractual Liability in European Private Law* (Cambridge University Press, 2008), Ch.5. For discussion of some non-European systems, see E.H. Hondius, *Precontractual Liability: Reports to the XIIIth Congress International Academy of Comparative Law* (Deventer: Kluwer, 1991), Chs 13 (Japan), 16 (Puerto Rico).

[62]   Cartwright and Hesselink, *Precontractual Liability in European Private Law*, see para.2-13 f n.61, pp.457–460.

in good faith. There is therefore a fundamental difference of principle in this area between English law and its continental neighbours.[63]

III. Potential Sources of Liability During the Negotiations

(1) Tort

Limited scope for pre-contractual liability in tort Although English law does 2-14
not admit general duties between parties negotiating a contract,[64] and does not have
a general principle of tortious liability which can govern the pre-contractual stage,[65]
a party's behaviour during the negotiations may give rise to liability under one of
the established torts. The most likely circumstance in which such liability may arise
is where one party makes a misrepresentation on which the other party has relied
and has suffered loss. Lord Ackner, making clear that there is no general duty to
negotiate in good faith, also said that misrepresentation during the negotiations may
give rise to liability[66]:

> "Each party to the negotiations is entitled to pursue his (or her) own interest, so long as
> he avoids making misrepresentations ..."

Misrepresentation during the pre-contractual stage may give rise to an action in
the tort of deceit, or the tort of negligence.[67] There are also limited circumstances
in which a claim may be brought in either deceit or negligence on the basis not that
the defendant made an active misrepresentation but that he failed to disclose
information.

Misrepresentation: the tort of deceit A person to whom a false representation 2-15
was made may recover damages in the tort of deceit from the person by whom (or
on whose behalf) the representation was made, if he can show that the representation was made fraudulently, with the intention that the claimant act upon it, and that
the representation in fact constituted an inducement to his own actions as a result
of which he suffered loss.[68] "Fraud" is established only if there is proof[69] that the
false representation was made knowingly, or without belief in its truth, or reck-
lessly (careless whether it be true or false): that is, there was no honest belief in its
truth.[70] "Loss" in the context of the tort of deceit means loss calculated on the tort
measure: the diminished financial position in which the claimant finds himself as
a consequence of relying on the false representation.[71] All losses which flow directly

---

[63]   Cartwright and Hesselink, *Precontractual Liability in European Private Law*, see para.2-13 fn.61,
      pp.485–488.
[64]   See para.2-04.
[65]   See para.2-11.
[66]   *Walford v Miles*, see para.2-04 fn.8, at 138; see generally para.2-06.
[67]   Where the contract is concluded, a claim for damages may be brought under Misrepresentation Act
      1967 s.2(1); see para.2-31.
[68]   Chitty, paras 7-047 to 7-073; Anson, pp.342–345. For a detailed account of the tort of deceit in the
      pre-contractual context, see Cartwright (Misrepresentation), Ch.5.
[69]   On proof of fraud to the civil standard, see Cartwright (Misrepresentation), para.5-46.
[70]   *Derry v Peek* (1889) 14 App. Cas. 337, HL, at 374.
[71]   Even where the fraudulent misrepresentation induces the claimant to enter into a contract which is
      less profitable than he had been led by the misrepresentation to expect, the lost profits of that contract
      are not recoverable since a claim based on the profits that the claimant would have received if the

from the fraudulent misrepresentation are recoverable, even if the defendant could not reasonably have foreseen them[72]; and although there is a duty on the claimant to mitigate his loss once he has discovered the fraud,[73] he cannot be met by a defence of contributory negligence[74] nor does the common law allow a representor to exclude his liability for his own fraud.[75] The action of deceit applies to pre-contractual misrepresentations, as long as the claimant can establish that he suffered loss in reliance on the false statement. If the misrepresentation induced him to enter into the contract, the loss will typically be calculated by reference to the loss suffered by reason of entering into the contract.[76] But the action of deceit is not limited to the case where a contract is entered into, and therefore it can be brought where the negotiations fail, as long as the claimant can establish that the fraudulent misrepresentation was a cause[77] of his taking some action[78] which resulted in loss. Typically, this will involve a claim that he pursued the negotiations in reliance on the defendant's fraudulent misrepresentation about his intention to conclude the contract, and in consequence he was led to incur expenditure that has been wasted, and perhaps to lose other opportunities for alternative contracts with third parties.[79] Given that a "misrepresentation" need not be made explicitly by words but is any falsehood communicated by the defendant to the claimant, including inferences from the defendant's words or conduct,[80] the tort of deceit provides a remedy for the claimant to recover his wasted expenditure, or other losses, where the defendant began or continued negotiations although he had no serious intention to finalise the contract, but by his words or actions led the claimant to believe that he was serious: that is, negotiations which (on the defendant's side) were either a sham

---

statement had been true is the normal measure of damages in contract, not tort: Cartwright (Misrepresentation), paras 2-08 to 2-10. However, if the claimant has been induced by the misrepresentation to tie up his capital unprofitably, he may be able to include in his claim an element for the hypothetical profit he could have made in investing that capital elsewhere: *East v Maurer* [1991] 1 W.L.R. 461, CA; Cartwright (Misrepresentation), para.5-39.

[72] *Doyle v Olby (Ironmongers) Ltd* [1969] 2 Q.B. 158, CA, at 167; *Smith New Court Securities Ltd v Scrimgeour Vickers (Asset Management) Ltd* [1997] A.C. 254, HL, at 266–267, 282.

[73] *Smith New Court Securities Ltd v Scrimgeour Vickers (Asset Management) Ltd* [1997] A.C. 254, HL, at 266.

[74] *Standard Chartered Bank v Pakistan National Shipping Corp (Nos 2 and 4)* [2002] UKHL 43; [2003] 1 A.C. 959 at [10]–[18].

[75] *S Pearson & Son Ltd v Dublin Corp* [1907] A.C. 351, HL, at 353, 362; *HIH Casualty and General Insurance Ltd v Chase Manhattan Bank* [2003] UKHL 6; [2003] 2 Lloyd's Rep. 61 at [16], [76], [122]. The position may be different in relation to fraud of agents or employees: see different views expressed in *HIH Casualty and General Insurance Ltd v Chase Manhattan Bank* at [16], [76]–[82], [98], [122].

[76] e.g. *Smith New Court Securities Ltd v Scrimgeour Vickers (Asset Management) Ltd*, see para.2-15 fn.72 (false statement by broker about competing bids for purchase of shares induced claimant to over-bid and therefore to enter into contract for purchase of shares at a loss; the recoverable loss was increased by the fact that were also other losses as a result of a fraud which had been perpetrated on the company and which when later discovered caused the share price to fall).

[77] It need be only *a* cause, not *the* cause: *Attwood v Small* (1838) 6 Cl. & Fin. 232 at 502, 7 E.R. 684 at 785.

[78] A misrepresentation does not generally cause loss directly; it is relied on, i.e. believed and acted upon by a person who then suffers loss by having acted upon it: Cartwright (Misrepresentation), para.3-51.

[79] e.g. if the claimant is the seller of an asset, and by being encouraged to remain in fruitless negotiations loses an opportunity to sell his asset to a third party and can now obtain only a lower price in the market, the reduction could fall within his (tort measure) loss.

[80] *Bradford Third Equitable Benefit Building Society v Borders* [1941] 2 All E.R. 205, HL, at 211; Cartwright (Misrepresentation), para.5-06.

from the outset, or later became a sham.[81] Since, however, there must be a causal link between claimant's reliance on the misrepresentation and the loss he can recover, only expenditure incurred after that reliance is in principle recoverable. If, therefore, the claim is based on the defendant's having changed his mind during the course of the negotiations but then having fraudulently given the impression that he was still serious in negotiating, only losses incurred from that point in the negotiations will be recoverable.

Misrepresentation: the tort of negligence If there is no evidence of fraud, but the claimant can show that a misrepresentation made by the defendant during the negotiations caused him to suffer loss, he may seek to hold the defendant liable for that loss in the tort of negligence.[82] This requires the claimant to establish that the defendant owed him a duty to take reasonable care in the negotiations, and breached that duty causing him the loss.[83] It is established that one party negotiating a contract may owe a duty to the other party in relation to the provision of information or advice, as long as in providing the information or advice he has assumed a responsibility to the recipient for its accuracy, or he knows or ought to know that that the recipient is likely to rely on it for a foreseeable purpose without verifying it.[84] Although the circumstances in which pre-contractual misrepresentations are actionable in the tort of negligence are more likely to be where the inaccurate information causes the claimant to enter into an unprofitable contract,[85] it is in principle also possible for a claim to be brought successfully, as in the tort of deceit,[86] where the negotiations were not completed and defendant's careless statement caused the claimant to suffer loss.[87] "Loss" in the tort of negligence is assessed on the same basic measure as in deceit—the diminished financial position in which the claimant finds himself as a consequence of relying on the false representation[88] —although here it is limited to loss which is within the scope of

2-16

---

[81] This is a core case of *culpa in contrahendo* within the general doctrine of pre-contractual liability as it has developed in continental European jurisdictions: see, e.g. Cartwright and Hesselink, *Precontractual Liability in European Private Law*, see para.2-13 fn.61, Case 1. It is also identified as a specific example of failure to negotiate in good faith in PICC art.2.1.15(3), PECL art.2:301(3) and DCFR art.II.–3:301(4).

[82] Where the loss flows from the claimant having entered into the contract with the defendant in reliance on his (non-fraudulent) misrepresentation, in practice a better claim will be that under Misrepresentation Act 1967 s.2(1): see para.2-31 fn.196.

[83] Chitty, paras 7-074, 7-086 to 7-097; Anson, pp.346–347. For a detailed account of the tort of negligence in the pre-contractual context, see Cartwright (Misrepresentation), Ch.6.

[84] *Esso Petroleum Co Ltd v Mardon* [1976] Q.B. 801, CA, applying to the context of pre-contractual negotiations the principles established by *Hedley Byrne & Co Ltd v Heller & Partners Ltd* [1964] A.C. 465, HL. See also *Caparo Industries Plc v Dickman* [1990] 2 A.C. 605, HL, at 638.

[85] As in *Esso Petroleum Co Ltd v Mardon* [1976] Q.B. 801, CA (carelessly inaccurate estimate by landlord of likely profitability of petrol station of which the other party took a lease and suffered losses: duty owed because landlord held itself out as having knowledge and skill not possessed by the prospective tenant).

[86] In the case of a non-fraudulent misrepresentation, however, the scope is narrower than in the tort of deceit since the claim in negligence does not cover misrepresentations about the defendant's intentions as to the future negotiations.

[87] In *Walford v Miles* see para.2-04 fn.8, the trial judge awarded damages for negligent misrepresentation to cover wasted costs of the negotiations, which was affirmed by the Court of Appeal but was not in issue in the House of Lords: see [1992] 2 A.C. 128, HL, at 133–136

[88] Cartwright (Misrepresentation), para.2-09. However, if the claimant has been induced by the misrepresentation to tie up his capital unprofitably, he may (as in the tort of deceit) be able to include in his claim an element for the hypothetical profit he could have made in investing that capital

the duty undertaken by the defendant,[89] and which is of a kind that the defendant could reasonably have foreseen when he committed the tort[90]; and in this tort the claimant may be met by the defence of contributory negligence.[91]

2-17   **Non-disclosure: the tort of deceit**   There is no general duty of disclosure in English law,[92] and no tort is committed even where one negotiating party deliberately withholds information which he knows would reveal to the other party that he is making a mistake about the subject-matter of the contract,[93] or the circumstances surrounding the contract, which would significantly affect his decision on what terms to agree or even whether to enter into the contract at all. An active misrepresentation, even an inference of false or misleading information from some act done by the defendant, could (if fraudulent) give rise to a claim in deceit.[94] However, there is a fundamental difference in principle between a misunderstanding which the defendant caused the claimant to make, and one made independently by the claimant which the defendant failed to correct.[95] The latter is only an omission, and until recently the courts have generally refused to allow non-disclosure to give rise to liability in deceit.[96] However, it is well established that in certain circumstances one party may be subject to a defined duty of disclosure, either because of the nature of the contract or because of the pre-existing relationship between the parties,[97] and that a failure to comply with such a duty of disclosure may render the ensuing contract voidable at the instance of the aggrieved party. The Court of Appeal has said that where the defendant was subject to such a duty of disclosure during the negotiations for a contract that was concluded, the fraudulent failure to disclose not only renders the contract voidable by the other party but also

---

elsewhere: *Esso Petroleum Co Ltd v Mardon*, [1976] Q.B. 801, CA at 821–822; *South Australia Asset Management Corp v York Montague Ltd* [1997] A.C. 191 at 216–217; Cartwright (Misrepresentation), para.6-58.

[89]   *South Australia Asset Management Corp v York Montague Ltd*, [1997] A.C. 191; Cartwright (Misrepresentation), para.6-55.

[90]   *The Wagon Mound* [1961] A.C. 388, PC; *Hughes v Lord Advocate* [1963] A.C. 837, HL (Sc).

[91]   Law Reform (Contributory Negligence) Act 1945 s.1(1).

[92]   See para.2-10.

[93]   The position is different if the misunderstanding is about the terms on which the contract is to be concluded, or the identity of the other party (where the identity is fundamental to the contract), because in the absence of agreement (objectively determined) between the parties on the terms or identity, the contract is void. If, therefore, one party knows that the other is mistaken about the terms on which he proposes to enter into the contract, then he may not be able to hold the other to those terms: *Hartog v Colin & Shields* [1939] 3 All E.R. 566 at 568; *Smith v Hughes*, see para.2-10 fn.51, at 609–610 (Hannen J); Cartwright (Misrepresentation), para.13-21. Or if the mistake is about the terms of the document in which the contract is to be embodied, there may be a unilateral mistake giving rise to a claim by the mistaken party for rectification: *Commission for the New Towns v Cooper (Great Britain) Ltd* [1995] Ch. 259, CA, at 292; Cartwright (Misrepresentation), para.13-47. For mistake of identity, see generally Cartwright (Misrepresentation), Ch.14.

[94]   e.g. *Gordon v Selico Ltd* [1985] 2 E.G.L.R. 79 (concealment of defects in property by landlord covering them up); Cartwright (Misrepresentation), para.5-06.

[95]   Cartwright (Misrepresentation), paras 1-03, 16-03 to 16-06.

[96]   *Peek v Gurney* (1873) L.R. 6 H.L. 377, HL, at 403; *Bradford Third Equitable Benefit Building Society v Borders* see para.2-15 fn.80, at 211; Cartwright (Misrepresentation), para.17-43.

[97]   e.g. where the negotiations are for a contract of partnership: Cartwright (Misrepresentation), para.17-26; or where the parties are in a fiduciary relationship: Cartwright (Misrepresentation), paras 17-39 to 17-42. The common law duty to disclose information when entering into a contract of insurance has now been superseded by statute (and the statutory duty of disclosure now extends only to non-consumer contracts of insurance): Cartwright (Misrepresentation), paras 17-06 to 17-25.

allows him to bring an action in the tort of deceit for loss caused, on the basis that fraudulent non-disclosure should in such circumstances be assimilated to fraudulent misrepresentation.[98] This decision raises certain difficulties which have not yet been addressed,[99] but its scope is in any event limited to those situations where a party negotiating a contract fails to fulfil a duty of disclosure imposed by law, and it does not change the general position that a mere fraudulent non-disclosure is not actionable. There is, however, a question about whether it applies even in the case where the negotiations fail and there is no contract concluded. This must be doubtful. The duty is to disclose information which is material to the other party's decision in entering into the contract; and the breach of duty occurs and becomes actionable at the moment when the contract is entered into. If the negotiations do not reach the stage of a concluded contract, the party who seeks a remedy for loss flowing from the break-off of the negotiations will not be able to attribute his loss to any breach of a duty of disclosure.

Non-disclosure: the tort of negligence   One negotiating party may owe the other   **2-18**
a duty of care during the negotiations, although we have seen this does not constitute a general duty of care to respect the other party's interest during the negotiations.[100] There can be a duty to take reasonable care in providing information or advice, but only where there is an assumption of responsibility by one party in favour of the other in relation to its accuracy.[101] It may not be very difficult to identify the assumption of responsibility from the act of providing information or advice in circumstances where the party providing it knows or ought to know that that the recipient is likely to rely on it for a foreseeable purpose without verifying it.[102] It is much more difficult to show that one negotiating party assumed a responsibility to take reasonable care to provide information: such a duty is a positive one (since non-disclosure is an omission) and the courts are reluctant to impose positive duties to speak through imposing duties of care in the tort of negligence, particularly in the context of negotiations for an ordinary commercial contract.[103] The mere fact that the negotiations are for a contract which in law gives rise to duties of disclosure, such as an insurance contract, is not sufficient to impose a duty of care in tort during the negotiations.[104] However, it is possible for there to be a

---

[98] *Conlon v Simms* [2006] EWCA Civ 1749; [2008] 1 W.L.R. 484 at [130] (Jonathan Parker LJ: "Non-disclosure where there is a duty to disclose is tantamount to an implied representation that there is nothing relevant to disclose"). See also Lawrence Collins J at first instance: [2006] EWHC 401 (Ch); [2006] 2 All E.R. 1024 at [202].

[99] Neither the trial judge nor CA appeared to take into account contrary authority, and the scope of what was decided is unclear, since if it is based on the general proposition that breach of a duty to disclose is to be assimilated to misrepresentation, it is not evident that this will not also extend to other remedies for misrepresentation, such as under Misrepresentation Act 1967 s.2(1): Cartwright (Misrepresentation), para.17-43 and esp. n.196; Chitty, para.7-156. The only case which appears to have followed *Conlon* in the proposition that deliberate silence gives rise to an actionable misrepresentation is *Cavell USA Inc v Seaton Insurance Co* [2008] EWHC 3043 (Comm); [2008] 2 C.L.C. 898 at [84].

[100] See para.2-11 fn.54.

[101] See para.2-16.

[102] *Caparo Industries Plc v Dickman*, see para.2-16 fn.84, at 638.

[103] *Banque Keyser Ullmann SA v Skandia (UK) Insurance Co Ltd* [1990] 1 Q.B. 665, CA, at 798–805; *Martel Building Ltd v Canada*, see para.2-10 fn.47.

[104] *Banque Keyser Ullmann SA v Skandia (UK) Insurance Co Ltd* [1990] 1 Q.B. 665, CA, at 800–801; *HIH Casualty and General Insurance Ltd v Chase Manhattan Bank* [2001] EWCA Civ 1250; [2001] 2 Lloyd's Rep. 483 at [59]–[74].

duty to take reasonable care to provide information, where the relationship between the negotiating parties is such that one party can be shown on the facts to have assumed a responsibility to the other, or where the law attaches to their relationship such a duty (such as a fiduciary relationship).[105]

(2) Contract

2-19   **Pre-contractual contracts**   Although the parties have not yet concluded the negotiations for their intended principal contract, they may in certain circumstances enter into a separate (pre-contractual) contract which is designed to govern some particular aspect of the negotiations, or to provide for the eventuality that the negotiations for the principal contract do not succeed.[106] Any such pre-contractual contract must comply with the requirements for the creation and validity of any contract,[107] and will generally have to be an express contract with clearly evidenced terms since, given the general approach of English law to allow negotiating parties freedom from mutual obligations,[108] there is a risk that anything less than an express contract imposing pre-contractual obligations would undermine this essential approach to the otherwise "adversarial" nature of the negotiating process.[109] There are certain well-established forms of pre-contractual contract available to parties negotiating a contract: option contracts, rights of pre-emption and "lock-out" contracts.[110] Parties also commonly use documents described as "letters of intent", or "comfort letters" during the negotiations which may contain contractual obligations. Exceptionally, however, the courts have been willing to imply pre-contractual contracts, particularly in the context of tendering. Each of these will be considered in the following paragraphs.

2-20   **Option contract**   An option contract is a contract under which one party is given the right to enter into a defined contract if he so chooses: if he "opts" to do so.[111] In order to satisfy the requirements of certainty,[112] the terms of the contract for which the beneficiary of the option has the right to call, as well as the circumstances in which he has the right to exercise the option, must be sufficiently clear.[113] Such a contract has sometimes been characterised as an irrevocable offer to enter into a

---

[105] cf. *Banque Keyser Ullmann SA v Skandia (UK) Insurance Co Ltd* [1990] 1 Q.B. 665, CA, at 804–805; Cartwright (Misrepresentation), para.17-44.

[106] It may be negligent for a professional adviser to fail to advise his client to enter into a formal contract to cover work being undertaken: *Harlequin Property (SVG) Ltd v Wilkins Kennedy* [2016] EWHC 3188 (TCC); [2017] 4 W.L.R. 30 at [415] (accountant/business adviser).

[107] Agreement, through offer and acceptance (see Ch.3); consideration (see Ch.8) if not executed as a deed (see Ch.7); intention to create legal relations (see para.3-09).

[108] See paras 2-04 to 2-07.

[109] *Walford v Miles* [1992] 2 A.C. 128, HL, at 138; see para.2-04.

[110] For confidentiality agreements, designed to protect a party who discloses sensitive information during the negotiations, see para.2-29.

[111] Where the grantee of the option has an option to purchase property, he may be said to have a "call option", the right to call upon the grantor to sell the property to him: e.g. *Spiro v Glencrown Properties Ltd* [1991] Ch. 537. The option may, however, be an option to sell—a "put option", the right to require the grantor of the option to purchase the property from him: e.g. *Active Estates Ltd v Parness* [2002] EWHC 893 (Ch); [2003] L. & T.R. 21 at [55].

[112] See paras 3-14 to 3-18.

[113] *Teekay Tankers Ltd v STX Offshore and Shipbuilding Co Ltd* [2017] EWHC 253 (Comm); [2017] 1 Lloyd's Rep. 387.

contract,[114] which also typically[115] defines the time within which and the manner in which the offeree (the option holder) can accept the offer and thereby create the contract. Since an offer is in principle revocable, and even a "firm offer'"—that is, an offer which the offeror expresses to be open for acceptance for a defined period—can be revoked at will by the offeror,[116] the option contract is the mechanism in English law[117] by which one party can bind himself to keep open an offer, and therefore give the offeree the right to decide whether the principal contract should be formed. However, an option contract is useful only when the terms of the principal contract have been settled, and so is generally limited to the case where the negotiations are complete.

Right of pre-emption   A right of pre-emption[118] is a contractual right to be given   **2-21**
an opportunity to enter into negotiations, or even to enter into a contract if the terms of the pre-emption are already stated with sufficient certainty to enable a contract to be formed,[119] but only if the party granting the pre-emption decides to proceed

---

[114] *Helby v Matthews* [1895] A.C. 471, HL, at 477, 479–480; *Beesly v Hallwood Estates Ltd* [1960] 1 W.L.R. 549 at 555–556; *Yates Building Co Ltd v RJ Pulleyn & Sons (York) Ltd* [1976] 1 E.G.L.R. 157, CA, at 157; *J Sainsbury Plc v O'Connor* [1990] S.T.C. 516 at 532; *Re Gray (Deceased)* [2004] EWHC 1538 (Ch), [2005] 1 W.L.R. 815 at [25]. For statements to the effect that an option to purchase constitutes a conditional contract of sale, see *Helby v Matthews* at 482; *Griffith v Pelton* [1958] Ch. 205, CA, at 225, criticised in *Beesley v Hallwood Estates Ltd* at 556. In the context of option contracts relating to land, a particular issue arises because a contract for the sale or other disposition of an interest in land must satisfy the formality requirements of LP(MP)A 1989 s.2 (below, para.5-09); and an option to purchase land (as long as it is not personal to the parties) already creates an equitable interest in the land in favour of the grantee of the option: *London and South Western Railway Co v Gomm* (1882) 20 Ch. D. 562, CA, at 581; M. Dray, A. Rosenthal, C. Groves, *Barnsley's Land Options*, 6th edn (Sweet & Maxwell, 2016), paras 2-068 to 2-071; Cheshire and Burn, pp.983–985; Megarry and Wade, para.15-012. It has been decided that, for the purposes of the 1989 Act, the analogy of the conditional contract is the more appropriate, and therefore the grant of the option, rather than its exercise, is the "contract" which must satisfy the formality requirements: *Spiro v Glencrown Properties Ltd*, see para.2-19 fn.111.

[115] Where the option prescribes the method by which it is to be exercised in terms which are mandatory, the exercise is only good if it complies with the stated requirements: *Yates Building Co Ltd v RJ Pulleyn & Sons (York) Ltd* [1976] 1 E.G.L.R. 157, CA; *Siemens Hearing Instruments Ltd v Friends Life Ltd* [2014] EWCA Civ 382; [2014] 2 P. & C.R. 5. This is an application of established principles relating to offers which prescribe a mode of acceptance (see para.3-37). The other rules of offer and acceptance will similarly apply except in so far as they are varied by the terms of the option; e.g. a well-drafted option will specify the time and manner of its exercise, but if there is no fixed period within which the option is to be exercised, it will be implied that it should be a reasonable period (on the analogy of an offer lapsing after a reasonable period for acceptance: see para.3-30).

[116] Law Com. WP No.60, *Firm Offers* (1975).

[117] The principal difficulty in relation to giving binding force to a firm offer in English law is the doctrine of consideration: Law Com. WP No.60, paras 15 to 18, 20. In civil law jurisdictions which do not require consideration in order to make a promise or an agreement binding, a firm offer can more easily become a contractually binding undertaking; alternatively, breach of an undertaking to keep open an offer may give rise to pre-contractual liability, in tort or under the doctrine of *culpa in contrahendo*: K. Zweigert and H. Kötz, *An Introduction to Comparative Law*, 3rd edn (trans. T. Weir, Clarendon Press, 1998), pp.357–363. But again this is not possible in English law because a party has no duty of good faith in negotiating, and is free to withdraw an offer at any time in the absence of a contractually binding agreement to keep the offer open: see para.3-30.

[118] Or a right of "first refusal": *AstraZeneca UK Ltd v Albemarle International Corp* [2011] EWHC 1574 (Comm); [2011] 2 C.L.C. 252 at [34]–[35] (a right to be given the opportunity to match any third-party offer which the grantor of the right might be otherwise minded to accept).

[119] cf. *Speciality Shops v Yorkshire and Metropolitan Estates Ltd* [2002] EWHC 2969 (Ch); [2003] 2

with the transaction.[120] Unlike an option contract, by which the party granting the option has put it within the beneficiary's power to decide whether to enter into the contract in question by exercising the option, a right of pre-emption does not give the beneficiary more than the hope that he may in due course be given the right to conclude the contract or (depending on the terms of the pre-emption) at least to enter into negotiations for the contract. The party granting the pre-emption can decide not to proceed at all with such a transaction; but the force of the right of pre-emption is that, if he does decide to proceed, he must first do what he undertook to do—initiate the negotiations, or offer to enter into the contract with the beneficiary. To be binding, and therefore to give rise to any possible remedy if the offer is made to a third party rather than to the beneficiary of the pre-emption, the right of pre-emption must take effect as a contract.[121] However, if the terms of the pre-emption are only that the grantor undertakes to give the grantee the first opportunity to enter into the contract, it is not necessary (unlike in the case of an option[122]) for the terms of the future contract yet to be finally settled.[123] It has been said, however, that the grantor must act bona fide in setting the terms on which he is willing to enter into the transaction,[124] and so he cannot frustrate the operation of the right of pre-emption by making an unreasonable offer in order to provoke a rejection by the beneficiary of the pre-emption with a view to being able in fact to enter into the transaction with a third party.

2-22   **Lock-out contract**   A "lock-out" contract is a contract by which one or both parties undertake not to enter into a contract with a third party, or not to negotiate with a third party: they "lock" themselves "out" of competing contracts or parallel negotiations. The content of the "lock-out" obligation will always depend on the terms of the agreement,[125] but given that there is no inherent duty on a negotiating party to conduct the negotiations in good faith, and each party is in principle free to pursue his own interest so long as he avoids making misrepresentations,[126] a

---

P. & C.R. 31 at [25]–[29], where Park J set out different types of pre-emption ("more possibilities may exist") and emphasised that it is necessary to consider carefully the precise terms of the agreement in any particular case.

[120] For discussion of the nature of a right of pre-emption, contrasted with options, in the context of contracts for the sale of land, see *Pritchard v Briggs* [1980] Ch. 338, CA, at 418 (unregistered land); *Barnsley's Land Options*, see para.2-20 fn.114, para.1-006 and Ch.6; Cheshire and Burn, pp.985–986; Megarry and Wade, paras 15-012 to 15-013, 15-062 to 15-065. In registered land, since 31 October 2003, a right of pre-emption has effect as an interest in the land: LRA 2002 s.115(1), and so must be created in writing signed by both parties: LP(MP)A 1989 s.2; *Barnsley's Land Options*, para.6-035; and can be protected by the entry of a notice and/or a restriction in the register: *Barnsley's Land Options*, para.6-053; *Law v Haider* [2017] UKUT 212 (TCC) (right of pre-emption in Tomlin order).

[121] See para.2-19 fn.107.

[122] See para.2-19 fn.111.

[123] *Brown v Gould* [1972] Ch. 53 at 58; *Smith v Morgan* [1971] 1 W.L.R. 803 at 808 (right of pre-emption does not require price of future sale contract to be fixed, but can impose on grantor the obligation to make an offer at the price at which she is in fact willing to sell).

[124] *Smith v Morgan* [1971] 1 W.L.R. 803 at 808. A challenge to the grantor's bona fides may not be easy to establish: ibid.

[125] The agreement may be simply not to enter into a contract during the lock-out period: e.g. *Encyclopaedia of Forms and Precedents*, 5th edn (ed. Lord Millett, LexisNexis Butterworths), Vol.4(3) (2017 reissue), para.[209]. Or it may be not to negotiate with third parties: e.g. *Encyclopaedia of Forms and Precedents*, Vol.38(1) (2012 reissue), para.[1501]; R. Christou, *Boilerplate: Practical Clauses*, 7th edn (Sweet & Maxwell, 2015), para.3-024.

[126] *Walford v Miles* [1992] 2 A.C. 128, HL; at 138; see para.2-04.

"lock-out" contract must be expressly agreed by the parties. It is a useful form of contract for a party who is concerned to obtain exclusive contracting or negotiating rights[127]:

> "There is clearly no reason in the English contract law why A, for good consideration, should not achieve an enforceable agreement whereby B, agrees for a specified period of time, not to negotiate with anyone except A in relation to the sale of his property. There are often good commercial reasons why A should desire to obtain such an agreement from B. B's property, which A contemplates purchasing, may be such as to require the expenditure of not inconsiderable time and money before A is in a position to assess what he is prepared to offer for its purchase or whether he wishes to make any offer at all. A may well consider that he is not prepared to run the risk of expending such time and money unless there is a worthwhile prospect, should he desire to make an offer to purchase, of B, not only then still owning the property, but of being prepared to consider his offer. A may wish to guard against the risk that, while he is investigating the wisdom of offering to buy B's property, B may have already disposed of it or, alternatively, may be so advanced in negotiations with a third party as to be unwilling or for all practical purposes unable, to negotiate with A."

However, it is important to note that the contract can only lock the other party *out* of a contract or of negotiations with third parties; it cannot lock him *in* to negotiating. It is therefore negative in substance, since there can be no positive duty to negotiate,[128] and therefore the party granting the "lock out" is entitled simply to decline to negotiate further, and to wait until the end of the "lock out" period when he becomes again entitled to contract with, or negotiate with, any third party he may choose. Indeed, he can go further and announce to the other party during the "lock out" period that he will not negotiate further, or enter into a contract with, the beneficiary of the "lock-out" and that he will seek to a contract with third parties after its expiration.[129] Moreover, in order to satisfy the requirement of contractual certainty, the period of the "lock out" must be fixed or ascertainable.[130]

"Letter of intent", "comfort letter", "memorandum of understanding" and "heads of agreement"　　It is not uncommon for one negotiating party to ask for a "letter of intent" from the other in order to give an assurance, or "comfort", that the negotiations are proceeding seriously, and sometimes to act as an encouragement for the party requesting such a letter that he can safely incur expenditure in order to negotiate the contract or even in preparation for the hoped-for contract. The parties may also sometimes enter together what they describe as a "memorandum of understanding" or "heads of agreement" about the future contract which they are

2-23

---

[127] *Walford v Miles* [1992] 2 A.C. 128, HL at 139 (Lord Ackner).

[128] *Walford v Miles* [1992] 2 A.C. 128, HL at 139 (Lord Ackner); see para.2-05.

[129] *Moroney v Insofoam Investments SA* unreported 5 December 1997 (J. Sher QC). In practice, the minimal content of a "lock out" contract may be supported by other terms, such as, in the case of negotiations for a sale contract, a provision for reimbursement of a purchaser's expenditure on legal and surveying fees should the vendor pull out of the transaction for no good reason: ibid.; see para.2-25.

[130] *Moroney v Insofoam Investments SA* unreported 5 December 1997; cf. *Pitt v PHH Asset Management Ltd* [1994] 1 W.L.R. 327 (agreement not to consider offers from third parties for two weeks held valid); *Global Container Lines Ltd v Black Sea Shipping Co* [1997] C.L.Y. 4535 ("lock-out" agreement enforceable where, although it does not state its duration, it is subject to implied term that the contract is terminable on reasonable notice or where duration is ascertainable by reference to the happening of an outside event).

negotiating, setting out what they have agreed in outline. However, "letter of intent"[131] and "comfort letter"[132] are not terms of art, and their scope is much less clearly definable than the other forms of pre-contractual contract discussed earlier in this section. Indeed, a "letter of intent" often has no contractual force at all, either because it does not contain sufficiently clear obligations to satisfy the requirement of contractual certainty, or because it is expressed to be non-binding and only for the comfort of the other party, or its language is such that the party giving the letter assumes not a legal liability but only a moral responsibility.[133] Sometimes, however, under the heading of a "letter of intent", the parties may enter into contractually binding obligations, such as where one party agrees to pay for some particular pre-contract work to be undertaken by the other, or agrees to reimburse the other for certain expenses which he incurs if the principal contract is not in due course concluded.[134] Such a contract is designed to protect one party against the risk of wasted expenditure, and is generally entered into where the party agreeing to make the payment has an interest in the other party beginning work so as to allow the principal contract, when its terms are settled, to be performed without delay. It is designed to reverse the normal risk allocation during the negotiations: that pre-contract expenditure is at the risk of the party who incurs it.[135] Similarly, a "memorandum of understanding" or "heads of agreement" may simply express the parties' non-binding present intentions as to the future contract,[136] or it may not yet contain sufficient terms to constitute a binding contract, or may even make clear that there are certain matters still to be decided which therefore prevents there being a sufficient contract.[137] However, a "memorandum" may be expressed to be, or may be construed (objectively[138]) as being, sufficient to form a binding contract, either as to the particular limited matters which it contains, or even as to the whole project in the case of a more extensive document.[139]

---

[131] *British Steel Corp v Cleveland Bridge and Engineering Co Ltd* [1984] 1 All E.R. 504 at 509; *Cunningham v Collett and Farmer* [2006] EWHC 1771 (TCC), (2006) 113 Con. L.R. 142 at [82]–[84].

[132] *Kleinwort Benson Ltd v Malaysia Mining Corp Bhd* [1989] 1 W.L.R. 379, CA, at 391.

[133] cf. *Kleinwort Benson Ltd v Malaysia Mining Corp Bhd*, [1989] 1 W.L.R. 379, CA (statement in comfort letter by parent company that "it is our policy to ensure that" subsidiary could meet its liabilities was only statement of present fact and did not constitute contractual guarantee).

[134] A request by one negotiating party that the other start work may, if it does not have contractual force, sometimes give rise to a claim in unjust enrichment for the value of the work done: see para.2-27.

[135] See para.2-07 and para.2-26. For the terms which can usefully be included in such a contract, see para.2-33.

[136] The parties may make this clear, e.g. by expressing the document to be "subject to contract": *BSkyB Ltd v HP Enterprise Services UK Ltd* [2010] EWHC 86 (TCC); [2010] B.L.R. 267 at [479]; see para.2-08. Or it may be the (objective) construction of the document: *Donegal International Ltd v Zambia* [2007] EWHC 197 (Comm); [2007] 1 Lloyd's Rep. 397 at [110]–[114]; *Mehboob Travel Ltd v Pakistan International Airlines Corp* unreported 5 July 2013, QB.

[137] *Dhanani v Crasnianski* [2011] EWHC 926 (Comm); [2011] 2 All E.R. (Comm) 799 at [81], [95] (objectively construed, term sheet was intended to be binding, but left so much to be agreed that it was in reality an agreement to agree with no indication of any objective criteria by reference to which agreement was to be reached on those matters which had not been agreed). For a "heads of agreement" clause see Christou, see para.2-21 fn.125, paras 3-007 to 3-024.

[138] See paras 3-07, 3-08.

[139] *Simtech Advanced Training and Simulation Systems Ltd v Jasmin Simtec Ltd* [1995] F.S.R. 475 at 486 (obligations in memorandum of understanding contractually binding, pending negotiation of full sub-contract); *ICS Incorporation Ltd v Michael Wilson & Partners Ltd* [2005] EWHC 404 (Ch); [2005] B.P.I.R. 805 at [17], [19] ("Binding Memorandum of Understanding" recording parties' agreement to form an incorporated joint venture).

Implied contract; duty to consider tenders   Since a negotiating party may   **2-24**
reverse by contract the general rule[140] that he has no duty to act in the other party's
interest during the course of the negotiations, it is possible that a court might find
that such a (pre-contractual) contractual obligation has been entered into impliedly,
rather than in express terms. However, it will not generally be easy to establish such
an implied contract.[141] One context in which implied contracts have been found,
however, is tendering.

An invitation to tender is generally not an offer, but only an invitation to potential
bidders to submit offers each of which the party inviting tenders is free to accept
or reject: there is no implication that the best bid will be accepted,[142] although if the
terms of the invitation to tender go further and provide that the contract will be
given to the bidder who submits the bid that satisfies some objectively definable
criterion (such as the lowest or highest price), the general rule is displaced and the
invitation becomes an offer which is accepted by the submission of the relevant
conforming bid.[143] However, where the invitation to tender does not constitute such
an offer, the question still arises whether it at least carries an implied undertaking
in relation to the treatment of the bids which are submitted in accordance with the
invitation. There are broader decisions in other common law jurisdictions which
have accepted that (subject always to the terms of the invitation to tender) there can
be an implied contractual[144] duty to treat all bids fairly,[145] and that this can be
characterised as a duty of good faith and fair dealing.[146] In English law, however,

---

[140] See para.2-04.

[141] *Blackpool and Fylde Aero Club Ltd v Blackpool BC* [1990] 1 W.L.R. 1195, CA at 1202 (Bingham
LJ: "contracts are not to be lightly implied"). This will be particularly so in relation to pre-
contractual contracts, given the starting-point of English law that there is normally no duty to act
in the other party's interest during negotiations.

[142] *Spencer v Harding* (1870) L.R. 5 C.P. 561, C.Pl.; see para.3-29. There is also a separate question of
what would constitute the "best" bid: such a term would have to be objectively definable to satisfy
the requirement of contractual certainty: cf. *Sidey Ltd v Clackmannanshire Council* [2011] CSOH
194, 2012 S.L.T. 334, OH, at [25].

[143] *Harvela Investments Ltd v Royal Trust Co of Canada (CI) Ltd* [1986] A.C. 207, HL; see para.3-29.

[144] The contract arises from an implied offer contained in the invitation to tender which is accepted by
the submission of a conforming bid. Claims that there is also a breach of a duty of care in tort in
failing properly to consider the bid have been met by the objection that the tort duty, even if it exists, is defined by the scope of the contractual duty: *Martel Building Ltd v Canada*, see para.2-10
fn.47 at [106]–[107]; *Blackpool and Fylde Aero Club Ltd v Blackpool BC*, [1990] 1 W.L.R. 1195,
CA at 1203 (Bingham LJ, tentatively of that opinion, but it was not necessary for the decision; at
1204 Stocker LJ declined to consider "the difficult questions which arise on the claim formulated
in tort").

[145] *Martel Building Ltd v Canada*, see para.2-10 fn.47, at [84]–[85], citing an established line of cases
(Canada). A clause reserving the right not to accept the lowest or any bid was held at [89] not to
exclude the obligation to treat all bidders fairly.

[146] *Pratt Contractors Ltd v Transit New Zealand* [2003] UKPC 83; [2004] B.L.R. 143 at [44]–[47] (New
Zealand). Such a duty is, however, a *contractual* duty to *act* in good faith, not a *pre-contractual* duty
to *negotiate* in good faith, and it required the party receiving the bids only to treat the tenders equally,
and act honestly, with no duty to act judicially or accord bidders a hearing: at [47]. It was accepted
by the parties that such a duty existed in the case, and PC at [45] declined to discuss the "somewhat
controversial question" as to whether the duty in cases of preliminary procedural contracts for dealing with tenders is a manifestation of a more general obligation to perform any contract fairly and
in good faith (as stated by Finn J in *Hughes Aircraft Systems International v Airservices Australia*
(1997) 146 A.L.R. 1, FCA, at 36–37). For the Canadian cases, see Waddams, para.41; and in
Australia, see Seddon and Bigwood, para.3.35 (noting that, particularly outside government tenders,
"the implications of [the] decisions are serious because they remove a degree of flexibility in the
tendering process").

the approach has been rather more cautious. In *Blackpool and Fylde Aero Club Ltd v Blackpool Borough Council*[147] it was held that, where tenders are solicited from selected parties, all of them known to the invitor, and where the invitation to tender prescribes a clear, orderly and familiar procedure, the invitee is protected at least to the extent that if he submits a conforming tender before the deadline he is entitled as a matter of contractual right to be sure that his tender will be considered, or at least will be considered if other tenders are.[148] However, it was also emphasised that the duty is only to consider the tender[149]; and in finding that there was a duty the judges emphasised that, on the facts, tenders were invited from a small class of selected bidders and there was a very detailed procedure set out for the submission of tenders. In this case the party inviting tenders was a public authority, although the decision does not appear to be limited to cases involving public bodies.[150] However, this may be a context in which a duty to consider conforming tenders can more easily be found,[151] and a number of other cases following the decision have also involved invitations by public authorities, with similarly detailed bidding procedures.[152]

2-25   **Remedies for breach of pre-contractual contracts**   Even if the claimant can establish the existence of one of the pre-contractual contracts referred to above, and that the other party has acted in breach of contract, there can sometimes be a question about whether the breach entitles him to a sufficiently useful remedy.

An *option contract* gives the beneficiary of the option a contractual right to a defined contract if he chooses to exercise the option. If, therefore, the other party in breach of the option contract causes the beneficiary not to obtain the contract to which he is entitled, for example by simply refusing to proceed with the contract or by entering into a competing contract with a third party, the beneficiary's claim for damages for breach of the option contract will in principle cover the loss he suffers by not obtaining his contract, including the profits he would have made from

---

[147] [1990] 1 W.L.R. 1195, CA.

[148] [1990] 1 W.L.R. 1195, CA at 1201. The invitee therefore had an action for breach of contact where it had posted a conforming tender into the invitor's letter box before the deadline but a member of the invitor's staff had failed to empty to the letter box before the bids were considered. For the problems of assessing the damages for such a breach of contract, however, see para.2-25, and para.2-25 fn.162.

[149] [1990] 1 W.L.R. 1195, CA at 1201 (Bingham LJ: "it has never been the law that a person is only entitled to enforce his contractual rights in a reasonable way").

[150] *J & A Developments Ltd v Edina Manufacturing Ltd* [2006] NIQB 85 at [49]; Chitty, para.11-044; S. Arrowsmith, *The Law of Public and Utilities Procurement*, 3rd edn, Vol.1 (Sweet & Maxwell, 2014), para.2.164. In the case of public procurement contracts, however, there is statutory regulation of tendering which may on the facts prevent the implication of a contract to consider tenders: *Harmon CFEM Facades (UK) Ltd v Corporate Officer of the House of Commons* (2000) 67 Con. L.R. 1 at [209]; given that the statutory regulations create their own regime, no contract will be implied: *J Varney & Sons Waste Management Ltd v Hertfordshire CC* [2010] EWHC 1404 (QB); [2010] Eu. L.R. 669 at [233]; *Willmott Dixon Partnership Ltd v Hammersmith and Fulham LBC* [2014] EWHC 3191 (TCC) at [242]. See generally Chitty, paras 11-051 to 11-052; Arrowsmith, *The Law of Public and Utilities Procurement*. The regulation of the award of public contracts is now contained in the Public Contracts Regulations 2015 (SI 2015/102) (implementing the Public Contracts Directive, Directive 2014/24/EU).

[151] *Natural World Products Ltd v ARC 21* [2007] NIQB 19 at [5].

[152] e.g. *Fairclough Building Ltd v Port Talbot BC* (1992) 62 B.L.R. 82; *Harmon CFEM Facades (UK) Ltd v Corporate Officer of the House of Commons* (2000) 67 Con. L.R. 1; *Natural World Products Ltd v ARC 21* [2007] NIQB 19; *Sidey Ltd v Clackmannanshire Council*, see para.2-24 fn.142 at [24]–[25]; *JBW Group Ltd v Ministry of Justice* [2012] EWCA Civ 8; [2012] 2 C.M.L.R. 10 at [61].

the contract (subject always, of course, to the usual limitations on the recovery of damages for breach of contract, such as the rules of remoteness and mitigation).[153] In a case where the contract can still be performed, and where the damages are an inadequate remedy,[154] the court might even order specific performance of the option contract to enable the beneficiary in fact to obtain the contract.[155]

The remedies available for breach of a contractual *right of pre-emption* will depend on the terms of the pre-emption, since the claimant must show that he suffered loss in consequence of the breach. If the pre-emption granted the beneficiary the right to an already-defined contract, such as the right to purchase a specific asset at an agreed or ascertainable price if (but only if[156]) the grantor chose to sell, then in the event that the grantor in breach of the pre-emption sells to a third party, the beneficiary will be able to establish his loss on normal contractual principles as that which flows from his failure to obtain the contract on the terms to which he was entitled.[157] However, if the pre-emption granted the claimant only the right to engage in negotiations, it may be more difficult to quantify the value which he has lost by being excluded from the negotiations, although where there is evidence of the terms on which the grantor of the pre-emption was prepared to sell, that will form a basis for the valuation of the contract that he has lost.[158]

We have seen that a *"lock-out" contract* does not impose a duty to negotiate, but only prohibits a party from contracting with or (depending on its terms) negotiating with third parties during a defined period. Even if the party who granted the "lock out" breaches it by, for example, engaging in negotiations with a third party, the courts will not normally issue an injunction to restrain the third-party negotiations for the period of the "lock-out" contract, since damages are said to be an adequate remedy.[159] In the context of negotiations for the sale of land, a "lock-

---

[153] Chitty, Ch.26; Furmston, Ch.8, s.B; Treitel, Ch.20; Anson, Ch.17; Cheshire, Fifoot and Furmston, pp.743–795; N. Andrews, M. Clarke, A. Tettenborn and G. Virgo, *Contractual Duties: Performance, Breach, Termination and Remedies*, 2nd edn (Sweet & Maxwell, 2017), Chs 20–26.

[154] Jones and Goodhart, pp.31–38.

[155] e.g. *Peña v Dale* [2003] EWHC 1065 (Ch); [2004] 2 B.C.L.C. 508 at [129]–[139] (specific performance of option to acquire shares in private company for which there was no ready market); *Coles v Samuel Smith Old Brewery (Tadcaster)* [2007] EWCA Civ 1461; [2008] 2 E.G.L.R. 159 (specific performance of tenant's option to purchase freehold land even where landlord had already sold to a wholly-owned subsidiary in attempt to frustrate exercise of option). There are many cases involving options to purchase land, where an additional dimension is added to the analysis by reason of the rule that the grant of an option to purchase already creates in the grantee an equitable interest in the land: see para.2-20 fn.113.

[156] It is the nature of a right of pre-emption that the beneficiary obtains only the hope of a future contract, or future negotiations for a contact, which remains entirely within the grantor's power to decide whether to initiate: see para.2-21.

[157] In the case of a pre-emption in relation to registered land, the grantee obtains not merely a contractual right but also an equitable interest in the land from the time of creation of the right of pre-emption: Land Registration Act 2002 s.115(1); the position is less clear in relation to unregistered land: Cheshire and Burn, pp.985–986; Megarry and Wade, para.15-065.

[158] In the case of a pre-emption right in relation to the sale of land where the pre-emption imposes on grantor only the obligation to sell at a price acceptable to both parties, and therefore to make an offer only at the price at which she is in fact willing to sell, then if the grantor proposes to sell by auction the price to be specified in the offer would be the intended auction reserve; or if it is a sale by private treaty the price would be the price intended to be named in the estate agent's particular, or the lower price, if any, to which the grantor is in fact prepare to descend: *Smith v Morgan*, see para.2-21 fn.124 at 808.

[159] *Tye v House* (1998) 76 P. & C.R. 188 at 190 (Evans-Lombe J, discharging ex parte injunction that he had earlier ordered).

out" contract may be used to protect the prospective purchaser from incurring substantial costs in getting ready to complete and at the last minute losing the property because the vendor elects to sell to somebody else: it has been said that in such a case the measure of damages for breach of the "lock out" would be the costs thrown away.[160] However, this does not mean that the claimant's costs will necessarily be recoverable. They may have been incurred anyway, even if the other party had fulfilled his duty not to contract with, or negotiate with, third parties during the "lock-out" period, since the claimant may still not have obtained the contract himself. The calculation of the loss that the claimant can establish as flowing from the breach of the "lock-out" contract will therefore depend upon the terms of the "lock out", and the facts as established at trial about the state of the parties' negotiations and any third-party negotiations, and in particular whether the claimant can show that he lost a real or substantial, not merely a speculative, chance of entering into the contract which he claims he lost.[161]

It may also be difficult to demonstrate that any loss flowed from the breach of a contractual *duty to consider the other party's tender* or (if it can be found) a higher duty to act fairly in considering the tender. Unless it can be shown that there is a substantial chance that the tender, if properly considered, would have led to a contract, and the value of that hypothetical contract can be ascertained, there may be no claim for substantial damages. The fact that the bidder has incurred costs in preparing the tender does not mean that they should be recoverable, since they may always have been wasted if the tender had not been accepted, and in general damages are only awarded on the basis of breach of contract for wasted expenditure if the expenditure would have been recouped had the contract been performed (or, at least, if there is no evidence that the expenditure would not have been recouped).[162]

As we have seen, the form of a so-called *letter of intent* and other similar documents will vary, and even if it contains contractually binding provisions, the content of the contractual obligations will vary.[163] Given that there may be difficulties in finding suitable general remedies for breach of other forms of pre-contractual contracts discussed above, the practical solution in using any form of contract in order to regulate pre-contractual negotiations involves the careful drafting of provisions which are appropriate to the particular negotiations, and to the remedies that one or other party might need if the negotiations fail, such as express clauses providing for the reimbursement of expenses incurred. Whether such clauses are

---

[160] *Tye v House* (1998) 76 P. & C.R. 188 at 190.

[161] *Dandara Holdings Ltd v Co-operative Retail Services Ltd* [2004] EWHC 1476 (Ch); [2004] 2 E.G.L.R. 163 at [13]–[14] (in that case, breach of the "lock-out" did not cause purchaser's loss, because there was a strong probability the vendor would have remarketed the property anyway: at [84]). In *Walford v Miles* [1990] 1 E.G.L.R. 212 at 215 the trial judge held that the "lock-out" agreement was binding, and its breach had caused the claimants to lose the opportunity of the principal contract, which it was "probable" they would have entered into. However, no assessment of damages was in fact made because CA ([1991] 2 E.G.L.R. 185) and HL ([1992] 2 A.C. 128, see para.2-22) held that there was no binding "lock-out" contract. There was a breach of a "lock-out" agreement in *Pitt v PHH Asset Management Ltd* [1994] 1 W.L.R. 327, CA, but the assessment of damages is not reported.

[162] *CCC Films (London) Ltd v Impact Quadrant Films Ltd* [1985] Q.B. 16; *Omak Maritime Ltd v Mamola Challenger Shipping Co Ltd* [2010] EWHC 2026 (Comm); [2011] 2 All E.R. (Comm) 155; Chitty, paras 26-024, 26-028; Treitel, para.20-028; Anson, pp.573–574; Burrows (Remedies), Ch.5. CA in *Blackpool and Fylde Aero Club Ltd v Blackpool BC*, see para.2-24 fn.148, did not comment on the measure of damages.

[163] See para.2-23.

characterised as part of a contractually binding "letter of intent", or are simply additional clauses within another contract such as a "lock-out" contract, is not of real significance. Matters to be considered in drafting such clauses are considered below.[164]

(3) Unjust Enrichment

Work done in anticipation of a contract Pre-contract expenditure can be incurred in various circumstances. For example, a party may incur costs—sometimes very substantial costs—in order to be able to submit a tender in response to an invitation to tender: in such a case, the cost is part of the overhead expenses of the business which the tenderer hopes will be met out of such contracts as are won in response to the tenders submitted for a range of possible contracts.[165] Or he may incur other costs during the course of the negotiations for the purpose of putting himself in a position to obtain and then perform the contract as soon as it is concluded. The party who incurs such expenditure cannot normally expect it to be reimbursed by the other party if the negotiations fail.[166] In the absence of a pre-contractual contract,[167] or evidence that the other party has committed a tort during the negotiations,[168] the expenditure is at the spending party's risk[169]: it is a gamble.[170]

2-26

However, where work is done by one party at the other party's request, or under an arrangement[171] between the parties where the other receives the benefit of work

---

[164] See para.2-33.

[165] *William Lacey (Hounslow) Ltd v Davis* [1957] 1 W.L.R. 932 at 934; *Countrywide Communications Ltd v ICL Pathway Ltd* [2000] C.L.C. 324 at 340–341; *MSM Consulting Ltd v United Republic of Tanzania* [2009] EWHC 121 (QB), (2009) 123 Con. L.R. 154 at [171].

[166] *Regalian Properties Plc v London Docklands Development Corp* [1995] 1 W.L.R. 212 at 230; *Jennings and Chapman Ltd v Woodman, Matthews & Co* [1952] 2 T.L.R. 409, CA (tenant of premises doing works at prospective sub-tenant's request took risk of whether landlord would give consent for sub-letting).

[167] See paras 2-19 to 2-25.

[168] Such as the tort of deceit which has induced the claimant, in reliance on the other party's fraudulent misrepresentation, to incur the costs which he claims: see para.2-15.

[169] See para.2-07. The reason for the break-down of the negotiations, and in particular whether it is the fault of the claimant or the defendant, may sometimes be relevant in assessing the risk: *Jennings and Chapman Ltd v Woodman, Matthews & Co*, see para.2-26 fn.166; *Countrywide Communications Ltd v ICL Pathway Ltd*, see para.2-26 fn.165, at 349; *MSM Consulting Ltd v United Republic of Tanzania*, see para.2-26 fn.165, at [177]. For criticism of the use of "fault" in this context, see Goff & Jones, para.16-15. In *Sabemo Pty Ltd v North Sydney Municipal Council* [1977] 2 N.S.W.L.R. 880 at 902–903 Sheppard J said that a negotiating party who does work beneficial for the project, which he would not expect to do gratuitously, will be entitled to compensation or restitution if the other party unilaterally decides to abandon the project not for any reason associated with bona fide disagreement concerning the terms of the contract, but for his own (however valid) reasons; but cf. *Regalian Properties Plc v London Docklands Development Corp*, see para.2-26 n.166, at 230–231 (Rattee J, not applying this to the case where the negotiations were conducted on terms that each party is free to withdraw at any time).

[170] *William Lacey (Hounslow) Ltd v Davis*, see para.2-26 fn.165, at 934; *Regalian Properties Plc v London Docklands Development Corp*, see para.2-26 fn.166, at 231.

[171] Many cases involve an express request by the defendant do undertake work, but sometimes the basis on which the work is done is an agreement between the parties which falls short of a binding contract where the courts do not analyse the cause of action in terms of work done in response to the other party's (implied) request: e.g. *Cobbe v Yeoman's Row Management Ltd* [2008] UKHL 55; [2008] 1 W.L.R. 1752 at [2], [40]–[44] (agreement between landowner and developer that developer would make and prosecute application for planning permission, with a view to development under which

done in circumstances where both understand that it is not intended to be gratuitous if the contract under negotiation does not materialise, then even if there is no (pre-contractual) contract under which the work is to be remunerated,[172] the other party may be required to pay for the work that has been done, as long as he had not made clear during the negotiations that such costs would remain at the other party's risk unless the negotiations resulted in a successfully concluded contract.[173]

2-27   **Work done pursuant to the other party's request**   If a negotiating party does work at the request of the other party, and the latter promises to pay for the work, whether by reimbursing the expenses incurred or on some other basis, there will generally be a (pre-contractual) contract covering the work and the enquiry will be simply into the terms of the contract: the scope of the work agreed to be done, and the rate at which payment is to be made.[174] Even if there is no express promise to pay for the work, the request by one party that the other undertake some specific work may be construed as carrying the implication that it is to be paid for and therefore an implied promise to pay may be found.[175] However, if such an implied promise is to form the basis of a contractual obligation, the price must be sufficiently certain.[176] A court may sometimes be able to determine the price that the parties have (impliedly) agreed, and if the parties are silent as to price the law may imply a reasonable price.[177]

---

it would obtain share in profit of development: developed entitled to quantum meruit for value of services).

[172] See para.2-27 fn.174.

[173] e.g. by a "subject to contract" condition which has not been withdrawn or waived: see para.2-08; merely asking the other party to undertake expenditure will not constitute waiver of the condition: *Regalian Properties Plc v London Docklands Development Corp*, see para.2-08 fn.166. cf. *Brewer Street Investments Ltd v Barclays Woollen Co Ltd* [1954] 1 Q.B. 428, CA (negotiations for lease were "subject to contract", but there was a binding contract (or, per Denning LJ at 436, a claim in restitution) for cost of pre-contract works executed by landlord which had been specifically requested and agreed to be paid for by prospective tenant).

[174] e.g. *Brewer Street Investments Ltd v Barclays Woollen Co Ltd*, see para.2-26 fn.173 (alterations to premises by landlord at prospective tenant's request, but lease negotiations then failed; majority held that there was a contract, based on tenant's agreement to be responsible for the cost of the alterations, although Denning LJ at 435–436 analysed the claim as one in restitution); *Laserbore Ltd v Morrison Biggs Wall Ltd* unreported 25 August 1993, QB (agreement to "reimburse ... fair and reasonable payment for all work executed and agreed under this interim arrangement" held by Official Referee to be the fair commercial rate for the services provided, using (on the facts) the reasonable rates for the work done, rather than a "cost plus" calculation); *Serck Controls Ltd v Drake & Scull Engineering Ltd* (2000) 73 Con. L.R. 100 (contract to pay "all reasonable costs incurred" construed at [36]–[39] to mean reasonable remuneration for executing the work, and not to exclude profit element and perhaps overheads).

Where parties are negotiating a long-term contract, still "subject to contract" (see para.2-08), but one party begins performing and the other pays, it is unlikely that the parties have entered into an interim contract on terms which include the terms still subject to negotiation, and the better analysis is that there is no contract but a restitutionary remedy to the extent that one party has been unjustly enriched: *Whittle Movers Ltd v Holywood Express Ltd* [2009] EWCA Civ 1189; [2009] 2 C.L.C. 771 at [14] (Waller LJ, following *British Steel Corp v Cleveland Bridge and Engineering Co Ltd*, see para.2-27 fn.180).

[175] *William Lacey (Hounslow) Ltd v Davis*, above, see para.2-26 fn.165, at 935 (but Barry J in fact decided the case on the basis of "quasi-contract"—restitution of unjust enrichment—rather than contract: see at 936).

[176] See para.3-14.

[177] Supply of Goods and Services Act 1982 s.15 (non-consumer contract for the supply of a service; consumer contracts are covered by Consumer Rights Act 2015 s.51).

Where, however, there is no contract, express or implied, governing the pre-contract work, the fact that the defendant requested the claimant to do the work may give rise to a claim for payment on the basis that the defendant would otherwise be unjustly enriched at the claimant's expense. The issue then becomes how to value the unjust enrichment of which the defendant is required to make restitution.[178] Where the work has conferred a valuable benefit on the defendant, it is within the normal principles of unjust enrichment that the defendant may be required to pay the value of that benefit.[179] There are, however, cases where the courts have not identified an objectively valuable benefit in the hands of the defendant, but have held that the fact that the claimant did work at the defendant's request, in circumstances where (although there was no contract) the work was not intended to be done gratuitously, was itself a benefit for which the defendant must pay[180] —and the benefit may be valued by the costs incurred by the claimant,[181] or the price that the defendant could reasonably have been expected to pay for the work done,[182] sometimes using evidence from the negotiations themselves as to the price where the work would have been covered by the contract price had the negotiations suc-

---

[178] For the difficulties involved in valuing the enrichment, as well as the theoretical basis of the claim, see Goff & Jones, Ch.16, esp. paras 16-02, 16-17, 16-19; A. Burrows, *The Law of Restitution* 3rd edn (Oxford University Press, 2011), pp.371–380; G. Jones, "Claims Arising Out of Anticipated Contracts Which Do Not Materialize" (1979–1980) 18 U.W. Ontario L. Rev. 447; E. McKendrick, "Work done in Anticipation of a Contract which does not Materialise" in W.R. Cornish, R. Nolan, J. O'Sullivan and G. Virgo (eds), *Restitution: Past, Present & Future* (1998), 163, and response by S. Hedley at 195; J. Edelman, "Liability in Unjust Enrichment where a Contract Fails to Materialize" in A. Burrows and E. Peel (eds), *Contract Formation and Parties* (2010), 159; J. Dietrich, "Classifying precontractual liability: a comparative analysis" (2001) 21 L.S. 153 (comparing also the German doctrine of *culpa in contrahendo*, see para.2-13).

[179] cf. *Cobbe v Yeoman's Row Management Ltd*, see para.2-26 fn.171 at [40]–[41] (property owner enriched by grant of planning permission as a result of developer's services for which it had to pay nothing, but the value of the enrichment received unjustly at the expense of the developer was not the increase in property value (which was only unlocked by the planning permission) but the value of the services received without payment).

[180] Such cases look rather more like implied contracts than restitution of an unjust enrichment: cf. *William Lacey (Hounslow) Ltd v Davis*, see para.2-26 fn.165 at 935–936 (Barry J, basing his reasoning on the old analysis of unjust enrichment as based on implied contract (quasi-contract)); cf. however, *British Steel Corp v Cleveland Bridge and Engineering Co Ltd* [1984] 1 All E.R. 504 at 509 (Goff J: "In most cases, where work is done pursuant to a request contained in a letter of intent, it will not matter whether a contract did or did not come into existence, because, if the party who has acted on the request is simply claiming payment, his claim will usually be based on a quantum meruit, and it will make no difference whether that claim is contractual or quasi-contractual. Of course, a quantum meruit claim (like the old actions for money had and received and for money paid) straddles the boundaries of what we now call contract and restitution, so the mere framing of a claim as a quantum meruit claim, or a claim for a reasonable sum, does not assist in classifying the claim as contractual or quasi contractual").

[181] *Brewer Street Investments Ltd v Barclays Woollen Co Ltd*, see para.2-26 fn.173, at 437 (Denning LJ: "the prospective tenants ought to pay all the costs thrown away. The work was done to meet their special requirements and was prima facie for their benefit and not for the benefit of the landlords"; the majority, however, held that the tenants' agreement to take responsibility for the costs created a contractual, rather than restitutionary, right of recovery of the costs incurred: see para.2-27 fn.174).

[182] *William Lacey (Hounslow) Ltd v Davis*, above, n.165 at 939; *British Steel Corp v Cleveland Bridge and Engineering Co Ltd*, see para.2-27 fn.180, at 511; *Vedatech Corp v Crystal Decisions (UK) Ltd* [2002] EWHC 818 (Ch) at [76] (Jacob J: valuation depends on position taken by parties in the failed negotiations: often a fee on the basis of time will be appropriate, but things may be different where a party provides a benefit on the express basis that he is to have a "share in the action").

ceeded and there is sufficient evidence about what price would have been finally agreed.[183]

2-28   **Unjust enrichment claim as a partial substitute for absence of a general principle of pre-contractual liability**   In *Countrywide Communications Ltd v ICL Pathway Ltd*[184] Nicholas Strauss QC recognised the difficulty in reconciling the cases in which courts have made awards on the basis of work done in anticipation of a contract where the negotiations fail, but identified the existing principles as a partial substitute for the absence of a general principle of pre-contractual liability in English law:

> "I have found it impossible to formulate a clear general principle which satisfactorily governs the different factual situations which have arisen, let alone those which could easily arise in other cases. Perhaps, in the absence of any recognition in English law of a general duty of good faith in contractual negotiations, this is not surprising. Much of the difficulty is caused by attempting to categorise as an unjust enrichment of the defendant, for which an action in restitution is available, what is really a loss unfairly sustained by the plaintiff. There is a lot to be said for a broad principle enabling either to be recompensed, but no such principle is clearly established in English law. Undoubtedly the court may impose an obligation to pay for benefits resulting from services performed in the course of a contract which is expected to, but does not, come into existence. This is so, even though, in all cases, the defendant is ex hypothesi free to withdraw from the proposed contract, whether the negotiations were expressly made 'subject to contract' or not. Undoubtedly, such an obligation will be imposed only if justice requires it or, which

---

[183]   *Way v Latilla* [1937] 3 All E.R. 759, HL, at 764 (Lord Atkin: "the court may take into account the bargainings between the parties, not with a view to completing the bargain for them, but as evidence of the value which each of them puts upon the services"); cf. *Benedetti v Sawiris* [2013] UKSC 50; [2014] A.C. 938 (value of services, for purposes of restitutionary award on basis of unjust enrichment, is normally market value of services, with possibility of defendant's subjective devaluation; but at least in relation to agreed price as being evidence of market value, the decision in *Way v Latilla* remains intact: see at [56] (Lord Clarke), [168] (Lord Neuberger)). For an argument that the claim in *Benedetti* (and similar cases) should be based on contract, rather than unjust enrichment, see P. Jaffey (2014) 77 M.L.R. 983.

[184]   See para.2-26 fn.165, at 349-350; approved by Christopher Clarke J. in *MSM Consulting Ltd v United Republic of Tanzania*, para.2-26 fn.165, at [171], adding also "(a) Although the older authorities use the language of implied contract the modern approach is to determine whether or not the circumstances are such that the law should, as a matter of justice, impose upon the defendant an obligation to make payment of an amount which the claimant deserved to be paid (quantum meruit): see *William Lacey (Hounslow) Ltd v Davis* [para.2-26 fn.165]; ... (b) Generally speaking a person who seeks to enter into a contract with another cannot claim to be paid the cost of estimating what it will cost him, or of deciding on a price, or bidding for the contract. Nor can he claim the cost of showing the other party his capability or skills even though, if there was a contract or retainer, he would be paid for them. The solicitor who enters a 'beauty contest' in the course of which he expresses some preliminary views about the client's prospects cannot, ordinarily expect to charge for them. If another firm is retained, he runs the risk of being unrewarded if unsuccessful in his pitch. (c) The court is likely to impose such an obligation where the defendant has received an incontrovertible benefit (e.g. an immediate financial gain or saving of expense) as a result of the claimant's services; or where the defendant has requested the claimant to provide services or accepted them (having the ability to refuse them) when offered, in the knowledge that the services were not intended to be given freely. (d) But the court may not regard it as just to impose an obligation to make payment if the claimant took the risk that he or she would only be reimbursed for his expenditure if there was a concluded contract; or if the court concludes that, in all the circumstances the risk should fall on the claimant: see the *Jennings and Chapman* case [para.2-26 fn.166]. (e) The court may well regard it as just to impose such an obligation if the defendant who has received the benefit has behaved unconscionably in declining to pay for it".

comes to much the same thing, if it would be unconscionable for the plaintiff not to be recompensed.

Beyond that, I do not think that it is possible to go further than to say that, in deciding whether to impose an obligation and if so its extent, the court will take into account and give appropriate weight to a number of considerations which can be identified in the authorities. The first is whether the services were of a kind which would normally be given free of charge. Secondly, the terms in which the request to perform the services was made may be important in establishing the extent of the risk (if any) which the plaintiffs may fairly be said to have taken that such services would in the end be unrecompensed. What may be important here is whether the parties are simply negotiating, expressly or impliedly 'subject to contract', or whether one party has given some kind of assurance or indication that he will not withdraw, or that he will not withdraw except in certain circumstances. Thirdly, the nature of the benefit which has resulted to the defendants is important, and in particular whether such benefit is real (either 'realised' or 'realisable') or a fiction, in the sense of Traynor C.J.'s dictum.[185] Plainly, a court will at least be more inclined to impose an obligation to pay for a real benefit, since otherwise the abortive negotiations will leave the defendant with a windfall and the plaintiff out of pocket. However, the judgment of Denning L.J. in the *Brewer Street* case[186] suggests that the performance of services requested may of itself suffice amount to a benefit or enrichment. Fourthly, what may often be decisive are the circumstances in which the anticipated contract does not materialise and in particular whether they can be said to involve 'fault' on the part of the defendant, or (perhaps of more relevance) to be outside the scope of the risk undertaken by the plaintiff at the outset. I agree with the view of Rattee J.[187] that the law should be flexible in this area, and the weight to be given to each of these factors may vary from case to case.

There is in my view considerable doubt whether an obligation can be imposed in a case in which the plaintiff has not provided a benefit of any kind, even of the 'fictional' kind discussed earlier of performing services at the request of the defendant albeit without enriching him in any real sense. Thus I doubt whether an obligation can be imposed on a contracting party to repay a plaintiff for expense incurred, reasonably or even necessarily, in anticipation of a contract which does not materialise, where this is not in the course of providing services requested by the defendant. Such an obligation would not be restitutionary, and there is no English authority which would clearly support its imposition, except perhaps in circumstances similar to those suggested in the *Humphreys Estate* and *Walton's* cases where the defendant is precluded by estoppel from deriving the existence of a binding contract.[188] If it were otherwise, there would often be a remedy, against gazumpers, against whom it could always or at least usually be said that the buyer did not take the risk of expenditure wasted through the seller's decision to withdraw, having earlier accepted an offer 'subject to contract', not for a reason connected with the negotiation of the contract, but because he had been offered more by someone else."

(4)   Equity

Breach of confidence   During the course of pre-contractual negotiations, one **2-29** party may provide information to the other that is commercially sensitive, but which

---

[185] [*Coleman Engineering Co v North American Aviation* (1966) 420 P 2d 713 at 729: "in fact the performance of services has conferred no benefit on the person requesting them, and it is pure fiction to base restitution on a benefit conferred".]

[186] [See para.2-27 fn.181.]

[187] [In *Regalian Properties Plc v London Docklands Development Corp*, see para.2-26 fn.166, at 231.]

[188] [*Attorney General of Hong Kong v Humphreys Estate (Queen's Gardens) Ltd* [1987] A.C. 114, PC; *Walton's Stores (Interstate) Ltd v Maher* (1988) 164 C.L.R. 387, HCA; but promissory estoppel has not been developed as a general remedy for the break-down of pre-contractual negotiations in English law: see para.2-30. cf., however, para.10-50.]

the recipient of the information requires in order to decide whether, or on what terms, to proceed with the negotiations and the eventual contract. For example, a party negotiating to purchase a company will need to have access to the company's financial and other records in order to assure himself that the investment is good, and to fix the price and the other terms on which he is prepared to buy. Although the seller does not have a duty to disclose information,[189] in practice disclosure of key information is often necessary if the negotiations are to proceed, although a party will be willing to disclose sensitive information only if the law provides sufficient protection against its misuse. The practical solution here, as so often in relation to potential problems that can be anticipated in the pre-contractual negotiations,[190] is for the parties to enter into a confidentiality agreement which has the force of contract, and which can define the scope of permitted use of information that is to be supplied.[191] However, in a case where the parties have not regulated this by a (pre-contractual) contract, the party providing confidential information may be protected under the general rules of equity[192] which are designed to remedy actual or threatened breach of confidence. Where a party makes (or threatens to make) unauthorised use or disclosure of information which is confidential and which he received in circumstances which imported the obligation of confidence,[193] he may be restrained by injunction from breaching the obligation, and may be required to pay damages for loss suffered by the other party, or to account for profits he himself has made, from the improper use of the information.[194]

2-30   **Promissory estoppel and proprietary estoppel**   The doctrine of estoppel may offer a potential source of remedy in equity for one negotiating party who relies on the other's representation that he will complete the contract, or on some other specific promise or representation made during the negotiations which ultimately fail. The equitable doctrine of *proprietary estoppel* may in certain circumstances give a remedy to a party who relies on the other party's representation to the effect that he has, or will acquire, an interest in the latter's land. At present, however, in English law the equitable doctrine of *promissory estoppel* has not been developed to allow a party a remedy based on his reliance on the other party's representation during the negotiations.[195]

---

[189] See para.2-10.

[190] See paras 2-32 to 2-34.

[191] For various precedents of confidentiality clauses and agreements, see *Encyclopaedia of Forms and Precedents*, 5th edn (ed. Lord Millett, LexisNexis Butterworths), Vol.12(3), *Confidentiality* (2017 reissue); and (in the context of research and development projects) Vol.32 (2016 reissue), paras [311]–[337].

[192] The duty is not based on implied contract: "It depends on the broad principle of equity that he who has received information in confidence shall not take unfair advantage of it": *Seager v Copydex Ltd* [1967] 1 W.L.R. 923, CA, at 931 (Lord Denning M.R.). For further discussion of the protection of confidential information by equity, see Snell, Ch.9.

[193] *Saltman Engineering Co Ltd v Campbell Engineering Co Ltd* (1948) 65 R.P.C. 203, CA, 213.

[194] *Peter Pan Manufacturing Corp v Corsets Silhouette Ltd* [1964] 1 W.L.R. 96 (injunction and account of profits); *Seager v Copydex Ltd* (No.2) [1969] 1 W.L.R. 809, CA (on the analogy of the quantification of loss in the tort of conversion, damages based on market value of confidential information on a sale between a willing seller and a willing buyer, and when the judgment for damages is satisfied, the information belongs to the defendant).

[195] See para.2-12 and Ch.10.

IV. CLAIMS BASED ON PRE-CONTRACTUAL MISCONDUCT WHERE THE CONTRACT IS CONCLUDED

Remedies where the negotiations succeed, rather than fail The discussion in this chapter has focused on the duties owed by one party to the other during the negotiations for a contract, and the remedies that might be available in the case where one party breaches such a duty. The typical case therefore involves losses suffered by the claimant where the negotiations fail. If, however, the negotiations succeed, and the contract is entered into, the claimant's perspective changes. His complaint is no longer the loss of the hoped-for contract, or the costs of the failed negotiations which he has wasted, but the fact that the other party's misconduct has caused him to suffer loss even though he obtained the concluded contract. The typical complaint here is that, without the defendant's misconduct, he would not in fact have entered into the contract at all, or would have entered into it on more advantageous terms. Here we enter into a different field: claims that the contract may be avoided, and/or that the claimant has a cause of action in damages for having entered into a contract of which the value is less than he paid,[196] or is less than was promised.[197] The relevant causes of action are misrepresentation, failure to disclose information which there was a legal duty to disclose, duress, undue influence and unconscionable conduct, and breach of contract (for misrepresentations incorporated into the contract). Detailed discussion of these areas—the so-called vitiating factors—must be sought elsewhere.[198]

2-31

V. PRACTICAL SOLUTIONS TO THE PROBLEMS OF THE PRE-CONTRACTUAL STAGE

Contractual solutions for the pre-contractual stage We have seen that there are a number of potential problems in the pre-contractual stage. Particularly where the negotiations may be long and complex, or where one party may incur significant costs in order to participate in the negotiations, perhaps the most general issue is whether the party can obtain sufficient certainty in relation to the management of the risk allocation of the negotiations: whether the negotiations will be pursued by the other party with sufficient vigour to merit incurring pre-contract expenditure, as well as spending time and effort, and what the risks may be of the negotiations collapsing even at a very late stage before the contract was going to be concluded.

2-32

---

[196] Tort-measure damages, designed to compensate the loss suffered by the claimant by reason of the tort, e.g. his reliance on the defendant's fraudulent or negligent misrepresentation in entering into the contract: Cartwright (Misrepresentation), para.2-09. Where the contract is concluded, there is also a special statutory cause of action under Misrepresentation Act 1967 s.2(1) for loss caused by a precontractual misrepresentation where the defendant cannot prove that he honestly and on reasonable grounds believed his (mis)representation, an action which is in practice more advantageous for a claimant than an action in either fraud or negligence: Cartwright (Misrepresentation), para.7-47.

[197] Contract-measure damages, designed to compensate the loss suffered by the claimant by reason of the fact that the contract has not been performed, e.g. where during the negotiations the defendant made a representation which he then warranted in the contract to be true: Cartwright (Misrepresentation), para.2-08.

[198] Cartwright (Misrepresentation), Pts 1 (misrepresentation) and 3 (non-disclosure); N. Enonchong, *Duress, Undue Influence and Unconscionable Dealing*, 2nd edn (Sweet & Maxwell, 2012); Chitty, Chs 7 and 8; Treitel, Chs 9 and 10; Anson, Chs 9 and 10. A claimant may sometimes seek to establish that the contract is void for mistake, but this does not rest on his showing any pre-contractual misconduct by the defendant: Cartwright (Misrepresentation), Pt 2; Chitty, Chs 3 and 6; Treitel, Ch.8; Anson Ch.8.

There are issues about access to sufficient information from the other party in order to make a proper assessment of the proposed contract, as well as whether the other party will respect the confidential nature of information that the negotiating party must himself provide in order to take part seriously in seeking to obtain the contract. Given that the starting-point in English law is that each party is free to act in his own interest during the negotiations as long as he does not make misrepresentations,[199] and that in consequence each party generally bears the risk of the breakdown of the negotiations, some of these issues can be covered only by express contractual provision in the form of a pre-contractual contract. A party has no implied duty not to undertake parallel negotiations with third parties, and has no duty to maintain an offer even if he has expressed it to be firm and open for acceptance for a defined period, so we have seen that a negotiating party wishing to guard against these risks needs to secure a lock-out contract,[200] or the grant of an option.[201] Even where there are general rules of law which can sometimes provide a solution in relation to other risks of the negotiations—such as the rules of unjust enrichment which may sometimes allow a negotiating party to obtain a sum to cover expenses he has incurred or the value of a benefit he has conferred on the other party,[202] and the equitable rules governing confidentiality,[203] or where the courts may sometimes be able to find a solution by implying a (pre-contractual) contract[204] —a specific contractual provision governing such matters is still preferable, not only because the (pre-contractual) contract can reduce argument about the basis of any such claim by providing in clear terms for the circumstances in which duties are to arise and the remedies which may be available for their breach, but also because the whole range of risks that the parties may need to cover in relation to the negotiations and their break-down can be brought together in a single document. To expect parties negotiating for a contract always to enter into a fully thought-through pre-contractual contract designed to manage all the relevant risks is of course unrealistic. The very nature of negotiations is that they may start tentatively and without the parties yet wishing to formalise their discussions, and at a later stage they may already have advanced too far before the parties are in a position to take steps to manage the risk allocation expressly. However, such a pre-contractual allocation of the negotiation risks by contract is clearly desirable where it is possible, and from the outset of negotiations, particularly complex contractual negotiations, it is therefore important to bear in mind the range of provisions that may be included in a pre-contractual contract.

2-33   **Provisions to be considered in drafting pre-contractual contracts** No contractual term can validly require a party to engage in negotiations,[205] nor to negotiate in good faith, nor even to use his best (or reasonable) endeavours to enter into a contract with the other party.[206] A contract may, however, prohibit a party from entering into a contract with a third party, or from negotiating with a third party,

---

[199] *Walford v Miles* [1992] 2 A.C. 128, HL, at 138; see para.2-04.
[200] See para.2-22.
[201] See para.2-20.
[202] See paras 2-26 to 2-28.
[203] See para.2-29.
[204] e.g. in the case of a tender process contract: see para.2-24.
[205] See para.2-05.
[206] See para.2-06.

as long as the time period of the "lock out" is sufficiently certain.[207] And a contract may provide that an offer is to be kept open for a particular period (an option)[208] or that the other party shall have the right of first refusal to enter into, or at least to negotiate, a contract in particular circumstances (a pre-emption).[209] However, given that such obligations are essentially one-sided in nature, it must be remembered that if the "lock-out", option or pre-emption contract is not executed as a deed it must be supported by consideration if it is to be contractually binding.[210]

The provisions which need to be considered carefully in drafting pre-contractual contracts also include those which are designed to protect one party against suffering losses by reason of the fact that the negotiations do not result in a concluded contract. Whether they take the form a separate agreement (often referred to as a "letter of intent"[211]) relating to the costs incurred in beginning work before the contract has been finalised, or as part of another provision such as a "lock-out" contract, terms may govern the financial consequences of the negotiations breaking down.[212] Taking, however, the general case of an agreement which is designed to make contractual provision to allow one party to undertake pre-contract work in the confidence that the costs of doing so will not be thrown away if the negotiations do not succeed, the following provisions certainly need to be considered:

(1) *The work to be done.* The contract should specify the work which the party is being asked to undertake, and this may be done by reference to the proposed plan of work for the contract which is still under final negotiation, if there is already sufficient detail to provide certainty of terms in the pre-contractual contract. The fact that there is a contractual duty to perform will allow the implication of duties relating to standard of work,[213] but this opens up the possibility of later dispute which can be reduced if the required standards can also be set out in the contract; again, this may sometimes be done by reference to the draft final contract itself.

(2) *Calculation of the payment.* The appropriate mechanism for calculating the payment due for the work to be done will vary from one contract to another. It might be set by reference to the proposed payment arrangements of the draft final contract; or by some other specific criterion such as the cost incurred by the party doing the work. The scope of the payments may be defined by reference to a standard of "reasonableness"—such as the

---

[207] See para.2-22.

[208] See para.2-20.

[209] See para.2-21.

[210] See para.7-18.

[211] See para.2-23.

[212] In the case of a lock-out agreement there can be difficulties in showing the losses caused by breach of the agreement: see para.2-25. The terms of the agreement may seek to address this by impose liability on the party in breach for the other party's wasted expenditure, or by using a liquidated damages clause relating to the costs and expenses which are genuinely estimated at the time of the lock-out contract to be likely to be wasted in the event of breach: R. Christou, *Boilerplate: Practical Clauses*, 7th edn (Sweet & Maxwell, 2015), para.3-024, although care must be taken to ensure that this is an (enforceable) liquidated damages clause rather than an (unenforceable) penalty clause: Chitty, 2nd supplement (2017), paras 26-178 to 26-216M (revised to take into account the significant developments made by *Cavendish Square Holding BV v Makdessi, ParkingEye Ltd v Beavis* [2015] UKSC 67; [2016] A.C. 1172; Anson, pp.598–604. See also Treitel, paras 20-129 to 20-146 (not yet, however, including discussion of the *Cavendish Square Holding* case).

[213] *Laserbore Ltd v Morrison Biggs Wall Ltd*, see para.2-27 fn.174.

"reasonable costs incurred",[214] or a "reasonable price" for the work done—which is sufficiently certain for a court to enforce,[215] although such a formulation is not without problems since a court may have some difficulty in determining what constitutes a reasonable price for pre-contract works where the final risk allocation of the contract is not yet settled.[216] It is, however, important to ensure that the contract makes provision for the price to be paid: although, if it is clear that the work is to be done under a (pre-contractual) contract, the court would imply and determine a reasonable price, there is a risk that the request for work to be done, without it being clear that there is a contractual undertaking to pay for it, will give rise to a restitutionary quantum meruit in which there is less certainty about how a court will quantify the sum (if any) to be paid.[217]

(3) *Conditions attached to payment.* The agreement may attach conditions to the scope of the payment due, or the circumstances in which it is to be payable. For example, there may be limit on the total sum payable.[218] Or the payment may be due only if the failure of negotiations for the principal contract cannot be attributed to the party undertaking the work.[219]

(4) *Relationship to the final contract.* If the negotiations are successful and the final contract is later entered into, work done and payments made in advance of the contract may be treated retrospectively as having been done and paid under the final contract. Such an intention may be implied,[220] but it is better that the parties (if they so intend) make express provision in the pre-contractual contract under which the pre-contract work is to be done, since such a provision avoids any argument about whether pre-contract performance which does not in fact comply with the terms of the final contract constitutes a breach of contract, or militates against the implication of an agreement as to retrospective effect.[221]

---

[214] However, in *Serck Controls Ltd v Drake & Scull Engineering Ltd* (2000) 73 Con. L.R. 100 at [36]–[39] H.H. Judge Hicks QC construed a contract to pay "all reasonable costs incurred" to mean reasonable remuneration for executing the work, and not to exclude profit element and perhaps overheads.

[215] If the contract provides for services to be performed, but is silent as to the price to be paid, a "reasonable charge" will be implied, and what is a reasonable charge is a question of fact: Supply of Goods and Services Act 1982 s.15(1), (2) (non-consumer contract for the supply of a service; consumer contracts are covered by Consumer Rights Act 2015 s.51).

[216] *Laserbore Ltd v Morrison Biggs Wall Ltd*, see para.2-27 fn.174 (H.H. Judge Bowsher: "The allocation of the risk is simply a matter of negotiation and the price would normally be adjusted accordingly, also as a matter of negotiation. In considering the implication of terms, it must be borne in mind that there is no reason why it is more fair that the risk should be borne by one party rather than the other. The same consideration makes it particularly difficult to assess fair and reasonable remuneration").

[217] See para.2-27.

[218] A limit may have the effect of encouraging the parties to finalise the negotiations, particularly in the case of a broad scope of work; there is otherwise a risk that the party who has the right to perform and be paid under the pre-contractual contract will simply do that rather than completing the contractual negotiations.

[219] *Serck Controls Ltd v Drake & Scull Engineering Ltd*, see para.2-33 fn.214: "In the event that we are unable to agree satisfactory terms and conditions in respect of the overall package, we would undertake to reimburse you with all reasonable costs incurred, *provided that any failure/default can reasonably be construed as being on our part*".

[220] *Trollope & Colls Ltd v Atomic Power Constructions Ltd* [1963] 1 W.L.R. 333.

[221] *Trollope & Colls Ltd v Atomic Power Constructions Ltd* [1963] 1 W.L.R. 333 at 340.

(5) *Provision for termination of the (pre-contractual) contract.* Since the work is being undertaking pending the conclusion of the negotiations, it may become clear during the course of the work that the negotiations will not succeed. The party who has asked for the work to be done may need a wide freedom to decide whether to call off the work; and supplementary provisions may also be needed, such as the right to require the other party to vacate the premises in a case where the pre-contract works have involved entry to land. Provisions defining payments that will be due for work already done by the time of termination must be drafted carefully.[222]

Such provisions should be set out expressly: if there is an agreement to pay for preliminary works which are to be carried pending the conclusion of the negotiations for the principal contract, it is likely to constitute only a separate, simple contract which will not incorporate terms (such as limitations on liability) that are still in the course of negotiation for the principal contract.[223]

A pre-contractual contract is not a substitute for the finally negotiated   2-34
contract Although a well-drawn pre-contractual contract may offer good protection to the parties in relation to the risks involved in the negotiations, and in particular where one or both parties need to begin to incur expenses in preparation for, or even in the performance of, the intended final contract, it should always be remembered that the pre-contractual contract is no substitute for the finally negotiated contract. There may be a temptation, once work begins under a pre-contractual contract, to allow a significant portion—or even the whole—of the intended work to be done under its terms. However, this may leave gaps in the protections for one or other party that would probably have been negotiated into the final contract, such as where a building project proceeds under the terms of a series of pre-contractual contracts which, given their short-term nature, do not contain a provision for liquidated damages for delay in the final completion of the project.[224] Discussing the dangers of the (very common) use of letters of intent in the construction industry, His Honour Judge Peter Coulson QC said[225]:

> "letters of intent are used unthinkingly in the UK construction industry, and ... they can create many more problems than they solve. In my view, the principal problem with letters of intent is a practical one: once they have been sent, and the contractor has started work pursuant to that letter of intent, all those involved, including the professional team, can easily take their eye off the ball and forget about the importance of ensuring that the full contract documents are signed as quickly as possible. Everybody is then so busy dealing with the day-to-day problems being thrown up by the commencement of the works themselves that the task of signing off an often complicated set of contract documents is relegated to an item of secondary importance. Then, very often, something goes wrong on site and, in the absence of a full contract to regulate the parties' rights and obligations in such circumstances, the result is confusion and acrimony."

---

[222] cf. *Almacantar (Centre Point) Ltd v Sir Robert McAlpine Ltd* [2018] EWHC 232 (TCC).

[223] *Arcadis Consulting (UK) Ltd v AMEC (BSC) Ltd* [2016] EWHC 2509 (TCC); (2016) 169 Con. L.R. 41.

[224] *Trustees of Ampleforth Abbey Trust v Turner & Townsend Project Management Ltd* [2012] EWHC 2137 (TCC); (2012) 144 Con. L.R. 115 (construction project manager liable to owner for breach of its duty of reasonable skill and care in failing to take sufficient steps to ensure that the final contract was concluded).

[225] *Cunningham v Collett and Farmer* [2006] EWHC 1771 (TCC); (2006) 113 Con. L.R. 142 at [88]. See also para.2-23.

VI. NEGOTIATIONS FOR THE VARIATION OF AN EXISTING CONTRACT

2-35 **The starting point: the rules governing pre-contractual negotiations apply to negotiations for the variation of a contract** The variation of an existing contract by agreement of the parties, whether it supersedes the initial contract (e.g. by novation) or simply modifies one or more terms of the contract, must satisfy the same rules as are set for the formation of the initial contract, at least if the varied contract is to have the same binding force as the initial contract.[226] The starting-point for the negotiations for the variation of an existing contract is therefore the same as the negotiations for the initial contract: there is no general duty between the parties to negotiate the variation "in good faith" and the parties are in principle free to act in their own individual interests in the negotiations,[227] subject, of course, to the general law which might impose liability by reason of their conduct during the negotiations, such as misrepresentation or breach of confidence.[228]

2-36 **The difference: an existing (contractual) relationship, which may have already been partly performed** The variation of an existing contract is, however, significantly different from the formation *de novo* of a contractual relationship between two parties. In the latter case, there is not yet a legal relationship between the parties which can frame a duty in relation to the conduct of the negotiations[229]; but where there is a *re*-negotiation of an *existing* context, the variation is to be made within the context of the existing (contractual) relationship. This does not in itself impose a duty of conduct in the (re-)negotiations: in English law,[230] no duty is implied by law into all contracts to perform the contract in good faith, although in some contracts such a duty may be implied on the facts,[231] and therefore might act as the framework for a more particularised duty in relation to the (re-)negotiations where the circumstances require the parties to agree the variation of one or more terms in order to make its continued performance workable. However, the courts have not yet developed even this limited context in which a duty to renegotiate in good faith might be found.

There may, however, be a clause in the initial contract which imposes an express duty to renegotiate in defined circumstances. It is in such contexts that the courts have shown themselves most keen to give effect to the duty, drawing on two strands of argument: first, that it would frustrate the clearly-expressed intentions of the parties if the clause cannot be enforced[232]; and secondly, that where the contract has

---

[226] See para.1-02.
[227] cf. para.2-04.
[228] cf. paras 2-14, 2-29.
[229] cf. para.2-03.
[230] Civil law systems commonly recognise duties to perform contracts in good faith: e.g. France: c.civ. art.1104; Germany: BGB §242 (obligations, including contracts). This is not, however, limited to the civil law systems: e.g. in the United States, see UCC §1–304.
[231] *Yam Seng Pte Ltd v International Trade Corp Ltd* [2013] EWHC 111 (QB); [2013] 1 C.L.C. 662 at [134]–[142] (Leggatt J). This has not been universally welcomed, but cf. *Al Nehayan v Kent* [2018] EWHC 333 (Comm) at [168] (Leggatt LJ: "Although the observations that I made in the *Yam Seng* case about the scope for implying duties of good faith in English contract law have provoked divergent reactions, there appears to be growing recognition that such a duty may readily be implied in a relational contract").
[232] *Petromec Inc v Petroleo Brasileiro SA* [2005] EWCA Civ 891; [2006] 1 Lloyd's Rep. 121 at [121] (Longmore LJ: "It would be a strong thing to declare unenforceable a clause into which the parties have deliberately and expressly entered"); followed in *Secretary of State for Defence v Turner Estate*

already been partly performed, the courts should strive to uphold it.[233] This does not result in a different view of the technical obstacle to giving a sufficiently certain legal meaning to a duty to negotiate "in good faith": the Court of Appeal[234] has said that, in giving effect to an express duty to renegotiate in good faith, as much as in the case of initial negotiations for a contract, it is bound by the decision of the House of Lords in *Walford v Miles*.[235] But in their interpretation of such a duty, the courts have often readily found an objective meaning which they have been able to enforce, particularly where the duty to re-negotiate is included in a clause which provides a mechanism for settling the terms if the negotiations break down, or by construing the clause as itself providing objective criteria which the court can apply (such as a "reasonable" price in a clause for the renegotiation of the price).[236]

Solutions Ltd [2015] EWHC 1150 (TCC); [2015] B.L.R. 448 at [104].

[233] *Mamidoil-Jetoil Greek Petroleum Co. SA v Okta Crude Oil Refinery AD* [2001] EWCA Civ 406; [2001] 2 Lloyd's Rep. 76 at [69] (Rix LJ: "Particularly in the case of contracts for future performance over a period, where the parties may desire or need to leave matters to be adjusted in the working out of their contract, the Courts will assist the parties to do so, so as to preserve rather than destroy bargains, on the basis that what can be made certain is itself certain. Certum est quod certum reddi potest. This is particularly the case where one party has either already had the advantage of some performance which reflects the parties' agreement on a long term relationship, or has had to make an investment premised on that agreement"); *Associated British Ports v Tata Steel (UK) Ltd* [2017] EWHC 694 (Ch); [2017] 2 Lloyd's Rep. 11 at [34].

[234] *Petromec Inc v Petroleo Brasileiro SA*, [2005] EWCA Civ 891; [2006] 1 Lloyd's Rep. 121 at [120]. cf. *Knatchbull-Hugessen v SISU Capital Ltd* [2014] EWHC 1194 (QB) at [23] (Leggatt J), quoted at para.2-06 fn.27, which goes too far on the current authorities.

[235] [1992] 2 A.C. 128, HL, at 138; see paras.2-04 to para.2-05.

[236] cf. the examples (some involving initial negotiation, others re-negotiation) given at para.2-06 fnn.28, 29; and paras 3-14, 3-16.

CHAPTER 3

FINDING THE AGREEMENT[1]

I.   THE MEANING OF "AGREEMENT"

"Agreement" at the core of contract   One common and very natural way of   **3-01**
viewing a contract is as an agreement which has the force of law. The derivation
of the word "contract", and its common usage even outside the technical context
of the English private law of obligations, carries the idea of the parties coming
together in a mutual und(1862) 11 C.B. (N.S.) 869; 142 E.R. 1037.erstanding or
agreement.[2] However, even if we take as a starting-point[3] the proposition that a
contract is based on the agreement of the parties, and that the formation of a contract
therefore requires an agreement between the parties to that contract, a range of questions emerge which have to be answered in order to understand the true context in
which English lawyers can properly describe a contract as an agreement. Most obvious, perhaps, is the question what is meant by "agreement": are we referring to a
subjective meeting of the minds of the parties, or is the existence and scope of the
parties' agreement to be tested from some other, *objective* perspective? Indeed, how
does the use of the language of "agreement", and its subjective or objective
interpretation, impact on the proposition that a party, by entering into a contract,
"intends" to be bound: what is the role of *intention* in the formation of a contract?
Moreover, even if we accept that there must be an agreement between the parties
in order to find a contact, what must they have agreed about? In other words, what
rules does the law set as to the *minimum content* of an agreement in order for it to

---

[1]   Chitty, Ch.2; Furmston, Ch.2, s.C; Treitel, Chs 2, 4; Anson, Ch.2; Cheshire, Fifoot and Furmston,
      Chs 3, 5; Furmston & Tolhurst, Chs 1–6; Burrows (Restatement) ss.7, 9, 10; Andrews, arts 2, 13-
      29, 31, 39-43.
[2]   OED Online, March 2018, "contract, n.": "1.a. A mutual agreement between two or more parties that
      something shall be done or forborne by one or both; a compact, covenant, bargain; *esp.* such as has
      legal effects …; a convention between states". "Contract" derives from Latin verb *contrahere* ("to
      draw or bring several objects together, to collect, assemble"; used also in Roman law to mean "to
      make a contact, conclude a bargain, to contract": C.T. Lewis and C. Short, *A Latin Dictionary*
      (Oxford University Press, 1879), "contraho". *The Oxford Latin Dictionary*, 2nd edn (Oxford
      University Press, 2012) gives as the specialist legal meanings of "contraho" "To establish or enter
      into (any formal relationship, e.g. between husband and wife, creditor and debtor) by mutual agree-
      ment … to enter into an agreement or contract, do business, have dealings (with)".
[3]   For an alternative analysis of contract as a set of enforceable *promises*, and for the case where a bind-
      ing unilateral obligation can come into existence through being made in the form of a deed, without
      the agreement of the other party, see para.1-03 and para.7-02.

be recognised as a binding contract? These questions will be considered in this section of this chapter, before we move on to consider in detail the practical analysis of the formation of the contract through the analysis of the parties' communications.

(1) Subjective and Objective Tests of Agreement

3-02 **"Subjective" and "objective" agreement** To say that two persons are in agreement might normally suggest that their actual understandings correspond: they are subjectively in agreement. However, given that the evidence for the existence of the agreement will be based at least partly on what the parties said or did at or before the moment when they came to their agreement, a court in making a legal determination which requires proof of the existence of the agreement will inevitably have to consider and interpret the external signs of the alleged agreement. If the court uses the external (objective) evidence only for the purpose of corroborating or disproving the parties' assertions about whether they (subjectively) agreed, the test itself may still be subjective—the search for the parties' actual shared understanding. However, the law may take a different approach, and define the existence and content of the agreement as that which is established by the external evidence. On such a test—an objective test—a person is in law taken to agree not what he intended to agree, but what his words or conduct show that he agreed, even if the court knows that his subjective understanding was in fact different. As we shall see, English law generally rejects a subjective test of agreement, and prefers an objective test for the purpose of establishing whether a contract has been formed, and what terms are contained within the contract. However, some issues are not entirely settled in this area.

3-03 **"Subjective" agreement** A subjective test for the existence of a sufficient agreement to form a contract would require both parties in fact to share the same understanding about the existence and terms of the contract: there would be no contract unless both parties in fact had that same understanding; or, as it is sometimes put, a mistake by either party about the terms of the contract prevents the formation of the contract.[4] Some legal systems adopt this subjective understanding of the notion of "agreement" as their underlying principle in contact law, generally basing their contract law theory on the proposition that a contractual obligation is undertaken voluntarily, and therefore the subjective will of the party should be its defining characteristic.[5] However, a subjective test of agreement in the forma-

---

[4] Mistake is a subjective matter: Cartwright (Misrepresentation), para.12-03. Apart from the case where there is a written document, agreed to (and, typically, signed) by both parties, which one party claims does not in fact reflect what he understood the agreement to be, it is generally rather difficult to refer to a party being mistaken about the terms of the contract: to speak of the "terms of the contract" presupposes the existence of a contract, but if the parties were not in fact in agreement, then there was no contract at all: Cartwright (Misrepresentation), para.13-02. The topics discussed in this section belong in the discussion of the formation of a contract, but are also often considered in relation to the (separate) topic of mistake: see e.g. Cartwright (Misrepresentation), Ch.13 (but see para.13-02); Furmston, Ch.4, s.C; Treitel, Ch.8 (but see para.8-054); Anson Ch.8 (but see p.272); Cheshire, Fifoot and Furmston, Ch.8 (but see p.297); cf. Chitty, Ch.3 (and note paras 3-001 to 3-003); R. Brownsword, *Smith & Thomas: A Casebook on Contract*, 13th edn (Sweet & Maxwell, 2015), Ch.5; E. McKendrick, *Contract Law*, 12th edn (Palgrave Macmillan, 2017), Ch.4; S.A. Smith, *Atiyah's Introduction to the Law of Contract*, 6th edn (Clarendon Press, 2006), pp.76–85.

[5] e.g. French law: see Cartwright (Misrepresentation), para.12-13 fn.37.

tion of a contract presents not only practical difficulties of proof of the parties' subjective states of mind, but also poses a threat to the security of contracts: to allow a party to escape an apparent contract because in fact he misunderstood the terms intended by the other party would deprive the other party of a contract even where the latter reasonably—objectively—believed that there was an agreement[6]; and the very existence of a general subjective test gives rise to the risk that individual contracts may be more difficult to establish and so such a test might be said to pose a threat to security of contract generally.[7] For such reasons, English law rejects the subjective test for the formation of a contract, and adopts a form of objective test. However, it should be noted that the rejection of the subjective test does not require the court to ignore the parties' subjective agreement if it can in fact be established. Although a subjective agreement between the parties about the existence and terms of their intended contract is not *necessary* in order to find a contract, it should at least be *sufficient*.[8] If this is not so, the operation of the objective test will have the effect of overriding the actual shared intentions of the contracting parties. Some statements by the courts in recent cases express this rather extreme position, but they do not appear to have considered the case where there is in fact a subjective agreement between the parties.[9]

"Objective" agreement   An objective test for the existence of a sufficient agreement to form a contract considers not what the parties actually intended but what the outward signs of their words and conduct demonstrates about their intentions; and traditionally English law tests objective standards by reference to the interpretation that would be given by the "reasonable man".[10] In the context of the formation of a contract, therefore, English law generally asks whether a reasonable person would conclude that the parties had agreed with each other. However, such a simple formulation is deceptive and hides a number of questions which must be borne in mind when constructing and applying the proper objective test of formation of the contract. These questions are considered in outline in the following paragraphs.[11]
3-04

(2)   Objectivity within English Contract Law

What perspective should the reasonable man have?   The (notional) reasonable man uses evidence of the parties' intentions, such as what the parties said and did, in order to determine whether they were in agreement. His conclusion, however, will depend at least in part on what evidence he is allowed to see: is it only that which passed between the parties? Or may he also take into account, for example, evidence of what one of the parties said to a third party, which casts light on what that party can be taken (objectively) to have been thinking? There have
3-05

---

6   Cartwright (Misrepresentation), para.12-15.
7   Cartwright (Misrepresentation), para.12-14.
8   Cartwright (Misrepresentation), para.13-10.
9   See para.3-06.
10   A hypothetical construct, used in many areas of English law simply to describe an objective standard expected in relation to some particular rule of law: the "reasonable man" of contract law is not necessarily the same anthropomorphised concept as the "reasonable man" of tort law or criminal law: cf. *R. v Smith* [2001] 1 A.C. 146, HL, at 188; J. Cartwright, "The Fiction of the 'Reasonable Man'" in A.G. Castermans and others (eds), *Ex libris Hans Nieuwenhuis* (Deventer: Kluwer, 2009), p.142.
11   For more detailed discussion, see Cartwright (Misrepresentation), Ch.13.

been suggestions in some cases[12] that the perspective should be that of a wholly external observer, apparently not limiting the relevant materials to those which passed between the parties. However, this has not been adopted as the general approach[13] —and in principle one would expect that only the communications between the parties should be relevant, or at least only the words and conduct of one party which could be heard or seen by the other party. An "agreement" is not just a coincidence of ideas, but requires a sharing of those ideas and an appreciation by each party that they understand each other.[14] This is a reason, no doubt, that the normal mechanism for finding a contractual agreement is through the analysis of the successive communications which passed between the parties, until it can be shown that one party accepted the offer of the other.[15] The search for the existence and meaning of the agreement should therefore normally be based on the interpretation of those communications; and, indeed, it could be said that the purpose of the objective test is to serve as a tool to interpret the communications passing between the parties during the formation of the contract.[16] As stated by Slade LJ[17]:

"It is a well-established principle of the English law of contract that an offer falls to be interpreted not subjectively by reference to what has actually passed through the mind of

---

12 Lord Denning was a particular proponent of this view: e.g. *Solle v Butcher* [1950] 1 K.B. 671, CA, at 691; *Frederick E Rose (London) Ltd v William H Pim Jnr & Co Ltd* [1953] 2 Q.B. 450, CA, at 460; *Oscar Chess Ltd v Williams* [1957] 1 W.L.R. 370, CA, at 373–374. In *Gibson v Manchester City Council* [1978] 1 W.L.R. 520, CA, at 523–524, Lord Denning took into account the fact that the Council put the house on its (internal) list of owner-owned houses, and that Mr Gibson did work on the house, as part of the evidence that there was a concluded contract of sale; the case was reversed by HL on the basis that there was no complete offer and acceptance: [1979] 1 W.L.R. 294; see para.3-24. The "detached" objective view was also supported by W. Howarth, "The Meaning of Objectivity in Contract" (1984) 100 L.Q.R. 265; (1987) 103 L.Q.R. 527.

13 For criticism of Howarth (see para.3-05 fn.12), see J.P. Vorster, "A Comment on the Meaning of Objectivity in Contract" (1987) 104 L.Q.R. 274. In *RTS Flexible Systems Ltd v Molkerei Alois Müller GmbH & Co KG* [2010] UKSC 14; [2010] 1 W.L.R. 753 at [45] SC made clear that the test is not subjective but objective, based on a consideration of the parties' communications; the distinction between detached and party-relative objectivity was not explored, but the application at [86], [87] assumes that the test is what a reasonable honest businessmen in the parties' positions would have concluded. For the approach generally adopted (outside the context of written contracts) see para.3-07.

14 Cross-offers therefore do not make a contract: *Tinn v Hoffman & Co* (1873) 29 L.T. 271 at 277; see para.3-35. Similarly, communications to third parties of which the other party is not aware should normally be irrelevant: *Wood v Scarth* (1858) 1 F. & F. 293, 175 E.R. 733 (communication by party to his own agent, not to the other party); *Felthouse v Bindley* (1862) 11 C.B. N.S. 869 at 876, 142 E.R. 1037 at 1040, see para.3-40 (communication to auctioneer). Silence is not normally sufficient, because it does not communicate an objectively ascertainable meaning: *Allied Marine Transport Ltd v Vale do Rio Doce Navegacao SA (The Leonidas D)* [1985] 1 W.L.R. 925, CA, at 941; see para.3-39.

15 See para.3-19.

16 J.R. Spencer, "Signature, Consent, and the Rule in L'Estrange v Graucob" [1973] C.L.J. 104, 106; Cartwright (Misrepresentation), para.13-11.

17 *Centrovincial Estates Plc v Merchant Investors Assurance Co Ltd* [1983] Com. L.R. 158 at 158; *Harvela Investments Ltd v Royal Trust Company of Canada (CI) Ltd* [1986] 1 A.C. 207, HL, at 225 (Lord Diplock: in unilateral contract, construction of obligation depends on what the words used by promisor would reasonably convey to promisee). In the case of an offer addressed to the public the question is how the public would understand it: "How would an ordinary person reading this document construe it?": *Carlill v Carbolic Smoke Ball Co* [1893] 1 Q.B. 256, CA, at 266 (Bowen LJ). The application of the objective test to interpret the parties' communications presupposes that there is sufficient evidence of what the parties in fact said: *Hadley v Kemp* [1999] E.M.L.R. 589 at 621–623.

the offeror, but objectively, by reference to the interpretation which a reasonable man in the shoes of the offeree would place on the offer."

Is the test wholly objective?   At least in the case where the enquiry is as to **3-06** whether the parties' discussions have led to a sufficient agreement to form a contract,[18] the test is not wholly objective. In the first place, if the parties are both in fact in (subjective) agreement on the existence and terms of the contract, then the court ought to hold the contract to have been concluded on those terms: the objective test ought not to be used to override what has in fact been agreed by both parties, but is to be used in the case where there is no subjective agreement but one party might be held to have (objectively) agreed with the other.[19] Secondly, the courts do not ask how a detached third party observer would interpret the communications, but how a reasonable person in the position of the party receiving the communication would interpret it: there is therefore a party-oriented perspective to the application of the objective test.[20] But the courts go further and ask not only how a reasonable person would have interpreted a communication, but how the recipient *in fact* understood it: that is, there is a subjective element to the test. So where one party is claiming that there is a contract on terms [x], and this is denied by the other party, the claimant can succeed only if (a) a reasonable person would have thought that the defendant was agreeing to a contract on terms [x], and (b) the claimant in fact (subjectively) so thought. This was made clear by Blackburn J in *Smith v Hughes*[21]:

> "if one of the parties intends to make a contract on one set of terms, and the other intends to make a contract on another set of terms, or, as it is sometimes expressed, if the parties are not ad idem, there is no contract, unless the circumstances are such as to preclude one of the parties from denying that he has agreed to the terms of the other. The rule of law is that stated in *Freeman v Cooke*.[22] If, whatever a man's real intention may be, he so conducts himself that a reasonable man would believe that he was assenting to the terms proposed by the other party, and that other party *upon that belief* enters into the contract with him, the man thus conducting himself would be equally bound as if he had intended to agree to the other party's terms."

---

[18] For the separate case where the question is how to interpret a written contract to which both parties have given their assent, see para.3-08.

[19] Cartwright (Misrepresentation), para.13-10 and authorities discussed there; Vorster, see para.3-05 fn.13; Chitty, para.3-014. There are, however, a few cases and dicta against this: *Upton-on-Severn Rural DC v Powell* [1942] 1 All E.R. 220, CA (neither party thought that there was a contract, but CA held that they must have intended to form a contract; however, this might be better explained as a case of restitution: *William Lacey (Hounslow) Ltd v Davis* [1957] 1 W.L.R. 932 at 938–939; J.R. Spencer [1973] C.L.J. 104, 111–112); *Furness Withy (Australia) Pty Ltd v Metal Distributors (UK) Ltd (The Amazonia)* [1990] 1 Lloyd's Rep. 236, CA, at 243 (Staughton LJ: "If the parties' correspondence and conduct shows ... an intention [to make a contract] it will not, or may not, matter that neither privately intended to make a contract"). cf. *RTS Flexible Systems Ltd v Molkerei Alois Müller GmbH & Co KG*, see para.3-05 fn.13, at [45] (contract "depends not upon [the parties'] subjective state of mind" but an objective consideration of their communications and conduct; but the point discussed here was not considered).

[20] See para.3-05.

[21] (1871) L.R. 6 Q.B. 597 at 607 (emphasis added). See also *Paal Wilson & Co A/S v Partenreederei Hannah Blumenthal (The Hannah Blumenthal)* [1983] 1 A.C. 854, HL, at 924 (Lord Brightman: "The test in my opinion is not wholly objective").

[22] (1848) 2 Exch. 654 at 663, 154 E.R. 652 at 656.

3-07 **The test used in interpreting communications between the parties** Under the test as applied in English law,[23] a party can therefore only enforce a contract—can only establish that the parties came to an "agreement" which forms the basis of a contract—on terms which he himself in fact at the time understood to have been agreed; and as long as his understanding would have been shared by a reasonable person in his position. It should be noted that the misunderstanding between the parties may be so great that each of them misinterpreted the other's communications, and in such a way that each was (from his own perspective) equally reasonable. In an extreme case of this kind there is no contract, because the lack of subjective agreement cannot be resolved by the objective test in favour of one or other of the parties.[24]

3-08 **The test used in interpreting a written contract** The negotiations between the parties may take various forms: oral or written communications, or a combination of the two. They may be relatively simple, with only a few short exchanges to come to a concluded agreement, but in complex negotiations the communications may be numerous, with each party successively responding to what has been said by the other, sometimes summarising the whole set of terms adding his own most recent variation to what has gone before, but sometimes only expressly mentioning a particular term which he wishes to vary and leaving it understood that the other terms already discussed remain in place.[25] It is for negotiations involving successive communications between the parties that the courts have developed the rules of offer and acceptance which are discussed later in this chapter[26]; and it is in such negotiations that the test discussed above for the formation of a contract is used— the "objective" test from the perspective of the reasonable person in each party's position in interpreting the other's communications, but also requiring the party in fact (subjectively) to have understood the agreement in the terms which he asserts.

Where, however, the existence and terms of the parties' agreement does not depend upon the construction of the separate communications during the negotiations, but is based on a single written document agreed, and typically signed, by both parties,[27] the nature of the inquiry—and the perspective adopted in the inquiry—is different. Unless there is some challenge to the document itself, such as that it was not in fact agreed at all,[28] or contains some mistake in drafting which means that the document fails to reflect the agreement which the parties had reached before the document was drawn up,[29] there is no doubt that there is an agreement

---

[23] For a summary of the test, see Cartwright (Misrepresentation), para.13-19; and for its practical application, focusing in particular on cases where one party claims to have made a mistake about the other's intention as to the existence or terms of the contract, see ibid., paras 13-20 to 13-29. See also Chitty, paras 3-013 to 3-035, esp. para.3-018; Treitel, paras 8-047 to 8-053; Anson, pp.273–278.

[24] Cartwright (Misrepresentation), paras 13-18, 13-20.

[25] *Golden Ocean Group Ltd v Salgaocar Mining Industries Pvt Ltd* [2012] EWCA Civ 265, [2012] 1 W.L.R. 3674 at [22].

[26] *Gibson v Manchester City Council* [1979] 1 W.L.R. 294 at 297; see para.3-24.

[27] Or identical documents, each signed by or on behalf of one of the parties, as commonly practised in the case of exchange of contracts for the sale of land: LP(MP)A 1989 s.2(1), (3), see para.5-20; Cheshire and Burn, pp.958–959; Megarry & Wade, para.15-036.

[28] e.g. under the plea of non est factum: Cartwright (Misrepresentation), paras 13-55 to 13-60; Chitty, paras 3-049 to 3-056; Furmston, paras 4.113 to 4.117; Treitel, paras 8-079 to 8-086; Anson, pp.279–282; Cheshire, Fifoot and Furmston, pp.333–340.

[29] e.g. a claim for rectification of the document to bring it into conformity with the parties' agreement: Cartwright (Misrepresentation), paras 13-38 to 13-54; Chitty, paras 3-057 to 3-104; Furmston, paras

between the parties on the terms of the document[30]: "where there is a writing, into which the terms of any agreement are reduced, the terms are to be regulated by that writing".[31] The inquiry is therefore limited to the interpretation of the content of the agreement, through an interpretation of the document itself—a matter of law.[32] And, once the agreement is contained in a single, agreed document, it less obvious that the perspective of one or other party should be used in the interpretation of the words used in that document. The interpretation of written contracts does sometimes take into account which party proposed, or benefits from, a particular term which was included in the document.[33] But in general the courts adopt the position that the test for interpretation of a written document is wholly objective, in the sense that the understanding of both parties as to the meaning of the words is regarded as irrelevant, and the question is how a reasonable person—having the background knowledge (the "context") which would reasonably have been available to the parties at the time of the contract—would interpret it.[34] The pre-contractual negotia-

---

4.118 to 4.129; Treitel, paras 8-059 to 8-078; Anson, pp.282–287. The claim may be based on either a common mistake (the document fails to reflect the parties' shared understanding of the terms of their contract), or unilateral mistake (the document fails to reflect the claimant's understanding, even though it may in fact represent the defendant's understanding). In either case, one would expect the question of whether there was (apart from the document, which is itself subject to challenge) an agreement which differs from that contained in the document, is to be tested by the same general approach as is used in finding the parties' agreement in the case of successive communications (see para.3-07): D. McLaughlan, "The 'Drastic' Remedy of Rectification for Unilateral Mistake" (2008) 124 L.Q.R. 608, 614–617, 640. However, in the case of common mistake, it has been said that the parties' agreement (to which the document is to be rectified) is to be determined as the "objective observer" would decide, which apparently excludes any consideration of a shared subjective agreement of the parties themselves: *Chartbrook Ltd v Persimmon Homes Ltd* [2009] UKHL 38; [2009] 1 A.C. 1101 at [60]; but this is controversial: Cartwright (Misrepresentation), para.13–40; Chitty, paras 3-077 to 3-082.

[30] The document is the record of the contract and normally the exclusive evidence of its terms: for the parol evidence rule, see generally H.M. Malek (ed.), *Phipson on Evidence*, 19th edn (Sweet & Maxwell, 2017), Ch.42; Lewison, para.3.11; Furmston, paras 3.4 to 3.6; Chitty, paras 13-099 to 13-136; Treitel, paras 6-014 to 6-031; Anson, pp.146–148; Cheshire, Fifoot and Furmston, pp.168–169.

[31] *Harris v Great Western Railway Co* (1876) 1 Q.B.D. 515 at 530 (Blackburn J, who went on to say that by giving his assent to the document, the party represents to the other that he has made himself acquainted with its contents and the other party relies on that representation by in turn giving his own assent. That analysis is relevant to the argument about why a party should be bound if he did not understand, or did not even read, the document, although it has been doubted: *McCutcheon v David MacBrayne Ltd* [1964] 1 W.L.R. 125, HL, at 134 (Lord Devlin) "when a party assents to a document forming the whole or a part of his contract, he is bound by the terms of the document, read or unread, signed or unsigned, simply because they are in the contract; and it is unnecessary and possibly misleading to say that he is bound by them because he represents to the other party that he has made himself acquainted with them").

[32] *Carmichael v National Power Plc* [1999] 1 W.L.R. 2042, HL, 2049. Where, however, the parties' agreement has to be ascertained wholly or partly from their oral exchanges and conduct, the interpretation of the terms of the contract is a matter of fact: ibid., or inference from primary fact: *Thorner v Major* [2009] UKHL 18; [2009] 1 W.L.R. 776 at [82]; Lewison, paras 4.01, 4.02.

[33] The *contra proferentem* rule: Lewison, para.7.08. This rule now has a very limited role in relation to commercial contracts, negotiated between parties of equal bargaining power: *Persimmon Homes Ltd v Ove Arup & Partners Ltd* [2017] EWCA Civ 373; [2017] P.N.L.R. 29 at [52] (Jackson LJ).

[34] *Investors Compensation Scheme Ltd v West Bromwich Building Society* [1998] 1 W.L.R. 896 at 912–913 (Lord Hoffmann). This objective test of interpretation of written contracts and other instruments is firmly established in the cases at the highest level: see, e.g. *Mannai Investment Co Ltd v Eagle Star Life Assurance Co Ltd* [1997] A.C. 749 at 775 and 779–780 (Lord Hoffmann); *Chartbrook Ltd v Persimmon Homes Ltd* [2009] UKHL 38; [2009] 1 A.C. 1101 at [14] (Lord Hoffmann: "There is no dispute that the principles on which a contract (or any other instrument or

tions are irrelevant for the purposes of interpreting the document,[35] and although, if there are two possible constructions of a term in the document, the court may choose between them, it does so on the basis of preferring the construction which is "consistent with business common sense", rather than, it appears, by asking what either or both of the parties in fact intended.[36]

(3)   The Role of Intention in Contract Formation

3-09   **The requirement of "intention to create legal relations"**   If a contract is to be viewed as an agreement which has the force of law,[37] it is necessary to decide which agreements fall within the protection of the law, in the sense of being legally binding and so supported by remedies in the event of their non-performance, and which agreements fall outside that protection, having at most only moral force. The general question of which agreements, or promises, are legally binding, is the common theme of this book,[38] and we shall see in the following chapters that English law sometimes uses formality to distinguish between enforceable and unenforceable transactions[39]; but the general doctrine which is applied to make that distinction is the doctrine of consideration.[40] The significance of a party's *intention to be legally bound* as a principle within, or lying behind, the use of formalities and the doctrine of consideration will be considered in those later chapters.[41] However, since the later

---

utterance) should be interpreted are those summarised by the House of Lords in *Investors Compensation Scheme Ltd v West Bromwich Building Society*. They are well known and need not be repeated"); *Rainy Sky SA v Kookmin Bank* [2011] UKSC 50; [2011] 1 W.L.R. 2900 at [14]; *Arnold v Britton* [2015] UKSC 36; [2015] A.C. 1619 at [15]; *Wood v Capita Insurance Services Ltd* [2017] UKSC 24; [2017] A.C. 1173 at [10]; Lewison, Ch.1. Lord Hoffmann has made clear that it is a test of "detached objectivity" (see para.3-05 fn.12): *Chartbrook* at [39] (a "reasonable outside observer", by contrast with the French determination of the subjective intentions of the parties). Where the document was addressed to, or would normally be read by, a particular kind of person, that person's (objective) perspective may be particularly relevant: *Mannai Investment Co Ltd v Eagle Star Life Assurance Co Ltd*, above (unilateral notice: recipient's perspective); *Homburg Houtimport BV v Agrosin Private Ltd (The Starsin)* [2003] UKHL 12; [2004] 1 A.C. 715 at [75], [188] (bill of lading addressed to banker who would not (like a lawyer) read the back to identify the carrier); *Cherry Tree Investments Ltd v Landmain Ltd* [2012] EWCA Civ 736; [2013] 1 Ch. 305 (third party inspecting document registered at Land Registry).

35   *Chartbrook Ltd v Persimmon Homes Ltd*, see para.3-08 fn.34, at [28]–[41]. This is, however, largely for "reasons of practical policy": *Investors Compensation Scheme Ltd v West Bromwich Building Society*, see para.3-08 fn.34, at 913 (Lord Hoffmann); "it would not be inconsistent with the English objective theory of contractual interpretation to admit evidence of previous communications between the parties as part of the background which may throw light upon what they meant by the language they used": *Chartbrook* at [33] (Lord Hoffmann).

36   *Rainy Sky SA v Kookmin Bank*, see para.3-08 fn.34, at [21] (Lord Clarke JSC). This does not allow "commercial common sense" to displace the clear (objective) interpretation of a term: *Arnold v Britton*, see para.3-08 fn.34, at [17], [76]–[77]; and see Lord Neuberger at [20]: "while commercial common sense is a very important factor to take into account when interpreting a contract, a court should be very slow to reject the natural meaning of a provision as correct simply because it appears to be a very imprudent term for one of the parties to have agreed, even ignoring the benefit of wisdom of hindsight. The purpose of interpretation is to identify what the parties have agreed, not what the court thinks that they should have agreed".

37   See para.3-01.

38   See para.1-04.

39   See Pt II.

40   See Pt III. For the possible use of the doctrine of promissory estoppel, see Ch.10.

41   See paras 4-03, 4-05, 5-30, 7-07, 8-16, 8-27, 8-28, 9-14, 9-15.

nineteenth century[42] it has become common to say that, in addition to the existence of an agreement (generally established through offer and acceptance) and consideration, the formation of an informal contract requires evidence of an "intention to create legal relations"—that is, there is a substantive additional requirement that the parties intend their agreement to have legally binding force.[43] A brief discussion of this topic belongs in this present chapter because the question of intention to be bound naturally belongs with the notion of the parties' agreement forming the basis of the contract: we can say that one element of the agreement is the parties' common intention which is directed at the creation of their respective contractual obligations. Each party agrees not only to the terms of the contract,[44] but agrees to it *being a contract*.[45] The Supreme Court has made this clear[46]:

"Whether there is a binding contract between the parties and, if so, upon what terms depends upon what they have agreed. It depends not upon their subjective state of mind, but upon a consideration of what was communicated between them by words or conduct, and whether that leads objectively to a conclusion that they intended to create legal relations and had agreed upon all the terms which they regarded or the law requires as essential for the formation of legally binding relations."

"Intention to create legal relations" as a subsidiary test Some legal systems give a primary focus to the requirement of the parties' intention in forming a contract, and therefore say that the key factor which distinguishes a legally binding promise, or agreement, from one which is only morally or socially binding is that the party made the promise, or gave his assent to the other party by way of agreement, with the intention to create legally binding obligations.[47] English law, however, gives primary focus to the doctrine of consideration, which in large

3-10

---

[42] The introduction of the requirement of contractual intention followed from the incorporation into English law during the 19th century of continental ideas of contract based on the will theory: D. Ibbetson, *A Historical Introduction to the Law of Obligations* (Oxford University Press, 1999), pp.233–234; A.W.B. Simpson, "Innovation in Nineteenth Century Contract Law" (1975) 91 L.Q.R. 247, 263–265. See, e.g. F. Pollock, *Principles of Contract*, 1st edn (Stevens, 1876), p.2 ("The intention of the parties must ... be an intention directed to legal consequences"), drawing explicitly on F.C. von Savigny, *System des heutigen römischen Rechts* (Berlin: Veit und Comp., 1840), Vol.3, §140, p.307.

[43] Chitty, paras 2-167 to 2-199; Furmston, paras 2.172 to 2.198; Treitel, Ch.4; Anson, pp.73–77; Cheshire, Fifoot and Furmston, Ch.5; cf. S. Hedley, "Keeping Contract in its Place—Balfour v Balfour and the Enforceability of Informal Agreements" (1985) 5 O.J.LS. 391.

[44] For further discussion of what the parties must agree about, in order to form a contract—its minimum content and certainty—see paras 3-13 to 3-17.

[45] The tests of offer and acceptance also contain elements of the parties' intention to be bound: see para.3-28. Note also *Baird Textiles Holdings Ltd v Marks & Spencer Plc* [2001] EWCA Civ 274; [2002] 1 All E.R. (Comm) 737 at [59]–[64] (Mance LJ: a contract requires (judged objectively) (a) an agreement on essentials with sufficient certainty to be enforceable, and (b) an intention to create legal relations; but the requirements should be taken in that order, and the former raises a presumption of the latter).

[46] *RTS Flexible Systems Ltd v Molkerei Alois Müller GmbH & Co KG*, see para.3-05 fn.13, at [45].

[47] e.g. German law, in which the contract is based on the parties' declarations of intention: B.S. Markesinis, H. Unberath and A. Johnston, *The German Law of Contract: A Comparative Treatise*, 2nd edn (Hart Publishing, 2006), p.87. See also PECL art.2:101(1) ("A contract is concluded if: (a) the parties intend to be legally bound, and (b) they reach a sufficient agreement, without any further requirement"); DCFR art.II.-4:101 ("A contract is concluded, without any further requirement, if the parties: (a) intend to enter into a binding legal relationship or bring about some other legal effect; and (b) reach a sufficient agreement"; see Notes for comparative discussion of a range of national laws).

measure removes the need to have a primary doctrine of intention to create legal relations,[48] although the parties' intention does play at least a subsidiary role. An agreement (formed through the acceptance of an offer) supported by consideration will still not be a contract unless there was also an intention to create legal relations. It should be noted that the test of "intention to create legal relations" is objective; and the way in which it is used in practice depends on the context in which the agreement is formed—a commercial agreement is in this sense viewed very differently from a non-commercial agreement.

3-11   **"Intention" tested objectively**   Since the interpretation of the parties' communications to each other, which form the basis of the agreement, is tested objectively,[49] it should not be surprising that the test of whether those communications evince an intention to be legally bound should also be tested objectively. The question should be how a reasonable person in each party's position would have interpreted the other party's intention based on his interpretation of the communications, as well as how the party receiving the communications in fact interpreted them.[50] One party should not be able to hold the other to a contractual agreement unless he could reasonably, and did in fact, believe that the other was making a contractual commitment.[51]

---

[48] See para.3-12. cf. para.3-09 fn.42 (Pollock's use of Savigny created an inevitable tension within his account of English law). In America, the Restatement of Contracts (2d), §21 goes so far as to say that "Neither real nor apparent intention that a promise be legally binding is essential to the formation of a contract", although it adds that "manifestation of intention that a promise shall not affect legal relations may prevent the formation of a contract" and it appears that the effect of this is not wholly different from the English law approach set out at para.3-12: cf. Farnsworth, para.3.7.

[49] See para.3-07.

[50] *RTS Flexible Systems Ltd v Molkerei Alois Müller GmbH & Co KG*, see para.3-05 fn.13, at [86]–[87]; cf. *Edwards v Skyways Ltd* [1964] 1 W.L.R. 349 at 355–356; *Maple Leaf Macro Volatility Master Fund v Rouvroy* [2009] EWCA Civ 1334; [2010] 2 All E.R. (Comm) 788 at [17]; *Novus Aviation Ltd v Alubaf Arab International Bank BSC(c)* [2016] EWHC 1575 (Comm); [2017] 1 B.C.L.C. 313 at [56] ("The extent of any such qualification to the objective test, and whether it exists at all, is far from clear. Moreover, whether it is theoretically justifiable to apply a different test in deciding whether parties intended to undertake contractual obligations from the test applied in determining the scope of those obligations is open to doubt": Leggatt J, discussing the interpretation of written contracts: cf. para.3-08).

[51] cf. para.3-06. See also *Pennyfeathers Ltd v Pennyfeathers Property Co Ltd* [2013] EWHC 3530 (Ch) at [36] (Rose J: "In order to establish that there was a binding contract, the Defendants must show both that the parties had the subjective intention of forming a binding contract and that what occurred between them would lead objectively to the conclusion that they intended to create legal relations: see *The Hannah Blumenthal* [see para.3-06 fn.21] (where the House of Lords held that a contract to abandon an arbitration did not arise from the lengthy inaction of both parties in prosecuting the arbitration because the sellers did not actually believe that the inaction of the buyers was an offer to abandon it) and *RTS Flexible Systems Ltd v Molkerei Alois Müller GmbH* [see para.3-05 fn.13] as to the objective assessment of words and conduct"). The application of the objective test to interpret the parties' communications in relation to the intention to create legal relations presupposes that there is sufficient evidence of what the parties in fact said: *Hadley v Kemp*, see para.3-05 fn.17, at 623. The test of intention to be legally bound is also tested objectively, determined from the party's statements or conduct as they were reasonably understood by the other party, under PECL art.2:102 and DCFR art.II.–4:102. In the case of a written contract, the parties' assent to the document (e.g. by their signature) is sufficient objective evidence of intention to be bound; as in the interpretation of the terms of the document, neither party's perspective needs to be privileged: see para.3-08.

Presumptions for and against intention In many types of transaction it would   **3-12**
be surprising to find that the agreement was not intended by both parties to be
legally binding: for example, where there is a sufficient agreement (embodying an
exchange[52]) between two commercial parties; or even where there is an agreement
between a consumer and a business or professional party for the provision of goods
or services to the consumer. Given that the test of intention is objective,[53] each party
to such a transaction will normally be entitled to assume that a legally-binding
agreement—a contract—has been formed, and so the courts will normally accept
that there is a contract as long as the agreement, supported by consideration, is
established: they do not require affirmative proof of the parties' intention and,
indeed, they will presume the intention unless there is proof that there was no such
intention. It has been said that, in a purely commercial transaction, the party who
asserts that no legal effect was intended has a heavy onus.[54] The context in which
the commercial parties came to their agreement must, however, be taken into
account.[55] Furthermore, we have seen that one way in which parties may indicate

---

[52]   i.e. supported by consideration: see para.8-15.
[53]   See para.3-11.
[54]   *Edwards v Skyways Ltd*, see para.3-11 fn.50, at 355 (Megaw J: agreement between board of airline
company and employee to make "ex gratia" payment on redundancy was binding: "ex gratia" did
not imply that it was not to be legally binding). cf. Hedley, see para.3-09 fn.43, p.412 ("Where the
parties are dealing at arms' length, the rule is simple: there is no requirement of intention to create
legal relations. It is open to one party to show that legal liability was excluded, though it will take
strong words to do this"); S.A. Smith, *Atiyah's Introduction to the Law of Contract*, 6th edn
(Clarendon Press, 2005), pp.98–99. For other cases involving arm's-length transactions, see *Esso
Petroleum Co Ltd v Customs and Excise Commissioners* [1976] 1 W.L.R. 1, HL ("free" world cup
coins, of little intrinsic value, included with petrol: majority held that Esso intended to create legal
obligation to supply the coins, but minority held no contractual intention in relation to the coins);
Edmonds v Lawson [2000] Q.B. 501, CA, at [21]–[23] (contract to engage pupil barrister: there is
no reason why a binding contract cannot be made for education and training, and the fact that the
relationship was covered by the disciplinary rules of the Bar Council, and that chambers would be
most unlikely to sue if pupil defaulted, did not point against the existence of a contract); *Barbudev
v Eurocom Cable Management Bulgaria EOOD* [2012] EWCA Civ 548; [2012] 2 All E.R. (Comm)
963 at [30], [37]–[38] (Aikens LJ: "side letter" was clearly intended to legally binding because
drafted by lawyers and legal language, even though it was not enforceable because only an "agreement to agree"); *Attrill v Dresdner Kleinwort Ltd* [2013] EWCA Civ 394; [2013] 3 All E.R. 607 at
[80] (variation of employment contract: "where a term is being introduced into a pre-existing
contractual relationship there will be a very strong presumption that it is intended to be legally
binding": Elias LJ). However, "there is no rule of law about it. Rather, it is a generalisation about
how the courts will expect the facts normally to be. The generalisation can be displaced in a particular
case": *Hadley v Kemp*, see para.3-05 fn.17, at 624 (Park J); *Sax v Tchernoy* [2014] EWHC 795
(Comm) at [62]–[67] (Hamblen J: the test of whether there is an intention to create legal relations
is objective, and it has been said that in a commercial context the onus is on the party who asserts
that no legal effect is intended: this may often be so but it must depend on the facts and circumstances
of the particular case); *Assuranceforeningen Gard Gjensidig v International Oil Pollution Compensation Fund* [2014] EWHC 3369; [2014] 2 C.L.C. 699 at [102] (Hamblen J: not appropriate to use
presumption in a hybrid case where the alleged contract involved a combination of what the parties
said and did and no expressly stated offer to contract).
[55]   *MacInnes v Gross* [2017] EWHC 46 (QB) (agreement over a dinner at which business matters were
not always to the fore: "The mere fact that the discussion took place over dinner in a smart restaurant
does not, of itself, preclude the coming into existence of a binding contract. A contract can be made
anywhere, in any circumstances. But I consider that the fact that this alleged agreement was made
in a highly informal and relaxed setting means that the court should closely scrutinise the conten-
tion that, despite the setting, there was an intention to create legal relations": Coulson J at [81]; the
alleged contract failed also because it was incomplete and uncertain). See also *Blue v Ashley* [2017]
EWHC 1928 (Comm) at [81] (no contractual offer made during an evening of drinking in a pub).

expressly that they do not (yet) intend to be legally bound is by expressing pre-contractual negotiations to be "subject to contract".[56] But even when the negotiations between commercial parties are complete, they may include in their agreement a provision making clear that it carries no legal commitment.[57]

In a domestic, family or social context, by contrast, one might not normally expect an agreement, even if it embodies an apparent bargain between parties, to be intended to be sued upon. The courts have therefore generally taken as the starting-point that an agreement between family members[58] or friends[59] is not contractually binding unless there is evidence of an intention to be bound, either in express terms or by necessary implication from the circumstances of the parties and the transaction generally.[60] In that sense, the domestic, family or social context raises the presumption that there is no intention to create legal relations.[61]

---

[56] See para.2-08. The negotiations may also be *impliedly* "subject to contract": see para.2-08 fn.34. A party who expressed the negotiations to be "subject to contract" may later withdraw or waive that condition, and therefore become legally bound; again the test is objective: see para.2-08 fn.39.

[57] *Rose and Frank Co v JR Crompton & Bros Ltd* [1925] A.C. 445, HL (agreement by which American firm were constituted sole agents of English firm in US and Canada, subject to "honourable pledge" clause which made clear that the arrangement was not a formal or legal agreement, nor subject to the American or English courts); *Kleinwort Benson Ltd v Malaysia Mining Corp Bhd* [1989] 1 W.L.R. 379, CA (statement in comfort letter by parent company that "it is our policy to ensure that" subsidiary could meet its liabilities was only statement of present fact and did not constitute contractual guarantee).

[58] *Balfour v Balfour* [1919] 2 K.B. 571, CA (separation agreement between husband and wife; see Atkin LJ at 597: "Agreements such as these are outside the realm of contracts altogether. The common law does not regulate the form of agreements between spouses. Their promises are not sealed with seals and sealing wax"); *Jones v Padavatton* [1969] 1 W.L.R. 328, CA (mother's agreement to pay maintenance to adult daughter who gave up job to read for the Bar).

[59] *Coward v Motor Insurers' Bureau* [1963] 1 Q.B. 259, CA (agreement to give fellow workman a lift to work on motorcycle on regular basis in return for weekly sum).

[60] *Balfour v Balfour* see para.3-12 fn.58, at 574 (Warrington LJ). For examples of cases in which the courts have found contracts between family members, see *Haggar v De Placido* [1972] 1 W.L.R. 716 (binding contractual agreement between tetraplegic and his mother and brother to provide care); *Tanner v Tanner* [1975] 1 W.L.R. 1346, CA (implied contractual licence for defendant, unmarried mother of claimant's twin children, to occupy house bought by claimant); *Hardwick v Johnson* [1978] 1 W.L.R. 683, CA (contractual licence where mother purchased house for son and his wife to live in); *Rollerteam Ltd v Riley* [2015] EWHC 1545 (Ch) at [41] (Robert Englehart QC: "This is not a case of trusting family relations and informal arrangements. On the contrary, the background here is one of bitter commercial disputes and arms length litigation". The case was appealed on other issues: [2016] EWCA Civ 1291; [2017] Ch. 109). In relation to agreements between married couple or civil partners, overriding rules within family law may limit the binding force of agreements on divorce or dissolution, even if the parties had expressly intended the agreements to be binding: cf. *Granatino v Radmacher* [2010] UKSC 42; [2011] 1 A.C. 534 (ante-nuptial agreement), although the Law Commission has recommended the introduction by statute of "qualifying nuptial agreements" which would allow parties (subject to certain procedural safeguards) to enter into enforceable contracts relating to certain arrangements about the financial consequences of divorce or dissolution: Law Com. No.343, *Matrimonial Property, Needs and Agreements* (2014).

[61] *Jones v Padavatton*, see para.3-12 fn.58, at 332 (Salmon LJ: "as a rule when arrangements are made between close relations, for example, between husband and wife, parent and child or uncle and nephew in relation to an allowance, there is a presumption against an intention of creating any legal relationship. This is not a presumption of law, but of fact. It derives from experience of life and human nature which shows that in such circumstances men and women usually do not intend to create legal rights and obligations, but intend to rely solely on family ties of mutual trust and affection. ... There may, however, be circumstances in which this presumption, like all other presumptions of fact, can be rebutted").

(4)   Agreement About What? Minimum Content and Certainty

An agreement must be complete   In order to form a contract, not only must the **3-13** parties be in agreement (objectively determined[62]), but they must have agreed on a sufficient body of terms that the law can recognise as a contract. This does not mean that the parties must have come to an express agreement about all the terms of their contract: implied terms are designed for the very purpose of filling gaps between the terms which the parties have expressly agreed.[63] And even if certain terms have not yet been finalised, the parties may already have agreed on sufficient terms to form a contract, and may have intended the contract to be binding leaving the subsidiary and inessential terms to be decided later[64]: it is generally for the parties to decide which terms are essential for their contract to be complete.[65] It is not even necessary that the parties agree expressly on the detail of every term which the law regards as essential to the type of contract which the parties intend to form, as long as there is a sufficiently certain mechanism by which detail can be completed: for example, agreement on the price is an essential term in a contract of sale of goods,[66] but if the parties' agreement is silent as to the ascertainment of the price, as long as there is agreement on the goods the property in which is to be transferred, and on any other terms the parties have decided should form part of their contract of sale,[67] the buyer must pay a "reasonable price".[68] However, a gap in the parties' agreement which prevents the agreement being sufficient to form a contract cannot be filled by implying a term[69]:

"It is of course the case that the court may imply terms into a concluded contract. But that assumes that there is a concluded contract into which terms can be implied. It is not legitimate, under the guise of implying terms, to make a contract for the parties. That is to put the cart before the horse."

---

[62]   See paras 3-07 and 3-08.

[63]   For implied terms, see generally Chitty, Ch.14; Furmston, Ch.3, s.B; Treitel, paras 6-032 to 6-050; Anson, pp.161–178; Cheshire, Fifoot and Furmston, pp.183–203. A term will be implied into a detailed commercial contract only if it satisfies the test of business efficacy, not merely because it is fair or reasonable; and the implication is based not on the actual intentions of the parties, but on what would have been agreed by notional reasonable people in the position of the parties at the time at which they were contracting: *Marks & Spencer Plc v BNP Paribas Securities Services Trust Co (Jersey) Ltd* [2015] UKSC 72; [2016] A.C. 742; at [17], [21], [24], [77], explaining *Attorney General of Belize v Belize Telecom Ltd* [2009] UKPC 10; [2009] 1 W.L.R. 1988.

[64]   *RTS Flexible Systems Ltd v Molkerei Alois Müller GmbH & Co KG*, see para.3-05 fn.13, at [45]; *Pagnan SpA v Feed Products Ltd* [1987] 2 Lloyd's Rep. 601, CA.

[65]   *Pagnan SpA v Feed Products Ltd*, see para.3-13 fn.64, at 619.

[66]   Sale of Goods Act 1979 s.2(1).

[67]   It will be necessary to show that the parties intended the transaction to be a contract of sale, i.e. that there was to be a money consideration, even though they have been silent about what the consideration should be.

[68]   Sale of Goods Act 1979 s.8(1); what is a reasonable price is a question of fact dependent on the circumstances of each particular case: s.8(3). This provision applies only if the parties have been silent as to the price: if they are in disagreement over the price, or if they have agreed a formula for the price which is not sufficiently certain (see para.3-14), there is no implied term: *May and Butcher Ltd v R.* [1934] 2 K.B. 17, HL. For the similar "reasonable charge" in a contract for the supply of a service where the contract is silent about the consideration for the service, see Supply of Goods and Services Act 1982 s.15(1).

[69]   *Wells v Devani* [2016] EWCA Civ 1106; [2017] Q.B. 959 at [19] (Lewison LJ: agreement for commission did not identify trigger on which commission was payable: this was an essential term, and could not be supplied by implication: at [37]).

3-14   **An agreement must be certain**   In practice, however, the apparent absence of a sufficiently complete agreement most commonly becomes an issue not of completeness but of certainty, since the parties do not generally leave gaps which the courts cannot complete by implying suitable terms, but they may include in their agreement terms which are not sufficiently clear and precise. If the agreement contains elements which are not objectively certain, nor capable of being defined without further negotiation between the parties, the agreement cannot form a contract,[70] although the courts will look carefully at the words used, in their context, to determine whether the term can be given a sufficiently certain meaning, and particularly in the context of a commercial contract where the parties clearly believe that they have concluded a contract, and have even acted on it, a court will be reluctant to decide that their agreement is not sufficiently certain.[71] Moreover, if the parties include a clause which is meaningless, and which can be severed from the agreement without affecting its completeness and certainty, the court may ignore the clause and hold the contract to be validly concluded.[72]

---

[70]   *G Scammell and Nephew Ltd v HC and JG Ouston* [1941] A.C. 251, HL ("balance of purchase price can be had on hire-purchase terms over a period of two years" so vague that it required further agreement to be reached between the parties before there would be a complete consensus ad idem: Viscount Simon LC at 254).

[71]   *Hillas & Co Ltd v Arcos Ltd* (1932) 147 L.T. 503, HL, at 511–512, 514; *G Scammell and Nephew Ltd v HC and JG Ouston*, see para.3-14 fn.70, at 255, 268; *Brown v Gould* [1972] 1 Ch. 53 at 56; *Cudgen Rutile (No.2) Pty Ltd v Chalk* [1975] A.C. 520, PC, at 537; *National Transport Co-operative Society Ltd v Attorney General of Jamaica* [2009] UKPC 48 at [60]. See also *Foley v Classique Coaches Ltd* [1934] 2 K.B. 1, CA (sale of petrol "at a price to be agreed by the parties in writing and from time to time" in contract which contained arbitration clause to resolve price dispute and had been acted on by the parties for three years: implied term that petrol be supplied at a reasonable price, which could be resolved under the arbitration clause); *Corson v Rhuddlan BC* (1990) 59 P. & C.R. 185, CA, at 194 (option to renew lease "at a rental to be agreed (but such rental shall not in any event exceed the rental hereby reserved)": contractual intention of the parties was clear that landlord should be under obligation to grant new lease and it was just and necessary to imply the provision for the rent to be a fair rent, not exceeding original rent); *Mamidoil-Jetoil Greek Petroleum Co. SA v Okta Crude Oil Refinery AD* [2001] EWCA Civ 406; [2001] 2 Lloyd's Rep. 76 at [69]; *MRI Trading AG v Erdenet Mining Corporation LLC* [2013] EWCA Civ 156; [2013] 1 Lloyd's Rep. 638 at [18]; *Astor Management AG v Atalaya Mining Plc* [2017] EWHC 425 (Comm); [2017] Bus. L.R. 1634 at [64] (Leggatt J: "The role of the court in a commercial dispute is to give legal effect to what the parties have agreed, not to throw its hands in the air and refuse to do so because the parties have not made its task easy. To hold that a clause is too uncertain to be enforceable is a last resort or, as Lord Denning MR once put it, 'a counsel of despair': see *Nea Agrex SA v Baltic Shipping Co Ltd* [1976] 1 QB 933, 943"); *Associated British Ports v Tata Steel (UK) Ltd* [2017] EWHC 694 (Ch); [2017] 2 Lloyd's Rep. 11 at [31]–[34]; *Openwork Ltd v Forte* [2018] EWCA Civ 783 at [25]. cf. *Baird Textiles Holdings Ltd v Marks & Spencer Plc* [2001] EWCA Civ 274; [2002] 1 All E.R. (Comm) 737 at [24]–[30] (lack of certainty over future contractual terms in long-term commercial relationship confirmed absence of intention to create legal relations in relation to alleged claim that there was a contract to effect that the relationship would continue long term and would be terminable only on reasonable notice; distinguishing *Hillas & Co Ltd v Arcos*).

[72]   *Nicolene Ltd v Simmonds* [1953] 1 Q.B. 543, CA ("the usual conditions of acceptance apply", but there were no usual conditions of acceptance, so the words were meaningless. See Denning LJ at 551–552: "It would be strange indeed if a party could escape from every one of his obligations by inserting a meaningless exception from some of them. ... The contract should be held good and the clause ignored. The parties themselves treated the contract as subsisting. They regarded it as creating binding obligations between them; and it would be most unfortunate if the law should say otherwise. You would find defaulters all scanning their contracts to find some meaningless clause on which to ride free").

An "agreement to agree" is uncertain We have already seen that the courts have **3-15** rejected the notion of a legally enforceable duty to negotiate on the basis that it would be uncertain.[73] The courts cannot themselves complete the contract for the parties because whether there would have been an agreement at all, and (if so) what terms would have been agreed, depends upon the parties themselves,[74] and each party is free to negotiate in his own interests without being subject to any overriding obligation to negotiate fairly, or in good faith, or to seek to come to an agreement.[75] An agreement for the sale of goods at a price which "shall be agreed upon from time to time" is therefore uncertain and does not create a contract.[76]

Objective criteria for determining the content of a term which has not been **3-16** **finalised** Where, however, the parties have agreed on a term which contains (expressly[77] or impliedly[78]) an objective standard for its determination, the courts will generally be able to give effect to that standard so as to complete the contract. We have already seen that, in the case of silence about the price in a contract for the sale of goods, it will be implied that the price is to be "reasonable".[79] What constitutes a "reasonable price" is a question of fact dependent on the circumstances of each particular case,[80] and the courts regard themselves as equipped to undertake an assessment of what constitutes a reasonable price—what reasonable parties[81] would have agreed in the circumstances—as long as there is sufficient evidence on which to base their determination. Similarly, if the contract provides a mechanism for the outstanding terms to be determined, such as determination by an identified

---

[73] See para.2-05. This is not saved by simply formulating the duty as one to use reasonable (or best) endeavours to negotiate, or to negotiate in good faith: see para.2-06.

[74] *Courtney & Fairbairn Ltd v Tolaini Brothers (Hotels) Ltd* [1975] 1 W.L.R. 297, CA, at 301 (Lord Denning MR: "no one can tell whether the negotiations would be successful or would fall through: or if successful, what the result would be"). cf. *Corson v Rhuddlan BC*, see para.3-14 fn.71, at 198 (Staughton LJ, obiter: obligation on parties to negotiate with view to fair rent, where contract set upper limit of the rent and the tenant was willing to pay that upper limit, could give rise to obligation on landlord to agree that figure).

[75] See para.2-06; *Walford v Miles* [1992] 2 A.C. 128, HL, at 138.

[76] *May and Butcher Ltd v R.*, see para.3-13 fn.68; *King's Motors (Oxford) Ltd v Lax* [1970] 1 W.L.R. 426 (option for lease renewal "at such a rental as may be agreed upon between the parties").

[77] *Didymi Corp v Atlantic Lines and Navigation Co Inc (The Didymi)* [1988] 2 Lloyd's Rep. 108, CA ("the hire shall be equitably decreased by an amount to be mutually agreed between the owners and the charterers"); *Petromec Inc v Petroleo Brasileiro SA* [2005] EWCA Civ 891; [2006] 1 Lloyd's Rep. 121 (agreement to pay reasonable extra costs, and to negotiate those extra costs in good faith); *Tramtrack Croydon Ltd v London Bus Services Ltd* [2007] EWHC 107 (Comm) at [90]–[91] ("parties shall in good faith agree (acting reasonably)" sums payable); *Anderson Properties Ltd v Blyth Liggins* [2017] EWHC 24 (Ch) at [25] (precise area of development land for lease and underleaseback was left to be settled after consultation with planning authority, but agreement to make planning application could not unreasonably be withheld, which indicated objective criteria). For the problems of the agreement to negotiate in good faith, see para.2-06 fn.26.

[78] *Foley v Classique Coaches Ltd*, see para.3-14 fn.71; *Sudbrook Trading Estate Ltd v Eggleton* [1983] 1 A.C. 444, HL (option to purchase at price to be agreed by parties' valuers construed as agreement to sell at fair and reasonable price); *Queensland Electricity Generating Board v New Hope Collieries Pty Ltd* [1989] 1 Lloyd's Rep. 205, PC, at 210 (price to be renegotiated after five years of 15-year supply contract: "it is implicit in a commercial agreement of this kind that the terms of the new price structure are to be fair and reasonable as between the parties"); *Corson v Rhuddlan BC*, see para.3-14 fn.71 (implied term that rent be a fair rent).

[79] See para.3-13.

[80] Sale of Goods Act 1979 s.8(3). Similarly, Supply of Goods and Services Act 1982 s.15(2).

[81] The courts can determine what *reasonable persons* in the parties' position would have agreed, but not what the *parties themselves* would have agreed: cf. para.3-15 and fn.74.

or identifiable third party[82] or for any disagreement between the parties to be settled by arbitration[83] or some other form of dispute resolution, it may be sufficient to render the agreement certain as long as the mechanism is sufficiently clearly defined.[84]

3-17   **Time at which the term must be certain**   A term is sufficiently certain if its content will be ascertainable by the time that it comes due to be performed. For example, the price payable under an option contract for the sale of publicly-quoted shares may be defined by reference to the market value of the shares,[85] or the rent payable under an option to renew a lease may be defined by the market value of the premises (taking into account also factors such as alterations made by the tenant to the premises),[86] at the time when the option falls to be exercised. In such cases the term is sufficiently certain as long as the market value can be ascertained at the time set by the contract.

3-18   **Summary of the courts' approach to arguments based on uncertainty**   A useful (non-exhaustive[87]) summary of the general approach to the problems which arise from potential uncertainty of contract terms was set out by Chadwick LJ[88]:

"First, each case must be decided on its own facts and on the construction of the words used in the particular agreement. Decisions on other words, in other agreements, construed against the background of other facts, are not determinative and may not be of any real assistance.

Secondly, if on the true construction of the words which they have used in the circumstances in which they have used them, the parties must be taken to have intended to leave some essential matter, such as price or rent, to be agreed between them in the future—on the basis that either will remain free to agree or disagree about that matter—there is no bargain which the courts can enforce.

Thirdly, in such a case, there is no obligation on the parties to negotiate in good faith about the matter which remains to be agreed between them—see *Walford v Miles*.[89]

---

82   *Lloyds Bank Ltd v Marcan* [1973] 1 W.L.R. 1387, CA ("best rent that can reasonably be obtained at the date hereof regard being had to the circumstances of the case" the rent to be fixed by a person chosen by the president of the Royal Institution of Chartered Surveyors). cf. Sale of Goods Act 1979 s.9(1) (agreement to sell at price fixed by valuation of third party who cannot or does not make the valuation, is avoided).

83   *Foley v Classique Coaches Ltd*, see para.3-14 fn.71; *Mamidoil-Jetoil Greek Petroleum Co. SA v Okta Crude Oil Refinery AD*, see para.3-14 fn.71 at [69] (Rix LJ: "The presence of an arbitration clause may assist the Courts to hold a contract to be sufficiently certain or to be capable of being rendered so, presumably as indicating a commercial and contractual mechanism, which can be operated with the assistance of experts in the field, by which the parties, in the absence of agreement, may resolve their dispute").

84   For examples and further discussion, see para.2-06 fn.28.

85   Note, however, that the "market value" of shares in a private company may not in itself be objectively certain if there are different bases on which the valuation might be made: *Gillatt v Sky Television Ltd* [2000] 1 All E.R. (Comm) 461, CA.

86   *Brown v Gould*, see para.3-14 fn.71.

87   *Mamidoil-Jetoil Greek Petroleum Co. SA v Okta Crude Oil Refinery AD*, see para.3-14 fn.71, at [69].

88   *BJ Aviation Ltd v Pool Aviation Ltd* [2002] EWCA Civ 163; [2002] 2 P. & C.R. 25 at [20]–[24], summarising principles set out earlier by Rix LJ in *Mamidoil-Jetoil Greek Petroleum Co. SA v Okta Crude Oil Refinery AD*, see para.3-14 fn.71, at [69]. These two summaries were applied in *MRI Trading AG v Erdenet Mining Corporation LLC*, see para.3-14 fn.71, and by Walker J in *Teekay Tankers Ltd v STX Offshore and Shipbuilding Co Ltd* [2017] EWHC 253 (Comm); [2017] 1 Lloyd's Rep. 387 at [133] ("the Rix/Chadwick principles").

89   [1992] A.C. 128 at 138G [see para.3-15 fn.75].

Fourthly, where the court is satisfied that the parties intended that their bargain should be enforceable, it will strive to give effect to that intention by construing the words which they have used in a way which does not leave the matter to be agreed in the future incapable of being determined in the absence of future agreement. In order to achieve that result the court may feel able to imply a term in the original bargain that the price or rent, or other matter to be agreed, shall be a 'fair' price, or a 'market' price, or a 'reasonable' price; or by quantifying whatever matter it is that has to be agreed by some equivalent epithet. In a contract for sale of goods such a term may be implied by section 8 of the Sale of Goods Act 1979.[90] But the court cannot imply a term which is inconsistent with what the parties have actually agreed. So if, on the true construction of the words which they have used, the court is driven to the conclusion that they must be taken to have intended that the matter should be left to their future agreement on the basis that either is to remain free to agree or disagree about that matter as his own perceived interest dictates there is no place for an implied term that, in the absence of agreement, the matter shall be determined by some objective criteria of fairness or reasonableness.

Fifthly, if the court concludes that the true intention of the parties was that the matter to be agreed in the future is capable of being determined, in the absence of future agreement, by some objective criteria of fairness or reasonableness, then the bargain does not fail because the parties have provided no machinery for such determination, or because the machinery which they have provided breaks down. In those circumstances the court will provide its own machinery for determining what needs to be determined—where appropriate by ordering an inquiry (see *Sudbrook Trading Estate Ltd v Eggleton*[91])."

II.   THE MECHANICS OF CONTRACT FORMATION: OFFER AND ACCEPTANCE

(1)   "Offer and Acceptance" as a Rule?

Finding the agreement from the parties' communications   Where the contract is alleged to have been formed through the parties' communications,[92] it is natural to look to those communications in order to establish the existence and content of the agreement. It is therefore not surprising that it is common to find in many legal systems an analysis of the formation of a contract based on the "acceptance" of an "offer", given that the unqualified acceptance by one party of the other party's offer shows that they are in agreement.[93] The formal significance of such an "offer and acceptance" analysis, and the approach taken to interpreting particular types of communication (or even lack of communication[94]) as "offer" or as "acceptance" varies, however, from one legal system to another.[95] When considering the ap-

3-19

---

[90]   [See para.3-16 fn.80.]

[91]   [1983] A.C. 444 [see para.3-16 fn.78].

[92]   In the case of a written contract, the formation of the contract generally occurs when the two parties give their assent to the document, typically by signing it. Different considerations therefore apply in relation to finding and interpreting the contract in such a case: see para.3-08, by contrast with para.3-07, although even in relation to written contracts it may be necessary to undertake an analysis of the formation of the agreement which preceded its being expressed in the written document, e.g. where it is claimed that the document fails to give effect to the common intention of the parties and should therefore be rectified: see para.3-08 fn.29 (although note the controversy mentioned there about how the parties' common intention is to be determined for the purpose of the remedy of rectification).

[93]   *Gibbon v Manchester City Council* [2010] EWCA Civ 726; [2010] 1 W.L.R. 2081 at [6] (Moore-Bick LJ: "Such concepts are part of the landscape in which everyone conducts their daily life"; cf. however para.3-30 fn.173).

[94]   For the problem of agreement alleged to have been formed through silence, see para.3-39.

[95]   See, e.g. K. Zweigert and H. Kötz, *An Introduction to Comparative Law*, 3rd edn (trans. T. Weir,

proach taken in English law it is important to bear in mind that the interpretation of the parties' communications is objective, each party assessing the significance of the other's words and conduct as a reasonable person in his position would do.[96] The interpretation of the communications between the parties is a matter of fact,[97] but, as we shall see, the development of the "offer and acceptance" analysis through decisions in cases which fit standard fact-patterns[98] has led the English common law to elevate the use of "offer and acceptance" analysis to the status of a legal rule. Not only have the courts recognised what types of communication will normally constitute offers which may be accepted and so form a contract, but they have also generally taken the view that "offer and acceptance" are not simply useful tools to establish the existence of the agreement, but are normally required as part of the legal analysis of the existence of the contract; without communications that can be analysed as the acceptance of an offer, there can be no contract. This last point, however, merits some discussion.

3-20 **"Offer and acceptance" is very often an artificial analysis** In the case of a simple contract one party may make an offer ("will you buy this bicycle for £100?"), which the other party accepts by just saying "yes". Or even in the case of long and complex negotiations one of the parties may make a firm proposal to set-tle their outstanding differences on a particular set of terms, and the other party as-sents to that as their final deal. In such cases we may quite easily find the offer and the acceptance, and therefore the formation of the contract. But such cases are not exhaustive of the formation of contracts—indeed, they may not even be typical. There are many situations in which the parties can certainly be said to have agreed to enter into a contract, but it is difficult or even artificial to identify the particular communications which constituted the offer and the acceptance. This point was made by Lord Wilberforce[99]:

> "It is only the precise analysis of this complex of relations into the classical offer and ac-ceptance, with identifiable consideration, that seems to present difficulty, but this same difficulty exists in many situations of daily life, e.g., sales at auction; supermarket purchases; boarding an omnibus; purchasing a train ticket; tenders for the supply of goods; offers of rewards; acceptance by post; warranties of authority by agents; manufacturers' guarantees; gratuitous bailments; bankers' commercial credits. These are all examples which show that English law, having committed itself to a rather technical and schematic doctrine of contract, in application takes a practical approach, often at the cost of forcing the facts to fit uneasily into the marked slots of offer, acceptance and consideration."

A contract has clearly been concluded when a customer leaves the supermarket having paid for the goods, or when a passenger has boarded a bus and paid the fare,[100] or has taken a ride in a taxi,[101] or when a person purchases goods in response

---

Clarendon Press, 1998), Ch.26; and for sources within European jurisdictions: H. Beale, B. Fauvarque-Cosson, J. Rutgers, D. Tallon and S. Vogenauer, *Cases, Materials and Text on Contract Law*, 2nd edn (Hart Publishing, 2010), Ch.6.

[96] See para.3-07.

[97] See para.3-08 fn.32.

[98] e.g. see paras 3-22, 3-26, 3-29, 3-42.

[99] *New Zealand Shipping Co Ltd v AM Satterthwaite & Co Ltd (The Eurymedon)* [1975] A.C. 154, PC, at 167. For the difficulty of finding consideration in some of the cases mentioned by Lord Wilberforce, see para.8-41.

[100] In the case of a bus of a kind where the fare is paid not to the driver on entry but to a conductor dur-

to a newspaper advertisement. But it may not be obvious to the parties involved in those transactions that one was making an offer which the other accepted. Indeed, we shall see that the law superimposes on such transactions not only an analysis based on offer and acceptance, but a standard legal analysis of a typical transaction which determines which of the parties is to be taken to have made the offer.[102]

Given that the purpose of the analysis is not only to determine that a contract has been formed, but also what are its (express) terms,[103] an analysis based on offer and acceptance can also be misleadingly simple. Even if one of the parties at the end of their negotiations clearly makes an offer to compromise on some outstanding matter, and the other accepts it and thereby all the intended terms are agreed so as to form the contract, the wording of the offer may be hopelessly inadequate to determine the contract terms. Issues which the parties have already agreed upon may have been left aside, and the active discussions continued expressly on only the unresolved matters; to determine what has been agreed by the acceptance of the final offer may therefore involve some retrospective analysis of the negotiations.[104] Moreover, the words of the offer itself, as they would be understood by a reasonable person in the position of the offeree, may be coloured by the discussions which the parties have already conducted. Even if an "offer and acceptance" analysis is adopted, it is therefore still necessary to take the whole of the negotiations into consideration for the purpose of interpreting those final communications—and therefore for the purpose of seeing whether the parties are agreed on all the material points.[105] In the case of a contract which is wholly or partly oral, evidence of what the parties said and did *after* the contract was concluded are admissible to determine what they agreed.[106]

"Offer and acceptance" is sometimes an impossible analysis   There are some situations in which it is impossible to analyse the formation of the contract through "offer and acceptance". For example, the members of an unincorporated association, such as a social club, may bind themselves together by contract on the terms

3-21

---

ing the course of the journey, the contract is formed by the passenger's conduct in getting into the bus: *Wilkie v London Passenger Transport Board* [1947] 1 All E.R. 258, CA, at 259.

[101] *Albert v Motor Insurers' Bureau* [1972] A.C. 301, HL, at 339 (Lord Cross: "If I get into a taxi and ask the driver to drive me to Victoria Station it is extremely unlikely that either of us directs his mind to the question whether we are entering into a contract. We enter into a contract not because we form any intention to enter into one but because if our minds were directed to the point we should as reasonable people both agree that we were in fact entering into one").

[102] See paras 3-22, 3-29. For the particular difficulty of finding the offer and acceptance in a "battle of forms", see paras 3-23, 3-47.

[103] See para.3-22.

[104] cf. *Golden Ocean Group Ltd v Salgaocar Mining Industries Pvt Ltd* [2012] EWCA Civ 265; [2012] 1 W.L.R. 3674 at [22].

[105] cf. *G Scammell and Nephew Ltd v HC and JG Ouston*, see para.3-14 fn.70, at 255; *Destiny 1 Ltd v Lloyds TSB Bank Plc* [2011] EWCA Civ 831 at [15]. The necessary use of evidence from the negotiations in order to find and interpret the key communications by which the parties came to their agreement contrasts sharply with the limited use that may be made of the negotiations as evidence in order to interpret a *written* contract: see para.3-08.

[106] *BVM Management Ltd v Roger Yeomans (t/a Great Hall at Mains)* [2011] EWCA Civ 1254 at [23]; *Maggs v Marsh* [2006] EWCA Civ 1058; [2006] B.L.R. 395 at [24]–[26]; *Crema v Cenkos Securities Plc* [2010] EWCA Civ 1444; [2011] 1 W.L.R. 2066 at [34]; Lewison, para.3.19. Post-contract evidence is generally not admissible to interpret a *written* contract, which is a matter of law: Lewison, para.3.19.

of their constitution[107]; this may constitute a web of individual contracts, or a single multi-party contract, but on either analysis each member does not make an offer to the others. Although there may be an offer and acceptance between each new member and the secretary (or other officer) of the club with whom the member agrees the terms of his membership, and the secretary may be said to be acting on behalf of the other members for the purposes of entering into their contracts, such an analysis is not only artificial but breaks down altogether where there are multiple applications for new membership dealt with together by the secretary.[108] In the case of such multi-party contracts, the courts appear simply to have recognised the existence of the contract from the parties' intention to be mutually bound, without seeking to find the offer and the acceptance.[109]

3-22   **Advantages of "offer and acceptance" analysis**   In spite of the evident artificiality of sometimes "forcing the facts"[110] to fit the analysis of "offer and acceptance", the courts have long accepted it as an appropriate general analysis for the formation of contracts.[111] The advantages of such an analysis are centred around the certainty and predictability of the rules for the formation of contracts.

The English courts have developed rules to determine what normally constitutes an offer, and an acceptance, in certain typical situations, such as in contracts formed in supermarkets, or at auction, or following other public advertisements, and in cases where the parties communicate at a distance. We shall see that these rules are not arbitrary, but are often set by reference to underlying principles indicating the circumstances in which parties should reasonably expect to be bound.[112] But the particular rules are not necessarily what the parties themselves might have thought

---

[107] *Re Recher's Will Trusts* [1972] Ch. 526 at 538–539.

[108] Treitel, para.2-076. It is different where there is no mutuality of obligation amongst the multiple parties, e.g. where an insurer issues a policy intended to benefit each of a number of individual persons, but not all are yet identifiable (such as a policy designed to cover those involved in a construction project, where the class of beneficiaries is only ascertained as the project progresses). Such a case may be analysed as a standing offer to insure persons who are subsequently ascertained: J. Birds, B. Lynch. S. Milnes, *MacGillivray on Insurance Law*, 13th edn (London: Sweet & Maxwell, 2015), para.1–197. Such an analysis also avoids difficulties of purported ratification in advance within in the law of agency: P.G. Watts and F.M.B. Reynolds, *Bowstead and Reynolds on Agency*, 21st edn (London: Sweet & Maxwell, 2017), para.2–049.

[109] *Re Recher's Will Trusts*, see para.3-21 fn.107; *Clarke v Earl of Dunraven (The Satanita)* [1897] A.C. 59, HL (contract between participants in a yacht race; see Lord Herschell at 63: "I cannot entertain any doubt that there was a contractual relation between the parties to this litigation. The effect of their entering for the race, and undertaking to be bound by these rules to the knowledge of each other, is sufficient, I think, where those rules indicate a liability on the part of the one to the other, to create a contractual obligation to discharge that liability"); *Hadley v Kemp* [1999] E.M.L.R. 589 at 626 (mutual obligations between all members of the band Spandau Ballet on the principle of *The Satanita*). In the case of a company formed and registered under the Companies Acts, the relationship between a company and its members (shareholders, in the case of a company with a share capital) is based on a statutory contract—as if there were covenants on the part of the company and of each member to observe the provisions of the company's constitution: Companies Act 2006 s.33(1); G. Shirazi, "To what extent does the section 33 contract differ from an orthodox contract?" [2013] Comp. Law. 36.

[110] *New Zealand Shipping Co Ltd v AM Satterthwaite & Co Ltd (The Eurymedon)*, see para.3-20 fn.99.

[111] *Adams v Lindsell* (1818) 1 B. & Ald. 681, 106 E.R. 250. The language of "offer and acceptance" became common in the cases and textbooks during the 19th century as the common law adopted the will theory of contract: Ibbetson, see para.3-09 fn.42, pp.222–223; Simpson, see para.3-09 fn.42, pp.258–262.

[112] For the rules determining what constitutes an offer, see paras 3-27 onwards; for acceptance, see paras 3-34 onwards.

about the mechanics of the formation of their contract (indeed, the parties often give no thought to such matters) and there is not always a single answer as to how one could determine whether the offer is made by, for example, the advertiser or the person who responds to the advertisement, in the case of a newspaper or other public advertisement; or the time at which an acceptance takes effect, where the parties communicate at a distance.[113] Therefore, the selection of a rule may be based on principle but may to some extent also be rather more pragmatic. But by devising rules for such standard cases—or, at least, *default* rules so that the parties' legal advisers and the courts have a common starting-point for the analysis of the formation of the contract in the event of dispute—the courts inject predictability into the law. A general test such as "were the parties in agreement?" becomes a broad inquiry into the facts; a test which analyses the formation of the contract in terms of offer and acceptance, and which also provides at least a default rule as to what (in the type of case under consideration) constitutes an offer, or an acceptance, directs the parties and the court to make a more focused inquiry into the facts in relation to the application of the legal rule in question. The parties can predict more accurately how the court will analyse their disagreement, and may therefore be able more easily to come to a settlement.

Beyond the general predictability that is offered by a rule-based analysis of "offer and acceptance", there are more particular advantages by way of certainty, especially in a commercial context.[114] If we analyse the formation of the contract by the acceptance of an offer, the acceptance is the critical communication. Finding the acceptance of the offer not only establishes that there is a contract, but also identifies the parties to the contract,[115] the express terms of the contract,[116] the time at which the contract comes into existence,[117] and the place of the contract.[118]

---

[113] Legal systems adopt different approaches to these questions: e.g. there is a greater willingness in French law to characterise public proposals as offers rather than just invitations to treat, but the difference from English law can be attributed to a different view both of principle and of the balance of convenience: B. Nicholas, *The French Law of Contract*, 2nd edn (Clarendon Press, 1992), pp.63–65.

[114] See, e.g. *Tekdata Interconnections Ltd v Amphenol Ltd* [2009] EWCA Civ 1209; [2010] 1 Lloyd's Rep. 357 at [25] (Dyson LJ: offer and acceptance should continue to be used in a case of battle of forms, see para.3-47: it "has the great merit of providing a degree of certainty which is both desirable and necessary in order to promote effective commercial relationships"); *LJ Korbetis v Transgrain Shipping BV* [2005] EWHC 1345 (QB) at [12] (Toulson J: "Rules about offer and acceptance ought to be clear, so that parties may know where they stand").

[115] i.e. the persons by or on whose behalf the offer and the acceptance were communicated. This may be relevant to determine whether a person is a party or a third party who must therefore establish a claim to enforce a term of the contract under the Contracts (Rights of Third Parties) Act 1999; or if the offeror claims that the person who purported to accept the offer was not the person to whom it was addressed, and so that there was a mistake of identity rendering the contract void: Cartwright (Misrepresentation), Ch.14.

[116] In principle these will be contained, or referred to, in the offer since the acceptance must be unequivocal. However, in practice the offer must be read in the context of the prior negotiations: see para.3-20.

[117] This may be relevant if, e.g. the contract period, or the time for performance of some obligation within the contract, is defined by reference to its commencement; or if the contract is one under which property or risk passes at the moment of its formation; or if there are two competing contracts for the same asset and the court needs to be able to identify the first in order to give it priority in enforcement: *Potter v Sanders* (1846) 6 Hare 1, 67 E.R. 1057.

[118] This may be relevant to questions of jurisdiction in case of disputes arising under the contract: *Taylor v Jones* (1875) 1 C.P.D. 87; *Entores Ltd v Miles Far East Corp* [1955] 2 Q.B. 327, CA; *Brinkibon Ltd v Stahag Stahl und Stahlwarenhandelsgesellschaft mbH* [1983] 2 A.C. 34, HL.

3-23   **Rejection of "offer and acceptance" analysis by Lord Denning**   From time to time the artificiality of the "offer and acceptance" analysis has been noted and criticised,[119] and in the modern law Lord Denning sought to move away from the formal analysis and to formulate a broader legal test which would simply ask whether the parties had agreed and, if so, on what terms[120]:

> "In many of these cases our traditional analysis of offer, counter-offer, rejection, acceptance and so forth is out of date. This was observed by Lord Wilberforce in *New Zealand Shipping Co. Ltd v A. M. Satterthwaite & Co. Ltd*.[121] The better way is to look at all the documents passing between the parties—and glean from them, or from the conduct of the parties, whether they have reached agreement on all material points—even though there may be differences between the forms and conditions printed on the back of them."

Lord Denning was here speaking by way of obiter dictum[122] in the context of a "battle of forms" where it can be particularly difficult to establish the formation of the contract through an analysis of "offer and acceptance". However, he repeated it in a later case, *Gibson v Manchester City Council*,[123] to hold that a local authority had contracted to sell a house to one of its sitting tenants, but in circumstances where it did not appear possible to identify an offer and acceptance.[124]

3-24   **Reinstatement of "offer and acceptance" analysis by the House of Lords**   In this latter case, however, the House of Lords on appeal emphatically rejected Lord Denning's approach. Since there was no acceptance of an offer there was no contract; and Lord Diplock made clear that it is not possible normally to substitute a broader test based on finding the parties' agreement from their correspondence and conduct[125]:

> "My Lords, there may be certain types of contract, though I think they are exceptional, which do not fit easily into the normal analysis of a contract as being constituted by offer

---

[119] Ibbetson, see para.3-09 fn.42, p.246, noting criticisms by Pollock in the 1880s.

[120] *Butler Machine Tool Co Ltd v Ex-Cell-O Corp (England) Ltd* [1979] 1 W.L.R. 401, CA, at 404.

[121] [See para.3-20 fn.99.]

[122] All members of the court in the *Butler Machine Tool* case agreed in the result, but the majority applied the traditional rule—Bridge LJ referred (at 407) to "the classical doctrine that a counter-offer amounts to a rejection of an offer and puts an end to the effect of the offer"—and CA has more recently reaffirmed that in the context of a battle of forms the analysis must normally be based on finding an acceptance of an offer: *Tekdata Interconnections Ltd v Amphenol Ltd*, see para.3-22 fn.114. For the difficulties involved in analysing a "battle of forms", see para.3-47.

[123] *Gibson v Manchester City Council* [1978] 1 W.L.R. 520, CA, at 523–524. No reference, however, was made to the *Butler Machine Tool* case see para.3-23 fn.120. Ormrod LJ agreed with Lord Denning MR, both on his broader ground of finding an agreement between the parties and by construing the documents passing between the parties so as to find an offer which was accepted (at 527). Geoffrey Lane LJ dissented.

[124] There was disagreement on this amongst the judges: the document which was relied on as an offer was one in which the Council told Mr Gibson that it "may be prepared to sell" the house to him; this was construed by Ormrod LJ in CA as "are prepared to sell" and therefore to constitute an offer. This was rejected by Geoffrey Lane LJ in CA, and by HL, see para.3-22 fn.118.

[125] *Gibson v Manchester City Council* [1979] 1 W.L.R. 294, HL, at 297. Lord Edmund-Davies rejected Lord Denning's answer to the case without apparently criticising his general approach; Lord Russell in a short opinion rejected "the relevance to the case of general references to consensus in the judgments below. There was no oral evidence". Lord Fraser agreed with Lord Diplock and Lord Russell, and Lord Keith agreed with Lord Diplock. The explicit rejection of Lord Denning's approach was therefore not unanimous but Lord Diplock's reasoning had the general support of a majority of the House.

and acceptance; but a contract alleged to have been made by an exchange of correspondence between the parties in which the successive communications other than the first are in reply to one another, is not one of these. I can see no reason in the instant case for departing from the conventional approach of looking at the handful of documents relied upon as constituting the contract sued upon and seeing whether upon their true construction there is to be found in them a contractual offer by the corporation to sell the house to Mr Gibson and an acceptance of that offer by Mr Gibson. I venture to think that it was by departing from this conventional approach that the majority of the Court of Appeal was led into error."

Summary of the significance of "offer and acceptance" in the modern law   It   **3-25**
appears that Lord Denning's attempt to replace the strict "offer and acceptance" analysis by a broader test of whether the parties were in agreement, has not survived the emphatic rejection by Lord Diplock in *Gibson v Manchester City Council*. However, Lord Diplock made clear that there may be certain exceptional types of contract which do not fit easily into the "offer and acceptance" analysis. Such cases may include the multi-party cases discussed above,[126] since the one situation in which Lord Diplock made clear that there must be an acceptance of an offer if there is to be a contract, is where the contract is "alleged to have been made by an exchange of correspondence between the parties in which the successive communications other than the first are in reply to one another": that is, a bilateral contract by correspondence. This has been accepted in later cases,[127] and it has also been suggested that another exception is a contract which is alleged to have come into existence as a result of performance.[128]

The general rule that offer and acceptance must be found to form a contract does not mean that the court should simply stop its analysis if it finds two communications which might be so analysed: it must still look at the broader negotiations to be sure that it has correctly identified the offer and acceptance which form the agreement, and that there is no evidence from the continuing communications and dealings between the parties which indicates that they had not yet in fact come to a concluded agreement on all matters which they regard as essential.[129] This applies whether the negotiations are conducted in writing, orally, or by conduct (or by a combination of those means of communication).[130]

Where a claim is based on a contract, the particulars of claim must contain the basis of the contract, whether the claim is based on a written agreement, an oral agreement or an agreement by conduct.[131]

---

126 See para.3-21.
127 *G Percy Trentham Ltd v Archital Luxfer Ltd* [1993] 1 Lloyd's Rep 25, CA, at 27; *Tekdata Interconnections Ltd v Amphenol Ltd*, see para.3-22 fn.114, at 361.
128 *G Percy Trentham Ltd v Archital Luxfer Ltd*, see para.3-25 fn.127, at 27 (Steyn LJ, citing *Brogden v Metropolitan Railway Co* (1877) 2 A.C. 666, HL, although in that case it appears that the offeree's conduct may have constituted acceptance: see para.3-36, and esp. fn.240.
129 *Hussey v Horne-Payne* (1879) 4 App. Cas. 311 (HL); *RTS Flexible Systems Ltd v Molkerei Alois Müller GmbH & Co KG*, see para.3-05 fn.13, at [45], [49]; *Pagnan SpA v Feed Products Ltd*, see para.3-13 fn.64, at 619; *Gibbs v Lakeside Developments* [2016] EWHC 2203 (Ch) at [16].
130 *Global Asset Capital Inc v Aabar Block Sarl* [2017] EWCA Civ 37; [2017] 4 W.L.R. 163 at [31].
131 CPR PD 16 paras 7.3 (written agreement: a copy of the document and any incorporated general conditions of sale), 7.4 (oral agreement: the contractual words used, stating by whom, to whom, when and where they were spoken), 7.5 (agreement by conduct: the conduct relied on, stating by whom, when and where the acts constituting the conduct were done). In the case of an alleged oral agreement which depends on conflicting evidence of the parties, the mere fact that one of the two parties does not make himself available for cross-examination at trial does not mean that the court should

Since the normal method of analysis of the formation of a contract remains the conventional search for the unequivocal acceptance of an offer, it is necessary to consider in some detail the rules which the courts have developed to determine what constitutes an offer and an acceptance.

3-26 **The significance of particular cases on "offer" and "acceptance"** The rules on offer and acceptance are to be drawn from the cases. As always in the common law, the significance of a case which was concerned with, for example, whether one party's communication to the other did or did not constitute in law an offer, may extend beyond the particular case and be authority for a general proposition about when a communication constitutes an offer. Moreover, in devising the rules about what constitutes an offer, or an acceptance, the courts have sometimes taken an overtly pragmatic or policy-based approach, and have based their reasoning on a general consideration of the type of case. We therefore have lines of cases involving particular fact patterns—for example, authorities on how to analyse the communications made to the general public in newspaper advertisements, at auction, in shops (self-service or otherwise), and so on.

As we shall see in the following sections, some of the cases which are still relied upon in defining an offer and an acceptance go back to the nineteenth century, when the courts had to grapple with the analysis of new forms of communication. Where contracts are formed by oral exchanges between the parties or their agents, or even by written exchanges where the letters are carried by the parties' agents, the analysis focuses on the words as they passed between the parties at the moment that the parties (or their agents) participated in the formation of the alleged contract. But with the arrival of the mail and telegraph services as independent carriers of messages, with the potential for delays, miscommunications and even the loss of communications which might be the fault of neither party, the courts had to begin to formulate rules to deal with the new challenges of analysing whether a contract was formed, and in particular when and where the contract was concluded. Technology continues to develop, and just as the courts in the nineteenth century had to decide how to respond to the new postal and telegram services as means of forming a contract, so the development of other forms of communication has over the years given rise to similar new questions: telephone; telex; fax; email; text messaging—no doubt the list is not yet complete as new forms of communication develop. The traditional common law approach to the development of the law comes into its own here.[132] We discover the law from the cases: the ratio decidendi of the case is the legal reason for the decision on the facts, so that when similar facts arise in future cases, we know the (legal) answer because the *ratio* of the previous case is necessarily applicable. But when a different but similar case arises, the court will consider the *ratio* of previous cases not because they apply so as to answer the case, but because the general principle which underlay the case in giving the answer to those particular facts may be able to direct the court in how to answer the new case. The extension of the law is by analogy: the underlying principle of the existing decided case or cases may apply directly to the new case, or may show how a new discrete answer can be given to the new case. Sometimes, then, the old cases will give direct

---

prefer the evidence of the other party, but it should test both parties' evidence by reference to any contemporaneous documents and the inherent probabilities before deciding where the truth lies: *Harb v Aziz* [2016] EWCA Civ 556 at [24].
[132] R. Cross and J.W. Harris, *Precedent in English Law*, 4th edn (Clarendon Press, 1991), Ch.VI.

answers to solve a new case; but sometimes the significance of the established cases is to provide the evidence for the court, or the parties' legal advisers, about how to develop the rules on offer and acceptance to cover new situations as they arise. In any event, it is not only the results of previous cases that are significant, but also the reasoning of the judges.

(2) Offer

An "offer" is a proposal which is capable of forming a contract by simple acceptance   Given that a contract is formed through the acceptance of an offer, and that an acceptance is a simple, unequivocal assent to the terms proposed by the offer,[133] it is clear that an offer must satisfy a number of requirements. In the first place, it must be a sufficiently clear and complete proposal, communicated to the offeree,[134] that the court can hold that the offeree's acceptance of it will form a contract. Since the parties must agree on a sufficient body of terms that the law can recognise as a complete contract, even if gaps may be filled by implied terms,[135] the offer must contain sufficient detail as to the terms of the proposed contract, and the terms of the offer must be sufficiently certain for the court to give contractual effect to them if they are accepted.[136] Furthermore, the proposal must be a proposal *for a contract*, rather than a proposal for discussion with a view to a possible contract: it must be more than an "invitation to treat"[137] and must constitute an expression of willingness to be bound to the terms proposed. However, in English law the communications of the parties are tested objectively: not what the offeror intends his communication to mean, but what a reasonable person in the offeree's position would understand it to mean.[138] This further allows the courts to form general rules about the circumstances in which particular types of communication constitute an offer, since they can generalise about whether a reasonable recipient of such a communication might expect it to be intended to be binding on simple acceptance, or might expect it to give rise only to further negotiations before a contract is concluded.

3-27

---

[133] See para.3-34.

[134] For exceptional cases where the offer and acceptance may be inferred by the prolonged silence and inactivity of both parties, see para.3-39.

[135] See para.3-13.

[136] See paras 3-14 to 3-18.

[137] "Invitation to treat" is the most common general term used by contrast with "offer for sale": e.g. *Partridge v Crittenden* [1968] 1 W.L.R. 1204 at 1209; *Pharmaceutical Society of Great Britain v Boots Cash Chemists (Southern) Ltd* [1952] 2 Q.B. 795, CA, at 801; *Fisher v Bell* [1961] 1 Q.B. 394 at 399. It has also been referred to as an "offer to chaffer" or more simply an "offer to negotiate", an "offer to receive offers": *Carlill v Carbolic Smoke Ball Co* [1893] 1 Q.B. 256 at 268.

[138] See para.3-07. In addition, the offeree must in fact have understood the contract in the same sense as the reasonable person (see para.3-06), and so if he knows that the offeror is not in fact intending to propose a firm set of terms, it cannot yet constitute an offer. The language of the proposal is not conclusive: e.g. what is called an "offer" may in fact be an invitation to treat: *Spencer v Harding*, see para.3-29 fn.161 ("We are instructed to offer to the wholesale trade for sale by tender" was not an offer to sell to the person who made the highest tender); *Clifton v Palumbo* [1944] 2 All E.R. 497, CA ("I ... am prepared to offer you ... my ... estate for £600,000" was not, in all the circumstances, an offer to sell); and what is called an "agreement" may be only an offer: *Dickinson v Dodds* (1876) 2 Ch. D. 463 at 471, 473 (signed memorandum: "I hereby agree to sell" was offer, but in fact this was made clear by postscript which referred to "This offer").

3-28   **Distinguishing an "offer" from an "invitation to treat", "sales talk" etc**   Various kinds of statement may be made by one party with a view to leading the other to enter into a contract but without being intended to become legally binding by simple acceptance. A proposal for a possible contract, even if it already contains sufficient detail to form a contract, may yet be intended to be only the first stage in negotiations. A statement may appear to be an inducement to the other party to a contract but may not be intended to have legal consequences even if the other party acts upon it. Sometimes the question is whether there is a contract at all when the other party responds affirmatively: for example, is a person who "accepts" a proposal in a newspaper advertisement thereby concluding a contract, or only taking the negotiations for a possible contract to the next stage? Sometimes the question is whether statements which were made by one party to the other during the course of their discussions became part of the contract which was concluded by their agreement: for example, when the seller of a good makes statements to the potential buyer about the qualities of the good which he then agrees to buy. In the first case, the question is whether there was yet an offer at all to be accepted; in the second case the question is what the offer contained—that is, although it is clear that there was an offer, because the seller undoubtedly agreed to enter into a binding contract to sell the good to the buyer, it may be disputed whether the seller's statements about the good were part of the offer. These may seem to be different issues, one relating to the formation (or not) of the contract, the other relating to the terms of the contract which has been formed; but given that the contract is formed by acceptance of an offer, and that the (express) terms of the contract will be those which have been agreed upon (i.e. they were in the offer which was accepted), they are in fact part of the same enquiry, and one would expect similar principles to be applied in relation to both.[139]

The common principle sometimes articulated by the courts is the *intention* of the party making the statement that his words have legal consequences. Whether a statement made during the course of negotiations for a contract becomes a term of the contract depends on the parties' intention[140]; and criteria by reference to which this enquiry is conducted include the significance of the statement (its importance for the other party, whether it is just "sales talk" or a "mere puff" relating to the good), and whether the party making the statement holds himself out to be in a superior position of knowledge about what he says.[141] Given that intention is tested objectively, the essential question is whether the claimant in fact believed, and reasonably could in the circumstances believe, that the defendant intended to make a binding promise in the contract as to the accuracy of his statement.[142] This in turn is part of a broader principle underlying the remedies for pre-contractual misrepresentation: in order to be actionable, the statement must have been one on which the claimant was entitled to rely: it must be reasonable for him to have taken

---

[139] Where there is a written contract, the test for its interpretation is different: see para.3-08; but see *Crest Nicholson (Londinium) Ltd v Akaria Investments Ltd* [2010] EWCA Civ 1331; [2010] All E.R. (D) 269 (Nov) at [25].

[140] *Heilbut, Symons & Co v Buckleton* [1913] A.C. 30, HL. In the case of a consumer contract for goods, digital content or services, many pre-contractual statements are by statute treated as included as terms of the contract: Consumer Rights Act 2015 ss.11, 12, 36, 37, 50; Cartwright (Misrepresentation), paras 8-16 to 8-19.

[141] For a detailed discussion, see Cartwright (Misrepresentation), paras 8-04 to 8-12.

[142] Cartwright (Misrepresentation), para.8-06; see para.3-07.

it as seriously intended by the other party.[143] It is suggested that this is the same broad principle that underlies the question whether a proposition is an "offer" or only an invitation to treat. It can be seen in a case such as *Carlill v Carbolic Smoke Ball Co*,[144] where the advertisement in a newspaper of the "carbolic smoke ball" included a statement that the manufacturer would pay "£100 reward ... to any person who contracts the increasing epidemic influenza, colds, or any disease caused by taking cold, after having used the ball three times daily for two weeks according to the printed instructions supplied with each ball. £1000 is deposited with the Alliance Bank, Regent Street, shewing our sincerity in the matter". This was held to be intended to be not just a "mere puff" or a mere expression of confidence in the product,[145] but an offer to pay £100 to anyone who satisfied the stated conditions, because that is how a reasonable person would read it, given the assurance that money had been set aside to pay claims.[146] Since the smoke ball was bought by the claimant not directly from the manufacturer but from a retailer, this was a collateral, unilateral[147] contract on the terms of the newspaper advertisement. But where the communications are aimed at a simple bilateral contract the question whether a proposal is an offer, or only a preliminary indication of possible terms, can be answered using a similar objective approach[148]:

> "In determining [the question]—was there a proposal made by one party (A) which was capable of being accepted by the other (B)—the correct approach is to ask whether a person in the position of B (having the knowledge of the relevant circumstances which B had), acting reasonably, would understand that A was making a proposal to which he intended to be bound in the event of an unequivocal acceptance."

Proposals to the public contrasted with proposals directed at individuals   Where a party claims that he has accepted the defendant's offer and thereby formed a contract, the claimant must first show on the facts that the defendant made an offer. Sometimes the offer may be evident: the defendant may have made clear by his language that his proposal was open for acceptance. If this is not explicit, the claimant may show that, on the facts of the case, he was reasonably entitled to believe that the defendant was making a proposal that constituted an offer.[149] Where a proposal is directed at the claimant alone, the question is normally simply a matter of construction of the communication from the perspective of the claimant as its recipient. It can be more problematic, however, where the proposal was directed more widely, either at a group which included the claimant, or even at the public in general. It is in the context of such public communications that the courts have identified certain standard fact-patterns—newspaper advertisements, shop displays, invitations to tender, auctions, and so on—in order to develop rules as to how to draw a distinction between an "offer" and an "invitation to treat". Such rules are based not only on what a recipient might normally (objectively) expect to constitute

3-29

---

[143] Cartwright (Misrepresentation), paras 3-12 to 3-19 (distinction between statements of fact and statements of opinion, or "sales talk").

[144] See para.3-27 fn.137.

[145] [1893] 1 Q.B. 256 at 261, 266, 273.

[146] [1893] 1 Q.B. 256 at 266–267. See also at 262, 273.

[147] On the formation of unilateral contracts generally, see paras 3-32, 3-38.

[148] *Crest Nicholson (Londinium) Ltd v Akaria Investments Ltd*, see para.3-28 fn.139 at [25], drawing on *Harvey v Facey* [1893] A.C. 552, PC; *Schuldenfrei v Hilton (Inspector of Taxes)* [1998] S.T.C. 404 and [1999] S.T.C. 821, CA; and Chitty 30th edn (2008), para.2-003.

[149] See para.3-28.

an offer, or only an invitation to treat; but also on broader principles of business practice and convenience. They are, however, only default rules which give way to express stipulation to the contrary, and therefore the final analysis depends on the facts of the particular case (and, in particular, the language of the communication in question).

If the proposal is directed not at an individual but at the public or a section of the public, it will generally be held to be only an invitation to treat. The reasons given for this have varied according to the context.[150] Where there is a public advertisement for the sale of goods in a newspaper,[151] or in a journal with a specialist readership,[152] or in a circular sent round generally to potential buyers,[153] then at least where the proposal relates to goods of which the seller has a limited stock, it is "common sense"[154] that it is not an offer which could be accepted by every person who decided to take it up. This argument does not apply in the case of on-the-spot purchases in response to a shop display where the stock is visible to the buyer, but it is well established that a display is normally only an invitation to treat, whether the display is in a shop window[155] or on the shelves of a supermarket.[156] In such cases varying reasons have been given. It has been said that the shopkeeper should be free to decide whether to sell at the marked price or to the particular person who wishes to buy[157] —a reason which is unlikely to hold water today, at least if the

---

[150] It should be noted that this question has often arisen not in the context of a claim between the parties to an alleged contract, but to determine whether a party has committed a criminal offence by reason of the manner in which he has published his proposal: see, e.g. *Stainthorpe v Bailey*, see para.3-29 fn.151; *Partridge v Crittenden*, see para.3-29 fn.152; *Fisher v Bell*, see para.3-29 fn.155; *Pharmaceutical Society of Great Britain v Boots Cash Chemists (Southern) Ltd*, fn.156, and *British Car Auctions Ltd v Wright*, see para.3-29 fn.162. However, this context does not detract from the force of these cases as precedents in a purely contractual context, since the courts clearly apply the contract law rules, even where they would prefer to interpret language such as "offer to sell" more broadly for the purposes of the criminal statutes (see, e.g. *Partridge v Crittenden* at 1209; *Fisher v Bell* at 399); and where they "regret" the implications of the contract law rules for their decisions on the criminal law (see Lord Widgery CJ and Melford Stevenson J in *British Car Auctions v Wright* at 1525).

[151] *Stainthorpe v Bailey* [1980] R.T.R. 7 (advertisement of a second-hand car in the Manchester Evening News).

[152] *Partridge v Crittenden* [1968] 1 W.L.R. 1204 (advertisement for "bramblefinch cocks, bramblefinch hens ... 25s. each" in classified advertisements in specialist periodical, "Cage and Aviary Birds").

[153] *Grainger & Son v Gough* [1896] A.C. 325, HL (circular, including price list, sent to potential trade buyers of wine by wine merchant).

[154] *Partridge v Crittenden*, see para.3-29 fn.152, at 1210 (Lord Parker CJ), quoting Lord Herschell in *Grainger & Son v Gough*, see para.3-29 fn.153, at 334 ("The transmission of such a price-list does not amount to an offer to supply an unlimited quantity of the wine described at the price named, so that as soon as an order is given there is a binding contract to supply that quantity. If it were so, the merchant might find himself involved in any number of contractual obligations to supply wine of a particular description which he would be quite unable to carry out, his stock of wine of that description being necessarily limited").

[155] *Timothy v Simpson* (1834) 6 C. & P. 499, 172 E.R. 1337 (dress displayed in shop window marked with price); *Fisher v Bell* [1961] 1 Q.B. 394 (knife displayed in shop window with price displayed on ticket).

[156] *Pharmaceutical Society of Great Britain v Boots Cash Chemists (Southern) Ltd* [1952] 2 Q.B. 795 (medicines displayed on shelves in single-room self-service shop).

[157] *Timothy v Simpson*, see para.3-29 fn.155, (shopkeeper's employees were entitled to refuse to sell to the claimant and to turn him out of the shop, making him a trespasser: the evidence was that they first demanded 7s. 6d., rather than the marked price of 5s. 11d.; and then refused the individual because he was a Jew).

grounds of refusal of an individual constitute unlawful discrimination[158] or an unfair commercial practice.[159] But it is also said to be in accordance with "ordinary principles of common sense and of commerce" to hold that the display in a shop is only an invitation to treat: if it were an offer, the customer who picked up a good might be construed as accepting the offer and thereby concluding the contract— which would pass the property to the customer who could insist on taking the good, but could also then no longer change his mind and replace it on the shelf without remaining liable to pay for it.[160] An invitation to tender is normally only an invitation to submit offers: the party inviting tenders is then free to decide which (if any) tender to accept.[161] And in an auction it is the bidder that makes the offer, which is accepted by the fall of the auctioneer's hammer: advertising the goods for sale at auction is not therefore itself an offer, but only an invitation to submit bids in the auction.[162]

Although the advertisement, shop display, invitation to submit tenders and advertisement of goods for sale at auction do not normally constitute offers, this default position may be reversed if it so appears on the facts of the case. If the language of an advertisement makes clear that it can be accepted by anyone who chooses to reply, or anyone who fulfils some condition set by the advertisement, then it will be an offer: this is the basis on which the advertisement was held to be an offer of the "reward" in *Carlill v Carbolic Smoke Ball Co.*[163] This may even result in multiple contracts if the language of the proposal is sufficiently clear that it is an offer and that it can be accepted by more than one person.[164] On principle, it is possible for a person with only one good available, or only a limited stock, to make an offer which can be accepted only by the first person to respond, or only as long as the stock lasts.[165] An invitation to submit tenders can be an offer if it is

---

[158] cf. *Quinn v Williams Furniture Ltd* [1981] I.C.R. 328, CA (requirement for married woman to provide guarantor for hire-purchase contract which would not have been required of a married man was unlawful discrimination under Sex Discrimination Act 1975 ss.1(1)(a), 29); *Gill v El Vino Co Ltd* [1983] 1 Q.B. 425, CA (refusing to allow female customers at a wine bar to be served and drink at the bar, when it was allowed for male customers, was unlawful discrimination under Sex Discrimination Act 1975 ss.1(1)(a), 29). The Equality Act 2010 now makes provision for a wider range of protected characteristics, and a wider range of prohibited conduct in relation to both direct and indirect discrimination.

[159] e.g. a misleading price indication constitutes an unfair commercial practice under Consumer Protection from Unfair Trading Regulations 2008 (SI 2008/1277) reg.3(4)(d), Sch.1 para.5.

[160] *Pharmaceutical Society of Great Britain v Boots Cash Chemists (Southern) Ltd*, see para.3-29 fn.156, at 802 (Lord Goddard CJ). This argument still holds in relation to purchases from open shelves in a modern supermarket, although the assumption on which the decision in the *Pharmaceutical Society of Great Britain* case was made—that the offer is made by the customer at the till to the employee of the supermarket who may accept it or reject it—is artificial in the context of modern self-scan tills.

[161] *Spencer v Harding* (1870) L.R. 5 C.P. 561.

[162] *British Car Auctions Ltd v Wright* [1972] 1 W.L.R. 1519 (drawing an analogy with the cases on shop displays and newspaper advertisements); *Harris v Nickerson* (1873) L.R. 8 Q.B. 286 (rejecting the argument that advertising goods for auction constitutes an offer which is accepted by everyone who attends the auction giving rise to an action for their expenses in attending the auction if the item is not in fact put into the auction on the day).

[163] See para.3-28.

[164] *Carlill v Carbolic Smoke Ball Co*, see para.3-27 fn.137, at 268.

[165] cf. *Lefkowitz v Great Minneapolis Surplus Store* 86 N.W. 2d 689 (1957), SC Minnesota (newspaper advertisements in form such as "Saturday 9 A.M. Sharp 3 Brand New Fur Coats Worth to $100.00 First Come First Served $1 Each" were offers to sell to plaintiff who was the first to present himself in accordance with the advertisement).

sufficiently clear that the contract will go to the highest bidder, although because the terms of the contract are not themselves contained in the invitation to tender but will depend on the terms contained in the highest bid, it is generally best analysed as a unilateral offer to enter into a bilateral contract with the person who submits the highest bid.[166] Even if the person inviting tenders does not undertake to accept the highest (or, indeed, any) tender, he may in certain narrowly defined circumstances be held to have made an offer, implied in his invitation to submit tenders, at least to consider such conforming tenders as are submitted.[167] And although the auction contract is formed by the auctioneer's acceptance of the bidder's offer, it is possible for the auctioneer to guarantee that the highest bid will be accepted by, for example, advertising that the auction will be "without reserve", although in this case there is a collateral contract with the auctioneer which is breached if he accepts a bid from or on behalf of the seller, or if he fails to knock down the item to the person who in fact submits the highest bid.[168]

3-30   **Period during which the offer may be accepted**   The contract can come into existence only if the offer is validly accepted. The offer may make express provision for the time and manner of a valid acceptance. The manner of acceptance is considered below[169]; here we consider the force of an express stipulation as to the time of acceptance, and how to determine the time within which the offer may be accepted if there is no express stipulation.

An express stipulation of the period of validity of an offer may be either positive or negative; that is, it may either promise to keep the offer open for a period within which the offeree is entitled to accept, or it may provide that the offer will lapse after a specified period if it has not in fact been accepted. In the absence of express stipulation, the question is whether there is an (implied) period within which the offeree has a guaranteed minimum period for reflection, and whether the offer will (impliedly) lapse after some specified period.

Even if the offer stipulates a period within which it can be accepted and contains an express promise that the offer will not be withdrawn within that period, the of-

---

[166] *Spencer v Harding*, see para.3-29 fn.161, at 563 (Willis J: "If the circular had gone on, 'and we undertake to sell to the highest bidder', the reward cases would have applied"). It must be certain what will constitutes the "highest bid", and as always the interpretation of the offer contained in the invitation to tender will depend on the objective test from the point of view of the recipient of the invitation: *Harvela Investments Ltd v Royal Trust Co of Canada (CI) Ltd* [1986] 1 A.C. 207, HL, at 225 (Lord Diplock: "what legal obligation would the words used by the promisor reasonably convey to the promisee that it was the intention of the promisor to assume towards him?"; on construction, only fixed bids, not referential bids, were invited). Where there are a number of potential variables in determining what constitutes the "highest bid" (e.g. in a works contract where there are many more issues than just the price) there may be a difficulty in determining whether the undertaking to accept the "best bid" is sufficiently certain: cf. *Sidey Ltd v Clackmannanshire Council* [2011] CSOH 194, 2012 S.L.R. 334, OH, at [25]. Where the tenders relate to public procurement contracts, special rules apply under EU law: Chitty, paras 11-051 to 11-052; S. Arrowsmith, *The Law of Public and Utilities Procurement*, 3rd edn (Sweet & Maxwell, 2014) Vol.1.

[167] *Blackpool and Fylde Aero Club Ltd v Blackpool BC* [1990] 1 W.L.R. 1195, CA; see para.2-24 for the limitations on such an implied contract.

[168] *Warlow v Harrison* (1859) 4 El. & El. 309, 120 E.R. 925; *Barry v Davies* [2000] 1 W.L.R. 1962, CA. Accepting a bid from the seller subverts the offer to sell "without reserve"; and "withdrawing the lot from sale because it has not reached the level which the auctioneer considers appropriate is tantamount to bidding on behalf of the seller. The highest bid cannot be rejected simply because it is not high enough": *Barry v Davies* at 1965 (Sir Murray Stuart-Smith).

[169] See paras 3-36 to 3-40.

feror is still free to withdraw the offer at any moment unless he has bound himself contractually not to do so. This is the force of an *option contract*: a contract by which one party (the offeree) is given the right to enter into a defined contract (on the terms of the offer) if he so chooses by simply accepting the offer in accordance with its terms.[170] But the grant of such an option, if it is not contained in a deed, requires consideration to be provided by the offeree.[171] A "firm offer" is not in itself binding as to the period which it purports to be open for acceptance.[172] Given that even an express promise to keep an offer open is not binding in the absence of a deed or a contract supported by consideration, it is not surprising that English law does not impose an implied duty on the offeror to allow the offeree a minimum period for reflection. An offer may be made one second and withdrawn the next without the offeror incurring any legal liability for the withdrawal.[173]

Where the offer is expressed to be open only for a defined period, the offer lapses automatically at the end of that period.[174] However, if there is no express stipulation on the matter, an offer cannot sensibly be held to be open for ever, but will lapse after such time as is "reasonable" in the circumstances.[175] It has been suggested that

---

[170] See para.2-20.

[171] *Dickinson v Dodds* (1876) 2 Ch. D. 463, CA, at 472 (James LJ: "it is clear settled law, on one of the clearest principles of law, that this promise [to keep offer open until a specified time], being a mere *nudum pactum*, was not binding, and that at any moment before the complete acceptance by Dickinson of the offer, Dodds was as free as Dickinson himself"). See also *Cooke v Oxley* (1790) 3 T.R. 653 at 653–654, 100 E.R. 785 at 786; *Offord v Davies* (1862) 12 C.B. (N.S.) 748, 142 E.R. 1336; *Routledge v Grant* (1828) 4 Bing. 653, 130 E.R. 920; *Stevenson, Jaques & Co v McLean* (1880) 5 Q.B.D. 346 at 351.

[172] For criticism, see Law Com. WP No.60, *Firm Offers* (1975). Civil law systems, which do not require consideration to make a promise or agreement binding, can more easily find a mechanism for giving binding force to an undertaking to keep an offer open, or at least to provide a remedy for a wrongful breach of such an undertaking: see para.2-20 fn.117.

[173] For how an offer is validly withdrawn, see para.3-31. In civil law systems which recognise a general doctrine of good faith in the formation of contracts, the making of an offer may carry an implied duty not to withdraw it contrary to good faith: K. Zweigert and H. Kötz, *An Introduction to Comparative Law*, 3rd edn (trans. T. Weir, Clarendon Press, 1998), pp.359–363. Where the offer is an offer to settle under CPR Pt 36, the provisions of the CPR apply to determine whether the offer may be withdrawn or its terms changed without the permission of the court and how an offeror may withdraw or change the terms of his offer (CPR r.36.9(2): "by serving written notice ... on the offeree" which excludes implied revocation or rejection of an offer as might occur under the common law rules of offer and acceptance: *Gibbon v Manchester City Council* [2010] EWCA Civ 726; [2010] 1 W.L.R. 2081 at [16]).

[174] An acceptance which arrives outside the period therefore does not bind the offeror and form the contract, although if the offeror wishes still to enter into the contract he may do so by accepting the (new) offer which has been made by the offeree's "acceptance". An offer to settle under CPR Pt 36 cannot be time-limited, and in that context (contrary to the normal, objective meaning of the words) a reference to the offer being "open for 21 days" is to be construed not as meaning that the offer will lapse after 21 days, but that the offeror will not attempt to withdraw it for that period: *C v D* [2011] EWCA Civ 646; [2012] 1 W.L.R. 1962.

[175] *Ramsgate Victoria Hotel Co Ltd v Montefiore* (1866) L.R. 1 Ex. 109 (application for shares in June; allotment in November was too late to constitute acceptance); *Re Bowron, Baily & Co* (1868) L.R. 3 Ch. App. 592 (application for shares in October; allotment in February was too late); *Manchester Diocesan Council for Education v Commercial & General Investments Ltd* [1970] 1 W.L.R. 241 at 247 (offer to purchase property made in August could still be accepted in January because offeree had indicated in September his intention to accept). The offer may also lapse on the death of the offeree before acceptance, although this should depend on the proper construction of the offer, for example whether it was personal to the offeree: *Reynolds v Atherton* (1921) 125 L.T. 690, CA, at 695–696 (Warrington LJ, noting that there was no judicial authority but textbook writers favour the view that an offer is personal); cf. (1922) 127 L.T. 189, HL, at 191 (Lord Dunedin, not deciding

the implied lapse of the offer is better seen as based not on an implication that the offer is made upon terms that, if not accepted within a reasonable time, it must be treated as withdrawn, but rather on an implication that if the offeree does not accept the offer within a reasonable time, he must be treated as having refused it.[176] The choice between these two different bases of implication is significant: the former asks what would have been reasonable to set as a period for acceptance at the moment when the offer was made, whereas the latter involves an assessment of whether, on the facts, the offeree should be regarded as having refused the offer: that is, the conduct of the parties after the offer has been made are relevant in the latter interpretation but not the former.[177] However, the terms of the offer ought in principle to be ascertainable when the offer is first made; and the better approach would be to say that an offer, when made, is to be interpreted as open for acceptance only for such time as then appears reasonable; whether on the facts the offeree can be held impliedly to have rejected the offer earlier than the expiry of that reasonable time will take into account the circumstances, and the offeree's conduct, as they appear to the offeror[178] during the period when the offer is open.[179]

Independently of any period for acceptance set by its terms, the offer can no longer be accepted once it has been terminated by revocation by the offeror, or by rejection by the offeree. These cases are considered in the following paragraphs.

3-31   **Termination (revocation) of offer by the offeror: general**   If the offeror revokes the offer, it can no longer be accepted.[180] The question is therefore what is necessary in order successfully to revoke an offer. In a legal system which requires a subjective meeting of the parties' minds in order to form a contract, it may be sufficient for the offeree to demonstrate that he had changed his mind and done some act which shows that he had decided to withdraw the offer without necessarily having to show that the other party knew or ought to have known of his decision.[181]

---

whether the offer, had it been addressed to individuals, could have been accepted by an offeree's personal representatives); *Sommerville v National Coal Board* 1963 S.L.T. 334, IH (offer of damages for personal injury could not be accepted after death where damages included future loss of earnings; court declined to decide whether an offer falls automatically on the death of the offeree). The purported acceptance by the personal representatives, if it does not constitute an acceptance binding the offeree's estate, may be a new offer by the representatives personally, which is then open for acceptance by the original offeror: *Re Cheshire Banking Co, Duff's Executors' Case* (1886) 32 Ch. D. 301, CA.

[176] *Manchester Diocesan Council for Education v Commercial & General Investments Ltd*, see para.3-fn.175, at 247.

[177] *Manchester Diocesan Council for Education v Commercial & General Investments Ltd*, see para.3-30 fn.175, at 247–248.

[178] The objective test will be applied, as always, to determine what the offeree can reasonably be taken to have intended, viewed from the perspective of the other party (the offeror): see para.3-07.

[179] The consequence of taking this interpretation of the basis of the implied lapse of the offer is that the offeree's conduct during the period of the offer can constitute his implied rejection of the offer, but cannot in itself extend the period of the offer beyond that which was reasonable when the offer was first made.

[180] *Routledge v Grant* (1828) 3 C. & P. 267 at 273, 172 E.R. 415 at 417–418; (1828) 4 Bing. 653, 130 E.R. 920. This is so even where the offer is expressed to be open for a fixed period, as long as the offeror is not contractually bound to keep the offer open: see para.3-30; *Byrne & Co v Leon van Tienhoven & Co* (1880) 5 C.P.D. 344 at 347; *Stevenson, Jaques & Co v McLean* (1880) 5 Q.B.D. 346 at 351.

[181] cf. *Byrne & Co v Leon van Tienhoven & Co*, see para.3-31 fn.180, at 347 (Lindley J, rejecting in English law the opinion attributed to "Pothier and some other writers of celebrity". "The reason for this opinion is that there is not in fact any such consent by both parties as is essential to constitute a

However, given the objective approach taken generally in determining the formation of a contract in English law,[182] one would expect that, given that the existence and meaning of an offer is to be determined by reference to the perspective of a reasonable person in the position of the offeree, the question whether the offer has been validly revoked should be similarly determined. Only if there is sufficient objective evidence, visible to the offeree,[183] that the offer has been revoked should the revocation be complete. We shall see below that there are circumstances in which the acceptance of an offer can take effect even though it has not yet been communicated to the offeree, under the so-called "postal rule".[184] However, given that the offeree has been led by the offeror to believe that there is an offer open for acceptance, the offeree is entitled to receive communication of its revocation and so the "postal rule" does not apply to communications by which the offeror seeks to revoke his offer.[185]

Under the objective test the question is not only what a party ought reasonably to know about the other party's intentions from the latter's words and conduct, but also what he in fact knows or believes: A can hold B to a contract on the terms that B's conduct would indicate to a reasonable person in A's position, regardless of what B in fact intended, but not if A actually knows of B's real intentions.[186] It is said that one cannot "snap up" an offer if one knows that the offeror is mistaken about its terms.[187] Similarly, if the offeree knows that the offeror has in fact changed his mind and no longer wishes to contract on the terms of the offer, he should not be entitled to accept it even if the offeror has not yet directly communicated revocation of his offer.[188] It will be a matter of evidence as to whether the offeree can be held to have known that the offeror must have decided to withdraw the offer and, given that in general the burden is on the offeror to take sufficient steps to revoke his offer, one would expect the courts to be cautious in so holding except where the evidence is clear. It has been so held in a case where the offer was to sell property which the

---

contract between them"); *Stevenson, Jaques & Co v McLean*, see para.3-31 fn.180, at 352 (Lush J: "the doctrine of Pothier ... which is undoubtedly contrary to the spirit of English law, has never been affirmed in our Courts"). The French civil code was amended in 2016, and now contains detailed provisions on offer and acceptance: arts 1113–1122 c.civ. For the position in modern French law before the reform, see B. Nicholas, *The French Law of Contract*, 2nd edn (Clarendon Press, 1992), pp.66-69; and for the 2016 amendments generally, see J. Cartwright and S. Whittaker (eds), *The Code Napoléon Rewritten: French Contract Law after the 2016 Reforms* (Hart Publishing, 2017); S. Rowan, "The New French Law of Contract" (2017) 66 I.C.L.Q. 805.

[182] See para.3-07.

[183] For the difficulty of revoking an offer which was not addressed to an individual, such as the public offer of a reward, see para.3-32.

[184] See para.3-42.

[185] *Byrne & Co v Leon van Tienhoven & Co*, see para.3-31 fn.180, at 348-349 (Lindley J: "both legal principles, and practical convenience require that a person who has accepted an offer not known to him to have been revoked, shall be in a position safely to act upon the footing that the offer and acceptance constitute a contract binding on both parties"); *Stevenson, Jaques & Co v McLean*, see para.3-31 fn.180; *Henthorn v Fraser* [1892] 2 Ch. 27, CA, at 31-32.

[186] See para.3-06; Cartwright (Misrepresentation), paras 13-13, 13-21.

[187] *Tamplin v James* (1880) 15 Ch. D. 215 at 221 (James LJ); *Hartog v Colin & Shields* [1939] 3 All E.R. 566 at 567.

[188] *Dickinson v Dodds*, see para.3-30 fn.171, at 473 (James LJ: "before there was any attempt at acceptance by the Plaintiff, he was perfectly well aware that Dodds had changed his mind ... It is impossible, therefore, to say that there was ever that existence of the same mind between the two parties which is essential in point of law to the making of an agreement"). See also Mellish LJ at 474.

offeree actually discovered (before acceptance) had since been sold to a third party.[189]

The death of the offeror, before the offer is accepted, can also constitute revocation of an offer. However, following the principles set out above, the offer should be revoked only where the offeree knows, or ought reasonably to know, of the death.[190] As long as the offer was not expressly or impliedly terminable by the offeror's death,[191] and death creates no other legal obstacle to the formation of the contract,[192] the offeree ought to be protected where he accepts the offer; and the contract which is thereby formed will bind the offeror's estate and his personal representatives.

3-32 **Termination (revocation) of offer by the offeror: the problem of unilateral contracts** In a "unilateral" contract only one party comes under an obligation.[193] The other party creates the contract by doing something which the offeror[194] has set as the condition for his obligation arising: the obligation arises *if* the offeree performs the condition set by the offer.[195] Two problems may arise in the case of

---

[189] *Dickinson v Dodds*, see para.3-30 fn.171.
[190] *Coulthart v Clementson* (1879) 5 Q.B.D. 42 (continuing guarantee revoked as to subsequent advances by notice of death of guarantor); cf. *Dickinson v Dodds*, see para.3-30 fn.171, at 475 (Mellish LJ, not referring to the offeree's knowledge of the death, but drawing a parallel with the case where the offeree knows that the property offered for sale has been sold to someone else). If the offer could not have been revoked by the offeror, even notice of the death will not revoke it: *Errington v Errington*, see para.3-30 fn.205, at 295 (offer of unilateral contract during period offeree is attempting to complete performance).
[191] Such a term is unlikely in an offer except in the case of continuing offers, e.g. a continuing guarantee: *Coulthart v Clementson*, see para.3-31 fn.190; *Harriss v Fawcett* (1873) L.R. 8 Ch. App. 866.
[192] e.g. where the contract was for services to be performed personally, and therefore is impossible: cf. *Taylor v Caldwell* (1863) 3 B. & S. 826 at 835-836, 122 E.R. 309 at 313 (Blackburn J, discussing circumstances where death of one party may frustrate a contract for personal services).
[193] The simplest case of a unilateral contract is the payment of a reward in return for doing some specified task: e.g. *Williams v Carwardine* (1833) 4 B. & Ad. 621, 110 E.R. 590 (£20 reward for information leading to conviction of murderer); *Carlill v Carbolic Smoke Ball Co* [1893] 1 Q.B. 256, CA (£100 payment to any person who contracted influenza after using "smoke ball"); but it is also possible for the obligation which arises to go beyond simple unilateral performance and be an undertaking to enter into a bilateral contract: e.g. *Harvela Investments Ltd v Royal Trust Co of Canada (CI) Ltd* [1986] 1 A.C. 207, HL, at 224-225 (promise to sell to highest bidder analysed as unilateral contract which would give rise to synallagmatic contract in the case of the highest bidder); *New Zealand Shipping Co Ltd v AM Satterthwaite & Co Ltd (The Eurymedon)* [1975] A.C. 154, PC, at 167-168 ("the bill of lading brought into existence a bargain initially unilateral but capable of becoming mutual, between the shipper and the appellant, made through the carrier as agent. This became a full contract when the appellant performed services by discharging the goods"); *Daulia Ltd v Four Millbank Nominees Ltd* [1978] Ch. 231, CA (unilateral contract to enter into contract of sale of land if purchaser procured banker's draft and attended at vendor's office at specified time with signed contract, although it was unenforceable because of failure to comply with LPA 1925 s.40); *Habibsons Bank Ltd v Standard Chartered Bank (Hong Kong) Ltd* [2010] EWCA Civ 1335, [2011] Q.B. 943 at [23] (offer to contract by way of novation with any financial institution which complies with specific provisions).
[194] The analysis of unilateral contracts in terms of offer and acceptance dates from the 19th century when "offer and acceptance" analysis was introduced generally into the English law of contract, although earlier cases had analysed them as promises in consideration of an act not yet performed: A.W.B. Simpson, "Innovation in Nineteenth Century Contract Law" (1975) 91 L.Q.R. 247, 261-262.
[195] Unilateral contracts are therefore sometimes referred to as "'if' contracts", following the terminology of Diplock LJ in, e.g. *United Dominions Trust (Commercial) Ltd v Eagle Aircraft Services Ltd* [1968] 1 W.L.R. 74, CA, at 83. The performance of the condition is also the consideration provided by the offeree for the offeror's promise: see paras 8-13, 8-18.

the attempt by the offeror to revoke the offer of a unilateral contract: a practical difficulty in knowing how revocation is to be effected, and a legal question about whether there may be a restriction on the power to revoke.

We have seen that revocation of an offer normally requires communication of the revocation to the offeree.[196] In the case of unilateral contracts there can sometimes be a practical difficulty in knowing how to revoke the offer because of the difficulty of finding the offeree in order to communicate the revocation, where the offer was not made to an individual or to a defined set of individuals but to a wide group or even to the public at large. This is not a problem limited to unilateral contracts, since it is possible, though not common, for a proposal of a bilateral contract which is made to the public to constitute an offer rather than just an invitation to treat.[197] Nor does it apply in the case of all unilateral contracts, since an offer may be made to an individual or a limited group of individuals.[198] However, an offer to the public will commonly be the offer of a unilateral contract, as in the case of the offer of a reward.[199] In such a case, it is likely that a court would hold that it is sufficient for the offeror to take such steps as are reasonable in the circumstances to seek to communicate to the same audience as that to which the offer had been addressed.[200] This is in accordance with the general principle for the objective interpretation of offers and their revocation[201]: given that the offeree did not receive notice of the offer directly and individually from the offeror, he cannot reasonably expect to receive direct and individual revocation, but ought to realise that any revocation might be made by similar means.[202]

A more particular legal difficulty may arise in relation to the power to revoke an offer of a unilateral contract. In principle, an offer may be revoked freely by the offeror if it has not yet been accepted, unless the offeror has undertaken to keep it open for a defined period—and such an undertaking must normally itself have contractually binding force by being supported by consideration or by being expressed as an obligation in a deed.[203] The fact that, in the case of a unilateral contract, the offeree must perform an act set by the offeror as the condition of acceptance creates a difficulty where the act may take some time, and the offeror wishes to revoke his offer once performance has begun but has not yet been completed. The contract is not complete until the condition has been satisfied, whether it involves simply the performance of the prescribed act, or also the notification to the offeror that the act has been done.[204] On the other hand, once the offeree has begun to perform, unless in the circumstances the offeree should reasonably have realised that the offer might be revoked and therefore any performance (short of its completion) is at his risk, it will generally not be acceptable to allow the offeror to revoke his acceptance without at least giving the offeree the op-

---

[196] See para.3-31.
[197] See para.3-29.
[198] e.g. *Daulia Ltd v Four Millbank Nominees Ltd*, see para.3-32 fn.193.
[199] e.g. *Williams v Carwardine* and *Carlill v Carbolic Smoke Ball Co*, see para.3-32 fn.193.
[200] There appears to be no English authority; cf. *Shuey v United States* 92 U.S. 73 (1875) at 76 (offer of reward made in public newspapers and other public proclamation was "withdrawn through the same channel by which it was made" although it was not read by person who later sought to accept it).
[201] See para.3-31.
[202] *Shuey v United States*, see para.3-32 fn.200, at 77.
[203] See para.3-30.
[204] On the interpretation of the offer in the case of a unilateral contract, see para.3-38.

portunity to complete the performance. Most recently, Longmore LJ has said[205]:

"This is a classic unilateral contract of the *Carlill v Carbolic Smoke Ball Co*[206] or the 'walk to York'[207] kind. Once the promisee acts on the promise by inhaling the smoke ball, by starting the walk to York or (as here) by not suing for the maintenance to which she was entitled, the promisor cannot revoke or withdraw his offer. But there is no obligation on the promisee to continue to inhale, to walk the whole way to York or to refrain from suing. It is just that if she inhales no more, gives up the walk to York or does sue for her maintenance, she is not entitled to claim the promised sum."

This is put in terms of an implied obligation not to revoke the offer once the offeree has begun performance. Goff LJ has said that there is also a positive obligation on the offeror not to prevent the completion of performance[208]:

"Whilst I think the true view of a unilateral contract must in general be that the offeror is entitled to require full performance of the condition which he has imposed and short of that he is not bound, that must be subject to one important qualification, which stems from the fact that there must be an implied obligation on the part of the offeror not to prevent the condition becoming satisfied, which obligation it seems to me must arise as soon as the offeree starts to perform. Until then the offeror can revoke the whole thing, but once the offeree has embarked on performance it is too late for the offeror to revoke his offer."

In none of the cases on this subject, however, is the basis of the implied obligation not to revoke the offer made clear. It has been suggested that the offeror cannot revoke because acceptance is complete when the offeree begins performance, although he does not satisfy the condition against which the offeror must perform his own obligation unless he actually completes performance[209]; this is in effect treating the unilateral contract as an implied offer of an option[210] which is accepted (and consideration is provided) by the offeree acting on the offer by beginning to perform.[211] Another way of seeing it is that the offer is not accepted until

---

[205] *Soulsbury v Soulsbury* [2007] EWCA Civ 969; [2008] Fam. 1 at [49]. See also *Offord v Davies* (1862) 12 C.B. (N.S.) 748 at 757, 142 E.R. 1336 at 1340 (Erle CJ: "This promise by itself creates no obligation. It is in effect conditioned to be binding if the plaintiff acts upon it, either to the benefit of the defendants, or to the detriment of himself. But, until the condition has been at least in part fulfilled, the defendants have the power of revoking it"); *Errington v Errington* [1952] 1 K.B. 290, CA, at 295 (Denning LJ: "The father's promise was a unilateral contract—a promise of the house in return for [his son and daughter-in-law's] act of paying the instalments [due on the mortgage]. It could not be revoked by him once the couple entered on performance of the act, but it would cease to bind him if they left it incomplete and unperformed").

[206] See para.3-32 fn.193.

[207] This is a reference to a traditional example: *Rogers v Snow* (1573) Dalison 94, 123 E.R. 301 at 302; *Great Northern Railway Co v Witham* (1873) L.R. 9 C.P. 16 at 19.

[208] *Daulia Ltd v Four Millbank Nominees Ltd*, see para.3-32 fn.193 at 239. See also Buckley LJ at 245.

[209] This was the solution, to resolve differences in the cases, proposed by Law Revision Committee, Sixth Interim Report, *Statute of Frauds and the Doctrine of Consideration* Cmd.5449 (1937), para.39 (promise should be binding as soon as promisee has entered on performance of the act, unless promise includes express or implied term allowing promisor to revoke; but no recovery unless performance is completed). cf. P.H. Winfield, *Pollock's Principles of Contract*, 13th edn (Stevens, 1950), p.19 ("surely the acceptance is complete as soon as B has made an unequivocal beginning of the performance requested, a 'commencement d'exécution' to use the term familiar in French law. Whether anything is payable before the whole of the work is done depends on the terms express or implied of A's offer on which B acts"); *Blue v Ashley* [2017] EWHC 1928 (Comm) at [50].

[210] On option contracts, see para.2-20.

[211] cf. Restatement of Contracts (2d) §45: "(1) Where an offer invites an offeree to accept by rendering a performance and does not invite a promissory acceptance, an option contract is created when

performance is complete, but that there is an implied promise not to revoke the offer if the offeree begins performing—in effect, a subsidiary, implied, unilateral contract.[212] On either analysis, however, we have to imply a contractual structure (offer, acceptance and consideration) which the parties have not articulated in order to obtain what the courts clearly (and, it is submitted, rightly) view as the correct conclusion. This is an example of our having to fit within the modern rules of offer and acceptance a transaction which does not really fit.[213]

Termination (rejection) of offer by the offeree   If the offeree rejects the offer, it has gone for good[214] and a new offer must be made by one of the parties, and accepted by the other, for a contract to come into existence. The rejection of the offer may be express, whether or not accompanied by a new offer; or it may be implied, typically by the offeree's making a proposal for the contract on different terms—that is, a counter offer[215] which has the effect of both rejecting the old offer and making a new offer which is then open for acceptance by the other party (the former offeror).[216] Not every response to an offer is a rejection if it does not unequivocally accept the offer. It may be merely an inquiry, asking for further details of the offer, or even asking for guidance about whether the offer is final or whether the offeror might be willing to consider some variation to the terms of the

3-33

---

the offeree tenders or begins the invited performance or tenders a beginning of it. (2) The offeror's duty of performance under any option contract so created is conditional on completion or tender of the invited performance in accordance with the terms of the offer".

[212] Anson, p.58; cf. Treitel, para.2-053 (such an analysis is artificial). In *Morrison Shipping Co Ltd v The Crown* (1924) 20 Ll. L. Rep. 283 at 287 Viscount Cave LC doubted whether a contract is yet formed when performance begins, but that "when work is done and expense incurred on the faith of a conditional promise, the promisor comes under an implied obligation not to revoke his promise, and if he does so may be sued for damages or on a quantum meruit".

[213] See para.3-20; cf. Simpson, see para.3-32 fn.194, pp.261–262. It should be noted that the analysis of option contracts is similarly difficult (sometimes seen as conditional contracts, sometimes as irrevocable offers: see para.2-20 fn.114). In the present context, however, the additional difficulty is not only in working out when the offer is accepted, but in implying the consideration for the "option" or the irrevocable offer. Where an option contract is entered into expressly, the need for consideration (or a deed) is clear.

[214] *Hyde v Wrench* (1840) 3 Beav. 334 at 337, 49 E.R. 132 at 133 (Lord Langdale MR: defendant's offer for sale of property at £1,000 was rejected by counter offer: "the Plaintiff made an offer of his own, to purchase the property for £950, and he thereby rejected the offer previously made by the Defendant. I think that it was not afterwards competent for him to revive the proposal of the Defendant, by tendering an acceptance of it"); *Trollope & Colls Ltd v Atomic Power Constructions Ltd* [1963] 1 W.L.R. 333 at 337 (Megaw J: "If an offer is rejected, there may be a counter-offer, but the counter-offer kills the original offer. The offeree cannot revert to the original offer and purport to accept it"). An offer is similarly rejected by a (counter-)offer made by the offeree in the form of a Pt 36 offer to settle, in spite of the fact that CPR Pt 36 is a self-contained code, which operates in other respects differently from the common law principles of offer and acceptance: *Gibbon v Manchester City Council*, see para.3-30 fn.173; *DB UK Bank Ltd v Jacobs Solicitors* [2016] EWHC 1614 (Ch); [2016] 4 W.L.R. 184 at [23]–[27].

[215] The term was in use by the second half of the 19th century: see, e.g. *Taylor v Laird* (1856) 1 H. & N. 266 at 273, 156 E.R. 1203 at 1206; *Tyrrell v Bank of London* (1862) 10 H.L. Cas. 26 at 57, 11 E.R. 934 at 946; *Canning v Farquhar* (1886) 16 Q.B.D. 727, CA, at 733; *Jones v Daniel* [1894] 2 Ch. 332 at 335 (Romer J: "He does not accept what I may call the counter offer of the Plaintiff"). In *Hyde v Wrench*, see para.3-33 fn.214, at 132, at 336, counsel referred to a "proposal" and "counter proposal".

[216] *Jones v Daniel*, see para.3-33 fn.215 (offer to buy property for £1,450; "acceptance" which included new terms relating to payment of deposit, date for completion, provision limiting title to be shown by vendor and other conditions, was only a counter offer).

offer.[217] No doubt if the response is of this latter kind, particularly where the response sets out some particulars on which the offeree is asking whether the offer might be varied, it will be more difficult to show that it was only an inquiry and not a counter offer. However, whether it is a counter offer or merely an inquiry depends upon the interpretation of the response—and here, as always,[218] the question is how the addressee of the communication ought reasonably to have interpreted it.[219]

We shall see below[220] that where a response from the offeree is expected to be made by a non-instantaneous method such as the post, the time at which the response takes effect is the time of posting, at least where the response is an acceptance of the offer. This is the so-called "postal rule" for acceptances. The question may be asked whether the rejection of an offer in similar circumstances takes effect on posting or only on receipt. One would generally expect that the postal rule should not apply to a rejection, whether it takes the form of a simple rejection or a counter offer.[221] The postal rule is said to protect the offeree, who is entitled upon dispatch of his acceptance to know that he has a contract and can therefore act upon it, as he has been led by the offeror to believe[222]; but in the case of rejection of an offer he has no need for such protection. On the other hand, there is also said to be an argument of policy in favour of finality, by which the offeree, having committed himself to the contract by posting his acceptance, cannot take advantage of the time before the acceptance is delivered to the offeror in order to change his mind and actually communicate his rejection of the offer.[223] If this argument has force, it might similarly be an argument against the offeree being able to post a rejection or counter offer, yet successfully change his mind and in fact communicate an acceptance before his posted response arrives. Given, however, that the offeror is not prejudiced by such conduct, and is able to hold the offeree to the contract on the basis of his actual communicated acceptance, any earlier posted rejection or counter offer ought to be irrelevant. Indeed, the offeror would be prejudiced by the fact that there is an earlier rejection of which he does not know, since he ought to be able to take the actual communication of acceptance by the offeror as giving rise to a binding contract where he has no notice of any rejection or counter offer.

---

[217] *Stevenson, Jaques & Co v McLean*, see para.3-31 fn.180 (offer by defendants to sell warrants for iron "for 40s., nett cash, open till Monday"; plaintiffs response "Please wire whether you would accept forty for delivery over two months, or if not, longest limit you would give" was inquiry, not counter offer).

[218] See para.3-07. See also *Jones v Daniel*, see para.3-33 fn.215, at 335 (Romer J: response was counter offer not acceptance based on objective test: "what would anybody when he received that letter fairly understand to be the meaning of it?").

[219] *Stevenson, Jaques & Co v McLean*, see para.3-31 fn.180, at 349–350.

[220] See para.3-42.

[221] The offer contained in the counter offer cannot take effect until it is communicated: *Henthorn v Fraser*, see para.3-31 fn.185, at 37 (Kay LJ: "An offer to sell is nothing until it is actually received"; statements to the contrary in *Taylor v Jones* (1875) 1 C.P.D. 87 at 91 were unnecessary because the place of a contract depends on the place of the acceptance, not the offer). It does not necessarily follow that the rejection cannot already have taken place on sending, even if the new offer does not take effect until receipt, where there are in law two different communications in the same letter which have different effect: *Henthorn v Fraser* at 37; although here it is not a single letter containing two separate propositions, but a single proposition which has two legal effects.

[222] See para.3-42.

[223] The argument against the offeree "blowing hot and cold": see para.3-43.

(3) Acceptance

"Acceptance" is the unequivocal assent to the terms of the offer, and must normally be communicated to the offeror   Acceptance is the unequivocal assent on the part of the offeree[224] to the terms proposed by the offeror in his offer. The subjective decision on the part of the offeree to accept an offer is not in itself sufficient, but the offeree must respond to the offer overtly, demonstrating objectively to the offeror his intention to accept.[225] Even if the proposed contract might be obviously in an offeree's interest the English courts are not prepared to infer acceptance from his silence without finding at least some outward sign of his agreement.[226] As we shall see, there are cases where the offeree may successfully accept an offer without in fact communicating his acceptance to the offeree, where the offeror has expressly or impliedly authorised him to do so: by performing a condition set out in the offer, such as in the case of a unilateral contract[227]; or where the posting of an acceptance is sufficient before it arrives or even if it never

3-34

---

[224] An unauthorised communication which does not bind the offeree under the general principles of agency has no more effect than if the offeree had decided to accept but had reserved the right to change his mind: *Powell v Lee* (1908) 99 L.T. 284 (unauthorised private communication by one of the members of a committee).

[225] For general discussion of the objective approach in the interpretation of the communications between the parties forming a contract in English law, see paras 3-05 to 3-07. Even in a legal system which bases its theory of the formation of a contract on the subjective meeting of the minds of the parties, some outward communication of the subjective intentions is generally required at least for practical reasons of proof: see, e.g. Nicholas, see para.3-31 fn.181, p.72; art.1118 c.civ. (2016 amendment [see para.3-31 fn.181]: acceptance is the manifestation of the will of the offeree to be bound on the terms of the offer). English law goes further by applying an objective test for the formation of an agreement (and not simply external evidence of the shared subjective intentions): see, e.g. *Paal Wilson & Co A/S v Partenreederei Hannah Blumenthal (The Hannah Blumenthal)* [1983] 1 A.C. 854, HL, at 915 (Lord Diplock: "the intention of each *as it has been communicated and understood by the other* (even though that which has been communicated does not represent the actual state of mind of the communicator)"). The objective test for the formation of a contract by offer and acceptance therefore requires communication to the other party, not simply evidence visible to a reasonable observer or a third party: see, e.g. *Hebb's Case* (1867) L.R. 4 Eq. 9 at 11 (entry by directors of person's name in allotment book is not acceptance of his application for shares); *Felthouse v Bindley* (1862) 11 C.B. (N.S.) 869, 142 E.R. 1037, see para.3-40 (evidence that the offeree (the nephew) had decided to accept the offer from his uncle by telling the auctioneer to withdraw the horse from the auction, was not sufficient: there was no communication to the uncle, and it did not constitute conduct which the uncle had prescribed for acceptance).

[226] See further para.3-39; but see *Attrill v Dresdner Kleinwort Ltd* [2013] EWCA Civ 394; [2013] 3 All E.R. 607 at [98] (Elias LJ: variation of employment contracts by adding discretionary bonus pool: "it is plain that the employer has dispensed with the need for any response to the offer at all. This was a promise without any disadvantage, actual or potential, of any kind to the employees. Nobody hearing the promise made in this announcement would for one moment expect the employee to be able to benefit from it only if he or she positively accepted the offer. It would be a wholly formal and unnecessary exercise; the only sensible implication is that all employees who might potentially benefit from the promise would be deemed to have accepted it"). The French civil code has a rule that appears similar: art.1120 c.civ. (2016 amendment [see para.3-31 fn.181]: silence does not count as acceptance unless so provided by legislation, usage, business dealings or other particular circumstances). However, the French courts have been more willing to decide, as a matter of fact in the particular case, that silence constituted acceptance where the offer was made in the exclusive interest of the offeree: Nicholas, see para.3-31 fn.181, pp.74–76, although this is controversial amongst French writers: J. Bell, S. Boyron and S. Whittaker, *Principles of French Law*, 2nd edn (Oxford University Press, 2008), p.304.

[227] See paras 3-37, 3-38.

arrives.[228] But, except in these or similar cases where the offeror can be held to have waived the right to be notified of the acceptance,[229] the general rule is that acceptance, being the decision of the offeree to enter into the contract on the terms of the offer, is to be communicated to the offeror[230] in such a form that the offeror can reasonably understand that his offer has matured into a binding contract.

3-35 **Acceptance must relate to the offer**   Before a communication can constitute an acceptance, it must be made in response to an offer. This is the reason why so-called "cross-offers" do not make a contract. The fact that two parties have individually decided at the same time that they wish to enter into a contract with each other on the same set of terms, and each sends an identical proposal to the other, does not yet form a contract even though each party now knows that they both wish the same contract: "there must be an offer which the person accepting has had the opportunity of considering, and which when he accepts he knows will form a binding contract".[231] An offer does not take effect until it is received[232]; the acceptance must necessarily follow receipt of the offer, even if the offeree responds very quickly.

Since a person can only claim to be a party to a contract on terms which he not only reasonably could believe are intended by the other party but also in fact does so believe,[233] in principle a person cannot claim to have accepted an offer of which he had no knowledge.[234] The operation of this principle can present some practical difficulties in the case of public offers of rewards, since as long as the offer has been made available to the public and the claimant in fact satisfies the condition set for the payment of the reward, there is little merit in the offeror refusing to pay, although there is no clear authority which would prevent the offeror from so doing where he can show that the offeree had not in fact heard of the advertisement and so could not have been responding to it when he did the act which apparently satisfied the condition. Such cases may well be unlikely in practice because of the difficulty of proof, given the fact that the claimant who makes a claim under the terms of the offer is by then responding to the offer of which he has knowledge.[235]

---

[228] See para.3-42.

[229] On the difficulties of waiving the right to be notified, especially where the acceptance is said to have been effected by silence and inactivity cf. however, see paras 3-39, 3-40.

[230] *Carlill v Carbolic Smoke Ball Co* [1893] 1 Q.B. 256, CA, at 262.

[231] *Tinn v Hoffman and Co* (1873) 29 L.T. 271 at 277 (Grove J); see also at 275 (Archibald J), 278 (Brett J, Keating J), 279 (Blackburn J: "Such grave inconvenience would arise in mercantile business if people could doubt whether there was an acceptance or not, that it is desirable to keep to the rule that an offer that has been made should be accepted by an acceptance such as would leave no doubt on the matter"). Honyman J at 275 disagreed ("The parties are *ad idem* at one and the same moment").

[232] *Henthorn v Fraser*, see para.3-31 fn.185, at 37.

[233] See para.3-07.

[234] *Taylor v Allon* [1966] 1 Q.B. 304 at 311-312 (driver could not show contract for renewal of insurance if he could not show that he knew of temporary insurance cover note and relied on it in taking car on the road).

[235] For difficulties associated with identifying the acceptance of an offer in the case of a unilateral contract, see para.3-38. *Gibbons v Proctor* (1891) 64 L.T. 594 is sometimes said to show that an offer of a reward can be accepted by a person who satisfies the conditions in the offer yet did not know of the offer, but it appears that, by the time that the condition in that case was satisfied (provision of information leading to conviction, effected by the claimant through an agent) the claimant did know of the offer: see report at (1891) 55 J.P. 616; and in *Great Eastern Shipping Co Ltd v Far East Chartering Ltd (The Jag Ravi)* [2011] EWHC 1372 (Comm); [2011] 2 Lloyd's Rep. 309 at [44]-

Similarly, if the claimant does know of the offer of the reward it is very difficult to argue that he did not accept that offer where he did the very act which was set in the offer as the condition for payment, although in a rare case the offeror may be able to show that the claimant's act was done without any reference to the offer.[236]

Acceptance by words or by conduct communicated to the offeror   The accept-   **3-36**
ance may be made by words, whether oral or written, addressed to the offeree. In the simplest case the offeree may just use the one word, "yes"; but in other cases there may be a question about how to interpret the words used in order to check that they are an acceptance and not, for example, a counter offer.[237] However, as in all cases where the law requires some particular form of communication, there may be no words, or not just words, but conduct or a combination of words and conduct which have to be interpreted.[238] What matters is whether the offeree has, by words or conduct, communicated to the offeror his unequivocal assent to the terms of the offer. An example of acceptance by conduct is where the offeree performs in accordance with the terms of the offer, and where there is nothing to indicate to the offeree that the performance is otherwise than in response to the offer—such as where a coal supplier proposed new terms of supply to a customer with which it had done regular business; and after negotiations the customer's agent put the draft contract, sent by the supplier, into a drawer without signing it but without making any objection as to its terms, and thereafter ordered supplies of coal on terms which could only be explained on the assumption that it was agreeing to the terms set out in the draft.[239] In practice, however, such a contract may often be found not only

---

[47] Judge Mackie QC thought that the better argument was that a party claiming under a unilateral contract must have performed the requested act with knowledge of the offer, but that the issue was open under English law, and he did not need to decide it. cf. however, A.H. Hudson, "Gibbons v. Proctor Revisited" (1968) 84 L.Q.R. 502, arguing that a publicly announced offer of a reward should be capable of acceptance by a person who has not read the offer, distinguishing this from the case of bilateral contracts such as *Taylor v Allon*, see para.3-35 fn.234.

[236] In *Williams v Carwardine* (1833) 5 Car. & P. 566 at 571, 172 E.R. 1101 at 1103, counsel argued (unsuccessfully) at trial that a reward in return for information leading to conviction should not be payable to a person who had provided the information for motives other than in order to obtain the reward, on the basis that it was "a case of what in the civil law is called policitation, that is, an offer by one party not accepted by the other". The King's Bench decided the case simply on the basis that the plaintiff had satisfied the condition set in the advertisement: (1833) 4 B. & Ad. 621, 110 E.R. 590. cf. *R. v Clarke* (1927) 40 C.L.R. 227, HCA, where the person claiming the reward gave information relating to a crime in order to clear his own name, and not in order to earn the reward, and so was held not to have accepted the offer. The merits of the claim may have influenced the court's analysis ("He has … neither a legal nor a moral claim to the reward": Isaacs A.C.J. at 231; cf. the claimant in *Williams v Carwardine* who gave the information after receiving a severe beating, believing that she had not long to live and to ease her conscience) but is based on principle: see, e.g. Higgins J at 241 drawing an analogy with cases where a claimant cannot obtain remedies for misrepresentation where he did not in fact rely on the defendant's false statement.

[237] See para.3-33. The interpretation is objective, from the perspective of the offeror: ibid.

[238] cf. the requirement of a false "representation" in order to give rise to remedies for misrepresentation, but where the misrepresentation may be wholly or partly by conduct: Cartwright (Misrepresentation), para.3-04; and see, e.g. *Walters v Morgan* (1861) 3 De G.F. & J. 718 at 724, 45 E.R. 1056 at 1059 (Lord Campbell L.C.: a "nod or a wink, or a shake of the head, or a smile from the purchaser"). Conduct will be interpreted objectively, from the perspective of the offeror: *Brogden v Metropolitan Railway Co* (1877) L.R. 2 App. Cas. 666 at 686 (Lord Hatherley: "a course of action on the part of the Plaintiffs of such a character as necessarily to lead to the inference on the part of the Defendants that the agreement had been accepted on the part of the Plaintiffs").

[239] *Brogden v Metropolitan Railway Co*, see para.3-36 fn.238, at 677–678; see, however, see para.3-36 fn.240. Where the offer is to vary an existing contract, it is particularly important to check that the

as a result of the acceptance by means of the offeree's conduct, but by the conduct of both parties, from whose mutual dealings it can be inferred that they have both agreed to proceed on the terms which are in fact evidenced by their dealings, without needing to identify separately the offer and the acceptance.[240] This is also the basis on which the parties may both be shown by their conduct to have agreed to enter into a contract which has not been formalised even though they clearly indicated at an earlier stage of their negotiations that they would not be bound until a formal contract was signed.[241]

3-37 **Prescribed form of acceptance** It is well established that the offeror may in the terms of his offer prescribe the form of a valid acceptance.[242] This rule is less straightforward in its application than at first appears, however, and various aspects must be considered.

It is first important to see whether the offeror has prescribed a mandatory form of acceptance, or only a permissive form. It may be that what appears to be the required form is, on proper construction, only an indication of one way in which the offer may be accepted, and therefore there is no "prescribed" form of accept-

---

continued performance is unequivocally referable to the new terms, rather than simply continued performance of the original terms: see, e.g. *Khatri v Cooperatieve Centrale Raffeisen-Boerenleenbank BA* [2010] EWCA Civ 397; [2010] I.R.L.R. 715; this will be easier to infer where the new terms are more favourable than the old: *Attrill v Dresdner Kleinwort Ltd* [2012] EWHC 1189 (QB); [2012] I.R.L.R. 553 at [170] (but CA held that there was in fact no need to communicate acceptance in this case: see para.3-34 fn.226). For other examples of acceptance by conduct, see *Wilkie v London Passenger Transport Board* [1947] 1 All E.R. 258, CA, at 259 (Lord Greene MR (obiter): passenger on a London bus of a kind which can be entered without yet having paid does not accept offer of carriage simply by taking hold of the rail and putting his foot on the bus, but by his conduct in putting his foot on the platform or inside the bus); *AE Yates Trenchless Solutions Ltd v Black and Veatch Ltd* [2008] EWHC 3183 (TCC); (2008) 124 Con. L.R. 188 at [5] (Akenhead J: "a contractor who commences work after receipt of an order to commence may well have its conduct in commencing the work objectively construed as an acceptance of the order, because objectively sensible business people would expect that commencement without reservation suggested acceptance of the order"); *Finmoon Ltd v Baltic Reefers Management Ltd* [2012] EWHC 920 (Comm); [2012] 1 C.L.C. 813 at [26] (offer nominating vessel was accepted by loading cargo). In a case of a "battle of forms" (see para.3-47) the contract may sometimes come into existence on the terms of the last document exchanged (the "last shot", which forms the offer) which is accepted by the other party's conduct in beginning performance.

[240] This is therefore a possible exception to the general rule that a contract must be formed through acceptance of an offer: see para.3-25; *G Percy Trentham Ltd v Archital Luxfer Ltd* [1993] 1 Lloyd's Rep. 25, CA, at 27 (Steyn LJ: "it is true that the coincidence of offer and acceptance will in the vast majority of cases represent the mechanism of contract formation. … But it is not necessarily so in the case of a contract alleged to have come into existence during and as a result of performance"). In *Brogden v Metropolitan Railway Co*, see para.3-36 fn.238, their Lordships identified different possible analyses of the formation, some pinpointing the acceptance of an offer, others relying rather on a broader evidence of agreement from the conduct of both parties: the customer beginning a course of dealing in response to the supplier's letter (Lord Cairns at 680); the payment of the first invoice at the new price (Lord Hatherley at 686); the placing of a first order supported by continuing evidence of the parties' conduct on the basis of the new terms (Lord Selborne at 689); the supply over a period on the new terms which evidenced a new contract (Lord Blackburn at 696).

[241] *Brogden v Metropolitan Railway Co*, see para.3-36 fn.238, at 672, 693; *RTS Flexible Systems Ltd v Molkerei Alois Müller GmbH & Co KG* [2010] UKSC 14; [2010] 1 W.L.R. 753 at [55], [86]–[87]. On "subject to contract" negotiations, see para.2-08;

[242] See, e.g. statements in *Brogden v Metropolitan Railway Co*, see para.3-36 fn.238, at 691; *Carlill v Carbolic Smoke Ball Co*, see para.3-34 fn.230, at 269; *Manchester Diocesan Council for Education v Commercial & General Investments Ltd*, see para.3-37 fn.245 at 245.

ance at all.[243] Even if the offeror requests acceptance in a particular form, it may still be only an indication that acceptance in that form will be valid without excluding the possibility that other forms will suffice. It has been said, for example, that if an offer made by post requests an acceptance "by return of post" it "does not mean exclusively by letter by return of post, but you may reply by telegram or by verbal message, or by any means not later than a letter written and sent by return of post would reach us".[244] An offeror who intends to go further and insist that he shall be bound only if the offer is accepted in a particular form, has the burden of making that clear; and in the absence of such a clear stipulation the offeree is entitled to accept by another means which is no less advantageous to the offeror.[245]

Where the offeror clearly prescribes a mandatory form of acceptance, this is in principle effective to exclude any other form that would otherwise have been sufficient to conclude the contract[246] even, it seems, where the form used by the offeree does not disadvantage the offeror.[247] Just as a party to a contract is free to set strict conditions of performance required of the other party within a contract,[248] so in forming a contract an offeror is free to set strict conditions as to the circumstances in which he will be bound by the other party's acceptance. However, a party who sets conditions for the other party's performance in a contract may waive the strict requirements, or may waive his rights which flow from the other party's failure to comply[249]; and similarly an offeror who prescribed a mandatory form of acceptance may waive it[250] and allow an acceptance which is in fact communicated in an

---

[243] *Maple Leaf Macro Volatility Master Fund v Rouvroy* [2009] EWCA Civ 1334; [2010] 2 All E.R. (Comm.) 788 at [16] (Longmore LJ: "The fact that the agreement envisages a signature and leaves a space for those signatures is not a 'prescription' that the agreement can only become binding on the appending of signatures", so one person could by email become party to the contract which was signed by the other parties). cf. *Novus Aviation Ltd v Alubaf Arab International Bank BSC(c)* [2016] EWHC 1575 (Comm); [2017] 1 B.C.L.C. 313 at [102]–[111] (on construction, counter-signature was not required to show acceptance of terms of commitment letter, but management agreement took effect only when signed by both parties). The word "prescribed" can itself be ambiguous as to whether it refers to a required or only a permitted procedure: cf. OED Online, March 2018, "prescribed, adj.": "1. Laid down or fixed beforehand; ordained, appointed, decreed; set, defined".

[244] *Tinn v Hoffman and Co*, see para.3-35 fn.231, at 274 (Honyman J).

[245] *Manchester Diocesan Council for Education v Commercial & General Investments Ltd* [1970] 1 W.L.R. 241 at 246. There, the condition that the successful tenderer "shall be informed of the acceptance of his tender by letter sent to him by post addressed to the address given in his tender and every letter sent shall be deemed to have been received in due course of post" did not preclude informal communication of acceptance by letter to the tenderer's surveyor.

[246] e.g. where an acceptance by post would have been sufficient to conclude the contract, a stipulation that the acceptance must in fact be communicated will exclude the "postal rule": *Holwell Securities Ltd v Hughes* [1974] 1 W.L.R. 155, CA, at 161 (but cf. para.3-42 fn.307).

[247] *Manchester Diocesan Council for Education v Commercial & General Investments Ltd*, see para.3-37 fn.245, at 246.

[248] e.g. *Holwell Securities Ltd v Hughes*, see para.3-37 fn.246, at 159 (Lawton LJ: "the grantee of an option must comply strictly with the conditions set for its exercise: see *Hare v Nicholl* [1966] 2 Q.B. 130"); *Union Eagle Ltd v Golden Achievement Ltd* [1997] A.C. 514, PC (time set for completion of contract to purchase flat was of the essence of the contract: 10 minute delay in tendering purchase price entitled vendor to rescind and forfeit deposit).

[249] Wilken and Ghaly, paras 4.27, 4.30.

[250] A prescribed form of acceptance is normally inserted into the offer by the offeror, designed to protect his own interests, and therefore the question is whether he can be shown to have waived the condition of the offer which required the particular form of acceptance. In a case, however, where the source of the condition which was eventually stipulated in the offer was not the offeror but the offeree, it will be for the *offeree* to decide whether to waive it, as long as his waiver does not prejudice the offeror: *Reveille Independent LLC v Anotech International (UK) Ltd* [2016] EWCA Civ 443;

alternative form to be sufficient. Such a waiver of the prescribed form of acceptance may be express or implied (for example, by the offeror's conduct in treating
it as sufficient),[251] and will result in the contract being formed, or being deemed to
have been formed, at the moment when the non-conforming acceptance was in fact
made.[252]

The fact that the offeror may prescribe a particular form of acceptance, and that
he may waive any particular requirements he has set as to acceptance, raises further
questions. Can he prescribe the doing of an act by the offeree which would not (but
for the terms of the offer) constitute a valid acceptance because the acceptance has
not been communicated to the offeror? This issue arises commonly in relation to
"unilateral" contracts.[253] And can he not only waive the right to communication of
acceptance, but set as the required form of acceptance that the offeree shall do nothing at all—i.e. can he prescribe silence as the form of acceptance?[254]

3-38   **Acceptance by conduct without communication; acceptance in unilateral
contracts**   The offeror may prescribe a form of acceptance by conduct which does
not necessarily require communication to the offeror[255]:

> "when an offer is made to another party, and in that offer there is a request express or
> implied that he must signify his acceptance by doing some particular thing, then as soon
> as he does that thing, he is bound."

In such a case the offer may be of a bilateral contract[256] but a unilateral contract[257]
is the paradigm case of a prescribed form of acceptance by conduct: the offer
defines what a person must do in order to obtain the benefit of the offeror's obligations, and only if that is done, strictly in accordance with the terms of the offer, does
the contract come into existence.[258] However, there can be some difficulties of

---

(2016) 166 Con. L.R. 79 at [41]. This may happen, for example, where the form of acceptance is
prescribed in the general terms of a tender, inserted by the party who invites tenders but who will
then be not the offeror but the offeree when the contract is entered into following submission of
tenders: see para.3-29; *Manchester Diocesan Council for Education v Commercial & General Investments Ltd*, see para.3-37 fn.245, at 246. If a requirement (e.g. of a signature on a document) is for
the benefit of both parties, it must be clear that both parties have waived it: *Novus Aviation Ltd v
Alubaf Arab International Bank BSC(c)*, see para.3-37 fn.243, at [107]. The rules for waiving
prescriptions as to the form of acceptance are therefore not peculiar to the rules for formation of
contracts, but part of the general rules on waiver of conditions which a party has inserted into a
transaction for his own benefit.

[251] *Manchester Diocesan Council for Education v Commercial & General Investments Ltd*, see
para.3-37 fn.245, at 246.

[252] *Manchester Diocesan Council for Education v Commercial & General Investments Ltd*, see
para.3-37 fn.245, at 246, (the contract was formed not on posting, as would have been the case if
the prescribed form had been followed, but when the acceptance was actually communicated to the
offeror).

[253] See para.3-38.

[254] See para.3-39.

[255] *Brogden v Metropolitan Railway Co* (1877) 2 A.C. 666, HL, at 691 (Lord Blackburn).

[256] Lord Blackburn (see para.3-38 fn.255) went on to give as two examples the acceptance of an offer
to buy goods at a specified price to be accepted by shipping of the goods; and the acceptance of an
offer by post. On acceptance by post, see para.3-41.

[257] See para.3-32.

[258] *Friends Life Ltd v Siemens Hearing Instruments Ltd* [2014] EWCA Civ 382; [2015] 1 All E.R.
(Comm) 1068 at [65] (Lewison LJ: "I do not accept that in the field of unilateral (or 'if' contracts)
there is any room for the notion of substantial compliance. As Diplock LJ said in *United Dominions*
[see para.3-32 fn.195 at 84] the question is whether the relevant event has occurred. That question

analysis in identifying the "acceptance" in the case of a unilateral contract. It is clear that the condition set by the offer may be the performance of an act which can be completed, and therefore the offeror's obligation comes into existence, without communication of that fact to the offeror. This may be put in terms of the offeror dispensing with the requirement of communication of acceptance[259]:

"One cannot doubt that, as an ordinary rule of law, an acceptance of an offer made ought to be notified to the person who makes the offer, in order that the two minds may come together. Unless this is done the two minds may be apart, and there is not that consensus which is necessary according to the English law—I say nothing about the laws of other countries—to make a contract. But there is this clear gloss to be made upon that doctrine, that as notification of acceptance is required for the benefit of the person who makes the offer, the person who makes the offer may dispense with notice to himself if he thinks it desirable to do so, and I suppose there can be no doubt that where a person in an offer made by him to another person, expressly or impliedly intimates a particular mode of acceptance as sufficient to make the bargain binding, it is only necessary for the other person to whom such offer is made to follow the indicated method of acceptance; and if the person making the offer, expressly or impliedly intimates in his offer that it will be sufficient to act on the proposal without communicating acceptance of it to himself, performance of the condition is a sufficient acceptance without notification."

It is a matter of construction of the offer whether notification is required: if nothing is stated expressly, it depends on whether the reasonable reader of the offer would believe, given the nature of the transaction, that the performance of the condition is sufficient without communication of either the decision to accept or even of the fact that the required act has been done. For example, an offer of a reward for finding a lost animal cannot sensibly require everyone reading the advertisement to communicate their decision to go and look for it[260]; but it may also, depending on its construction, mean that the obligation to pay the reward arises at the moment that the animal is found, rather than when the offeror is notified, although of course no claim can be made to enforce the obligation without notification of the fact that the condition has been satisfied.[261]

Acceptance by silence   In the cases discussed above, the acceptance takes effect when the offeree does whatever is prescribed by law in order to conclude the contract (the unequivocal communication of assent to the offeror)[262] except where the law or the offeror has devised an alternative form of acceptance, such as a prescribed form of actual communication,[263] or a prescribed form of conduct which

3-39

---

is to be answered 'Yes' or 'No'. It cannot be answered 'Almost'").
[259] *Carlill v Carbolic Smoke Ball Co* [1893] 1 Q.B. 256, CA, at 269–270 (Bowen LJ), following *Harris' Case* (1872) L.R. 7 Ch. App. 587 (Mellish LJ, explaining and justifying the "postal rule": see para.3-42) and *Brogden v Metropolitan Railway Co*, see para.3-38 fn.255.
[260] *Carlill v Carbolic Smoke Ball Co*, see para.3-38 fn.259, at 270 (Bowen LJ).
[261] *Carlill v Carbolic Smoke Ball Co*, see para.3-38 fn.259, at 269–270 (Bowen LJ: if the offer so provides, performance can be sufficient acceptance without notification); 274 (A.L. Smith LJ: performance of the condition by using the smoke ball was an acceptance of the offer); cf. Lindley LJ at 262–263 (the offeror did not expect or require notice of the acceptance *apart from notice of the performance*). See also *Brogden v Metropolitan Railway Co*, see para.3-38 fn.255, at 691 (undertaking to enter into contract to buy goods if the offeree ships them immediately is complete on shipping the cargo even if they are then lost).
[262] See para.3-36.
[263] See para.3-37; esp. *Manchester Diocesan Council for Education v Commercial & General Invest-*

can be effective without actual communication to the offeror.[264] Where a particular form of acceptance is prescribed by the offeror he is entitled to insist upon it, but may also waive the requirement and hold the offeree to the contract where the offeree has in fact chosen to accept by an alternative form of communication.[265] In none of these cases, however, is it sufficient for the offeree to *say and do nothing*— that is, silence and inactivity are not in themselves sufficient to constitute acceptance. There are two situations, however, in which it may be claimed that an offer has been accepted by silence: where the offeree's silence is said to have been sufficient in itself to show that he accepted the offer; and where the offeror in his offer prescribed silence as a form of acceptance. Both present difficulties for the reason that silence in itself presents a difficulty in the formation of a contract.

The refusal generally to accept that silence and inactivity can constitute acceptance follows from, or at least is closely connected to, the general objective approach in English law. Mere mental assent is insufficient to constitute acceptance[266]; and it is not even sufficient that there may be evidence of the offeree's decision to accept which has not been communicated to the offeror, since in principle the offeror is entitled to know whether the contract has been concluded.[267] It has also been said that the principal problem with silence as a means of acceptance is that it does not constitute a sufficiently unequivocal communication of the offeree's assent: "silence and inaction are of their nature equivocal, for the simple reason that there can be more than one reason why the person concerned has been silent and inactive".[268] However, this does not exclude all possibility of "silence and inaction" constituting communication of a person's intention if, in the circumstances, the silence is not in fact unequivocal. Such a case does not involve the waiver of the requirement of communication of acceptance; rather, the silence itself communicates acceptance—acceptance *by silence*. It is evident that this will be very rare, for the very reason that we have already noted: a person's failure to respond may be attributed to a range of reasons, and the offeror is not generally entitled to assume that the silence does in fact indicate assent. Even if the offer appears to be very favourable to the offeree, that is not in itself sufficient to entitle the offeror to assume that silence indicates assent.[269]

In a number of cases the courts have been prepared to hold that silence and

---

ments Ltd, see para.3-37 fn.245.

[264] See para.3-38; and see esp. Lord Blackburn in *Brogden v Metropolitan Railway Co*, see para.3-38 fn.255. The "postal rule" (see para.3-41) is also an example where the law or the offeror permits acceptance without actual communication.

[265] See para.3-37; *Manchester Diocesan Council for Education v Commercial & General Investments Ltd*, see para.3-37 fn.245.

[266] See para.3-34 and fn.225.

[267] See para.3-34.

[268] *Allied Marine Transport Ltd v Vale do Rio Doce Navegacao SA (The Leonidas D)* [1985] 1 W.L.R. 925, CA, at 941 (Robert Goff LJ, discussing the requirements of an "unequivocal representation" for the purposes of equitable estoppel: see para.10-22. See also at 937 for a similar rejection of the argument that a contract was formed through both an offer by silence ("We have all been brought up to believe it to be axiomatic that acceptance of an offer cannot be inferred from silence, save in the most exceptional circumstances") and acceptance by silence; cf. however, see para.3-39 fn.271.

[269] e.g. I offer by letter to sell you my car (which has a market value of £20,000) for £10. Your silence may be because you did not in fact receive the offer; or you did not take it seriously (perhaps you thought that I must have made a mistake or that I am crazy); or you positively decided not to reply because you do not drive and have no use for the car; cf. para.3-34 fn.226. If I *told you* in the offer that you need not reply if you wish to accept it, then different problems arise: see para.3-40.

inactivity constituted a sufficient communication of assent, but the context of such decisions is distinctive: where the parties are already in a contract which imposes on them duties which they fail to observe, or at least where the other party has a reasonable expectation that there will be some particular form of activity, and where the inactivity goes beyond mere breach of contract and becomes an indication of a proposal to abandon the contract altogether, and the other party's corresponding silence and inactivity becomes also an indication of assent to that proposal.[270] In other words, both the offer and the acceptance of the abandonment of a contract may be inferred by silence and inactivity of both parties. The period of silence must be long in order to show sufficiently clearly that there is an intention to abandon, although in an appropriate case this may be established.[271] However, such a situation cannot easily be carried across to the normal case of the formation of a contract between parties who are not already contractually bound[272]: the silence of the offeree may in some circumstances be taken as an indication of his intention to reject an offer,[273] but not to accept it for the very reason that there is no duty to com-

---

[270] The case may be the reverse, and the parties' silence may communicate an assent to a new contract, if the terms of the contract provide expressly or impliedly that the contract will be renewed if neither party has given notice before a particular term: e.g. the implied continuation of a periodic tenancy from one period to the next until either party gives notice to quit: *Prudential Assurance Co Ltd v London Residuary Body* [1992] 2 A.C. 386, HL, at 394; *Hammersmith and Fulham LBC v Monk* [1992] 1 A.C. 478, HL, at 491. This is, however, the operation of the terms of the contract itself.

[271] For cases where the courts have held that abandonment of the contract was to be inferred from the silence and inactivity of both parties, see *Pearl Mill Co Ltd v Ivy Tannery Co Ltd* [1919] 1 K.B. 78 (contract of sale of specific quantity of goods, "delivery as required": delivery of part, but "inordinate" delay in requesting delivery of remaining goods indicated abandonment; interpreted, however, as a decision only on repudiation by CA in *Allied Marine Transport Ltd v Vale do Rio Doce Navegacao SA*, see para.3-39 fn.268); *André et Compagnie SA v Marine Transocean Ltd (The Splendid Sun)* [1981] Q.B. 694, CA (arbitration to resolve dispute under contract was abandoned by eight years' total inactivity by both parties); *Excomm Ltd v Guan Guan Shipping (Pte) Ltd (The Golden Bear)* [1987] 1 Lloyd's Rep. 330 (arbitration abandoned by nearly eight year's total silence); *Tankreederei Ahrenkeil GmbH v Frahuil SA (The Multitank Holsatia)* [1988] 2 Lloyd's Rep. 486 (arbitration abandoned by over six years' inactivity). For cases where the courts have rejected arguments of abandonment based on silence and inactivity, see *Paal Wilson & Co A/S v Partenreederei Hannah Blumenthal (The Hannah Blumenthal)* [1983] 1 A.C. 854, HL (during period of delay in arbitration proceedings both parties communicated with each other and were still actively trying to obtain evidence for use in the arbitration); *Allied Marine Transport Ltd v Vale do Rio Doce Navegacao SA*, see para.3-39 fn.268 (five years' inactivity by charterers did not indicate offer to abandon arbitration, and "was a matter of pure speculation as to which different persons, acting for the owners, could well have reached different conclusions": at 940); *Food Corp of India v Antclizo Shipping Corp (The Antclizo)* [1987] 2 Lloyd's Rep. 130, CA (eight years' inactivity in this arbitration explicable by parties' awaiting outcome of decisions in their other disputes).

[272] One particular difficulty in applying the conventional principles of offer and acceptance to the abandonment of a contract by silence is that the offeree must normally intend to accept the offer (see para.3-35) whereas in a case of abandonment the offeree (or, indeed, both parties) may generally simply have forgotten about the contract. See *Tankreederei Ahrenkeil GmbH v Frahuil SA (The Multitank Holsatia)*, see para.3-39 fn.271 at 493 (Phillips J: "to demonstrate consensual abandonment of an arbitration by silence and inactivity a respondent must show: (i) That the clear inference to be drawn by the respondent from the inactivity of the claimant was that the claimant did not wish or intend to proceed with the arbitration provided that the respondent consented to its abandonment; (ii) That the clear inference to be drawn by the claimant from the inactivity of the respondent was that the respondent consented to the abandonment of the arbitration; (iii) That these inferences represented, *or at least did not conflict with*, the respondents' understanding of the position" (emphasis added)).

[273] cf. para.3-30 fn.176.

municate a rejection nor even any reasonable expectation on the part of the offeror that the offeree will communicate if he wishes to reject.

3-40   **Silence as a prescribed form of acceptance**   A more difficult question arises,
however, in a case where the offeror does indicate in his offer that the offeree may
accept by silence: he does not prescribe any form of acceptance by conduct, but
expressly waives the requirement of communication of acceptance. If in such
circumstances the offeree decides to accept the offer, but takes the offeror at his
word and does not do or say anything in reply, can he be taken in law to have accepted? According to the decision of the Court of Common Pleas in *Felthouse v
Bindley*[274] there is no contract in such circumstances. In that case, negotiations
between an uncle and his nephew for the sale of the nephew's horse, where the
remaining issue was whether the price should be £30 or 30 guineas (i.e. £30 and
30 shillings, £31 10s), concluded with the uncle writing to the nephew "If I hear
no more about him, I consider the horse mine at £30 15s." The nephew did not
reply, but instructed an auctioneer, who was due to conduct an auction of all his
farming stock, to reserve the horse because it was sold. It was held that there was
no contract at that point, and therefore when the auctioneer in error included the
horse amongst the nephew's goods sold in the auction the uncle had no claim
against the auctioneer for conversion of the horse since, there being no contract of
sale in his favour, he had no title to it and so no right to possession. This is a difficult case since part, at least, of the underlying reasoning of the court appears to
be designed to protect the nephew whereas the nephew was not himself resisting
the contract. In argument, Byles J said[275]: "What right had the plaintiff to impose
upon the nephew the trouble of writing a letter to decline or to assent to the
contract?"; counsel's response, to the effect that it was enough to show that the
nephew did assent to the contract, was met by the Judge's answer that this was not
sufficient without delivery or acceptance—that is, silent assent, even if it could be
shown, was not in law sufficient to form the contract. The judgments follow the
same line; Willes J said[276]:

> "it is ... clear that the uncle had no right to impose upon the nephew a sale of his horse
> for £30 15s. unless he chose to comply with the condition of writing to repudiate the offer.
> The nephew might, no doubt, have bound his uncle to the bargain by writing to him: the
> uncle might also have retracted his offer at any time before acceptance. It stood an open
> offer: and so things remained until the 25th of February, when the nephew was about to
> sell his farming stock by auction. The horse in question being catalogued with the rest of
> the stock, the auctioneer (the defendant) was told that it was already sold. It is clear,
> therefore, that the nephew in his own mind intended his uncle to have the horse at the price
> which he (the uncle) had named,—£30 15s.: but he had not communicated such his inten-
> tion to his uncle, or done anything to bind himself. Nothing, therefore, had been done to
> vest the property in the horse in the plaintiff down to the 25th of February, when the horse
> was sold by the defendant."

It might seem unfair to the offeree that he should fail to obtain the contract when
has done (or, rather, not done) the very thing that the offeror has prescribed.[277] If

---

[274] (1862) 11 C.B. (N.S.) 869; 142 E.R. 1037.
[275] (1862) 11 C.B. (N.S.) 869 at 873; 142 E.R. 1037 at 1039.
[276] (1862) 11 C.B. (N.S.) 869; 142 E.R. 1037 at 875–876, at 1040. Byles J agreed with Willes J.
[277] This may have been recognised by Keating J who said at 877, at 1040: "Had the question arisen as

the rejection of silence as acceptance, even when prescribed by the offeror as sufficient, is based on the protection of the offeree, it is curious that the offeree should be prejudiced by the rule. However, it appears that there is more than that: we have already seen that the recognition of silence as acceptance is problematic in the contract of the objective test generally adopted by English law[278]; and given that the requirement of offer and acceptance is founded on a search for certainty, a test under which the existence, time and place of the contract can be identified by parties and the court through the analysis of the facts of the case,[279] there is an inherent problem in allowing the mere mental assent of the offeree to constitute acceptance even if it has been so permitted by the offeror: at what moment does the contract come into existence,[280] and how do we know—until the offeree takes some further (objectively evidenced) action[281] —that he has irrevocably made up his mind?

A possible solution to this potential problem of unfairness to the offeree is to say that, whilst the silence and inactivity of the offeree cannot in law constitute acceptance so as to form a bilateral contract at the moment when the offeree decides to accept yet does nothing, the offeror may none the less be estopped from denying that there is a valid contract, at least where the offeree can show that he has relied on there being a contract. Such an analysis has the attraction of allowing the offeree to take advantage of the right not to communicate acceptance, as expressly permitted by the offeror—in effect, a waiver, given in advance, of the legal consequences of the failure to communicate acceptance in the manner prescribed by law[282] —but not imposing on the offeree any duty to communicate in the case of a decision not to accept[283]; of binding only the offeror and not third parties[284];

---

between the uncle and the nephew, there would probably have been some difficulty".

[278] See para.3-39.

[279] See para.3-22.

[280] This concern typically arises in a case where the contract may have the effect of transferring the title to goods and impact on the rights of third parties. In *Felthouse v Bindley*, see para.3-40 fn.274, the question was whether there was a contract which had transferred title to the uncle, and therefore whether he had title to sue the auctioneer in conversion. This context may have influenced the judges in Felthouse to take a restrictive approach: cf. Willes J, see para.3-40 fn.276 ("Nothing, therefore, had been done to vest the property in the horse in the plaintiff down to the 25th of February...")

[281] One solution would be to say that it is not the mere silent assent of the offeree which forms the contract, but his doing an overt act which unequivocally shows that he has decided to accept: here telling the auctioneer that he has sold the horse to his uncle: cf. C.J. Miller, "*Felthouse v Bindley* Re-Visited" (1972) 35 M.L.R. 489, 491, suggesting that there was a contract, and noting that on the Exchequer Chamber (1863) 7 L.T. 835, 11 W.R. 429, which appears to have rested its rejection of an appeal from the Common Pleas emphasised not on the absence of acceptance but on the lack of a written memorandum of sale for the purposes of the Statute of Frauds. However, recognising as acceptance collateral conduct, neither requested by nor communicated to the offeror, does not fall within the normal requirements for (nor the normal rationale of) acceptance: see paras 3-36 to 3-37.

[282] cf. para.3-37.

[283] This is, of course, an important position to maintain: there can be no question of the offeror imposing on the offeree the duty to take positive steps to reject the offer. The desire to protect the offeree in such circumstances, but also to place the risk on the offeror and to provide clarity for the purposes of contract and the law of property, can also be shown by the statutory exemption of the consumer from any obligation to provide consideration for products supplied in the course of inertia selling, and the right to use, deal with or dispose of unsolicited goods as if they were an unconditional gift: Consumer Protection from Unfair Trading Regulations 2008 (SI 2008/1277) reg.27M, inserted by Consumer Contracts (Information, Cancellation and Additional Charges) Regulations 2013 (SI 2013/3134) reg.39, and renumbered by Consumer Protection (Amendment) Regulations 2014 (SI 2014/870) reg.4(2) (implementing Directive 2011/83/EU art.27, and replacing Consumer Protection (Distance Selling) Regulations 2000 (SI 2000/2334) reg.24, itself replacing earlier provisions of the

and of allowing the offeree to hold the offeror to the putative contract only where he can show not merely that he in fact decided to accept, but also that he has acted in reliance on there being a contract.[285] Such an argument has been suggested in some textbooks[286] but does not appear to have been adopted in any case.[287]

3-41   **Time and place of acceptance: normally, when acceptance is communicated**   Where the contract is formed by the acceptance of an offer, the normal rule is that, since the acceptance must normally be communicated in order for it to take effect,[288] the contract is formed when, and where, the acceptance is actually received. In many cases the time and place of the contract are not significant, and the only question is whether the contract was formed. But it has often been in cases where the time[289] or place[290] of the contract is significant for the resolution of the dispute between the parties that the courts have not only stated explicitly the general rule that an acceptance must be communicated in order to form a contract, but have also considered whether there may be an exception to the general rule.[291] We shall see in the following paragraphs that there are two broad exceptions: first, where the general rule is displaced by an exception (often termed the "postal rule") that the sending of the acceptance concludes the contract (and therefore the time and place of the sending of the acceptance constitutes the time and place of the contract); secondly, a general exception by which the outcome of the application of the normal rule of acceptance (or even of the "postal rule") is varied to take account of the fault of one or other party which caused a delay in the actual communication.

3-42   **Time and place of acceptance: exceptionally, when sent; the "postal rule"**   The offeror may prescribe as the form of acceptance the posting of an acceptance, waiving the right to receive actual communication before the contract is concluded[292]:

> "where ... a person writes a letter and says, I offer to take an allotment of shares, and he expressly or impliedly says, If you agree with me send an answer by the post, there, as soon as he has sent that answer by the post, and put it out of his control, and done an

---

Unsolicited Goods and Services Act 1971 s.1, and implementing Directive 97/7/EC art.9).

[284] An estoppel normally binds only the representor, although for circumstances in which the representor's successor in title may be bound, see Spencer Bower (Estoppel), paras 6.24 to 6.46.

[285] For the requirement of reliance to give rise to an estoppel by representation, see para.10-06; Spencer Bower (Estoppel), Ch.5.

[286] Chitty, para.2-073; Treitel, para.2-046; Cheshire, Fifoot and Furmston, p.67, n.101.

[287] An argument along these lines was rejected very briefly by Kerr J in *Fairline Shipping Corp v Adamson* [1975] 1 Q.B. 180, although that case has not been further cited on this point. The grounds of rejection of the estoppel argument were partly based on the facts, and that there was no reliance by the offeree, but also the proposition that "the plaintiffs' cause of action against the defendant cannot be grounded on estoppel". This would not, however, be a case of promissory estoppel (in which it is said that a cause of action cannot be grounded on the estoppel: see paras 10-08, 10-38); but estoppel by representation where the defendant (offeror) would not be allowed to lead evidence that the offeror had not in fact accepted the offer, or that there is a properly-concluded contract: see para.10-06.

[288] See para.3-34.

[289] See para.3-22 fn.117.

[290] See para.3-22 fn.118.

[291] e.g. *Entores Ltd v Miles Far East Corp* [1955] 2 Q.B. 327, CA, at 335, 336; *Brinkibon Ltd v Stahag Stahl und Stahlwarenhandelsgesellschaft mbH* [1983] 2 A.C. 34, HL, at 41, 43, 48; *Holwell Securities Ltd v Hughes* [1974] 1 W.L.R. 155, CA, 157.

[292] *Brogden v Metropolitan Railway Co*, see para.3-38 fn.255, at 691 (Lord Blackburn), referring to *Harris' Case*, see para.3-42 fn.302.

extraneous act which clenches the matter, and shews beyond all doubt that each side is bound, I agree the contract is perfectly plain and clear."

Lord Blackburn refers here to the offeror *expressly or impliedly* prescribing the posting of reply as the form—and the time—of acceptance. An express prescription would be clear (although still subject to the construction of the language of the offer[293]) but likely to be found only in the case of more formal invitations to contract. The courts have, however, developed the notion of an implied prescription as to the use of the post in order to accept an offer, to the point where it is now generally referred to as the postal *rule*.[294] It is important to remember that this so-called rule is itself an exception to the general rule that acceptance must be communicated, and therefore it should be applied only where it is clear that acceptance by post is sufficient on the facts to displace the normal requirement of communication; and although the "postal rule" has its origin in the case of acceptance communicated by the public postal service,[295] it is not in fact limited to cases where the postal service is used but also applies to other forms of long-distance and non-instantaneous communication.[296]

The difficulties which the law here seeks to address are those flowing from the inevitable delay in the transmission of communications between parties who do not deal directly (whether in person or through an agent). The offeror may have changed his mind, and may even have sent a revocation of his offer, before the offeree dispatches his acceptance in ignorance of the offeror's change of mind.[297] Not achieving their object immediately, communications passing through media such as the postal service go into a kind of limbo, out of the control of both parties,[298] and there may be a failure in the communication—delay beyond that which would be expected by the normal operation of the post, or even the loss of the letter by the postal service.[299] The law determines which party should run the risks associ-

---

[293] See para.3-37.

[294] The idea of a "rule" is as early as *Dunlop v Higgins* (1848) 1 H.L. Cas. 381 at 400, 9 E.R. 805 at 813 (Lord Cottenham LC: "Common sense tells us that transactions cannot go on without such a rule, and [*Adams v Lindsell*, see para.3-42 fn.301, and *Stocken v Collin* (1841) 7 M. & W. 515, 151 E.R. 870] seem to be the leading cases on the subject").

[295] See esp. S. Gardner, "Trashing with Trollope: A Deconstruction of the Postal Rules in Contract" (1992) 12 O.J.L.S. 170.

[296] See para.3-43.

[297] On revocation of an offer by the offeror, see para.3-31.

[298] If the communication is handed by the sender to his own agent, there is clearly no communication yet, and the sender could still recall it: *Hebb's Case* (1867) L.R. 4 Eq. 9 at 12 (Lord Romilly MR); this will generally be the case where a party uses a private courier as his own agent rather than a general postal service. Similarly, a communication to the authorised agent of the recipient would be complete on delivery to the agent: ibid. It has been said that the postal service is the agent of both parties, and that this explains why placing the acceptance in the hands of the postal service forms the contract: ibid.; *Household Fire and Carriage Accident Insurance Co Ltd v Grant* (1879) 3 Exch. D. 216 at 221; *Byrne & Co v Leon van Tienhoven & Co* (1880) 5 C.P.D. 344 at 348. The better view, however, is that the postal service has the authority of neither party in relation to the receipt of contractual communications: *Henthorn v Fraser* [1892] 2 Ch. 27, CA, at 35–36 (Kay LJ: "The Post Office are only carriers between them. They are agents to convey the communication, not to receive it. The communication is not made to the Post Office, but by their agency as carriers. The difference is between saying 'Tell my agent A., if you accept,' and 'Send your answer to me by A.' In the former case A. is to be the intelligent recipient of the acceptance, in the latter he is only to convey the communication to the person making the offer which he may do by a letter, knowing nothing of its contents. The Post Office are only agents in the latter sense").

[299] *Dunlop v Higgins*, see para.3-42 fn.294 at 395, at 810–811 (delay in delivery by reason of severe

ated with such problems. We have seen that the revocation of an offer does not generally take effect until it is received by the offeree, in accordance with the objective test which protects the offeree in circumstances where he has been led by the offeror, in the terms of the offer and the circumstances in which it was made, reasonably to believe that there is still an offer to accept.[300] The same rationale applies to the postal rule of acceptance: if the offeror, by the terms of the offer and the circumstances in which it was made, has led the offeree reasonably to believe that there is an offer to be accepted and that the dispatch of his acceptance by the postal service is the way (or, at least, *a way*) in which the contract can be concluded, then the posting of the acceptance is the form (and the time and place) of acceptance.[301] This not only fits the objective model of contracting in English law, but also provides a commercially sensible rule, allocating the risk appropriately so that if the offeror wishes to retain the right to change his mind, or to receive actual notification of acceptance, he must do so sufficiently clearly in the offer; but if in context the post would normally be a suitable form of acceptance the offeree is entitled to rely on it. The policy argument was set out by Mellish LJ[302]:

"When a person in one part of the country writes to a person in another part of the country a letter containing an offer, and either directly or impliedly tells him to send his answer by post, and an answer accepting that offer is returned by post, when is a complete contract made? Is it made at the time when the letter accepting the offer is put into the post, or is it not made until that letter is received? It was contended before us that it is not made until

---

frost); *Duncan v Topham* (1849) 8 C.B. 225 at 227; 137 E.R. 495 at 496–497 (Cresswell J, directing the jury that contract would be complete even if acceptance letter lost by negligence of post-office authorities), cited in *Harris' Case*, see para.3-42 fn.302, at 596 (Mellish LJ, criticising reasoning supporting the opposite view in *British & American Telegraph Co Ltd v Colson*, see para.3-42 fn.302, but accepting at 597 that "although the contract is complete at the time when the letter accepting the offer is posted, yet it may be subject to a condition subsequent that if the letter does not arrive in due course of post, then the parties may act on the assumption that the offer has not been accepted"; James LJ at 592 declined to express an opinion on the point); *Household Fire and Carriage Accident Insurance Co Ltd v Grant*, see para.3-42 fn.298 (acceptance letter posted but not received).

300 See para.3-31.

301 The earliest explanation was that "The defendants must be considered in law as making, during every instant of the time their letter was travelling, the same identical offer to the plaintiffs; and then the contract is completed by the acceptance of it by the latter": *Adams v Lindsell* (1818) 1 B. & Ald. 681 at 683, 106 E.R. 250 at 251, which "looks suspiciously like a borrowing from Pothier": Simpson, see para.3-32 fn.194, p.261; repeated in *Dunlop v Higgins*, see para.3-42 fn.294 at 400, at 813; *Henthorn v Fraser*, see para.3-42 fn.298 at 31.

302 *Harris' Case* (1872) L.R. 7 Ch. App. 587 at 593–594. See also *Household Fire and Carriage Accident Insurance Co Ltd v Grant*, see para.3-42 fn.291 at 223–224, 232; *Brinkibon Ltd v Stahag Stahl und Stahlwarenhandelsgesellschaft mbH*, see para.3-41 fn.291 at 41, 48. For the opposite argument, see *British & American Telegraph Co Ltd v Colson* (1871) L.R. 6 Ex. 108 (the postal acceptance rule "would be such as to work great and obvious injustice in a variety of mercantile transactions of constant occurrence" because the offeror could not know whether the contract has been concluded: Kelly C.B. at 112; the offeree takes the risk on himself by using the post, which should be seen as his agent: Bramwell B at 118, but allowing at 119 that "if the person addressed had agreed that posting a letter should suffice, like a delivery of goods to a carrier, he would be bound. But it seems to me that when nothing more appears than that the post may be resorted to, the mere posting should not bind the person written to; because, in all cases, unless the contrary appears by express stipulation, the post may be resorted to". Bramwell B's view of the postal service as the offeree's agent has not been accepted: cf. para.3-42 fn.298. As Bramwell LJ, he maintained his objection to the postal rule in a dissenting opinion in *Household Fire and Carriage Accident Insurance Co Ltd v Grant*, above).

the letter is received; so that until it is received the contract may be revoked by the person who has made the offer.

Now throughout the argument I have been forcibly struck with the extraordinary and very mischievous consequences which would follow if it were held that an offer might be revoked at any time until the letter accepting it had been actually received. No mercantile man who has received a letter making him an offer, and has accepted the offer, could safely act on that acceptance after he has put it into the post until he knew that it had been received. Every day, I presume, there must be a large number of mercantile letters received which require to be acted upon immediately. A person, for instance, sends an order to a merchant in *London* offering to pay a certain price for so many goods. The merchant writes an answer accepting the offer, and goes that instant into the market and purchases the goods in order to enable him to fulfil the contract. But according to the argument presented to us, if the person who has sent the offer finds that the market is falling, and that it will be a bad bargain for him, he may at any time, before he has received the answer, revoke his offer. The consequences might be very serious to the merchant, and might be much more serious when the parties are in distant countries."

The explanation given by Mellish LJ still starts from the assumption that the offeror "directly or impliedly tells [the offeree] to send his answer by post": the question, therefore, is when there is an implied prescription of post as the form of acceptance. It is not sufficient that the offeree can and does use the post in order to communicate his acceptance[303]; whether the postal rule applies—and so the posting itself constitutes the acceptance—depends on whether post was an acceptable form of communication, and whether the offeree was reasonably entitled, in the circumstances, to believe that the offeror was prepared to be bound by the sending of the acceptance.[304] The most obvious situation in which this applies is where the offer itself came by post and gave no indication that it could not be similarly accepted.[305] But it is not only in the case of an offer received by post that the postal rule will apply[306]; and the courts will be careful to check that there is nothing in the

---

[303] *Holwell Securities Ltd v Hughes*, see para.3-43 fn.307.

[304] The postal rule allows the offeree to bind the offeror by posting his acceptance; if the offeror had no reason to expect the post to be used, and had not acted in such a way as to entitle the offeree to believe that acceptance would be binding on posting, an acceptance which is in fact posted should not take effect until it is received by the offeror. See *Dunlop v Higgins*, see para.3-42 fn.294, at 398, at 812 (postal reply was the "usage of trade"); *Household Fire and Carriage Accident Insurance Co Ltd v Grant*, see para.3-42 fn.298, at 228 (Baggallay LJ: the postal rule "is limited in its application to cases in which by reason of general usage, or of the relations between the parties to any particular transactions, or of the terms in which the offer is made, the acceptance of such offer by a letter through the post is expressly or impliedly authorized"); *Henthorn v Fraser*, see para.3-42 fn.298, at 33 (Lord Herschell: "I am not sure that I should myself have regarded the doctrine that an acceptance is complete as soon as the letter containing it is posted as resting upon an implied authority by the person making the offer to the person receiving it to accept by those means. ... I should prefer to state the rule thus: Where the circumstances are such that it must have been within the contemplation of the parties that, according to the ordinary usages of mankind, the post might be used as a means of communicating the acceptance of an offer, the acceptance is complete as soon as it is posted"); and see at 36 (Kay LJ: "Posting an acceptance of an offer may be sufficient where it can fairly be inferred from the circumstances of the case that the acceptance might be sent by post").

[305] e.g. *Household Fire and Carriage Accident Insurance Co Ltd v Grant*, see para.3-42 fn.298, at 223, 224; *Dunlop v Higgins*, see para.3-42 fn.294; *Bruner v Moore* [1904] 1 Ch. 305 at 316 (parties were American citizens, together in London when contract was signed, but obviously contemplated that they would thereafter separate and visit various parts of Europe and communicate by letter and telegram to exercise option created by the contract).

[306] *Henthorn v Fraser*, see para.3-42 fn.298 (offer handed to offeree, but open for acceptance for 14 days and the parties lived in different towns, so acceptance by post was in parties' contemplation).

offer, even one received by post, which displaces the postal rule and reinstates the general rule that the acceptance should be communicated.[307]

3-43   **Retractation of posted acceptance**   If the postal rule applies to a particular communication of acceptance, the contract is in principle complete on posting. However, the offeree may change his mind and in fact communicate his rejection of the offer before the posted letter has reached the offeror, and the question in such a case is whether the offeree has successfully prevented the formation of the contract. There is no authority on this in English law,[308] and the arguments are balanced. It is said that to allow the offeree to retract his acceptance (or to disclaim reliance on the posted acceptance and instead to reject the offer by an alternative means of communication) is wrong because it allows him to "blow hot and cold"—to post the acceptance in the safe knowledge that the contract will be formed at that moment unless he takes advantage of the delay involved in using the postal service to change his mind if, to use the classic example, the contract was for shares where the market price moved against him between posting of the acceptance and his actual communication of rejection.[309] On the other hand, given that the postal rule is designed for the benefit of the offeree, to give him certainty that the contract is concluded on posting where it was reasonable for him so to believe,[310] it can be said that he should be allowed to waive reliance on the rule at least where this does not prejudice the offeror; and given that the offeror is not prejudiced by acting on the first communication which he actually receives (the rejection), the better view is to allow the communicated rejection to take effect rather than the already-posted acceptance.[311]

---

[307] e.g. *Holwell Securities Ltd v Hughes* [1974] 1 W.L.R. 155, CA ("option shall be exercised by notice in writing to the intending vendor": notification could be made by post, but "notice in writing" indicated that it would not take effect until communicated. The interpretation of language can be quite subtle: if it had said "the offer ... may be accepted in writing" the acceptance would have been effective on posting: Russell LJ at 158; but "notice in writing" is familiar conveyancing language, and the word "notice" carries the inference that it must be made known to someone: Lawton LJ at 160).

[308] In Scotland, *Dunmore v Alexander* (1830) 9 S. 190, IH, is sometimes cited as showing the retractation is permitted, but commentators differ as to whether this was retractation of an offer or an acceptance: W.W. McBryde, *The Law of Contract in Scotland*, 3rd edn (Thomson, 2007), para.6-06, criticising W.M. Gloag, *The Law of Contract*, 2nd edn (1929, reprint Caledonian Books, 1985), p.38; H.L. MacQueen and J. Thomson, *Contract Law in Scotland*, 4th edn (Bloomsbury, 2016), para.2.34 (noting that *Dunmore v Alexander* was decided before the postal acceptance rule had been transplanted into Scots law, and that it was doubted in *Thomson v James* (1855) 18 D. 1, IH). In *Morrison v Thoelke* 155 So. 2d 889 (1963) District CA of Florida held that posting of acceptance prevailed over a communicated retractation; and in *Soldau v Organon Inc* 860 F.2d 355 (1988), the 9th Circuit of the US Court of Appeals held that an acceptance of an offer was effective when mailed even though acceptance was later retrieved from the mail box (per curiam at 356: "The so-called 'mailbox' or 'effective when mailed' rule was adopted and followed as federal common law by the Supreme Court ... we could not change the rule, and there is no reason to believe the Supreme Court would be inclined to do so. It is almost universally accepted in the common law world. It is enshrined in the Restatement (Second) of Contracts §63(a), and endorsed by the major contract treatises").

[309] This is the approach taken by Anson, p.55; Chitty, para.2-059, Furmston, para.2.251 and Treitel, para.2-038, appear to lean in favour of this argument, but Cheshire, Fifoot and Furmston, pp.72–73 are neutral.

[310] See para.3-42.

[311] A.H. Hudson, "Retractation of Letters of Acceptance" (1966) 82 L.Q.R. 169 prefers to allow retractation, arguing that the offeror has taken the risk that a posted letter may be overtaken by a speedier means of communication, unless he has prescribed actual communication of the acceptance or has

Scope of operation of the "postal rule"; novel forms of communication What 3-44
has been said above about the inevitable delays involved in the sending of communications through the postal service applies equally to any other communication through a non-instantaneous medium which is outside the control or
responsibility of both parties, such as telegram[312]; but this does not apply in the case
of telephone[313] or telex[314] where, even though the parties are separated in space and
have to rely on third-party technology in order to communicate, there is not the
same separation of time as in the case of the postal service, and the offeree responds
in a form where he can detect whether the acceptance has been received
successfully. He therefore does not need to rely on the mere sending of the communication but can know whether his message has come to the offeror's attention.[315]
The "postal rule" was developed to deal with the problems arising from acceptance by a means which is not instantaneously discoverable by the offeror, and cases
have settled the scope of operation of the rule to certain forms of communication:
the general postal service[316] and telegram.[317] But new forms of communication
continue to be devised, and the question will be whether the postal rule applies to
allow the sending of an acceptance by some novel form of communication to be sufficient to conclude the contract. This is an area in which the common law technique
of reasoning by analogy from previous cases comes into its own: the existing cases
dealing with the applicability (or not) of the postal rule, and the general principles
which underlie the reasoning in those cases can be used to answer how a court
should deal with novel cases.[318] The most obvious new forms for which the courts
will need to find answers are electronic, such as email and internet contracts.[319] For
example, a court might need to determine whether a contract was concluded where

---

specified that retractation will not be allowed; and suggests that the reasonable man might well suppose that a letter of acceptance could be retracted. For the opposite case, where the offeree first posts
a rejection, but then accepts by a speedier means of communication, see para.3-33.

[312] *Bruner v Moore*, see para.3-42 fn.305, at 316. In the UK telegrams are no longer available as part
of the public postal service, although the service still exists through a private company: *http://
www.telegramsonline.co.uk*.

[313] cf. *Entores Ltd v Miles Far East Corp* [1955] 2 Q.B. 327, CA, at 332.

[314] *Entores Ltd v Miles Far East Corp*, see para.3-44 fn.313, at 333, 335, 337; *Brinkibon Ltd v Stahag
Stahl und Stahlwarenhandelsgesellschaft mbH*, see para.3-41 fn.291, at 42.

[315] *Entores Ltd v Miles Far East Corp*, see para.3-44 fn.313, at 333; *Brinkibon Ltd v Stahag Stahl und
Stahlwarenhandelsgesellschaft mbH*, see para.3-41 fn.291, at 43 (Lord Fraser: "a party (the accep-
tor) who tries to send a message by telex can generally tell if his message has not been received on
the other party's (the offeror's) machine, whereas the offeror, of course, will not know if an unsuccessful attempt has been made to send an acceptance to him. It is therefore convenient that the ac-
ceptor, being in the better position, should have the responsibility of ensuring that his message is
received").

[316] If an offeree uses not the general postal service but a private courier, the courier is likely to be seen
as his agent and therefore the postal rule would not apply merely by handing the acceptance to the
courier: see para.3-42 fn.298.

[317] See para.3-44 fn.312.

[318] See para.3-26. Note also *Brinkibon Ltd v Stahag Stahl und Stahlwarenhandelsgesellschaft mbH*, see
para.3-41 fn.291, at 42 (Lord Wilberforce, quoted at para.3-45).

[319] D. Nolan, "Offer and Acceptance in the Electronic Age" in A. Burrows and E. Peel, *Contract Formation and Parties* (Oxford University Press, 2010), p.61; A. Davidson, *The Law of Electronic Commerce* (Port Melbourne: Cambridge University Press, 2009), Ch.3, discussing principally Australian and New Zealand law, and the UNCITRAL Model Law of Electronic Commerce (1996, amended
1998), which has been adopted in many jurisdictions although not in the UK except for Crown
Dependencies and overseas territories: see *http://www.uncitral.org/uncitral/en/uncitral_texts/
electronic_commerce/1996Model_status.html*.

the evidence is that an email acceptance was properly sent but through some electrical fault failed to be read by the offeror—such as where it was received by the server on which the offeror's emails are stored, but was then deleted in error by some cause not attributable to the offeror. In this discussion an analogy might be the telex cases (an instantaneous form of electronic communication where the sender knows whether the communication has been successful),[320] suggesting that as long as the email is not rejected by the offeror's server, the time at which it would take effect would be when received by the server (and so the postal rule does not apply). However, if the sender of an email knows that there may be a delay before his message would be retrieved, and therefore knows that there is a likely delay in actual communication, a court might say that an email acceptance (in the absence of language in the offer to prescribe the method or time of acceptance[321]) would take effect when the offeror in fact reads it or, if earlier, when the offeree would reasonably have expected the offeror to read it.[322]

3-45 **Delays in the communication of acceptance: attribution of fault** The "postal rule" not only allows the offeree by the posting of his acceptance to fix the time and place of the formation of the contract; it also allocates to the offeror the risk of failure of the communication—the delay or even the loss of the letter by the postal service.[323] However, this only covers the case where the delay in communication is not attributable to either party. If the reason for the acceptance being received by the offeree late, or not at all, is within the sphere of risk and responsibility of one or other of the parties—and so (to that extent) the party's "fault"—it is natural that the delay should be held to operate against that party.[324] Where such a case is alleged, it is necessary first to determine at what moment, but for the fault of the party in question, the acceptance would have been taken to be effective in law; and then, secondly, to consider whether that answer should be varied by reason of the fact that one party was at fault in relation to the delay.

If the "postal rule" applies by reason of the terms of the offer and the

---

[320] See para.3-44 fn.314.

[321] Note that, in the case of internet contracts, it is common for the online retailer to include conditions defining the method and timing of acceptance: Nolan, see para.3-44 fn.109, pp.85–86, giving examples from the online retailer Amazon.co.uk.

[322] Nolan, see para.3-44 fn.319, pp.70–76, favours the time of receipt by the server. If the reason that the offeree did not see the message was within his sphere of risk, it should in any event count against him: see para.3-45. See also Davidson, *The Law of Electronic Commerce*, see para.3-44 fn.319, pp.59–60, arguing that the question is not what single rule of acceptance should apply to any particular form of electronic communication such as email, but how the parties in fact use that form: "Email is sometimes used as a chat room or instant messaging. Two users may send and receive numerous emails within a matter of minutes. It may be conversational, with questions and answers clarifying each other's position before a formal offer and acceptance occurs. This use of communications should be regarded as instantaneous ... However, some users utilise electronic mail like standard mail. A given office's protocol may be to access email once per day and then carefully draft a reply for sending later in the day. Such an office may require a supervisor to check the contents of all mail before it is sent, whether it is standard or electronic mail ... this use would be more akin to standard mail. The focus of the application of the rule should be on the use, bearing in mind Wilberforce's threefold test [*Brinkibon Ltd v Stahag Stahl und Stahlwarenhandelsgesellschaft mbH*, quoted at para.3-45] of intention, sound business practice and risk".

[323] See para.3-42 fn.299.

[324] *LJ Korbetis v Transgrain Shipping BV* [2005] EWHC 1345 (QB) at [11] (Toulson J: "Common sense dictates that it is unfair to the intended recipient that he should be bound by something which he is unlikely to receive because of the fault of the sender").

circumstances in which it was made,[325] then the contract would have been formed at the moment when the acceptance was dispatched. If, therefore, there was a delay in its dispatch which was caused by some act or event which is attributable to the offeror—within his sphere of responsibility—the contract should be taken to have been formed at the moment at which, but for that act or event, the acceptance would have been dispatched and if a contract would thereby have been formed the offeror cannot deny the contract.[326] Or if there was some act or event attributable to the offeree which delayed the delivery of the communication after its dispatch, the offeree should not be able to hold the offeror to the contract on the basis of his sending of the acceptance but only (if at all[327]) on the basis of the facts taking into account his own responsibility for the delay.[328] If, by contrast, the "postal rule" did not apply to the sending of the acceptance, and therefore in the normal course the contract would have been concluded only on its receipt, the question is whether there is some act or event attributable to the offeror which caused him to fail to receive it—in which case he should not be entitled to claim that he did not receive it[329]; or an act or event attributable to the offeree, in which case he cannot complain that there was a delay in the communication which may thereby delay or even prevent the formation of the contract: in such a case the offeree has simply not accepted the offer until his reply in fact (if ever) arrives.

In determining whether one party was at fault the courts will take into account normal business practice, and what each party is reasonably entitled to expect of the other.[330] Discussing variations to the standard case of long-distance communication which give rise to delays in transmission, some of which involve fault by one

---

[325] See para.3-42.

[326] *Adams v Lindsell* (1818) 1 B. & Ald. 681 at 683, 106 E.R. 250 at 251 (offer, requesting "answer in course of post", was sent by fault of offeror to Bromsgrove, Leicestershire instead of Bromsgrove, Worcestershire. Acceptance sent by offeree after delayed receipt was valid: "as to the delay in notifying the acceptance, that arises entirely from the mistake of the defendants, and it therefore must be taken as against them, that the plaintiffs' answer was received in course of post").

[327] It may be that the failure means that the communication is not a valid "acceptance" at all.

[328] *LJ Korbetis v Transgrain Shipping BV*, see para.3-45 fn.324, at [11] (where, however, it was assumed that a faxed acceptance, which was misdirected, would otherwise have attracted the postal rule; cf. para.3-44).

[329] *Entores Ltd v Miles Far East Corp* [1955] 2 Q.B. 327, CA, at 333 (Denning LJ: offeror who realises that there is a failure of communication by offeree should ask offeree to repeat it where the offeree "reasonably believes that his message has been received. The offeror in such circumstances is clearly bound, because he will be estopped from saying that he did not receive the message of acceptance. It is his own fault that he did not get it"); *Townsend's Case* (1871) L.R. 13 Eq. 148 at 155 (Malins VC "he who has caused the mistake is not the person entitled to take advantage of it", applying *Adams v Lindsell*, see para.3-45 fn.326, in case where it was assumed that the acceptance had to be received, and not just posted: see at 153); cf. *Tenax Steamship Co Ltd v The Brimnes (Owners) (The Brimnes)* [1975] Q.B. 929, CA (exercise by owners of contractual right of withdrawal of vessel for late payment by charterer; telex sent during ordinary business hours regarded has having been received that day even if not read; see Megaw LJ at 966–967: "if a notice arrives at the address of the person to be notified, at such a time and by such a means of communication that it would in the normal course of business come to the attention of that person on its arrival, that person cannot rely on some failure of himself or his servants to act in a normal businesslike manner in respect of taking cognisance of the communication so as to postpone the effective time of the notice until some later time when it in fact came to his attention").

[330] See, e.g. *Brinkibon Ltd v Stahag Stahl und Stahlwarenhandelsgesellschaft mbH*, see para.3-41 fn.291, at 43 (Lord Fraser: "once the message has been received on the offeror's telex machine, it is not unreasonable to treat it as delivered to the principal offeror, because it is his responsibility to arrange for prompt handling of messages within his own office"). This is another example of the application of the general objective test in the formation of contracts: see para.3-07.

or other party, Lord Wilberforce said[331]: "No universal rule can cover all such cases: they must be resolved by reference to the intentions of the parties, by sound business practice and in some cases by a judgment where the risks should lie". However, this should not be seen creating a general discretion in the court to determine each case: the facts may vary, but the underlying principles by reference to which the rules of offer and acceptance are determined must be clear.[332]

III. PRACTICAL ISSUES RELATING TO FINDING THE AGREEMENT

(1) Finding the Agreement through Offer and Acceptance

3-46   **Using the offer and acceptance to find the agreement**   We have seen that the English courts have developed a rule to the effect that, at least in the case where the parties negotiate by mutual successive communications, there must normally be an offer by one, accepted unequivocally by the other, if a contract is to come into existence. "Offer and acceptance" are not simply a useful tool to determine whether the parties have in fact agreed, but have been elevated to the status of a legal rule for the formation of a contract.[333] There can be difficulties in fitting many day-to-day transactions into the "offer and acceptance" model, but in most cases this is not because there is any doubt that there is a contract but rather because the parties do not in practice think in terms that one of them is making an offer, and the other accepting it; there may be some difficulties of legal analysis but such cases do not generally raise practical problems.[334] In very many cases the case law will provide direct solutions for the interpretation of the facts in order to determine the formation of the contract[335]; and although new cases can emerge, we have seen that the courts will apply the existing cases by analogy,[336] bearing in mind Lord Wilberforce's statement that new cases "must be resolved by reference to the intentions of the parties, by sound business practice and in some cases by a judgment where

---

[331] *Brinkibon Ltd v Stahag Stahl und Stahlwarenhandelsgesellschaft mbH*, see para.3-41 fn.291, at 42 (Lord Wilberforce, giving a range of variants to the standard case of acceptance by telex: "The senders and recipients may not be the principals to the contemplated contract. They may be servants or agents with limited authority. The message may not reach, or be intended to reach, the designated recipient immediately: messages may be sent out of office hours, or at night, with the intention, or upon the assumption, that they will be read at a later time. There may be some error or default at the recipient's end which prevents receipt at the time contemplated and believed in by the sender. The message may have been sent and/or received through machines operated by third persons. And many other variations may occur"); see also Lord Brandon at 50.

[332] *LJ Korbetis v Transgrain Shipping BV*, see para.3-45 fn.324, at [12] (Toulson J: "Mr. Lewis submitted that in such situations there should be no firm rule of law, as in the ordinary posting rule, but that it should be for the court to decide on a case by case basis what result most fairly suited the facts. I do not accept that submission. Rules about offer and acceptance ought to be clear, so that parties may know where they stand. A situation in which it is unclear whether or not a contract has been formed until a court decides in the exercise of some form of general discretion whether or not a contract has been formed would be unsatisfactory").

[333] See paras 3-19, 3-24.

[334] See para.3-20; note particularly Lord Wilberforce's comment that the courts take a "practical approach, often at the cost of forcing the facts to fit uneasily into the marked slots of offer, acceptance, and consideration": *New Zealand Shipping Co Ltd v AM Satterthwaite & Co Ltd (The Eurymedon)* [1975] A.C. 154, PC, at 167.

[335] See the many different fact-patterns in which the courts have determined what constitutes an "offer" and an "acceptance", discussed in the earlier paragraphs of this chapter.

[336] See para.3-26.

the risks should lie".[337] This approach might seem potentially uncertain, but it provides guidance for how the courts should deal with novel cases to seek to obtain a predictable result, and as far as possible to give effect to what the parties intended, and to find a commercially sensible solution.

The general rules on offer and acceptance are, in effect, default rules, designed to apply in cases where the parties have not addressed more particularly the formation of their contract.[338] If the precise details of the formation of the contract are important for the parties—for example, where the place or time at which the contract is to be concluded is critical, rather than leaving it to the courts' interpretation of where or when the "offer" was "accepted"[339]—the parties are entirely free to make this explicit. A party can prevent a communication being an offer at all, if he makes clear that it is only an enquiry, or an invitation to treat, and not yet an offer which could bind him by the other party's simple acceptance.[340] Or he can make an offer which prescribes the method or time of reply for a valid acceptance.[341] Broadly speaking, a party making a proposal for a contract can set the basis on which he is willing to be bound—but of course this requires the parties to think carefully in advance and to be well advised about the language they use in their communications to ensure that there is no ambiguity which could result in an unplanned outcome.

The problem of a "battle of forms"   One situation can, however, present a   **3-47**
significant practical difficulty: where the parties do take positive steps to regulate the formation of their contract but do so in such a way that they each present conflicting documents to the other. This is commonly referred to as a "battle of forms", given that it typically arises in a case where two commercial parties are negotiating for a contract, and each has its own standard terms of business and is willing to contract only on its own terms. The parties' communications take the form of each reiterating that the contract is on its own terms, not on the terms that it has received from the other party, and so there never appears to be any acceptance by one party of the set of terms proposed by the other.

This is a sufficiently common—and commercially difficult—issue that many legal systems have developed special rules providing that a reply which contains terms additional to or different from those contained in the offer can conclude the contract, and the contract will include those additional or different terms as long as they are not material and the offeror does not raise an objection. The United Nations Convention on Contracts for the International Sale of Goods, for example, has the following provision[342]:

---

[337] *Brinkibon Ltd v Stahag Stahl und Stahlwarenhandelsgesellschaft mbH*, see para.3-45 fn.331.

[338] See para.3-22.

[339] The time and place of the contract are normally the time and place at which the acceptance in law takes effect: see para.3-22.

[340] See para.3-28.

[341] See paras 3-30, 3-37. The "postal rule" of acceptance is only a default rule and so will not override the clear terms of the offer as to the method and time of acceptance: *Holwell Securities Ltd v Hughes* [1974] 1 W.L.R. 155, CA, see para.3-42 fn.307.

[342] United Nations Convention on Contracts for the International Sale of Goods (Vienna, 1980) ("CISG") art.19. Very many states have ratified the Convention (see *http://www.uncitral.org/uncitral/ en/uncitral_texts/sale_goods/1980CISG_status.html*), but the UK has not done so, and therefore this rule forms no part of English law.

   PICC art.2.1.11 has substantially the same text as art.19(1), (2) CISG but omits to define "material" alterations. However, the Comment on art.2.1.1. says "What amounts to a "material" modifica-

"(1) A reply to an offer which purports to be an acceptance but contains additions, limitations or other modifications is a rejection of the offer and constitutes a counter-offer.

(2) However, a reply to an offer which purports to be an acceptance but contains additional or different terms which do not materially alter the terms of the offer constitutes an acceptance, unless the offeror, without undue delay, objects orally to the discrepancy or dispatches a notice to that effect. If he does not so object, the terms of the contract are the terms of the offer with the modifications contained in the acceptance.

(3) Additional or different terms relating, among other things, to the price, payment, quality and quantity of the goods, place and time of delivery, extent of one party's liability to the other or the settlement of disputes are considered to alter the terms of the offer materially."

Such a provision departs from the strict offer and acceptance rule in only a limited way since it will only resolve a battle of forms in a case where the difference between the offer and the purported acceptance is non-material. However, in English law even this is not possible. Lord Denning's attempt in *Butler Machine Tool Co Ltd v Ex-Cell-O Corp (England) Ltd*[343] to move away from the formal analysis by offer an acceptance and instead to look for "agreement on all material points—even though there may be differences between the forms and conditions printed on the back of them" was later rejected by the House of Lords.[344] Although the House of Lords did not discuss the problems associated with battles of forms,[345] the Court of Appeal has made clear more recently in *Tekdata Interconnections Ltd v Amphenol Ltd*[346] that there is no special rule for such cases. There might be situations in which the terms of the contract would be found from the conduct of the parties rather than from the normal offer and acceptance analysis but this would be

tion cannot be determined in the abstract but will depend on the circumstances of each case. Additional or different terms relating to the price or mode of payment, place and time of performance of a non-monetary obligation, the extent of one party's liability to the other or the settlement of disputes, will normally, but need not necessarily, constitute a material modification of the offer. An important factor to be taken into account in this respect is whether the additional or different terms are commonly used in the trade sector concerned and therefore do not come as a surprise to the offeror".

See also UCC §2-207:

"(1) A definite and seasonable expression of acceptance or a written confirmation which is sent within a reasonable time operates as an acceptance even though it states terms additional to or different from those offered or agreed upon, unless acceptance is expressly made conditional on assent to the additional or different terms.

(2) The additional terms are to be construed as proposals for addition to the contract. Between merchants such terms become part of the contract unless:

   (a)   the offer expressly limits acceptance to the terms of the offer;
   (b)   they materially alter it; or
   (c)   notification of objection to them has already been given or is given within a reasonable time after notice of them is received."

[343] [1979] 1 W.L.R. 401, CA, at 404; see para.3-23. At 405 Lord Denning added: "The terms and conditions of both parties are to be construed together. If they can be reconciled so as to give a harmonious result, all well and good. If differences are irreconcilable—so that they are mutually contradictory—then the conflicting terms may have to be scrapped and replaced by a reasonable implication".

[344] *Gibson v Manchester City Council* [1979] 1 W.L.R. 294 at 297; see para.3-24.

[345] The *Butler* case involved a battle of forms; in the *Gibson* case the House of Lords did not discuss the difficulties of such cases, since it was not a battle of forms case, and the statement of Lord Denning which the House of Lords there rejected was from the Court of Appeal in *Gibson*, and no mention was made of the fact that the same point had been raised earlier in the *Butler* case: see generally paras 3-23, 3-24.

[346] [2009] EWCA Civ 1209, [2010] 1 Lloyd's Rep. 357 at [25].

rare,[347] and in principle the court must find the acceptance of an offer if there is to be a contract. The importance of maintaining the general rule was stated by Dyson LJ[348]:

"the rules which govern the formation of contracts have been long established and they are grounded in the concepts of offer and acceptance. So long as that continues to be the case, it seems to me that the general rule should be that the traditional offer and acceptance analysis is to be applied in battle of the forms cases. That has the great merit of providing a degree of certainty which is both desirable and necessary in order to promote effective commercial relationships."

In practice, in a case involving a battle of forms, either the court will find that there was never any concluded contract—which it will be reluctant to do at least in a case where the parties have both acted on the assumption that there was a contract, even if their assumptions differed as to whose standard form terms were the basis of the contract[349]—or the terms contained in the document put forward by one or other party will be found to be the terms of the contract.[350] The difficulty here is the arbitrary outcome: there must have been an unequivocal acceptance if there is a contract, and this must generally be found not in the documents which the parties exchanged but in the fact that one of the parties, having received a (counter-)offer to his own proposal, took some step which can be construed as his acceptance by conduct.[351] This is why it is sometimes said that the "last shot" wins: there is no rule to that effect, but in practice when one party begins performing the court may be able to say that the last communication from the other party which was not explicitly rejected was the offer that has been accepted by conduct. This approach is in accordance with the objective test which English law adopts for the interpretation of the parties' communications, as each would reasonably understood the other[352]; if we required subjective agreement we would have to admit that there was simply no contract. But the uncertainty over the interpretation that the courts will place on the parties' conduct as potential acceptance presents a risk for the parties who are negotiating and seeking to insist on their own terms. At the least, parties must be advised to ensure that if they do take steps that could be construed as acceptance, they do so with the explicit caveat that it does not constitute an acceptance but a continued assertion of their own terms as the basis of the contract.

---

[347] [2009] EWCA Civ 1209, [2010] 1 Lloyd's Rep. 357 at [21] ("although I am not saying that the context of a long-term relationship and the conduct of the parties can never be so strong as to displace the result which a traditional offer and acceptance analysis would dictate, I do not consider the circumstances are sufficiently strong to do so in this present case. Indeed I think it will always be difficult to displace the traditional analysis, in a battle of forms case, unless it can be said there was a clear course of dealing between the parties"). See also Pill LJ at [39]. In the *Tekdata* case the parties had been doing business for many years, but the analysis of the particular contract was still based on the documents relating to its formation.

[348] [2009] EWCA Civ 1209, [2010] 1 Lloyd's Rep. 357 at [25]; followed in *Claxton Engineering Services Ltd v TXM Olaj-És Gázkutató Kft* [2010] EWHC 2567 (Comm); [2011] 1 Lloyd's Rep. 252 at [52].

[349] The conflict may become evident only some time after the contract has been formed and when it has been already partly performed, e.g. where the term which one party seeks to rely on (and which the other party claims was not in the contract because it was not part of "his" terms) is triggered only by later events, such as the price increase clause relied on by the sellers in the *Butler* case.

[350] For an unusual case where there was a contract, but on neither party's terms, see *Transformers & Rectifiers Ltd v Needs Ltd* [2015] EWHC 269 (TCC); (2015) 159 Con. L.R. 33.

[351] See para.3-36.

[352] See para.3-07.

(2) Finding the Agreement in a Written Contract

3-48 **Finding the agreement in a written contract** We have seen that in the case of a written contract—where the parties at the end of the negotiations agree a single written document as their contract—the issues are quite different from those discussed in relation to finding the agreement where it is formed through offer and acceptance.[353] Assuming that there is no challenge to the validity of the document itself, there is no doubt that there is a contract, nor what its (express) terms are: they are contained in the document, and so the analysis turns instead to its interpretation. However, certain practical issues arise in relation to written contracts which must be borne in mind during the negotiations.

First, it is important to be clear at the outset that the contract, when finally negotiated, will be the written document. In principle—except in the unusual case where there is a statutory requirement of writing for the type of contract in question[354] —the contract would be concluded when there is an agreement formed by the unequivocal acceptance of an offer; and in the case of a written contract there will typically be such an agreement before the final written text is signed by the parties. In order, therefore, to ensure that no prematurely binding contact is concluded through the exchanges, whether oral or written, by which the parties come to their agreement, it should be made clear that the parties will not be bound until they have both signed a written document which will itself form the contract. The simplest way to achieve this is to make the negotiations expressly subject to contract.[355]

Secondly, although it is obvious that the clear and unambiguous drafting of the written contract is crucial to avoid dispute about the interpretation of the written contract, it should be remembered that evidence of the negotiations cannot be used in the process of interpreting the written document.[356] Before the document is finalised it must therefore be checked that it records the agreement with sufficient clarity, and that there will be no need to look back at the negotiations in order to understand it properly.

---

[353] See para.3-08.

[354] e.g. a contract for the sale or other disposition of an interest in land, under LP(MP)A 1989 s.2: see Ch.5.

[355] See para.2-08.

[356] *Chartbrook Ltd v Persimmon Homes Ltd* [2009] UKHL 38; [2009] 1 A.C. 1101; see para.3-08.

PART II CONTRACT FORMALITIES

CHAPTER 4

THE ROLE OF FORMALITY[1]

I. FORMALITY IN GENERAL

The use of "formality" in private law transactions   All legal systems make use   **4-01**
of formalities within private law. The law sets the requisame functions as a requirement of formrements for the validity and enforceability of transactions entered into
by private parties, and sometimes the requirements for a particular type of transaction will include formality requirements—that is, the requirement that the transaction be effected in a particular form. The key element of a legal formality is the way
in which an act is done[2]: the procedure which the party or parties must follow in
order to give legal effect to the transaction, independently of other substantive
requirements. The nature of such formalities may vary: for example, one or both
parties may be required to use particular words; or use writing; or use writing in a
particular form; and the procedure may be effected by just the parties themselves
or may also involve the participation of one or more third parties. The formality
requirement may be set as a *substantive* legal condition of the intended transaction; or it may be a condition of its enforceability—an *evidential* requirement.
Moreover, the use of the formality may be optional, in the sense that it provides an
alternative way of achieving a transaction where the formality substitutes for some
other substantive requirement which the law would otherwise set for the transaction in question; or where it adds some further legal advantage for the party or parties over an informal transaction of the same kind. Using examples drawn from different aspects of private law (property law, family law and succession as well as
contract, and drawing on the approach taken in other legal systems as well as within
English private law), the following paragraphs of this section will consider in
general terms the use of legal formalities: the reasons why legal systems set formality requirements at all (the function of formality); the different types of formality
which can be adopted and the different uses which may be made of formality
requirements (substantive or evidential formalities, mandatory or optional); and the
consequences for the validity and enforceability of the transaction where the parties fail to comply with the required formality. The following section will then

---

[1]   Within the books dealing with the law of contract, see Chitty, paras 5-001 to 5-009; Furmston, paras
      2.266 to 2.273; Treitel, paras 5-001 to 5-003, 5-028; Anson, pp.79-80, 94-95; Cheshire, Fifoot and
      Furmston, Ch.7; Burrows (Restatement) s.11; Andrews, art.32. For formalities in relation to real
      property law, see Cheshire and Burn, Ch.25.
[2]   cf. OED Online, March 2018, "formality, n.": "8. A ceremony; a formal act or observance; a legal,
      authorized, or customary procedure".

outline the use of formalities within the English law of contract, by way of introduction to the detailed discussion which follows in Chapters 5, 6 and 7.

(1)   The Function of Formality Requirements

4-02   **Formality is the exception rather than the rule**   It would not be sensible for a legal system to require all private law transactions to be entered into formally: even minimal formality would make everyday transactions difficult to effect.[3] Although the contract for the sale of goods in a shop, and the transfer to the buyer of property in the goods, necessitate some outward conduct by the parties, such as the offer and acceptance of the contract and the physical delivery of the goods to the buyer, these are not formalities but are simply the way in which the sale is necessarily effected. Even if the law sets the requirements of offer and acceptance in order to form a contract,[4] the offer and acceptance are still informal: they may be done orally or in writing without any other particular requirement as to their form.[5] The delivery of tangible goods may be a means of transferring property in the goods, but it is not a formality in the sense that no particular act of delivery is required nor, indeed, is physical delivery required at all.[6] Such oral and informal transactions must be capable of having legal effect without the addition of any requirement of form, otherwise common everyday transactions would not have the legal force that society expects. Although there may be practical reasons for the parties to adopt some outward sign of their transaction, in order to demonstrate that it has taken place and thereby to evidence it in the case of later challenge—in the case of the simplest contract of sale, the provision of a receipt for the transaction by the seller—this is not a formality set by the law in order to validate the transaction but is adopted merely as a matter of convenience and practice.[7]

---

[3]   F. Pollock, *Principles of Contract*, 1st edn (Stevens, 1876), pp.116-126, suggests that the modern approach is the reverse of the original position, under both English law and Roman law, that formal contracts were the rule, informal contracts the exception. For a more nuanced discussion, see J.H. Baker, *An Introduction to English Legal History*, 4th edn (Butterworths, 2002), Chs 18, 19 (and noting at p.320 that informal agreements were enforceable in the local courts: "one could not put every covenant into writing; but then one should not be able to bother the king's central courts with every unwritten covenant").

[4]   See paras 3-24, 3-25. For the suggestion that the requirement of consideration is a requirement of form, or at least is designed to fulfil the same functions as a requirement of form, see para.4-16 fn.116.

[5]   The common law draws no distinction between oral and written contracts; a deed is a particular form of written instrument with certain different effects (see paras 4-05, 4-10), and statute may require writing, or even a deed, in particular circumstances (see para.4-05). But at common law all contracts (oral or written) which are not executed as deeds are said to be "by parol": *Beckham v Drake* (1841) 9 M. & W. 79 at 92, 152 E.R. 35 at 40.

[6]   Transfer of property in goods may be effected by delivery, but may also be effected by the intention of the parties pursuant to a contract of sale; or by deed; or by an informal declaration of trust: M. Bridge, *Personal Property Law*, 4th edn (Oxford University Press, 2015), Ch.5.

[7]   The law could, of course, require a receipt. In Italy not only is the shopkeeper required to issue receipts, but until 2003 even customers could be fined if they could not produce, within the vicinity of the shop, valid receipts showing the correct price: Decreto legge 471/1997 art.11, para.16, repealed by Decreto legge 269/2003 art.33, para.16. However, the purpose of the law was not to validate the contract but to ensure that shopkeepers recorded transactions for the purpose of taxation, and so to use the customer to put pressure on the shopkeeper to do so. H. Kötz, *European Contract Law*, 2nd edn (trans. G. Mertens and T. Weir, Oxford University Press, 2017), p.74, says that "really the only contracts which are still made orally are everyday transactions when the parties perform on the spot. In almost all other cases the parties sign a form" either to provide evidence for firms' business

Certain transactions require formality for the protection of the parties, or of third parties, or of a broader public interest All legal systems recognise that there are various circumstances in which it is justifiable to impose formality requirements for private law transactions; and the justifications for the imposition of formality requirements are commonly linked to the protection of the parties, or of third parties, or of a broader public interest, the particular formality being tailored to achieve the purpose for which it is imposed. The Law Commission, discussing formalities in the context of the use of deeds in English law, said that there are three main aims, of equal importance[8]:

> "(a) cautionary: that is, trying to ensure that the maker does not enter into the transaction without realising what he is doing;
> (b) evidential: providing evidence that the maker did enter into a transaction, and evidence of its terms;
> (c) labelling[9]: making it apparent to third parties what kind of a document it is and what its effect is to be."

This is not an exhaustive list of the functions of formality in private law transactions; and of course the nature of formality will relate to the nature of the transaction. Where the transaction affects in principle only the parties—typically, therefore, in the case of a contract which creates rights in personam—the reason for imposing formality may focus on the protection of the parties themselves, designed both to ensure that a weaker party fully understands the transaction and is not subject to undue pressures, and to provide clear evidence of the transaction and its formal validity in the case of later dispute. Which contracts merit the imposition of formality will depend on the view taken about the need to protect one or both parties. If the legal system allows gratuitous contracts, formality may be imposed for the purpose of protecting the consent of the donor, given that (one might argue) the nature of a donation itself demonstrates an imbalance between the parties calling for justification. Or the potentially weaker position of one of the parties may call for protective formalities—such as in the case of contracts concluded by

4-03

---

transactions, or because firms wish to use their own detailed standard terms. However, even where written contracts are used for such reasons, they are not a legal formality, but only a matter of convenience for one or both parties.

[8] Law Com. WP No.93, *"Transfer of Land: Formalities for Deeds and Escrows"* (1985), para.3.2. The Law Commission referred also to "interesting discussions of the general problems raised by formality requirements in T.G. Youdan, 'Formalities for trusts of land' [1984] C.L.J. 306 at pp.314–15 and the articles referred to there at nn.42 and 44". These articles include L.L. Fuller, "Consideration and Form" (1941) 41 Colum. L.Rev. 799, 800-806 (a seminal article which identified the "evidentiary", "cautionary" and "channeling" functions performed by legal formalities in general, but discussed them in the particular context of contractual formalities); A.G. Gulliver and C.J. Tilson, "Classification of Gratuitous Transfers" (1941) 51 Yale L.J. 1, 5-13 ("ritual", "evidentiary" and "protective" functions of the Statutes of Wills); J.H. Langbein, "Substantial Compliance with the Wills Act" (1975) 88 Harv. L.Rev. 489, 492–497 ("evidentiary", "channeling", "cautionary", "protective [against imposition]" functions of Wills Act formalities); J.M. Perillo, "The Statute of Frauds in the Light of the Functions and Dysfunctions of Form" (1974) 43 Fordham L.Rev. 39, 43-69 ("magical, sacramental and psychological", "earmarking and classifying", "cautionary", "clarifying", "managerial", "publicity", "educational", "regulatory and taxation", "evidentiary" functions of contractual formalities). See also Law Com. No.164, *Formalities for Contracts etc of Land* (1987), paras 2.7-2.12 (evidential, cautionary and channelling functions, as well as certainty and the protection of third-party interests in the case of land).

[9] [Commonly referred to in the language of Fuller, see para.4-03 fn.8 at p.801, as the "channel(l)ing function", making clear that it is not only a matter of identification of the transaction to outsiders but also providing to parties themselves the legal framework into which they may fit their actions—channel their intentions in order to achieve their objects.]

consumers, where it can be efficient to provide a general protection by way of formality without having to examine the particular weakness of the individual party.[10] It should be noted that a formal contract protects *both* parties: by requiring the "weaker" party to comply with formalities, the "stronger" party is thereby provided with greater security against challenge to the validity of the transaction.

Where the transaction is of the nature that could affect third parties—typically, therefore, in the case of a property transaction which operates in rem—there may be an additional concern to protect third parties, who need to be able to know that the transaction has taken place, and that it is legally valid and enforceable, if they are to be affected by it.[11] It is therefore not surprising that it is in the case of property transactions—and, in particular, transactions relating to those forms of property that are of the greatest social or economic significance, such as land—that we tend to see more stringent and detailed formalities for the validity of transactions in private law.[12] This is not to say that there is not still a need to use formalities also to protect the parties themselves involved in property transactions: a good example is the will, where there is an obvious concern to ensure that the testator's intentions are properly recorded and given effect.[13]

There may also be broader public concerns about private law transactions which translate into the use of formalities in particular circumstances. For example, if the state subjects a particular type of transaction between private parties to taxation, one way of securing the state's interest is to subject every such transaction or its enforceability to a formality which ensures that the tax is collected.[14] There may also be a public interest in the validity and lawfulness of private law transactions, going

---

[10] Individual weaknesses will be protected through other doctrines, such as duress, undue influence and "unconscionable bargains": Chitty, Ch.8; Treitel, Ch.10; Anson, Ch.10; Cheshire, Fifoot and Furmston, pp.394-414. Those doctrines may also have general protective rules; e.g. presuming that one party was capable of influencing the other in certain relationships: *Royal Bank of Scotland Plc v Etridge (No.2)* [2001] UKHL 44; [2002] 2 A.C. 773 at [18].

[11] Contracts can also sometimes affect third parties, who can therefore have an interest in the certainty and security of the contract; e.g. if the third party takes as assignee of one of the contracting parties, or if the contract is one which by its nature has potential proprietary effect, such as a lease or a contract for the creation or disposition of an interest in land which creates equitable property rights under the doctrine of *Walsh v Lonsdale*, see para.4-18 fn.129. In the latter case, LP(MP)A 1989 s.2 imposes the formality of writing for the creation of the contract: see para.4-18.

[12] In English law the reluctance to impose formalities for the formation of contracts contrasts with the much more significant level of formality in the case of property, notably in the case of land: not only is a deed required to convey or create most legal estates or interests in land (LPA 1925 s.52) but also in many cases the disposition does not operate at law until the statutory requirements for registration have been complied with: Land Registration Act 2002 s.27 and Sch.2. It is significant that the type of contract which attracts the strictest formality rules in modern English law is the contract relating to land: see para.4-18; Ch.5.

[13] Strong formalities are justifiable in the case of a will not only because it is gratuitous, but also the testator must not be influenced by potential beneficiaries, and in the event of a challenge post mortem the testator will of course not be available to testify as to his or her intentions. Wills of land were included in the Statute of Frauds 1677 s.5, and given stronger formality requirements than other transactions such as contracts (to be "attested and subscribed in the Presence of the said Devisor by three or four credible Witnesses, or else they shall be utterly void and of none Effect").

[14] e.g. in English law, stamp duty land tax is payable on the transfer of land where the price is above a certain threshold; the transaction must be notified to HM Revenue and Customs (HMRC), and without a certificate from HMRC that the transaction has been declared (and, where appropriate, the tax paid) the transfer cannot be registered at the Land Registry: Finance Act 2003 s.79. Until 2003 stamp duty was charged on certain documents transferring property, and a stamp was physically impressed on the document to show that the duty had been paid: under Stamp Act 1891 s.14 an unstamped instrument which is required by law to be stamped cannot be received in evidence in civil proceedings (including arbitration). Similarly, after the death of a person a grant of probate or

beyond the protection of the consent of the individual parties, and identifying a state interest in verifying the legality of the transaction. This is said to be a justification for the practice, known in civil law systems but not in the common law, of subjecting certain transactions of economic or social significance to a formality of "authentication" by a third party such as a notary, as a condition of validity.[15]

(2) Different Types of Formality, and Different Uses of Formality Requirements

Different types of formality: acts, words and writing   Legal systems use dif-   **4-04**
ferent types of formality for private law transactions, although the nature of the formality will generally reflect the principles discussed in para.4-03: the formality will require the parties to take positive steps to achieve it, and its use will provide clarity about the transaction and evidence that it has been properly accomplished, and will mark out the transaction as in some sense special, more than just an everyday transaction. Sometimes the law requires a particular act to be done or particular words to be spoken in order to accomplish a legal transaction,[16] but formalities in modern private law tend to focus around the use of writing[17] which,

---

administration cannot be made without production of documents showing whether inheritance tax is payable in relation to the estate, and after the grant the relevant information is passed by the probate registry to the Revenue: Senior Courts Act 1981 ss.109, 110. In France there is a broader regime of taxation of inter vivos gifts. A *notaire* must be involved to authenticate a donation between private parties (c.civ. art.931), as well as to effect charges over land (c.civ. art.2416) and more generally to authenticate transactions relating to the disposition of land as a condition of their being able to be registered in the public register which gives them effect as against third parties, but he acts as public officer, independent of the parties, to ensure that the transaction is notified to the tax authorities and the tax collected: see generally *http://www.notaires.fr/notaires/principaux-domaines-d-intervention*.

[15] "Preventive justice": Council of the Notariats of the European Union, *Comparative Study of Authentic Instruments*, prepared for the European Parliament's committee on Legal Affairs (2008), para.2.2 (available at *http://www.europarl.europa.eu/document/activities/cont/200811/20081127ATT43123/20081127ATT43123EN.pdf*). See generally J. Cartwright, "'Authenticity' and 'Authentic Instruments': the Perspective of English Law" in L. Aynès (ed.), *L'authenticité* (Paris: La documentation Française, 2013), pp.201–205.

[16] e.g. a public oral declaration, before a registrar and at least two witnesses, using a formula of words prescribed by law, as part of the ceremony of marriage: Marriage Act 1949 ss.44, 45, 45A, 46B, as amended by Marriage Ceremony (Prescribed Words) Act 1966. However, the oral declaration is necessary but not sufficient since the marriage must also be recorded in a publicly searchable register: ibid., Pt IV.

[17] Kötz, European Contract Law, see para.4-02 fn.7, pp.76–77. In ancient legal systems, formalities were often oral, or involved overt acts which would demonstrate clearly that the transaction was being entered into. Such formalities were appropriate, in particular, in societies where parties entering into private law transactions could not be expected to use writing as in the modern world. In Roman law by the 5th century BC the transfer of certain assets of significance in the early agricultural economy (land and houses, slaves, working animals of draught and burden (e.g. oxen, horses, mules and asses) and rights of way and water, collectively termed "*res mancipi*") could be transferred only by a formal conveyance ("*mancipatio*") which involved the presence of the parties, a scale-bearer (to weigh out the price to be paid—pre-coinage) and five other witnesses, and particular words had to be spoken as the asset was delivered to the transferee: see B. Nicholas, *An Introduction to Roman Law* (Clarendon Press, 1962), p.104. In the later law this was no longer practised; long before it was formally abolished in the 6th century AD, it fell out of use because the law was developed to allow this formality to be evaded in practice by simple delivery: see Nicholas, *An Introduction to Roman Law*, pp.116–117; J. Cartwright, "Equity's Connivance in the Evasion of Legal Formalities" in E. Koops and W.J. Zwalve (eds), *Law and Equity: Approaches in Roman Law and Common Law* (Leiden and Boston: Martinus Nijhoff, 2014), pp.111, 121–124; and see para.4-13 fn.103).

even if it has the advantage of (in principle) permanence and therefore use as evidence in the event of disputes, is not, however, a very significant hurdle for a party to meet: writing is an everyday medium of communication which may not mark out the transaction nor make the parties stop and think much more than any other form of communication. Indeed, if we include electronic communications such as text messages, email and internet-based messaging as modern developments of writing,[18] the cautionary function is even more diluted, given the well-developed social practice of everyday communication by such means from mobile telephones. More than just "writing" may therefore be required: the writing may have to take a particular form, use particular words, bear the party's signature, have the signature attested by one or more witnesses, or be deposited in a public registry.[19] In each different case the formality will be chosen, at the time when it is introduced as a requirement, with a view to providing the level of protection deemed to be required for the parties and (if appropriate) for third parties and/or the public interest: that is, the introduction of a particular formality requirement is a positive step, generally designed to meet some specific perceived need. In order to understand why the law uses a particular formality it is therefore necessary to examine why it was introduced. Sometimes there is a change in the law relating to the formalities required for a particular type of transaction, either a reduction or an increase in the level of formality, which is similarly the recognition of a new understanding of the need for formalities for the particular transaction. But we shall also see that, rather than making a positive change in the formality requirements for some particular transaction, the law may acquiesce in the failure of parties to comply with the formality requirements, and may find ways of indirectly giving legal effect to a transaction that does not (or does not fully) comply with the formality requirements. In such cases, too, it is important to assess the original rationale for the formality requirement in question, to determine the circumstances (if any) in which it can be acceptable to allow its circumvention.[20]

4-05   **Formality involving writing**   For some purposes, it may be sufficient to set as the formality that the parties use writing, or at least that the party against whom the transaction is to be enforced does so (either in effecting the transaction or in acknowledging it).[21] It is perhaps natural also to require the party or parties to *sign* the written document: a signature can be seen as adding an element of seriousness to the transaction, giving clearer evidence of the individual's intention to be bound

---

Similarly, the early Roman contractual formality of the *stipulatio* (an oral form of contract) required the use of particular words, although spoken, not written: Nicholas, p.193. In due course the strictness of the particularity of words was relaxed, and in practice writing was later used as a substitute: Nicholas, pp.194–196. For a particularly unusual and antique formality for serious agreements, see Herodotus, *Histories*, iv.70 ((trans. A. de Sélincourt, Penguin, 1954), p.264: oath or solemn compact by Scythians sealed by parties' blood, mixed with wine and, after prayers and other rituals, drunk by the contracting parties and their chief followers).

[18]   See para.4-06.
[19]   See paras 4-05 to 4-08.
[20]   See paras 4-12 to 4-15.
[21]   Writing alone as the formality is unusual in the modern law: signature is commonly the minimum additional requirement. See, however, Financial Collateral Arrangements (No.2) Regulations 2003 (SI 2003/3226), implementing Directive 2002/47/EC, which requires a financial collateral arrangement to be evidenced in writing (reg.3(1)), but disapplies other statutory requirement which might impose either the substantive requirement of writing, or a signature (reg.4).

by the writing and in that sense authenticating it.[22] This model was adopted by the Statute of Frauds 1677, which introduced the requirement of writing, signed by the party or parties (or his or their agents), as a condition of the validity or enforceability of various private law transactions—no doubt those transactions relating to property and contract which were thought at the time to be particularly important to protect.[23] It was a reaction to difficulties encountered in the enforceability of certain transactions: the rule which at that time precluded the parties from giving evidence in their own cause meant that in the absence of written transactions, or at least written evidence of transactions on the part of the parties themselves, the jury did not have appropriate evidence on which to act, and might even be faced with perjured evidence by hired witnesses.[24] There is no longer the same justification for the use of writing; and, indeed, as times change we may take different views about which transactions should be singled out for protection by the use of formalities. The formality requirements set up by the Statute of Frauds in relation to property transactions have, broadly, been retained in a modern form in newly enacted provisions,[25] but in England[26] the provisions of the Statute in relation to most forms of

---

[22] *J Pereira Fernandes SA v Mehta* [2006] EWHC 813 (Ch); [2006] 1 W.L.R. 1543 at [27] (Judge Pelling QC: "a party can sign a document for the purposes of s.4 [of the Statute of Frauds 1677] by using his full name or his last name prefixed by some or all of his initials or using his initials, and possibly by using a pseudonym or a combination of letters and numbers (as can happen for example with a Lloyds slip scratch), providing always that whatever was used was inserted into the document in order to give, and with the intention of giving, authenticity to it. Its inclusion must have been intended as a signature for these purposes"). For the significance of signature as showing assent to the terms of a written document, cf. *L'Estrange v F Graucob Ltd* [1934] 2 K.B. 394, DC, at 403 (Scrutton LJ: "When a document containing contractual terms is signed, then, in the absence of fraud, or, I will add, misrepresentation, the party signing it is bound, and it is wholly immaterial whether he has read the document or not"); *Peekay Intermark Ltd v Australia and New Zealand Banking Group Ltd* [2006] EWCA Civ 386; [2006] 2 Lloyd's Rep. 511 at [43] (Moore-Bick LJ: "It is an important principle of English law which underpins the whole of commercial life; any erosion of it would have serious repercussions far beyond the business community"). For signature by the operation of a signature writing machine, without the need for the party to "sign the document with a pen held in his own hand" see *Ramsay v Love* [2015] EWHC 65 (Ch) at [7].

[23] Including the grant of leases exceeding three years and freehold interests out of land (ss.1, 2: to have the force of estates at will if not in signed writing; the predecessor to LPA 1925 ss.53(1)(a), 54); declarations of trust of land (ss.7, 8: to be manifested and proved by signed writing, otherwise void and of no effect, unless trust arises "by implication or construction of law" or "by an act or operation of law"; the predecessor to LPA 1925 s.53(1)(b), (2)); assignments of trusts (s.9: to be done in a signed writing or by will, otherwise void and of no effect; the predecessor to LPA 1925 s.53(1)(c)); and certain promises, agreements and contracts (promise by executor or administrator to pay damages from his own estate, promise of guarantee, agreement entered into in consideration of marriage, contract for the sale of land or any interest in land, and agreement that was not to be performed within a year of its formation: s.4: no action to enforce unless the agreement, or a memorandum, is in signed writing; contract of sale of goods of at least the value of £10: s.17: contract "not good" unless the buyer had accepted the goods, given a deposit or paid in part, or both parties or their authorised agents have signed a memorandum). See W.S. Holdsworth, *A History of English Law*, Vol.VI, 2nd edn (Methuen, 1937), pp.391–392 (explaining the inclusion of the particular contracts which "at first sight … do seem to be selected in a very arbitrary fashion").

[24] Baker, see para.4-02 fn.3, pp.348-350; Holdsworth, see para.4-05 fn.23, pp.387–389. The full title of the Statute of 1677 is "An Act for Prevention of Frauds and Perjuries", and its opening words are "For prevention of many fraudulent practices, which are commonly endeavoured to be upheld by perjury and subornation of perjury, Be it enacted …"

[25] LPA 1925 s.53; see para.4-05 fn.23. For the formalities in property law generally, see Cheshire and Burn, Ch.25.

[26] Many other common law jurisdictions adopted the English Statute of Frauds, either directly or in their own particular versions, and many have amended those provisions over the years: see, e.g. in

contract have now been repealed.[27] However, new formality requirements have been set for different types of contract for which the functions of formality are deemed to be necessary in the modern law—in particular, certain categories of consumer contract.[28]

The writing (whether signed or not) may be required to include certain words, generally designed to fulfil one or more of the functions of formality discussed above: for example, the requirement that the business party provide the consumer with specified information in certain types of contract such as distance[29] or doorstep ("off-premises")[30] contracts, or regulated consumer credit and consumer hire contracts,[31] ensures that the consumer is informed of the nature of the contract and reinforce the consumer's right to reflect on the wisdom of entering into the transaction.[32] Similarly, some jurisdictions have required parties not merely to sign

---

Australia: Seddon and Bigwood, para.16.6 (and table at p.882 showing which provisions are in force in each State); in Canada: Fridman, pp.203–204 (and esp. fn.4 for list of local statutes which replaced the Statute of Frauds in various provinces); in New Zealand: Burrows, Finn & Todd, para.9.2; in Singapore: Phang and Goh, pp.54–55. The United States added further types of contract to the list in the Statute of Frauds, and those provisions (including those which have since been repealed in England) are still in force today in many States: Farnsworth, §6.1.

27 Law Reform (Enforcement of Contracts) Act 1954 (enacting Law Revision Committee, Sixth Interim Report, *Statute of Frauds and the Doctrine of Consideration*, Cmd.5449 (1937), as varied by Law Reform Committee, First Report, *Statute of Frauds and Section 4 of the Sale of Goods Act, 1893*, Cmd.8809 (1953)) repealed all except the provision in s.4 requiring a signed memorandum in order to enforce a guarantee; the provision requiring a signed memorandum in relation to contracts for the sale of land or any interest in land was replaced by a similar provision in LPA 1925 s.40, see para.5-06, itself repealed but replaced by a stronger formality requirement as a condition of existence of the contract by LP(MP)A 1989 s.2, see paras 4-18, 5-09. In proposing the repeal of s.4 the Law Revision Committee in 1937 thought that its provisions were (inter alia) outdated, arbitrary, out of accord with the way business is done, lopsided in their operation and badly drafted: see Sixth Interim Report, para.9. The Law Reform Committee in 1953, agreeing with those criticisms except in relation to contracts of guarantee (see para.6-06), did not think that there should be any delay in reform by reason of the fact that the Statute had been retained by the United States and all Commonwealth countries (except for New Zealand, where a reform committee was considering the issue): "we believe that this is a matter on which the countries concerned might well be prepared to follow the lead of this country" (First Report, 1953, para.5).

28 e.g. see para.4-05 fnn.29-31.

29 Consumer Contracts (Information, Cancellation and Additional Charges) Regulations 2013 (SI 2013/3134) regs 13, 14 (implementing, with effect from 13 June 2014, Directive 2011/83/EU and replacing Consumer Protection (Distance Selling) Regulations 2000 (SI 2000/2334) regs 7, 8, amended by SI 2005/689 and implementing Directive 97/7/EC); reg 13 was amended by SI 2015/1629 with effect from 1 October 2015. See para.5-33.

30 Consumer Contracts (Information, Cancellation and Additional Charges) Regulations 2013 (SI 2013/3134) reg.10 (implementing, with effect from 13 June 2014, Directive 2011/83/EU and replacing Cancellation of Contracts made in a Consumer's Home or Place of Work etc. Regulations 2008 (SI 2008/1816), revoking SI 1987/2117 and reimplementing Directive 85/577/EEC); and amended by SI 2015/1629 with effect from 1 October 2015. See para.5-33.

31 Consumer Credit Act 1974 Pt V and Consumer Credit (Agreements) Regulations 1983 (SI 1983/1553), amended by SI 2004/1482, which contain detailed requirements as to the form of notices and their signature. See para.5-32.

32 Failure on the part of the business to comply with these various requirements to provide information sometimes extends the consumer's "cooling off period" (i.e. his right to cancel the contract), but sometimes renders the contract unenforceable without an order of the court, which may also require the court to exercise a discretion before allowing enforcement: see paras 5-32, 5-33. Consumer Contracts (Information, Cancellation and Additional Charges) Regulations 2013 (SI 2013/3134) reg.9 (and amended by SI 2015/1629 with effect from 1 October 2015) also requires a trader to provide certain information to a consumer in any other contract (i.e. in a contract which is neither a distance contact nor an off-premises contract), although in this case there is no requirement that it

contractual documents, but to add a manuscript formula above the signature to emphasise that the signature imports consent.[33]

The written document may itself be required to take some particular form: for example, at common law a deed had to be written on paper or parchment, and the seal of any party to the deed had to be attached.[34] In the modern law these aspects of the formality requirements for deeds have been relaxed: there is now no rule restricting the substances on which a deed may be written,[35] nor that an individual seal a deed,[36] but the new formalities still satisfy the cautionary, evidentiary and labelling functions[37] of the old formalities. The instrument must now make clear on its face that it is intended to be a deed by the person making it, or the parties to it, and the valid execution by an individual requires him to sign it in the presence of a witness who attests the signature (or a third party to sign at his direction and in his presence and the presence of two attesting witnesses), and to deliver it as a deed.[38]

Formalities in the electronic age   The development of electronic forms of com-   **4-06**
munication raises significant questions in relation to private law transactions. If parties wish to use electronic means in order to enter contracts or to effect transfers of property, the law must determine how to give effect to their transactions, how to develop existing rules to take account of the electronic form of transactions[39] and, indeed, whether to allow the parties' electronic communications to have the same effect as traditional paper transactions. It is in the case of formality requirements, where writing has been set as a core element of the formality, that these questions become particularly acute, and the law must determine whether, and how, an electronic document can fulfil the same or equivalent functions to those for which the written document was prescribed. There is inevitably a general trend in modern jurisdictions[40] to accept that electronic transactions must be allowed to substitute for traditional paper transactions, although in some contexts there may be greater

---

be in writing (or other durable medium).

[33]   There is still a practice in France of sometimes asking the party undertaking an obligation to write *"bon pour accord"* or *"lu et apprové"* before signing the document, although this now has only a practical, psychological force and since 1980 is not a legal requirement: M. Fabre-Magnan, Droit des obligations, I—Contrat et engagement unilatéral, 4th edn (Paris: Presses universitaires de France, 2016), p.345.

[34]   *Goddard's Case* (1584) 2 Co. Rep. 4b, 5a: "There are but three things of the essence and substance of a deed, that is to say, writing in paper or parchment, sealing and delivery"; Co. Lit. 35b: "A deed cannot be written upon wood, leather, cloth, or the like, but only upon parchment or paper, for the writing upon them can be least vitiated, altered or corrupted".

[35]   LP(MP)A 1989 s.1(1)(a): see para.7-06. This allows a deed to be written on more durable material than paper, such as fire- and flood-proof metal and non-biodegradable plastic: Emmet, para.20.002. It also opens up the possibility of electronic deeds: see para.4-06.

[36]   LP(MP)A 1989 s.1(1)(b); for this, and for execution of deeds by corporations, see para.7-09.

[37]   See para.4-03.

[38]   LP(MP)A 1989 s.1(3), for instruments delivered as deeds from 31 July 1990: s.1(11), SI 1990/1175. The use of a seal is now neither necessary nor sufficient for the execution of an instrument as a deed by an individual; nor does the fact that it is executed under seal in itself make clear that the document is intended to be a deed: LP(MP)A 1989 s.1(2A), added by SI 2005/1906 art.8. The requirement that an individual sign (or place his mark on) a deed was first added by LPA 1925 s.73, for deeds executed after commencement of that Act (1 January 1926).

[39]   cf. para.3-44 (accommodation of new technologies in the rules of offer and acceptance in the formation of contracts). For the disclosure of electronic documents in civil proceedings, see CPR, PD 31B (in force since 1 October 2010).

[40]   e.g. the electronic notarial instrument was introduced in France by decree no.2005-973 of 10 August 2005. See generally *L'authenticité*, see para.4-03 fn.15, paras 116-126.

caution about whether the state of electronic communications is yet sufficiently developed to allow a full substitution: for example, where there is a concern over the security of electronic transmissions and the verifiability and storage of electronic documents, or where at least there is not yet sufficient public confidence in such matters.[41]

In English law, there has been little intervention in the traditional rules to cover electronic formality requirements, although this reflects in part the fact that many of the existing formality rules may already cover most of the forms of electronic communication currently in use. In advice published in 2001 the Law Commission[42] expressed the view that emails (including both the electronic message and any electronic documents which may be attached) and transactions conducted through a website will generally satisfy the definition of "writing" in the Interpretation Act

---

For European provisions designed to facilitate electronic transactions, see Directive 2000/31/EC of 8 June 2000 on electronic commerce, which requires, inter alia, that (art.9) "Member States shall ensure that their legal system allows contracts to be concluded by electronic means" although a Member State may exclude certain particular contracts from this requirement (contracts that create or transfer rights in real estate, except rental rights; contracts requiring by law the involvement of courts, public authorities or professions exercising public authority; contracts of suretyship and collateral security granted by non-professionals; contracts governed by family law or by the law of succession). Regulation (EU) No.910/2014 of 23 July 2014 on electronic identification and trust services for electronic transactions in the internal market provides for mutual recognition of Member States' electronic identification and authentication schemes (art.6), and the recognition of electronic signatures from other Member States (arts 25-34), and also deal with electronic seals (arts 35-40), electronic time stamps (arts 41-42), electronic registered delivery services (arts 43-44), website authentication (art.45) and electronic documents (art.46); but it does not affect national or EU law related to the conclusion and validity of contracts or other legal or procedural obligations relating to form (art.2.3). This Regulation repealed and replaced Directive 1999/93/EC on a Community framework for electronic signatures.

See also United Nations Commission on International Trade Law UNCITRAL) Model Law on Electronic Commerce (1996, amended 1998), and Model Law on Electronic Signatures (2001), both discussed by the Law Commission, see para.4-06 fn.42, Pt 2; United Nations Convention on the Use of Electronic Communications in International Contracts (2005). The UNCITRAL Model Law of Electronic Commerce has been adopted in many jurisdictions although not in the UK except for Crown Dependencies and overseas territories: *http://www.uncitral.org/uncitral/en/uncitral_texts/electronic_commerce/1996Model_status.html*. See also A. Davidson, *The Law of Electronic Commerce* (Port Melbourne: Cambridge University Press, 2009), Ch.3 ("Electronic commerce and the law of contract), discussing principally Australian and New Zealand law, and the UNCITRAL Model Law as enacted there.

[41] e.g. the land register is held in electronic form; Land Registration Act 2002 s.91, provides for certain electronic documents to be regarded as if they had been executed as deeds for the purposes of dispositions of land; and systems have been developed to allow parties to submit documents electronically to the Registry, and conveyancers who have a "Network Access Agreement" are authorised to make certain simple changes to the register online (such as removing the name of a deceased joint owner). However, the full system of "e-conveyancing", designed to allow direct access by parties (or their solicitors or licensed conveyancers) to the electronic register so that they can register their rights directly without the intervention of Land Registry staff was deferred indefinitely by the Land Registry in 2011: Land Registry *Report on responses to e-conveyancing secondary legislation part 3* (July 2011), citing public and professional unease about proceeding at the present time: *http://webarchive.nationalarchives.gov.uk/20140709094354/http://www.landregistry.gov.uk/__data/assets/pdf_file/0006/3102/econveyancing_cons.pdf*. In 2016 the Law Commission accepted that "the goals of electronic conveyancing need to be adjusted in response to the technical limitations that have become clear since the LRA 2002 came into force in order to provide a more realistic framework for a future electronic conveyancing system": Consultation Paper No.227, *Updating the Land Registration Act 2002*, (2016), para.20.11. The final proposals are contained in Law Com. No.380, Updating the Land Registration Act 2002 (2018), Ch.20.

[42] Law Commission Advice, "*Electronic Commerce: Formal Requirements in Commercial Transactions*" (December 2001), Pt 3.

1978[43] because they are visible on-screen both to the sender and to the recipient, and therefore no amendment needs to be made to any statutory provisions which set "writing" as a formality requirement in order to cover such forms of electronic communication.[44] Presumably this would also apply to other forms of electronic communication where the message appears on the screen of the sender during its composition and on the screen of the recipient to enable it to be read, although only if the message is stored in digital form.[45] The Commission also thought that digital signatures, scanned manuscript signatures,[46] typing one's name or initials into an electronic communication[47] and clicking on a website button[48] are all generally capable of satisfying a statutory signature requirement, on the basis that "it is the function, rather than form, which is determinative of the validity of a signature" and that each of these methods shows the authentication intention of the signatory.[49] Part

---

[43] Interpretation Act 1978 Sch.1: "'Writing' includes typing, printing, lithography, photography and other modes of representing or reproducing words in a visible form". cf. *El Majdoub v CarsOnTheWeb.Deutschland GmbH* EU:C:2015:334; [2015] 1 W.L.R. 3986 (CJEU) ("Any communication by electronic means which provides a durable record of the agreement shall be equivalent to 'writing'" in art.23(2) of Council Regulation (EC) No 44/2001 of 22 December 2000 on jurisdiction and the recognition and enforcement of judgments in civil and commercial matters (OJ 2001 L12, p 1) (the "Brussels I Regulation") is satisfied by "click-wrapping", where the communication did not appear on the party's computer screen but the party *could have* clicked on a hyperlink in order to print it and save it before the contract was concluded).

[44] This purposive approach was confirmed by *Golden Ocean Group Ltd v Salgaocar Mining Industries Pvt Ltd* [2012] EWCA Civ 265; [2012] 1 W.L.R. 3674 (contract of guarantee identified from sequence of emails was "agreement … in writing" for purposes of Statute of Frauds 1677 s.4); *J Pereira Fernandes SA v Mehta* [2006] EWHC 813 (Ch); [2006] 1 W.L.R. 1543 at [16] (email capable of being a sufficient note or memorandum for the purpose of s.4 because it was in writing), applied to Statute of Frauds (Amendment) Act 1828 s.6 by *Lindsay v O'Loughnane* [2010] EWHC 529 (QB); [2012] B.C.C. 153 at [95].

[45] This appears to be assumed by the Law Commission in para.3.8 of its Advice (see para.4-06 fn.42) ("Electronic communications generally have a dual form: first, their display on a screen; secondly, their transmitted/stored form as files of binary (digital) information"). If the electronic communication is a form of instant messaging which, although it appears on-screen, immediately disappears and does not leave a file which can later be retrieved, it seems more difficult to attribute to it the characteristics of "writing". (Perhaps a useful analogy is the distinction in the tort of defamation between libel (a statement in a permanent form) and slander: Winfield & Jolowicz, para.13-032).

[46] *Re a Debtor (No.2021 of 1995)* [1996] 2 All E.R. 345 at 351 (Laddie J: document composed on-screen with pre-scanned signature of author, and then sent by fax modem, is received as a document "signed" by its author).

[47] cf. the use of imprinting a name or initials in a hard-copy document which has been accepted as a "signature": *Goodman v J Eban Ltd* [1954] 1 Q.B. 550, CA (rubber-stamp signature for purposes of Solicitors Act 1932 s.65); *Brydges v Dix* (1891) 7 T.L.R. 215 (printed signature of clerk to local authority sufficient on notices under Public Health Act 1875). This is confirmed by *Golden Ocean Group Ltd v Salgaocar Mining Industries Pvt Ltd*, see para.4-06 fn.44 (forename of authorised agent, appended to emails, sufficient to constitute signature).

[48] The Law Commission recognised that it might be said that the website click differs from other accepted forms of signature, but they drew an analogy with the making of a signature by marking "X": see para.4-06 fn.42, paras 3.37 to 3.38.

[49] Law Commission, see para.4-06 fn.42, para.3.39. The insertion into the electronic communication of the sender's name in a form which does not demonstrate an authenticating intention is therefore not a "signature": *J Pereira Fernandes SA v Mehta* see para.4-06 fn.44 (email address inserted automatically by internet service provider on transmission was not signature within Statute of Frauds 1677 s.4). For further discussion of the practical difficulties involved in the electronic execution of deeds and contracts for which there is a statutory requirement of a signed document (so-called "virtual signings" or "virtual execution"), see paras 5-23 (contracts for the sale, etc. of land) and 7-08 (deeds).

II of the Electronic Communications Act 2000[50] provides for the admissibility of electronic signatures in evidence in relation to any question as to the authenticity of a communication with which the signature is incorporated or logically associated,[51] and it permits the modification by statutory instrument of any enactment or subordinate legislation for the purpose of authorising or facilitating the use of electronic communications or electronic storage (instead of other forms of communication or storage) for any of a range of specified purposes which include the doing of anything which is required to be or may be done or evidence in writing or otherwise using a document, notice or instrument, or which is required to be or may be authorised by a person's signature or seal, or is required to be delivered as a deed or witnessed.[52] This therefore allows the modification of any statutory formality requirements which involve signed documents or deeds in order to facilitate the use of electronic communications, although the statutory instruments so far made under this Act have not yet changed the statutory formalities governing contracts or deeds mentioned in para.4-05.[53] The Law Commission's advice in 2001[54] took a purposive approach to the interpretation of "writing" and "signature" in the existing formality requirements in private law—an approach which is entirely justifiable[55] —and, whilst recognising that their views were not universally accepted, they recommended against a general reform under the powers given by the Electronic Communications Act 2000 because of the difficulties and risks associated with attempting a global solution.[56] However, they acknowledged that there will be some forms of electronic communication which will not fall within the existing definition of "writing"—such as "electronic document interchange" where the digital information is exchanged between computer systems and is intended to be acted upon without any human intervention (and is therefore not visible on-screen to the sender and to the recipient)[57]; and that there are some statutory formalities

---

50   Amended by Electronic Identification and Trust Services for Electronic Transactions Regulations 2016 (SI 2016/696), implementing Regulation (EU) No.910/2014; the original text of Part II of the 2000 Act implemented, inter alia, Directive 1999/93/EC (repealed and replaced by Regulation (EU) No.910/2014): see generally see para.4-06 fn.40. See also Electronic Commerce (EC Directive) Regulations 2002 (SI 2002/2013), implementing Directive 2000/31/EC, which require (reg.9) certain information to be provided where contracts are concluded by electronic means except in the case of non-consumer parties who have agreed otherwise.

51   Electronic Communications Act 2000 s.7.

52   Electronic Communications Act 2000 s.8(1), (2)(a), (c).

53   Two types of contract for which English law imposes formality requirements can be excluded from the implementation of Directive 2000/31/EC, see para.4-06 fn.40: real estate contracts (excluding rental contracts) and sureties granted by non-professionals; however, LP(MP)A 1989 s.2, also covers contracts to grant leases; and Statute of Frauds 1677 s.4, also covers guarantees granted by professionals, so there can be no blanket exclusion of electronic contracts in relation to those statutory provisions. Email already satisfies the "writing" requirement of the Statute of Frauds (see para.4-06 fn.44), although the formality required for land contracts is more detailed and special provision may be desirable: see see para.4-07 fn.63.

54   See para.4-06 fn.42.

55   cf. *Victor Chandler International Ltd v Customs and Excise Commissioners* [2000] 1 W.L.R. 1296, CA (prohibition on circulation of "advertisement or other document" in Betting and Gaming Duties Act 1981, using statutory language which first appeared in 1952, should be interpreted as including direct electronic transmission by teletext to take account of technological advances since 1952, and to use established principle that statute should be interpreted "as always speaking": F.A.R. Bennion, *Statutory Interpretation: a Code*, 3rd edn (Butterworths, 1997), s.288, p.686 (see now 7th edn (ed. D. Bailey and L. Norbury), LexisNexis, 2017, Ch.14).

56   Law Commission, see para.4-06 fn.42, para.3.43.

57   Law Commission, see para.4-06 fn.42, paras 3.19 to 3.20.

which are worded in such a way as to exclude electronic communications, which should be amended.[58]

In 2017 the Law Commission announced that it would include in its next **4-07** programme of law reform a project on electronic signatures, designed to address any uncertainty as to the validity of electronic signatures in all types of contract.[59] The Commission will also consider "smart contracts"—self-executing contracts using blockchain technology, which automatically trigger various processes according to their terms—in order to ensure that the English legal and regulatory framework facilitates their use.[60]

There is one formality, discussed in detail in Chapter 5, where special provision remains to be made for electronic transactions. Under section 2 of the Law of Property (Miscellaneous Provisions) Act 1989, contracts for the sale or other disposition of an interest in land must be in writing and signed by both parties[61]: even if the requirements of "writing" and "signature" may be satisfied by common forms of electronic communication, as argued by the Law Commission in 2001,[62] there have been plans eventually to make specific provision for electronic contracts in registered conveyancing when "e-conveyancing" is introduced.[63]

One might have expected some general mechanism to be developed to allow deeds to be made in electronic form. However, rather than amending the general

---

[58] Law Commission, see para.4-06 fn.42, para.3.48, giving the example of the Consumer Credit Act 1974 ss.63 and 64, which then required a copy of an executed agreement and the notice of cancellation rights to be sent by post. This was amended to require sending "by an appropriate method" by SI 2004/3236 (an order made under the Electronic Communications Act 2000).

[59] Law Com. No.377, *The 13th Programme of Law Reform* (2017), paras 2.11 to 2.13. In January 2018, the Law Commission began the project under the title "electronic execution of documents" and issued a Consultation Paper (No.237) on 21 August 2018: *https://www.lawcom.gov.uk/project/electronic-execution-of-documents/*. The Law Society has published a practice note, developed by a joint working party of the Law Society Company Law Committee and the City of London Law Society Company Law and Financial Law Committees, on *Execution of a document using an electronic signature*: see *https://www.lawsociety.org.uk/support-services/advice/practice-notes/execution-of-a-document-using-an-electronic-signature/*.

[60] Law Com. No.377, see para.4-07 fn.59, para.2.39 ("For example, historical data recorded in blockchain code cannot be erased or rewritten. Although this is usually presented as an advantageous feature of blockchain, it also means that a third party arbiter (such as a court) cannot correct any perceived mistakes, or unfairness in the contract in the same way. There are questions about how this feature would interact with contract law concepts such as implied terms or contracts which are held to have been void from the outset. There are also questions about data protection law."). This project is due to commence in late summer 2018: see *https://www.lawcom.gov.uk/project/smart-contracts/*.

[61] See paras 5-09 to 5-23.

[62] See para.4-06 fn.42. Digital signatures have recently been used for the first time in the exchange of contracts for a residential sale and purchase: Law Com. No.380, see para.4-06 fn.41, para.20.11.

[63] In 2001 the Lord Chancellor's Department published proposals for a draft order under the Electronic Communications Act 2000 to introduce a new s.2A into the 1989 Act to enable an electronic contract to be as effective for the purposes of s.2 (and any other enactment) as an equivalent paper contract: LCD Consultation Paper 05/2001 (March 2001). This has not been implemented, and was not taken into the reform of registered land in the Land Registration Act 2002, but in 2007 the Land Registry published a revised version of the proposed s.2A which would be limited to contracts relating to registered land: Land Registry Consultation Paper, *"E-conveyancing Secondary Legislation Part I"* (February 2007). Any reform has been delayed until later in the programme by which electronic conveyancing is to be introduced: Land Registry, *"Report on Responses to E-conveyancing Secondary Legislation Part I"* (2007), p.26; but note that the introduction of e-conveyancing has now been deferred indefinitely: see para.4-06 fn.41. However, it is not now intended to require contracts for registered land to be in electronic form, even after the introduction of e-conveyancing: Law Com. No.380, see para.4-06 fn.41, para.20.40.

statutory requirements for a deed, which would allow parties in any context to use electronic instruments to give to a transaction the same effect as the traditional hard-copy deed, there has been an amendment to deal with the use of electronic transactions in one particular context: registered land. Under the Land Registration Act 2002, a document in electronic form which purports to effect certain dispositions relating to registered land for which a deed would otherwise be required is to be regarded as a deed if it fulfils certain requirements.[64]

4-08 **Formality requiring third-party participation** Some formalities may require the participation of third parties; the purpose may be to provide independent verification of the transaction, to reinforce the protection of the party entering into it, or to provide a broader public element to the transaction and its effects.

A common requirement for third-party participation is in the form of a witness to the transaction: a person who does not participate in the transaction itself, but is present and can confirm that it took place.[65] In the context of private law transactions, the purpose of a witness is generally only to verify the fact of its execution, sometimes adding an attestation clause, which the witness signs to confirm the method of execution.[66] There is, however, no requirement of witnessing in the case of simple contracts in English law, even those required to be in, or evidenced in, writing signed by the parties or their agents. However, where the parties use a deed in order to create contractual obligations,[67] the formalities of a valid deed executed by an individual include the requirement that the signature of the party be witnessed.[68] The use of witnesses in this context may reflect a desire to impose a higher level of formality with a reinforced cautionary function,[69] given especially that the requirement of witnessing of deeds executed by individuals was introduced at the time when the requirement of sealing was abolished.[70] Moreover, the deed is not simply a method of creating obligations but is also (and, indeed, primarily) used in relation to the creation and disposition of property rights, notably interests

---

[64] Land Registration Act 2002 s.91: it must make provision for the time and date when it takes effect, have the certified electronic signature of each person by whom it purports to be authenticated, and satisfy such other conditions as may be provided by rules; and to fall within the section the document must purport to give effect to a disposition of a registered estate or charge, or a disposition of an interest which is the subject of a notice in the register, or a disposition which triggers the requirement of registration, which is of a kind specified by rules. This section was first applied to electronic legal charges (SI 2008/1750, revoked by SI 2018/70 r.6) but since 6 April 2018 it applies to electronic dispositions of registered estates or charges: Land Registration Rules 2003 (SI 2003/1417) rr.54A-54D (inserted by SI 2018/70 r.11) as long as the disposition satisfies certain conditions, and only after the registrar is satisfied that adequate arrangements have been made or will be in place for dealing with documents in electronic form that purport to effect a disposition of that kind and has given notice publicising the fact.

[65] OED Online, March 2018, "witness, n.": "5. a. One who is called on, selected, or appointed to be present at a transaction, so as to be able to testify to its having taken place: spec. one who is present at the execution of a document and subscribes it in attestation thereof; more definitely, *attesting or subscribing witness*".

[66] e.g. the two witnesses to a will normally sign an attestation clause to confirm that they were both present at the same time when the testator signed the will, as required by Wills Act 1837 s.9, substituted by Administration of Justice Act 1982 ss.17, 73(6); but they have no business knowing the contents of the will. If there is no attestation clause, or an insufficient clause, before the will can be admitted to probate the witnesses may be required to confirm by sworn affidavit that the will was duly executed: Non-Contentious Probate Rules 1987 (SI 1987/2024) r.12.

[67] See para.7-18.

[68] See para.4-05 fn.38. For deeds executed by corporations, see para.7-05.

[69] See para.4-03.

[70] See para.4-05, text to fn.38.

in land,[71] and it is in the context of property transactions that formalities tend to be stronger. Witnessing—by two witnesses who have no interest in the estate of the testator—is also a requirement for a valid will.[72]

In some cases the third-party involvement in a transaction is even stronger: not simply to witness the transaction but to become involved in it. In this case the identity of the third party indicates the purpose of the third-party intervention, usually a person who acts in some public capacity on behalf of the State to provide a public dimension to the transaction. In legal systems which require certain transactions to take the form of a notarised "authentic instrument", the function of the notary is to "authenticate" the document: not only to provide a higher degree of proof than the legal system would normally afford to an instrument entered into privately, and to provide a reinforced cautionary and protective function for the parties,[73] but also to afford additional benefits to the instrument. Sometimes the "authentication" permits direct enforceability of the transaction in the event of the failure of one party to perform duties set out in the instrument, without having first to obtain authority from a court to invoke the civil enforcement process; sometimes it provides a record which can be entered directly into public registers; sometimes it provides a measure of public control and oversight of the transaction recorded in the instrument for such purposes as verifying its legality and the collection of taxation due in respect of the transaction.[74] Such "authentic instruments" are typically used in civil law jurisdictions for certain property transactions (notably land law and in the law of succession), for certain declarations and agreements made in the context of family law, and for certain obligations (notably donations).[75]

English law does not use notaries or "authentic instruments" on the civil law model. Many of the transactions which are required to be notarised in civil law jurisdictions can be effected in England by a private transaction between the parties, with at most the participation of a witness.[76] However, there is also a different form of third-party public intervention in private law transactions where public registration of the transaction is required in order to complete the transaction, or to give it its full effect. Many legal systems use public registers in order to protect the interests of third parties to transactions—typically, in the case of property law, where a third party can be bound by the effects of a transaction relating to property only if it was recorded in a publicly-searchable register.[77] In English law, the strong-

---

71 LPA 1925 s.52.
72 See para.4-08 fn.66.
73 Sometimes referred to as "preventive justice": an *ex ante* control of the transaction by a public authority, designed to minimise *ex post* judicial disputes in relation to the parties' understanding of their transaction: see para.4-03 fn.15.
74 See generally Council of the Notariats of the European Union, *Comparative Study of Authentic Instruments*, see para.4-03 fn.15; and for French law in particular, see *L'authenticité*, see para.4-03 fn.15.
75 For a comparative summary (published in 2008) in relation to France, Germany, Poland, Romania (which do use a system of notarisation of authentic instruments), and England and Sweden (which do not), see Council of the Notariats of the European Union, *Comparative Study of Authentic Instruments*, see para.4-03 fn.15, pp.21-25.
76 e.g. a promise of a donation, made by a deed: above.
77 e.g. in French law, although a contract for the sale of land can be created by informal agreement between the parties, and the transfer of the property itself is effected by the authentic instrument drawn up by the notary (who, although acting as a public officer, authenticates the transaction in a private meeting with the two parties), third parties can only, in principle, be affected by the transfer and other rights over it (such as charges over the property) by the public registration which follows

est requirement of this kind is in the case of land,[78] where the old system of unregistered title, under which the title to land could be transferred by a (privately-executed) deed, has been replaced by a system under which the deed of transfer does not convey the legal title but must be completed by registration.[79] This system of registration of title not only provides security of title for the registered proprietor, and notice to third parties of the title (and of any third-party interests registered against it) but also provides a mechanism for the verification by a public authority[80] of the title itself and the identities of the parties involved in any transfer of title[81]; and there is an indirect control over the tax payable on inter vivos transfers of land, since the Land Registry will not register a transfer without a certificate from HM Revenue and Customs to the effect that the relevant information relating to liability to stamp duty land tax has been provided to them.[82]

4-09   **Formality as evidence to support enforceability**   Formality requirements can be used for different purposes. It may be that some particular formality is set by the law only as a condition for the judicial enforceability of the transaction, rather than as a substantive condition of the existence or validity of the transaction itself. The reason for using an evidential formality requirement clearly focuses on the

---

the notarisation: J. Bell, S. Boyron and S. Whittaker, *Principles of French Law*, 2nd edn (Oxford University Press, 2008), pp.280-283.

[78] The transfer of title to shares, constituting the transferee a member of the company, also generally depends upon the registration of a proper instrument of transfer in the register of members of the company (or in the central register kept by the registrar, in the case of a private company which has made an election to keep information on the central register): CA 2006 ss.770, 112(2), 128A (introduced by Small Business, Enterprise and Employment Act 2015 Sch.5, para.3). For other examples of the use of formalities including registration as a condition of validity of a transaction in relation to third parties, see Bills of Sale Acts 1878 and 1882 s.8 (bill of sale to be attested and registered otherwise void in respect of personal chattels comprised in it); CA 2006 s.859H, substituted for original s.874 by SI 2013/600 (unregistered company charges void against liquidator, administrator and creditor).

[79] Indeed, the registration confers the legal title to the property, in the sense that it cures any defect in the title: Land Registration Act 2002 s.58(1). Subject to the possibility of rectification of the register to correct a mistake (not normally granted against a registered proprietor in possession who has not caused or substantially contributed to the mistake by fraud or lack of proper care: Land Registration Act 2002 s.65, Sch.4 paras 3 and 6), the State guarantees the title as registered and indemnifies those who (without fraud or lack of care on their own part) suffer loss in consequence of any mistake in registration or official documents issued by the Land Registry in relation to the registration: Land Registration Act 2002 s.103, Sch.8. For registration of title generally, see generally Cheshire and Burn, Ch.28; Megarry and Wade, Ch.7; *Ruoff and Roper on the Law and Practice of Registered Conveyancing* (Sweet & Maxwell, looseleaf); and for proposed reform, see Law Com. No.380, see para.4-06 fn.41.

[80] The Land Registry forms part of the Department for Business, Energy and Industrial Strategy: see generally: *https://www.gov.uk/government/organisations/land-registry/about*.

[81] Before the title is first placed on the register, the Registry verifies the title from the (unregistered) deeds of title: Land Registration Act 2002 Pt 2. For verification of identity, see Land Registry Practice Guide 67, "Evidence of identity - conveyancers": *http://www.landregistry.gov.uk/professional/guides/practice-guide-67*; and Inland Revenue Forms ID1: Verify identity: citizen: *https://www.gov.uk/government/publications/verify-identity-citizen-id1* and ID2: Verify identity: corporate body: *https://www.gov.uk/government/publications/verify-identity-corporate-body-id2*.

[82] Finance Act 2003 s.79; see also para.4-03 fn.14. This applies to "notifiable land transactions", defined in s.77, and the duty to deliver a land transaction return is contained in s.76. A contract for a land transaction is not itself a land transaction, but in certain circumstances the contract can be treated as if it were the completion transaction, or may be taken together with the later completion transaction, for the purpose of the charge to tax: s.44.

evidential function of formality[83]: to encourage parties to formalise their transaction in order to provide reliable evidence in the event of dispute or any other context where it must be enforced. The production of an evidential formality may also have the effect of furthering the other functions of formality: it may make the parties stop and consider the transaction (the "cautionary" function) as they take part in the formality designed to ensure that there is the required evidence, and if the requirement is for a particular form of evidence (e.g. writing in a particular form) its production will also evidence ("label") the intended nature of the transaction, and may also provide other benefits such as documents which can be used for the purposes of registration or taxation. However, an evidential formality may not have such other broad benefits, depending on how the law defines the requirement.[84] For example, in English law the general approach of the Statute of Frauds was to set as the formality requirement for the enforceability of certain contracts that the agreement, or a memorandum of it, be in writing signed by the party to be sued or by his authorised agent; but if the contract was oral, the memorandum could be a document which was signed later, and may not be signed with the same care and thought that one would expect of a formality of writing associated with the entry into the transaction itself.[85] It has even been held that the written memorandum could be signed earlier than the contract which is concluded orally, as long as it is a document which acknowledged the contract and its terms.[86] Moreover, a formality requirement which is merely evidential does not in itself deny the substantial validity of the transaction entered into without the required formality, and the law may be able to recognise its effects in certain circumstances even if the transaction could not be enforced directly. For example, property may pass under a contract for which an evidential requirement of writing is not satisfied; and the contract itself may be indirectly enforced if some rule of law prevents the defendant from raising objection to the lack of evidence.[87]

---

[83] See para.4-03, for this and other aims of formality.

[84] e.g. French law requires either a notarised instrument or a (privately) signed written document for contracts exceeding a certain value (set by decree from time to time: it was fixed at €1,500 by Décret no.80-533, 15 July 1980): c.civ. art.1359 (formerly art.1341). However, this is not as rigid a requirement as might first appear, since it does not apply generally to contracts covered by commercial law, and other general exceptions have been created by the courts: B. Nicholas, *The French Law of Contract*, 2nd edn (Clarendon Press, 1992), p.61.

[85] For an extreme example, see *Barkworth v Young* (1856) 4 Drew 1, 62 E.R. 1 (acknowledgement in writing 14 years after oral contact); and see Kindersley VC at 13-14, at 6, listing a number of cases in which the courts have held that documents not created for the purposes of acknowledging the oral agreement could none the less constitute a memorandum for the purposes of the Statute of Frauds on the basis that a wide interpretation was appropriate to meet the object of the Statute (see para.4-05 fn.24) since any document signed by the person to be sued on the (oral) contract should be sufficient to avoid the mischief of perjury.

[86] e.g. a written offer which is then accepted orally. For a general discussion of the authorities, see *Tiverton Estates Ltd v Wearwell* [1975] Ch. 146 at 165-167 (Stamp LJ); and for general discussion of the approach taken by the courts finding a memorandum which satisfied the Statute of Frauds (and, later, LPA 1925 s.40) in relation to contracts for the sale or other disposition of land or an interest in land, see Cheshire and Burn, pp.962–963; Megarry and Wade, 5th edn (Stevens, 1984), pp.575–584. For guarantees see para.6-12.

[87] A deposit paid under an oral contract for the sale of land could still be forfeited if the purchaser defaulted, and the absence of written memorandum under LPA 1925 s.40 had to be specifically pleaded since it was a matter of procedure, not substance: Law Com. No.164, *Formalities for Contracts etc of Land* (1987), para.1.3 (for a similar issue under the new formality set by LP(MP)A s.2, see *Sharma v Simposh Ltd* [2011] EWCA Civ 1383, [2013] Ch. 23). The requirement to produce a written memorandum could be avoided in the case of a contract relating to land by a claimant who

4-10   **Formality as a substantive condition of legal effect**   Where a formality is set not merely as an evidential condition for the enforceability of a transaction, but as a substantive condition of the existence or validity of a transaction, it appears to be a more serious formality, designed to further also the other functions of formality such as the cautionary function, or a broader public function in ensuring that there is a document, or the entry on a register, before the transaction has its full legal effect. This is not to say that the law might not in the case of such formalities still sometimes admit exceptions, or allow a transaction which has not been properly formalised to have some legal effect, or even the full legal effect for which the transaction was required by law to be formalised.[88] But a formality set as a substantive condition is generally designed to provide a higher level of protection of the transaction and of the parties (and, where appropriate, third parties). For example, when the Law Commission proposed to replace the evidential formality required for land contacts by a substantive formality, it did so consciously intending to affirm not only the evidential function, but also the cautionary and channelling function of written formalities in the case of land, and the need to provide a simple rule which provides greater clarity and certainty.[89]

Some formalities are not simply evidential but, although not required in order to give the transaction legal effect, may limit some aspect of the validity of the transaction if they are not complied with. There are several types of contract, for example, where a business party dealing with a consumer is required to issue certain notices as part of the formation of the contract. The failure to issue the required notice is not fatal to the contract's coming into existence and into force, but increases the rights of the consumer or limits the rights of the business party—such as where the consumer is given a fixed period within which he can cancel the contract (a "cooling-off period") but the business party's failure to issue the required notice extends the period.[90]

4-11   **Formality as choice**   We generally see formality as a requirement—mandatory in

---

satisfied the requirements of part performance (developed by equity after the Statute of Frauds, but later recognised in the legislation when s.40 replaced it in 1925: s.40(2)). For part performance, see Cheshire and Burn, pp.963–965; Megarry and Wade, 5th edn (Stevens, 1984), pp.587–597; and see para.5-06. For the argument that a party may be estopped from pleading the Statute of Frauds, see para.4-13 and para.6-18.

88   See paras 4-13 to 4-14.

89   Law Com. No.164, *Formalities for Contracts etc of Land* (1987), paras 2.7-2.12, 4.2.

90   Some such rights of "cancellation" or "withdrawal" originally had a purely domestic origin in English law, but have now been replaced to implement more recent European legislation: Consumer Credit Act 1974 s.67 (new provision, and new s.66A, substituted by SI 2010/1010, implementing Consumer Credit Directive 2008/48/EC art.14); Timeshare Act 1992 s.5, repealed and replaced by SI 2010/2960 reg.20, implementing Timeshare Directive 2008/122/EC art.6 (replacing 1994/47/EC art.5). Most, however, follow simply from the implementation of European Directives, e.g. Consumer Rights Directive 2011/83/EU art.9 (replacing Doorstep Selling Directive 1985/577/EC art.5 (implemented by SI 1987/2117 reg.5, and reimplemented by SI 2008/1816 reg.7) and Distance Selling Directive 1997/7/EC art.6 (implemented by SI 2000/2334 reg.10)), implemented by Consumer Contracts (Information, Cancellation and Additional Charges) Regulations 2013 (SI 2013/3134); Distance Marketing of Financial Services Directive 2002/65/EC art.6, implemented by SI 2004/2095 reg.9; Solvency II Directive 2009/138/EC art.186 (replacing Life Assurance Directive 2002/83/EC art.35); R. Schulze and J. Morgan, "The Right of Withdrawal" in G. Dannemann and S. Vogenauer (eds), *The Common European Sales Law in Context* (Oxford University Press, 2013), pp.294-340. Such a formality is obviously designed to protect the consumer, and is aimed principally at the cautionary function of formality: without receiving the notice, the consumer is taken not to have a full understanding of his rights and duties under the contract and therefore he may not have had a sufficient opportunity to (re)consider his decision to enter into it.

particular transactions. However, in certain circumstances the use of formality is a choice: it provides a formal mechanism for a transaction which the parties will follow if they wish their transaction to have certain effects, although they could carry out the transaction without the formality. In the case of contracts there is no requirement that the parties use a deed,[91] although the choice of a deed may be a way of securing particular advantages such as a longer period of limitation in the event of a claim for breach of the contract contained within the deed,[92] or to obtain different benefits by way of evidence or procedure.[93]

(3) Failure to Comply with Formality Requirements

The law's response to failure of formality Formalities are set by the law for particular transactions, in order to further particular aims.[94] However, it may happen that parties to such a transaction fail to follow the requirements to the letter, and the question is whether the law should condone the failure by still giving effect to the transaction, or at least some partial effect; or should insist on the formality requirement and refuse to give effect to the transaction. The answer to this question is not straightforward, and may depend on such things as whether the failure of formality was by ignorance, by accident or by design; how far the parties have fallen short of meeting the formality requirement (e.g. substantial compliance being treated as if it were complete); and even how seriously the court views the particular formality requirement, and whether it is satisfied that the purpose for which the formality was imposed for that type of transaction can none the less be sufficiently fulfilled by the actual transaction entered into with lesser formality, or even without any of the required formality. This question is one which all legal systems face: wherever the law sets formality requirements, parties have sought to avoid them.[95] And once the law starts to condone the failure of formality, this may encourage parties to continue not to take the trouble to comply, which in turn may sow the seeds of a reform of the particular formality rule, or at least may create a generally-recognised exception to it.[96]

4-12

Many examples could be given of the ways in which English law has responded to parties' failure to comply with formality requirements. Here we shall just give some examples of the circumstances in which the law appears to have condoned

---

[91] A deed is required for certain *property* transactions, such as the creation or conveyance of a legal estate in land: LPA 1925 s.52; see para.7-03.

[92] 12 years (Limitation Act 1980 s.8) rather than six years in the case of actions founded on simple contract (Limitation Act 1980 s.5): see para.7-19.

[93] See, e.g. estoppel by deed; see para.7-20. A deed also removes the need to show consideration for a promise, which saves the parties to what is in substance a gratuitous promise having to devise some form of (even nominal) consideration in order to make the promise binding; another way of looking at this, however, is to say that a deed is a mandatory formality to give binding force to a gratuitous promise (a truly gratuitous promise, with nothing at all requested in return): see paras 4-18, 7-18.

[94] See para.4-03.

[95] In Roman law, for example, the strict and cumbersome formality of *mancipatio* required for the transfer of property in certain important assets (see para.4-04 fn.17) was ignored in favour of an informal delivery of the property (*traditio*): see Cartwright in Koops and Zwalve, see para.4-04 fn.17, pp.121–124. And in French law, the requirement of notarisation of a donation (c.civ. art.931) may be sometimes avoided by a *donation déguisée*: Nicholas, see para.4-09 fn.84, pp.147–148.

[96] e.g. the doctrine of part performance, first developed by the courts to justify enforcing a contract which was not evidenced in writing as required by Statute of Frauds 1677 s.4, was later formally recognised in the re-enactment of the Statute of Frauds in relation to contracts for the sale or other disposition of land or an interest in land, in LPA 1925 s.40(2).

the failure by giving effect (wholly or partly) to private law transactions (contract or property), and the reasoning which the courts have used to justify their approach. Further detail of the law's response to the avoidance of the formalities required for contracts will be discussed at the appropriate point in the following chapters.[97]

4-13 **Failure of formality by ignorance, accident or design** One might expect the courts to be less strict towards parties who have good reason not to have realised that they should have entered into the particular formalities required by the law for their transaction—and, by contrast, the deliberate failure to use the required formality should not be viewed with sympathy. This is sometimes the courts' approach—for example, taking the view that a commercial party who knows, or ought to know, that the formality is required should not expect the law to recognise the transaction which does not conform[98]; yet being more open to finding remedies which in practice give effect to transactions which non-commercial parties have entered into without realising the need for formality.[99] A court can also be influenced by an inequality between the parties as regards their knowledge or experience, and in particular by the fact that the party resisting the claim does so by now seeking to take advantage of the formality requirement in circumstances where the claimant did not know of the requirement and has acted reasonably in reliance on the defendant's assurances about the transaction. This is an example of the operation of the maxim that "Statute should not be an engine of fraud"[100] —under which equitable doctrines have been developed to give effect to transactions which do not

---

[97] See paras 5-24 to 5-29 (LP(MP)A 1989 s.2); 6-15 to 6-18 (Statute of Frauds 1677 s.4); 7-14 to 7-16 (formalities for a deed).

[98] e.g. *Cobbe v Yeoman's Row Management Ltd* [2008] UKHL 55; [2008] 1 W.L.R. 1752 at [27] (Lord Scott: "It would be an unusually unsophisticated negotiator who was not well aware that oral agreements relating to such an acquisition [of an interest in land] are by statute unenforceable and that no express reservation to make them so is needed. Mr Cobbe was an experienced property developer and Mrs Lisle-Mainwaring gives every impression of knowing her way around the negotiating table"); see also Lord Walker at [71], [81] ("the general principle that the court should be very slow to introduce uncertainty into commercial transactions by over-ready use of equitable concepts such as fiduciary obligations and equitable estoppel"), [91] ("Mr Cobbe's case seems to me to fail on the simple but fundamental point that, as persons experienced in the property world, both parties knew that there was no legally binding contract"); followed by *Generator Developments Ltd v Lidl UK GmbH* [2018] EWCA Civ 396 at [78] (Lewison LJ: no equitable claim based on "*Pallant v Morgan* equity" in case of commercial parties, legally advised). For further discussion of *Cobbe* and other cases where the question has been whether the formalities for a contract for the sale of land can be avoided through the doctrines of proprietary estoppel and constructive trust, see paras 5-27, 5-28.

[99] e.g. *Thorner v Major* [2009] UKHL 18; [2009] 1 W.L.R. 776 at [96]–[97] (Lord Neuberger: "the analysis of the law in *Cobbe's* case [see para.4-13 fn.98] was against the background of very different facts. The relationship between the parties in that case was entirely arm's length and commercial, and the person raising the estoppel was a highly experienced businessman ... In this case, by contrast, the relationship between Peter and David was familial and personal, and neither of them, least of all David, had much commercial experience. Further, at no time had either of them even started to contemplate entering into a formal contract as to the ownership of the farm after Peter's death"). See also Lord Neuberger of Abbotsbury, "The Stuffing of Minerva's Owl? Taxonomy and Taxidermy in Equity" [2009] C.L.J. 537 at 544 ("Where parties can reasonably be expected to regulate their relationship by a binding contract if they want to do so, equity should fear to tread").

[100] This was used in direct (and ironic) reference to the Statute of Frauds: the Statute was designed to guard against fraud, and should not itself be allowed to become an instrument of fraud (or, as it is sometimes put, an "engine of fraud"). See, e.g. judgment of Lord Mansfield in 1774 reported at Lofft 620 at 622, 98 E.R. 831 at 831 ("I shall say to the rule what the Court of Chancery said of the Statute of Frauds, that no rule shall be made an instrument of fraud; nor employed contrary to the ends for which it was made. Frustra legis auxilium implorat qui legem ipsam subvertere conatur. Ratio est anima legis"); *Forster v Hale* (1798) 3 Ves. Jr. 696 at 713, 30 E.R. 1226 at 1234; *Maddison v*

comply with formalities required by statute, where the party seeking to rely on the statutory formality should not in conscience be allowed to do so: it is "fraudulent", in the broad sense used by equity, to insist on the strict requirement of formality.[101] When the court responds in such a way it does not claim to ignore the statute, but to impose an independent remedy which operates outside the statute[102]: the legal right to the property, for example, may not have been transferred in the absence of the required formality, but an equitable remedy is granted which has largely the same effect as if the formality had been observed. In this case, the courts may formally respect the statute, whilst in substance undermining it.[103] Indeed, in the case of many statutory formalities the statute itself recognises the potential hardship of an absolute requirement of formality, and leaves open a door to allowing an informal transaction to have effect, notably by excluding from its own requirements the "creation or operation of resulting, implied or constructive trusts".[104]

Alderson (1883) 8 App. Cas. 467, HL, at 474; *Hodgson v Marks* [1971] Ch. 892 at 908; *Steadman v Steadman* [1976] A.C. 536, HL, at 558. However, the maxim is also used in relation to other statutes which impose formality requirements: e.g. *McCormick v Grogan* (1869) L.R. 4 H.L. 82 at 97; *Blackwell v Blackwell* [1929] A.C. 318, HL, at 336–337 (Wills Act 1837); *Lyus v Prowsa Developments Ltd* [1982] 1 W.L.R. 1044 at 1054–1055 (Land Registration Act 1925); and, indeed, has become more generally applied to statutes outside the context of formality requirements (see, e.g. *R. (Welwyn Hatfield Council) v Secretary of State for Communities and Local Government* [2010] EWCA Civ 26; [2010] 2 P. & C.R. 10 at [46]; on appeal, [2011] UKSC 15; [2011] 2 A.C. 304 at [66]–[67]).

[101] In the context of disposition of property, in particular, there are many cases in which parties have been allowed to avoid legal formalities through the operation of the equitable doctrines of proprietary estoppel and constructive trust: e.g. *Pascoe v Turner* [1979] 1 W.L.R. 431, CA (proprietary estoppel: mistress, a widow with invalidity pension and modest capital, believed statement by plaintiff, a businessman who invested in property, that the house was hers and spent money on redecoration, improvements and repairs); *Rochefoucauld v Boustead* [1897] 1 Ch. 196, CA, at 206 (constructive trust); *Blackwell v Blackwell*, see para.4-13 fn.100 (secret trust). For the suggestion that these are all emanations of a single general principle, see *Re Basham (Deceased)* [1986] 1 W.L.R. 1498 at 1503–1504 (Nugee QC, who made similar points in argument as counsel in *Ottaway v Norman* [1972] Ch. 698 at 701–702). See generally Cheshire and Burn, pp.1011–1017.

[102] This is most often stated in relation to the circumvention of the formalities required on death, e.g. secret trust: *Jones v Badley* (1868) L.R. 3 Ch. App. 362 at 364 (Lord Cairns: "the Court does not violate the spirit of the statutes; but for the same end, namely prevention of fraud, it engrafts the trusts on the devise by admitting evidence which the statute would in terms exclude, in order to prevent a devisee from applying property to a purpose foreign to that for which he undertook to hold it"); *Blackwell v Blackwell*, see para.4-13 fn.100 at 335 (Viscount Sumner: "For the prevention of fraud equity fastens on the conscience of the legatee a trust, a trust, that is, which otherwise would be inoperative; in other words it makes him do what the will in itself has nothing to do with; it lets him take what the will gives him and then makes him apply it, as the Court of conscience directs, and it does so in order to give effect to wishes of the testator, which would not otherwise be effectual"); *donatio mortis causa*: *Duffield v Elwes* (1827) 1 Bligh (N.S.) 497 at 530, 4 E.R. 959 at 971; *Sen v Headley* [1991] Ch. 425, CA; mutual wills: *Re Cleaver* [1981] 1 W.L.R. 939 at 947. It was also said that under the doctrine of part performance "the defendant is really 'charged' upon the equities resulting from the acts done in execution of the contract, and not (within the meaning of the statute) upon the contract itself": *Maddison v Alderson*, see para.4-13 fn.100 at 475 (Lord Selborne LC).

[103] This is not unlike the way in which the Praetor in Rome granted remedies which had the effect of undermining formality requirements set by the civil law for the transfer of property, although in the case of Rome the result was more absolute since the Praetor, who had control of court procedure, could simply apply his remedies in place of the civil law. In English law, the courts have never sought to override and disregard statutory legal formalities relating to property but have created equitable rights which have a more nuanced and limited effect, notably in not binding a third party who purchases the property without notice of the defect in title or the equitable right. See generally Cartwright in Koops and Zwalve, see para.4-04 fn.17.

[104] In the modern law, see LPA 1925 s.53(2); LP(MP)A 1989 s.2(5). There is some debate whether this

The common law doctrine of estoppel by representation may sometimes provide a similar solution. A party who has not complied with the formality may not be able to rely on the lack of formality to deny effect to the transaction where he has represented some fact to the other party which (if true) would mean that the transaction has been perfected, and the other party has relied on that representation.[105]

4-14   **Substantial compliance**   In some circumstances the courts may treat a transaction which does not fully comply with the formality requirement as if it did, particularly if the substantial (but not complete) compliance fulfils the purpose of the formality, and therefore the spirit of the legal requirement. Indeed, if there is regular acceptance of such transactions there may become either an established exception to the former requirement, or even a variation in what the law sets as the required formality. For example, when the common law used to require a deed to bear the seal of an individual party in order to bind him to it, parties sometimes failed to use a seal (in the strict sense as expected by the law) and instead used a symbolic wafer attached to the instrument as if it were a seal; or even indicated by a mark on the instrument where the seal should be affixed even if they did not affix either a seal or a substitute such as a wafer. As long as the other requirements for the execution of a deed were satisfied, the courts began to accept such instruments as validly executed deeds.[106] However, this did not allow the courts to go so far as to dispense altogether with the seal; reciting in the document that it had been sealed was not enough without some physical sign,[107] although such a recital could

---

can extend to cases of proprietary estoppel, or whether estoppel can in any event operate as an independent exception to the formality requirement, outside the statute: see para.5-28. The Statute of Frauds itself contained an exception in s.8 for "where any conveyance shall be made of any lands or tenements by which a trust or confidence shall or may arise or result by the implication or construction of law". The requirement under s.4 of a written memorandum for a contract relating to land was undermined by the courts' development of the doctrine of part performance; this was then made an express exception in the re-enactment of s.4 by LPA 1925 s.40(2).

[105]   e.g. *TCB Ltd v Gray* [1986] Ch. 621 at 633 (document drafted as deed, containing representation of the fact that it was sealed, although this was not the case. Reliance on the document as a deed gave rise to estoppel); *Shah v Shah* [2001] EWCA Civ 527; [2002] Q.B. 35 (witness to signature on deed was not in fact present when signed in accordance with requirements of LP(MP)A 1989 s.1(3), see para.4-05 fn.38, but signatory was estopped from denying validity as against other party who did not know of defect and relied on the document). However, not all formality requirements can be circumvented by the operation of the doctrine of estoppel: see para.4-15.

If both parties shared the misapprehension that the transaction had been validly executed, this could give rise to an estoppel by convention, rather than an estoppel by representation. In this context, there is therefore a similarity in effect between estoppel by representation (statement of fact which, if true, results in the transaction being valid, relied on by the claimant), estoppel by convention (common assumption that the transaction has been validity executed, acted on by both parties including the claimant) and proprietary estoppel (representation that an interest in land has been or will be transferred, acted on by the claimant): the transaction is not formally valid, but has effect as if it had, based not simply on the claimant's belief but on his acting on it to his detriment. For these different forms of estoppel, see further paras 10-05 to 10-07.

[106]   *Stromdale & Ball Ltd v Burden* [1952] Ch. 223 at 230 (Danckwerts J: " Meticulous persons executing a deed may still place their finger on the wax seal or wafer on the document, but it appears to me that, at the present day, if a party signs a document bearing wax or wafer or other indication of a seal, with the intention of executing the document as a deed, that is sufficient adoption or recognition of the seal to amount to due execution as a deed"); *First National Securities v Jones* [1978] Ch. 109, CA (circle pre-printed on document containing letters "L.S." ["*Locus Sigilli*", the place for the seal], across which party signed: sufficient to constitute a deed).

[107]   *TCB Ltd v Gray*, see para.4-13 fn.105, at 633 (Sir Nicolas Browne-Wilkinson VC: "I would not only be flying in the face of what actually happened, but also disregarding the statutory requirement that

open up another way of avoiding the formality: reliance on the doctrine of estoppel by representation.[108]

Considering the purpose of the formality   In all cases where the court is asked   **4-15**
to give effect, directly or indirectly, to a transaction for which the law prescribes a
formality which has not in fact been complied with, it should examine the underlying purpose of the particular formality in order to determine whether it would
undermine that purpose to give effect to the transaction in spite of the failure of
formality. For example, in determining whether a party may be estopped from relying on the lack of formality it has been said[109]:

> "The general principle that a party cannot rely on an estoppel in the face of a statute
> depends upon the nature of the enactment, the purpose of the provision and the social
> policy behind it"

and the courts have examined particular statutory provisions in light of the evidence
of the statute itself,[110] the circumstances in which, and reasons for which, it was
enacted,[111] and any broader issues of policy which they have been able to identify
in relation to the underlying purpose of the formality.[112]

There may even be an argument that it would undermine the purpose of the
formality requirement *not* to find a means of giving it effect: as we have seen, the
courts took the view that, given that the Statute of Frauds was designed to avoid
parties fraudulently claiming to assert rights by requiring at least evidence in writing of the relevant transaction with which the defendant could properly be charged,

---

the document should be sealed. I think it would be wrong to extend the legal fiction any further and
I decline to do so").

[108] *TCB Ltd v Gray*, see para.4-13 fn.105, at 634.

[109] *Yaxley v Gotts* [2000] Ch. 162, CA, at 191 (Beldam LJ); see also Robert Walker LJ at 175 and Clarke
LJ at 182.

[110] e.g. where the statute contains an exception to the formality requirement such as in the case of the
"creation or operation of resulting, implied or constructive trusts" this can be relevant to determining whether other similar exceptions would be appropriate, such as proprietary estoppel: *Yaxley v
Gotts*, see para.4-15 fn.109, although this has been controversial: *Cobbe v Yeoman's Row Management Ltd*, see para.4-13 fn.98 at [29] (Lord Scott, obiter; not however referring to the decision in
Yaxley v Gotts nor other cases which followed it). For criticism of the approach of Lord Scott, and
approval of the decision in *Yaxley* in allowing proprietary estoppel as an exception to the requirement of writing in LP(MP)A 1989 s.2, see *Whittaker v Kinnear* [2011] EWHC 1479 (QB) at [28]–
[29]; *Muhammad v ARY Properties Ltd* [2016] EWHC 1698 (Ch) at [47]–[47]; and see further para.5-
28.

[111] e.g. considering the Law Commission Report which proposed LP(MP)A 1989 s.2 and referred
expressly to estoppel as a means of giving effect to an agreement which would not comply with the
formality: Law Com No.164, *Formalities for Contracts etc of Land* (1987), paras 5.1–5.5; discussed
extensively in *Yaxley v Gotts*, see para.4-15 fn.109. In *Whittaker v Kinnear*, see para.4-15 fn.110,
at [29] Bean J noted that Beldam LJ, one of the members of the court in *Yaxley*, had been Chairman
of the Law Commission when it proposed what became s.2, and "Like Hengham C.J.C.P. who in
oral argument on a point of statutory interpretation in a case in 1307 (*Aumeye v Anon* YB 33-35
Edw.1 82) said to counsel 'do not gloss the statute, for we know it better than you: we made it', he
was in a good position to say what the Commission had in mind". See also *Shah v Shah*, see
para.4-13 fn.105, at [23]–[25] (Pill LJ, considering the Law Commission report which proposed
LP(MP)A 1989 s.1, but concluding that the reference in the Report to estoppel was too slender to
base his decision on it).

[112] e.g. *Shah v Shah*, see para.4-13 fn.103, at [30] (Pill LJ: "I can detect no social policy which requires
the person attesting the signature [to a deed in order to satisfy LP(MP)A 1989 s.1] to be present when
the document is signed. The attestation is at one stage removed from the imperative out of which
the need for formality arises. It is not fundamental to the public interest, which is in the requirement for a signature").

this was sometimes applied *e contrario* so that if there was clearly a transaction which it would be fair to allow a party to enforce, the defendant should not be allowed to plead the Statute to avoid being bound where to do so, given his conduct, would itself be fraudulent.[113]

II. FORMALITY IN THE ENGLISH LAW OF CONTRACT

4-16   **The general rule: informality**   The general rule in English law is that the formation of a contract does not require any formality. A contract is said to be formed by the (objective) agreement of the parties, normally established through the acceptance by one of an offer made by the other,[114] and supported by consideration.[115] Consideration may sometimes be thought to substitute for formality,[116] but it is not in itself a formality requirement since it looks to *what* the parties have agreed (the contract must, broadly, embody a bargain under which the party seeking to enforce a contract has promised or done something at the other party's request) rather than *how* they have agreed it.[117] The terms of the contract may be laid out in a written document which both parties agree and, typically, sign. But even where they decide during the negotiations that their contract will be complete only when the document is settled and signed,[118] the written document, and their signatures on it, do not constitute a formality required by the law but are merely the parties' own way of securing a clear and well-evidenced contract.[119]

4-17   **Exceptional cases justify the use of formality**   There are exceptions to the general rule, where English law does set formality requirements as conditions of the enforcement, or even the existence, of certain types of contract. Given that the social significance of different types of contract varies over time, and the advantages which formality can be seen to bring to different contracts will also similarly vary, it is not surprising to find that the law has varied the use of such formalities over the years. Formalities which were once introduced for good reason may no longer need to be maintained, giving perhaps the overall impression of a trend in the modern law to reduce the requirements of formality; but we shall see that formality has also been increased, or new formalities introduced, to meet new concerns about particular types of transaction for which the functions of formality provide positive benefits, in the interests of the parties or to further a wider third-party or public interest.[120]

Some reductions in formality requirements are designed simply to remove anomalies. For example, at common law a corporation was able to enter into a

---

[113] See para.4-13 fn.100.

[114] See Ch.3.

[115] See Ch.8.

[116] e.g. *Vantage Navigation Corp v Suhail and Saud Bahwan Building Materials LLC (The Alev)* [1989] 1 Lloyd's Rep. 138 at 147 (Hobhouse J: "Ultimately the question of consideration is a formality as is the use of a seal or the agreement to give a peppercorn"); O.W. Holmes, *The Common Law* (Boston: Little, Brown & Co, 1881), p.273 ("In one sense, everything is form which the law requires in order to make a promise binding over and above the mere expression of a promisor's will. Consideration is a form as much as a seal"); cf. L.L. Fuller, "Consideration and Form" (1941) 41 Colum. L.Rev. 799. See further para.8-27.

[117] See para.4-01 and fn.2.

[118] e.g. where the negotiations are "subject to contract": see para.2-08.

[119] To this extent, the parties may choose to use writing, and signatures, in order to fulfil the same aims for which the law imposes requirements of form: see para.4-03.

[120] cf. para.4-03.

contract only by an instrument under its seal. This was a significant restriction on contractual capacity, and exceptions were created first by statute and at common law for particular types of corporation,[121] and then by a general enactment in 1960 it was provided that all other bodies corporate could make, vary or discharge contracts through their authorised agents in the same manner as private persons, thus consigning this particular formality to history.[122] Perhaps the most significant reduction in formalities came in the repeal of most of the requirements set by the Statute of Frauds for contracts to be evidenced by signed writing. As we have seen,[123] in 1677 a number of types of contract were regarded as sufficiently important to be subjected to this new, special formality; by 1954 most were no longer seen as deserving this special treatment, and only contracts of guarantee and contracts for the sale of land or an interest in land were retained.[124]

Examples of contracts subject to formality requirements in the modern 4-18
law   These reductions in contract formalities have, however, been matched in the modern law by increased formalities for other types of contract, as well as the retention of certain other established formal requirements. Here we just mention some key examples of the contracts which are now subject to formality requirements.

No contracting party is now required as a matter of law to use a deed in order to enter into contracts,[125] but in certain circumstances parties must use a deed if they are to give their agreements full binding force. The notable example is where the agreement is gratuitous—unilateral, in the sense not only that only one party is to

---

[121]   The common law allowed an exception in the case of trading corporations; Companies Clauses Consolidation Act 1845 s.97, created a general exception for companies registered under the Companies Acts (carried into successive Companies Acts; see now CA 2006 s.43, using a simpler formulation than in the earlier Acts, e.g. CA 1948 s.32). LPA 1925 s.74(2), which permits the signature of an authorised agent on behalf of a company, was held not to constitute a general reform: *AR Wright & Son Ltd v Romford BC* [1957] 1 Q.B. 431 (where Lord Goddard CJ reviewed the law generally and drew attention to its unsatisfactory state).

[122]   Corporate Bodies' Contracts Act 1960 s.1, implementing Eighth Report of the Law Reform Committee, *Sealing of Contracts Made by Corporate Bodies* (HMSO, 1958) Cmnd.622; see [1959] C.L.J. 28 and [1961] C.L.J. 12 (H.W.R. Wade). This Act complemented the existing legislation: companies formed and registered under the CA 1948 were excluded by s.2 because they were already covered by the earlier Act (see para.4-17 fn.121); see now s.2 as substituted by SI 2009/1941 (excluding (a) a company registered under CA 2006, (b) a company incorporated outside the UK; (c) a limited liability partnership, all of which are now covered under other provisions: see CA 2006 s.43; SI 2009/1917 reg.4 and SI 2009/1804 reg.4, applying CA 2006 s.43 to overseas companies and limited liability partnerships respectively).

[123]   See para.4-05.

[124]   Law Reform (Enforcement of Contracts) Act 1954, deleting from Statute of Frauds 1677 s.4 promises by executors or administrators to pay damages from their own estate, agreements entered into in consideration of marriage, and agreements not to be performed within a year of their formation; and repealing Sale of Goods Act 1893 s.4, which had already replaced the provision in Statute of Frauds 1677 s.17 by an amended version rendering unenforceable a contract for the sale of goods of at least the value of £10 unless the buyer had accepted and received part of the goods, given a deposit or paid in part, or the party enforcing the contract (or his authorised agent) had signed a memorandum. The provision of s.4 requiring a written memorandum for a contract for the sale of land or an interest in land had already been replaced by LPA 1925 s.40, so all that remained of s.4 itself after the 1954 reform was the requirement that a guarantee be evidenced in writing. Other common law jurisdictions have retained some or all of the original provisions of the Statute of Frauds s.4, or have introduced their own substitute provisions; and (particularly in the US) have even extended the scope of s.4: see para.4-05 fn.26.

[125]   See para.4-17 fn.122, for the abolition of this requirement for corporate bodies.

be bound,[126] but also that the other party is to receive a pure benefit without being asked to give or do anything in return. The deed is a formality which renders enforceable the instrument containing a promise which is not supported by consideration and which, but for the deed, would not be a legally binding promise. One way of looking at this is to say that, in English law, a deed is a formality required by the law in order to make a gratuitous undertaking binding.[127] It may also be said that a lease granted for a term exceeding three years is an example of a contract which must be executed as a deed.[128] However, this is better seen as a rule of the law of property, which requires the lease to satisfy the statutory formality if it is to have full proprietary effect in creating not just a contract between the parties but a legal estate in the land.[129]

The contract for the sale or other disposition of an interest in land is, however, certainly a contract which is required by law to satisfy formality: the Statute of Frauds required a written memorandum to ensure its enforceability,[130] and this was one of the original list of formal contracts for which the formality was retained when the formality requirements for most were removed in 1954.[131] But this is a type of contract for which the required formality has now been increased. Since 1989 a contract for the sale or other disposition of an interest in land must be in writing, either in one document incorporating all the expressly-agreed terms, signed by both parties, or in identical documents, each signed by one party and exchanged.[132] The requirement of writing is now a substantive condition of existence of the contract, rather than as evidence for its enforceability, and reflects a decision to reinforce formality in the case of land contracts, given the benefits which the written contract affords.[133]

Other types of contract have particular requirements of writing as a matter of

---

[126] In a "unilateral contract" as recognised in English law, such as the offer of a reward for finding a lost pet, only one party (the person who offered the reward) undertakes an obligation; but it is not gratuitous because the offeree has to provide consideration in finding and returning the animal and thereby *earning* the reward: see para.3-32 and para.8-13.

[127] Seen this way, it brings the common law closer to the civil lawyer's notion of contract: typically, civilians admit gratuitous agreements within their general notion of contract, although it is not uncommon then to subject the gratuitous contract to some special formality, such as the requirement of notarisation in the case of a *donation* in French law: see para.4-03 fn.14. For comparative discussion of the enforceability of "gift promises", see R. Hyland, *Gifts: A Study in Comparative Law* (New York: Oxford University Press, 2009), Ch.5. However, the tradition in English writing, based naturally on its different history, is to see a contract by deed in the modern law as a legal category of contract separate from a "simple" contract: see para.7-01.

[128] Treitel, para.5-005.

[129] LPA 1925 ss.52(1), (2)(d), 54(2). "A lease is a hybrid, part contract, part property": *Linden Gardens Trust Ltd v Lenesta Sludge Disposals Ltd* [1994] 1 A.C. 85, HL, at 108 (Lord Browne-Wilkinson). A lease which is not executed as a deed may still have effect between the parties as a contract for lease—but only, given that it is an agreement for the disposition of an interest in land, if it satisfies the requirement of writing under LP(MP)A 1989 s.2(1); below. If it does take effect as a contract for lease it will have proprietary effect *in equity* under the doctrine of *Walsh v Lonsdale* (1882) 21 Ch. D. 9, CA, and may therefore bind third parties under the general rules for the binding force of equitable interests in registered or unregistered land: see Cheshire and Burn, pp.215–220.

[130] Statute of Frauds 1677 s.4, replaced by LPA 1925 s.40.

[131] See para.4-17.

[132] LP(MP)A 1989 s.2(1), in force since 27 September 1989. For detailed discussion, see paras 5-09 to 5-29.

[133] Law Com. No.164, *Formalities for Contracts etc of Land* (1987), paras 2.7–2.12 (certainty, as well as the evidential, cautionary and channelling functions discussed at para.4-03, and the importance of land as a unique asset, and the benefits of protection of third-party interests in the case of land).

substantial validity: a long-established example is the bill of exchange[134]; much more recent are the raft of consumer contracts for which particular written forms are required.[135] There are still types of contract in the modern law which require some form of written evidence in order to support their judicial enforceability. The main example is the contract of guarantee, the last remnant of the original provisions of section 4 of the Statute of Frauds 1677.[136]

More detail of these contracts will be given in the following chapters.

---

[134] Bills of Exchange Act 1882 s.3(1); see para.5-36.
[135] See para.4-05 fnn.29–31; see paras 5-30 to 5-35.
[136] See paras 6-05 to 6-18. See also Marine Insurance Act 1906 s.22 (contract of marine insurance); see para.6-19.

CHAPTER 5

SPECIFIC FORMALITIES: SUBSTANTIVE CONDITIONS OF A BINDING CONTRACT[1]

I. THE USE OF FORMALITY AS A SUBSTANTIVE CONDITION OF LEGAL EFFECT

Formality as a condition of existence or validity of a contract   In Chapter 4 we **5-01** saw some of the purposes for which formality is used in private law, and the advantages for the parties, or for third parties or the broader public interest, in requiring the transaction to be entered into in particular form.[2] And we saw that, whilst the law may sometimes impose a requirement of formality by way of evidence to support the enforceability of a transaction, a rule which imposes not simply an evidential requirement but a substantive condition for the transaction itself—which in principle denies that the transaction has its intended legal effect if it is not followed—is designed to afford stronger protection to the party or parties in question, and to any other interests that merit protection.[3] In this chapter, we consider in more detail contracts for which the law sets a requirement of form as a substantive condition of a binding contract. Chapter 6 will consider contracts for which the formality requirement is not substantive, but only evidential.

Statutory regulation of particular types of contract   The examples discussed **5-02** in this chapter are all formality requirements set by statute.[4] This has certain implications. First, the ways in which the formalities are defined are not general but specific to particular types of contract. The common law lays down general rules

---

[1]   Chitty, Ch.4; Furmston, paras 2.300 to 2.357; Treitel, paras 5-006 to 5-012; Anson, pp.82–83, 88–95; Cheshire, Fifoot and Furmston, pp.288–291.

[2]   See esp. para.4-03.

[3]   See paras 4-09, 4-10.

[4]   The deed is a common law formality (albeit one which has been amended by statute: see para.7-05), which may be used in order to make a gratuitous promise binding. However, this is not to be analysed as a formality requirement set by the common law, but rather an instrument which can be used to make binding a promise or an agreement that would not otherwise be a contract at all, lacking one of the fundamental elements for the formation of a contract (i.e. consideration: see para.7-18; Ch.8). Deeds are discussed in Ch.7.

for the formation of contracts and their validity; legislative intervention into the law of contract can be general[5] but tends to be particular, aimed at particular types of contract and therefore allowing the formality (its requirements and the consequences of non-compliance) to be tailored to the needs of each type of contract. Secondly, given the nature of legislative texts, we find detailed provisions setting out the required formalities, any exceptions that may have been allowed by the legislator, and the consequences for the contract if the formality is not used. Thirdly, many cases which raise questions about statutory formalities will require the courts to engage in interpretation of the statute and to consider how to respond to questions which are not apparently dealt with in the terms of the statute themselves. We shall see, for example, that questions may arise about the meaning of the words of a statute which sets a formality where there is a later development in social practices associated with the type of contract in question—such as where the statute was drafted in an age where the words "writing" and "signature" naturally connoted physical forms but the court has to consider to what extent electronic communications can satisfy the requirements.[6] A difficulty can also arise for the courts to determine whether exceptions can be made to the apparently strict requirements of the statute—either by interpretation of the words of the statute itself, or by admitting the operation of some doctrines of the common law or equity outside the statute. This raises a potential clash between the authority of the statute, and the courts' desire to address new problems as they arise.[7]

5-03　**Form as an additional requirement**　In the contracts discussed in this chapter, the statutory formality is required in addition to the normal requirements set by the common law for the formation of the contract: agreement (normally formed through the acceptance of an offer) and consideration.[8] The formality is an extra hurdle; a simple agreement, embodying a bargain, is not enough to constitute a contract in the case of these transactions. Rather, the requirements for the formation of these contracts are agreement (through offer and acceptance), consideration and the formality as defined by the statute for the particular type of contract.[9] It must therefore be remembered, in reading this chapter, that only the addition requirement of form is here being discussed, and that the contracts must in addition satisfy the normal requirements for the formation of a contract.[10]

5　e.g. legislative variation of the common law rules of contract, applied to contracts generally—although even in the case of apparently general legislative reform in the field of contract law it is common for the application of the legislation to exclude certain types of contract: e.g. Law Reform (Frustrated Contracts) Act 1943 (exclusions at s.2(5)); Contracts (Rights of Third Parties) Act 1999 (exclusions at s.6).

6　See para.5-18.

7　e.g. the discussion in *Cobbe v Yeoman's Row Management Ltd* [2008] UKHL 55; [2008] 1 W.L.R. 1752 and later cases about whether the absence of writing required by LP(MP)A 1989 s.2, can be circumvented by the doctrine of proprietary estoppel: see para.5-28.

8　See Ch.3 (agreement); Ch.8 (consideration).

9　See, e.g. Law Com. No.164, *Transfer of Land: Formalities for Contracts for Sale etc. of Land* (1987), para.4.6.

10　For the need to find an agreement which satisfies the common law requirements of a contract, in addition to satisfying the requirement of writing under LP(MP)A 1989 s.2, see *Commission for the New Towns v Cooper (Great Britain) Ltd* [1995] Ch. 259, CA, at 293; see para.5-17.

The contracts which require writing as substantive condition of legal effect   The requirement of form as a condition of legal effect is exceptional in English law,[11] but in the modern law it has been extended to apply to some very significant types of contract: in particular, contracts relating to land and many consumer contracts. In these cases the requirement takes the form of writing, although the writing required in each case varies, as do the consequences of failure to comply with the formality requirement. In the following sections of this chapter we consider types of contract for which statute now sets substantive formality requirements, focusing most particularly on contracts relating to land.[12]   **5-04**

II.   CONTRACTS FOR THE SALE OR OTHER DISPOSITION OF AN INTEREST IN LAND

(1)   Section 2 of the Law of Property (Miscellaneous Provisions) Act 1989: Background and Context

The imposition of formality requirements for contracts relating to land   The statutory provision which currently sets the formality requirements for contracts relating to land is s.2 of the Law of Property (Miscellaneous Provisions) Act 1989. However, this provision cannot be fully understood in isolation from its historical background, and its context as part of the wider set of formality rules relating to land transactions in the modern law.   **5-05**

The predecessors to section 2: section 4 of the Statute of Frauds and section 40 of the Law of Property Act 1925   The Statute of Frauds first imposed formality requirements for "any contract or sale of lands, tenements or hereditaments, or any interest in or concerning them".[13] This was not an isolated provision, however, but one which introduced formality requirements for a range of contracts, as well as for property transactions and wills.[14] There are therefore two dimensions to the original introduction of formality requirements for contracts relating to land: the need to provide the protection of formality for parties entering into certain types of contract which were deemed to be significant[15]; and the need to provide the protec-   **5-06**

---

[11] cf. paras 4-02, 4-09, 4-10: formality is the exception, rather than the rule; and within formality requirements, substantive (rather than evidential) requirements have also generally been the exception.

[12] A "construction contract" (broadly, an agreement to carry out construction operations relating to land or buildings, or to arrange their carrying out or to provide labour for their carrying out) does not have to be in writing, but the Housing Grants, Construction and Regeneration Act 1996 s.107 required the contract to be in writing if the provisions of Pt II of the Act were to apply to it—in particular, the right to adjudication of disputes (s.108) and a range of provisions relating to payment, such as the contractor's right to stage payments and the employer's right to withhold payment. The requirement of writing created difficulties in practice, and s.107 was repealed by Local Democracy, Economic Development and Construction Act 2009 with effect from 1 November 2011, so that now Pt II of the 1996 Act applies to construction contracts in any form, although s.108 was amended to require the contract still to contain certain particular provisions in writing if the right to refer a dispute to adjudication is to arise (failing which adjudication provisions prescribed by the Minister in the "Scheme for Construction Contracts" will apply by way of implied term in the contract: ss.108(5), 114). See S. Furst, V. Ramsey, *Keating on Construction Contracts*, 10th edn (London: Sweet & Maxwell, 2016), paras 18-019, 18-020 and generally Ch.18.

[13] Statute of Frauds 1677 s.4.

[14] See para.4-05.

[15] The protection was against the risk of being held liable under a contract to which one had not in fact agreed, by a jury which might even act on the basis of perjured evidence: see para.4-05 fn.24.

tion of formality for transactions relating to property, and in particular relating to land. Contracts relating to land are at the intersection of these concerns, and it is not surprising that they should be included for specific regulation by way of formality.

Under the Statute of Frauds, the formality for contracts was writing, but as evidence rather than as a substantive condition of validity.[16] When land law was substantially reformed and modernised in 1925, this provision was maintained, but was moved into the Law of Property Act 1925, which provided in s.40(1)[17]:

> "No action may be brought upon any contract for the sale or other disposition of land or any interest in land, unless the agreement upon which such action is brought, or some memorandum or note thereof, is in writing, and signed by the party to be charged or by some other person thereunto by him lawfully authorised."

An addition was made, however, which did not appear in the Statute of Frauds: that the section "does not affect the law relating to part performance".[18] After the passing of the Statute of Frauds the courts of equity began to develop the doctrine of part performance, a doctrine peculiar to this type of contract, but based on the broader principle that the statute should not be used as an instrument of fraud to deny enforceability to a transaction, even though it did not satisfy the statutory formality requirement, where it would be against conscience to do so.[19] The details of the doctrine of part performance, as it continued to be developed until the repeal in 1989[20] of s.40 of the Law of Property Act 1925, do not concern us here.[21] Broadly, however, the doctrine allowed a party who had performed some or all of his obligations under the contract to bring an action in equity to enforce the obligations of the other party under the contract, even if the contract was not evidenced in writing as required by the Statute. It treated the claimant's performance not simply as evidence of the contract in place of the statutory formality of writing, but as giv-

---

[16] Statute of Frauds 1677 s.4: "no action shall be brought whereby ... to charge any person ... upon [the contract] unless the agreement on which such action shall be brought, or some memorandum or note thereof, shall be in writing, and signed by the party to be charged therewith, or some other person thereunto by him lawfully authorized".

[17] The language is very similar to the Statute of Frauds, see para.5–06 fn.16; in so far it is different it was intended to give effect to judicial interpretation of the Statute, and not to make any substantive change: see B.L. Cherry, J. Chadwick and J.R.P. Maxwell, *Wolstenholme and Cherry's Conveyancing Statutes*, 11th edn (Stevens, 1925), p.193. Sir Benjamin Cherry drafted the greater part of LPA 1925: *Cadogan Estates Ltd v McMahon* [2001] 1 A.C. 378, HL, at 391–392.

[18] LPA 1925 s.40(2).

[19] See para.4-13. This development began within a decade after the passing of the Statute of Frauds: see *Maddison v Alderson* (1883) 8 App. Cas. 467 at 477–480 (Earl of Selborne LC, referring to *Hollis v Edwards* (1683) 1 Vern. 159, 23 E.R. 385 and *Butcher v Stapely* (1685) 1 Vern. 363, 23 E.R. 524, as well as later cases which continued to develop the doctrine).

[20] LP(MP)A 1989 ss.2(8) and 4; Sch.2.

[21] For further discussion, see Cheshire and Burn, pp.963–965; *Megarry and Wade*, 5th edn (Stevens, 1984), pp.587–597; J. Williams, *The Statute of Frauds, Section Four, in the Light of its Judicial Interpretation* (Cambridge University Press, 1932), Pt III, Ch.7. Given the time which has now elapsed since the reform of 1989, in practice questions relating to the enforcement of contracts governed by the old law rarely arise; however, for an example of such a case in 2004 see *Inglorest Investments Ltd v Campbell* [2004] EWCA Civ 408; [2004] 2 P. & C.R. DG7 (contract entered into in 1968). cf. *TCG Pubs Ltd v The Master and Wardens or Governors of the Art of Mystery of the Girdlers of London* [2017] EWHC 772 (Ch) at [42]–[47] (court had to decide how to interpret provisions for option to be granted in 2015 under terms of a lease executed in 1987, now that the 1989 Act would apply to it).

ing rise to an equity in favour of the party who had acted in performance of the contract, against the other party who had stood by and let him incur expense or prejudice his position on the faith of the agreement being valid, and so could not in conscience assert that the agreement was unenforceable.[22] This was therefore an equitable claim, said by the courts to be outside the operation of the Statute itself,[23] and was not as secure for the claimant as if he held a memorandum, signed by or on behalf of the defendant, which would give him an undisputed right to enforce the contract by reason of the Statute.[24] But, in cases where it applied, it had the effect of circumventing the statutory formality. We shall see below that, although s.2 of the Law of Property (Miscellaneous Provisions) Act 1989 operates in a significantly different way from these earlier provisions in now requiring writing not merely as evidence but as a substantive condition of binding effect for contracts relating to land, some similar questions have arisen as to whether equitable doctrines, similar to the old doctrine of part performance, can justify a court giving effect to an agreement which does not comply with the statutory formality for the creation of a contract.[25]

The background to the 1989 reform   The replacement of s.40 of the Law of   **5-07**
Property Act 1925 by s.2 of the Law of Property Miscellaneous Provisions Act 1989 followed a study made by the Law Commission, and the 1989 Act implemented in substance the recommendations of the Commission's Report.[26] The principal defects in the old law were said to be that it created injustice and uncertainty: the operation of s.40 was not necessarily mutual (if only one party signed a written

---

[22]   *Steadman v Steadman* [1976] A.C. 536, HL, at 540.
[23]   e.g. *Maddison v Alderson*, see para.5–06 fn.19, at 474–475 (Earle of Selborne LC: "the defendant is really 'charged' upon the equities resulting from the acts done in execution of the contract, and not (within the meaning of the statute) upon the contract itself").
[24]   As an equitable doctrine, part performance was subject to limitations applicable to claims in equity, such as the fact that only equitable remedies would be given; if specific performance or injunction could not be granted, the claimant had no useful remedy. Even after the Court of Chancery was given the power by Chancery Amendment Act 1858 s.2 (see now Senior Courts Act 1981 s.50) to award damages in addition to, or in substitution for, specific performance and injunction, this would not avail the claimant where specific performance was not available: *Lavery v Pursell* (1888) 39 Ch. D. 508, 519.
[25]   See paras 5-26 to 5-29.
[26]   Law Com. No.164, *Transfer of Land: Formalities for Contracts for Sale etc. of Land* (1987), following consultation after the publication of their WP No.82 (1985). The version introduced into Parliament and enacted (below, para.5-09) was worded differently from the principal provision in the draft Bill attached to the Law Commission's Report. The Law Commission's version was: "No contract for the sale or other disposition of an interest in land shall come into being unless the contract is in writing and—(a) all the express terms of the contract are incorporated (whether expressly or by reference) in one document or each of two or more documents; and (b) that document or, as the case may be, one of those documents (though not necessarily the same one) is signed by or on behalf of each party to the contract". For comments on the significance of the difference in wording of the Act, see *Commission for the New Towns v Cooper (Great Britain) Ltd* [1995] Ch. 259, CA, at 283–289; *McCausland v Duncan Lawrie Ltd* [1997] 1 W.L.R. 38, CA, at 46–47; *North Eastern Properties Ltd v Coleman* [2010] EWCA Civ 277, [2010] 1 W.L.R. 2715 at [41]–[42].
        cf. Lord Neuberger of Abbotsbury, "The Stuffing of Minerva's Owl? Taxonomy and Taxidermy in Equity" [2009] C.L.J. 537 at 545 ("that misconceived piece of legislation, s.2 of the Law of Property (Miscellaneous Provisions) Act 1989. ... Section 40 of the Law of Property Act 1925, which s.2 was designed to replace, had its quirks, but it worked perfectly well. Now that the Law Commission, by needlessly meddling, Parliament, with misconceived drafting, and the courts, through inconsistent decisions, have had their wicked ways with s.2, we are worse off than we ever were with s.40").

memorandum, the contract could be enforced against him, whilst he could not enforce it against the other); and the case-law demonstrated difficulties over the interpretation of s.40 and of its scope of operation, and created uncertainty in the doctrine of part performance.[27] The Commission considered removing altogether the formality requirements relating to land contracts,[28] but rejected this because it received no support during its consultation process.[29] Rather, the Commission took the view that contracts for land should continue to receive special treatment, given the benefits which follow from the use of formalities[30]; and that the formality requirements should be strengthened to require the contract not simply to be evidenced in writing but to be in writing. This was designed to provide clarity and certainty[31]:

> "We believe that the present law, which allows oral contracts to be binding but unenforceable and which may later become enforceable, is indefensibly confusing. Such contracts can become enforceable inadvertently, or people who have genuinely contracted can escape their contractual obligations.[32] A simple, straightforward rule that contracts concerning land cannot be made orally would remove all these causes of confusion. More importantly, such a rule should incidentally suppress the injustice inherent in the present provision enabling enforcement at one party's option in appropriate circumstances: we consider this potential lack of mutuality to be especially indefensible."

The Law Commission was very critical of the doctrine of part performance.[33] It did, however, say that the increase in formality should not give rise to unacceptable hardship in individual cases of non-compliance, and noted a range of possible remedies to enable justice to be achieved, including not only common law remedies in tort or restitution where no contract is concluded[34] but also equitable doctrines[35]; and they noted in particular that doctrines of estoppel might be used, and might sometimes achieve results very similar to those of part performance.[36]

---

27 Law Com. No.164, see para.5–07 fn.26, paras 1.7–1.10, referring to more detailed discussion in WP No.92, Pt III.

28 Law Commission WP No.92, paras 5.10, 5.11.

29 Law Com. No.164, para.2.6 ("there was absolutely no support for this proposal. In fact, some on consultation went so far as to call it irresponsible").

30 Certainty, provided by the evidential function of writing; protection of the parties provided by the cautionary function; clarity of the transaction and its validity provided by the "channelling" function; and the "general uniqueness of land" gives rise to the need to avoid confusion, for the benefit of the parties and of third parties, about who owns what: Law Com. No.164, paras 2.7–2.12. They also investigated other legal systems, and noted that most other jurisdictions require more formality for contracts relating to land than for other contracts: paras 2.13–2.21 (see also App.C for a comparative table). For a general discussion of the functions which formalities can perform see para.4-03.

31 Law Com. No.164, para.4.2.

32 As in *Tiverton Estates Ltd v Wearwell Ltd* [1975] Ch. 146, CA [discussed in para.1.4 of the Report].

33 Law Commission WP No.92, paras 3.23–3.26; Law Com. No.164, paras 1.8, 1.9, 4.13, 5.4; see para.5-06.

34 For possible claims in tort, contract, unjust enrichment and equity where negotiations for a contract fail, see paras 2-14 to 2-30.

35 Law Com. No.164, Pt V.

36 Law Com. No.164, para.5.1. "We see no cause to fear that the recommended repeal and replacement of the present section as to the formalities for contracts for sale or other disposition of land will inhibit the courts in the exercise of the equitable discretion to do justice between parties in individual otherwise hard cases": para.5.5.

This aspect of the new law, by comparison with the old, is considered further below.[37]

Contracts for the sale of land in the context of land transactions generally   Contracts relating to land generally do not stand alone, but form part of more complex transactions which include the creation or disposition of interests in land— i.e. transactions involving property rights, to which the contract is commonly the precursor. The policies which lie behind the approach taken by the law to contracts relating to land will often therefore be informed and influenced by the policies applicable to land transactions more generally; and there will be a need to ensure that the legal regulation of contracts makes their use consistent with the property transactions to which they relate. This may explain, for example, the desire to subject land contracts to the requirement of writing, in order to provide the protective functions of formality[38] for the benefit not only of the parties themselves but also for third parties, given that a contract for the sale of land can be of particular relevance to third parties since in equity it can have proprietary effect.[39] The creation and disposition of interests in land are subject to formalities which are notably more stringent than in the case of transactions relating to most other property rights, no doubt because of the benefits afforded by formality to landowners and third parties as well as in the broader public interest[40]; it is not surprising that contracts relating to land are similarly singled out. There are also practical matters to consider, such as to ensure that the particular formality rule adopted for the contract relating to land is consistent with that used in a transaction which also involves a property transaction. If there are reasons for exempting certain property transactions from formality, it may give similar reasons for exempting contracts relating to those property transactions.[41] And when electronic property transactions are introduced allowing the completion of a transaction to be effected in electronic form rather than by a physical deed submitted to the Land Registry for registration, one would expect that the preliminary stage of the transaction—the contract—should similarly be capable of taking an electronic form.[42] The Law Commission's proposals for reform which led to the enactment of s.2 of the Law of Property (Miscellaneous Provisions) Act 1989 were themselves part of a broader review of the system of conveyancing which was undertaken with a view to its modernisation and simplification[43]; the section, and any issues arising in relation to its drafting and its interpretation, must be seen in this context.

The provisions of section 2 of the Law of Property (Miscellaneous Provisions) Act 1989   For ease of reference, the provisions of s.2 are first set out here in full in their current form. Key elements of the section will be discussed in the following paragraphs.

5-08

5-09

---

[37] See paras 5-28, 5-29.
[38] See para.4-03.
[39] Under the doctrine of *Walsh v Lonsdale* (1882) 21 Ch. D. 9, CA; Cheshire and Burn, pp.215-220, 978-983.
[40] Cheshire and Burn, Ch.25; see paras 4-03, 4-07.
[41] e.g. contracts for leases not exceeding three years are excluded from the requirement of writing (LP(MP)A 1989 s.2(5)(a)) because the grant of such a lease is itself excluded from the requirement of writing by LPA 1925 s.54(2) and from the requirement of a deed by LPA 1925 s.52(2)(d).
[42] See para.5-23.
[43] Law Com. No.164, para.1.2.

"**2.**—(1)   A contract for the sale or other disposition of an interest in land can only be made in writing and only by incorporating all the terms which the parties have expressly agreed in one document or, where contracts are exchanged, in each.

(2)   The terms may be incorporated in a document either by being set out in it or by reference to some other document.

(3)   The document incorporating the terms or, where contracts are exchanged, one of the documents incorporating them (but not necessarily the same one) must be signed by or on behalf of each party to the contract.

(4)   Where a contract for the sale or other disposition of an interest in land satisfies the conditions of this section by reason only of the rectification of one or more documents in pursuance of an order of a court, the contract shall come into being, or be deemed to have come into being, at such time as may be specified in the order.

(5)   This section does not apply in relation to—

   (a)   a contract to grant such a lease as is mentioned in s.54(2) of the Law of Property Act 1925 (short leases);

   (b)   a contract made in the course of a public auction; or

   (c)   a contract regulated under the Financial Services and Markets Act 2000, other than a regulated mortgage contract, a regulated home reversion plan, a regulated home purchase plan or a regulated sale and rent back agreement[44];

and nothing in this section affects the creation or operation of resulting, implied or constructive trusts.

(6)   In this section—

   "disposition" has the same meaning as in the Law of Property Act 1925;
   "interest in land" means any estate, interest or charge in or over land[45];
   "regulated mortgage contract", "regulated home reversion plan", "regulated home purchase plan" and "regulated sale and rent back agreement" must be read with—

      (a)   s.22 of the Financial Services and Markets Act 2000,
      (b)   any relevant order under that section, and
      (c)   Schedule 2 to that Act.[46]

(7)   Nothing in this section shall apply in relation to contracts made before this section comes into force.[47]

(8)   Section 40 of the Law of Property Act 1925 (which is superseded by this section) shall cease to have effect."

(2)   Contracts Within the Scope of Section 2

5-10   **The section applies to contracts, not dispositions**   Section 2 applies to "a contract for the sale or other disposition of an interest in land"—i.e. a contract for sale, or *a contract for* some other disposition.[48] It does not apply to the disposition of an interest in land itself, for which separate formalities are prescribed by other

---

[44]   Substituted by SI 2001/3649 art.317(2); further amended by SI 2009/1342 art.24(a).

[45]   The words "or in or over the proceeds of sale of land" at the end of the definition of "interest in land" were repealed by Trusts of Land and Appointment of Trustees Act 1996 Sch.4 para.1.

[46]   Definition inserted by SI 2001/3649 art.317(3), and further amended by SI 2006/2383 art.27(b) and SI 2009/1342 art.24(b).

[47]   i.e. 27 September 1989: LP(MP)A 1989 s.5(3).

[48]   By s.2(6) "disposition" has the same meaning as in LPA 1925, which contains a very wide definition at s.205(1)(ii): "'Conveyance' includes a mortgage, charge, lease, assent, vesting declaration, vesting instrument, disclaimer, release and every other assurance of property or of an interest therein by any instrument, except a will; ... and "disposition" includes a conveyance and also a devise, bequest, or an appointment of property contained in a will ...".

statutes.[49] A contract for the sale of land, or for the creation of an interest in land, may have the effect of creating an equitable interest,[50] but the contract itself need comply only with s.2 of the 1989 Act and not with the formalities required for dispositions of interests in land.[51] Similarly an instrument which effects a disposition of an interest in land without the intervention of a contract, need not comply with s.2, but only with the formalities required for dispositions.[52]

"Interest in land" Section 2 applies to contracts for the sale or other disposition of an "interest in land", which means "any estate, interest or charge in or over land".[53] This is a wide definition,[54] which covers equitable interests in the land as well as legal estates, interests and charges. Even if the interest has arisen informally, such as under a resulting or constructive trust, a contract to dispose of it is required

5-11

---

[49] LPA 1925 ss.52 (deed required to convey or create most legal estates), 53(1)(a), (b), 54 (writing required for creation or disposition of most interests in land, and for declaration of trust respecting land); LRA 2002 s.27 and Sch.2 (many dispositions do not operate at law until requirements for registration complied with). See generally Cheshire and Burn, Ch.25.

[50] Under the doctrine of *Walsh v Lonsdale*, see para.5-08 fn.39.

[51] *McLaughlin v Duffill* [2008] EWCA Civ 1627, [2010] Ch. 1 at [25]–[26].

[52] *Target Holdings Ltd v Priestley* (2000) 79 P. & C.R. 305 (mortgage; Judge Hicks QC at [53]: "contracts *of* disposition, as distinct from executory contracts *for* disposition, are not caught [by s.2]"); *Helden v Strathmore Ltd* [2011] EWCA Civ 542; [2011] Bus. L.R. 1592 (mortgage: Lord Neuberger at [27]: "Mr Helden's case on s.2 is hopeless. It proceeds on a fundamental misunderstanding of the reach and purpose of that section, a misunderstanding, it is fair to say, which appears to be not uncommon. Section 2 is concerned with contracts for the creation or sale of legal estates or interests in land, not with documents which actually create or transfer such estates or interests"); *Joyce v Rigolli* [2004] EWCA Civ 79; [2004] 1 P. & C.R. DG22 (boundary agreement: Arden LJ at [31] contract *for* sale is one whose purpose is to sell or dispose of interest, not where that is merely its effect), followed in *Yeates v Line* [2012] EWHC 3085 (Ch); [2013] Ch. 363 at [29]; *Eagle Star Insurance Co Ltd v Green* [2001] EWCA Civ 1389 at [15] (deed of mortgage must satisfy LP(MP)A 1989 s.1 (see para.7-05), but not s.2); *Rollerteam Ltd v Riley* [2016] EWCA Civ 1291; [2017] Ch. 109 at [45] (unilateral contract for settlement agreement completed by express declarations of trust: immediate disposition of interests in land, not a contract for disposition at any future time). Where the property right arises *by virtue of* the contract, such as under the doctrine of *Walsh v Lonsdale*, see para.5-08 fn.39, the contract must comply with s.2: e.g. the creation of an equitable mortgage over land by deposit of title deeds, which before 1989 arose informally under the theory that the deposit amounted to part performance of an oral contract for the mortgage, must now be in writing and satisfy s.2: *United Bank of Kuwait Plc v Sahib* [1997] Ch. 107, CA, at 139, 143 (although note that now, under registered land, there are no physical documents of title that could be used in this manner: Cheshire and Burn, p.811); *Bank of Scotland Plc v Waugh* [2014] EWHC 2117 (Ch); [2015] 1 P. & C.R. DG3 (purported grant of mortgage not effective because not executed as a deed, but satisfied s.2 and so took effect as equitable mortgage).

[53] s.2(6).

[54] As first enacted, it was even wider: "any estate, interest or charge in or over land *or in or over the proceeds of sale of land*" but the italicised words were deleted by Trusts of Land and Appointment of Trustees Act 1996; see para.5-09 fn.45. The interest of a beneficiary under a trust for sale of land (e.g. the beneficial interest of a co-owner) was said, at least for some purposes, to be an interest in the proceeds of sale rather than in the land itself by virtue of the doctrine of conversion, and the original wording of s.2 was designed to ensure that contracts relating to such interests were included within its scope. Since the reform of trusts of land by the 1996 Act, beneficial interests under a trust of land are interests in the land and therefore contracts for such interests are caught by s.2: see generally Cheshire and Burn, pp.465–466, 477; Megarry and Wade, paras 10-029 to 10-032, 12-006. However, the effect of the reform of s.2 by the 1996 Act is that an agreement to grant a charge over the proceeds of sale of land is no longer within the statute. See also *Young v Lauretani* [2007] EWHC 1244 (Ch); [2007] 2 F.L.R. 1211 (agreement to apply proceeds of sale of grandmother's property not covered by s.2).

to satisfy the formality requirements of s.2.[55] Taken with the wide definition of "disposition",[56] this means that s.2 covers a contract to enter into any transaction which involves the creation or transfer of any interest, legal or equitable, in land, such as a contract to transfer the freehold estate or an equitable interest under a trust of land, to grant or assign a lease,[57] and to grant a mortgage,[58] an easement or a profit à prendre.[59] However, if the contracts relates to land, but not to the sale or disposition of an interest in the land, s.2 will not apply—such as a contractual licence to occupy land, since a licence is not an interest in land.[60] The following paragraphs give further particular examples of types of contract which have been held to fall, or not to fall, within the scope of the section.

5-12   **Examples of contracts within the scope of the section**   Section 2 clearly applies in the most common land contracts: the contract for the sale of the freehold legal estate in land, where the contract generally precedes the execution of the deed of transfer of title to the estate[61]; or the contract to assign the leasehold estate, if a contract is similarly used in anticipation of the deed of assignment.[62] The creation and surrender of a lease are dispositions of an interest in land, and therefore the contract to grant a new lease[63] and the contract to surrender an existing lease[64] are subject to the requirements of s.2. Similarly a legal or equitable mortgage or charge over land create an interest in the land and so an agreement to grant such a mortgage or charge must satisfy s.2 if it is to be a binding contractual undertaking.[65] The section applies not only where the party who undertakes in the contract to transfer an interest in land, or to create a new interest in the land, already has the interest which he is to transfer or out of which he is to create a new interest: the agreement to

---

[55]   Law Com. No.164, see para.5–07 fn.26, para.4.4.

[56]   See para.5–10 n.48.

[57]   Except certain short leases by virtue of the exception in s.2(5)(a); see para.5-13.

[58]   Except certain contracts regulated under the Financial Services and Markets Act 2000, by virtue of the exception in s.2(5)(c); see para.5-13.

[59]   These are all estates or interests in, or charges over, land: Cheshire and Burn, Ch.6 (fee simple); Ch.14 (equitable concurrent interests); Ch.8 (leases); Ch.21 (mortgages); Ch.18 (easements and profits); Megarry and Wade, paras 3-035 to 3-069 (fee simple); Ch.11 (beneficial interests under trust of land), Ch.17 (leases), Ch.24 (mortgages), Ch.27 (easements and profits).

[60]   Cheshire and Burn, pp.930–933; Megarry and Wade, paras 34-016 to 34-019. For the distinction between a lease (which is an estate in the land) and a licence (which is not), see *Street v Mountford* [1985] A.C. 809, HL; Cheshire and Burn, pp.185-196; Megarry and Wade, paras 17-013 to 17-032.

[61]   The contract is not necessary but is generally used in order to bind the parties to the transaction but to allow time for further searches and enquiries to be made before completion of the transaction by a deed and registration at the Land Registry: see F. Silverman, *The Law Society's Conveyancing Handbook*, 24th edn (Law Society, 2017) Pt E2.

[62]   *Singh v Sanghera* [2013] EWHC 956 (Ch) at [19]–[20].

[63]   *Thursby v Eccles* (1900) 70 L.J.Q.B. 91 (contract to grant lease of furnished flat was contract concerning an interest in land and so within Statute of Frauds 1677 s.4); *Wright v Robert Leonard (Developments) Ltd* [1994] N.P.C. 49 (agreement to grant 125-year lease).

[64]   *Commission for the New Towns v Cooper (Great Britain) Ltd* [1995] Ch. 259, CA, at 283; *Proudreed Ltd v Microgen Holdings Plc* (1996) 72 P. & C.R. 388, CA, at 393. The express surrender of a lease requires a deed under LPA 1925 s.52(1), but an informal surrender may be implied, by operation of law: LPA 1925 s.52(2)(c); the agreement for a (future) surrender must, however, be in writing in compliance with LP(MP)A 1989 s.2, if it is to be a binding contract: *Ealing Family Housing Association Ltd v McKensie* [2003] EWCA Civ 1602; [2004] L. & T.R. 15 at [12], [17].

[65]   *Kinane v Mackie-Conteh* [2005] EWCA Civ 45; [2005] 2 P. & C.R. DG3 (but saved on the facts by constructive trust under s.2(5)); *United Bank of Kuwait Plc v Sahib*, see para.5–10 fn.52.

[150]

dispose of a future-acquired interest is also caught by the section.[66] Nor need the undertaking be unconditional: a contract which defines with sufficient certainty the circumstances in which, if at all, one party will sell or otherwise dispose of an interest in land in favour of the other party is also required to satisfy the requirements of s.2.[67] This is the basis on which it has been held that the document by which an option to purchase land is granted must satisfy the requirements of the section, rather than the document by which the option is exercised: at least for the purposes of s.2, the option to buy land can properly be described as a contract for the sale of that land conditional on the exercise of the option.[68]

The requirements of s.2 can be a trap for the unwary practitioner or contracting party who does not identify an agreement as one for the disposition of an interest in land, where it is predominantly a different type of agreement or a transaction whose focus is not on interests in land—for example, an agreement for the winding-up of a partnership where the partnership assets include land[69]; or a family settlement where the family home is one of the assets[70]; or an agreement for mutual wills where the wills are to include bequests of land.[71] Any agreement for the future disposition of assets which include land must satisfy the formality

---

[66] *Singh v Beggs* (1996) 71 P. & C.R. 120, CA (agreement to grant lease out of freehold if it was acquired in the future).

[67] *Singh v Beggs*, see para.5–12 fn.66.

[68] *Spiro v Glencrown Properties Ltd* [1991] Ch. 537 at 541 (Hoffmann J). This was a purposive construction: "An option is not strictly speaking either an offer or a conditional contract. It does not have all the incidents of the standard form of either of these concepts. To that extent it is a relationship sui generis. But there are ways in which it resembles each of them. Each analogy is in the proper context a valid way of characterising the situation created by an option. The question in this case is not whether one analogy is true and the other false, but which is appropriate to be used in the construction of s.2 of the Law of Property (Miscellaneous Provisions) Act 1989" (Hoffmann J at 544). The option in *Spiro* was a call option; applied in *Re Gray (Deceased)* [2004] EWHC 1538 (Ch); [2005] 1 W.L.R. 815 at [18] (testamentary option not contractually binding because no signed documentation satisfying s.2). The principle was extended to a put option by Neuberger J in *Active Estates Ltd v Parness* [2002] EWHC 893 (Ch); [2003] L. & T.R. 21 at [55]. For option contracts, see further para.2-20.
  The grant of a right of pre-emption, however, is not a contract which gives the beneficiary the right to call for the property, and it may not even set out the terms of a future contract since it will commonly give the beneficiary the right of first refusal but without yet stating the price or other terms which will form the basis of any possible future contract. It cannot therefore be characterised as a contract for the sale or other disposition of an interest in land and so it is the *implementation* of the pre-emption that must satisfy s.2—which creates a difficulty for the beneficiary if the parties are not alert to the need to create a document which complies with the section: see *Bircham & Co Nominees (No.2) Ltd v Worrell Holdings Ltd* [2001] EWCA Civ 775; (2001) 82 P. & C.R. 34 (s.2 not complied with); *Butts Park Ventures (Coventry) Ltd v Bryant Homes Central Ltd* [2003] EWHC 2487 (Ch); [2004] B.C.C. 207 (both grant of pre-emption and its exercise complied with s.2). For rights of pre-emption, see further para.2-21.

[69] *Healy-Upright v Bradley* [2007] EWHC 3161 (Ch) at [33].

[70] *Green v Collyer-Bristow* [1999] Lloyd's Rep. P.N. 798; but not where the agreement is to compromise ancillary relief proceedings, which does not give rise to a contract enforceable in law, and is characterised not as an agreement for the disposition of an interest in land, but an agreement to avoid the expense and stress of a contested hearing: *Xydhias v Xydhias* [1999] 2 All E.R. 386 at 394, 396–397, applied in *Cox v Cox* [2006] EWHC 1077 (Ch); [2006] B.C.C. 890 at [44]. On the exclusion from the operation of s.2 of contracts designed to settle legal proceedings, see further para.5-15.

[71] *Healey v Brown* [2002] EWHC 1405 (Ch); [2002] N.P.C. 59 at [19]; but not if the agreement is for a testamentary disposition which does not dispose of an interest in land as such: *Re Walters* [2007] EWHC 3060 (Ch) at [29]–[31] (direction to executors to dispose of residue after conversion of estate (which included land); distinguishing *Healey v Brown*). cf. *Legg v Burton* [2017] EWHC 2088 (Ch); [2017] 4 W.L.R. 186 at [23], [26]–[27] (Judge Paul Matthews: distinction between agreement for

---

[151]

requirements of s.2 if it is to be contractually binding.[72] Section 2 also applies to an agreement to vary—although not to rescind—a term material to a contract which was itself subject to the formality requirements of the section[73]; this can also create a pitfall for conveyancers since the variation must be by a document which itself complies fully with the section.[74]

5-13   **Contracts excluded by the section from its the scope**   Section 2 contains within its own terms certain exclusions from its scope in relation to contracts where it would be impractical to insist on writing, and which will be valid and enforceable even if made orally.[75] It does not apply to a contract to grant[76] a lease taking effect in possession for a term not exceeding three years (whether or not the lessee is given power to extend the term) at the best rent which can be reasonably obtained without taking a fine[77]; nor to a contract made in the course of a public auction[78]; nor to a contract regulated under the Financial Services and Markets Act 2000 (other than a regulated mortgage contract, a regulated home reversion plan, a regulated home purchase plan or a regulated sale and rent back agreement).[79] It is also stated expressly that nothing in the section affects the creation or operation of resulting,

---

mutual wills relating to particular interest in land or gift of residue "does seem rather capricious, even unprincipled", and a solution might be found in the doctrine of proprietary estoppel, which takes effect without a contract and does not require writing).

[72]   A contract may be severable, but where a composite transaction includes a contract for the sale or other disposition of an interest in land the contract as a whole must satisfy s.2: *Kilcarne Holdings Ltd v Targetfollow (Birmingham) Ltd* [2004] EWHC 2547 (Ch); [2005] 2 P. & C.R. 8 at [189]; see para.5-14.

[73]   See para.5-40.

[74]   e.g. it must contain all the expressly agreed terms (as varied): see para.5-19; see E. Slessenger, "Varying land contracts" [2008] Conv. 7.

[75]   Law Com. No.164, see para.5-07 fn.26, para.4.9.

[76]   Contracts to *assign* short leases are not excluded; this was a deliberate decision by the Law Commission: Law Com. No.164, para.4.10, and is consistent with the rule that the actual assignment of a short lease must also satisfy the formality rules for the disposition of interests in land: *Crago v Julian* [1992] 1 W.L.R. 372.

[77]   LP(MP)A 1989 s.2(5)(a), incorporating this same exception from formality as applies to the formality rules for the creation of such a lease under LPA 1925 s.54(2); see *Looe Fuels Ltd v Looe Harbour Commissioners* [2008] EWCA Civ 414; [2009] L. & T.R. 3 (s.2 satisfied: rent was the best that could reasonably be obtained); *Hutchison v B&DF Ltd* [2008] EWHC 2286 (Ch); [2009] L. & T.R. 12 (oral agreement for five-year lease: s.2 not satisfied, but entry into possession on payment of rent created a periodic tenancy).

[78]   LP(MP)A 1989 s.2(5)(b). Such a contract will be formed on the fall of the hammer, as in the case of all auction contracts: it would undermine the system of contracting at auction if the parties to a contract for the sale of land were still free to refuse to sign the written contract. Under LPA 1925 s.40 (see para.5-06), the parties had to sign a memorandum to render the contract enforceable, although the auctioneer had irrevocable authority to sign on their behalf after the fall of the hammer: *UK 2000 Ltd v Weis* [2004] EWHC 2830 (Ch) at [47]–[48]; Law Com No.164, para.4.11.

[79]   LP(MP)A 1989 s.2(5)(c). This is the current formulation, as substituted by SI 2001/3649 art.317(2) and amended by SI 2009/1342 art.24(a); definitions of "regulated mortgage contract", "regulated home reversion plan", "regulated home purchase plan" and "regulated sale and rent back agreement" were inserted by SI 2001/3649 art.317(3), by reference to the Financial Services and Markets Act 2000, and were further amended by SI 2006/2383 art.27(b) and SI 2009/1342 art.24(b). The section originally provided simply for the exclusion of "a contract regulated under the Financial Services Act 1986". The Law Commission's view was that debentures and other investments (e.g. unit trusts investing in land) "are so distanced from the land itself that the arguments against formality outweigh those in favour of formality": Law Com No.164, para.4.12.

implied or constructive trusts; this very significant exception is considered further below.[80]

Beyond these express exclusions, the courts have had occasion to identify other types of contract to which s.2 does not apply by reason of the interpretation of the statute.

Contracts outside the scope of the section: separate, or collateral, con- **5-14**
tracts The Law Commission, when it proposed the new rule that contracts for the sale or other disposition of land must be in writing, noted that "the collateral contract may in substance be regarded as [a] way of enforcing a term omitted from what purports to be a contract in writing".[81] If the court is satisfied that what appears to be a single agreement is in fact two separate contracts, one for the sale or other disposition of an interest in land, the other a contract which does not relate to land, it may be able to enforce the latter, even if it is not contained in a document which satisfies the requirements of s.2—whilst at the same time saving also the land contract, since it is fatal to the whole agreement if it involves the disposition of an interest in land but the signed document does not contain all the agreed terms.[82] However attractive such a solution may be, some judges have sounded a note of caution about it. Lewison J has said[83]:

> "Although it may be possible for parties to hive off parts of their arrangements into separate and distinct contracts,[84] the court should be wary of artificially dividing what is in truth a composite transaction.[85] If part of a composite transaction is a contract for the sale or other disposition of an interest in land, then the contract as a whole must satisfy the statutory requirements."[86]

However, if there is a clearly separate agreement, not containing an agreement

---

[80] See para.5-27.
[81] Law Com. No.164, see para.5–07 fn.26, para.5.7.
[82] See para.5-19.
[83] *Kilcarne Holdings Ltd v Targetfollow (Birmingham) Ltd*, see para.5–12 fn.72 at [189]. The appeal in this case ([2005] EWCA Civ 1355; [2006] 1 P. & C.R. DG20) did not relate to this issue. See also *Business Environment Bow Lane Ltd v Deanwater Estates Ltd* [2007] EWCA Civ 622; [2007] L. & T.R. 26 at [42]–[43] (Sir Andrew Morritt C: "The law relating to collateral contracts is well-established but in connection with sales or leases of land needs to be applied with caution ... those who assert a collateral contract in relation to a term not so contained must show that it was intended to have contractual effect separate from the normal conveyancing documents. Otherwise it will be invalidated by s.2").
[84] *Tootal Clothing Ltd v Guinea Properties Ltd Management Ltd* (1992) 64 P. & C.R. 452 [CA; contract for lease of commercial premises, including tenant's obligation to carry out shop-fitting works to premises and receive rent-free period for works to be done; supplemental agreement, made on same day but in separate document, by which landlord agreed to make contribution to cost of tenant's shop-fitting works was a separate agreement which was not caught by s.2; the principal reason given for the decision in the case was however that the land contract had been completed and so s.2 no longer applied: see para.5–14 fn.92, but cf. see para.5–14 fn.93].
[85] *Grossman v Hooper* [2001] EWCA Civ 615; [2001] 3 F.C.R. 662 [contract for transfer of title to house to former co-habitee; separate agreement that transferee would discharge debt to a third party was not a term of the land contract and therefore was not required to be in writing. For criticism of the language and analysis of "collateral contracts" see at [19] (Chadwick LJ) and [33] (Sir Christopher Staughton, who asked at [35]: "If the parties are allowed by a simple device [of hiving off parts of their agreement into a separate non-land contract] to avoid the effects of s.2, what was the point of Parliament enacting it?"].
[86] *Godden v Merthyr Tydfil Housing Association* [1997] N.P.C. 1; (1997) 74 P. & C.R. D1 [CA; Simon Brown LJ: "there was in this case but one single unified agreement—an agreement under which the defendants undertook to purchase from the plaintiff land which in the first place he was to acquire, prepare and develop to their order. It seems to me entirely unreal to attempt to separate that out into

to sell or dispose of an interest in land even if it is related to the land contract—such as a side-letter containing a warranty as to the vendor's title alongside but separate from the contract for the sale of the land, but issued in order to induce the purchaser to enter into the land contract[87]—the courts will give effect to it without requiring it to satisfy the requirements of s.2.[88] Some judges have even emphasised that the court should lean in favour of holding the parties' agreements valid and binding, rather than being too astute to apply s.2 to strike them down.[89] Briggs J sought to reconcile the cases[90]:

"(i) Nothing in s.2 of the 1989 Act is designed to prevent parties to a composite transaction which includes a land contract from structuring their bargain so that the land contract is genuinely separated from the rest of the transaction in the sense that its performance is not made conditional upon the performance of some other expressly agreed part of the bargain. Thus, in Chadwick LJ's example in *Grossman v Hooper*,[91] parties may agree to the sale and purchase both of a house and of its curtains and carpets in a single composite transaction. None the less it is open to them to agree either (a) that completion of the purchase of the house is dependent upon the sale of the carpets and curtains or (b) that it is not. They are free to separate the terms of a transaction of type (b) into two separate documents (one for the house and the other for the carpets and curtains) without falling foul of s.2. They may also agree to structure a transaction which includes the sale of two or more parcels of land by way of separate contracts for each, so that none of the land contracts is conditional upon the performance of any of the others. (ii) By contrast, the parties to a composite transaction are not free to separate into a separate document expressly agreed terms, for example as to the sale of chattels or the provision of services, if upon the true construction of the whole of the agreement, performance of the land sale is conditional upon the chattel sale or service provision. That would, albeit for reasons which seem to me to frustrate rather than serve the purposes for which the 1989 Act was passed, fall foul of s.2(1), however purposively construed. So would a series of separate contracts for the sale of separate parcels of land, if each was conditional upon the performance of the other. (iii) Since the splitting into separate contracts of parts of a composite transaction is inherently likely to give rise to uncertainties as to whether

---

two discrete, or even distinct, agreements—one involving the disposition of land, the other not. Rather, all the obligations between the parties were integral to each other, part and parcel of a single scheme"].

[87] In such a case the side letter creates a collateral contract for which the consideration is entering into the main (land) contract: Cartwright (Misrepresentation), para.8–07; Chitty, paras 13–004 to 13–006.

[88] *Record v Bell* [1991] 1 W.L.R. 853 at 861–862 (offer by vendor of warranty as to what appeared on land register regarding vendor's title where up-to-date office copies of Land Registry entries had not been obtained, made to induce purchaser to exchange contracts and thereby to accept offer of (collateral) contract regarding state of title. "It would be unfortunate if common transactions of this nature should nevertheless cause the contracts to be avoided. It may, of course, lead to a greater use of the concept of collateral warranties than has hitherto been necessary" (Judge Paul Baker QC at 862)).

[89] *Hanoman v Southwark LBC* [2008] EWCA Civ 624; [2009] 1 W.L.R. 374 at [56] (Arden LJ: "I do not consider that the court needs to interpret a collateral contract so far as possible to bring it *within* s.2 of the 1989 Act: on the contrary, on general principle the court should so far as possible interpret it so that it can be enforced and party autonomy respected"; criticising Sir Andrew Morritt C. in *Business Environment Bow Lane Ltd v Deanwater Estates Ltd*, see para.5–14 fn.83; the issue was not raised on appeal at [2009] UKHL 29; [2009] 1 W.L.R. 1367).

[90] *North Eastern Properties Ltd v Coleman* [2010] EWCA Civ 277; [2010] 1 W.L.R. 2715 at [54]–[55]; see also Longmore LJ at [81] ("This section is not intended to be a charter for those wishing to disown apparent contracts for the sale of property to go behind the document and search for statements made in pre-contract negotiations, then to claim that they were intended to be terms of the contract and thus bring the whole contractual edifice crashing to the ground").

[91] [See para.5–14 fn.85.]

performance of the one is conditional upon performance of the other, the parties are free, and in my opinion should positively be encouraged, to make plain by express terms whether or not that conditionality exists. To do so serves rather than evades or frustrates the purposes of s.2, an important part of which is to encourage clarity rather than uncertainty in land transactions. An obvious way of providing expressly that performance of the terms of a separate contract are not to operate as a condition for the performance of the land contract where they form parts of a composite transaction, is for the parties to insert an appropriately worded entire agreement clause in the land contract."

It has been said that s.2 applies only to executory contracts; and that where all the land elements of an agreement which fails to comply with the section have been performed, the remaining (non-land) elements may be examined without reference to s.2 and therefore enforced.[92] However, this has been rejected by the Court of Appeal which has made clear that the only question is whether the non-land elements are part of the contract which is subject to the requirements of s.2, or are contained in a separate agreement. If the former, the fact that the land elements of the contract have been completed does not affect the fact that the agreement for the non-land elements remains void by virtue of the operation of the statute.[93]

Examples of other contracts outside the scope of the section In various contexts the courts have made clear that s.2 will not apply to compromises of disputes. In a dispute between the vendor and purchaser under a contract for the sale of land which the purchaser refused to complete, a compromise agreement which required the purchaser to put the property on the market and sell it to a third party if a new purchaser could be found, did not itself constitute a contract for the sale of land, which would be formed only when the property had been marketed.[94] Where the compromise agreement settles a boundary dispute by way of a demarcation agreement which is designed to identify the boundary, rather than to change it, it may not fall within the section either because the agreement is not one "for" the disposition of an interest in land even if its effect was that some small parcels of land were to be conveyed to complete the agreement,[95] or because Parliament could not have intended the section to apply to demarcating agreements under which trivial transfers were involved.[96] And a compromise agreement which contains an agreement for the sale or other disposition of an interest in land, which

5-15

---

92 *Kilcarne Holdings Ltd v Targetfollow (Birmingham) Ltd*, see para.5–12 fn.72, at [198] (Lewison J, interpreting this as the binding ratio of CA in *Tootal Clothing Ltd v Guinea Properties Ltd Management Ltd*, see para.5–14 fn.84); *Campden Hill Ltd v Chakrani* [2005] EWHC 911 (Ch); [2005] N.P.C. 65 at [49]–[50]; *Mirza v Mirza* [2009] EWHC 3 (Ch); [2009] 2 F.C.R. 12 at [143]; *North Eastern Properties Ltd v Coleman*, see para.5–14 fn.90, at [49].

93 *Keay v Morris Homes (West Midlands) Ltd* [2012] EWCA Civ 900; [2012] 1 W.L.R. 2855 at [44]–[48]. See Rimer LJ at [47]: "The proposition that a void contract can, by acts in the nature of part performance, mature into a valid one is contrary to principle and wrong".

94 *Nweze v Nwoko* [2004] EWCA Civ 379; [2004] P. & C.R. 33, distinguishing *Jelson Ltd v Derby City Council* [1999] 3 E.G.L.R. 91, where it was held at [43] that an agreement under which one party can be required to convey land to a third party nominated by the other is a contract within s.2 because it was in effect an option; cf. para.5–12 fn.68.

95 cf. para.5–10 fn.52 (distinction between disposition, which is not covered by s.2, and contract for disposition, which is).

96 *Joyce v Rigolli* [2004] EWCA Civ 79; [2004] 1 P. & C.R. DG22 at [31]–[32] (Arden LJ), interpreted and applied in *Yeates v Line* [2012] EWHC 3085 (Ch); [2013] Ch. 363 at [29]–[30] ("Arden LJ was of the opinion that a demarcation agreement which has a disposing effect does not fall foul of s.2(1) unless it has a disposing purpose *and* more than a trivial amount of land is disposed of"); *Chadwick v Abbotswood Properties Ltd* [2004] EWHC 1058 (Ch); [2005] 1 P. & C.R. 10 at [64]; *Styles v Smith*

arises following the acceptance of an offer made under Pt 36 of the Civil Procedure Rules, is binding and enforceable by the Court by virtue of its inherent jurisdiction even if it does not create a contract which complies with s.2 of the 1989 Act.[97] Similarly, other agreements which arise by virtue of statutory authority, even if they have the appearance of contracts for the sale or other disposition of an interest in land, may not be required to satisfy s.2 if it appears that Parliament must have intended the statutory contract to be valid and enforceable in its own right.[98] It has also been held that a "lock-out" contract, by which a party to negotiations for the sale of property agrees, in return for good consideration, not to negotiate with a third party for a defined or definable period,[99] is not covered by s.2 because, even though it forms part of the negotiations towards a sale of the land, it is plainly not a contract for the sale of any interest in land.[100]

(3)   The Requirements of Section 2

5-16   **Summary of the requirements**   The requirements of s.2 are set out in subss.(1) to (3):

> "**2.**—(1)   A contract for the sale or other disposition of an interest in land can only be made in writing and only by incorporating all the terms which the parties have expressly agreed in one document or, where contracts are exchanged, in each.
> (2)   The terms may be incorporated in a document either by being set out in it or by reference to some other document.
> (3)   The document incorporating the terms or, where contracts are exchanged, one of the documents incorporating them (but not necessarily the same one) must be signed by or on behalf of each party to the contract."

There must therefore be an agreement which (apart from the formality of writing, an additional requirement under the statute) constitutes a *contract*; the contract must be *made in writing* which *incorporates all the expressly-agreed terms* in a *single document* (or in each of exchanged documents) containing the terms or *incorporating them by reference*; and the document (or the exchanged documents) must be *signed by or on behalf of each party*. These requirements will be discussed in the following paragraphs of this section. The consequences of the failure to comply are considered in the following section.[101]

5-17   **"A contract"**   Section 2 does not give a complete definition of the requirements for a valid contract for the sale or other disposition of an interest in land, but merely adds to the common law requirements for the formation of a contract the require-

---

[2005] EWHC 3224 (QB) at [14]; *Melhuish v Fishburn* [2008] EWCA Civ 1382 at [22].

[97]   *Orton v Collins* [2007] EWHC 803 (Ch); [2007] 1 W.L.R. 2953. The court can order the parties to sign a single document incorporating the terms of the settlement to enable their agreement to have the necessary contractual effect within s.2: at [63]. For another context in which the courts have not applied s.2 because the agreement to settle proceedings is not a "contract" within the meaning of the section, see *Xydhias v Xydhias* [1999] 2 All E.R. 386 at 394, 396–397, applied in *Cox v Cox* [2006] EWHC 1077 (Ch); [2006] B.C.C. 890 at [44] (compromise of ancillary relief application). See also T. Watkin, "The Compromise of Property Disputes" [2007] Conv. 544.

[98]   *Llanelec Precision Engineering Co Ltd v Neath Port Talbot CBC* [2000] 3 E.G.L.R. 158 (compulsory purchase).

[99]   For "lock-out" contracts see further para.2-22.

[100]   *Pitt v PHH Asset Management Ltd* [1994] 1 W.L.R. 327, CA.

[101]   See paras 5-24 to 5-29.

ment of writing.[102] The contract must therefore satisfy the normal common law definition of a contract: it must embody an agreement, normally formed through the acceptance of an offer[103] and consideration[104]; the terms must be sufficiently complete and certain[105]; and there must be sufficient contractual intention so that, for example, if the parties' negotiations are conducted under a "subject to contract" condition, their putting the proposed terms into writing which satisfies s.2 will not constitute a binding contract until the condition is withdrawn or waived.[106]

"can only be made in writing" This is the fundamental element of s.2: if the putative contract, which fulfils all the other requirements for a contract at common law,[107] is not "made in writing" it is not a contract.[108] We shall see that there may be other ways to give such an agreement some effect,[109] but this cannot be *as a contract* since the statute prevents the contract being formed if the requirement of writing is not satisfied. This is the most significant difference between s.2 and the former provisions of s.40 of the Law of Property Act 1925 and, before that, s.4 of the Statute of Frauds 1677.[110] Those provisions used the normal rules of the common law to determine whether there was a contract, but made its enforcement dependent upon a memorandum in writing signed by or on behalf of the party against whom it was to be enforced.

5-18

The Law Commission took the view that "most people, whether or not lawyers, will readily understand what is meant by a contract in writing and have little difficulty in recognising such a contract when they see one".[111] It made clear that a "written contract", or a "contract in writing" is one where it is "a contractual instru-

---

[102] See para.5-03.

[103] See Ch.3 (agreement); *Commission for the New Towns v Cooper (Great Britain) Ltd* [1995] Ch. 259, CA, at 293 (Evans LJ: "It is axiomatic ... that the communications shall have culminated in the unqualified acceptance by or on behalf of one party of an offer or counter-offer made by or on behalf of the other party. Otherwise, there would be no agreement. It follows, in my judgment, that the exchange of documents which is necessary in order to constitute a contract under the Act cannot take place until the agreement has been concluded by offer, or counter-offer, and final acceptance in this way"); *McNicholas Construction (Holdings) Ltd v Endemol UK Plc* [2003] EWHC 2472; [2003] 43 E.C. 136 (C.S.) (parties had shaken hands but there was no sufficient agreement yet, so question of application of LP(MP)A 1989 s.2 did not arise); *Re Stealth Construction Ltd* [2011] EWHC 1305 (Ch); [2012] 1 B.C.L.C. 297 at [47] (emails between the parties not sufficient to form contract).

[104] See Ch.8 (consideration); *Newell v Tarrant* [2004] EWHC 772 (Ch) at [38] (no consideration for contract to create charge; but document not properly signed for purposes of s.2 anyway: see para.5-22).

[105] See paras 3-13 to 3-18; *Cox v Cox* [2006] EWHC 1077 (Ch); [2006] B.C.C. 890 at [39] (divorce agreement was too uncertain, although as a contract to compromise ancillary relief proceedings it was not anyway a contract for the disposition of an interest in land: at [44]; see para.5-15 fn.97); *Westvilla Properties Ltd v Dow Properties Ltd* [2010] EWHC 30 (Ch); [2010] 2 P. & C.R. 19 (agreement not uncertain, when properly interpreted).

[106] See para.2-08; Law Com. No.164, see para.5-07 fn.26, para.4.15.

[107] See para.5-17.

[108] The question is whether the contract was made in writing in conformity with the statute, not whether the original document can be produced—although if the document is lost, and its existence or its compliance with the statute is disputed, the court must be satisfied on the evidence that it was properly entered into: *Butts Park Ventures (Coventry) Ltd v Bryant Homes Central Ltd* [2003] EWHC 2487; [2004] B.C.C. 207 at [9] (inference from circumstances; "common sense and ordinary business usage" indicated probability that document had been properly signed); *Park Lane Ventures Ltd v Locke* [2006] EWHC 1578 (Ch) (copy of document with witness evidence in support).

[109] e.g. through the doctrine of constructive trust: see para.5-27.

[110] See para.5-06.

[111] Law Com No.164, see para.5-07 fn.26, para.4.5. The Act does not follow the language of the draft Bill presented by the Law Commission, and in some respects this affects the interpretation of a

ment which the parties agree or intend is to contain the whole of their contract".[112] Although the concept of "writing" may at first seem clear, it is inevitable that situations will arise where the court needs to determine whether the particular form of communication constitutes "writing" within the meaning of s.2. The Interpretation Act 1978 provides some assistance, by providing that in any Act (unless the contrary intention appears) "'Writing' includes typing, printing, lithography, photography and other modes of representing or reproducing words in a visible form".[113] This therefore applies for the purposes of s.2, although further questions inevitably arise as to how this extended definition of the meaning of "writing" should be interpreted where a document is created in hard-copy form but is transmitted through electronic means (e.g. in the case of transmission by fax), or is created and stored in electronic form (e.g. email). We have already seen the general approach taken by the law to the use of electronic forms of communication in circumstances where a written formality has traditionally been required by the law; and that it appears that the requirement of "writing" may be satisfied by emails and website transactions where the communication is visible on-screen to both parties even if it is stored in digital form.[114] In the case of s.2, however, there are further issues to consider: in addition to writing, there are the requirements of signature[115] and (in many cases) exchange of contracts[116] for which new provision may need to be made in order to facilitate electronic contracts. This will be considered further below.[117]

5-19   **"only by incorporating all the terms which the parties have expressly agreed"**   The express terms of the contract[118] must be included in the written document. In the case of a contract for the sale of land, the terms must include the property, the parties and the price, and the parties' mutual obligations to buy and sell[119] but there will generally be other express terms, often set out in special conditions of sale which are incorporated into the contract.[120] What the parties expressly agreed, and therefore whether the document includes them, is a question of fact which may require a full consideration of the evidence at trial and may therefore

---

contract "in writing" because the Commission had a less strict view of the requirements for exchange of contracts: see para.5-20. However, its general statements about what constitutes an agreement "in writing" are still valuable.

[112] Law Com No.164, see para.5–07 fn.26, para.4.5, adopting the meaning of "written contract", given by D.W. McLauchlan, *The Parol Evidence Rule* (1976), p.39.

[113] Interpretation Act 1978 s.5, Sch.1.

[114] See para.4-06.

[115] See para.5-22.

[116] See para.5-20.

[117] See para.5-23.

[118] This includes a variation of a contract which is subject to s.2, and so the new contract must set out the agreed terms in their entirety: *HL Estates Ltd v Parker-Lake Homes Ltd* [2003] EWHC 604 (Ch). However, the simplest method of achieving this is for the variation to incorporate all the terms of the original contract (except in so far as they are varied) by express incorporation: see para.5-21.

[119] Cheshire and Burn, p.950; Megarry and Wade, paras 15-027 to 15-031. *Firstpost Homes Ltd v Johnson* [1995] 1 W.L.R. 1567, CA, at 1573 (Peter Gibson LJ: "a contract must contain mutual obligations and a commitment by each party").

[120] A contract which specifies merely the parties, the property and the price is an "open contract" into which certain (rather limited) obligations will be implied; it is therefore customary to use standard-form conditions of sale which have been developed in the conveyancing industry for both residential and commercial sales, although the parties commonly vary the standard conditions expressly when they incorporate them into their contract, or add their own particular terms: Cheshire & Burn, pp.953–954; Megarry and Wade, paras 15-001, 15-047, 15-050.

be unsuitable for decision on summary judgment.[121] The omission of an agreed express term prevents the contract coming into existence,[122] although as long as all the express terms are included there is no obstacle to the validity of the contract if other terms have to be implied. The terms which must be included within the written document are the express terms of the contract which is subject to s.2—that is, the contract for the sale or other disposition of an interest in land. If there are expressly agreed terms which can properly be characterised as forming part of a separate, or collateral, contract which is not itself subject to the requirements of s.2, their omission from the written document is irrelevant.[123] However, if there is no such collateral contract, the failure to include *any* expressly agreed term is fatal, even if the term is not one which relates to the interest in land,[124] although it may sometimes be possible for the court to remedy an omission from the written document by rectifying it.[125] An "entire agreement" clause, drafted so as to deny contractual force to any representations or agreements which the parties may have made before the document is signed, can be helpful in avoiding argument that there are expressly agreed terms which are not contained in the document.[126]

---

[121] *Keay v Morris Homes (West Midlands) Ltd* [2012] EWCA Civ 900; [2012] 1 W.L.R. 2855 at [27], [33]. This raises a similar question of fact as to whether an agreed term was part of the contract for the sale of land, or was a separate contract: *Grossman v Hooper*, see para.5–14 fn.85, at [21].

[122] e.g. *Rudra v Abbey National Plc* (1998) 76 P. & C.R. 537, CA (name of vendor could be established only by extrinsic evidence, so s.2 not satisfied); *Francis v F Berndes Ltd* [2011] EWHC 3377 (Ch); [2012] 1 E.G.L.R. 117 at [26] (document referred only to party being "prepared to sell" the property and did not include the obligations to sell and buy which the parties had in fact agreed, so s.2 not satisfied); *Re Stealth Construction Ltd*, see para.5–17 fn.103 at [48] (emails were not sufficient to show a contract for a legal charge (see para.5-17), but nor did they contain the agreed terms relating to the amount of the loan to be secured by the charge, the date of repayment, the rate of interest and dates for payment of interest); *Oun v Ahmad* [2008] EWHC 545 (Ch); [2008] 2 P. & C.R. DG3 (written contract failed to include parties' agreed apportionment of price between building, goodwill, and fixtures and fittings. See Morgan J at [31]: "There cannot be a binding contract for only those terms which have been incorporated because they are not the complete set of terms which were expressly agreed").

[123] For the courts' approach to finding a separate, or collateral, contract, see para.5-14.

[124] *Wright v Robert Leonard (Developments)* [1994] N.P.C. 49, CA (single contract for flat and its furnishings, but document failed to mention the furnishings; however, the contract was rectified to include the furnishings). The Law Commission in its Working Paper preferred requiring only the "main terms" to be in writing, but rejected this in its final Report in favour of the "simplicity and certainty" of requiring all the agreed terms to be in writing: Law Com. No.164, see para.5–07 fn.26, para.4.7.

[125] *Wright v Robert Leonard (Developments)* [1994] N.P.C. 49, CA; see para.5-25.

[126] cf. *McGrath v Shah* (1987) 57 P. & C.R. 452 at 459 (Chadwick QC, commenting on the similar point in relation to the requirements formerly set by LPA 1925 s.40, see para.5-06: "One can see why such a provision is included in a contract for the sale and purchase of land. All material terms of a contract for the sale of land must be evidenced by some memorandum in writing signed by the party to be charged—see section 40(1) of the Law of Property Act 1925. Accordingly, it is highly undesirable to have any scope for argument whether the written terms of a contract for the sale of land do, in fact, constitute the entire contract"). However, whether an "entire agreement" clause has this effect will depend upon its drafting: cf. *Sutcliffe v Lloyd* [2007] EWCA Civ 153; [2007] 2 E.G.L.R. 13 (clause which referred to the written agreement representing the "entire understanding" in relation to the "matters dealt with" in the document was not engaged in relation to matters not mentioned in it). For varieties of "entire agreement" clauses, see generally R. Christou, *Boilerplate: Practical Clauses*, 7th edn (Sweet & Maxwell, 2015), Ch.10; Cartwright (Misrepresentation), paras 9-06, 9-07; Lewison, para.3.16.

5-20 **"in one document or, where contracts are exchange, in each"** The document which the parties both sign, or each document which the parties (separately) sign,[127] must contain all the express terms. "One document" is straightforward. The meaning of "exchange of contracts" may be less obvious, however—and it is critical since if there is no "exchange" within the meaning of s.2 there will be no contract in the absence of the single document bearing both parties' signatures.[128] It is now clear that a contract formed by a simple exchange of letters, is not sufficient[129]; the Court of Appeal has made clear that an "exchange of contracts" has the normal meaning as understood by conveyancing practitioners. Stuart-Smith LJ said[130]:

"In my opinion, the authorities show that, even if the expression 'exchange of contracts' is not a term of art, it is a well-recognised concept understood both by lawyers and laymen which has the following features.

1. Each party draws up or is given a document which incorporates all the terms which they have agreed, and which is intended to record their proposed contract. The terms that have been agreed may have been agreed either orally or in writing or partly orally or partly in writing.

2. The documents are referred to as 'contracts' or 'parts of contract,' although they need not be so entitled. They are intended to take effect as formal documents of title and must be capable on their face of being fairly described as contracts having that effect.

3. Each party signs his part in the expectation that the other party has also executed or will execute a corresponding part incorporating the same terms.

4. At the time of execution neither party is bound by the terms of the document which he has executed, it being their mutual intention that neither will be bound until the executed parts are exchanged.

5. The act of exchange is a formal delivery by each party of its part into the actual or constructive possession of the other with the intention that the parties will become actually bound when exchange occurs, but not before.

6. The manner of exchange may be agreed and determined by the parties. The traditional method was by mutual exchange across the table, both parties or their solicitors being present. It also commonly takes place by post, especially where the

---

127 See para.5-22.
128 The requirement of "exchange" in s.2 is stricter than that proposed by the Law Commission in Law Com. No.164, see para.5–07 fn.26, which "would have permitted a contract contained in one or each of two documents, whether or not exchanged as a contract. This suggests that Parliament intended to require greater formality in the creation of a contract for the sale of land than that suggested by the Law Commission": *McCausland v Duncan Lawrie Ltd* [1997] 1 W.L.R. 38, CA, at 46–47 (Morritt LJ); *Commission for the New Towns v Cooper (Great Britain) Ltd* [1995] Ch. 259, CA, at 287 (Stuart-Smith LJ: the Law Commission's draft Bill was "wide enough to encompass offer and acceptance in the course of correspondence").
129 *Valentine v Allen* [2003] EWCA Civ 915 at [25]; see also para.5–20 fn.128. An earlier decision of CA in *Hooper v Sherman* [1994] N.P.C. 153, which (Morritt LJ dissenting) had accepted that an exchange of letters by which the parties confirmed an earlier oral agreement could satisfy s.2, and in which CA relied on statements in the Law Commission's Report (see para.5–20 fn.128), was not followed in *Commission for the New Towns v Cooper (Great Britain) Ltd*, see para.5–20 fn.128, at 289, 295.
130 *Commission for the New Towns v Cooper (Great Britain) Ltd*, see para.5–20 fn.128 at 285 (deriving these propositions from *Eccles v Bryant and Pollock* [1948] Ch. 93 at 99–100; *George Trollope & Sons v Martyn Bros* [1934] 2 K.B. 436 at 455; *Domb v Isoz* [1980] Ch. 548 at 557; *Harrison v Battye* [1975] 1 W.L.R. 58); see also Evans LJ at 295 ("when there has been a prior oral agreement, there is only an 'exchange of contracts' within s.2 when documents are exchanged which set out or incorporate all of the terms which have been agreed and when, crucially, those documents are intended, by virtue of their exchange, to bring about a contract to which s.2 applies"). The definition of "exchange" given by Stuart-Smith LJ was applied in *De Serville v Argee Ltd* [2001] N.P.C. 82 at [28]; *Sharif v Sadiq* [2004] EWHC 1913 at [16].

parties or their solicitors are at a distance. In such a case exchange is sequential and does not take place until the second document to be dispatched has been received or posted.[131] Exchange can also take place by telephone, in which case it will be simultaneous.[132]"

In a case where there are more than two parties, it will similarly be possible for the contract to be concluded either by a single document or by the exchange of separate documents, although the method of "exchange" of multiple documents will evidently be more complex.[133]

We have already seen that, in the case of an option to purchase land, it is the document by which the option is granted that must satisfy the requirements of the section, rather than the document by which the option is exercised.[134]

"The terms may be incorporated ... by reference to some other document"   5-21   The signed document need not itself contain all the agreed terms if it refers to another document which contains those terms which do not appear in the signed document. This permits the normal contractual practice of incorporation of other written terms into a signed document.[135]

The signed document must identify the other document which is to be incorporated.[136] This seems to require express reference. Under the former provisions of s.40 of the Law of Property Act 1925 a document to which there was implied reference in the signed memorandum of the agreement could be read together with the signed document.[137] However, the requirements of s.2 of the Law of Property (Miscellaneous Provisions) Act 1989 are intended generally to be stricter.[138]

---

[131] *Eccles v Bryant and Pollock* [1948] Ch. 93 at 97–98 (Lord Greene MR).

[132] *Domb v Isoz* [1980] Ch. 548 at 558 (Buckley LJ). [The Council of the Law Society has issued advice on exchange by the parties' solicitors by telephone, fax or telex, reproduced in F. Silverman, *The Law Society's Conveyancing Handbook*, 24th edn (Law Society, 2017), App.III.2. On exchange of contracts see generally *The Law Society's Conveyancing Handbook*, Pt C; Emmet, paras 2.020 to 2.022.]

[133] As in the case of two parties, it will be for the parties to agree what constitutes exchange by delivery of (actual or constructive) possession of the documents: see para.5 of the list set out by Stuart-Smith LJ above). For the purposes of the validity of the contract within s.2 it is not significant which party retains the signed document(s) after exchange has taken place, although there will be practical concerns for the purposes of enforcement for each party to hold or have access to a copy signed by the other(s).

[134] See para.5-12.

[135] *Courtney v Corp Ltd* [2006] EWCA Civ 518 (signature on contract for legal charge, which referred to lender's standard terms and conditions, was sufficient even though borrower had not seen the document containing the terms and conditions).

[136] *Record v Bell* [1991] 1 W.L.R. 853 at 860 Judge Paul Baker QC: "There are two ways they could be incorporated. They could be set out at length in the contract for sale, or the contract for sale could refer to some other document in which these terms were to be found. The document referred to need not itself be signed, but it has to be identified in the document which is signed".

[137] Cheshire and Burn, p.963 (and see further Cheshire and Burn, 16th edn (Butterworths, 2000), pp.120–121; Megarry and Wade, 5th edn (Stevens, 1984), pp.578–580; J. Williams, *The Statute of Frauds, Section Four, in the Light of its Judicial Interpretation* (Cambridge University Press, 1932), Pt II, Ch.7; *Timmins v Moreland Street Property Co Ltd* [1958] Ch. 110, CA). The courts' interpretation of LPA 1925 s.40 also allowed incorporation by reference to a document *or transaction*: *Timmins v Moreland Street Property Co Ltd* at 130, but LP(MP)A 1989 s.2 is also narrower in allowing only reference to a *document*.

[138] cf. *Record v Bell*, see para.5–21 fn.136, at 859; *Firstpost Homes Ltd v Johnson* [1995] 1 W.L.R. 1567, CA, at 1571.

5-22 **"signed by or on behalf of each party to the contract"** Without the signature by or on behalf of each party[139] on the same document, or on separate documents which are then exchanged, the contract does not come into existence.[140] The signature may be of the party or his agent, and there is no requirement for the agent to receive written authority to sign: the normal principles of agency apply,[141] and so authority may be conferred orally as well asin writing.[142] It should also be noted that it is the parties to the contract who must sign: if the contract requires one of the parties to create or transfer an interest in the land in favour of a third party, the third party is not a party to the contract and his signature is not necessary.[143]

It is the "document incorporating the terms" (or each of the exchanged[144] documents incorporating the terms) which must be signed.[145] This is natural: the document incorporating the terms is the principal contractual document, and if there is a separate document which is incorporated by reference into the contract[146] it is neither necessary nor sufficient within the statute for the incorporated document to be signed.[147]

Section 2 does not define "signature", nor give any indication as to the manner in which the contractual document is to be signed. In the case of hard-copy documents, the Court of Appeal has decided that a party "signs" a document within the

---

[139] As long as a valid contract has come into force as between A and B, both of whom have signed the contract, notwithstanding that a third contemplated party C has not signed the contract, the requirements of the statute are satisfied by the signatures of A and B alone: *Rabiu v Marlbray Ltd* [2016] EWCA Civ 476; [2016] 1 W.L.R. 5147 at [65].

[140] This is a marked change from the position under LPA 1925 s.40, under which if there was a memorandum signed by only one party (or his agent) the contract (which came into existence by virtue of the offer and acceptance without formality) could be enforced against that party but not by him against the non-signing party. This lack of mutual enforceability of the contract was heavily criticised by the Law Commission, which saw the new requirement of a signature by *both* parties as a way of remedying the injustice: Law Com. No.164, see para.5–07 fn.26, para.4.8.

[141] Including later ratification relating back to the time of an (unauthorised) signature: *OPM Property Services Ltd v Venner* [2004] EWHC 427 (Ch) at [46], following *Koenigsblatt v Sweet* [1923] 2 Ch. 314 (a similar decision in relation to the Statute of Frauds 1677 s.4); and the rule under CA 2006 s.51 (formerly CA 1985 s.36C) that a person purporting to contract for or as agent for a company which has not yet been formed is personally liable on the contract: *Braymist Ltd v Wise Finance Co Ltd* [2002] EWCA Civ 127; [2002] Ch. 273 at [67].

[142] *McLaughlin v Duffill* [2008] EWCA Civ 1627; [2010] Ch. 1 at [23]–[24]. This is unchanged from the position under LPA 1925 s.40, which (following the same rule under the Statute of Frauds 1677 s.4) required the memorandum to be signed by the party "or by some other person thereunto by him lawfully authorised". For formalities relating to the creation and disposition of interests in land, however, and dispositions of equitable interests and trusts, LPA 1925 ss.53(1)(a), (c) and 54(a) (again following earlier provisions in the Statute of Frauds) require an agent who signs to be authorised in writing (or by will). In *McLaughlin v Duffill* CA left open at [14] the question of which party has the burden of proof that the agent had (or had no) authority.

[143] *RG Kensington Management Co Ltd v Hutchinson IDH Ltd* [2002] EWHC 1180; [2003] 2 P. & C.R. 13 at [57] ("The closing words of s.2(3) require the contract, or the parts of the contract to be signed by 'each party to the contract', not by 'each party to the prospective conveyance or transfer'": Neuberger J, disapproving *Jelson Ltd v Derby City Council* [1999] 3 E.G.L.R. 91); followed in *Milebush Properties Ltd v Tameside MBC* [2010] EWHC 1022 (Ch); [2010] 2 E.G.L.R. 93 at [66] (s.2 did not require signature of third-party beneficiary of an agreement under Town and Country Planning Act 1990 s.106: such an interpretation of s.2 "would substantially frustrate the statutory scheme contained in s.106 of the 1990 Act").

[144] See para.5-20.

[145] s.2(3).

[146] See para.5-21.

[147] *Firstpost Homes Ltd v Johnson* [1995] 1 W.L.R. 1567, CA (letter agreeing to sell "land shown on the enclosed plan"; parties' signature on the plan but not on the letter was not sufficient because the plan was a separate document incorporated by reference into the letter).

meaning of the section only if he writes his own name with his own hand on the document in such a way as to authenticate the document[148]; and in particular that typing is insufficient even if it is done by the party himself since further evidence would then be required at trial to establish that the party had typed his name with the necessary authenticating intent.[149] The application of s.2 in the context of electronic contracts (including electronic signatures) is considered in the following section.

Electronic contracts within section 2   We have already seen that the law is developing its formality requirements in response to the development of electronic forms of communication.[150] In the context of s.2, there are three issues which need to be addressed in considering what forms of electronic communication will be sufficient: the requirements of writing, and of a signature; and what constitutes—in electronic terms—a single document or (where the parties do not use a single document) exchange of contracts.

5-23

In general any statutory requirement of *writing* as a formality will be satisfied by emails because they take a form visible to sender and recipient[151]; this has been applied in the context of s.2, following a similar decision on s.4 of the Statute of Frauds 1677.[152] The same would apply for other forms of electronic transmission which are visible to both parties and are stored in either physical or digital form.[153]

Signatures may take an electronic form as digital signatures, scanned manuscript

---

[148] *Firstpost Homes Ltd v Johnson* [1995] 1 W.L.R. 1567, CA at 1575, adopting the statement of Denning LJ in *Goodman v J Eban Ltd* [1954] 1 Q.B. 550 at 561. If a party signs the document in two capacities, one signature suffices as long as the signature is expressed to authenticate the document in both capacities: *Redcard Ltd v Williams* [2011] EWCA Civ 466; [2011] 4 All E.R. 444 (directors signing on behalf of company as authorised signatories under CA 2006 s.44 and in their own personal capacities). A party may sign a document by writing only his initials on it, but only if is clear that he intended to authenticate the full terms of the document: *Newell v Tarrant* [2004] EWHC 772 (Ch) at [47]–[49] (initialling of corrections to document in its margin insufficient).

[149] *Firstpost Homes Ltd v Johnson* [1995] 1 W.L.R. 1567, CA at 1575–1576 (Peter Gibson LJ) and 1577 (Balcombe LJ), rejecting the argument that a broader interpretation of what constituted signature on a memorandum for the purposes of LPA 1925 s.40 and Statute of Frauds 1677 s.4, should be adopted. See Peter Gibson LJ at 1576: "I do not see why it is right to encumber the new Act with so much ancient baggage, particularly when it does not leave the 'signed' with a meaning which the ordinary man would understand it to have".

[150] See para.4-06.

[151] Thus satisfying the definition of "writing" in the Interpretation Act 1978, see para.5–18 fn.113; Law Commission Advice, "*Electronic Commerce: Formal Requirements in Commercial Transactions*" (December 2001), Pt 3.

[152] *Re Stealth Construction Ltd* [2011] EWHC 1305 (Ch); [2012] 1 B.C.L.C. 297 at [44] (the emails were in electronic form, printed only in the context of the subsequent dispute), following *J Pereira Fernandes SA v Mehta* [2006] EWHC 813 (Ch); [2006] 1 W.L.R. 1543 (guarantee within Statute of Frauds s.4); see now also *Golden Ocean Group Ltd v Salgaocar Mining Industries Pvt Ltd* [2012] EWCA Civ 265; [2012] 1 W.L.R. 3674 at [16] (guarantee within Statute of Frauds s.4; sequence of emails sufficient).

[153] In the case of fax transmissions, a physical document produced by the receiving machine will be "writing" (*Bircham & Co Nominees (No.2) Ltd v Worrell Holdings Ltd* [2001] EWCA Civ 775; (2001) 82 P. & C.R. 34 at [16]; it is also presumably within the extended definition of "writing" in the Interpretation Act 1978, see para.5–18 fn.113, which includes printing and photography); if the fax transmission is stored digitally and viewed on-screen rather than being printed, it will be "writing" for the same reason as email. If, however, the communication is only transient, and is not stored, it appears not to satisfy the requirement of "writing" even if at the moment of transmission it is visible to the sender and the recipient: see para.4-06 fn.45. The Law Commission's view is that a transmission which passes only between computer systems and is not intended to be read and acted upon by humans ("electronic document interchange"), is not "writing": para.4-06 fn.57.

signatures,[154] or the party's name or initials or some other identifying mark[155] typed into an electronic communication such as an email,[156] as long as the signatory intends the electronic "signature" to authenticate the document.[157] It seems, therefore, that such forms of electronic signature, when used in appropriate cases, will satisfy the requirement of "signature" in s.2. However, in 2001 the Lord Chancellor's Department published proposals[158] to introduce a new s.2A into the Law of Property (Miscellaneous Provisions) Act 1989, to deal specifically with electronic signatures on contracts falling within s.2 and to enable an electronic contract to be as effective for the purposes of s.2 (and any other enactment) as an equivalent paper contract. This proposal was not taken further, but in 2007 the Land Registry published a revised version of the earlier proposals, designed to deal only with contracts relating to registered land, and to be introduced as part of the planned broader implementation of electronic conveyancing.[159] However, since the introduc-

---

[154] Either a manuscript signature on a document which is then scanned and sent in digital form, or a pre-scanned signature inserted into an electronic document such as an email, in each case to be received by the addressee as a signed document: *Bircham & Co Nominees (No.2) Ltd v Worrell Holdings Ltd*, see para.5–23 fn.153, at [61] (faxed document confirmed with LP(MP)A 1989 s.2); see also general discussion by Laddie J in *Re a Debtor (No.2021 of 1995)* [1996] 2 All E.R. 345 at 351 (scanned signature inserted into proxy form for purposes of Insolvency Rules 1986 (SI 1986/1925) r.8.2(3); revoked and replaced by Insolvency (England and Wales) Rules 2016 (SI 2016/1024)).

[155] *J Pereira Fernandes SA v Mehta*, see para.5–23 fn.152, at [27] (Judge Pelling QC: "a party can sign a document for the purposes of s.4 [of the Statute of Frauds] by using his full name or his last name prefixed by some or all of his initials or using his initials, and possibly by using a pseudonym or a combination of letters and numbers (as can happen for example with a Lloyds slip scratch), providing always that whatever was used was inserted into the document in order to give, and with the intention of giving, authenticity to it").

[156] *Re Stealth Construction Ltd*, see para.5–23 fn.152, at [44] (parties inserting their names at end of emails had signed them for purposes of s.2, although contract failed for other reasons); cf. *J Pereira Fernandes SA v Mehta*, see para.5–23 fn.152, at [29]–[30] (email address automatically inserted by internet service provider is not a signature for Statute of Frauds 1677 s.4, because it does not have authenticating intention; and its appearance divorced from the main body of the text of the message emphasised this to be so).

[157] Law Commission Advice, see para.5–23 fn.151, para.3.39, adding also that clicking on a website button may be a signature; see para.4-06.

[158] LCD Consultation Paper 05/2001, *Electronic Conveyancing—A draft order under s.8 Electronic Communications Act 2000* (March 2001). For Pt II of the Electronic Communications Act 2000, see para.4-06.

[159] Land Registry Consultation Paper, *E-conveyancing Secondary Legislation Part I* (February 2007). The revised proposal was for a new s.2A which would read:

    2A.—(1)   This section applies to a document in electronic form where—
        (a)   the document purports to be a contract which falls within subsection (2), and
        (b)   the conditions in subsection (3) are met.
    (2)   A contract falls within this subsection if it is—
        (a)   to make a disposition which falls within s.91(2) LRA 2002; and
        (b)   one to which s.2 above applies.
    (3)   The conditions referred to above are that—
        (a)   all the terms which the parties have expressly agreed are incorporated in the document (whether by being set out in it or by reference to some other document),
        (b)   the document makes provision for the time and date when the contract takes effect,
        (c)   the document has the electronic signature of each person by whom it purports to be authenticated, and
        (d)   each electronic signature is certified.
        (e)   each electronic signature is one required by a network access agreement, and

tion of electronic conveyancing has itself been deferred indefinitely,[160] it is unlikely that further legislative steps will be made for the time being in relation to electronic contracts for the sale of land.[161]

The final question is how a *single document* in electronic form can be signed by both parties in order to comply with s.2; or, alternatively, how the parties can effect an *exchange* of electronic contracts. In some cases it will be straightforward to have a single document which is transmitted by electronic means: for example, where one party signs a contract containing all the terms, scans it or sends it by fax to the other party who then prints it and adds his own signature.[162] It has even been said that an email by one party to the other, to which the latter replies, can form a single document (and therefore the parties' signatures written into their respective emails are the two signatures on the single document), at least where the second email is sent as a reply and so creates a string, as opposed to being simply a new

---

     (f)   the document contains such information and is in such electronic form as may be specified in directions made and published by the registrar.

    (4)   A document to which this section applies is to be regarded for the purposes of s.2 above and any other enactment as—

     (a)   in writing, and

     (b)   signed by each individual, and sealed by each corporation, whose electronic signature it has.

    (5)   If subsection (4) of section 36A of the Companies Act 1985 (execution of documents) applies to a document because of subsection (4) above, subsection (6) of that section (presumption of due execution) shall have effect in relation to the document with the substitution of 'authenticated' for 'signed' (and subsection (8) of that section, in so far as it relates to the document, shall be read accordingly).

    (6)   If subsection (3) of section 29C of the Industrial and Provident Societies Act 1965 (execution of documents) applies to a document because of subsection (4) above, subsection (5) of that section (presumption of due execution) shall have effect in relation to the document with the substitution of 'authenticated' for 'signed'.

    (7)   In this section—

     (a)

         'network access agreement' means an agreement for the purposes of paragraph 1(1) of Schedule 5 to the Land Registration Act 2002, and

         'registrar' means the Chief Land Registrar of Her Majesty's Land Registry, and

     (b)   references to an electronic signature and to the certification of such a signature are to be read in accordance with section 7(2) and (3) of the Electronic Communications Act 2000."

[160] See Ch.4 para.4-06 fn.41.

[161] It is not now intended to require contracts for registered land to be in electronic form, even after the introduction of e-conveyancing: Law Com. No.380, see para.5-23 fn.160, para.20.40.

[162] *Bircham & Co Nominees (No.2) Ltd v Worrell Holdings Ltd*, see para.5-23 fn.153, at [61] (so said by Sir Richard Scott VC at first instance; not pursued on appeal). Note that it is not advisable to send just the signature page of the document for countersignature: the signature should be on the whole document. See *R. (on the application of Mercury Tax Group) v Revenue and Customs Commissioners* [2008] EWHC 2721 (Admin); [2009] S.T.C. 743 at [39], where Underhill J held that, in the case of a deed (see para.7-08), the document to be signed must exist as a discrete physical entity, whether in a single version or in a serious of counterparts, at the moment of signing. The Law Society has issued a Practice Note, *Execution of documents by virtual means* (February 2010) recommending that the same method of execution should be made for the purposes of LP(MP)A 1989 s.2, and therefore in the case of "virtual execution" each party should send the whole document in electronic form, together with the signature page: see *https://www.lawsociety.org.uk/support-services/advice/practice-notes/execution-of-documents-by-virtual-means/*.

email referring to an earlier email. "It is the electronic equivalent of a hard copy letter signed by the sender being itself signed by the addressee".[163] If there is no single document, each party should attach his (electronic) signature to a separate (electronic) document containing all the agreed terms, and the parties should then exchange the documents.[164]

(4) Failure to Comply with the Requirements of Section 2

5-24 **Consequences of agreement failing to comply with section 2** An agreement which falls within the scope of the formality requirements set by s.2 of the Law of Property (Miscellaneous Provisions) Act 1989, but which does not comply with those requirements, is not a contract. This is the fundamental difference from the rule as it was previously under s.40 of the Law of Property Act 1925 (and before that s.4 of the Statute of Frauds 1677), which did not prevent the formation of a contract but provided that the contract could not be enforced against a party who had not signed a memorandum which satisfied the statute. We have already seen that the lack of formality under s.2 of the 1989 Act may have implications not only for the intended contract between the parties, but also for their property rights, if the contract (had it come into existence under s.2) would in itself have had proprietary consequences.[165] However, there are some possible solutions to the problems arising from the failure to satisfy s.2. Some aspects of a transaction, which do not themselves hinge on the existence of a valid contract, may still take effect—such as the deposit paid under an agreement for the sale of land, where the property may pass by reference to the parties' intentions at the time of payment.[166] And a document which fails to satisfy the formality requirements for a contract for the sale of land may satisfy the formality requirements for a disposition of land, which will therefore allow dispositive provisions to take effect.[167] Sometimes it may even be possible to correct the lack of contractual formality by obtaining rectification of documents which formed part of the parties' transaction in order to comply with s.2.[168] Or, although the agreement itself does not take the form required by the statute, it may be possible to use other doctrines such as constructive trust, or some form of estoppel, to give the parties' agreement some effect, or even broadly the same substantive effect as it would have had if the formality requirements had been satisfied.[169]

5-25 **Rectification of documents to comply with section 2** Section 2(4) contemplates the possibility of a contract for the sale or other disposition of an interest in land satisfying the conditions of the section by reason only of the rectification of one or

---

[163] *Re Stealth Construction Ltd*, see para.5-23 fn.152, at [45] (David Richards J).

[164] See para.5-20.

[165] e.g. under the doctrine of *Walsh Lonsdale* (1882) 21 Ch. D. 9, CA, such as an equitable mortgage which used to arise by the contract implied by a deposit of title deeds: see para.5-08 fn.39 and para.5-10 fn.52.

[166] *Sharma v Simposh Ltd* [2011] EWCA Civ 1383; [2013] Ch. 23.

[167] *Murray v Guinness* [1998] N.P.C. 79 (grant of equitable charge, where document sufficient to comply with s.53(1) LPA 1925, but not LP(MP)A 1989 s.2 because it was signed only by one party (the disponor)), discussed in *Kinane v Mackie-Conteh* [2004] EWHC 998 (Ch); [2004] 19 E.G. 164 (C.S.) at [37] and [2005] EWCA Civ 45, [2005] 2 P. & C.R. DG3 at [18].

[168] See para.5-25.

[169] See paras 5-26 to 5-29.

more documents in pursuance of an order of a court. This does not in itself provide the framework for rectification, which will depend on the general law on the equitable remedy of rectification.[170] Section 2 does, however, make clear that if a court orders rectification of a document so as to satisfy the conditions of the section, the court specifies in the order the time at which the contract comes into being or is deemed to have come into being. This varies the normal rule that, if rectified, a contact has effect in the rectified form ab initio, and the provision in s.2 is designed to avoid injustice which might flow from a retrospective validation of the contract affecting third-party transactions which have taken place in the meantime.[171]

The purpose of rectification is not to correct the parties' agreement, but to correct the expression of their agreement in a document which fails accurately to record the agreement which the parties had made (common mistake) or which fails accurately to record what one party believed the contract to be in circumstances where the other party cannot in conscience insist on the version as written (unilateral mistake). In a case, for example, where the written document does not incorporate all the terms which the parties expressly agreed, a court may order its rectification to include all the agreed terms and thereby to comply with s.2.[172] However, if the document reflects what the parties intended, even though they made some mistake of fact or law in relation to their transaction as it was recorded in the document, rectification is not available. This means that where the parties agree that one of the terms shall not be recorded in the document it cannot be rectified so as to include the term—even if the parties were mistaken as to the legal requirements for a valid contract and so believed that it was unnecessary for them to record that term in the written document.[173]

Equitable doctrines allowed to circumvent the statutory formalities We have already seen that under s.40 of the Law of Property Act 1925 (replaced by s.2 of the Law of Property (Miscellaneous Provisions) Act 1989) the requirement of a written memorandum, signed by the defendant, for the enforceability against him of a contract for the sale or other disposition of an interest in land could be circumvented by the claimant having partly performed the contract, although this equitable doctrine of part performance did not, strictly, allow the claimant to enforce the contract, but rather gave him an equitable claim which operated outside the   **5-26**

---

[170] For detailed discussion, see Cartwright (Misrepresentation), paras 13-38 to 13-54; D. Hodge, *Rectification*, 2nd edn (Sweet and Maxwell, 2016), paras 9-21 to 9-28.
[171] Law Com. No.164, see para.5-07 fn.26, para.5.6; Cartwright (Misrepresentation) para.13-54; *Oun v Ahmad* [2008] EWHC 545 (Ch); [2008] 2 P. & C.R. DG3 at [36]. See also *WG Mitchell (Gleneagles) Ltd v Jemstock One Ltd* [2006] EWHC 3644 (Ch) at [24] (Sir Andrew Morritt C., criticising the interpretation placed by the Inland Revenue on s.2(4)).
[172] See para.5-19. For cases where rectification has been ordered, see *Wright v Robert Leonard (Developments)* [1994] N.P.C. 49, CA; *Peters v Fairclough Homes Ltd* unreported, 10 December 2002 at [26]–[27].
[173] *Oun v Ahmad*, see para.5-25 fn.171, at [55] (Morgan J: the "express agreement to omit the term means that there is no defect or mistake in the recording of, or the expression of, the arrangement and it is beyond the ambit of rectification to write into the written agreement a term which the parties expressly agreed should not be so recorded": parties agreed on apportionment of price between the property, goodwill, and fixtures and fittings, but also agreed not to record it in the written document which therefore failed to comply with s.2); followed in *Francis v F Berndes Ltd* [2011] EWHC 3377 (Ch); [2012] 1 E.G.L.R. 117 at [41].

contract (and outside the statute).[174] Section 2 of the 1989 Act operates differently: if the statutory formalities are not complied with, there is no contract at all which can be partly performed; the doctrine of part performance has therefore not been carried over into the new provisions for formalities for land contracts.[175] However, the 1989 Act makes a rather similar provision that[176]

> "nothing in this section affects the creation or operation of resulting, implied or constructive trusts."

As did the provisions which it replaced, the 1989 Act expressly contemplates the operation of equitable doctrines outside the operation of s.2 itself—not now part performance, but the same equitable doctrines as are expressly allowed to operate outside the scope of statutory formality provisions relating to property.[177] Although the detail may differ, there is a consistency here in the policies relating to formalities for private law transactions: the statute lays down certain requirements (whether evidential or substantive,[178] and more or less onerous) but also contemplates[179] that there may be certain situations in which a party, not being able to demonstrate that the formalities have been effected, ought in fairness none the less to be able to enforce a transaction—if not *the* transaction, at least *a* transaction which may have the same or similar effect. And even if the statute makes clear by its language that such an exception to its requirements is possible, it is not the statute but Equity that forms the basis of the exception.

5-27   **Resulting, implied or constructive trusts**   Given the terms of s.2, it is clear that a transaction which finds its validity through the doctrines of resulting, implied or constructive trusts can have effect regardless of the fact that it could also be analysed as an agreement which failed to satisfy the formality requirements of the section for the creation of a valid contract. Such multiple characterisation of the

---

[174]   See para.5-06.

[175]   In *Singh v Beggs* (1996) 71 P. & C.R. 120, CA, at 122 Neill LJ doubted whether the doctrine of part performance had been abolished, on the basis that it was an equitable doctrine which could survive the repeal of LPA 1925 s.40; and see *Actionstrength Ltd v International Glass Engineering IN.GL.EN. SpA* [2003] UKHL 17; [2003] 2 A.C. 541 at [22]–[23] (Lord Hoffmann, noting that part performance was justifiable (i) as a form of estoppel, and (ii) as a substitute for the written memorandum as evidence of the contract). cf. *Yaxley v Gotts* [2000] Ch. 162, CA, at 172 (Robert Walker LJ: "it is clear that it has not survived"); Law Com No.164, see para.5-07 fn.26, para.6.4: "Contracts failing to comply with the formalities we recommend would be void and not merely enforceable. The doctrine of part performance would therefore cease to have effect in contracts concerning land ... but other remedies and doctrines would remain available as indicated, in particular equitable estoppel, rectification and collateral contracts".

[176]   LP(MP)A 1989 s.2(5).

[177]   LPA 1925 s.53(2) (allowing trusts as an exception to the formality requirements in s.53(1) for the creation or disposition of interests in land, a declaration of trust of land, and a disposition of an equitable interest or trust).

[178]   See paras 4-09, 4-10.

[179]   The Statute of Frauds 1677 s.4, did not expressly contemplate the doctrine of part performance which was developed by the courts of Equity soon after the Statute of Frauds itself, but this was then expressly mentioned in LPA 1925 s.40(2): see para.5-06. However, the exception for resulting, implied or constructive trusts, now found in LPA 1925 s.53(2) in relation to property formalities, was already mentioned in the Statute of Frauds s.8 ("where any conveyance shall be made of any lands or tenements by which at trust or confidence shall or may arise or result by the implication or construction of law, or be transferred or extinguished by an act or operation of law, than and in every such case such trust or confidence shall be of the like force and effect as the same would have been if this statute had not been made, anything herein before contained to the contrary notwithstanding").

factual (and therefore legal) basis of a transaction is not unusual in the context of land law: for example, there are cases where, on the facts, a permission to occupy land can be characterised as a contractual licence, which will have effect only as between the parties; or as giving rise to a constructive trust or an equity by estoppel (proprietary estoppel) which can bind third parties.[180]

This is not the place to discuss in detail the nature of trusts, nor the circumstances in which resulting, implied or constructive trusts may arise.[181] In brief, however, there will be such a trust where one party holds property which he is deemed in law[182] to hold on behalf or for the benefit of another. In the context of failed contracts for the sale of land it is constructive trusts which are most commonly in issue; and for such trusts there is no simple definition, and the range of circumstances in which they may arise is very wide. In general terms, however, it is where the legal holder of property cannot in conscience deny the other party's beneficial interest, typically because of the circumstances in which he has acquired it or because of what he has said and done in relation to the property on which the other party has acted so as to make it unconscionable to deny the latter's expectation of an interest in the property.[183] For our purposes, this is generally relevant where the parties have come to an agreement under which the holder of an estate in land is to create or transfer an interest in the land to the other, but that agreement fails to satisfy the requirements of s.2 of the Law of Property (Miscellaneous Provisions) Act 1989 and so cannot be enforced as a contract; but the intended recipient of the interest can show that he is entitled under a constructive trust to an interest—or even the very interest which he would have been entitled under the intended contract. In *Yaxley v Gotts*,[184] for example, the Court of Appeal held that a person who was promised an interest in a house if he undertook work on it could be granted the interest—or, at least, an interest which protected his expectation[185] —even though the arrangement was contained in an oral agreement which therefore failed to satisfy the requirements for a valid contract under s.2 of the 1989 Act. Other cases have accepted,[186] or rejected,[187] claims to an interest under a constructive trust on the application of the principles of equity for the creation of such trusts.

---

[180] e.g. *Re Sharpe* [1980] 1 W.L.R. 219 at 224, 225 (contractual licence would bind the other party but analysis as constructive trust necessary to bind other party's trustee in bankruptcy, or purchaser from the trustee); *Bannister v Bannister* [1948] 2 All E.R. 133, CA (undertaking by purchaser to permit vendor to occupy cottage rent-free created licence, but also gave rise to constructive trust; this might also be analysed as a case of proprietary estoppel); *Binions v Evans* [1972] Ch. 359, CA (undertaking to allow third party to occupy created licence but also constructive trust). See generally Cheshire and Burn, pp.933-935.

[181] See L. Tucker, N. Le Poidevin and J. Brightwell, *Lewin on Trusts*, 19th edn (Sweet & Maxwell, 2014, with supplements) Pt I, esp. Chs 7–9; Hanbury and Martin, Pt 2, esp. Chs 11 (Resulting Trusts), 12 (Constructive Trusts).

[182] i.e. by contrast with an express trust.

[183] Hanbury and Martin, para.12-001.

[184] [2000] Ch. 162, CA.

[185] The property was a house, converted into flats, which G was proposing to buy, and on which Y (a builder) was to do refurbishment works of the upper floors in return for getting the ground floor flat. The house was in fact bought by G's son, but he adopted the arrangements which his father had made with Y. The interest awarded by the trial judge (affirmed by CA) was a 99-year lease of the ground floor. CA held that Y's interest arose under a constructive trust, which therefore operated under LP(MP)A 1989 s.2(5): see at 177, 181, 193; but that it could also be analysed as proprietary estoppel: see para.5-28.

[186] *Kinane v Mackie-Conteh* [2005] EWCA Civ 45; [2005] 2 P. & C.R. DG3; *Oates v Stimson* [2006] EWCA Civ 548; [2006] All E.R. (D) 219 (May); *S v S* [2006] EWHC 2892 (Fam); [2007] F.L.R. 1123 at [56], [59] (constructive trust over equitable charge arising from parties' agreement (though

5-28   **Proprietary estoppel**   More controversial, however, is the claim to create an interest under the doctrine of proprietary estoppel in circumstances where the contract is void under s.2. The Court of Appeal in *Yaxley v Gotts*[188] held that the trial judge had been entitled to hold that the interest in the property arose under the doctrine of proprietary estoppel. In part, their argument was based on the close relationship between the doctrines of proprietary estoppel and constructive trust, and the idea that since s.2 itself allowed the operation of constructive trusts, this can itself justify the operation of proprietary estoppel, at least in a case where the facts could equally be resolved by the operation of the established principles of constructive trusts.[189] But the Court also took a broader perspective, and said that the doctrine of estoppel could operate outside the statute because it would not undermine the policy of the statute. Beldam LJ said[190]:

> "The general principle that a party cannot rely on an estoppel in the face of a statute depends upon the nature of the enactment, the purpose of the provision and the social policy behind it. This was not a provision aimed at prohibiting or outlawing agreements of a specific kind, though it had the effect of making agreements which did not comply with the required formalities void. This by itself is insufficient to raise such a significant public interest that an estoppel would be excluded."

---

void under s.2) which beneficiary relied on); *Ely v Robson* [2016] EWCA Civ 774; [2017] 1 F.L.R. 1704 (agreement to settle claim for declaration as to beneficial interests under Trusts of Land and Appointment of Trustees Act 1996 s.14); *Dowding v Matchmove* [2016] EWCA Civ 1233; [2017] 1 W.L.R. 749 at [28] ("common intention" constructive trust; criticised [2017] Conv. 146 at 89 (M. Dixon); 155–156 (T. Boncey and F. Ng): "when the Law Commission proposed s.2 in Law Com.164, they adopted the general principle that '[n]o reform should increase the likelihood of a contract for the sale (or other disposition) of land becoming binding before the parties have been able to obtain legal advice'. [Law Com 164 at [1.11]] The [common intention constructive trust] doctrine in its current form, however, creates a serious risk that parties who have every intention of involving lawyers in the transaction may enter into potentially binding agreements before they have a chance to consult them").

[187] *Ravenocean Ltd v Gardner* [2001] N.P.C. 44 (constructive trust unarguable: not inequitable to limit to restitutionary claim because unlike *Yaxley* it was a wholly executory contract under which nothing had been done other than incurring relatively small expenditure); *Newell v Tarrant* [2004] EWHC 772 (Ch) at [51]–[53] (equitable charge: no constructive trust because not unconscionable to rely on lack of formality under s.2 where contract would have been voidable for undue influence anyway); *Representative Body of the Church in Wales v Newton* [2005] EWHC 631 (QB), [2005] 16 E.G. 145 (C.S.) at [64] (agreement to assign lease: constructive trust cannot come into existence until conditions for transfer of beneficial interest fulfilled); *McGuane v Welch* [2008] EWCA Civ 785, [2008] 2 P. & C.R. 24 at [35] (constructive trust cannot be inferred or imposed contrary to the express agreement of the parties); *Singh v Sanghera* [2013] EWHC 956 (Ch), [2013] All E.R. (D) 187 (Apr) at [21] (agreement to create new lease or assign existing lease void under s.2; no constructive trust because landlord's conscience not affected).

[188] [2000] Ch. 162, CA.

[189] [2000] Ch. 162, CA at 180 (Robert Walker LJ: "the species of constructive trust based on 'common intention' ... is closely akin to, if not indistinguishable from, proprietary estoppel. Equity enforces it because it would be unconscionable for the other party to disregard the claimant's rights. Section 2(5) expressly saves the creation and operation of a constructive trust"), 193 (Beldam LJ "the provision that nothing in section 2 of the Act of 1989 is to affect the creation or operation of resulting, implied or constructive trusts effectively excludes from the operation of the section cases in which an interest in land might equally well be claimed by relying on constructive trust or proprietary estoppel"). cf. however, *Stack v Dowden* [2007] UKHL 17; [2007] 2 A.C. 432 at [37] (Lord Walker: "I am now rather less enthusiastic about the notion that proprietary estoppel and 'common interest' constructive trusts can or should be completely assimilated").

[190] [2000] Ch. 162, CA at 191. See also Robert Walker LJ at 174 and Clarke LJ at 182. This was later followed in the context of a failure to comply with the formalities of a deed under LP(MP)A 1989 s.1, in *Shah v Shah* [2001] EWCA Civ 527; [2002] Q.B. 35 at [19]–[20]; see para.7-16.

A further significant argument was that the Law Commission, in proposing the reform enacted in s.2, had expressly contemplated the proprietary estoppel should be available in appropriate cases as a means of giving effect to an agreement which would not satisfy the formality requirements.[191]

This general approach, accepting in principle that proprietary estoppel can apply to a case where a contract fails by virtue of s.2, was adopted by a number of cases after the decision in *Yaxley v Gotts*.[192] However, some doubt was cast on it by the decision of the House of Lords in *Cobbe v Yeoman's Row Management Ltd*[193] in which a claim for an interest under the doctrine of proprietary estoppel was rejected. This case was rather different from cases such as *Yaxley*, since it involved not a concluded agreement for the disposition of an interest in land, but a belief by the claimant, a property developer, that negotiations would lead to a concluded contract under which he would acquire an interest after obtaining planning permission for the proposed development of the property. The defendant refused to proceed after planning permission was granted, and no final agreement had yet been reached on all the terms of the proposed transaction: it was therefore a case where pre-contractual negotiations were broken off[194] rather than an agreement which had been made but failed for lack of formality under s.2 of the 1989 Act. The Court of Appeal in *Cobbe*[195] followed *Yaxley v Gotts* in accepting a case of proprietary estoppel; the House of Lords reversed this, emphasising that both parties were experienced in commercial transactions, knew that the contract was not yet binding and so took the risk of whether a contract had been concluded.[196] However, Lord Scott went further and appeared to reject the very possibility of proprietary estoppel being effective in a case where a contract fails for lack of formality under s.2[197]:

"Section 2 of the 1989 Act declares to be void any agreement for the acquisition of an interest in land that does not comply with the requisite formalities prescribed by the section. Subsection (5) expressly makes an exception for resulting, implied or constructive trusts. These may validly come into existence without compliance with the prescribed

---

[191] [2000] Ch. 162, CA at 182 (Clarke LJ), 190 (Beldam LJ); cf. Robert Walker LJ at 176. See Law Com. No.164, see para.5-07 fn.26, Pt V. The same point was made during the second reading of the Bill in the House of Lords: *Hansard* HL Vol.503, cols 603, 610.

[192] *Loubatieres v Mornington Estates (UK)* [2004] EWHC 825 (Ch) at [33] (but no estoppel on facts); *Kinane v Mackie-Conteh*, see para.5-27 fn.186, (proprietary estoppel applies at least where it overlaps with constructive trust); *Oates v Stimson*, see para.5-27 fn.186; *Scottish & Newcastle Plc v Lancashire Mortgage Corp Ltd* [2007] EWCA Civ 684; [2007] N.P.C. 84 at [55] (but there was no contract in this case anyway; the case was pleaded only on the basis of estoppel: at [53]); *McGuane v Welch*, see para.5-27 fn.187, at [37] (but no estoppel on the facts).

[193] [2008] UKHL 55; [2008] 1 W.L.R. 1752.

[194] See further Ch.2.

[195] [2006] EWCA Civ 1139; [2006] 1 W.L.R. 2964.

[196] [2008] UKHL 55; [2008] 1 W.L.R. 1752 at [18], [91]. However, since the claimant had, in obtaining planning permission which benefited the property, undertaken work beyond that normally expected in advance of a contract being concluded, he was entitled to a quantum meruit payment for his services: see at [42], [93]; see also paras 2-26, 2-27. See also *Thorner v Major* [2009] UKHL 18; [2009] 1 W.L.R. 776 at [92], [96] (Lord Neuberger, emphasising that the reason that the claim for estoppel failed in *Cobbe* was the fact that the parties had consciously not finalised their agreement, and that the party raising the estoppel was a highly experienced businessman); similarly Lord Neuberger of Abbotsbury, "The Stuffing of Minerva's Owl? Taxonomy and Taxidermy in Equity" [2009] C.L.J. 537 at 541-543; *Generator Developments Ltd v Lidl UK GmbH* [2018] EWCA Civ 396 at [78]–[79] (Lewison LJ: no equitable claim based on "*Pallant v Morgan* equity" in case of commercial parties, legally advised, who had not yet agreed terms and had expressed "subject to contract" qualification). See also para.4-13 fnn.98, 99.

[197] [2008] UKHL 55; [2008] 1 W.L.R. 1752 at [29].

formalities. Proprietary estoppel does not have the benefit of this exception. The question arises, therefore, whether a complete agreement for the acquisition of an interest in land that does not comply with the s.2 prescribed formalities, but would be specifically enforceable if it did can become enforceable via the route of proprietary estoppel. It is not necessary in the present case to answer this question, for the second agreement was not a complete agreement and, for that reason, would not have been specifically enforceable so long as it remained incomplete. My present view, however, is that proprietary estoppel cannot be prayed in aid in order to render enforceable an agreement that statute has declared to be void. The proposition that an owner of land can be estopped from asserting that an agreement is void for want of compliance with the requirements of s.2 is, in my opinion, unacceptable. The assertion is no more than the statute provides. Equity can surely not contradict the statute."

This goes too far: we have seen that the courts of Equity have been able in various contexts to admit remedies which, though operating outside the requirements set by a statute, have the effect of circumventing it.[198] Indeed, after *Cobbe*, courts have generally[199] continued to accept that, in a case where the facts are such that a claim based on proprietary estoppel could succeed, but for the existence of an agreement which constitutes a void contract by reason of failure to comply with s.2, the estoppel claim can succeed. However, this is sometimes still explained on the basis that it might in fact be covered by the exception in s.2(5) itself on the basis that proprietary estoppel in such cases operates through the mechanism of constructive trust.[200]

---

[198] e.g. the doctrine of part performance, developed after the Statute of Frauds 1677, although later incorporated in LPA 1925 s.40(2): see para.5-06; and see generally para.4-13 for the general equitable doctrine that a statute should not be an "engine of fraud".

[199] Lord Scott's statement was followed by Peter Smith J in *Hutchison v B&DF Ltd* [2008] EWHC 2286 (Ch); [2009] L. & T.R. 12 at [68].

[200] *Herbert v Doyle* [2008] EWHC 1950 (Ch) at [15] (Herbert QC: "Lord Scott's statement of his present view was avowedly obiter, and in my view it remains the case that, if all the requirements are otherwise satisfied for a claim based on proprietary estoppel to succeed, the claim will not fail solely because it also consists of an agreement which falls foul of s.2. The analysis of such a case may be that the court gives effect to the proprietary estoppel by recognising or imposing a constructive trust, and it is this which enables s.2(5) to apply"); *Brightlingsea Haven Ltd v Morris* [2008] EWHC 1928 (QB); [2009] 2 P. & C.R. 11 at [47] (Jack J: Lord Scott's rejection of the operation of proprietary estoppel in *Cobbe* at [29] "does not sit easily with those cases where it has been held that a proprietary estoppel may be given effect to by a constructive trust"); *Kinnear v Whittaker* [2011] EWHC 1479 (QB); [2011] 2 P. & C.R. DG20 at [28]–[29] (Bean J: "Lord Scott made it clear that these remarks were obiter. They are accordingly not binding on me. ... One of the members of the court in *Yaxley v Gotts* was Beldam LJ. He had been Chairman of the Law Commission at the time of its working paper and report on Formalities for Contracts for Sales of Land on which the 1989 Act was based. Like Hengham C.J.C.P. who in oral argument on a point of statutory interpretation in a case in 1307 (*Aumeye v Anon* YB 33-35 Edw.1 82) said to counsel 'do not gloss the statute, for we know it better than you: we made it', he was in a good position to say what the Commission had in mind"). See also Lord Neuberger of Abbotsbury [2009] C.L.J. 537 at 546 ("the very reason for mounting the proprietary estoppel claim is that there is no enforceable contract ... I suggest that s.2 offers no bar to a claim based in equity"); *Muhammad v ARY Properties Ltd* [2016] EWHC 1698 (Ch) at [47]–[49] (Master Matthews: proprietary estoppel is not about enforcing a contract at all, so s.2(5) [constructive trust] is a red herring); *Legg v Burton* [2017] EWHC 2088 (Ch); [2017] 4 W.L.R. 186 at [21]–[27] (Judge Paul Matthews); *Farrar v Miller* [2018] EWCA Civ 172 at [59]–[63] (Kitchin LJ, setting out arguments that a free-standing action based on proprietary estoppel does not frustrate the policy behind s.2); G. Owen and O. Rees, "Section 2(5) of the Law of Property (Miscellaneous Provisions) Act 1989: a Misconceived Approach?" [2011] Conv. 495 (arguing for the deletion of the reference in s.2(5) of the 1989 Act to resulting, implied and constructive trusts and for that section, if it is to be retained at all, to merely make reference to proprietary estoppel). For earlier

Other forms of estoppel   There are various different forms of estoppel.[201] The   **5-29**
most common form which may be raised by a party who seeks to give effect in
substance to an agreement which fails to comply with s.2 of the Law of Property
(Miscellaneous Provisions) Act 1989 is proprietary estoppel,[202] since it relates
specifically to interests in land, and can give effect not only to representations about
the parties' existing rights in land, but also to representations about future rights.[203]
There is therefore a possible overlap with facts giving rise to contracts for the
disposition of an interest in land. Other forms of estoppel may sometimes be
relevant. Promissory estoppel gives a remedy in certain circumstances to the party
who has relied on the other's non-contractual representation as to his future conduct,
but at present English law does not in principle allow promissory estoppel to create new obligations and so (except in the case of a modification of a contract) it is
not an alternative to a contract complying with s.2 of the 1989 Act.[204] Estoppel by
representation covers the case where one party makes a representation of present
fact (not the future[205]) on which the other relies, thereby barring the representor from
leading evidence in any later action to contradict his representation. Estoppel by
convention does not apply to representations about future rights, but to the parties' shared understanding or assumption about a state of facts or law, on which they
have acted and are then estopped from denying that state of facts of law. Although
there is no natural overlap between estoppel by representation or estoppel by
convention and the operation of s.2, there are situations where one party's statement of fact, or both parties' assumptions of fact or law, when acted upon, can have
the same effect as if their agreement had been properly formalised within s.2: for
example, if one party incorrectly represents that the contract has been signed in accordance with the section and the other party acts on the basis that the document
constitutes a valid contract.[206] However, the use of such forms of estoppel is limited,
and there is a similar concern here, as we have seen above,[207] not to allow the policy
of the statute to be undermined. For example, the mere fact that both parties think
that the agreement constitutes a valid contract when it does not comply with the section cannot give rise to an estoppel by convention,[208] although it is less clear whether

---

suggestions that proprietary estoppel may be analysed as a form of constructive trust, see *Re Basham*
[1986] 1 W.L.R. 1498 at 1504 (Nugee QC); Sir Christopher Slade, "The Informal Creation of
Interests in Land" (1984) Child & Co Oxford Lecture, 12.

[201] See generally paras 10-03 to 10-08.

[202] See para.5-28.

[203] Cheshire and Burn, pp.909–922.

[204] For the use of promissory estoppel in the modification of an existing contract, see Ch.10. For arguments about whether promissory estoppel might be developed to create new obligations, see paras
10-49 to 10-51.

[205] *Jorden v Money* (1854) H.L. Cas. 185 at 214-215, 226-227, 20 E.R. 868 at 882, 886.

[206] cf. *Shah v Shah*, see para.5-28 fn.190 (representation that deed had been executed in compliance with
requirements of LP(MP)A 1989 s.1).

[207] See para.5-28.

[208] *Godden v Merthyr Tydfil Housing Association* [1997] N.P.C. 1; (1997) 74 P. & C.R. D1 (Sir John
Balcombe: "At the end of the day it became apparent that he was seeking to rely on estoppel by
convention—that is that as both parties contracted in ignorance of the provisions of the Act, the association was estopped from relying on those provisions. This argument, if accepted, would drive a
coach and horses through a recent Act of Parliament enacted for very specific reasons of public
policy"), referred to by Clarke LJ in *Yaxley v Gotts*, see para.5-27 fn.184, at 182. For other cases
where estoppel by convention has been argued unsuccessfully in relation to s.2, see *McNicholas
Construction (Holdings) Ltd v Endemol UK Plc* [2003] EWHC 2472; [2003] 43 E.C. 136 (C.S.) at
[50]–[57] (no agreement, so no shared assumption to give rise to estoppel; it was only a hope that

one party's explicit representation of the validity of the contract, acted on by the other, might be able to give rise to an estoppel by representation.[209]

III. Consumer[210] Contracts for which Formalities are Required

5-30   **Formality as a means of consumer protection**   Of the aims commonly attributed to the use of formalities in private law transactions,[211] the one which particularly benefits the consumer is the *cautionary* aim: the use of formality to try to ensure that the party understands the transaction and considers it before becoming committed. Ways in which this can be achieved include requiring that the contract be not only in writing, signed by the consumer, but take a particular form,[212] designed to bring home to the consumer the nature of the transaction and any particular terms to which particular attention ought to be paid; and requiring the business party to provide information before or at the time of the contract, not only about the terms of the contract but also about other aspects of the transaction and its subject-matter. Such requirements fall within the scope of this chapter where the failure to comply has an impact on the validity or binding force of the contract, although as we shall see in the following paragraphs of this section the details of

---

there would be a deal in due course); *Scottish & Newcastle Plc v Lancashire Mortgage Corp Ltd*, see para.5-28 fn.192 (applied by trial judge as alternative to proprietary estoppel; CA rejected on facts because the parties' assumption related to a future (not existing) state of affairs: at [63]).

[209] Such an argument failed on the facts in *Peters v Fairclough Homes Ltd* unreported, 20 December 2002 at [24], but was in any event doubted by the judge (Gaunt QC) on the basis that non-compliance with s.2 may be only be excused by an estoppel in circumstances where there is a constructive trust within LP(MP)A 1989 s.2(5). cf. *Actionstrength Ltd v International Glass Engineering IN.GL.EN. SpA* [2003] UKHL 17; [2003] 2 A.C. 541 at [9], [51] (on facts, no representation that contract of guarantee, not evidenced by written memorandum with Statute of Frauds s.4, was enforceable; whether such a representation could found an estoppel was left open by Lord Hoffmann at [29] and Lord Clyde at [34]); see para.6-18.

[210] The definition of "consumer" varies, depending on its context and origin: it is not a term devised or defined by the common law, so its use in statutory texts depends on its definition in each statute. Many "consumer protection" provisions in English law result from the implementation of European directives, where "consumer" is generally defined as a natural person acting for purposes outside his trade, business or profession, although the detail of the definitions varies (see, e.g. see para.5-33 fn.245); but domestic legislation uses different definitions and sometimes even includes business activities: e.g. CCA 1974 defines a "consumer credit agreement" and a "consumer hire agreement" (see para.5-32) as one where the debtor is an "individual" (ss.8 (amended by CCA 2006 s.2(1)(a)), 15)—but there is no restriction to non-business purposes of the "individual", which includes a partnership of two or three persons, not all of whom are bodies corporate, and an unincorporated body of persons (s.189(1) (amended by CCA 2006 s.1). Thus, debtors and hirers who enter into the contract as sole traders, or small partnerships or unincorporated associations, are protected as much as private (non-business) parties.

[211] See para.4-03.

[212] Whether such forms achieve this cautionary aim is another matter and, no doubt, depends on what is required in any particular case. A form which is too detailed may well not in fact be read, even if the signature affirms that it has been; and a document which appears to be a standard approved form may be paid undue reverence without provoking the intended reflection on the transaction. In its proposals to reform the formalities for contracts for the sale or other disposition of an interest in land (Law Com. No.164, *Transfer of Land: Formalities for Contracts for Sale etc. of Land* (1987): see para.5-07) the Law Commission rejected the use of prescribed forms for contracts relating to land on the basis (inter alia) that "the cautionary role of prescribed forms appears fairly limited. In practice, warnings on prescribed forms, it is said, do not always have the desired effect. On the contrary, they may even lull a party into signing. People may be less cautious if they are signing what appears to them to be an 'approved' form" (Law Com. No.164, para.3.10).

this vary.[213] Other mechanisms of protection are used in relation to certain consumer contracts, such as giving consumers a time within which to change their mind and cancel the contract without penalty. Such a right of cancellation may not in itself be a requirement of form, but can be used in conjunction with formalities, and as one of the sanctions against the business party for failure to comply with the formality requirements.[214]

Formality is required only for particular consumer contracts Formality **5-31** requirements are the exception rather than the rule in English private law, and in the case of contracts each situation in which a particular formality is set for the creation of the contract has to be justified by reference to either the type of contract, or the type of party who needs the protection of the formality.[215] Even if consumers can be seen as a class requiring some form of general protection when dealing with businesses, it would not be appropriate to subject every consumer contract to a formality requirement.[216] Contracts for the sale of goods to consumers, for example, must be capable of being formed informally to allow for speedy, everyday purchases—although there are other mechanisms which the law can use in such contracts to provide protections for the consumer which do not delay or even prevent the formation of the contract itself in the way that setting formality rules might do.[217] However, there are certain types of contract where it is possible to say that consumers[218] deserve generally to be protected, either because of the significance of that type of transaction in itself for the average consumer or because it is a transaction in which there is an inherent risk that the business party will be able to take some form of advantage of the consumer in obtaining a quick and ill-considered decision on entering into the contract.[219] Types of contract which have been singled out by the law for protection of the consumer at the stage of forma-

---

[213] Some consumer protection regulations impose on the business party the duty to provide information at or before the time of the contract, but provides criminal sanctions for non-compliance, rather than affecting the validity of the contract: e.g. Package Travel and Linked Travel Arrangements Regulations 2018 (SI 2018/634), replacing with effect from 1 July 2018 the Package Travel, Package Holidays and Package Tours Regulations 1992 (SI 1992/3288), requires specific information to be provided (Pt 2), and sanctions the failure to provide the information (or the failure to provide it in the required form) by prosecution, and by implied condition in the contract which provides the consumer with a private remedy for non-compliance: see para.5-34, although the contract is not thereby void or unenforceable: reg.35.

[214] e.g. by providing that if the formality requirements are not satisfied, the period within which the consumer has the right to cancel the contract is extended: see para.5-33.

[215] See para.4-17.

[216] Consumer Contracts (Information, Cancellation and Additional Charges) Regulations 2013 (SI 2013/3134), Pt 2 imposes general requirements on contracts between a trader and a consumer in relation the provision of information by the trader; but there are exclusions of particular types of contract (e.g. gambling contracts, various forms of credit and financial services contracts, contracts relating to land, package travel contracts and timeshare contracts: reg.6; some of these will be subject to the duty to provide information under other provisions), although the duties in relation to contracts concluded on the trader's premises (reg.9) are more limited, and the information need not be given on paper or other durable form as in the case of off-premises contracts (reg.10(2)) or in a way appropriate to the means of distance communication in the case of a distance contract (reg.13(1)).

[217] e.g. by controlling the terms of the contract to protect the consumer against unfairness (Consumer Rights Act 2015 Pt 2), or by implying terms as to the quality of the goods which are not capable of exclusion as against the consumer (Consumer Rights Act 2015 ss.9, 31); or by providing better remedies for the consumer against a trader in the event of breach of contact (Consumer Rights Act 2015 s.19).

[218] On the meaning of "consumer", see para.5-30 fn.210.

[219] There are of course other general doctrines of contract law which can provide targeted protection

tion include consumer credit and consumer hire contracts,[220] transactions which are entered into in the consumer's home or place of work, or at a distance,[221] package travel contracts[222] and timeshare contracts.[223]

5-32   **Consumer credit contracts and consumer hire contracts**[224]   The Consumer Credit Act 1974 Pt V (as amended[225]) makes provision for the formation of regulated consumer credit and regulated consumer hire agreements,[226] and either by its own provisions or by regulations made under the Act[227] it requires certain specified information to be provided to the debtor or hirer both before[228] and after[229] the agreement has been entered into, and it regulates in considerable detail the form, content, and manner of execution of regulated agreements.[230] Sections 60[231] and 61, which require the detail of the form and content of agreements to be contained in

---

in particular cases, such as duress, undue influence and "unconscionable bargains": Chitty, Ch.8; Treitel, Ch.10; Anson, Ch.10; Cheshire, Fifoot and Furmston, pp.394–414. However, the prophylactic use of formality for types of contract where there may be potential risks of this kind enables a general solution which therefore does not require evidence of particular wrongdoing by the business party before the transaction can be challenged. On the question whether it is possible for the parties to contract *into* a statutory regime, such as the CCA, where their agreement does not otherwise fall within the Act, see *NRAM Plc v McAdam* [2015] EWCA Civ 751; [2016] Bus. L.R. 232.

[220] See para.5-32. The Consumer Credit Act 1974 was enacted following the *Report of the Committee on Consumer Credit* (HMSO, 1971), Cmnd.4596 (the Crowther Report), which conducted a wide-ranging review and concluded that there was a need for better protection for consumers in credit transactions: see R.M. Goode, *Consumer Credit Law* (Butterworths, 1989).

[221] See para.5-33.

[222] See para.5-34.

[223] See para.5-35.

[224] See further Chitty, Ch.39.

[225] This was originally a domestic provision but has been amended by (inter alia) SI 2010/1010 which implements Directive 2008/48/EC on credit agreements for consumers, and SI 2015/910 which implements Directive 2014/17/EU on credit agreements for consumers relating to residential immovable property.

[226] For the definitions of (regulated) consumer credit and (regulated) consumer hire agreements see CCA 1974 ss.8 (amended by CCA 2006 and SI 2015/910) and 15 (amended by CCA 2006 and SI 2013/1881) respectively. See also para.5-30 fn.210.

[227] Consumer Credit (Agreements) Regulations 1983 (SI 1983/1553), amended principally by SI 2004/1482; Consumer Credit (Agreements) Regulations 2010 (SI 2010/1014), implementing art.10 of Directive 2008/48/EC and imposing certain more stringent requirements in relation to consumer credit agreements within the meaning of the Directive (excluding credit wholly or predominantly for business purposes; see para.5-30 fn.210), amended by the Mortgage Credit Directive Order 2015 (SI 2015/910), implementing Directive 2014/17/EU. In consequence, the 1983 Regulations apply to hire agreements, and to credit agreements (where the debtor is an individual) secured on land, for credit in excess of £60,260 (other than renovation agreements), and "business" credit agreements; the 2010 Regulations apply to other regulated consumer credit agreements, although the creditor can choose to adopt the regime set by the 2010 Regulations in cases where it would not otherwise apply. See SI 1983/1553 art.8 (amended by SI 2010/1014); SI 2010/1014 reg.2; Chitty, para.39-076.

[228] See, e.g. for credit agreements, CCA 1974 s.55C (copy of draft agreement to be provided in advance on request), added by SI 2010/1010.

[229] CCA 1974 ss.61A (copy of executed agreement to be provided; added by SI 2010/1010); 64 (notice of cancellation rights where agreement is cancellable within s.67).

[230] See also CCA 1974 s.105 (security instruments in relation to regulated agreement to be in writing; form and content of documents to be prescribed by regulations (see Consumer Credit (Guarantees and Indemnities) Regulations 1983 (SI 1983/1556)), and security instrument not expressed in writing or improperly executed is enforceable against the surety on order of the court only).

[231] Section 60(1) was amended by SI 2013/1881 and SI 2013/1882.

regulations, and the signature of the agreement, make clear the cautionary function of the formality:

"**60.**—(1) The Treasury shall make regulations as to the form and content of documents embodying regulated agreements, and the regulations shall contain such provisions as appear to them appropriate with a view to ensuring that the debtor or hirer is made aware of—

(a) the rights and duties conferred or imposed on him by the agreement,

(b) the amount and rate of the total charge for credit (in the case of a consumer credit agreement),

(c) the protection and remedies available to him under this Act, and

(d) any other matters which, in the opinion of the Treasury, it is desirable for him to know about in connection with the agreement.

(2) Regulations under subsection (1) may in particular—

(a) require specified information to be included in the prescribed manner in documents, and other specified material to be excluded;

(b) contain requirements to ensure that specified information is clearly brought to the attention of the debtor or hirer, and that one part of a document is not given insufficient or excessive prominence compared with another.

61.—(1) A regulated agreement is not properly executed unless

(a) a document in the prescribed form itself containing all the prescribed terms and conforming to regulations under section 60(1) is signed in the prescribed manner both by the debtor or hirer and by or on behalf of the creditor or owner, and

(b) the document embodies all the terms of the agreement, other than implied terms, and

(c) the document is, when presented or sent to the debtor or hirer for signature, in such a state that all its terms are readily legible."

The regulations made under the Act set out very detailed requirements for the form of the agreement, provisions it must contain relating to the terms of the agreement itself, statements of protection and remedies available to debtors or hirers, and a signature box—and they even prescribe the order in which these things must be set out in the document and certain headings that must be used to draw the reader's attention, and require that information must be presented in a clear and concise manner, with wording easily legible and of a colour readily distinguishable from its background.[232] There are also detailed provisions for the method of signature.[233]

If an agreement fails to contain the required information, or to be signed in accordance with the statutory requirements, it is "not properly executed",[234] for which the sanction is that it is enforceable by the creditor against the debtor or hirer on

---

[232] Consumer Credit (Agreements) Regulations 1983, see para.5-32 fn.227, regs 2 (regulated consumer credit agreements) 3 (regulated consumer hire agreements), 6(2) (form of lettering on documents); Consumer Credit (Agreements) Regulations 2010, see para.5-32 fn.227, reg.3; all requiring agreements to include particular information and statements set out in Schedules to the respective Regulations.

[233] Consumer Credit (Agreements) Regulations 1983, see para.5-32 fn.227, reg.6; Consumer Credit (Agreements) Regulations 2010, see para.5-32 fn.227, reg.4. The agreement may be concluded by the use of electronic communications, and the signature may be an electronic signature: Consumer Credit (Agreements) Regulations 2010 reg.4(5); *Bassano v Toft* [2014] EWHC 377 (QB); [2014] E.C.C. 14 at [42]–[44].

[234] CCA 1974 s.61(1), above.

an order of the court only.[235] Section 127 provides that where there is an application to enforce the improperly executed agreement, the court must exercise a structured discretion[236]:

> "the court shall dismiss the application if, but only if, it considers it just to do so having regard to—
>
> (i) prejudice caused to any person by the contravention in question, and the degree of culpability for it; and
>
> (ii) the powers conferred on the court by subsection (2)[237] and sections 135 and 136.[238]"

In its original formulation, s.127 contained further provisions which severely limited the circumstances in which this discretion was available,[239] but these were repealed in 2007.[240]

5-33   **Distance or doorstep ("off-premises") contracts**   The Regulations governing distance contracts[241] and doorstep ("off-premises") contracts[242] operate rather differently from those governing consumer credit and consumer hire contracts discussed in para.5-32. The Regulations prescribe information which must be

---

[235] CCA 1974 s.65(1).

[236] CCA 1974 s.127(1)(a).

[237] [i.e. in making an enforcement order, the power to reduce or discharge sums due by the debtor or hirer as compensation for prejudice suffered as a result of the contravention.]

[238] [i.e. power to impose conditions on the order, or suspend its operation, and to amend any agreement or security.]

[239] See esp. CCA 1974 s.127(3), applied in *Dimond v Lovell* [2002] 1 A.C. 384, HL (consumer credit agreement not properly executed because it did not contain prescribed information, so it was "irredeemably unenforceable" under CCA 1974 s.127(3): Lord Hoffmann at 397). Although it had this automatic effect, s.127(3) was not incompatible with the European Convention on Human Rights: see *Wilson v First County Trust (No.2)* [2003] UKHL 40; [2004] 1 A.C. 816 where HL rejected claims that s.127(3) was incompatible with art.6 (on the basis that it restricted not procedural rights, but the substantive rights of the creditor by rendering an improperly executed agreement unenforceable) nor with art.1 of the First Protocol (on the basis that, although contractual rights are "possessions" within art.1, the agreement was unenforceable from the outset so the creditor had no contractual rights to which art.1 could apply; and the denial of remedies following an improperly executed agreement was a proportionate means of achieving a legitimate aim of consumer protection).

[240] CCA 2006 s.15, in force from 6 April 2007 (SI 2007/123), repealing subss.(3) to (5) of s.127 as it was originally enacted.

[241] Distance contracts for financial services are governed by Financial Services (Distance Marketing) Regulations 2004 (SI 2004/2095), as amended, implementing Directive 2002/65/EC; other distance contracts are governed by Consumer Contracts (Information, Cancellation and Additional Charges) Regulations 2013 (SI 2013/3134), as amended, implementing with effect from 13 June 2014 Directive 2011/83/EU and replacing Consumer Protection (Distance Selling) Regulations 2000 (SI 2000/2334), as amended, implementing Directive 97/7/EC. The 2013 Regulations are general, but exclude certain types of contract (e.g. gambling contracts (including the National Lottery), various forms of credit and financial services contracts, contracts relating to land, package travel contracts and timeshare contracts: reg.6), thus generally covering distance contracts for the supply of goods, digital content and services. The 2004 Regulations exclude from their operation provisions which would overlap with those which are already covered by other similar consumer protection provisions, such as the cancellation rights already provided for related agreements under SI 2013/3134, or for certain credit agreements under CCA 1974: SI 2004/2095 reg.11 as amended by SI 2013/3134.

[242] SI 2013/3134, see para.5-33 fn.241, replacing Cancellation of Contracts made in a Consumer's Home or Place of Work etc. Regulations 2008 (SI 2008/1816); the 2008 Regulations revoked SI 1987/2117 and reimplemented Directive 85/577/EEC.

provided by a business (or trader) concluding a distance contract[243] or an off-premises contract[244] with a consumer,[245] before the consumer is bound by the contract,[246] and require the business or trader to confirm the contract and to provide the information on paper or in another durable medium.[247] The information which must be provided includes such things as a description of the main characteristics of the goods or services or the financial service, and matters relating to the price which the consumer must pay, thereby ensuring that the consumer is provided with sufficient detailed information to take an informed decision on the contract.

The fact that the consumer has not had an opportunity in a distance contract to see the product or ascertain the value of the service before concluding the contract has been said[248] to be the justification for giving a right of cancellation, but in the case of both distance contracts and off-premises contracts the cancellation period is used also as a limited sanction for non-compliance with the duties to provide information. The consumer generally has the right to cancel a distance or off-premises contract without giving any reason and without incurring liability[249]; and

---

[243] SI 2013/3134, see para.5-33 fn.241, reg.5: "a contract [subject to exclusions in reg.6: see para.5-33 fn.241] concluded between a trader and a consumer under an organised distance sales or service-provision scheme without the simultaneous physical presence of the trader and the consumer, with the exclusive use of one or more means of distance communication up to and including the time at which the contract is concluded"; SI 2004/2095 reg.2: "any contract concerning one or more financial services concluded between a supplier and a consumer under an organised distance sales or service-provision scheme run by the supplier or by an intermediary, who, for the purpose of that contract, makes exclusive use of one or more means of distance communication up to and including the time at which the contract is concluded".

[244] SI 2013/3134, see para.5-33 fn.241, reg.5: "a contract [subject to exclusions in reg.6: see para.5-33 fn.241] between a trader and a consumer [where the payment to be made by the consumer is more than £42: reg.7(4)] which is any of these—(a) a contract concluded in the simultaneous physical presence of the trader and the consumer, in a place which is not the business premises of the trader; (b) a contract for which an offer was made by the consumer in the simultaneous physical presence of the trader and the consumer, in a place which is not the business premises of the trader; (c) a contract concluded on the business premises of the trader or through any means of distance communication immediately after the consumer was personally and individually addressed in a place which is not the business premises of the trader in the simultaneous physical presence of the trader and the consumer; (d) a contract concluded during an excursion organised by the trader with the aim or effect of promoting and selling goods or services to the consumer".

[245] "Consumer" is defined as an individual acting for purposes outside his business (SI 2004/2095 reg.2(1)) or wholly or mainly outside his trade, business, craft or profession (SI 2013/3134 reg.4; the words "wholly or mainly" have been added in the implementation and do not appear in Directive 2011/83/EU art.2(1), but accord with Recital 17 of the Directive); cf. para.5-30 fn.210.

[246] SI 2013/3134, see para.5-33 fn.241, regs 10 (off-premises contract), 13 (distance contract; and see reg.14 for additional requirements where the distance contract is concluded by electronic means); SI 2004/2095, see para.5-33 fn.241, reg.7 (distance financial services contract).

[247] SI 2013/3134, see para.5-33 fn.241, regs 12 (off-premises contract: paper or, if the consumer agrees, another durable medium) and 16 (distance contract: durable medium), to be provided within a reasonable time after the conclusion of the contract, if it was not already so provided before the contact was concluded; but in any event not later than the time of delivery of any goods supplied under the contract, and before performance begins of any service supplied under the contract; SI 2004/2095, see para.5-33 fn.241, reg.8 (distance financial services contract: either in good time prior to the consumer being bound by the contract or immediately after the conclusion of the contract). Directive 2011/83/EU Recital 23, explains that "durable media ... include in particular paper, USB sticks, CD-ROMs, DVDs, memory cards or the hard disks of computers as well as e-mails".

[248] See Directive 97/7/EC Recital 14.

[249] SI 2013/3134, see para.5-33 fn.241, reg.29 (distance or off-premises contract: certain limitations on the right are set out also in reg.28); SI 2004/2095, see para.5-33 fn.241, reg.9 (distance financial services contract: certain limitations on the right are set out also in reg.11).

the cancellation period is 14 days, normally beginning on day on which the contract is concluded but in the case of sales contracts this is varied to the day when the goods come into the physical possession of the consumer or his nominee.[250] Where, however, the business or trader has not complied with the duty to provide information—including the duty to inform the consumer of his right to cancel the contract[251]—the cancellation period is extended until 14 days after the consumer receives the required information. There is a long-stop period of 12 months for this extension, except for a distance contract for the provision of financial services for which is no long-stop period, so the cancellation right remains until 14 days from the day when the consumer receives the last of the required information.[252]

5-34   **Package travel contracts**   Contracts for package travel are required to comply with regulations as to their contents and form.[253] Before a package travel contract is concluded the non-consumer (the organiser or retailer of the package) must provide specified information in a clear, comprehensible and prominent manner and, where the information is provided in writing, in a legible form[254]; and must ensure that the package travel contract is in plain and intelligible language and, where the contract (or part of the contract) is in writing, the contract, or the part of the contract, is in a legible form, and sets out the full content of the package, including specified information.[255] The sanction for non-compliance is different from that in the case of the other consumer protection statutes discussed in the previous paragraphs of this section: here, it is an implied condition of the contract that the non-consumer (the organiser or retailer of the package) complies with the requirements as to contents and the form of the contract,[256] thus giving the consumer the right to be discharged from the contract.

5-35   **Timeshare and other holiday accommodation contracts**   Certain holiday accommodation contracts between a trader and a consumer—timeshare contract and long-term holiday contracts, contracts under which the trader assists the consumer

---

[250] SI 2013/3134, see para.5-33 fn.241, reg.30 (distance or off-premises contract); SI 2004/2095, see para.5-33 fn.241, reg.10 (distance financial services contract).

[251] SI 2013/3134, see para.5-33 fn.241, Sch.2 para.(l) (distance or off-premises contract); SI 2004/2095, see para.5-33 fn.241, Sch.1 para.13 (distance financial services contract).

[252] SI 2004/2095, see para.5-33 fn.241, reg.10. In the case of a distance contract relating to life insurance or a personal pension the period is 30 calendar days rather than 14 calendar days: SI 2004/2095 reg.10(5). Exceptions to the right to cancel are set out in reg.11 (including cases where the contract is cancelled, or there are cancellation rights, under other provisions: see para.5-33 fn.241). For a purposive interpretation of the earlier provisions (SI 2008/1816) to ensure that the trader's failure to give notice of the right to cancel did not deprive the consumer of the statutory right to cancel, see *Swift v Robertson* [2014] UKSC 50; [2014] 1 W.L.R. 3438.

[253] Package Travel and Linked Travel Arrangements Regulations 2018 (SI 2018/634), implementing Directive (EU) 2015/2302 (replacing with effect from 1 July 2018 the Package Travel, Package Holidays and Package Tours Regulations 1992 (SI 1992/3288), which implemented Directive 90/314/EEC), Pt 2 and Scheds. A "package travel contract" means a contract on a package as a whole or, if the package is provided under separate contracts, all contracts covering the travel services included in the package: reg.2(1); and a "package" means a combination of at least two different types of travel services for the purpose of the same trip or holiday: reg.2(5), which gives further definition.

[254] SI 2018/634 reg.5(4).

[255] SI 2018/634 reg.7(1), (2).

[256] SI 2018/634, regs 6(4), 7(10).9(3). Other requirements on the organiser or retailer to provide information, outside the contract itself, are sanctioned by criminal penalties, not by affecting the validity of the contract: see para.5-30 fn.213.

in buying or selling rights under such contracts, and timeshare exchange contracts—are required to comply with regulations in relation to their form.[257] The contract must be in writing and include specified key information, and a standard withdrawal form[258] to facilitate the exercise by the consumer of the right of withdrawal from the contract given by the regulations.[259] Failure to comply with the formality requirement renders the contract unenforceable against the consumer.[260] The consumer may exercise a right of withdrawal for 14 days from the date of the contract (or, if later, the date on which the consumer receives a copy of the contract) but only if the contract contains the standard withdrawal form and the required key information; there is a long-stop period for withdrawal of the later of three months and 15 days if the key information is not provided, and one year and 14 days if the standard withdrawal form is not included.[261] Again, therefore, the lengthened period for cancellation (here termed "withdrawal") is used as a sanction to encourage the trader to provide the information which the consumer needs in order to be properly informed about the transaction.

IV.   OTHER CONTRACTS FOR WHICH WRITING IS REQUIRED AS A SUBSTANTIVE FORMALITY

Bills of exchange and promissory notes   A bill of exchange, such as a cheque,   **5-36**
must be in writing,[262] signed by the person giving it; and the acceptance of the bill is invalid unless it is in written on the bill and signed by the drawee, or his agent, although the signature without additional words is sufficient to indicate acceptance.[263] A promissory note must also be made in writing and signed by the maker or his agent.[264] Corporations may execute such instruments either by the signature of an authorised agent, or by their corporate seal.[265]

---

[257] Timeshare, Holiday Products, Resale and Exchange Contracts Regulations 2010 (SI 2010/2960), implementing Directive 2008/122/EC. For the definitions of the types of contract covered by the Regulations, see Pt 2.

[258] Set out in SI 2010/2960 Sch.5.

[259] SI 2010/2960 reg.15.

[260] SI 2010/2960 reg.15(8), which also makes contravention a criminal offence. There are also requirements for the trader to provide key information to the consumer before entering into the contract, contravention of which is a criminal offence: reg.12, which is also actionable in civil proceedings and the civil liability cannot be excluded: art.35(1), (4), (5).

[261] SI 2010/2960 reg.21.

[262] Although a bill of exchange or promissory note must be in writing, provision is now made for cheques and other bills of exchange or promissory notes (other than banknotes) to be presented to a bank by electronic means, by the provision of an electronic image of both faces of the instrument instead of by presenting the physical instrument: Bills of Exchange Act 1882, Pt 4A, added by Small Business, Enterprise and Employment Act 2015 s.13.

[263] Bills of Exchange Act 1882 ss.3(1) ("A bill of exchange is an unconditional order in writing, addressed by one person to another, signed by the person giving it, requiring the person to whom it is addressed to pay on demand or at a fixed or determinable future time a sum certain in money to or to the order of a specified person, or to bearer"); 17(2) (acceptance by drawee); 91(1) (signature by agent). An instrument which does not comply with the conditions set by s.3(1) is not a bill of exchange: s.3(2). On bills of exchange generally, see Chitty, Ch.34; J.M. Phillips, I. Higgins and R. Hanke, *Byles on Bills of Exchange and Cheques*, 30th edn (Sweet & Maxwell, 2018).

[264] Bills of Exchange Act 1882 ss.83(1) ("A promissory note is an unconditional promise in writing made by one person to another signed by the maker, engaging to pay, on demand or at a fixed or determinable future time, a sum certain in money, to, or to the order of, a specified person or to bearer"); 91(1) (signature by agent). Bankers' cheques are bills of exchange, but are subject to certain special rules under Pt III of the Act. Promissory notes are subject to the provisions of the Act relat-

5-37   **Estate agents' contracts**   Where an estate agent enters into a contract to undertake work for a client, or the parties agree to vary an existing contract for estate agency work, the estate agent must first give the client prescribed information, in writing, about such matters as the client's potential liability to pay the agent under the contract; the sanction for non-compliance is that the contract is not enforceable by the agent without an order of the court.[266]

5-38   **Regulatory regimes; claims management contracts**   Some regulatory regimes also provide for the formality of written contracts as part of their regulatory rules. For example, a contract between a claims management company and a client must be in writing, signed by the client, and the company must not take payment from the client until the contract is signed; and the contract terms must be clear and prescribed information must be provided by the business to the client either in writing or electronically, before the contract is agreed.[267]

5-39   **Statutory requirements of writing which do not affect the substantive validity or enforceability of the contract**   There are various types of contract for which statute imposes a requirement of writing but without depriving the contract of its substantive validity or enforceability in the event of non-compliance. For example, the contract of employment need not be in writing, but no later than two months after the beginning of the employment the employer must give the employee a written statement of prescribed particulars of employment.[268] Failure by the employer to provide the written statement does not affect the validity of the contract, but the employee may require a reference to be made to an employment tribunal to determine what particulars ought to have been included.[269] However, an

---

ing to bills of exchange with certain modifications: s.89.

[265] Bills of Exchange Act 1882 s.91(2).

[266] Estate Agents Act 1979 s.18; Estate Agents (Provision of Information) Regulations 1991 (SI 1991/859). In such a case the court exercises a structured discretion: Estate Agents Act 1979 s.18(6): "(a) the court shall dismiss the application if, but only if, it considers it just to do so having regard to prejudice caused to the client by the agent's failure to comply with his obligation and the degree of culpability for the failure; and (b) where the court does not dismiss the application, it may nevertheless order that any sum payable by the client under the contract or, as the case may be, under the contract as varied shall be reduced or discharged so as to compensate the client for prejudice suffered as a result of the agent's failure to comply with his obligation". This is similar to the court's discretion in enforcing an improperly executed consumer credit agreement: see para.5-32. For the approach a court should take in exercising the discretion under the 1979 Act, see *Wells v Devani* [2016] EWCA Civ 1106; [2017] Q.B. 959 (where there was, however, no concluded contract between the agent and the prospective client).

[267] Ministry of Justice Claims Management Regulation Unit, Conduct of Authorised Persons Rules 2014, Client Specific Rule 11, made under Compensation (Claims Management Services) Regulations 2006 (SI 2006/3322): see *https://www.gov.uk/government/publications/claims-management-regulation-conduct-of-authorised-person-rules-2014*. The requirement of writing was introduced with effect from 8 July 2013 following a review and public consultation by the Ministry, in order to provide better information and other protection for consumers.

[268] Employment Rights Act 1996 s.1. If there are later changes to any of the particulars, a written statement must be given at the earliest opportunity, and not later than one month after the change: Employment Rights Act 1996 s.4.

[269] Employment Rights Act 1996 s.11. The written statement need not be the contract, and is only evidence of what the employer believes the terms to be: any question of interpretation of the terms of the contract is not for determination under s.11: *Owens v Multilux Ltd* [1974] I.R.L.R. 113, NIRC, at 114; M. Jefferson (ed.), Sweet & Maxwell's Encyclopedia of Employment Law (looseleaf), para.2H-7. However, the employer can satisfy the requirement to provide a written statement by giv-

apprenticeship agreement if it is to satisfy the statutory definition of such an agreement[270] must be in the form of a written statement of particulars of employment or a document in writing in the form of a contract of employment or letter of engagement.[271] In the case of the employment of seamen in a UK ship, there must be an agreement in writing signed by the employer and the employee[272]; non-compliance does not affect the validity of the contract of employment, but the crew agreement must be carried in the ship whenever it goes to sea, and the master or the person employing the crew are criminally liable (and the ship may be detained) if the ship goes to sea or attempts to go to sea in contravention of these requirements.[273] A commercial agent and his principal are each entitled to receive from the other, on request, a signed written document setting out the terms of the agency contract.[274] And the landlord must provide a rent book or similar document, containing prescribed information, to a tenant under a residential weekly tenancy.[275]

V. WRITING AS A SUBSTANTIVE FORMALITY FOR THE VARIATION OF A CONTRACT

Formalities required by law   The variation of an existing contract by agreement of the parties, whether it supersedes the initial contract (e.g. by novation) or simply modifies one or more terms of the contract, must satisfy the same rules as are set for the formation of the initial contract, at least if the varied contract is to have the same binding force as the initial contract.[276] Where the law sets a specific formality as a substantive condition for the formation of a contract of a particular type, as a general rule the same formality will be required for a contractual variation of such a contract. Section 2 of the Law of Property (Miscellaneous Provisions) Act 1989 therefore applies to an agreement to vary a term material to a contract which was itself subject to the formality requirements of the section.[277] It

5-40

---

ing the employee a document in writing in the form of a contract of employment or letter of engagement which contains the required information, given before or within the required period after the beginning of the employment: ss.7A, 7B, added by Employment Act 2002 s.37.

[270] Apprenticeships, Skills, Children and Learning Act 2009 s.32(1), (2)(b).

[271] Apprenticeships (Form of Apprenticeship Agreement) Regulations (SI 2012/844) reg.2.

[272] Merchant Shipping Act 1995 s.25: a "crew agreement", which is normally made as a single agreement with all the crew on a ship, but there may be more than one crew agreement for a ship, and a single crew agreement may relate to more than one ship.

[273] Merchant Shipping Act 1995 s.25.

[274] Commercial Agents (Council Directive) Regulations 1993 (SI 1993/3053) reg.13. Any purported waiver of the right is void (reg.13(2)) but non-compliance does not affect the validity of the agency contract itself.

[275] Landlord and Tenant Act 1985 ss.4, 5. Non-compliance does not affect the validity of the tenancy under which the landlord is still entitled to the rent: *Shaw v Groom* [1970] 2 Q.B. 504, CA; but the landlord and anyone demanding or receiving rent on behalf of the landlord commits a criminal offence: s.7.

[276] See para.1-02.

[277] *McCausland v Duncan Lawrie Ltd* [1997] 1 W.L.R. 38, CA at 49 (Morritt LJ: "There would be little point in requiring that the original contract comply with section 2 if it might be varied wholly informally"); *Kilcarne Holdings Ltd v Targetfollow (Birmingham) Ltd* [2004] EWHC 2547 (Ch); [2005] 2 P. & C.R. 8 at [198] (if contract falls within s.2 at its inception, any material variation must comply with s.2); *Keay v Morris Homes (West Midlands) Ltd* [2012] EWCA Civ 900; [2012] 1 W.L.R. 2855 at [31]. For this purpose, "material" terms include the completion date: *McCausland v Duncan Lawrie Ltd*; and any variation (even modest) to the price: *MP Kemp Ltd v Bullen Developments Ltd* [2014] EWHC 2009 (Ch) at [37]. In order to satisfy s.2, the variation need not spell out in detail why the parties have agreed to vary the original agreement, only that the new contract set

does not, however, apply to a contract which is designed not to vary the contract but only to rescind (or discharge) it.[278] Moreover, apart from the statute, the common law does not require any particular formality to be observed for a contract which discharges another existing contract.[279]

5-41   **Formalities required by the contract**   Sometimes the parties—particularly commercial parties—provide in their contract that any variation will not be effective unless it complies with a particular form, such as being set out in writing and signed by both parties. After some initial hesitation,[280] in 2016 the Court of Appeal held that such clauses do not bind the parties: first in a decision where the point was strictly obiter, although it had been subject to full argument[281]; and again by a differently-constituted court on a point of decision.[282] This was criticised by some academic writers, mainly on the basis that it failed to give effect to the parties' clearly expressed intentions in the original contract and therefore undermined certainty in commercial contracts,[283] although it is evident that the arguments are not one-sided. As one writer put it[284]:

> "There are strong commercial arguments in favour of giving effect to such clauses: they promote certainty, avoid false or frivolous claims of an oral agreement and can usefully prevent a person in a large organisation having a conversation or producing a document which unwittingly and unintentionally is inconsistent with a provision in a contract between the organisation and a counterparty... Conversely, there are strong counter-arguments of principle—freedom of contract means that parties cannot fetter their future conduct (reminiscent of topical arguments about parliamentary sovereignty)."

In 2018, however, the Supreme Court held by a majority that the law does give effect to a contractual provision requiring specified formalities to be observed for a variation: any purported variation by the parties in contravention of such a provision is therefore invalid.[285] This may be seen as a triumph of pragmatism (com-

---

out the agreed terms in their entirety: *HL Estates Ltd v Parker-Lake Homes Ltd* [2003] EWHC 604 (Ch) at [32].

[278] *Kilcarne Holdings Ltd v Targetfollow (Birmingham) Ltd*, see para.5-40 fn.277, at [208], applying *McCausland v Duncan Lawrie Ltd*, , see para.5-40 fn.277, and *Morris v Baron & Co* [1918] A.C. 1, HL.

[279] *Kilcarne Holdings Ltd v Targetfollow (Birmingham) Ltd*, see para.5-40 fn.277, at [208].

[280] In *I-Way Ltd v World Online Telecom UK Ltd* [2002] EWCA Civ 413, CA in an interlocutory appeal heard argument based on American authorities (and in particular the UCC which provides in §2–209(2) that "A signed agreement which excludes modification or rescission except by signed writing cannot otherwise be modified or rescinded") and concluded that the law in England is not settled, although appeared to lean in favour of the informal overriding of a clause excluding unwritten modification. Earlier, in *United Bank Ltd v Asif* unreported, 11 February 2000, CA had approved the judgment below which had concluded that no oral variation of the written terms could have any legal effect. Both cases were discussed and explained by Beatson LJ in *Globe Motors Inc v TRW Lucas Varity Electric Steering Ltd* [2016] EWCA Civ 396; [2016] 1 C.L.C. 712 at [102]–[105].

[281] *Globe Motors Inc v TRW Lucas Varity Electric Steering Ltd*, see para.5-41 fn.280, at [96].

[282] *MWB Business Exchange Centres Ltd v Rock Advertising Ltd* [2016] EWCA Civ 553; [2017] Q.B. 604.

[283] J. Morgan, "Contracting for Self-Denial: On Enforcing 'No Oral Modification' Clauses" [2017] C.L.J. 589.

[284] J. O'Sullivan, "Unconsidered Modifications" (2017) 133 L.Q.R. 191 at 196. See also E. McKendrick, "The Legal Effect of an Anti-oral Variation Clause" (2017) 32 J.I.B.L.R. 439.

[285] *MWB Business Exchange Centres Ltd v Rock Advertising Ltd* [2018] UKSC 24; [2018] 2 W.L.R. 1603 at [10], [15] (Lord Sumption, with whom Lady Hale, Lord Wilson and Lord Lloyd-Jones

mercial certainty, giving effect to the parties' original intentions[286]) over principle ("conceptualism"[287]), but it has now settled the matter.[288] The Court recognised that the enforcement of such clauses carries the risk that a party may act on the (invalid) variation, and then find itself unable to enforce it, and that in such a case the safeguard against injustice lies in some form of estoppel: although the variation is in law invalid, the other party may be estopped from relying on the invalidity. No detailed guidance was given on the operation of estoppel in this context, although the Court made clear that, at the very least, the other party would have to represent unequivocally by words or conduct that the variation was valid notwithstanding its informality, and that its mere informal agreement to the variation would not suffice.[289]

---

agreed); this was the appeal from *MWB Business Exchange Centres Ltd v Rock Advertising Ltd*, see para.5-41 fn.282. Lord Briggs agreed in the result, but his reasoning was significantly different: he held that the parties can agree to remove a "no oral variation" clause from their bargain, in a similar way to the parties' removal of a "subject to contract" condition from their negotiations (at [29]; cf para.2-08), but "[w]hat is conceptually impossible is for the parties to a contract to impose upon themselves such a scheme, but not to be free, by unanimous further agreement, to vary or abandon it by any method, whether writing, spoken words or conduct, permitted by the general law" (at [26]). However, such an agreement must be express (or by strictly necessary implication), and implied agreement cannot be found simply from the fact that that the parties agree orally on a variation of the substance of their relationship without saying anything at all about the clause: see at [24], [31].

286 *MWB Business Exchange Centres Ltd v Rock Advertising Ltd*, see para.5-41 fn.285, at [11]–[12] ("the effect of the rule applied by the Court of Appeal in the present case is to override the parties' intentions. ... There are many cases in which a particular form of agreement is prescribed by statute: contracts for the sale of land, certain regulated consumer contracts, and so on. There is no principled reason why the parties should not adopt the same principle by agreement. ... No Oral Modification clauses ... are very commonly included in written agreements.... There are at least three reasons for including such clauses. The first is that it prevents attempts to undermine written agreements by informal means, a possibility which is open to abuse, for example in raising defences to summary judgment. Secondly, in circumstances where oral discussions can easily give rise to misunderstandings and crossed purposes, it avoids disputes not just about whether a variation was intended but also about its exact terms. Thirdly, a measure of formality in recording variations makes it easier for corporations to police internal rules restricting the authority to agree them. These are all legitimate commercial reasons for agreeing [such] a clause ... I make these points because the law of contract does not normally obstruct the legitimate intentions of businessmen, except for overriding reasons of public policy. Yet there is no mischief in No Oral Modification clauses, nor do they frustrate or contravene any policy of the law").

287 *MWB Business Exchange Centres Ltd v Rock Advertising Ltd*, see para.5-41 fn.285, at [13] ("The reasons advanced in the case law for disregarding them are entirely conceptual..." noting that other legal systems such as the Vienna Convention on Contracts for the International Sale of Goods (1980) and the PICC give effect to such clauses). cf. Lord Briggs' different reasoning, see para.5-41 fn.285.

288 The attention will therefore now shift to the interpretation of the clause, to ascertain what the parties have agreed by way of restriction on their freedom to vary the contract.

289 *MWB Business Exchange Centres Ltd v Rock Advertising Ltd*, see para.5-41 fn.285, at [16], drawing an analogy with the use of estoppel in the event of failure to comply with the formality requirements of the Statute of Frauds 1677 s.4: *Actionstrength Ltd v International Glass Engineering IN. GL EN. SpA* [2003] UKHL 17; [2003] 2 A.C. 541 at [9], [51]; see para.6-18.

CHAPTER 6

SPECIFIC FORMALITIES: WRITTEN EVIDENCE AS A CONDITION OF ENFORCEABILITY[1]

I.   The Use of Formality as an Evidential Condition

Formality as an evidential condition of a contract   In Chapter 4 we saw that the   **6-01**
evidential function was one of the purposes for which formality is used in private
law: it is designed to provide reliable evidence that the party did enter into the
particular transaction, and may also provide evidence of the terms of the transaction itself.[2] There are also other purposes served by formality,[3] and in Chapter 5 we
have seen the use of various formalities as substantive conditions of types of
contract in which there is a desire to provide protection to the party or parties to the
contract as well as sometimes to other interests that merit protection. Where the
formality is imposed only as a matter of evidence, however, even if compliance with
the formality requirement may sometimes bring broader benefits, its purpose is
more limited.[4] In particular, if the formality is not complied with, such a formality
rule does not in principle deny the existence or validity of the contract but only its
legal enforceability—and it may be possible to recognise certain effects of the
contract without directly enforcing the contract itself. An evidential condition has
the character of a rule of procedure rather than one of substance, although the effect may often be similar.[5]

---

[1]   Chitty, paras 45-042 to 45-060; Furmston, paras 2.276 to 2.299; Treitel, paras 5-013 to 5-028; Anson, pp.84–88; Cheshire, Fifoot and Furmston, pp.270–288; G. Andrews and R. Millett, *Law of Guarantees*, 7th edn (Sweet & Maxwell, 2015), Ch.3; W. Courtney, J. Phillips and J. O'Donovan, *The Modern Contract of Guarantee*, 3rd English edn (Sweet & Maxwell, 2016), Ch.3; D. Marks and G. Moss, *Rowlatt on Principal and Surety*, 6th edn (Sweet & Maxwell, 2011), Ch.3.
[2]   See esp. para.4-03.
[3]   ibid.: e.g. cautionary and labelling (or "channelling"), as well as protection of third party and other broader public interests.
[4]   See para.4-09.
[5]   Failure to comply with some of the formalities discussed in Ch.5 had the consequence that the contract was "unenforceable"; however, these were not simply evidential formalities, but substan-tive requirements for the contract in question, sometimes giving the court a structured discretion whether to allow the contract to be enforced in the particular circumstances of the case: see paras 5-32, 5-35. For an analogous distinction between procedure and substance, cf. the operation of the Limitation Acts in generally barring actions rather than substantive rights: A. Burrows (ed.), *English*

6-02 **Similar issues arise in considering the operation of substantive and evidential requirements of form** Some of the issues which arise in relation to substantive formalities, and which we have seen in Chapter 5,[6] are equally relevant in the case of evidential formalities. Such formalities are again set by statute, not as general rules for contracts[7] but specific to particular types of contract; and the legislative texts make detailed provision for the required formalities, any exceptions that may have been allowed by the legislator, and the consequences for the contract if the formality is not used—but there are also questions about the interpretation of what the statute requires,[8] and whether exceptions can be made to the apparently strict requirements of the statute.[9]

6-03 **Form as a requirement independent of the conditions of formation of the contract** In the contracts discussed in this chapter, the statutory formality is required not as an additional condition for the formation of the contract,[10] but as an independent condition of its judicial enforceability. In principle, a simple agreement, embodying a bargain, is sufficient to constitute a contract, but no action can be brought to enforce it in the absence of a written document which satisfies the statutory requirement. The formality is an additional requirement; but not one which is a necessary element of the formation of the contract itself. Indeed, it is generally not necessary that the written document be created at the time when the contract is formed, and there are cases where the written acknowledgement of the contract, sufficient to render it enforceable, was signed significantly later than the contract itself.[11]

6-04 **The contracts which require writing as an evidential condition of legal enforceability** The requirement of form as a condition of enforceability of a contract is very unusual in modern English law. Formality is the exception, rather than the rule[12]; and although in the first significant legislative[13] introduction of formality requirements for private law transactions the Statute of Frauds 1677 adopted evidential formalities, rather than substantive formalities, for those types of contract which it identified as requiring writing, the contracts which are subject to evidential formality requirements have been significantly reduced in the modern law[14]; new formalities have generally focused on the substantive validity of the contract.[15] Of

---

Private Law, 3rd edn (Oxford University Press, 2013), para.22.15.

6   See para.5-02, and generally throughout Ch.5.

7   A legal system could set a general rule of evidence; e.g. signed writing for the enforcement of any contract above a certain value (cf. French law: see para.4-09 fn.84); however, English law has not adopted this approach.

8   e.g. over the meaning of "writing"; see paras 4-05, 4-06, 6-12 and 6-13.

9   See para.6-18.

10 cf. para.5-03 for substantive conditions of form.

11 e.g. *Barkworth v Young* (1856) 4 Drew 1, 62 E.R. 1 (acknowledgement in writing 14 years after oral contact). Such cases show that evidential formalities do not necessarily have the same cautionary purpose or benefit as substantive formalities: see para.4-09.

12 See para.4-02.

13 The deed was already in use in the thirteenth and fourteenth centuries as an evidential requirement at common law for the enforcement of certain promises: see para.7-01.

14 See para.6-05.

15 e.g. the replacement of the evidential formality of a written memorandum, contained in LPA 1925 s.40 (itself following the Statute of Frauds 1677 s.4), by the substantive formality of a written contract in LP(MP)A 1989 s.2(1): see para.5-07; and new formalities designed to provide consumer

the provisions of the Statute of Frauds dealing with contracts, the only remaining section is the portion of s.4 which regulates the formalities required for contracts of guarantee.[16] Under the Marine Insurance Act 1906 there is also a requirement of written evidence for the enforceability of a contract of marine insurance.[17] The principal focus of this chapter is the formality requirements for a contract of guarantee.

II.   Contracts of Guarantee

(1)   Section 4 of the Statute of Frauds 1677: Background and Context

The imposition of formality requirements for contracts by the Statute of Frauds, and the reduction of evidential formality requirements in the modern law   The Statute of Frauds imposed formality requirements for a range of contracts, as well as for property transactions and wills. Some (mostly relating to property transactions) required writing as a substantial condition of validity; others (including those relating to contracts) required writing as an evidential condition of actionability.[18] The reason for the introduction of these requirements for contracts was to protect the parties in a system of civil procedure where they risked being held liable under a contract to which they had not in fact agreed, by a jury which might even act on the basis of perjured evidence.[19] The justification for requiring written evidence of a contract before it can be enforced is clearly no longer the same today. There may be other justifications for retaining evidential formality requirements for contracts, but the general trend in England[20] has been to remove the categories of contract for which such evidence is mandatory, leaving the enforceability of most contracts simply to the application of the general rules of evidence. The list originally contained in s.4 of the Statute of Frauds required written evidence in order to enforce a range of promises, agreements and contracts[21]:

6-05

> "no action shall be brought whereby to charge any executor or administrator upon any special promise, to answer damages out of his own estate; (2) or whereby to charge the defendant upon any special promise to answer for the debt, default or miscarriages of another person; (3) or to charge any person upon any agreement made upon consideration of marriage; (4) or upon any contract or sale of lands, tenements or hereditaments, or any interest in or concerning them; (5) or upon any agreement that is not to be performed within the space of one year from the making thereof; (6) unless the agreement upon which such action shall be brought, or some memorandum or note thereof, shall be in writing, and signed by the party to be charged therewith, or some other person thereunto by him lawfully authorized"

---

protection and rendering certain consumer contracts void, or unenforceable, if the contract is not in writing, or if some form of written notice is not served in the formation of the contract: see paras 5-30 to 5-35.

16   In fact, this is the only remaining operative part of the whole of the Statute of Frauds, but some provisions which used to be found in the Statute have been taken into other modern statutes: e.g. LPA 1925 ss.53, 54; see para.4-05 fnn.23, 25.

17   See para.6-19.

18   See para.4-05 fn.23.

19   See para.4-05 fn.24.

20   For different approaches elsewhere in the common law, see para.4-05 fn.26.

21   Statute of Frauds 1677 s.4 (spelling and capitalisation of the words modernised).

and, by a separate provision[22]:

"no contract for the sale of any goods, wares and merchandizes, for the price of ten pounds sterling or upwards, shall be allowed to be good, except the buyer shall accept part of the goods so sold, and actually receive the same, or give something in earnest to bind the bargain, or in part of payment, or that some note or memorandum in writing of the said bargain be made and signed by the parties to be charged by such contract, or their agents thereunto lawfully authorized."

This last provision was replaced by a similar rule in the Sale of Goods Act 1893[23]; the provision within section 4 concerning contracts for the sale of land and interests in land was replaced by a similar rule in the Law of Property Act 1925.[24] All the remaining provisions of section 4, and the provision which had been taken over by the Sale of Goods Act 1893, were repealed by the Law Reform (Enforcement of Contracts) Act 1954, *except for* the provision of s.4 relating to guarantees. What now still remains of the original wording of the Statute of Frauds is therefore the following:

"no action shall be brought ... whereby to charge the defendant upon any special promise to answer for the debt, default or miscarriages of another person ... unless the agreement on which such action shall be brought, or some memorandum or note thereof, shall be in writing, and signed by the party to be charged therewith, or some other person thereunto by him lawfully authorized."

6-06   **The retention of evidential formality requirements for contracts of guarantee**   In retaining the evidential formality requirement for guarantees in s.4 of the Statute of Frauds, Parliament in 1954 acted upon the recommendations of the First Report of the Law Reform Committee.[25] This Committee reviewed the Sixth Interim Report of the Law Revision Committee,[26] which in 1937 had proposed the repeal of the whole of s.4, together with certain other statutes imposing evidential formality requirements for particular categories of contract,[27] on the basis that "Contemporary opinion is almost unanimous in condemning the Statute and favouring its amendment or repeal".[28] In the 1937 Report, the majority recommended that the provision requiring a written memorandum to support an action on a guarantee should be included in the repeal, on the basis that there is no such requirement for an indemnity, and the retention of the special rule for guarantees is unnecessary and

---

22   Statute of Frauds 1677 s.17.
23   s.4(1).
24   s.40; see para.5-06. This was then repealed and replaced by the stronger formality rule of LP(MP)A 1989 s.2, which requires a written contract as a substantive formality for a contract for the sale or other disposition of an interest in land: see para.5-07.
25   Law Reform Committee, First Report, *Statute of Frauds and Section 4 of the Sale of Goods Act, 1893*, Cmd.8809 (1953).
26   Law Revision Committee, Sixth Interim Report, *Statute of Frauds and the Doctrine of Consideration*, Cmd.5449 (1937).
27   Sale of Goods Act 1893 s.4, see para.6-05 fn.23; and Mercantile Law Amendment Act 1856, see para.6-12 fn.71. They did not consider LPA 1925 s.40, see para.6-05 fn.24, which was outside their terms of reference: Sixth Interim Report, see para.6-06 fn.26, para.4.
28   See para.6-06 fn.26, para.8. The criticisms were set out in detail by the Law Revision Committee, see para.6-06 fn.26, para.9; and summarised by the Law Reform Committee, see para.6-06 fn.25, para.2: the statutory provisions "had outlived the conditions which generated and, in some degree, justified them; that they operate in an illogical and often one-sided and haphazard fashion over a field arbitrarily chosen; and that on the whole they promote rather than restrain dishonesty".

would "perpetuate the artificial distinction between guarantee and indemnity".[29] However, a minority of the Committee dissented from this and recommended that a special requirement be retained for guarantees, on the basis that it is a special form of contract where the guarantor needs the protection that a requirement of writing can afford[30]:

> "We realise that most guarantees, such for instance as those given to a Bank, will, whether the section is repealed or not, always be contained in a written document; but, if oral contracts of guarantee are allowed, we feel that there is a real danger of inexperienced people being led into undertaking obligations that they do not fully understand, and that opportunities will be given to the unscrupulous to assert that credit was given on the faith of a guarantee which in fact the alleged surety had no intention of giving. A guarantee is in any case a special class of contract; it is generally one-sided and disinterested as far as the surety is concerned, and the necessity of writing would at least give the proposed surety an opportunity of pausing and considering, not only the nature of the obligation he is undertaking, but also its terms."

This minority recommendation emphasised the cautionary function of formality[31]; and the Law Reform Committee in 1953 preferred the minority view on this point and therefore recommended the retention of the words in s.4 of the Statute of Frauds relating to contracts of guarantee. Commentators remain of mixed views about the merits of retaining s.4 in its present form,[32] although there might even be a case for strengthening the formality to require the guarantee to be in writing, rather than merely evidenced by writing.[33]

(2)   Contracts Within the Scope of Section 4

The section applies to contracts of guarantee   Section 4 applies to "any special   **6-07** promise to answer for the debt, default or miscarriages of another person"—i.e. a contractually binding guarantee.[34] Since the section renders such a contract unenforceable in the absence of the requisite written evidence, it is fundamentally important to be able to define the contract of guarantee, and to distinguish it from other apparently similar or related contracts which are not within the scope of the

---

[29]   See para.6-06 fn.26, para.15. For the difficulties of distinguishing between a guarantee and an indemnity, see para.6-08.

[30]   See para.6-06 fn.26, p.33.

[31]   See para.4-03.

[32]   Andrews and Millett, *Law of Guarantees*, see para.6-01 fn.1, para.3-002 give judicial dicta on both sides of the argument. cf. *MyBarrister Ltd v Hewetson* [2017] EWHC 2624 (Ch) at [52] (Daniel Alexander QC: "while the application of the statute to guarantees may be thought to be of questionable continuing value in current commercial circumstances, it represents the law and courts should not strive to find ways of getting round it by seeking somewhat artificial characterisations of obligations to take them outside its provisions").

[33]   See para.6-18, esp. fn.114.

[34]   "Suretyship is the generic term given to contracts by which one person (the surety) agrees to answer for some existing or future liability of another (the principal) to a third person (the creditor), and by which the surety's liability is in addition to, and not in substitution for, that of the principal": Andrews and Millett, *Law of Guarantees*, see para.6-01 fn.1, para.1-001; see also Chitty, para.45-01. "Suretyship" can be used to refer to both guarantees and indemnities (e.g. Andrews and Millett, *Law of Guarantees*, para.1-003; Chitty, para.45-07), but the distinction between a contract of guarantee and a contract of indemnity is critical for the application of Statute of Frauds s.4 (see para.6-08). Most books tend to use the word "guarantee" as their primary term for discussion but will often refer to the guarantor as a "surety" or the contract as a contract of "suretyship".

statute,[35] as well as to be clear what kinds of guarantees are within the statute and which guarantees have been (exceptionally) held to fall outside it.[36]

6-08   **Distinguishing a guarantee from an indemnity**   A guarantee within section 4 is, as the statute puts it, a promise "to answer for" what "another person" owes or has done. It is a *secondary* undertaking, collateral to a separate contractual or other obligation owed by another person (the primary debtor), under which the guarantor is liable to the creditor of the guarantee because the primary debtor has not performed the obligations which he owes, or has committed some other wrong. There must be a primary debtor for a guarantee to exist.[37] In this respect the guarantee is commonly contrasted with an "indemnity", a primary undertaking under which any claim against the party giving the indemnity arises from his failure to perform his own undertaking, and is not dependent upon whether another person has undertaken a related obligation or has failed to perform it. In many cases a contract of indemnity will be linked to the failure of a third party to perform an obligation, such as where one person indemnifies another against loss flowing from a third party's misconduct, but such an indemnity is not in itself dependent upon the validity of the third party's obligation nor its breach[38]: in the case of an indemnity, the question is not whether the primary debtor has failed to perform, but whether the conditions for liability set by the contract of indemnity have been satisfied—the party is liable to pay under the indemnity simply because he promised in those circumstances to pay. There are many cases in which the courts have had to determine whether a particular contract constitutes a guarantee (secondary undertaking) or an indemnity (primary undertaking).[39] Many of them do not involve any discussion of s.4 of the Statute of Frauds because there is often a sufficient written agreement or memorandum to satisfy s.4 even if the contract is held to be one of guarantee, but, in addition to the formality requirements of that section, there are a number of special rules which apply to contracts of guarantee (but not to contracts of indemnity) and on which cases before the courts have turned.[40] However, all the

---

[35]   See para.6-08.

[36]   See paras 6-09, 6-10.

[37]   *Lakeman v Mountstephen* (1874) L.R. 7 H.L. 17 at 24 (Lord Selborne: "There can be no suretyship unless there be a principal debtor, who of course may be constituted in the course of the transaction by matters *ex post facto*, and need not be so at the time, but until there is a principal debtor there can be no suretyship. Nor can a man guarantee anybody else's debt unless there is a debt of some other person to be guaranteed").

[38]   The party who gave the indemnity may therefore (unlike the guarantor) still be liable even if the third party's liability is not enforceable because the obligation was void or voidable or has been discharged: e.g. *Yeoman Credit Ltd v Latter* [1961] 1 W.L.R. 828, CA (indemnity to cover potential losses from hire-purchase contract entered into by minor).

[39]   cf. *Yeoman Credit Ltd v Latter*, see para.6-08 fn.38, at 835 (Harman LJ: the distinction between a guarantee and an indemnity "seems to me a most barren controversy. It dates back, of course, to the Statute of Frauds, and has raised many hair-splitting distinctions of exactly that kind which brings the law into hatred, ridicule and contempt by the public. Nevertheless, this difficulty persists, and the decided cases on the subject are hardly to be reconciled").

[40]   e.g. the invalidity or discharge of the principal contract will prevent the guarantee being enforceable; there are certain duties of disclosure of unusual risks in the principal transaction in favour of a guarantor (but not a party giving an indemnity), and a bank taking a non-commercial guarantee is required to take steps to satisfy itself that the guarantor knows what he or she is doing: see the discussion by Lord Scott in *Royal Bank of Scotland Plc v Etridge (No.2)* [2001] UKHL 44; [2002] 2 A.C. 773 at [185]–[190]; any variation of the principal contract without the guarantor's consent, if it could affect the guarantor's liability, will discharge the guarantor: *Holme v Brunskill* (1877) 3 Q.B.D. 495,

cases which have drawn this distinction are relevant for our purposes of defining a contract of "guarantee" which will therefore be subject to the formality requirements of s.4.

In all cases the question is what the parties have in fact agreed by way of obligation, and therefore whether in substance the contract is one of guarantee or not.[41] The name the parties give to their obligation is not conclusive,[42] but a contract is generally a guarantee if in substance the party promises to perform a particular obligation (such as the payment of a sum of money) if another person does not perform that obligation, or if the party promises more generally to "see to it"[43] that another person will comply with his obligations.[44] The scope of the guarantor's obligations is normally coterminous with the obligations of the principal debtor to the beneficiary of the guarantee, and therefore where the nature and scope of the party's liability is not identical to that of the principal debtor under a separate contract to which it makes reference,[45] or where the undertaking is given not to the creditor of the principal debt but to another person who may suffer loss by reason of a default on the primary debt,[46] it will generally be an indemnity not a guarantee. It has also been said that if the promise in question is the central object of the contract, and the promise relates to another separate transaction in which the promi-

---

CA, at 505; so too will the release by the creditor of other guarantors who are jointly and severally liable with the guarantor: *Mercantile Bank of Sydney v Taylor* [1893] A.C. 317, PC; and the guarantor is entitled to be indemnified by the principal debtor in respect of the latter's liability to the creditor which the guarantor has discharged: see para.6-15 fn.97.

[41] *Moschi v Lep Air Services Ltd* [1973] A.C. 331, HL, at 344 (Lord Reid), 349 (Lord Diplock). A contract may contain clauses some of which contain guarantee obligations, others indemnities. For the problem of whether such clauses can be separated for the purposes of s.4, see para.6-17.

[42] *Moschi v Lep Air Services Ltd* [1973] A.C. 331, HL, at 349 (Lord Diplock); e.g. *Western Credit Ltd v Alberry* [1964] 1 W.L.R. 945, CA ("surety" gave "guarantee" which also included reference to "indemnity" but its terms pointed to it being a guarantee not indemnity); *Trafalgar House Construction (Regions) Ltd v General Surety & Guarantee Co Ltd* [1996] A.C. 199, HL (bond held on construction to be secondary guarantee); *Gold Coast Ltd v Caja de Ahorros del Mediterraneo* [2001] EWCA Civ 1806; [2002] 1 All E.R. (Comm) 142 ("guarantee" held on construction to be on-demand bond).

[43] The words must still be construed in their context to determine what they mean. See, e.g. *Lakeman v Mountstephen*, see para.6-08 fn.37 ("go on and do the work, and I will see you paid": should be left to jury to determine whether this constituted a primary undertaking rather than a secondary guarantee).

[44] *Moschi v Lep Air Services Ltd*, see para.6-08 fn.41, at 344–345 (Lord Reid, noting that where the a guarantee is a simple undertaking to pay any instalment that the principal debtor fails to pay, the guarantor is then liable in debt; but where it is an undertaking that the principal debtor will carry out his contract, the guarantor is liable for damages for breach of the contract of guarantee by virtue of the fact that the principal debtor breaks his own contract); *Associated British Ports v Ferryways NV* [2009] EWCA Civ 189; [2009] 1 Lloyd's Rep. 595 at [11]; *MyBarrister Ltd v Hewetson* [2017] EWHC 2624 (Ch) at [61] (Daniel Alexander QC: "'see to it' obligations are classic kinds of guarantee")..

[45] *Yeoman Credit Ltd v Latter*, see para.6-08 fn.38, at 832–833 (contract of indemnity where adult undertook to cover any loss suffered by hire-purchase company from contract with minor: the liability was not for any particular (or, indeed, any) breach by the minor, and might be more or less than the claim of the company against the minor under the contract).

[46] *Re Hoyle* [1893] 1 Ch. 84, CA, at 97, 99 (one partner "guaranteed" to his other partners in a firm that he would cover any loss to them (or to the firm) if his son defaulted on a debt to the firm: it was "not a promise to his partners to pay a debt due from a third party to those partners, but a promise to indemnify the other partners if the debtor did not pay the firm" (Bowen LJ at 99; A.L. Smith LJ at 100 thought that the agreement was "very near the line")).

sor has no direct personal interest, it is likely to be a guarantee.[47] And if there are other terms which are relevant only to a guarantor's liability, this will point towards it being a guarantee.[48]

The commercial context of the transaction can also be relevant to show what the parties must have intended to be the nature of the contract. For example, on-demand bonds[49] (primary liability) are common in the context of banking transactions, and an obligation to pay on presentation of a particular document or certificate rather than on proof of the underlying facts is indicative of such a bond rather than a guarantee[50]; on the contrary, however, it has been said that outside the context of a banking instrument there is a strong presumption against the parties having intended to create an on-demand bond and therefore a guarantee (secondary liability) is more likely unless there are sufficient indications in the wording of the instrument to displace the presumption.[51] But where the undertaking is given in support of a transaction which the parties know may itself be void or unenforceable the courts will incline in favour of construing it as an indemnity, since that must be the parties' intention otherwise the undertaking would be ineffective.[52]

---

[47] *Pitts v Jones* [2007] EWCA Civ 1301; [2008] Q.B. 706 at [32] ("the court should ask what was the object of the contract or transaction, and if the promisor's obligation to pay arose as an incident to the central object of the contract or transaction, that obligation would be an indemnity, whereas if it were the central obligation of the contract or transaction, it would be a guarantee": Smith LJ, interpreting Vaughan Williams LJ in *Harburg India Rubber Comb Co v Martin* [1902] 1 K.B. 778, CA, at 786 who, however, was not in that passage distinguishing between a guarantee and an indemnity, but was considering cases which, though they appear to fall within s.4, "have been held not to come within the object of the contract": see para.6-10).

[48] e.g. *Trafalgar House Construction (Regions) Ltd v General Surety & Guarantee Co Ltd*, see para.6-08 fn.42, at 205 (provision that no alteration in the terms of principal contract should release surety from liability: cf. above, n.40). However, if there is a written document the fact that it does *not* contain provisions commonly found in a well-drawn guarantee does not indicate that it is not a guarantee but is at best neutral: *Associated British Ports v Ferryways NV*, see para.6-08 fn.44, at [12].

[49] "In essence it is a particularly stringent contract of indemnity. It is a contractual undertaking by a person, usually a bank, to pay a specified amount of money to a third party on the occurrence of a stated event, usually the non-fulfilment of a contractual obligation by the principal to that third party. Sometimes the wording of the contract has the result that the liability of the person who has given the bond arises on mere demand by the creditor, notwithstanding that it may be evident that the principal is not in any way in default or even that the creditor himself is in default under his contract with the principal. It all depends on the wording of the instrument. It is often a difficult question to determine whether, on its true construction, a particular contract which provides for payment on demand is a performance or demand bond (where the obligation to pay is triggered by a demand alone or by a demand accompanied by the provision of specified documents) or whether it is a guarantee (strictly so called) where the obligation to pay is of the 'see to it' kind, i.e. conditional on proof by the creditor of default by the principal": *Vossloh AG v Alpha Trains (UK) Ltd* [2010] EWHC 2443 (Ch); [2011] 2 All E.R. (Comm) 307 at [29] (Sir William Blackburne).

[50] *Gold Coast Ltd v Caja de Ahorros del Mediterraneo*, see para.6-08 fn.42; *Meritz Fire & Marine Insurance Co Ltd v Jan de Nul NV* [2010] EWHC 3362 (Comm); [2011] 1 All E.R. (Comm) 1049, affirmed [2011] EWCA Civ 827; [2012] 1 All E.R. (Comm) 182; *Spliethoff's Bevrachtingskantoor BV v Bank of China Ltd* [2015] EWHC 999 (Comm); [2015] 1 C.L.C. 651 at [70] (Carr J, citing the "recent authoritative guidance" given by Longmore LJ in *Wuhan Guoyu Logistics Group Co Ltd v Emporiki Bank of Greece SA* [2012] EWCA Civ 1629; [2012] 2 C.L.C. 986 at [25]–[29]).

[51] *Marubeni Hong Kong and South China Ltd v Mongolian Government* [2005] EWCA Civ 395; [2005] 1 W.L.R. 2497 at [30]. For examples, see *Van der Merwe v IIG Capital LLC* [2008] EWCA Civ 542; [2008] 2 All E.R. (Comm) 1173 (presumption rebutted); *Vossloh AG v Alpha Trains (UK) Ltd*, see para.6-08 fn.49 (presumption not rebutted); *Wuhan Guoyu Logistics Group Co v Emporiki Bank of Greece SA*, see para.6-08 fn.50 (presumption not rebutted).

[52] *Yeoman Credit Ltd v Latter*, see para.6-08 fn.38, at 833, 835 (indemnity in support of contract in favour of minor); *Lakeman v Mountstephen*, see para.6-08 fn.37, at 24–25 (Lord Selborne: promise

Guarantees within section 4   The section applies to a promise to answer for the   **6-09**
"debt, default or miscarriages of another person". This covers not only the most
common case, guarantees of debts and defaults which arise out of contractual
obligations of another person, but also guarantees of liabilities arising out of tortious wrongs[53]:

> "I think the term miscarriage is more properly applicable to a ground of action founded
> upon a tort than to one founded upon a contract: for in the latter case the ground of ac-
> tion is, that the party has not performed what he agreed to perform; not that he has
> misconducted himself in some matter for which by law he is liable. And I think, that both
> the words miscarriage and default apply to a promise to answer for another with respect
> to the non-performance of a duty, though not founded upon a contract."

The section covers not only promises to pay an existing debt, and to cover the
liabilities arising out of an existing breach of duty, but also the promise to pay a debt
when it later falls due, and the promise that a third party will perform his obligations to the creditor (thus giving rise to a claim under the guarantee if the third party
later fails to perform).[54] As we have seen, however, it is only a guarantee within the
scope of the section if the undertaking is to answer for the debt, default or miscarriages of third party as it is owed by the third party to the creditor of the guarantee:
if the so-called guarantee is given to another person, not the creditor of the principal
obligation, even though that person may suffer loss in the event of non-performance,
it is not a guarantee at all.[55] Where a contract of guarantee is varied by the parties,
the contract as varied must comply with s.4, although the section does not apply
to an agreement to rescind (or discharge) the guarantee.[56]

Guarantees outside section 4   There are certain situations in which the courts   **6-10**
have held that, although the contract appears to fall within the wording of the statute
because it is, or includes, a promise to answer for another's debt or obligation, it
should not be held to be covered by the statute because the "guarantee" element is
only incidental to the contract, which has a different "object".[57] The two main

---

of payment given by chairman of Board to contractor in circumstances where he may not have
authority of the Board to do work: to treat as guarantee of future liability to be undertaken by the
Board "would be absolutely to defeat the whole purpose of the communication, which was to remove
a difficulty then pressing upon the mind of the contractor, as to whether or not he had sufficient
authority from any one to go on with the work; and the answer was given in terms *de praesenti* for
the express purpose of inducing him at once to go on").

[53] *Kirkham v Marter* (1819) 2 B. & Ald. 613 at 617, 106 E.R. 490 at 491 (Holroyd J; promise by third
party to pay damage caused by tort which resulted in death of claimant's horse).

[54] *Moschi v Lep Air Services Ltd*, see para.6-08 fn.41, at 344–345.

[55] *Re Hoyle*, see para.6-08 fn.46. Similarly, a contract *with the debtor* undertaking to cover his debt to
the creditor is not a guarantee, because the statute applies only to promises made to the person to
whom another is answerable: *Eastwood v Kenyon* (1840) 11 Ad. & El. 438 at 446, 113 E.R. 482 at
485.

[56] See para.6-20. The *assignment* of the benefit of a guarantee has no special formality requirements
but follows the normal rules for the assignment of debts and other choses in action: Chitty, Ch.19;
Treitel, Ch.15; Anson, Ch.22; Cheshire, Fifoot and Furmston, Ch.16; but the guarantee must itself
satisfy the requirements of s.4 if it is to be enforceable by the assignee.

[57] For a general discussion see *Harburg India Rubber Comb Co v Martin*, see para.6-08 fn.47, where
all three judges set out the exceptional situations in which a promise to answer for another's debt,
though not an indemnity (see para.6-08), has been held not to fall within s.4. The trial judge had applied the so-called "property exception" (see para.6-10 fn.58), but this was reversed on the facts by
CA.

examples are often referred to as the "property cases", where a person with an interest in property which is subject to some third-party right agrees to pay off the third party in order to obtain the property free of incumbrances[58]; and the "del credere" cases where the contract consists in employing a "del credere" agent who undertakes as part of his obligations the assurance that third parties with whom he contracts on behalf of the principal will pay any sums due under the contracts.[59] Vaughan Williams LJ put it as follows[60]:

> "Whether you look at the 'property cases' or at the 'del credere cases,' it seems to me that in each of them the conclusion arrived at really was that the contract in question did not fall within the section because of the object of the contract. In each of those cases there was in truth a main contract—a larger contract—and the obligation to pay the debt of another was merely an incident of the larger contract. As I understand those cases, it is not a question of motive—it is a question of object. You must find what it was that the parties were in fact dealing about. What was the subject-matter of the contract? If the subject-matter of the contract was the purchase of property—the relief of property from a liability, the getting rid of incumbrances, the securing greater diligence in the performance of the duty of a factor, or the introduction of business into a stockbroker's office—in all those cases there was a larger matter which was the object of the contract. That being the object of the contract, the mere fact that as an incident to it—not as the immediate object, but indirectly—the debt of another to a third person will be paid, does not bring the case within the section."

Some judges explain these exceptions from s.4 by saying that they are not guarantees but indemnities[61]; others, however, avoid that distinction, or even admit that the obligation is one within the statute (to "answer for" the debt of another), but say that they are outside the scope of the section because the guarantee is not the main object of the contract which is rather to protect a different interest of the party entering into it.[62]

For completeness, it should be added that a financial collateral arrangement

---

58 *Harburg India Rubber Comb Co v Martin*, see para.6-08 fn.47, at 783–784, 786, 791, 792–793; *Castling v Aubert* (1802) 2 East 325, 102 E.R. 393; *Fitzgerald v Dressler* (1859) 7 C.B.(N.S.) 374, 141 E.R. 861; distinguished in *Davys v Buswell* [1913] 2 K.B. 47, CA (fact that person guaranteeing debt due from company has floating charge on company's assets is insufficient: "I do not think that, in any sense in which the word 'interest' has been used in any of the prior cases on the subject, the plaintiff here had any such interest as would make it true to say that he gave the guarantee by reason of any liability or obligation which existed independently of the guarantee, or that he was contracting for the protection of any right. The case seems to me to be one of a guarantee pure and simple, and therefore to come within the statute": Vaughan Williams LJ at 55–56).
59 *Harburg India Rubber Comb Co v Martin*, see para.6-08 fn.47, at 784, 786, 790, 793; *Couturier v Hastie* (1852) 8 Ex. 40 at 56, 155 E.R. 1250 at 1257 (Parke B: "though it may terminate in a liability to pay the debt of another, that is not the immediate object for which the consideration is given"); extended in *Sutton & Co v Grey* [1894] 1 Q.B. 285, CA to case where plaintiff stockbrokers agreed to introduce clients to defendant, sharing commission equally and paying half of any losses. On del credere agency, see generally P.G. Watts (ed.), *Bowstead and Reynolds on Agency* (21st edn, 2017), paras 1-042, 9-022.
60 *Harburg India Rubber Comb Co v Martin*, see para.6-08 fn.47, at 787.
61 e.g. *Sutton & Co v Grey*, see para.6-10 fn.59, at 287 (Lord Esher MR); *Walker Crips Stockbrokers Ltd v Savill* [2007] EWHC 2598 (QB) at [72]–[75].
62 e.g. *Sutton & Co v Grey*, see para.6-10 fn.59 at 290 (Lopes LJ), 291 (Kay LJ); *Harburg India Rubber Comb Co v Martin*, see para.6-08 fn.47, at 786 (Vaughan Williams LJ), 792 (Cozens-Hardy LJ); *Davys v Buswell*, see para.6-10 fn.58, at 54 (Vaughan Williams LJ).

within the Financial Collateral Arrangements Directive[63] is excluded from the scope of section 4 even if it would otherwise fall within the section.[64]

(3) The Requirements of Section 4

Summary of the requirements The requirements of s.4 are that   **6-11**

"the agreement on which such action shall be brought, or some memorandum or note thereof, shall be in writing, and signed by the party to be charged therewith, or some other person thereunto by him lawfully authorized."

There must therefore be either a *written contract* or a *written memorandum or note* of it, which *need not be contemporaneous* with the contract, *signed by the party* against whom the action is to be brought, *or his lawfully authorised agent*. These requirements will be discussed in the following paragraphs of this section. The consequences of the failure to comply are considered in the following section.[65]

"the agreement ... or some memorandum or note thereof ..." The normal   **6-12**
rules of contract law apply in relation to the creation[66] and interpretation[67] of the contract of guarantee. Section 4 of the Statute of Frauds expressly contemplates that its formality requirements may be satisfied either by a written agreement of guarantee, or by a written "memorandum or note" of the agreement: that is, the guarantee may itself be in writing, or may be oral but rendered enforceable by a written memorandum which satisfies section 4.[68]

---

[63] Directive 2002/47/EC.
[64] Financial Collateral Arrangements (No.2) Regulations 2003 (SI 2003/3226) reg.4(1); such arrangements must be evidenced in writing (reg.3(1)) but need not comply with the other requirements of Statute of Frauds 1677 s.4 (such as signature).
[65] See paras 6-15 to 6-18.
[66] Agreement (normally formed through offer and acceptance: see Ch.3) and either consideration (see Ch.8) or the formality of a deed (see Ch.7). A deed may often be advisable (see para.7-18) because if the loan which is to be guaranteed has already been made, the guarantee cannot be made in consideration of the loan because that would be "past consideration" (see para.8-20).
      If the parties have reached agreement but do not intend their agreement to be binding until the written document is signed, the negotiations are not yet complete but remain "subject to contract": *Investec Bank (UK) Ltd v Zulman* [2010] EWCA Civ 536; *Harvey v Dunbar Assets Plc* [2013] EWCA Civ 952; [2013] 32 E.G. 57 (C.S.) (single composite guarantee for signature by four joint and several guarantors, not to be binding until all four had signed); cf. para.2-08.
[67] *Perrylease Ltd v Imecar AG* [1988] 1 W.L.R. 463 at 469–473 (objective extrinsic evidence admissible to interpret written contract of guarantee in same way as any other written contract; Statute of Frauds s.4 does not affect this); *Fairstate Ltd v General Enterprise and Management Ltd* [2010] EWHC 3072 (QB); [2011] 2 All E.R. (Comm) 497 at [75]–[76] (Salter QC: "extrinsic evidence may be relied upon to identify the guarantor, the creditor, the principal debtor or the obligation to be guaranteed, where any of these have been inadequately or ambiguously described in the relevant document. Where the evidence is sufficiently convincing (and the other conditions are met) for an order for rectification to be made, such evidence may even be used to supply a missing name or obligation." But "where there is a genuine dispute as to the existence of any agreement of guarantee, or as to precisely what has been agreed, the Court may need to consider the extrinsic evidence that is presented to it for these purposes with particular care. In such cases, the Court will be slow to deprive the defendant of a legitimate statutory defence on the basis of contested oral evidence alone").
[68] *Elpis Maritime Co Ltd v Marti Chartering Co Inc* [1992] 1 A.C. 21, HL, at 32. By contrast, a guarantee given in relation to the debtor or hirer's obligations under an agreement regulated under the CCA 1974 (see para.5-32) must be *in writing* in a form which complies with the Consumer Credit

The written agreement or the written memorandum must (either itself or by express or implied reference to another document or documents[69]) state all the material terms of the contract which the parties have expressly agreed,[70] except for any consideration which was given to make the guarantee contractually binding,[71] and contain an express or implied recognition that a contract was entered into.[72] Not only must the parties to the guarantee itself be clear,[73] but also the identity of the principal debtor, whose debt or other obligation is being guaranteed, is a material term, and its complete absence from the written document is "fatal non-compliance"[74] with the Statute. Any part of the agreement between the parties which impacts upon the guarantee and its scope must be included within the written, material terms.[75]

The written memorandum of an oral agreement need not be contemporaneous with the contract but need only be in existence when the action to enforce the contract is commenced.[76] It has even been held that the written offer of a guarantee

---

(Guarantees and Indemnities) Regulations 1983 (SI 1983/1556): CCA 1974 s.105.

[69] *Moat Financial Services Ltd v Wilkinson* [2005] EWCA Civ 1253 at [21]–[23] (variation of guarantee satisfied s.4 by express and implied reference to earlier documents; following *Timmins v Moreland Street Property Co Ltd* [1958] Ch. 110, CA (LPA 1925 s.40; see para.6-12 fn.70)).

[70] The rather more numerous cases on LPA 1925 s.40 (contracts for the sale or disposition of an interest in land entered into before 27 September 1989: see para.5-06) are relevant in interpreting s.4 in relation to contracts of guarantee, since s.40(1) reproduced the closing language of s.4 which states the requirements of a written memorandum. In relation to contracts for the sale of land, the courts held that a term which was not evidenced by the memorandum may sometimes be waived by a party if it was exclusively for his benefit (*Hawkins v Price* [1947] Ch. 645 at 659); and that the claimant could perform a term of the oral agreement, beneficial to the defendant, which was not included in the written memorandum and so cure its omission (*Martin v Pycroft* (1852) 2 De G. M. & G. 785, 42 E.R. 1079; *Scott v Bradley* [1971] Ch. 850). For further details, see Cheshire and Burn, pp.962–963.

[71] Mercantile Law Amendment Act 1856 s.3, reversing the earlier rule in *Wain v Warlters* (1804) 5 East 10 at 17, 102 E.R. 972 at 975; *Saunders v Wakefield* (1821) 4 B. & Ald. 595, 106 E.R. 1054. If the guarantee is contained in a deed, no consideration is necessary for its enforcement: see para.7-18.

[72] *Clipper Maritime Ltd v Shirlstar Container Transport Ltd (The Anemone)* [1987] 1 Lloyd's Rep. 546 at 556 (Staughton J), following similar statements in relation to LPA 1925 s.40, in *Tiverton Estates Ltd v Wearwell Ltd* [1975] Ch. 146 at 156, 160, 165.

[73] *G&H Montague GmbH v Irvani* [1990] 1 W.L.R. 667, CA (Statute did not apply to liability under bill of exchange; but if it did apply, bill of exchange, or correspondence between parties leading to making of bill of exchange, was sufficient evidence: "I see no reason to construe it so as to frustrate an obligation deliberately assumed, on the ground that the parties are not identified, when anyone familiar with the practice of negotiable paper could tell at a glance who was giving the promise and to whom" (Mustill LJ at 683–684)).

[74] *Union Bank (UK) Plc v Pathak* [2006] EWHC 2614 (Ch); [2006] All E.R. (D) 210 (May) at [58] (Briggs QC). If, however, there is at least a purported identification of the principal debtor it is a question of construction whether that purported identification does refer to the true principal debtor: ibid.; see para.6-12 fn.67.

[75] In *National Westminster Bank Plc v Binney* [2011] EWHC 694 (QB) Eder J declined to decide points of law concerning the admissibility of parol evidence of alleged oral agreements or representations relating to the scope of a written guarantee because, on the facts, there was no agreement or representation as alleged. Presumably, as in the case of contracts for the sale of land (see para.5-14), there can be a valid and enforceable collateral oral contract as long as its terms do not impact upon the terms of the guarantee which the Statute requires to be in, or evidenced in, writing: the question is whether the promise or agreement comprising the guarantee satisfies the Statute. cf. *Wood v Benson* (1831) 2 Cr. & J. 94, 149 E.R. 40 (two separate undertakings within the same contract, only one unenforceable by virtue of the Statute of Frauds); but *Chater v Beckett* (1797) 7 T.R. 201, 101 E.R. 931 (whole contract failed, so claimant could not enforce part not affected by the Statute; however, the court referred to the Statute of Frauds making the contract "void": cf. para.6-15).

[76] *Sievewright v Archibald* (1851) 17 Q.B. 103 at 107, 117 E.R. 1221 at 1223 (Statute of Frauds s.17);

can be a memorandum if it is accepted unconditionally[77] —thereby admitting a document created before the contract of guarantee was itself formed. The sequence of documents (including emails) passing between the parties during the negotiations, from which the agreement is deduced, can also satisfy the Statute.[78] Documents which have been held to constitute a sufficient memorandum of an oral agreement for the purposes of the Statute include a letter addressed to the guarantor's own agent,[79] a will referring in a recital to a guarantee entered into by the deceased,[80] and a page of a charterparty referring to the guarantee and signed by the guarantor.[81]

"in writing"; electronic contracts within section 4 We have already seen the general approach taken by the law to the use of electronic forms of communication in circumstances where a written formality has traditionally been required by the law; and that it appears that the requirement of "writing" may be satisfied by emails and website transactions where the communication is visible on-screen to both parties even if it is stored in digital form.[82] It has been held in the context of s.4 of the Statute of Frauds that an email could constitute a written note or memorandum,[83] and a sequence of emails by which the parties negotiated their agreement, could constitute an agreement in writing.[84]

6-13

"signed by the party to be charged therewith, or some other person thereunto by him lawfully authorized" It is not sufficient that the written agreement, or the written note or memorandum of the agreement, be produced by or on behalf of the guarantor; it must also be signed. The signature may be of the guarantor or his agent, and there is no requirement for the agent himself to receive written author-

6-14

Lucas v Dixon (1889) 22 Q.B.D. 357, CA (s.17); *Re Hoyle* [1893] 1 Ch. 84, CA, at 97 (s.4). If the signed, written document cannot be produced to the court, the creditor may prove its existence by other evidence: *Bank of Scotland v Hussain* [2011] EWHC 1934 at [40]–[44]; *Mitsui OSK Lines Ltd v Salgaocar Mining Ltd* [2015] EWHC 565 (Comm); [2015] 2 Lloyd's Rep. 518 at [41]; Andrews and Millett, *Law of Guarantees*, see para.6-01 fn.1, para.3-021.

[77] *J Pereira Fernandes SA v Mehta* [2006] EWHC 813 (Ch); [2006] 1 W.L.R. 1543 (but it was not a sufficient memorandum because it did not satisfy the requirements of s.4 as regards signature; see para.6-14).

[78] *Golden Ocean Group Ltd v Salgaocar Mining Industries Pvt Ltd* [2012] EWCA Civ 265; [2012] 1 W.L.R. 3674, applied in *Mitsui OSK Lines Ltd v Salgaocar Mining Ltd*, see para.6-12 fn.76, at [40].

[79] *Gibson v Holland* (1865) L.R. 1 C.P. 1: "a note or memorandum is equally corroborative, whether it passes between the parties to the contract themselves, or between one of them and his own agent" (Erle CJ at 5).

[80] *Re Hoyle* [1893] 1 Ch. 84, CA: "The Court is not in quest of the intention of parties, but only of evidence under the hand of one of the parties to the contract that he has entered into it. Any document signed by him and containing the terms of the contract is sufficient for that purpose ... A will is not only a document signed by the testator, but a document signed very solemnly; but I lay no stress on that, for any document signed by the party to be charged will do" (Bowen LJ at 99–100).

[81] *Elpis Maritime Co Ltd v Marti Chartering Co Inc*, see para.6-12 fn.68.

[82] See para.4-06.

[83] *J Pereira Fernandes SA v Mehta*, see para.6-12 fn.77, at [16].

[84] *Golden Ocean Group Ltd v Salgaocar Mining Industries Pvt Ltd*, see para.6-12 fn.78: "I can see no objection in principle to reference to a sequence of negotiating emails or other documents of the sort which is commonplace in ship chartering and ship sale and purchase. Whether the pattern of contract negotiation and formation habitually adopted in other areas of commercial life presents difficulty in adoption of the same approach must await examination when the problem arises. Nothing I have said is intended to discourage the obviously sensible practice of incorporating a guarantee either in a readily identifiable self-standing document or otherwise providing for it as part of the terms of a formally executed document. The Statute of Frauds must however, if possible, be construed in a manner which accommodates accepted contemporary business practice" (Tomlinson LJ at [22]).

ity to sign: the normal principles of agency apply,[85] and so authority may be conferred orally as well as in writing.[86]

If the agreement, or the memorandum, is not a single document but is two or more documents, the guarantor or his agent must sign one document which expressly or impliedly refers to the others in such a way that they can be read together.[87]

The Statute of Frauds does not define "signature", nor give any indication as to the manner in which the agreement or memorandum is to be signed. We have seen the same issue in relation to contracts for the sale or other disposition of an interest in land under s.2 of the Law of Property (Miscellaneous Provisions) Act 1989,[88] although in that context the Court of Appeal has said[89] that it will take a stricter view than the rather liberal interpretation of cases decided under the Statute of Frauds, under which a signature could be written anywhere on the agreement, provided that was intended to bind the party to the whole instrument[90]; and it could be just the guarantor's initials,[91] or even his printed name.[92] Signatures may also take an electronic form,[93] such as the party's name or initials or some other identifying

---

[85] Including later ratification relating back to the time of an (unauthorised) signature: *Koenigsblatt v Sweet* [1923] 2 Ch. 314 (contract for the sale of land within Statute of Frauds 1677 s.4); and the rule under CA 2006 s.51 (formerly CA 1985 s.36C) that a person purporting to contract for or as agent for a company which has not yet been formed is personally liable on the contract: *Braymist Ltd v Wise Finance Co Ltd* [2002] EWCA Civ 127; [2002] Ch. 273 at [67] (decision on signature by agent under LP(MP)A 1989 s.2; see para.5-22).

[86] *Heard v Pilley* (1869) L.R. 4 Ch. App. 549; *McLaughlin v Duffill* [2008] EWCA Civ 1627; [2010] Ch.1 at [17]–[19] (decision on LP(MP)A 1989 s.2, but drawing on decisions under Statute of Frauds). CA left open (at [14]) the question of which party has the burden of proof that the agent had (or had no) authority.

[87] On joinder of documents to satisfy the Statute of Frauds, see Cheshire & Burn, 16th edn (Butterworths, 2000), pp.120–121; Megarry and Wade, 5th edn (Stevens, 1984), pp.587–597; J. Williams, *The Statute of Frauds, Section Four, in the Light of its Judicial Interpretation* (Cambridge University Press, 1932), Pt III, Ch.7.

[88] See para.5-22.

[89] *Firstpost Homes Ltd v Johnson* [1995] 1 W.L.R. 1567, CA, at 1576 (Peter Gibson LJ).

[90] *Johnson v Dodgson* (1837) 2 M. & W. 653 at 659, 150 E.R. 918 at 921 (Lord Abinger CB); *Caton v Caton* (1867) L.R. 2 H.L. 127 (party's name appeared in different parts of the paper, but as a reference or description not in the form of promise or undertaking). See also *Lucas v James* (1849) 7 Hare 410 at 418–419, 68 E.R. 170 at 173 (writing in pencil can constitute a signature, if in the circumstances it appears to be intended to authenticate the document).

[91] *Hill v Hill* [1947] Ch. 231 (LPA 1925 s.40).

[92] *Cohen v Roche* [1927] 1 K.B. 169 at 174–176 (name printed on front page of auction catalogue), following *Saunderson v Jackson* (1800) 2 Bos. & P. 238, 126 E.R. 1257 and *Schneider v Norris* (1814) 2 M. & S. 286, 105 E.R. 388 (vendor's name printed on bill delivered to purchaser); *Leeman v Stocks* [1951] Ch. 941 (vendor's initials and surname inserted into standard form contract of sale by auctioneer before sale). cf. *Ramsay v Love* [2015] EWHC 65 (Ch) at [7] ("signature writing machine" operated by party or agent would suffice for guarantee, although this was a contract of indemnity and therefore not covered by s.4 of the Statute of Frauds. On this point the interpretation of "signature" for the purposes of LP(MP)A 1989 s.2 is stricter: see para.5-22. The 1989 Act requires the party to write his own name with his own hand on the document: typing or printing is insufficient: *Firstpost Homes Ltd v Johnson*, see para.6-14 fn.89, at 1575–1576 (Peter Gibson LJ) and 1577 (Balcombe LJ).

[93] For electronic signatures generally, see para.4-06. The Law Commission is undertaking a project on electronic signatures, designed to address any uncertainty as to the validity of electronic signatures in all types of contract: Law Com. No.377, *The 13th Programme of Law Reform* (2017), paras 2.11 to 2.13; Consultation Paper No.237 (2018). See para.4-07 fn.59.

mark[94] typed into an electronic communication such as an email, as long as the signatory intends the electronic "signature" to authenticate the document.[95]

(4) Failure to Comply with the Requirements of Section 4

Consequences of agreement failing to comply with section 4   Section 4 of the   **6-15**
Statute of Frauds does not prevent the formation of a contract to which it applies, but only provides that the contract cannot be enforced by action against a party who has not signed an agreement or a memorandum satisfying the section.[96] Any act of performance of the terms of the contract is therefore validly done even if it could not have been directly enforced because of a lack of writing: for example, where a guarantor against whom an (oral) guarantee could not have been enforced makes a payment to discharge his liability under the contract, the payment is validly made, and may give rise to the guarantor's right to be indemnified by the primary debtor.[97] However, an executor or administrator must not discharge an obligation undertaken by the deceased which is unenforceable by reason of the Statute of Frauds, since it does not create a debt or liability against the estate,[98] and the executor or administrator has an overriding duty to protect the estate against demands which by law cannot be enforced against it.[99]

Procedure and practice; pleading the Statute   Given that a contract which fails   **6-16**
to satisfy the requirements of s.4 is not void but "no action shall be brought upon" it, the section establishes a rule of procedure, not of substantive validity of the contract. It is for a party who wishes to rely on the Statute in order to deny the enforceability of a contract which he has made, to plead the Statute.[100]

---

94   *J Pereira Fernandes SA v Mehta*, see para.6-12 fn.77, at [27] (Judge Pelling QC: "a party can sign a document for the purposes of section 4 [of the Statute of Frauds] by using his full name or his last name prefixed by some or all of his initials or using his initials, and possibly by using a pseudonym or a combination of letters and numbers (as can happen for example with a Lloyds slip scratch), providing always that whatever was used was inserted into the document in order to give, and with the intention of giving, authenticity to it").

95   *J Pereira Fernandes SA v Mehta*, see para.6-12 fn.77, at [29]–[30] (email address automatically inserted by internet service provider is not a signature for Statute of Frauds 1677 s.4, because it does not have authenticating intention; and its appearance divorced from the main body of the text of the message emphasised this to be so).

96   *Maddison v Alderson* (1883) 8 App. Cas. 467 at 474 (Earl of Selborne LC: "the 4th section of the Statute of Frauds does not avoid parol contracts, but only bars the legal remedies by which they might otherwise have been enforced"); *Leroux v Brown*, see para.6-16 fn.101. Some earlier cases referred to the contract being "void": e.g. *Chater v Beckett* (1797) 7 T.R. 201 at 204, 101 E.R. 931 at 933 (Lord Kenyon CJ).

97   In the absence of an express right of indemnity against the primary debtor (the terms of which will determine its scope) there is an implied right to reimbursement by way of restitution to the extent that the payment has conferred a benefit on the primary debtor by discharging his liability to the creditor: Goff & Jones, paras 19-16 to 19-21. For the suggestion that it is open to debate whether the payment of money under a contract which could not be enforced by reason of the Statute of Frauds might be recoverable on the basis of a mistake of law, see Anson, p.87. However, this is against a statement by Lord Blackburn in *Maddison v Alderson*, see para.6-15 fn.96, at 490 that "when a parol promise is to answer for the default of another and credit is given on the faith of such a parol guarantee to one who makes default, the consideration cannot be restored, and cannot be compensated for except by fulfilling the contract of guarantee".

98   *Re Rownson* (1885) 29 Ch. D. 358, CA, at 364.

99   *Midgley v Midgley* [1893] 3 Ch. 282, CA, at 299.

100 *Cooth v Jackson* (1801) 6 Ves. Jun. 12 at 39, 31 E.R. 913 at 927 (Lord Eldon LC: "if the Defendant

The characterisation of the requirement of s.4 of the Statute as a matter of procedure has had a significant further consequence in relation to litigation in the English courts concerning foreign contracts. It was held in *Leroux v Brown*[101] that, since s.4 establishes a rule of procedure rather than of substantive validity of the contract, a contract entered into under the law of another jurisdiction, even if otherwise valid and enforceable in England under the rules of private international law, is not enforceable unless it satisfies the Statute. This decision has been said by the Court of Appeal still to be applicable,[102] although it has rightly been very heavily criticised.[103]

6-17   **Solutions for the absence of statutory formalities**   There are some possible solutions for problems arising from the failure to satisfy s.4. If the contract is severable, or if a contract collateral to the contract of guarantee can be established, those provisions which do not relate to the (unenforceable) guarantee may be enforced.[104] And it may be possible to obtain rectification of a document which fails to satisfy the formality requirements for an enforceable guarantee, in order to comply with s.4.[105] If the person giving a guarantee is subject to some other regulatory jurisdiction, it may be that there will be professional sanctions for non-compliance with the obligations even though they are strictly unenforceable by judicial action.[106] There

admits the agreement, but insists upon the benefit of the statute, the statute protects him: if he does not say any thing about the statute, then he must be taken to renounce the benefit of it"); *Clarke v Callow* (1876) 46 L.J.Q.B. 53, CA. The decisions in older cases depend on the application of the procedure rules then in force. Non-compliance with the Statute should now be raised as a matter of defence under CPR Pt 15. The existence of a potential defence under the Statute (which had been raised in the pleadings but then not pursued) does not deprive the court of jurisdiction to make a consent order settling the claim: *RM Legal Solicitors v TA Milano* [2014] EWHC 1251 (QB).
[101] (1852) 12 C.B. 801 at 824, 826, 138 E.R. 1119 at 1129, 1130 (oral agreement governed by French law failed to satisfy Statute of Frauds).
[102] *G&H Montague GmbH v Irvani* [1990] 1 W.L.R. 667, CA, at 684 (Mustill LJ (obiter) "it would take a good deal to persuade me that this court should now hold [*Leroux v Brown*] to be wrongly decided. On the contrary, the reasoning on the interpretation of the statute seems to me ... unassailable. The statute has twice been amended, since *Leroux v Brown* was decided, at times when the criticisms of the decision were current. Yet the opportunity was not taken to confine it to domestic contracts. In such circumstances, if the case is to be overturned, this should be undertaken by the House of Lords"); see Purchas LJ similarly at 690–691.
[103] See, e.g. Dicey, Morris and Collins, *The Conflict of Laws*, 15th edn (London: Sweet & Maxwell, 2017), paras 2-046, n.86 (the "decision was doubted by Willes J. in *Williams v Wheeler* (1806) 8 C.B. (N.S.) 299, 316, and *Gibson v Holland* (1865) L.R. 1 C.P. 1, 8 and condemned by nearly every writer who has discussed it"); 7-026 ("To characterise the section as procedural merely because it says 'no action shall be brought' is to regard the form of the section as more important than its substance. To characterise it as procedural for the purposes of the conflict of laws merely because it had previously been characterised as procedural for some purposes of English domestic law is to lose sight of the purpose of the characterisation"). At para.2-046 the editors contrast the similar characterisation by the English courts of limitation periods as procedural and therefore governed by the lex fori, but note that, for limitation periods, "fortunately, the false turn taken by the English courts was corrected by the Foreign Limitation Periods Act 1984, and the Contracts (Applicable Law) Act 1990 Sch.1, art.10(1)(d) and Rome I Regulation (Regulation (EC) 593/2008 art.15(h))"; and at para.7-030 they note that the effect of *Leroux v Brown* "has been greatly reduced by the Rome I Regulation, Art.18(2), which allows the proof of a contract by reference to the law governing the issue of formal validity as an alternative to the law of the forum".
[104] See para.6-12 fn.75.
[105] *Fairstate Ltd v General Enterprise and Management Ltd* [2010] EWHC 3072 (QB); [2011] 2 All E.R. (Comm) 497 at [75].
[106] For the exercise by the Court of its own jurisdiction to enforce an undertaking given to the Court

is also, however, a question whether it may be possible to use other mechanisms such as equitable doctrines, or some form of estoppel, to give effect to the guarantee even though it is not itself directly enforceable because of the lack of writing.[107]

Part performance and estoppel   We have already seen that in a range of different circumstances the courts have developed the means of giving at least some effect to transactions which fail to satisfy formality requirements set by the law, where there are good countervailing reasons to prevent a party insisting on the strict application of the formality rule.[108] In the case of s.4 of the Statute of Frauds, the courts devised the doctrine of "part performance" to circumvent the requirement of a written memorandum, signed by the defendant, for the enforceability against him of a contract for the sale or other disposition of an interest in land. This equitable doctrine of part performance did not, strictly, allow the claimant to enforce the contract, but rather gave him an equitable claim which operated outside the contract (and outside the Statute).[109] Part performance was developed only in relation to the provision in s.4 dealing with contracts relating to land,[110] but it was based on the general principle that the courts would not permit the Statute of Frauds itself to be made an instrument of fraud,[111] which is also the basis of other similar equitable doctrines developed by the courts to allow a party to circumvent the absence of a legal formality requirement.[112] It is therefore perhaps natural to consider whether a party might be able to invoke some similar doctrine, such as a form of estoppel, to prevent a party relying on the absence of formality in order to resist a claim under a contract of guarantee.

However, the suggestion that such ways can be found to circumvent the strict formality requirements must always be viewed cautiously, since they should not be permitted to undermine the purpose of the particular formality requirement set by the statute.[113] A contract of guarantee is a serious unilateral commitment, and the requirement of writing has a clear protective function; indeed, one might expect the formality requirement to be increased, rather than decreased, in order to give clear and verifiable protection to the guarantor.[114] When the tort of deceit was developed, and opened up the possibility of a claim being brought against a person who made a fraudulent statement about a person's creditworthiness, the use of the tort was seen

6-18

by an attorney, one of its own officers, see *Re Greaves* (1827) 1 Cr. & J. 374n., 148 E.R. 1466n.; *Evans v Duncombe* (1831) 1 Cr. & J. 372, 148 E.R. 1465.
[107] See para.6-18.
[108] See paras 4-12 to 4-15.
[109] See para.5-06.
[110] It was also referred to expressly in LPA 1925 s.40 when it replaced the provisions of Statute of Frauds s.4, relating to land. In *Clipper Maritime Ltd v Shirlstar Container Transport Ltd (The Anemone)* [1987] 1 Lloyd's Rep. 546 at 557 Staughton J contemplated (obiter) the possibility that acts of part performance by the party seeking to enforce a guarantee of which there is no sufficient memorandum in writing to satisfy s.4 might render the guarantee enforceable, but without any detailed consideration of the "difficult questions of law" involved.
[111] *Maddison v Alderson*, see fn.96, at 474 (Earl of Selborne LC).
[112] See para.4-13.
[113] See para.4-15; see esp. *Yaxley v Gotts* [2000] Ch. 162, CA, at 191 (Beldam LJ: "The general principle that a party cannot rely on an estoppel in the face of a statute depends upon the nature of the enactment, the purpose of the provision and the social policy behind it").
[114] cf. Anson, p.82, arguing that the "subtle distinctions" of the application of the Statute of Frauds s.4 should be removed and the formality increased to require the guarantee to be *in writing*. For the reasons given by the Law Reform Committee in 1953 to retain the provision in Statute of Frauds s.4, dealing with guarantees, see para.6-06.

to threaten the policy of the Statute of Frauds by allowing claims against a person making a fraudulent oral representation or assurance of creditworthiness which would not have been enforceable as a guarantee; Parliament responded in 1828 by providing a defence to the tort claim if the representation or assurance was not made in writing.[115] And Lord Blackburn, albeit obiter, commented in 1880 that Parliament has retained the requirement of written evidence for guarantees even though there are "constantly cases occurring in which it is felt that it is morally very wrong to set up such a defence, and in which, as has been sometimes said, the statute for the prevention of fraud operates as a statute to facilitate fraud".[116] In the modern law, judges have contemplated the possibility that there might be situations where a guarantor, whose obligation is in law unenforceable by reason of the lack of formality under s.4 of the Statute of Frauds, might act in such a way as to estop himself from relying on the statute,[117] although no such estoppel has yet been found in the decision in any reported case.[118] There can be no argument in favour of an estoppel to circumvent the absence of writing within s.4 unless the guarantor has said or done something which encourages the beneficiary erroneously to believe that the guarantee is legally binding, and where the beneficiary reasonably so believes and acts accordingly.[119] For example, one can imagine the case for an estoppel by representation where the guarantor incorrectly represents that the guarantee has been signed in accordance with s.4 and the beneficiary acts on the basis that the document constitutes a valid contract.[120] However, the House of Lords has made clear that the mere making of an oral promise of guarantee cannot be a representation sufficient to found an estoppel.[121]

---

[115] Statute of Frauds Amendment Act 1828 ("Lord Tenterden's Act") s.6: "No action shall be brought whereby to charge any person upon or by reason of any representation or assurance made or given concerning or relating to the character, conduct, credit, ability, trade, or dealings of any other person, to the intent or purpose that such other person may obtain credit, money, or goods upon, unless such representation or assurance be made in writing, signed by the party to be charged therewith". On the scope of application of this provision in the modern law, see Cartwright (Misrepresentation), para.5-30.

[116] *Steele v McKinlay* (1880) 5 App. Cas. 754, HL(Sc) at 769.

[117] *Bank of Scotland v Wright* [1990] B.C.C. 663 at 681 (Brooke J: "I would not exclude the possibility that circumstances might arise in which a guarantor might have acted in such a way as to create or influence the other party's mistaken belief in the effectiveness of his guarantee so that it would be unconscionable to allow him to rely on the Statute of Frauds. Such a finding would depend very much on the court's views, on the facts of any particular case of the personalities and attributes of the two parties between whom the alleged estoppel was alleged to have arisen. I am satisfied, however, that it would be quite wrong to do so on the facts of this case").

[118] *MyBarrister Ltd v Hewetson* [2017] EWHC 2624 (Ch) at [55] (speeches in *Actionstrength*, see para.6-18 fn.121, "show that there is a high hurdle to be overcome to establish an estoppel to reliance on the Statute of Frauds"), [77] (application to serve reply alleging that an estoppel to reliance on the Statute of Frauds had arisen faced "formidable hurdles").

[119] *Bank of Scotland v Wright*, see para.6-18 fn.117, at 681 ("Although I do not consider that Mr Wright was quite as naive as he would have me believe, he was not an acute, experienced, commercially minded businessman, and I can find nothing in his conduct throughout this affair which could properly be described as the active encouragement or influencing of the bank in its mistaken belief which the cases have shown are a necessary ingredient of this type of estoppel. If the bank, which ought to have been quite capable of knowing the law and of drawing up the guarantee properly, had failed to do so, while retaining the mistaken belief that it had looked after its interests properly, then in my judgment Mr Wright would have been quite entitled to rely on the Statute of Frauds".)

[120] cf. *Shah v Shah* [2001] EWCA Civ 527; [2002] Q.B. 35 (representation that deed had been executed in compliance with requirements of LP(MP)A 1989 s.1; see para.7-16).

[121] *Actionstrength Ltd v International Glass Engineering IN.GL.EN. SpA* [2003] UKHL 17; [2003] 2

III.   Other Contracts for which Writing is Required as an Evidential Formality

Contracts of marine insurance   A contract of marine insurance[122] is inadmissible in evidence unless it embodied in a marine policy in accordance with the Marine Insurance Act 1906.[123] The policy must comply with the requirements of the Act as to form and content,[124] and be signed by or on behalf of the insurer.[125] It need not itself be the contract,[126] but may be executed and issued either at the time when the contract is concluded, or afterwards.[127] The effect of this provision is that neither party can enforce the contract if there is no policy, complying with the Act, that can be used as evidence of it. This is a drastic consequence for the insured, in particular, who has no control over the issue of the policy; and the provision is anomalous in imposing a special formality requirement for marine insurance contracts which does not apply for other insurance contracts. The original purpose of the requirement of writing as evidence for the enforceability of a marine insurance contract was to ensure that stamp duty was paid. Stamp duty on such policies was abolished in 1970,[128] and the Law Commission has said that the requirement to have a policy in writing is now widely ignored, and should be abolished.[129]

6-19

A.C. 541 at [9] (Lord Bingham: "There was no representation by St-Gobain that it would honour the agreement despite the absence of writing, or that it was not a contract of guarantee, or that it would confirm the agreement in writing. Nor did St-Gobain make any payment direct to Actionstrength which could arguably be relied on as affirming the oral agreement or inducing Actionstrength to go on supplying labour. If St-Gobain were held to be estopped in this case it is hard to see why any oral guarantor, where credit was extended to a debtor on the strength of a guarantee, would not be similarly estopped. The result would be to render nugatory a provision which, despite its age, Parliament has deliberately chosen to retain". See also Lord Woolf at [12] and Lord Walker at [51]. Whether such a representation of the validity of the guarantee, even if made, could found an estoppel was left open by Lord Hoffmann at [29] and Lord Clyde at [34]).

[122]   "a contract whereby the insurer undertakes to indemnify the assured, in manner and to the extent thereby agreed, against marine losses, that is to say, the losses incident to marine adventure": Marine Insurance Act 1906 s.1.

[123]   Marine Insurance Act 1906 s.22. Contracts by which the Secretary of State or others undertake reinsurance of war risks are not governed by this provision, but have separate requirements (including being laid before each House of Parliament): Marine and Aviation Insurance (War Risk) Act 1952 ss.1, 7.

[124]   Marine Insurance Act 1906 ss.23, 26, 30. Sch.1 contains a non-mandatory form of policy.

[125]   Marine Insurance Act 1906 s.24(1). Corporations may execute such instruments either by the signature of an agent, or by their corporate seal: ibid.

[126]   Marine Insurance Act 1906 s.21 (contract concluded when proposal of assured accepted by insurer, whether policy then issued or not; slip or covering note may be referred to for purposes of showing when proposal accepted).

[127]   Marine Insurance Act 1906 s.22.

[128]   Finance Act 1970 s.32, Sch.7 para.1(2)(b).

[129]   Law Commission CP No.201, *Insurance Contract Law: Post Contract Duties and Other Issues* (2011), Ch.4; see also Law Commission Issues Paper 9, *The Requirement for a Formal Marine Policy: Should Section 22 Be Repealed?* (October 2010). Consultees were unanimously in support of the repeal of s.22. In Law Com. No.353, *Insurance Contract Law: Business Disclosure; Warranties; Insurers' Remedies for Fraudulent Claims; and Late Payment* (July 2014) para.1.15, the Law Commission noted that the requirement for a formal marine policy was not covered by that report, but said that they intended to publish a further (final) report by the end of 2014. However, no further proposal has yet been made. See generally *https://www.lawcom.gov.uk/project/insurance-contract-law/*.

IV. WRITTEN EVIDENCE AS A CONDITION OF ENFORCEABILITY OF A VARIATION OF A CONTRACT

6-20 **Formality set as an evidential condition for the enforceability of a contract applies also to its variation.** The variation of an existing contract by agreement of the parties, whether it supersedes the initial contract (e.g. by novation) or simply modifies one or more terms of the contract, must satisfy the same rules as are set for the formation of the initial contract, at least if the varied contract is to have the same binding force as the initial contract.[130] Where the law sets a specific formality as an evidential condition for the enforceability of a contract of a particular type, as a general rule the same formality will be required for a contractual variation of such a contract. Where a contract of guarantee is varied by the parties, the contract as varied must comply with s.4 of the Statute of Frauds.[131] although this may be by there being a signed memorandum which is sufficiently complete to satisfy the requirements of the section[132] by referring to other documents (and so the variation, if signed, may refer to the original form of guarantee).[133] The Statute does not, however, apply to a contract which is designed not to vary the contract but only to rescind (or discharge) it.[134]

---

[130] See para.1-02.
[131] See para.6-20.
[132] See para.6-12.
[133] *Moat Financial Services Ltd v Wilkinson* [2005] EWCA Civ 1253 at [21]–[23].
[134] *Morris v Baron & Co* [1918] A.C. 1; nor does the Statute apply where there is a mere forbearance to enforce it which is enforceable as a waiver or under the doctrine of estoppel: *Morris v Baron & Co* at 30–31; *Besseler Waechter Glover & Co v South Derwent Coal Co Ltd* [1938] 1 K.B. 408 at 416 (both cases dealing not with guarantees but with contracts for the sale of goods of the value of £10 or more under Sale of Goods Act 1893 s.4, replacing Statute of Frauds 1677 s.17).

CHAPTER 7

A GENERAL FORMALITY: THE DEED[1]

I. THE DEED AS A FORMAL INSTRUMENT IN ENGLISH LAW: HISTORY AND CONTEXT

Historical context for the use of deeds   The deed is an ancient form of instru-   **7-01**
ment in transactions between private parties in English law, and in many respects
its form and use in modern private law can be understood only from its history. The
detail of the origins and of the form and early uses of the deed must be sought in
specialist works on English legal history[2]; for present purposes it is sufficient to note
that the deed was a formal instrument on paper or parchment which a party sealed
and delivered to acknowledge that he was bound by the instrument[3]; and that it was
used to effect both dispositions of property and transactions creating, varying and
discharging obligations. It allowed parties to enter into transactions by affixing their
seal on a document even if they were unable to write or to read it and so relied on
others to relay its contents to them[4]; and it allowed parties to make use of documents in order to effect the grant or surrender of incorporeal interests in land (which
could not be effected by physical delivery)[5] and to accompany[6] (and, eventually, to

---

[1] Chitty, paras 1-113 to 1-144; Furmston, paras 2.136 to 2.137; Treitel, paras 3-170 to 3-173; Anson,
     pp.80–82; Halsbury, 5th edn, Vol.32 (2012); Burrows (Restatement) s.8(1); Andrews, art.33.
[2] See, e.g. A.W.B. Simpson, *A History of the Common Law of Contract* (Clarendon Press, 1987), Pt
     I, Chs 1, 2; J.H. Baker, *An Introduction to English Legal History*, 4th edn (Butterworths LexisNexis,
     2002), p.279, Ch.18; S.F.C. Milsom, *Historical Foundations of the Common Law*, 2nd edn (But-
     terworths, 1981), pp.246–262; F. Pollock and F.W. Maitland, *The History of English Law*, 2nd edn
     (Cambridge University Press, 1968), Vol.ii, Ch.V (Contract), esp. pp.219–220, 223–224 (on the
     origin and use of seals); W.S. Holdsworth *A History of English Law*, vol.iii, 5th edn (Methuen &
     Co, 1942), pp.226–234.
[3] *Goddard's Case*, see para.7-04 fn.38.
[4] If the document was not as represented to a party who in fact affixed his seal and delivered the instru-
     ment, he had recourse to the plea that the apparent deed (*factum*) was not his deed (*non est factum*):
     this was an extension from the primary use of the plea of *non est factum* in cases where a person
     had not in fact executed the instrument with the intent to make it his deed, or even at all (e.g. where
     a seal was misused to create a forged instrument). For the modern use of the plea of *non est factum*,
     see *Saunders v Anglia Building Society* [1971] A.C. 1004, esp. at 1024 (Lord Wilberforce, setting
     the modern law in its historical context); Cartwright (Misrepresentation), paras 13-55 to 13-60;
     Chitty, paras 3-049 to 3-056; Treitel, paras 8-079 to 8-086; Anson, pp.279–282; Cheshire, Fifoot and
     Furmston, pp.333–340.
[5] Co. Litt. 9a, 172a, 338a; A.W.B. Simpson, *A History of the Land Law*, 2nd edn (Clarendon Press,
     1986), pp.121–122; Holdsworth, see para.7-01 fn.2, pp.98–99.

substitute for[7]) physical delivery in the case of freehold estates in land.[8] In relation to obligations, the deed was in use in the thirteenth and fourteenth centuries—long before the development of the modern law of contract from different historical roots[9] —as an evidential requirement for the enforcement of an agreement by way of the writ of covenant in the King's courts[10]; and as evidence of a debt (either a sum of money or a quantity of fungible goods) in an action of debt.[11] Where there was a simple promise to pay a sum of money, a deed was required to enable the action of debt to be brought[12]; and a very significant form of deed was the "conditioned bond", an undertaking to pay a specific sum of money unless a specified condition was performed.[13]

The later development of the modern general law of contract, requiring consideration for the enforcement of a promise,[14] has not in itself affected the law on deeds which has continued to exist and to develop. Later in this chapter we shall see the place for deeds in modern English law,[15] and that the formality requirements for deeds have now been changed in various respects.[16] The result, however, is a modern law of deeds which is still based on its medieval origins; and which, in the context of the law of obligations, forms an alternative mechanism by which promises may be given binding force, even if the promise does not satisfy the requirements for a contract supported by consideration. It may therefore be said that there are two alternative bases of contractual obligation in modern English law: an informal (or "simple", or "parol"[17]) contract—an agreement, whether written or oral

---

[6]   Simpson, see para.7-01 fn.5, p.120; Holdsworth, see para.7-01 fn.2, pp.221–234.
[7]   Real Property Act 1845 s.2; Simpson, see para.7-01 fn.5, p.278. The requirement to use a deed to convey legal estates in land was finally imposed by LPA 1925 ss.51(1), 52(1).
[8]   Co. Litt. 49a.
[9]   The action of assumpsit: see paras 8-02, 8-03 and the works cited there.
[10] Informal agreements were enforced in the local courts; "by 1321, however, the royal judges had decided that the only acceptable evidence of a covenant in the royal court was a deed, a written document under seal": Baker see para.7-01 fn.2, p.319. See also D. Ibbetson, *A Historical Introduction to the Law of Obligations* (Oxford University Press, 1999), pp.24–28; Pollock and Maitland, see para.7-01 fn.2, pp.219–20; Holdsworth, see para.7-01 fn.2, pp.417–420; Simpson, *A History of the Common Law of Contract*, see para.7-01 fn.2, pp.9–17.
[11] In support of the writ of debt, the debt could be evidenced either by a deed or by proof of the fact of some other informal transaction which gave rise to the debt, such as a sale or loan: Baker, see para.7-01 fn.2, pp.321–322. See also Ibbetson, see para.7-01 fn.10, pp.28–30; Simpson, see para.7-01 fn.10, pp.53, 88, 136; Holdsworth, see para.7-01 fn.2, pp.417–420.
[12] Baker, see para.7-01 fn.2, p.322; Simpson, see para.7-01 fn.10, pp.88–90, 95 ("whatever the position may have been at an early period, the developed common law treated the instrument as dispositive—the instrument *was* the obligation").
[13] "Debt on an obligation", an action which continued in regular use until the 19th century when the forms of action were abolished, and in the context of which the courts developed the modern rules against penalties in order to limit the use of penal debts attached to performance conditions: Baker, see para.7-01 fn.2, pp.323–326; Ibbetson, see para.7-01 fn.10, pp.150–151, 213–214, 255–256; Simpson, see para.7-01 fn.10, pp.90–92, 118–125.
[14] See para.7-01 fn.9.
[15] See para.7-03 and section III.
[16] See, section II, esp. para.7-05.
[17] Contrary to its original and core meaning, the use by English lawyers of the word "parol" is not limited to words in their oral form, but includes any informal written or spoken agreement or evidence: see Skynner C.B. in *Rann v Hughes*, see para.7-01 fn.19; cf. OED Online, March 2018, "parol, n. and adj.".

or partly written and partly oral, supported by consideration; and a formal (or "specialty"[18]) contract—an agreement or undertaking contained in a deed.[19]

Deeds poll and indentures   A deed may be a unilateral instrument, or an instrument between two or more parties. If unilateral, it was traditionally called a "deed poll"; if between parties ("inter partes") it was traditionally an "indenture".[20] These names were used to reflect the physical form in which deeds used to be executed: if there were more than one party, the instrument was written in multiple parts and the parts cutting with jagged line ("indented") so that the several parts in the possession of each of the parties to the deed could be shown to form part of the same instrument.[21] A unilateral deed had no need to be cut to correspond in two or more parts, and so the top and sides were cut even ("polled").[22] This physical form of the indenture, rather than the fact that it was described in the instrument as an indenture, used to be part of the formality requirements of a deed inter partes,[23] but both the practice of indenting and the technical language has fallen largely into disuse.[24] Since 1845 it has been provided that a deed purporting to be an indenture shall have the effect of an indenture although not actually indented,[25] and it is not necessary to use the word "indenture".[26]

7-02

A "party" to a deed inter partes is simply one who joins in and executes the deed with the other party or parties, and thereby acquires a right to enforce terms which are expressed to be in his favour without having to demonstrate that he has provided consideration.[27] A deed can therefore embody a bilateral or multilateral transaction, with or without sufficient consideration to give rise to an enforceable contract

---

[18] See para.7-19 fn.215.

[19] *Rann v Hughes* (1778) 7 T.R. 350n, 101 E.R. 1014 (Skynner C.B.: "All contracts are, by the laws of England, distinguished into agreements by specialty, and agreements by parol; nor is there any such third class as some of the counsel have endeavoured to maintain, as contracts in writing. If they be merely written, and not specialties, they are parol, and a consideration must be proved"). On the significance of this case, see further para.8-02. See also *Foakes v Beer* (1884) 9 App. Cas. 605, HL, at 613 (Lord Selborne: "The distinction between the effect of a deed under seal, and that of an agreement by parol, or by writing not under seal, may seem arbitrary, but it is established in our law"). A deed does not require an "agreement" as in the case of an informal contract: see Ch.3, but can give effect to a unilateral promise, notably in the case of a deed poll: see para.7-02.

[20] Co. Litt. 35b ("Of deeds, some be indented, and some be deeds poll. Of indented, some be bipartite, some tripartite, some quadripartite, etc.").

[21] Co. Litt. 229a. The indentation was "formerly in acute angles, *instar dentium*, like the teeth of a saw, but at present in a waving line"; and originally (when deeds were "more concise") the parts of the deed were written on the same piece of parchment and were separated by cutting the indentation through words or letters written across the join: W. Blackstone, *Commentaries on the Laws of England*, 15th edn (Strahan, 1809), book II, pp.295–296.

[22] Co. Litt. 229a.

[23] Co. Litt. 229a (even if the document is called an indenture, if it is not in fact indented it is not in law an indenture: "it may be an indenture without words, but not by words without indenting").

[24] In modern usage, the term "deed poll" is most commonly used to refer to the deed executed in order to evidence a change of name: Halsbury, Vol.88 (2012) 5th edn, para.333; Enrolment of Deeds (Change of Name) Regulations 1994 (SI 1994/604).

[25] Real Property Act 1845 s.5; see now LPA 1925 s.56(2) ("A deed between parties, to effect its objects, has the effect of an indenture though not indented or expressed to be an indenture").

[26] LPA 1925 ss.56(2), 57.

[27] *Cannon v Hartley* [1949] Ch. 213 (volunteer was party to deed of separation and direct covenantee); *Pinnel's Case* (1602) 5 Co. Rep. 117a at 117b, 77 E.R. 237 at 238 ("if a man acknowledges himself to be satisfied by deed, it is a good bar [to enforcement of a debt], without any thing received"). This does not, however, apply for covenants in restraint of trade, for which consideration must be given even if executed as a deed: *Davis v Mason* (1793) 5 Term Rep. 118 at 120, 101 E.R. 69 at 70.

in the absence of a deed, but which is enforceable by its parties[28]; but it can also take effect as a unilateral, gratuitous instrument by which either a right of property or a contractual right is granted to a person identified in the deed as its beneficiary, and it is the formality of the deed which creates that enforceable right without the requirement for the beneficiary to accept it or even know about it.[29]

7-03 **The use of deeds in modern English private law** The deed remains a significant formal instrument within the modern law, in both property law and contract. It is in the property law context, however, and in particular land transactions, that deeds are most commonly encountered, and therefore we shall see during the course of this chapter that many of the judicial authorities relating to deeds come from the context of dispositions of interests in land. They can, however, generally be read as applicable to deeds as they may be used in any context.

In the context of property law, a legal estate or interest in or over land cannot generally be created or transferred without a deed.[30] Under the system of registration of title to legal estates in land, transfers of legal estates must still be effected by a deed of transfer, even though the transfer must itself be completed by registration in the (electronic) land register in order to operate at law.[31] A mortgage over land is also normally effected by deed, again subject to registration.[32] And outside the law of real property, deeds may be used in order to create or transfer property rights as an alternative to physical delivery in the case of tangible property.[33]

---

[28] Even where the deed is between parties, it is possible for a person who is not a party to enforce a covenant directly under LPA 1925 s.56(1) (reproducing and extending Real Property Act 1845 s.5), but only where the deed relates to real property, according to the interpretation of the majority in *Beswick v Beswick* [1968] A.C. 58, HL; and only if the person, though not himself a party, is identified as one *with whom* the covenant is made, according to Neuberger J in *Amsprop Trading Ltd v Harris Distribution Ltd* [1997] 1 W.L.R. 1025. On the effect of s.56 in the context of the law of real property, see Cheshire and Burn, pp.741–743; Megarry and Wade, paras 32-006 to 32-008. If the deed embodies a contract, whether or not relating to real property, a third party may have the right to enforce a term directly under the Contracts (Rights of Third Parties) Act 1999.

[29] The deed must be "delivered", but this does not require physical delivery to the beneficiary: see para.7-12, who may therefore remain in ignorance of its execution: *Macedo v Stroud* [1922] 2 A.C. 330, PC, at 337. If a contract is seen as based on agreement, the deed may not be characterised as a contract at all, but rather as a unilateral legal act given force by its form (cf. Treitel, para.3-170); *Prime Sight Ltd v Lavarello* [2013] UKPC 22; [2014] A.C. 436 at [30]); but it is more usual to see contract as covering the wider category of consensual legal obligations and therefore to include a contract by deed poll: e.g. Anson, p.79; Chitty, paras 1-113, 1-136.

[30] LPA 1925 s.52(1). The exceptions are set out in s.52(2); perhaps the most significant is the creation of a lease not exceeding three years at the best rent which can reasonably be obtained without taking a fine (a premium for the grant of the lease): ss.52(2)(d), 54(2).

[31] The parties and their solicitors do not have direct access to the electronic register to effect a change of title, but must transmit the deed of transfer to the Land Registry: the proposal to allow such direct access, in a system of "e-conveyancing", was deferred indefinitely by the Land Registry in 2011: see para.4-06 fn.41. There is, however, provision for certain documents in electronic form which purport to effect dispositions relating to registered land to be regarded as deeds, thereby allowing in effect a form of electronic deed but only in certain specified contexts: Land Registration Act 2002 s.91; see para.7-08, esp. fn.84. However, the submission of applications, and the transmission of many documents to the Land Registry (such as deeds of transfer), is now done routinely by the parties' legal advisers by the electronic transfer of scanned copies of the original documents through the Registry's electronic document registration service ("e-DRS").

[32] In registered land, a legal mortgage can be created only by a charge by deed expressed to be by way of legal mortgage (LPA 1925 s.85(1), Land Registration Act 2002 s.23(1)(a)); the charge may, however, be effected by an electronic transaction: see para.7-03 fn.31.

[33] M. Bridge, *Personal Property Law*, 4th edn (Oxford University Press, 2015), p.174.

In the context of contracts, the deed can be used an alternative to a simple, informal contract,[34] and therefore the parties to an agreement which constitutes a binding contract supported by consideration may choose to give effect to their agreement through the formality of a deed in order to obtain advantages which a deed may bring over a simple, informal contract.[35] But if the promise which it is sought to render enforceable is not supported by consideration, the deed is a mechanism by which it may be given force which it would otherwise not have.[36] We shall consider in more detail practical issues relating to the use of deeds in the context of modern contractual obligations later in this chapter.[37]

II.   THE FORMALITY REQUIREMENTS FOR A VALID DEED

(1)   Requirements Set by the Common Law and by Statute

The requirements of a valid deed at common law   The common law required   **7-04**
a deed to be written on paper or parchment, and sealed and delivered by the party or parties executing the deed.[38] A signature was not required; nor was a witness; and the deed did not need to be dated in order to be validly executed.[39] We shall see that the common law had to define what would constitute a sufficient "sealing"[40] and "delivery"[41] of the instrument, but it is clear that, if it was not in fact sealed, it was not a deed[42]; nor did the instrument take effect as a deed until it had been delivered within the meaning given by the common law to that term. These are therefore formality requirements set by the common law as substantive conditions of the legal effect of an instrument as a deed.[43]

The instrument which was executed by being sealed and delivered had to be a sufficient and complete document to give effect to the intention of the party executing it: for example, a document which, at the time of its execution, contained blanks in its terms which prevented the instrument constituting an effective transaction, could not become a valid and enforceable deed by the blanks later being filled in by a third party who had no authority to re-execute the deed on behalf of the parties.[44] And although there may be schedules annexed to the document which was

---

[34] See para.7-01 fn.17.

[35] e.g. a longer period of limitation of actions: see para.7-19.

[36] Even so, it may not have the same full force as a promise supported by consideration; e.g. the remedy of specific performance, though not often available for a contract supported by consideration, will not normally be granted at all in the case of a voluntary undertaking: see para.7-18.

[37] See paras 7-17 to 7-21.

[38] *Goddard's Case* (1584) 2 Co. Rep. 4b at 5a, 76 E.R. 396 at 398 ("there are but three things of the essence and substance of a deed, that is to say, writing in paper or parchment, sealing and delivery"). Coke added requirements as to the parties and the transaction to give a list of "ten things ... necessarily incident" to a deed, but the essential formality requirements are unchanged in his list (Co. Litt. 35b: "First, writing. Secondly, in parchment or paper. Thirdly, a person able to contract. Fourthly, by a sufficient name. Fifthly, a person able to be contracted with. Sixthly, by a sufficient name. Seventhly, a thing to be contracted for. Eighthly, apt words required by law. Ninthly, sealing. And tenthly, delivery".

[39] *Goddard's Case*, see para.7-04 fn.38.

[40] See para.7-09.

[41] See para.7-12.

[42] *National Provincial Bank of England v Jackson* (1886) 33 Ch. D. 1, CA, at 11.

[43] cf. para.4-10.

[44] *Hibblewhite v McMorine* (1840) 6 M. & W. 200 at 216; 151 E.R. 380 at 388 (Parke B., reviewing the authorities: "there is none that shews that an instrument, which when executed, is incapable of

itself sealed, so that the instrument as a whole, including the schedules, was executed as a deed, the schedules must be in existence and attached to the principal document at the time when it is sealed.[45]

7-05 **Changes to the common law made by statute; summary of the requirements of a valid deed in the modern law**   Changes have been made by statute to the common law requirements for a valid deed. Some are general changes applicable to all deeds, flowing from the desire to reform the formality requirements in order to meet modern circumstances; other changes distinguish in their effect between individuals and corporations executing deeds. The common law did not itself make any distinction in the formality requirements for deeds as between individuals and corporations[46]: the deed must be written on paper or parchment, and be sealed and delivered[47] by the individual or by the corporation,[48] or by an agent authorised (by deed[49]) to act on his or its behalf. However, as new forms of corporation have been created by statute, the requirements for the execution of deeds by corporations have sometimes also been varied in ways appropriate for each type of corporation.

Of the requirements set by the common law for a deed, only delivery remains unchanged.[50] The requirement that the deed be written on paper or parchment was changed in 1990 to allow a deed to be written on any substance[51] although writing

---

having any operation, and is no deed, can afterwards become a deed, by being completed and delivered by a stranger in the absence of the party who executed and unauthorized by instrument under seal"); cf. *Hudson v Revett* (1829) 5 Bing. 368; 130 E.R. 1103 (blanks at first left in deed on its sealing by one party but later completed in that party's presence, acknowledging the deed; it had either been delivered at first subject to a condition which was later satisfied, or was re-delivered). See also *Powell v Duff* (1812) 3 Camp. 181; 170 E.R. 1348 (bond subject to condition, but condition was added later because defendant was in a hurry to get away: not a deed); *Tayler v Great Indian Peninsula Railway Co* (1859) 4 De G. & J. 559; 45 E.R. 217 (transferee of shares left blank: transfer void); *Swan v North British Australasian Co* (1863) 2 Hurl. & C. 175; 159 E.R. 73, Ex.Ch. (share transfer executed in blank, completed later by third party fraudulently in relation to other shares than those intended: no deed; and no estoppel by negligence which may not apply to deeds but may be limited to negotiable instruments signed in blank); *France v Clark* (1884) 26 Ch. D. 257, CA (transferee of shares left blank); *Société Générale de Paris v Walker* (1885) 11 App. Cas. 20, HL (transferee of shares left blank and no act of re-delivery to perfect deed); *Powell v London and Provincial Bank* [1893] 2 Ch. 555, CA (transferee of shares left blank).

45   *Weeks v Maillardet* (1811) 14 East 568; 104 E.R. 719 (schedules not annexed to articles when they were executed, but were written and attached to the sealed document by the parties' agent soon after its execution: schedules not part of the deed, and the whole deed failed because the sealed document had no meaning without the schedules); cf. *West v Steward* (1845) 14 M. & W. 47; 153 E.R. 383 (schedules not annexed to deed at time of execution, but deed had effect by its terms without the schedules).

46   At common law, however, corporations were required to use deeds in order to enter into any contract, although exceptions were created by statute and at common law for certain types of corporation, and finally the Corporate Bodies' Contracts Act 1960 provided that all other bodies corporate could make, vary or discharge contracts through their authorised agents in the same manner as private persons: see para.4-17.

47   See para.7-04.

48   A corporation aggregate must therefore seal the deed in its capacity as the corporation, rather than by the seals of its individual members: *Cooch v Goodman* (1842) 2 Q.B. 580; 114 E.R. 228.

49   See para.7-13.

50   See para.7-12. However, the requirement that an agent be authorised by deed to *deliver* a deed on behalf of his principal was abolished by LP(MP)A 1989 s.1(1)(c): see para.7-13, esp. fnn.177, 178.

51   LP(MP)A 1989 s.1(1)(a); see para.7-06. Section 1 of the 1989 Act came into force on 31 July 1990: SI 1990/1175 art.2.

is still required.[52] There is a new requirement since 1990 that the instrument make clear on its face that it is intended as a deed.[53] But the most significant changes have been in the use of sealing, signatures and witnessing, and it in this context that distinctions have been drawn between deeds executed by individuals, and deeds executed by corporations.

From 1 January 1926 an individual executing a deed was required either to sign or to place his mark upon it: sealing was no longer deemed sufficient.[54] And in 1990 the requirement for an individual to seal a deed was abolished,[55] but he must now sign the deed in the presence of an attesting witness (or two witnesses if he directs someone to sign for him).[56] Corporations may still use their corporate seals in order to execute deeds, and some corporations must do so. A corporation sole[57] must use a seal, since there has been no change to that requirement of the common law in the case of corporations sole.[58] Whether a corporation aggregate must use its corporate seal depends on whether the particular kind of corporation has statutory authority to execute a valid instrument by some other means than by sealing it. Many statutes have permitted alternative methods of execution, typically by the signature of certain officers, although if the corporation has no such permitted alternative method, it must use a seal. In 1989 companies registered under the Companies Acts were permitted to execute a deed by the signatures of a director and the company secretary, or of two directors, in place of the common seal of the corporation[59]; since 2008 it is also sufficient for a deed to be signed on behalf of the company by one director in the presence of an attesting witness.[60] There are specific statutory provisions governing the execution of deeds by certain other corporations aggregate; for example, the provisions for limited liability partnerships mirror those now in force for companies registered under the Companies

---

[52] For the impact of the developing use of electronic transactions on the law of deeds, see para.7-08.

[53] LP(MP)A 1989 s.1(2)(a), in force from 31 July 1990: see para.7-05 fn.51 and 7-07.

[54] LPA 1925 s.73. This provision was repealed by LP(MP)A 1989 s.4, Sch.2 when the requirement of signature was absorbed into the broader reform effected by the 1989 Act: see para.7-05 fn.56.

[55] LP(MP)A 1989 s.1(1)(b), in force from 31 July 1990: see para.7-05 fn.51; para.7-09.

[56] LP(MP)A 1989 s.1(3)(a).

[57] e.g. the Crown; the holder for the time being of an ecclesiastical office such as dean of a cathedral, or vicar of a parish; certain ministers of the Crown (e.g. the Secretaries of State for Education (SI 2010/1836 art.3), Culture, Olympics, Media and Sport (SI 2010/1551 art.3), Business, Innovation and Skills (SI 2009/2748 art.3), Energy and Climate Change (SI 2009/229 art.3) and Justice (SI 2007/2128 art.3); and public officers who are designated as corporations sole by the legislative enactment which established them, such as the Official Custodian for Charities (Charities Act 2011 s.21, Sch.2 para.1); the Comptroller and Auditor General (Budget Responsibility and National Audit Act 2011 s.12(1)); the Public Trustee (Public Trustee Act 1906 s.1(2)) and the Treasury Solicitor (Treasury Solicitor Act 1876 s.1). See generally Halsbury, 5th edn, Vol.24 (2010), para.315.

[58] Corporations sole are not "individuals" within the meaning of LP(MP)A 1989 s.1: see s.1(10); and no other general statutory provision relating to the execution of deeds by corporations applies to corporations sole, although there are certain provisions relating to execution of deeds (by seal) by particular corporations sole such as Secretaries of State (Ministers of the Crown Act 1975 s.3) and the public officers designated as corporations sole by legislative enactment, listed above, n.57. In 1998 the Law Commission recommended against having a general statutory provision governing execution by corporations sole: Law Com. No.253, *The Execution of Deeds and Documents by or on behalf of Bodies Corporate* (1998), para.4.28.

[59] CA 1985 s.36A, added by CA 1989 s.130.

[60] CA 2006 s.44, in force since 6 April 2008. It is not necessary that the document contain words spelling out that the signatures are by or on behalf of the company where it is clear that the document is executed by the company: *Williams v Redcard Ltd* [2011] EWCA Civ 466; [2011] 4 All E.R. 444. Gore-Browne says at para.8[23] that the use of common seals has become comparatively unusual.

Acts[61]; the Companies Act is applied to overseas companies with modifications so that the company may execute a deed either by affixing its common seal or in such manner as is permitted by the laws of the territory in which the company is incorporated[62]; an incorporated body of charity trustees may either use its common seal (if it has one) or execute the instrument by the signatures of a majority of the charity trustees or of two or more authorised trustees[63]; an incorporated friendly society may either use its common seal (if it has one) or execute the instrument by the signatures of a member of its committee of management and its secretary, or of two members of the committee of management[64]; and a society registered under the Co-operative and Community Benefit Societies Act 2014 may either use its common seal (if it has one) or execute the instrument by the signatures of a member of its committee and its secretary, or of two members of its committee.[65]

In summary, therefore, the formalities necessary now for the valid execution of an instrument as a deed depend on whether the party executing the deed is an individual or a corporation. A deed executed by an individual must be written (on any substance) in a form which makes clear that it is intended to be a deed; signed by the individual in the presence of one attesting witness (or two witnesses if he directs someone to sign for him); and delivered by the individual or on his behalf. A deed executed by a corporation must be written (on any substance) in a form which makes clear that it is intended to be a deed; executed in the form required for the particular type of corporation (sealing in the case of a corporation sole; sealing or certain authorised signatures, with or without attesting witnesses, in the case of corporations aggregate) and delivered by or on behalf of the corporation. The details of these several requirements in the modern law will be considered in the following paragraphs.

(2)   The Form Required for a Deed

7-06   **The deed may be written on any substance**   The common law required a deed to be written on paper or parchment. This was said to provide the best medium to protect the deed against alteration or damage,[66] but in the modern age this is no longer so: other substances than paper may provide a more secure medium against damage and, indeed, it is not evident that all deeds need to have a permanent physical form. The Law Commission saw no good reason to maintain this restriction,[67] and their recommendation for its removal was enacted by section 1 of the Law of

---

[61]   Limited Liability Partnerships (Application of Companies Act 2006) Regulations 2009 (SI 2009/1804) reg.4 (common seal, or signature of two members, or signature of one member in the presence of an attesting witness).

[62]   Overseas Companies (Execution of Documents and Registration of Charges) Regulations 2009 (SI 2009/1917) reg.4.

[63]   Charities Act 2011 ss.260, 261.

[64]   Friendly Societies Act 1992 Sch.6 para.2.

[65]   Co-operative and Community Benefit Societies Act 2014 s.53.

[66]   Co. Litt. 35b ("A deed cannot be written upon wood, leather cloth, or the like, but only upon parchment or paper, for the writing upon them can be least vitiated, altered or corrupted").

[67]   Law Com. No.163, *Deeds and Escrows* (1987), para.2.3 ("Some paper is extremely flimsy, and all paper is at risk from fire or flooding. While it is highly desirable that deeds which have to be referred to many years later should be on a durable substance, other deeds have a very short life. Why should a deed be invalidated because it is on some other substance?").

Property (Miscellaneous Provisions) Act 1989[68] in relation to instruments delivered as deeds from the date when that section came into force.[69] The requirement of signature and writing will tend in practice to restrict the substances used,[70] but it is now possible for parties wishing to create deeds with a more durable physical form to choose an appropriate material.[71]

The instrument must "make clear on its face that it is intended to be a deed"   There is no rule requiring the deed to take any particular physical form, nor even to contain any particular words.[72] The common law required an indenture to be clear by its form (with indentations) or by its words of self-description as an indenture, but we have seen that such requirements were removed as early as 1845,[73] and any words which show that it is to take effect as a deed are sufficient. The Law of Property Act 1925 provides[74]:

7-07

> "Any deed, whether or not being an indenture, may be described (at the commencement thereof or otherwise) as a deed simply, or as a conveyance, deed of exchange, vesting deed, trust instrument, settlement, mortgage, charge, transfer of mortgage, appointment, lease or otherwise according to the nature of the transaction intended to be effected."

In addition, the Law of Property (Miscellaneous Provisions) Act 1989 has introduced a formal requirement that the document make clear on its face that it is intended to be a deed, although there is no prescribed form of words by which this is to be done[75]:

> "**1.**—(2)   An instrument shall not be a deed unless—
>   (a)   it makes it clear on its face that it is intended to be a deed by the person making it or, as the case may be, by the parties to it (whether by describing itself as a deed or expressing itself to be executed or signed as a deed or otherwise[76])
>   ..."

This followed the recommendation of the Law Commission, which sought not only to make it easier as a matter of practice to distinguish between deeds and other documents (even those which are also signed and witnessed), but also to bring home

---

[68]   s.1(1)(a): "(1) Any rule of law which—(a) restricts the substances on which a deed may be written ... is abolished".

[69]   i.e. 31 July 1990: SI 1990/1175 art.2.

[70]   Law Com. No.163, see para.7-06 fn.67, para.2.3; but for the possibility of using electronic means of "writing" and "signature", see para.7-08.

[71]   e.g. fire- and flood-proof metal or non-biodegradable plastic: Emmet, para.20.002.

[72]   The substantive terms of the deed must, of course, satisfy the requirements for the creation of the rights or obligations which the parties intend: e.g. the parties must be named, and the terms must be sufficiently certain to satisfy the normal rules for certainty of transactions. For the invalidity of a deed which leaves essential terms blank, see para.7-04 fnn.44, 45.

[73]   See para.7-02.

[74]   LPA 1925 s.57.

[75]   LP(MP)A 1989 s.1(2)(a). The document as a whole must be intended to be a deed: *Startwell Ltd v Energie Global Brand Management Ltd* [2015] EWHC 421 (QB) at [47].

[76]   [This formulation was intended to "give some indication of a general uniform practice which could usefully be adopted" but also "leave a court free to decide whether or not a document was intended to be a deed where a different formula was used, but only where there was evidence for such a finding within the document itself": Law Com. No.163, see para.7-06 fn.67, para.2.16.]

to the parties that it is a deed that is being executed.[77] In other words, the requirement is designed to fulfil the cautionary and labelling functions of formality.[78]

However, for the instrument to make clear on its face that it is intended to be a deed it must do so by its own language, and this will not be satisfied merely by the fact that the parties use formal language and have their signatures witnessed.[79] In particular, it is not sufficient for the party to use the old form of sealing as an indication that it is intended to be a deed.[80]

7-08 **Deeds in electronic transactions** We have seen that the law is developing its formality requirements in response to the development of electronic forms of communication.[81] A deed cannot, however, be made in electronic form. Although Pt II of the Electronic Communications Act 2000 allows the modification of any of statutory formality requirements in order to facilitate the use of electronic communications for purposes which include "the doing of anything which under any such provisions is required to be or may be authorised by a person's signature or seal, or is required to be delivered as a deed or witnessed"[82] no reform has been made to the general requirements for a deed,[83] although in the particular context of registered land there is provision that a document in electronic form which purports to effect certain dispositions relating to registered land for which a deed would otherwise be required is to be regarded as a deed if it fulfils certain requirements.[84]

A different question related to electronic documents also arises in practice: how a document, which is to be executed as a deed by more than one party, should be

---

[77] Law Com. No.163, see para.7-06 fn.67, para.2.16.
[78] See para.4-03.
[79] *HSBC Trust Co (UK) Ltd v Quinn* [2007] EWHC 1543 (Ch) at [51] (insufficient that the document, written by the parties without legal advice, said "we the undersigned", set out the price in numbers and words and gave the parties' full names and addresses, and their signatures were witnessed: "All that they show is that the parties intended it to be legally binding, and in my judgment this is plainly not enough; what is needed is something showing that the parties intended the document to have the extra status of being a deed" (Christopher Nugee QC)); *Startwell Ltd v Energie Global Brand Management Ltd*, see para.7-07 n.75, at [48] (Warbey J: the fact that there is a witness to the contract is not of itself enough to satisfy the "face value requirement" of s.1).
[80] LP(MP)A 1989 s.1(2A) ("an instrument shall not be taken to make it clear on its face that it is intended to be a deed merely because it is executed under seal"), added by SI 2005/1906 art.8 (in force from 15 September 2005).
[81] See para.4-06.
[82] Electronic Communications Act 2000 s.8(2)(c).
[83] In 1987 the Law Commission rejected (for the time being) the idea of allowing deeds to be in any form other than writing on some permanent substance: Law Com. No.163, see para.7-06 fn.67, para.2.3 cf., however, Law Commission Consultation Paper No.237 (2018) Ch.8.
[84] Land Registration Act 2002 s.91: it must make provision for the time and date when it takes effect, have the certified electronic signature of each person by whom it purports to be authenticated, and satisfy such other conditions as may be provided by rules; and to fall within the section the document must purport to give effect to a disposition of a registered estate or charge, or a disposition of an interest which is the subject of a notice in the register, or a disposition which triggers the requirement of registration, which is of a kind specified by rules. This section was first applied to electronic legal charges (SI 2008/1750, revoked by SI 2018/70 r.6) but since 6 April 2018 it applies to electronic dispositions of registered estates or charges: Land Registration Rules 2003 (SI 2003/1417) rr.54A-54D (inserted by SI 2018/70 r.11) as long as the disposition satisfies certain conditions, and only after the registrar is satisfied that adequate arrangements have been made or will be in place for dealing with documents in electronic form that purport to effect a disposition of that kind and has given notice publicising the fact. Deeds of transfer must therefore still be executed in paper form, although scanned copies of the physical deed are then used for the purposes of registration: see para.7-03 fn.31.

executed where the parties are not both present at the same time (a "virtual signing"). It has already been noted that the execution of a deed must be the execution of the whole instrument which is to take effect as a deed, and therefore all parts of the deed (including any schedules) must be in existence and attached to the principal document at the time when it is executed.[85] Parties who are not in the same place may execute separate identical counterparts. But an alternative is for one party to sign and send the whole document, including the signature page, by email (or in some other electronic form) for execution by the other party so that both execute the same set of terms.[86]

(3)   Execution as a Deed

Sealing   For the execution of deeds by individuals,[87] the requirement of the common law that the party execute an instrument as a deed by affixing his seal was abolished by s.1 of the Law of Property (Miscellaneous Provisions) Act 1989[88] in relation to instruments delivered as deeds from the date when that section came into force.[89] Sealing therefore now forms no part of the execution of deeds by individuals: it is neither necessary nor sufficient to mark out an instrument as the party's deed.[90]

7-09

In the modern law, even before the use of the seal by individuals was abolished, it had been seen as an anachronism, far removed from the historical practice of using seals to authenticate documents.[91] The Law Commission regarded sealing as a "meaningless exercise"[92]; Lord Wilberforce referred to it as "mumbo-jumbo"[93]; and in the House of Lords during the passage of the Bill which became the 1989 Act, it was described as "for most people, a meaningless formality"[94] and "legal mummery".[95] This reflected the fact that the courts had already in practice diluted the requirements for the sealing of deeds by individuals so that it was not necessary to use wax impressed with a seal, nor even any particular form of attachment

---

[85]   See para.7-04, esp. fn.45.

[86]   See Law Society Practice Note, *Execution of documents by virtual means* (February 2010) (*https://www.lawsociety.org.uk/support-services/advice/practice-notes/execution-of-documents-by-virtual-means/*) following the decision in *R. (on the application of Mercury Tax Group Ltd) v Revenue and Customs Commissioners* [2008] EWHC 2721 (Admin); [2009] S.T.C. 743 at [39], where Underhill J held that the document to be executed as a deed must exist as a discrete physical entity, whether in a single version or in a serious of counterparts, at the moment of signing. In such cases the first party to sign will generally deliver the deed in escrow, subject to the condition that the other party or parties also sign: see para.7-12.

[87]   This means individual natural persons: it does not include a corporation sole: LP(MP)A 1989 s.1(10).

[88]   s.1(1)(b): "(1) Any rule of law which—(a) requires a seal for the valid execution of an instrument as a deed by an individual ... is abolished".

[89]   i.e. 31 July 1990: SI 1990/1175 art.2.

[90]   Nor does it satisfy the requirement that the document make clear on its face that it is intended to be a deed: see para.7-07 fn.80.

[91]   "Sealing was no great chore: it corresponded to signing today, and, although the seal could be a grand affair, a blob of wax with some sort of impress on it sufficed": Simpson, see para.7-01 fn.10, p.90.

[92]   Law Commission WP No.93, *Formalities for Deeds and Escrows* (1985), para.4.2, referring to the statement of the *Law Revision Committee in its Sixth Interim Report* (1937), Cmd.5449, p.35 that "a seal nowadays is very much in the nature of a legal fiction".

[93]   HL Deb 25 February 1971, Vol.315, col.1213 (during the second reading of the Powers of Attorney Bill).

[94]   HL Deb 24 January 1989, Vol.503, col.599 (The Lord Chancellor, Lord Mackay, moving the second reading).

[95]   HL Deb 24 January 1989, Vol.503, col.605 (Lord Coleraine).

to the instrument (such as a red wafer glued to the document where the sealing wax might otherwise have been placed[96]). By 1871[97] the Court of Common Pleas was able to accept as a deed a document which bore no wax impression, but had pieces of green ribbon attached where the seals should be, with the usual form of attestation ("signed sealed and delivered") by the executing parties, who also later acknowledged the document was their deed, even though it was also evidenced that the ribbon was already attached before it was sent to the parties for signature. The court was prepared to assume that at the moment of execution the parties had done something that constituted the act of sealing, and Bovill CJ said[98]:

> "To constitute a sealing, neither wax, nor wafer, nor a piece of paper, nor even an impression, is necessary. Here is something attached to this deed which may have been intended for a seal, but which from its nature is incapable of retaining an impression."

The limits of this decision were debated by the later cases: some assumed that it could only be correct on the assumption that, for example, the parties at the moment of execution had pressed their fingers on the ribbon in order to acknowledge it as their seal,[99] and so where there was no sign of any kind on a document that a wax seal or anything else which could have substituted for it had in fact been attached at the moment of execution, and no such evidence from the document itself or from the attesting witnesses beyond a statement in the document that it had been sealed, the deed could not be assumed to have been duly sealed and was therefore not properly executed.[100] In *First National Securities v Jones*,[101] however, Buckley LJ thought that it was authority that[102] "for due execution of a deed it is not necessary to have any physical seal, nor even any impression on the paper, as long as the evidence establishes that the document has been delivered by the relevant party as his act and deed"; and the Court of Appeal there held that a printed document which was expressed to be a deed, with an attestation clause affirming that the party had sealed the document and a circle printed on the document containing the letters "L.S."[103] across which the party had signed his name, was a valid deed. Sir David Cairns went further and thought that, even if the signature had not been across the printed circle, it would still have been valid[104]:

---

[96] This had in fact become a common form of execution of deeds: small self-adhesive red circular stickers were sold by law stationers for the purpose.
[97] *Re Sandilands* (1871) 6 C.P. 411.
[98] *Re Sandilands* (1871) 6 C.P. 411 at 413. See also Byles J, ibid.: "The sealing of a deed need not be by means of a seal; it may be done with the end of a ruler or anything else. Nor is it necessary that wax should be used".
[99] *National Provincial Bank of England v Jackson* (1886) 33 Ch. D. 1, CA, at 11 (Cotton LJ). Lindley LJ (at 14) regarded *Re Sandilands* as "a good-natured decision, in which I am not sure that I could have concurred".
[100] *National Provincial Bank of England v Jackson*, see para.7-09 fn.99; *Re Smith* (1892) 67 L.T. 64, CA; *Re Balkis Consolidated Co Ltd* (1888) 58 L.T. 300 (where there was no seal or wafer on the document, but a circular mark on the paper with the words "place of the seal" printed within it; North J left open the possibility of further evidence of sealing, given the contradictory evidence as to whether the party executing the deed had put his finger on the printed seal).
[101] [1978] Ch. 109, CA.
[102] [1978] Ch. 109, CA at 115.
[103] "Locus sigilli", the place of the seal; cf. *Re Balkis Consolidated Co Ltd*, see para.7-09 fn.100.
[104] See para.7-09 fn.101, at 121. See also Goff LJ at 119 ("in this day and age, we can, and we ought to, hold that a document purporting to be a deed is capable in law of being such although it has no more than an indication where the seal should be").

"while in 1888[105] the printed indication of a locus sigilli was regarded as being merely the place where a seal was to be affixed, I have no doubt that it is now regarded by most business people and ordinary members of the public as constituting the seal itself. I am sure that many documents intended by all parties to be deeds are now executed without any further formality than the signature opposite the words 'Signed, sealed and delivered' usually in the presence of a witness, and I think it would be lamentable if the validity of documents so executed could be successfully challenged."

This decision did not dispense with the need for a seal, although it reduced the formality of sealing to the minimum; and so if a document bore no trace at all of anything (even a pre-printed indication of a seal) that could be regarded as the seal,[106] with no evidence of an act at the time of execution which could constitute the act of sealing the instrument, it could not be held to be validly executed as a deed.[107] Given the uncertainties created by these cases,[108] but also the general view that sealing is no longer a meaningful formality for individuals, the Law Commission recommended its abolition.[109]

Sealing remains, however, an indispensable requirement for the valid execution of an instrument as a deed by a corporation sole[110]; and it is one of the ways by which corporations aggregate may execute deeds.[111] However, at least in the case of corporations aggregate,[112] the formality of sealing does not raise the same difficulty which the law used to have in interpreting what should constitute a valid seal in the case of an individual. The formality for the valid execution of a deed by many categories of corporation aggregate is defined by statute, and generally the language of the statute requires the sealing to be by affixing the "common seal" of the

---

[105] [*Re Balkis Consolidated Co Ltd*, see para.7-09 fn.100. A pre-printed seal was sufficient to constitute a sealed order of justices in *R. v St Paul, Covent Garden Inhabitants* (1845) 7 Q.B. 232; 115 E.R. 476.]

[106] See also *Stromdale and Ball Ltd v Burden* [1952] Ch. 223 at 230 (Danckwerts J: "Meticulous persons executing a deed may still place their finger on the wax seal or wafer on the document, but it appears to me that, at the present day, if a party signs a document bearing wax or wafer or other indication of a seal, with the intention of executing the document as a deed, that is sufficient adoption or recognition of the seal to amount to due execution as a deed"), followed in *First National Securities v Jones*, see para.7-09 fn.101, at 118, 119, 120.

[107] *TCB Ltd v Gray* [1986] Ch. 621 at 633 (Sir Nicolas Browne-Wilkinson VC, referring to the "benign approach" of the line of cases culminating in *First National Securities v Jones*, see para.7-09 fn.101; but holding that, although the instrument was not executed as a deed, the party representing that he had so executed it was estopped from denying that it was a deed in favour of a person who relied on it as a valid deed; cf. para.7-16. The issues of law were not considered by CA on appeal: [1987] Ch. 458n.).

[108] See also D.C. Hoath, "The Sealing of Documents—Fact or Fiction" (1980) 43 M.L.R. 415.

[109] Law Com. No.163, see para.7-06 fn.67, para.2.4.

[110] See para.7-05 fnn.57, 58.

[111] Whether a corporation aggregate must use a seal depends on whether it is of a kind of corporation which is permitted by statutory authority to use some alternative method of execution: see para.7-05.

[112] Although many corporations sole will have a seal unique to the office (e.g. the Crown, and the Ministers of the Crown and the public officers, designated as corporations sole by legislative enactment, listed see para.7-05 fn.57), there is no requirement for every corporation sole to have a corporate seal, and so the person holding the office may need to execute a deed in right of the corporation in the same manner in which an individual executed an instrument as a deed before LP(MP)A 1989 s.1 came into force. In so far as he or she acts as the corporation, rather than as an individual, he remains bound by the common law requirements in executing an instrument as a deed: LP(MP)A 1989 s.1(10).

corporation.[113] It will therefore be clear on the face of the document whether the "common seal" has in fact been affixed.[114]

7-10   **Signature**   For the execution of deeds by individuals, the requirement that the person making it sign (or place his mark upon) the deed was first introduced as part of the mandatory formality by the Law of Property Act 1925,[115] although signature was already in fact common practice alongside sealing of the deed.[116] The reform of the formalities for deeds by the Law of Property (Miscellaneous Provisions) Act 1989 has continued the requirement of signature (or a mark[117]) but has also allowed the signature to be that of another person in the individual's presence, rather than of the individual himself.[118] The Act does not further define what is required to constitute a signature or mark. In other contexts, including the Statute of Frauds, the courts have given a wide interpretation to the requirement of a signature,[119] but in the interpretation of the requirement of s.2 of the 1989 Act that a contract for the sale or other disposition of an interest in land be signed by the parties, the Court of Appeal has decided that a party "signs" a document only if he writes his own name with his own hand on the document in such a way as to authenticate the document.[120] It seems that the reference to signature for the purposes of the execu-

---

[113] e.g. CA 2006 s.44(1)(a) (company regulated by CA 2006); there is no requirement for a company to have a common seal (CA 2006 s.45(1)) but if it does not it will execute deeds by the signature of its officers: s.44(1)(b); see para.7-10. See similarly Overseas Companies (Execution of Documents and Registration of Charges) Regulations 2009 (SI 2009/1917) reg.4 (overseas companies); Limited Liability Partnerships (Application of Companies Act 2006) Regulations 2009 (SI 2009/1804) reg.4 (limited liability partnerships); Charities Act 2011 s.260(2) (incorporated body of charity trustees).

[114] This does not, however, mean that something must be attached to the document: "affixing" the seal may involve the impressing of the seal onto the instrument without the addition of wax or a wafer; the seal must have its name engraved in legible characters on the seal: CA 2006 s.45(2); Gore-Browne at para.8[23]. If there is a challenge to the validity of the seal itself, this may sometimes be resolved in favour of a purchaser by LPA 1925 s.74(1), as substituted by SI 2005/1906: "In favour of a purchaser an instrument shall be deemed to have been duly executed by a corporation aggregate if a seal purporting to be the corporation's seal purports to be affixed to the instrument in the presence of and attested by—(a) two members of the board of directors, council or other governing body of the corporation, or (b) one such member and the clerk, secretary or other permanent officer of the corporation or his deputy".

[115] LPA 1925 s.73, repealed and replaced by LP(MP)A 1989 s.1; s.4, Sch.2.

[116] G.C. Cheshire, *The Modern Law of Real Property*, 1st edn (Butterworth & Co, 1925), p.595.

[117] LP(MP)A 1989 s.1(4)(b).

[118] LP(MP)A 1989 s.1(3)(a)(ii); in this case, two attesting witnesses are required: see para.7-11. The signature by a third party in the presence of the party is not, however, execution by an agent which requires authority to be given by deed: see para.7-13.

[119] e.g. rubber-stamp signature: *Goodman v J Eban Ltd* [1954] 1 Q.B. 550, CA (Solicitors Act 1932 s.65); the party's printed name on a memorandum to satisfy the Statute of Frauds: see cases cited at para.6-14 fn.92.

[120] *Firstpost Homes Ltd v Johnson* [1995] 1 W.L.R. 1567, CA, at 1575, adopting the statement of Denning LJ (dissenting) in *Goodman v J Eban Ltd*, see para.7-10 fn.119, at 561. It was said, in particular, that typing is insufficient even if it is done by the party himself since further evidence would then be required at trial to establish that the party had typed his name with the necessary authenticating intent: ibid., at 1575–1576 (Peter Gibson LJ) and 1577 (Balcombe LJ); cf. *Ramsay v Love* [2015] EWHC 65 (Ch) at [7] (Morgan J: "those statements were not designed to distinguish between signing by use of a pen held in the executing party's hand as distinct from the use of a signature writing machine"). In the case of a deed, the attesting witness could be called to support the claim that the deed was properly executed within LP(MP)A 1989 s.1 (for a contract within s.2 only the parties' signature is necessary, without a witness), but the same argument holds in favour of a simple formality of hand-written signatures which generally require no further evidence.

tion of a deed within s.1 of the 1989 Act should be interpreted similarly, to give it the more natural meaning,[121] at least in relation to hard-copy instruments. It should be noted that, although in other contexts a signature may take the form of a name typed into an electronic communication,[122] the fact that a deed cannot yet be made in electronic form[123] excludes the use of electronic signatures in the execution of deeds.[124]

We have seen that the formality of sealing has been retained for the valid execution of an instrument as a deed by corporations, although very many corporations aggregate have statutory authority to execute deeds by the use of signatures of one or more of their officers as an alternative to using the corporate seal.[125] For example, a company regulated by the Companies Act 2006 may execute a deed by the signature of two "authorised signatories",[126] or by a single director of the company in the presence of an attesting witness.[127] Such statutes do not define what must be done to constitute a "signature"; it seems likely that, as in the case of a deed executed by an individual, a court would give the words its natural meaning, and would require the officer of the corporation to write his own name with his own hand on the document in such a way as to authenticate it on behalf of the corporation.

Attestation   For the execution of deeds by individuals, attestation was introduced   **7-11**
as a formal requirement by the Law of Property (Miscellaneous Provisions) Act 1989, thereby adding an element of formality at the same time that the formality

---

[121]   The Law Commission intended the requirement to be for "some personal authentication of the document by hand-written signature or other individual mark", but also rejected the idea of giving an even more restrictive definition: Law Com. No.163, see para.7-06 fn.67, para.2.5. cf. *Firstpost Homes Ltd v Johnson*, see para.7-10 fn.120 at 1576 (Peter Gibson LJ: "I do not see why it is right to encumber the new Act with so much ancient baggage, particularly when it does not leave the 'signed' with a meaning which the ordinary man would understand it to have").

[122]   See para.4-06.

[123]   See para.7-08.

[124]   An electronic signature can be used on an electronic instrument effecting a disposition relating to land which, though not itself a deed, and is to be regarded as a deed within LRA 2002 s.91; see para.7-08 fn.84.

[125]   See para.7-05.

[126]   This does not, however, simply mean that the company can authorise any persons to sign; "authorised signatories" are defined in CA 2006 s.44(3) as being every director of the company and, in the case of a private company with a secretary or a public company, the secretary (or any joint secretary) of the company. The constitutional documents of a corporation may place their own internal regulation on how deeds and other documents are to be executed on behalf of the corporation, but for the purposes of the legal formality it is important to consider the statutory provisions which define the valid execution of a deed. Defects in the internal procedures of the corporation in relation to the execution of a deed may be solved in favour of third parties either by general rules relating to the protection of third parties against unauthorised acts by or on behalf of a corporation, or by statutory protections relating to the execution of deeds, either in relation to corporations generally (e.g. LPA 1925 s.74(1), substituted by SI 2005/1906 art.3: "in favour of a purchaser an instrument shall be deemed to have been duly executed by a corporation aggregate if a seal purporting to be the corporation's seal purports to be affixed to the instrument in the presence of and attested by (a) two members of the board of directors, council or the governing body of the corporation, or (b) one such member and the clerk, secretary or other permanent officer of the corporation or his deputy") or in relation to particular types of corporation (e.g. CA 2006 s.44(5): in favour of a purchaser, a document is deemed to have been duly executed if it purports to be signed in accordance with s.44(2)).

[127]   CA 2006 s.44(2). If the document is to be signed by the same person on behalf of more than one company (e.g. where group companies, represented by the same person, are parties to the same document), he must sign it separately in each capacity: CA 2006 s.44(6).

of sealing was removed,[128] although attestation was already in fact common practice alongside sealing of the deed.[129] Where an individual making a deed signs it himself, he must do so in the presence of one witness who attests the signature; if the deed is signed by someone else at the individual's direction and in his presence, it must be done in the presence of two witnesses who each attest the signature.[130] In the case of a deed made by a corporation which is authorised to execute deeds by signature rather than by its common seal,[131] the statute which grants that authority also defines whether and how the signatures must be attested. For example, a company regulated by the Companies Act 2006 may execute a deed by the signatures of two "authorised signatories"[132] without any further witness; but it may also be done by one director in the presence of a witness who attests the signature.[133]

These statutory provisions all make clear that the function of the witness is not only to see the signature being written on the instrument,[134] but also to "attest" the signature. There are conflicting older authorities as to what constitutes "attestation", and the statutes which impose the requirement of attestation of deeds give no definition,[135] but the better view seems to be that, in its modern legal sense, attestation involves the addition of the witness's own signature to the document with words of confirmation that the document was signed in his presence.[136] The witness may be called to give evidence of due execution if the validity of the deed is later challenged[137]; but the attesting witness need not be called even if he is still available, and the document and its signature may be proved by other means.[138]

---

[128] See para.7-09.

[129] Law Com. No.163, see para.7-06 fn.67, para.2.12, noting that certain deeds were already required to be attested: land registry transfers (under the rules then in force, Land Registration Rules 1925 Form 19) and powers of attorney executed under the Powers of Attorney Act 1971 or the Enduring Powers of Attorney Act 1985 (later repealed and replaced by lasting powers of attorney by Mental Capacity Act 2005).

[130] LP(MP)A 1989 s.1(3)(a).

[131] See para.7-05.

[132] See para.7-10 fn.126.

[133] CA 2006 s.44(2).

[134] cf. *Re Gibson* [1949] P. 434 at 436–37 (Pearce J: "In the light of common sense, and without any authority, I should be inclined to hold that for the purposes of [Wills Act 1837 s.9], a "witness" means, in regard to things audible, one who has the faculty of hearing, and in regard to things visible, one who has the faculty of seeing. The signing of a will is a visible matter. Therefore, I think that a will is not signed 'in the presence of' a blind person, nor is a blind person a witness for the purposes of the section").

[135] For a review, and criticism of the LP(MP)A 1989 s.1, for failing to provide a definition, see M. Dray, "Deeds speak louder than words. Attesting time for deeds?" [2013] Conv. 298.

[136] This was the understanding of the Law Commission, relying on *Re Selby-Bigge* [1950] 1 All E.R. 1009, where Hodson J discussed the meaning of "attestation" as evidenced by dictionaries and case-law, and drew a distinction between the general dictionary meaning and the meaning when used in relation to the execution of formal legal documents; see Law Com. No.163, see para.7-06 fn.67, para.2.13, fn.18. See *Darjan Estate Co Plc v Hurley* [2012] EWHC 189 (Ch); [2012] 1 W.L.R. 1783 at [12] (not possible to interpret the signature of an unidentified person as the attestation of the signatures of both parties to a lease).

[137] cf. *Re Smith*, see para.7-09 fn.100 (challenge to validity of deed on basis that it had not been duly sealed, in spite of an attestation clause which, although not formally required by the common law for the validity of a deed, stated that had been "signed, sealed and delivered" by the obligor: "the attesting witness has not been called to give evidence as to whether the bond was sealed or not, and there is absolutely nothing to show that it was actually sealed": Lindley LJ at 66); *Re Balkis Consolidated Co Ltd*, see para.7-09 fn.100 (attesting witness did not make affidavit of circumstances in which document was executed).

[138] Evidence Act 1938 s.3 ("an instrument to the validity of which attestation is requisite may, instead

There is, however, no prescribed form of attestation clause[139]; nor is there even any restriction on who may act as witness.[140] Unlike in the case of wills,[141] there is no bar on a witness to a deed being a person taking a benefit under the deed.[142]

Delivery Unless the instrument is "delivered" it does not take effect as a deed.[143]   **7-12**
The significance of delivery is therefore that, given that it cannot be delivered until after the other formality requirements[144] have been satisfied, it fixes the moment at which the instrument becomes binding as a deed.[145]

The delivery of the deed would therefore seem to be a very significant element in its creation. However, in 1985 the Law Commission proposed that delivery be abolished as a requirement[146] although they finally proposed that it should be retained,[147] and in relation to the execution of deeds by individuals, the Law of Property (Miscellaneous Provisions) Act 1989 includes the requirement of delivery as one element of valid execution[148]; similarly other statutes setting out the requirements for the valid execution of deeds by corporations aggregate include the requirement of delivery.[149] None of these statutes, however, defines "delivery": each

---

of being proved by an attesting witness, be proved in the manner in which it might be proved if no attesting witness were alive"); this reversed the former rule that the document was to be proved by calling the attesting witness, and applies to instruments generally, except for wills and other testamentary documents: ibid.; Phipson, paras 40-24 to 40-30.

[139] "Prescribing an attestation clause would have the considerable disadvantage that it could easily be written wrongly and thus an otherwise valid deed would be invalidated": Law Com. No.163, see para.7-06 fn.67, para.2.14.

[140] Phipson, para.40-27. However, a party to a deed cannot attest another party's signature: *Seal v Claridge* (1881) 7 Q.B. 516 at 519 (Lord Selborne LC); Phipson, para.40-28.

[141] Wills Act 1837 s.15 (gifts by attesting witness or spouse are void).

[142] The Law Commission considered, but rejected, such a restriction on who may be a witness to a deed when it proposed the new formalities for the execution of deeds by individuals: Law Com. No.163, see para.7-06 fn.67, para.2.13; and none of the statutes which permit corporations aggregate to execute deeds by attested signatures (e.g. CA 2006 s.44; see para.7-11 fn.133) restricts who may act as attesting witness.

[143] An earlier delivery which failed for some reason to give effect to the instrument may be cured by a later re-delivery: e.g. *Goodright d. Carter v Straphan* (1774) 1 Cowp. 201, 98 E.R. 1043 (re-delivery by widow after death of husband, at a period when a woman could not validly enter into deed during her marriage); or re-delivery of instrument which, because it was incomplete when first delivered, did not take effect as deed: see para.7-04, esp. fn.44).

[144] Sealing, or signature, with or without attestation: see paras 7-09 to 7-11.

[145] A deed need not bear a date; and even if it bears a false date, or an impossible date (e.g. 30 February), this does not affect its validity, which takes effect from delivery: *Goddard's Case* (1584) 2 Co. Rep. 4b at 5a, 76 E.R. 396 at 400 ("when a deed is delivered, it takes effect by the delivery, and not from the day of the date. And therefore be the deed without date, or of a false or impossible date, yet the deed is good"); *Cromwell v Grunsden* (1698) 2 Salk. 462 at 463; 91 E.R. 399 at 399–400. The date which appears on the deed will, however, be prima face evidence of the date of its execution: *Anderson v Weston* (1840) 6 Bing. N.C. 296 at 300–301; 133 E.R. 117 at 119; and even if it is shown the delivery was not made on the date which appears on the deed, references within the document to the "date" may be construed as the day of the expressed date, rather than of delivery: *Styles v Wardle* (1825) 4 B. & C. 908; 107 E.R 1297; cf. *Clayton's Case* (1584) 5 Co. Rep. 1a, 77 E.R. 48 ("from henceforth" within a deed referred not to the date on the deed but the date when it became effective, i.e. delivery). A party may also be estopped from denying that the date which he inserts into a deed is the date when it took effect: *Rudd v Bowles* [1912] 2 Ch. 60 at 65.

[146] Law Commission WP No.93, see para.7-09 fn.92, paras 4.4, 8.2.

[147] Law Com. No.163, see para.7-06 fn.67, paras 2.7 to 2.10.

[148] LP(MP)A 1989 s.1(3)(b).

[149] The general provision is in LPA 1925 s.74A(1)(b), added by SI 2005/1906 art.4. For specific provisions, see e.g. CA 2006 s.46(1)(b) (companies regulated by CA 2006), applied also to Limited Li-

simply carries forward the existing requirement already set by the common law for the valid execution of a deed.[150]

The main reason that the Law Commission had proposed the abolition of the requirement was that "delivery" does not bear the meaning which one would expect: an instrument which has not yet been physically handed over to the other party may in law already have been delivered and therefore takes irrevocable effect[151]:

"Originally delivery involved a physical handing over of the deed which obviously signified the intention of the grantor of the deed to be bound by it.[152] However, a deed is now effectively delivered in law 'as soon as there are acts or words sufficient to shew that it is intended by the party to be executed as his deed presently binding on him'[153]. It is thus essentially a question of the grantor's intention, but it does not matter whether this intention is communicated to the grantee provided it is in fact evinced by some sufficient act or words.[154] Since delivery no longer requires any physical handing over, a deed may be taken as delivered even when kept with the grantor's own papers if there is evidence that he evinced an intention to be bound by it.[155] Laymen might well think the word 'delivery' here to be a dangerous misnomer as it does not accord with their understanding of the word. This may lead them to believe that until the deed is handed over to 'the other side' it is still capable of recall."

However, after consultation, the Law Commission "somewhat reluctantly" recommended that delivery should remain one of the required formalities for a deed, since it serves a useful purpose in fixing the date when the deed takes effect,[156] particularly where it is desired to delay its effect until some time after it has been formally executed.[157] In the case of a deed made by a corporation the mere execu-

---

ability Partnerships by SI 2009/1804 reg.4; Charities Act 2011 s.260(4) (incorporated body of charity trustees); Friendly Societies Act 1992 Sch.6 para.2(5) (incorporated friendly society); Co-operative and Community Benefit Societies Act 2014 s.53(4) (registered society).

150 *Goddard's Case*, see para.7-12 fn.145, at 5a, at 398, quoted at para.7-04 fn.38.
151 Law Commission WP No.93, see para.7-09 fn.92, para.4.4.
152 D.E.C. Yale, "The Delivery of a Deed" [1970] C.L.J. 52. [This is a valuable discussion of the history of "delivery" of deeds, "not to criticise the existing law but to tell the story of the change in legal doctrine, how the old law which required an act of giving was replaced by the new law where all that is required is an appropriate declaration of intention. ... one legal content has been emptied out of 'delivery' and replaced by another. The wine has been changed (for better or worse) but the bottle bears the same label" (at pp.73–74).]
153 *Xenos v Wickham* (1867) L.R. 2 H.L. 296; *Alan Estates v WG Stores Ltd* [1982] Ch. 511 [CA].
154 Delivery may be inferred from conduct (*Keith v Pratt* (1862) 10 W.R. 296) and has been inferred from the mere facts of signing and sealing (*Hall v Bainbridge* (1848) 12 Q.B. 699 [116 E.R. 1032]); but cf. per Kay LJ in *Powell v London and Provincial Bank* [1893] 2 Ch. 555 [CA] at pp.565–566 [rejecting the argument that a party who has executed a deed with blanks intended it to be (re)delivered when the blanks were completed by a third party and the deed acted upon]. [See also *Hare v Horton* (1833) 5 B. & Ad. 715; 110 E.R. 954 (possession of deed by other party prima facie evidence that it had been delivered to him as a deed); *Shelton's Case* (1582) Cro. Eliz. 7, 78 E.R. 274 (parties came together for purpose of executing deed; instrument left behind and not countermanded was delivered in law)].
155 [*Doe d. Garnons v Knight* (1826) 5 B. & C. 671; 108 E.R. 250].
156 See para.7-12 fn.145.
157 Law Com. No.163, see para.7-06 fn.67, paras 2.8, 2.10. In the Working Paper, the proposal to abolish the requirement of delivery was linked to the proposal to reform the law of escrows (see para.7-12 fn.162) by abolishing the notion of delivery in escrow and allowing instead for the deed itself to contain (express) conditions for its operation: Law Com. WP No.93, see para.7-09 fn.92, paras 9.1, 9.2, 13.3. However, the proposals for the reform of escrows were not supported on consultation and the Law Commission did not recommend them in its final report, thus raising again the question of whether to delivery should itself also be retained: Law Com. No.163, paras 1.5, 2.7. In 1994 the Law

tion will itself raise a rebuttable presumption of delivery[158]; however, now that sealing no longer forms part of the formalities for the execution of a deed by an individual,[159] there appears to be no such presumption in the case of a deed made by an individual.[160]

A deed may in fact be "delivered", but in circumstances where it is not yet to have immediate effect: a condition[161] is attached to the delivery so that the deed becomes binding only when the condition is satisfied. Such a deed is delivered "in escrow".[162] This is common in conveyancing transactions where a party executes the document and hands it to his solicitor for later transmission to the other party at completion.[163] No particular form is necessary to attach the condition, which may

---

Commission again considered whether the requirement of delivery should be retained (CP No.143, paras 11.57–11.60), but decided again that it should: Law Com. No.253, *The Execution of Deeds and Documents by or on behalf of Bodies Corporate* (1998), para.6.22.

[158] It has been held that the manifestation of the intention to deliver a deed may be by the seal itself: *Hall v Bainbridge*, see para.7-12 fn.154; *Commercial Credit Services v Knowles* [1978] C.L.Y. 794; presumably this will apply to the case of the execution of a deed by a corporation sole, which must be by seal (see para.7-09). In the case of a corporation aggregate, LPA 1925 s.74A(2), added by SI 2005/1906 art.4, provides that an instrument is presumed to be delivered upon its being executed (by seal or signature, as prescribed: see para.7-05) as a deed, unless a contrary intention is proved. The statutes and regulations governing particular types of corporation aggregate, listed at para.7-12 fn.149, also contain similar provisions. LPA 1925 s.74(1) is dealing with a quite separate matter (protection of the purchaser: see para.7-10 fn.126) and even before the addition of s.74A did not dispense with the requirement of sealing by a corporation: *Bolton MBC v Torkington* [2003] EWCA Civ 1634; [2004] Ch. 66 at [45] (Peter Gibson LJ, criticising Buckley J in *D'Silva v Lister House Development Ltd* [1971] Ch. 17 at 29–30), although that addition, and other reforms made by SI 2005/1906, were designed to remove doubts, as well as some inconsistencies in the provisions then in force, on the recommendation of the Law Commission in Law Com. No.253, see para.7-12 fn.157.

[159] See para.7-09.

[160] *Bibby Financial Services Ltd v Magson* [2011] EWHC 2495 (QB) at [335] (H.H. Judge Richard Seymour QC: "The critical thing is that the person who has signed the deed must have separately indicated that he intends to be bound by the deed. Mere signature is not enough. Nor is it enough that what looks like a deed has been given to the person who appears to be the beneficiary of it").

[161] The condition cannot, however, be the death of the party executing the deed, since in that case the document becomes a testamentary disposition, the validity of which is determined by the Wills Act 1837: *Governors and Guardians of Foundling Hospital v Crane* [1911] 2 K.B. 367, CA, at 379, 382; *Vincent v Premo Enterprises (Voucher Sales) Ltd* [1969] 2 Q.B. 609, CA, at 621.

[162] Or "scroll": *Holford v Parker* (1618) Hob. 246, 80 E.R. 391 ("delivered .... as a scrole upon condition"). The OED gives as the etymology "> Anglo-Norman *escrowe, escrouwe*, Old French *escroe, escroue* scrap, shred, strip of parchment, scroll (modern French *écroue* entry of a name in a jail register) > medieval Latin type **scrōda*, of Germanic origin: compare Old High German *scrŏt* scrap, fragment > Old Germanic **skraudo* (whence English shred n.)": OED Online, March 2018, "escrow, n.".

[163] Originally an escrow involved a first (conditional) physical delivery to a third party, who would then effect a second (unconditional) delivery to the beneficiary of the deed, but this is no longer necessary: *Terrapin International Ltd v Inland Revenue Commissioners* [1976] 1 W.L.R. 665 at 669–670. However, it has long been held that if there is physical delivery to the other party to the deed, in that capacity, it cannot be an escrow: *Whyddon's Case* (1595) Cro. Eliz. 520; 78 E.R. 769; *Williams v Green* (1600) Cro. Eliz. 884; 78 E.R. 1109; *Thoroughgood's Case* (1612) 9 Co. Rep. 136b, 777 E.R. 925; *Coare v Giblett* (1803) 4 East 85 at 95, 102 E.R. 762 at 766; *Pym v Campbell* (1856) 6 E. & B. 370 at 374; 119 E.R. 903 at 905 (Crompton J: "delivery estops the parties to the deed; that is the technical reason why a deed cannot be delivered as an escrow to the other party"); cf. *London Freehold and Leasehold Property Co v Baron Suffield* [1897] 2 Ch. 608, CA, at 621 (if several grantees, and one is also solicitor of grantor and of the other grantees, delivery to him may be by grantor in escrow); *Watkins v Nash* (1875) L.R. 20 Eq. 262 at 266 (delivery in escrow to agent of grantee, in circumstances negativing intention to deliver yet to grantee himself). cf. *Terrapin International Ltd v Inland Revenue Commissioners* at 670 (Walton J: The escrow "may initially be

be express or implied, and by words or by conduct or even from the very nature of the transaction,[164] and the only question is whether the particular party executing the deed intended to impose a condition on his own delivery by way of escrow[165]: the other party need not concur to the delivery in escrow.[166] Once he has delivered the instrument in escrow, however, the party has committed himself to it: even though it is not effective as a deed until the condition is satisfied, the party who has executed it cannot in the meantime change his mind and recall it but must at least allow a reasonable time for the condition to be satisfied[167]; and, once the condition is satisfied, the deed relates back to the time at which it was delivered as an escrow, but only to the extent necessary to give it effect.[168]

---

delivered to the grantee, who in such a case will be restrained by equity from acting upon it until the condition has in fact been fulfilled").

[164] *Phillips v Edwards* (1864) 33 Beav. 440 at 446-447, 55 E.R. 438 at 441 (Romilly MR: escrow "in any case where the deed implies mutuality, that is when some important act is to be done by or on the part of the person to whom it is to be delivered, such as the payment of purchase-money or the execution of the counterpart"); *Glessing v Green* [1975] 1 W.L.R. 863, CA, at 867 ("inescapable inference" in general practice of sale of land that conveyance is executed by vendor as escrow conditional on completion, i.e. payment of purchase price and, where appropriate, execution by purchaser); *Bank of Scotland v King* [2007] EWHC 2747 (Ch); [2008] 1 E.G.L.R. 65 at [53] (payment of only part of purchase price at time of delivery of deed justifies inference that deed was delivered as escrow pending payment of balance); *Johnson v Baker* (1821) 4 B. & Ald. 440, 106 E.R. 998 (creditors agreed that deed giving effect to composition must be signed by all to be effective). Where the deed is executed at a time when the negotiations are still "subject to contract" (above, para.2-08), no delivery in escrow is implied: *Bolton MBC v Torkington*, see para.7-12 fn.158, at [53]; *Longman v Viscount Chelsea* (1989) 58 P. & C.R. 189, CA, at 198 (Nourse LJ: "it is only in exceptional cases that a 'subject to contract' qualification will be overtaken" by delivery in escrow).

[165] In the case of execution by a company, the relevant intention is of the officers who execute the instrument, rather than of others in the company, such as those who manage such transactions: *D'Silva v Lister House Development Ltd*, see para.7-12 fn.158, at 30.

[166] *Bentray Investments Ltd v Venner Time Switches Ltd* [1985] 1 E.G.L.R. 39 at 43 (Stuart-Smith J, relying on *Glessing v Green*, see para.7-12 fn.164, at 867–868).

[167] *Beesly v Hallwood Estates Ltd* [1961] 1 Ch. 105, CA, at 118 (Harman LJ), 120 (Lord Evershed MR, referring to *equitable* relief after a long delay); *Vincent v Premo Enterprises (Voucher Sales) Ltd*, see para.7-12 fn.161 (parties who had executed and delivered lease and counterpart to solicitors as escrow could not recall them; see Lord Denning MR at 619, contrasting contracts for the sale of land, where there is no binding contract until exchange, but "a deed it is different. A deed is binding on the maker of it, even though the parts have not been exchanged, as long as it has been signed, sealed and delivered"); *Kingston v Ambrian Investment Co Ltd* [1975] 1 W.L.R. 161, CA; *Glessing v Green*, see para.7-12 fn.164 at 869 (Sir John Pennycuick: "It seems to us that the time limit is in its nature an element, and a vitally important element, in the implied condition, and I see no reason to call in aid some equitable principle of imprecise application", preferring the approach in *Kingston v Ambrian Investment Co Ltd*); *Alan Estates v WG Stores Ltd* [1982] Ch. 511, CA, at 520–521.

[168] *Security Trust Co v Royal Bank of Canada* [1976] A.C. 503, PC, at 517 (Lord Cross of Chelsea: "On fulfilment of the condition subject to which it was delivered as an escrow, a deed is not taken to relate back to the date of its delivery for all purposes, but only for such purposes as are necessary to give efficacy to the transaction—ut res magis valeat quam pereat (see *Butler and Baker's Case* (1591) 3 Co. Rep. 25a). Thus the fact that the grantor has died before the condition of an escrow is fulfilled does not entail the consequence that the disposition fails"); *Thompson v McCullough* [1947] K.B. 447, CA (conveyance of reversion in escrow: satisfaction of condition did not retrospectively validate notice to quit issued by new landlord during period of escrow); *Terrapin International Ltd v Inland Revenue Commissioners* [1976] 1 W.L.R. 665, following *Wm Cory & Son Ltd v Inland Revenue Commissioners* [1965] A.C. 1088, HL (stamp duty chargeable at date when condition satisfied, not when deed delivered in escrow); *Alan Estates v WG Stores Ltd*, see para.7-12 fn.167, at 521, 528 (rent under lease delivered in escrow payable from date of initial delivery; Ackner LJ dissented at 524–525). The Law Commission considered whether this should be changed, e.g. so that the deed takes effect only when the condition is fulfilled, but decided that "while there may be good reasons

Execution of deed by an agent   Although there is no general rule requiring   **7-13**
formality for the creation of agency or the exercise of his authority by an agent,[169]
sometimes the law requires the agent's authority to be given in writing where the
agent is to have power to fulfil a formality in writing on behalf of the principal.[170]
At common law an agent could execute a deed on behalf of his principal, but only
if he was authorised by deed by the principal to do so,[171] and if the agent executed
the deed in the name of the principal rather than in his own name.[172] The rule that
the authority to execute a deed must itself be given by deed remains unchanged[173];
but an individual who is the donee of a power of attorney may now, if he thinks fit,
act in his own name as the agent of the donor of the power.[174]

Even if the instrument was executed by the party himself, but it was left to an
agent simply to undertake the final act of delivery which would make the instrument binding as a deed,[175] the common law required the agent to be authorised by
deed before he could validly deliver it as the party's agent. This proved, however,
very troublesome since it is common for a party to hand over a document, already
executed (apart from its delivery), to his solicitor in readiness for the completion
of a transaction, but without yet wishing to bind himself even by way of escrow[176]
because he wishes to retain the right to recall the deed if the final stages of negotiation are not successful, but with a view to the solicitor being given the authority at
a later stage to deliver it on his behalf. The requirement for the authority to deliver
a deed itself to be given by deed has now been abolished by the Law of Property

---

for preferring a date different from the present one, we are not satisfied that the present law is so
unsatisfactory in principle or practice as to warrant making any change": Law Com. No.163, see
para.7-06 fn.67, para.3.4.

[169] Chitty, Ch.31; Furmston, Ch.6, Pt B; Treitel, Ch.16; Anson, Ch.23; Cheshire Fifoot and Furmston,
Ch.15.

[170] e.g. LPA 1925 s.53(1)(c) (disposition of equitable interest "in writing signed by the person disposing of the same, or by his agent thereunto lawfully authorised in writing or by will"). However, the
authority to enter into contracts which have to be in, or evidenced in, writing can be given orally,
as well as in writing: see paras 5-22 (contract for the sale or other disposition of land under LP(MP)A
1989 s.2); 6-14 (guarantee under Statute of Frauds 1677 s.4).

[171] See, e.g. *Berkeley v Hardy* (1826) 5 B. & C. 355, 108 E.R. 132 (agent on behalf of individual);
Mayor, Alderman and Burgesses of Kidderminster v Hardwick (1873) L.R. 9 Exch. 13 at 24 (agent
on behalf of corporation).

[172] *Frontin v Small* (1726) 2 Ld Raym. 1418, 92 E.R. 423; *White v Cuyler* (1795) 6 Term Rep. 176, 101
E.R. 176.

[173] An instrument creating a power of attorney must be executed as a deed by the donor of the power:
Powers of Attorney Act 1971 s.1(1), amended by LP(MP)A 1989 s.1(8), Sch.1 para.7. A company
regulated by the Companies Act may, by instrument executed as a deed, empower a person as its
attorney to execute deeds or other documents on its behalf: CA 2006 s.47(1). A corporation aggregate must, of course, always act through its human officers, who do not act as attorneys when
their acts or signatures constitute the execution of the instrument as a deed by the company (e.g. in
affixing the seal, or in signing the deed on behalf of the company under CA 2006 s.44(1), (2)). The
power of attorney is necessary to confer the powers of agency on a person to execute instruments
independently of the execution by the company itself.

[174] Powers of Attorney Act 1971 s.7(1), as substituted by LP(MP)A 1989 s.1(8), Sch.1 para.7(1), and
amended by SI 2005/1906. LPA 1925 s.74(3) provides that a person authorised under a power of attorney or under any statutory or other power to convey an interest in property in the name or on
behalf of a corporation sole or aggregate may execute the conveyance by, inter alia, signing the name
of the corporation. The power given by the Powers of Attorney Act 1971 to the attorney to sign in
his own name is an alternative to this: see s.7(2) of the 1971 Act.

[175] See para.7-12.

[176] See para.7-12.

(Miscellaneous Provisions) Act 1989,[177] which also provides that, in favour of a purchaser, the party's lawyer is presumed to have such authority.[178]

(4)   Failure to Comply with the Requirements for a Valid Deed

7-14   **Consequences of agreement failing to comply with the requirements for a valid deed**   An instrument which is not executed as required by the common law[179] or (where the common law requirements have been changed by statute[180]) by any applicable statute, is simply not a deed. It does not therefore effect as a matter of law any transaction which it purports to effect in so far as a deed is required. A purported conveyance, not executed as a deed, will not pass legal title to land[181]; and a promise, for which there is no consideration, contained in an instrument which is not properly executed as a deed will not be binding.[182] However, if the instrument, or the transaction which is set out in the instrument, can take effect irrespective of whether it is executed as a deed, then the failure of formality will not prevent it. For example, an agreement between two parties which can take effect as a contract, supported by consideration, does not cease to be a contract because it is set out in a document which fails to be executed properly as a deed, as long as the fact that it was intended to be executed as a deed does not on the facts undermine the parties' intention to be bound to the contract.[183] If not properly executed, it will not have the advantages of a deed,[184] but it may still take effect as an informal written contract.[185]

7-15   **Protection of third parties where deed not validly executed**   In certain circumstances third parties will be protected by statute against the fact that there has been some defect in the execution of a deed, such as where a corporation's seal has been improperly affixed to an instrument which appears to be a valid deed. Section 74(1) of the Law of Property Act 1925 now provides[186]:

---

[177]   s.1(1)(c): "(1) Any rule of law which—(a) requires authority by one person to another to deliver an instrument as a deed on his behalf to be given by deed … is abolished".

[178]   s.1(5), amended by SI 2005/1906 and Legal Services Act 2007 Sch.21 para.81(a): "Where a relevant lawyer, or an agent or employee of a relevant lawyer, in the course of or in connection with a transaction, purports to deliver an instrument as a deed on behalf of a party to the instrument, it shall be conclusively presumed in favour of a purchaser that he is authorised so to deliver the instrument"; "relevant lawyer" is defined in s.1(6), and includes solicitors and licensed conveyancers.

[179]   See para.7-04.

[180]   See para.7-05.

[181]   LPA 1925 s.52(1).

[182]   For the deed as substitute for consideration, see para.7-18.

[183]   e.g. the intention to execute the written document as a deed might perhaps form the basis of an argument that the negotiations were still subject to contract, pending the execution of a valid deed.

[184]   e.g. a longer period of limitation which is reserved to "specialties": see para.7-19.

[185]   *Bank of Scotland Plc v Waugh* [2014] EWHC 2117 (Ch); [2015] 1 P. & C.R. DG3 (purported grant of mortgage not effective under LPA 1925 s.52 because not attested, but it satisfied LP(MP)A 1989 s.2 (see para. 5-09), and so took effect as equitable mortgage); *Darjan Estate Co Plc v Hurley*, see para.7-11 fn.136, at [12] (lease not executed as a deed because signatures not attested (see para. 7-11) but took effect as agreement for lease and therefore equitable lease under the doctrine of *Walsh v Lonsdale* (1882) 21 Ch. D. 9, CA).

[186]   Substituted by SI 2005/1906. For similar provisions which operate in favour of purchasers in relation to instruments which purport to satisfy the relevant formality requirements for the execution of a deed, see CA 2006 s.44(5); Limited Liability Partnerships (Application of Companies Act 2006) Regulations 2009 (SI 2009/1804) reg.4; Overseas Companies (Execution of Documents and Registration of Charges) Regulations 2009 (SI 2009/1917) reg.4; Charities Act 2011 s.260(5)

"In favour of a purchaser[187] an instrument shall be deemed to have been duly executed by a corporation aggregate if a seal purporting to be the corporation's seal purports to be affixed to the instrument in the presence of and attested by—

(a)   two members of the board of directors, council or other governing body of the corporation, or

(b)   one such member and the clerk, secretary or other permanent officer of the corporation or his deputy."

This allows a purchaser to rely on the apparently properly executed deed, whether or not it in fact bears the correct seal and whether or not it was in fact properly executed in the presence of the attesting witnesses.

Estoppel and other similar doctrines   The doctrine of estoppel can also in some   **7-16**
circumstances allow a party who relies on a false representation that the deed has been properly executed to plead an estoppel against the representor and thus to hold him to the terms of the deed as if it had been properly executed. However, an estoppel does not make the instrument into a deed: only the person who makes a representation that the instrument was validly executed as a deed can be estopped from denying its validity by virtue of the representee's reliance on the representation.[188] We have already seen that estoppel, and similar doctrines, have been applied in the context of other contractual formalities to prevent a party relying on the absence of formality in order to resist a claim against him under the contract.[189] In all cases the courts consider the underlying policy of the particular formality in order to determine whether it would undermine that purpose to give effect to the transaction in spite of the failure of formality.[190] In relation to the formalities set by the common law or statute for the execution of a deed, the courts have allowed a party to enforce the terms of an instrument that was not properly executed in two different respects: first, where the document was not in fact sealed, although the document stated in terms that it had been "signed, sealed and delivered" in the presence of an attesting witness, and it was relied on by the claimant as a valid deed[191]; and secondly, where an attesting witness was not in fact

---

(incorporated body of charity trustees); Friendly Societies Act 1992 Sch.6 para.2(6) (incorporated friendly society); Co-operative and Community Benefit Societies Act 2014 s.53(5) (registered society). See also para.7-09 fn.114 and para.7-10 fn.126.

[187]   Defined in LPA 1925 s.205(1)(xxi).

[188]   *Mowatt v Castle Steel and Iron Works Co* (1886) 34 Ch. D. 58, CA, at 63. See Spencer Bower (Estoppel), paras 6.24 to 6.46 for a discussion of the circumstances in which the representor's successors in title can be bound.

[189]   See para.5-06 (contracts for sale or other disposition of land or any interest in land: LPA 1925 s.40: equitable doctrine of part performance); paras 5-26 to 5-29 (contacts for sale or other disposition of an interest in land under LP(MP)A 1989 s.2: resulting, implied or constructive trusts; proprietary estoppel; and other forms of estoppel); cf. para.6-18 (contracts of guarantee under Statute of Frauds 1677 s.4); and for general discussion see paras 4-12 to 4-15.

[190]   *Yaxley v Gotts* [2000] Ch. 162, CA, at 191 (Beldam LJ); and generally see para.4-15.

[191]   *TCB Ltd v Gray* [1986] Ch. 621 at 633 (Sir Nicolas Browne-Wilkinson VC: "There is ... a representation of fact that it was in fact sealed. Mr Gray executed the document with the intention that it should be relied on as a power of attorney and knowing the TCB was going to rely on it as such. TCB in fact relied on it to their detriment, since they advanced money in reliance on documents executed under the power. The case therefore has all the necessary elements of a classic estoppel"); following Danckwerts J in *Stromdale and Ball Ltd v Burden* [1952] Ch. 223 at 230. *TCB Ltd v Gray* was decided when sealing was a requirement for the valid execution of a deed by an individual, and Sir Nicolas Browne-Wilkinson declined to relax even further the formal require-

present when the deed was signed although the attestation clause stated in terms that he had been, and it was relied on by the claimant as a valid deed.[192] In the latter case, Pill LJ said[193]:

> "I have … come to the conclusion that there was no statutory intention to exclude the operation of an estoppel in all circumstances or in circumstances such as the present. The perceived need for formality in the case of a deed requires a signature and a document cannot be a deed in the absence of a signature. I can detect no social policy which requires the person attesting the signature to be present when the document is signed. The attestation is at one stage removed from the imperative out of which the need for formality arises. It is not fundamental to the public interest, which is in the requirement for a signature. Failure to comply with the additional formality of attestation should not in itself prevent a party into whose possession an apparently valid deed has come from alleging that the signatory should not be permitted to rely on the absence of attestation in his presence. It should not permit a person to escape the consequences of an apparently valid deed he has signed, representing that he has done so in the presence of an attesting witness, merely by claiming that in fact the attesting witness was not present at the time of signature. The fact that the requirements are partly for the protection of the signatory makes it less likely that Parliament intended that the need for them could in all circumstances be used to defeat the claim of another party."

This suggests that not every aspect of the formality can be dispensed with by the operation of the doctrine of estoppel: Pill LJ appeared to say that a representation that the document had been signed could not found an estoppel. However, it is not clear that this is so: if the representation that an instrument was sealed could form the basis of an estoppel in the time before sealing was replaced by signature,[194] it is not clear why a representation that an instrument was signed should not be capable in an appropriate case[195] of similarly forming the basis of an estoppel today.

Another doctrine that can sometimes apply in the case of a deed which is not validly executed is the principle that a party who has taken the benefit of the terms of a deed cannot deny that he must be subject to its burdens.[196] This has been held to apply where a person who was described as a party, and assented to it by taking its benefits, had not himself executed it and so was not as such bound by covenants in the deed, but could still be sued on the covenants set out in it.[197]

---

ment of sealing: see para.7-09.

[192] *Shah v Shah* [2001] EWCA Civ 527; [2002] Q.B. 35. The instrument therefore failed to satisfy the requirements of attestation under LP(MP)A 1989, s.1(3)(a); see para.7-11. The Law Commission envisaged that estoppel could apply in such a case: Law Com. No.163, see para.7-06 fn.67, para.2.15. cf. *Briggs v Gleeds* [2014] EWHC (Ch) 1178; [2015] Ch. 212 at [43] (no estoppel because there was no attestation clause, so the document did not even appear to comply with the 1989 Act on its face), followed in *Bank of Scotland Plc v Waugh* [2014] EWHC 2117 (Ch); [2015] 1 P. & C.R. DG3 at [78].

[193] *Shah v Shah* [2001] EWCA Civ 527; [2002] Q.B. 35 at [30].

[194] *TCB Ltd v Gray*, see para.7-16 fn.191.

[195] Such a case might arise where the representation is that the signature on the document which is seen by the claimant is the defendant's signature (and it is not); or where the document is simply unsigned, but is not seen by the claimant (e.g. where the defendant tells the claimant that he has signed and delivered the deed, but in fact he has not done so, but the claimant then acts on the basis the deed is valid and binding).

[196] For the broader operation of this principle in the context of land law, allowing positive covenants in a deed to be enforced that would otherwise not be binding on a party, see Cheshire and Burn, p.730; Megarry and Wade, paras 32-024 to 32-026.

[197] *Webb v Spicer* (1849) 13 Q.B. 886 at 893; 116 E.R. 1502 at 1505.

III.   DEEDS IN PRACTICE

Use of deeds by choice   The law sets the formality of a deed as a mandatory   **7-17**
requirement in order to effect certain transactions: notably, the creation or transfer
of most legal estates and interests in land.[198] Parties wishing to create contractual
obligations do not, however, generally need to use a deed, although the choice of
a deed may secure particular advantages which make it worthwhile to take the
trouble to execute the contract as a deed. Indeed, the use of a deed may not be much
more troublesome than a simple written contract, particularly where the parties are
entering into a formal transaction with the aid of their legal advisers, given that the
formalities of a deed are not in practice very onerous now that a party can generally execute an instrument as a deed by means of a witnessed signature.[199] The use
of a deed is always a conscious choice, however: the general requirement that the
document make clear on its face that it is intended to be a deed,[200] and other
particular requirements for execution by different types of party,[201] mean that it
should not generally be possible to execute a document as a deed accidentally. This
is as it should be, given the functions of formality—including the "cautionary" function, designed to ensure that the maker does not enter into the transaction without
realising what he is doing.[202]

A deed avoids the need to show sufficient consideration   Within the context of   **7-18**
contractual obligations, the use of a deed can be said to have a number of potential
advantages; perhaps the most obvious is that a promise contained in a deed is
enforceable by a party to the deed (or, in the case of a deed poll, by the grantee of
the benefit of the deed)[203] without his having to show that he gave consideration for
it.[204] Even in a commercial context, there are many situations where parties wish
to enter into binding obligations without asking for anything in return that could be
characterised as sufficient consideration for the promise—such as where it is sought
to set up a binding obligation to effect a gratuitous property transfer between related
companies, or to assign without consideration a present or future debt or other chose
in action,[205] or to create a guarantee of a loan that has already been made,[206] or where

---

[198] LPA 1925 s.52(1); see para.7-03.

[199] Sealing is now required only for corporations sole and those corporations aggregate which do not
have statutory authority to execute a deed by signature: individuals and most corporations aggregate can execute deeds by attested signature(s): see para.7-05.

[200] See para.7-07.

[201] In particular, either sealing or the use of attesting witnesses: see paras 7-09, 7-11.

[202] See para.4-03.

[203] For the distinction between deeds inter partes and deeds poll, see para.7-02. A person named as a
beneficiary of a covenant in a deed inter partes, though not a party, may also be able to enforce it if
it relates to real property, and if he is identified as a person with whom the covenant is made: see
para.7-02 fn.28.

[204] See paras 7-01, esp. fn.19, 7-02, esp. fn.27; below, para.8-03.

[205] The legal assignment of a debt or chose in action does not require consideration: LPA 1925 s.136;
but the promise to make the assignment must have contractual force and therefore be either supported by consideration or made in a deed.

[206] A guarantee must be evidenced by a written memorandum if it is to be enforceable: see para.6-07;
but it must also satisfy the requirements of a contractually binding promises, i.e. it must either be
supported by consideration or be made in a deed. The guarantee may be given in consideration of
the promise to grant the loan, but if the loan has already been made, the consideration of the loan
itself will be "past consideration" (see para.8-20) and either other consideration must be provided,
or the guarantee should be executed as a deed.

the creditor of an existing debt agrees to release it in whole or in part.[207] Similarly, where there is a novation of a contract on a change of one of the parties, a deed is generally executed by the original parties and the new party, to ensure that all are bound in relation to both the release of the party leaving the contract and the binding of the new party. In any case where there is a possibility that a party to the contract might be met by an argument that he cannot enforce it because of insufficiency of consideration, it is therefore wise to use a deed.[208]

However, although a gratuitous undertaking will be legally binding by virtue of the deed, the remedies to enforce it may not be as full as in the case of an undertaking contained in a contract supported by consideration. The common law regarded the deed as sufficient to make the undertaking binding: common law remedies are therefore in principle available—not only damages for loss caused by breach,[209] but the claim in debt to enforce a liquidated sum owed by virtue of the deed.[210] However, the fact that the beneficiary of an obligation has not provided consideration for it will normally preclude his obtaining an order of specific performance, since it is an equitable remedy and the courts of equity did not normally enforce promissory undertakings, even if contained in a deed, in favour of a volunteer.[211] This may not, however, be a very serious limitation in most cases since the remedy of specific performance is of limited availability, although it is commonly available in the case of undertakings to transfer interests in land, and other specific and unique property.[212]

7-19   **A claim for breach of a contract executed as a deed has a longer limitation period**   An action founded on simple contact cannot be brought[213] after the expiration of six years from the date on which the cause of action accrued.[214] However, a deed is a "specialty",[215] and under the Limitation Act 1980[216]:

---

[207] Even the payment of part of an existing debt is not sufficient consideration for a promise not to enforce the balance, and so either separate consideration must be given or the release must be executed as a deed: *Pinnel's Case* (1602) 5 Co. Rep. 117a at 117b, 77 E.R. 237 at 238; see para.9-18.

[208] e.g. in the case of a novation, there will generally be consideration in the mutual release of the old obligations, and the creation of new, bilateral obligations: see para.9-05. But occasionally there might be doubts (e.g. where all the obligations on one side appear already to have been performed) so a deed will avoid any question about the enforceability of the novation.

[209] *Cannon v Hartley* [1949] Ch. 213 at 217.

[210] A debt arising from a gratuitous transaction is not distinguished from other debts for the purpose of proof and distribution in bankruptcy: although the courts of equity used to give priority to creditors for valuable consideration, since the Judicature Act 1875 s.10, all debts and liabilities, whether contracted for value or not, rank pari passu: *Re Whitaker* [1901] 1 Ch. 9, CA.

[211] *Colman v Sarrel* (1789) 1 Ves. Jun. 50, 30 E.R. 225; *Jefferys v Jefferys* (1841) Cr. & Ph. 138, 41 E.R. 443; *Meek v Kettlewell* (1843) 1 Ph. 342, 41 E.R. 662; *Re Ellenborough* [1903] 1 Ch. 697; *Cannon v Hartley*, see para.7-18 fn.209, at 217. See generally Jones and Goodhart, pp.24–25; N. Andrews, M. Clarke, A. Tettenborn and G. Virgo, *Contractual Duties: Performance, Breach, Termination and Remedies*, 2nd edn (Sweet & Maxwell, 2017), para.27-015; Chitty, para.27-039.

[212] Jones and Goodhart, Ch.4; Andrews, Clarke, Tettenborn and Virgo, see para.7-18 fn.211, paras 27-023 to 27-038; Chitty, paras 27-005 to 27-022; Furmston, para.8.166; Treitel, paras 21-017 to 21-028; Anson, pp.608–611.

[213] Proceedings are started when the court issues a claim form at the request of the claimant, CPR r.7.2(1), but where the claim form as issued was received in the court office earlier than the date on which it was issued by the court, the claim is "brought" for the purposes of the Limitation Act on that earlier date: CPR PD 7A, para.5.1.

[214] Limitation Act 1980 s.5. There are particular rules under the Act for actions on a contract of loan (s.6) and where the claim (including a claim in contract) is for damages for personal injuries (s.11).

"An action upon a specialty shall not be brought after the expiration of twelve years from the date on which the cause of action accrued."

In a claim for breach of contract, the cause of action accrues on breach.[217] Where the contract is executed as a deed, therefore, the claim for breach of contract has a limitation period of 12 years from the breach, double the length of the normal limitation period for breach of contract; this extended limitation period is an advantage for any party who might have a claim under a deed, and is therefore one reason that parties, including commercial parties, choose to use a deed even where the transaction does not otherwise require it.[218] In 2001 the Law Commission recommended a new regime for the law of limitation of actions[219] which would apply to claims for breach of contract without drawing any distinction between simple contracts and contracts executed as a deed, and would therefore remove the present advantage of deeds as regards limitation periods.[220] However, this reform is not being taken forward.[221]

For general provisions for extension of limitation periods in cases of the claimant's disability, see s.28, and in cases of deliberate concealment by the defendant or his agent of facts relevant to the claimant's right of action, see s.32(1)(b). Where the claim is for recovery of a debt or other liquidated pecuniary claim, the limitation period which is still running begins to run again on the debtor's written and signed acknowledgement or part-payment of the claim: s.29(5), (7); s.30. For a claim to contribution under the Civil Liability (Contribution) Act 1978 s.1 there is a special time-limit of two years from the accrual of the right to recover contribution: see Limitation Act 1980 s.10.

[215] "The obvious and most common case of an action upon a specialty is an action based on a contract under seal, but it is clear that 'specialty' was not originally confined to such contracts but extended also to obligations imposed by statute": *Collin v Duke of Westminster* [1985] Q.B. 581 at 601 (Oliver LJ). See Law Com. No.253, see para.7-12 fn.157, paras 2.35-2.43, where the Law Commission considered (but rejected) the argument that an instrument must bear a seal if it is to be a specialty, instead taking the view that if it is in law a deed (whether or not, under the modern law, it is sealed: see para.7-05) it constitutes a specialty.

[216] s.8(1). This does not affect any action for which a shorter period of limitation is prescribed by any other provision of the Act: s.8(2).

[217] *Battley v Faulkner* (1820) 3 B. & Ald. 288, 106 E.R. 668; *Gibbs v Guild* (1881) 8 Q.B.D. 296 at 302.

[218] For a case which turned on this issue, see *Startwell Ltd v Energie Global Brand Management Ltd* [2015] EWHC 421 (QB).

[219] Law Com. No.270, *Limitation of Actions* (2001), proposing a single, core limitation regime which would apply to most claims for a remedy for a wrong, claims for the enforcement of a right and claims for restitution: a primary limitation period of three years starting from the date on which the claimant knows, or ought reasonably to know (a) the facts which give rise to the cause of action; (b) the identity of the defendant; and (c) if the claimant has suffered injury, loss or damage or the defendant has received a benefit, that the injury, loss, damage or benefit was significant; and a long-stop limitation period of 10 years, starting from the date of the accrual of the cause of action (or, for those claims in tort where loss is an essential element of the cause of action, from the date of the act or omission which gives rise to the cause of action); but with special rules for claims in respect of personal injury.

[220] See Law Com. No.270, see para.7-19 fn.219, para.4.8 ("Under the current law, specialties perform a useful function, allowing a choice of a longer limitation period for breach of contract than the normal six years, but this will not be necessary when parties have an express power [under the Commission's proposed reforms] to choose an extended limitation period. The existence of separate limitation periods for claims for breach of a contract that has been executed as a deed, as opposed to a simple contract, creates needless complexity").

[221] The Government accepted the Report in principle in July 2002, and in 2008 it was announced that provisions on the subject would be included within a proposed Civil Law Reform Bill. However, in 2009 the Government announced that the limitation reforms would not, after all, be taken forward: Law Com. No.323, *Annual Report 2009-10*, paras 3.12 to 3.15.

7-20　　**Statements in a deed may give rise to an estoppel**　English law does not have a general rule by which certain instruments are accorded higher status by way of evidence,[222] but the fact that a deed is a solemn instrument has led to the courts taking a more serious view of statements made within it. As a matter of evidence, a party may be estopped in many contexts by a statement of fact (or, now, law[223]) on which he intends a person to rely and he in fact relies ("estoppel by representation")[224]; but in the context of deeds there is a stronger rule, developed by the common law, that a party is estopped, as against the other parties to the deed and their successors in title, from disputing the validity or effectiveness of his grant, including statements of fact made in either the recitals or the operative parts of the deed ("estoppel by deed").[225] The relationship between these forms of estoppel has been debated,[226] but one clear indication of the approach of the courts is seen in a statement by Lord Maugham[227]:

> "Estoppel by deed is a rule of evidence founded on the principle that a solemn and unambiguous statement or engagement in a deed must be taken as binding between parties and privies and therefore as not admitting any contradictory proof."

The courts of equity did not, however, give effect to an estoppel if there was a ground on which the deed would be rectified or rescinded in order to counter the representation which was alleged to form the basis of the estoppel; and in this context, the courts of equity did not treat a receipt clause in a deed as effecting an estoppel if the money has not in fact been paid.[228] However, by statute a receipt for consideration money or other consideration in the body of a deed or endorsed on the deed is sufficient evidence of full payment in favour of a later purchaser who has no notice of the fact of non-payment.[229]

7-21　　**Proof of contents of a deed**　At common law, the original deed had itself to be produced if a party wished to rely on it in proceedings. However, as with other documents the courts will now admit secondary evidence to establish the fact of an instrument and its contents.[230]

---

[222]　This so-called *"hiérarchie des preuves"* is established in French law, and the instrument authenticated by a *notaire* or other public officer forms stronger proof of its contents than other documents: L. Aynès (ed.), *L'authenticité* (Paris: La documentation Française, 2013); C. Deneuville and others, "La hiérarchie des preuves" in *La Semaine Juridique*, édition notariale et immobilière, February 1, 2013: JCP N 2013, No.5, 25–50.

[223]　*Briggs v Gleeds* [2014] EWHC (Ch) 1178; [2015] Ch. 212 at [35].

[224]　Spencer Bower (Estoppel), paras 1.18, 1.19; Phipson, para.5-29; Cooke, pp.16–32; see para.10-06. Coke referred to this as "estoppel *in pais*": Co. Litt. 352a: for the terminology, see para.10-03 fn.6.

[225]　Spencer Bower (Estoppel), para.1.29, 8.79 to 8.89; Phipson, para.5-14; Cooke, pp.6–8. Coke referred to this as "estoppel by matter in writing": Co. Litt. 352a, but all Coke's examples of "writing" are of deeds. See also *Prime Sight Ltd v Lavarello* [2013] UKPC 22; [2014] A.C. 436 at [30] (the suggestion in Chitty, 30th edn (2008), Vol 1 para.1-112, that there is little point in now preserving any separate category of estoppel by deed, since the basis of the estoppel appears now to be covered by estoppel by representation or by convention, "may be going too far"): this appears to be based on the assumption that promise enforceable by deed is not a "contract": cf. para.7-02 fn.29.

[226]　Phipson, para.5-09. *First National Bank Plc v Thompson* [1996] Ch. 231, CA, at 236.

[227]　*Greer v Kettle* [1938] A.C. 156, HL, at 171.

[228]　*Greer v Kettle* [1938] A.C. 156, HL; see also *Destine Estates Ltd v Muir* [2014] EWHC 4191 (Ch) at [90]–[94].

[229]　LPA 1925 s.68.

[230]　Phipson, para.41-27; *Barber v Rowe* [1948] 2 All E.R. 1050, CA (proof of loss of lease; evidence of contents from counterpart).

IV. VARIATION OF DEEDS

A deed may be varied by a simple contract We have seen that the variation of   **7-22**
an existing contract by agreement of the parties, whether it supersedes the initial
contract (e.g. by novation) or simply modifies one or more terms of the contract,
must satisfy the same rules as are set for the formation of the initial contract, at least
if the varied contract is to have the same binding force as the initial contract.[231] At
common law the rule was that a deed could be varied only by deed. However, in
equity a deed could be varied by a simple written or oral contract, and this now
prevails.[232]

---

[231] See para.1-02.
[232] *Berry v Berry* [1929] 2 K.B. 316. The parties to the deed may, however, include a term in the deed
requiring a formality (e.g. writing, or a deed) for its variation: *MWB Business Exchange Centres Ltd
v Rock Advertising Ltd* [2018] UKSC 24; [2018] 2 W.L.R. 1603; see para.5-41.

PART III THE DOCTRINE OF CONSIDERATION

CHAPTER 8

CONSIDERATION AS A CONDITION OF THE EXISTENCE OF A CONTRACT[1]

I.   THE DOCTRINE OF CONSIDERATION: HISTORICAL AND COMPARATIVE CONTEXT

Consideration is explained by its history, but criticised by comparison with   **8-01**
other systems   Consideration is one of the fundamental elements in the formation of a contract in English law and in other common law systems whose contract law is based historically on English law. Every legal system must draw a line between those promises or agreements which should be given legally binding force, and those which should be left outside the protection of the law and regulated simply by moral pressure or social sanctions[2]; the doctrine of consideration is the principal mechanism by which the courts of common law in England drew this line. It was not, however, a simple matter for the courts to develop the doctrine; and in the modern law there has been much criticism of its operation, and even of the very requirement of consideration for the formation of a contract. Some criticism is linked to comparisons with other legal systems which have developed their law of contract without reliance on such a doctrine. In later paragraphs of this chapter and in Chapter 9 we shall see some of the difficulties encountered by the operation of the doctrine, and some of the calls for its reform or abolition.[3] Here, however, by way of background of the doctrine as it exists in the modern English law, we first consider briefly its origins; and to set the comparative context, we also look briefly at ways in which other legal systems address through other doctrines the kind of issues which the English courts have sought historically to address through the doctrine of consideration.

---

[1]   Chitty, paras 4-001 to 4-076, 4-186 to 4-203; Furmston, Ch.2, s.B; Treitel, paras 3-001 to 3-055, 3-153 to 3-169; Anson, pp.96-116, 120-122; Cheshire, Fifoot and Furmston, pp.100-124; Burrows (Restatement) s.8; Andrews, arts 34-38.
[2]   See para.1-04.
[3]   See paras 8-40 to 8-43, 9-23.

(1)   Origins of the Doctrine of Consideration

8-02   **The origins of consideration, a doctrine settled by the end of the eighteenth century**   This is not the place to discuss in detail the historical development of the modern law of contract in general,[4] nor even of the doctrine of consideration in particular.[5] The modern contract can be traced back to the enforcement of promises by means of the action of *assumpsit*[6]; and in the context of *assumpsit* the language of "consideration" in pleadings as justifying the enforcement of an undertaking dates back to the sixteenth century.[7] The notion that it is the reciprocity embodied in an agreement that justifies the protection of the law is of very long-standing.[8] Many of the rules which we now identify as the principal building-blocks of the modern English law of contract were only developed and refined through judicial

---

[4]   Cheshire, Fifoot and Furmston, Ch.1 (A.W.B. Simpson, revised by D.J. Ibbetson), is a particularly good overview of the general historical development of English contract law, including (at pp.8–10) the doctrine of consideration; the most detailed account is in A.W.B. Simpson, *A History of the Common Law of Contract* (Clarendon Press, 1987) (and esp. Pt II, Chs 4–7 on consideration). See also J.H. Baker, *An Introduction to English Legal History*, 4th edn (Butterworths LexisNexis, 2002), Chs 19 and 20 (and esp. pp.339–341 and 351–352 on consideration); D. Ibbetson, *A Historical Introduction to the Law of Obligations* (Oxford University Press, 1999), Chs 5, 11 and 12 (and esp. pp.236–241 on consideration); S.F.C. Milsom, *Historical Foundations of the Common Law*, 2nd edn (Butterworths, 1981), Ch.12 (and esp. pp.356–360 on consideration); W.S. Holdsworth, *A History of English Law*, Vol.iii, 5th edn (Methuen, 1942), Ch.3 and Vol.viii, 2nd edn (Methuen, 1937), pp.2–42 on consideration; W.S. Holdsworth, *Essays in Law and History* (ed. A.L. Goodhart and H.G. Hanbury, Clarendon Press, 1946), pp.128–138 (and esp. pp.132–134 on consideration).

[5]   Although the broad picture is well established, there are controversies which have not been settled: "Whether the doctrine of consideration was an indigenous product, or in part derived from the doctrine of *causa promissionis* of canon or civil law, has long been a matter of controversy, and it cannot be said that its pedigree has yet been explained in a fully satisfactory way": A.W.B. Simpson (revised by D.J. Ibbetson) in Cheshire, Fifoot and Furmston, p.10, referring also to Simpson, *A History of the Common Law of Contract*, see para.8-02 fn.4, Pt II, Chs 4–7; J.H. Baker, "*Origins of the 'Doctrine' of Consideration, 1535–1585*" in M.S. Arnold and others (eds), On the Laws and Customs of England (Chapel Hill: University of North Carolina Press, 1981), p.336; D.J. Ibbetson, "*Consideration and the Theory of Contract in the Sixteenth Century Common Law*" in J.L. Barton (ed.), Towards a General Law of Contract (Berlin: Duncker & Humblot, 1990), p.67.

[6]   "originally an off-shoot of the actions of trespass and deceit, and, when it first made its appearance, it was a delictual action. It lay when a man had agreed (assumpsit) to do something, and had done it badly, with the result that the plaintiff was injured. Later it was extended to cases when a man agreed to do something, and had failed to do it, with the result that the plaintiff was injured, provided that the plaintiff, as the result of and relying upon the making of the agreement, had altered his position to his detriment. Finally, it was extended to cases where a man had promised to do something in return for a counter-promise by the other party—in other words it was extended to remedy the breach of purely executory contracts": Holdsworth, *Essays in Law and History*, see para.8-02 fn.4, p.132. For further discussion and analysis, see the works cited at para.8-02 fn.4.

[7]   Baker, *An Introduction to English Legal History*, see para.8-02 fn.4, p.340; A.W.B. Simpson (revised by D.J. Ibbetson) in Cheshire, Fifoot and Furmston, p.8, fn.23, cites *Joscelin and Shelton* (1557) 3 Leo. 4, 74 E.R. 503 as the earliest assumpsit case in the printed reports to mention consideration by name.

[8]   "Consideration, in the sense of reciprocity, had been for centuries the linchpin of the English law of contract": Ibbetson, *A Historical Introduction to the Law of Obligations*, see para.8-02 fn.4, p.236; see also pp.202–203. Although the doctrine of consideration grew within the action of assumpsit, rather than the earlier actions of covenant or debt, a similar idea was already developing in the earlier actions where an agreement could be enforced in the middle ages by the writ of debt if the claimant could show that he had given something to the defendant in return for the promise he sought now to enforce—a quid pro quo: Holdsworth, *Essays in Law and History*, see para.8-02 fn.4, pp.131–132.

decisions during the course of the nineteenth century,[9] but the requirement of consideration for an informal, or "simple",[10] contract was already settled before then, although during the eighteenth century there was some very significant judicial debate and disagreement about how to draw the line for legally-binding promises made otherwise than in a deed. In 1765, in the context of a mercantile transaction, Lord Mansfield said[11]:

"the ancient notion about the want of consideration was for the sake of evidence only: for when it is reduced into writing, as in covenants, specialties, bonds, etc., there was no objection to want of consideration. And the Statute of Frauds[12] proceeded upon the same principle"

and that a written promise to pay could therefore be enforced even in the absence of consideration being provided in return. Moreover, this was consistent with the law merchant: "it would be very destructive to trade, and to trust in commercial dealing" if the person who had made a firm promise in writing could renege on it.[13] The underlying idea here was that consideration is a sort of formality, or a substitute for formality[14]; and the writing fulfils the cautionary function of formality.[15]

However, the approach taken by Lord Mansfield was firmly rejected in 1778 in *Rann v Hughes*[16] where Skynner CB, giving the opinion of the judges in response to a reference by the Lord Chancellor when the case reached the House of Lords, said[17]:

"It is undoubtedly true that every man is by the law of nature, bound to fulfil his engagements. It is equally true that the law of this country supplies no means, nor affords any remedy, to compel the performance of an agreement made without sufficient consideration; such agreement is nudum pactum ex quo non oritur actio[18]... But it is said that if this promise is in writing that takes away the necessity of a consideration, and obviates the objection of nudum pactum ..."

---

9 A.W.B. Simpson, "Innovation in Nineteenth Century Contract Law" (1975) 91 L.Q.R. 247.
10 A "simple" or "parol" contract is one not contained in a deed: see para.7-01 and Skynner C.B. in *Rann v Hughes*, quoted at para.8-02 fn.17.
11 *Pillans v Van Mierop* (1765) 3 Burr. 1663 at 1669, 97 E.R. 1035 at 1038. See also Simpson, *A History of the Common Law of Contract*, see para.8-02 fn.4, p.618, suggesting the Lord Mansfield was "no innovator in legal matters, though the contrary is often supposed" and that his statements in *Pillans* were a repetition of views that were current earlier.
12 [See para.4-05. This statement must not be taken literally. The Statute of Frauds did not dispense with the requirement of consideration for a contract, but added an extra requirement for the enforceability of a contract; e.g. in the modern law, a contract of guarantee must be evidenced by a written memorandum to be enforceable; but, if not contained in a deed, it must also still satisfy the requirements for the formation of a contract, including consideration in return for the promise of guarantee: see para.6-12.]
13 *Pillans v Van Mierop*, see para.8-02 fn.11, at 1670, at 1038.
14 On this, see further para.8-27.
15 See para.4-03. See also Wilmot J in *Pillans v Van Mierop*, at para.8-02 fn.11, at 1671, at 1039, who found consideration, but held also that this was not necessary, because the promise, being "reduced into writing, is a sufficient guard against surprize".
16 (1778) 7 T.R. 350n, 101 E.R. 1014; (1778) 4 Bro. P.C. 27, 2 E.R. 18.
17 (1778) 7 T.R. 350n, 101 E.R. 1014. The trial judge in the case was Lord Mansfield; the jury had held that the promise was binding: (1778) 4 Bro. P.C. 27 at 29, 2 E.R. 18 at 20. This was reversed by the Exchequer Chamber, affirmed by the House of Lords after receiving the unanimous opinion given by the judges through Skynner C.B.
18 ["a bare agreement from which no action arises".]

All contracts are, by the laws of England, distinguished into agreements by specialty,[19] and agreements by parol; nor is there any such third class as some of the counsel have endeavoured to maintain, as contracts in writing. If they are merely written and not specialties, they are parol, and a consideration must be proved."

This settled the position: a promise contained in a deed may be enforced by virtue of the formality of the deed,[20] without the claimant having to show that he gave consideration for the promise; but if there is no deed, then consideration must be shown, and the fact that the promise is in writing, or in terms which show a clear intention to be legally bound, is not sufficient to dispense with the requirement of consideration. The developments in the doctrine of consideration since then have generally been aimed at refining the doctrine, sometimes by limiting the scope of consideration so as to narrow the range of legally enforceable agreements,[21] sometimes to relax its operation so as to allow promises to be binding.[22] But, so far at least, there has been no attempt to change it fundamentally to make the consideration merely a matter of evidence, and in that sense a substitute for a formal contract, in the manner which Lord Mansfield would apparently have preferred.[23]

8-03　**Consideration as alternative to a deed**　We have already noted that in the mediaeval period promises and agreements were enforced in the local courts and in the King's courts, and that the deed came to be required either as evidence of a promise or agreement before it could be enforced in the King's courts or as a requirement for the creation of a legally enforceable promise to pay a sum of money.[24] The common law developed around different forms of action, for which different writs were developed: and in the early period promises and agreements were enforced through actions of covenant, and of debt. The deed had therefore acquired its own significance as the formal element justifying the enforcement of an undertaking, before *assumpsit* was developed to provide a general form of action to enforce a promise, an action which a party could choose to use in preference to the action of debt to enforce payment of a sum of money, as well as to obtain a remedy for the other party's failure to fulfil any other promise.[25] Once this general

---

[19]　[i.e. deeds: see para.7-19.]

[20]　See also para.8-03.

[21]　e.g. in emphasising that consideration must be of economic value: *Thomas v Thomas* (1842) 2 Q.B. 851; 114 E.R. 330, and must not merely consist of the fulfilment of a pre-existing moral obligation: *Eastwood v Kenyon* (1840) 11 Ad. & El. 438 at 450–451; 113 E.R. 482 at 486–487 (Lord Denman CJ: if a moral obligation were sufficient consideration "the doctrine would annihilate the necessity for consideration at all, inasmuch as the mere fact of giving a promise creates a moral obligation to perform it. The enforcement of such promises by law, however plausibly reconciled by the desire to effect all conscientious engagements, might be attended with mischievous consequences to society...").

[22]　This is generally the more recent experience, given that the courts do not easily or comfortably come to the conclusion that an agreement, intended by the parties to be binding, should be in law unenforceable for lack of consideration, especially in a commercial context: see para.8-28.

[23]　Lord Mansfield's view was relied on by Law Revision Committee, Sixth Interim Report, *Statute of Frauds and the Doctrine of Consideration* Cmd.5449 (1937), para.29, in recommending that writing should become a substitute for consideration: see para.8-40. The Report was not, however, enacted; see para.9-23 fn.190.

[24]　See para.7-01.

[25]　The crucial development was in *Slade's Case* (1602), discussed in Baker, *An Introduction to English Legal History*, see para.8-02 fn.4, pp.344–345; A.W.B. Simpson (revised by D.J. Ibbetson) in Cheshire, Fifoot and Furmston, p.7.

contractual action had been established, it was developed quite separately from the law relating to deeds; but, as we have seen,[26] the law of deeds was itself also developed independently of the general law of (informal) contracts and without reference to the doctrine of consideration which became established as a core element of an informal contract. In the modern law, we have therefore inherited two independent legal bases for the enforcement of promises and agreements: the formality of a deed, by virtue of which an undertaking (either unilateral or bilateral[27]) may be enforced; and the informal promise which may be enforced only if the promisee has provided consideration in return for the promise.

(2) Comparisons with Other Legal Systems

Consideration is not known in the civil law tradition The jurisdictions of continental Europe have drawn their law of contract, in different ways, from the Roman law tradition—adopting not the ancient Roman law, but the Roman law as revived in the twelfth and thirteenth centuries and developed thereafter with strong influences of canon law.[28] One aspect of the civilian tradition was that the enforcement of a promise was justified by reference to its *causa*: the cause, or motivation for the promise, which could include moral, as well as economic, reasons.[29] Promises could be binding even if there was nothing in return: indeed, the moral duty to keep one's promise was seen as a strong factor behind the canon lawyers' development of the civil law from the middle ages onwards,[30] and therefore promises of gifts might be justifiably enforced as much as promises for which something was bargained in return. We do not need here to trace the development of the Roman and canon law principles through to the modern era,[31] although the fact that these are the origins helps to understand the way in which modern civil law systems draw their own line around those promises which the law will enforce.[32] There is no single answer given by the modern civil law systems, although they fall broadly into two groups: those which still include the requirement of a "cause" for the validity of a legally binding promise—such as systems which draw their inspiration from the French civil code of 1804[33] (although France

8-04

---

26 See Ch.7, esp. paras 7-01 to 7-05.
27 For the distinction between deeds poll and deeds inter partes, see para.7-02.
28 B. Nicholas, *An Introduction to Roman Law* (Clarendon Press, 1962), pp.46–50; Holdsworth, *Essays in Law and History*, see para.8-02 fn.4, pp.128–131; P. Stein *Roman Law in European History* (Cambridge University Press, 1999), esp. Ch.3; R.C. van Caenegem, *An Historical Introduction to Private Law* (Cambridge University Press, 1992), pp.45–67.
29 J. Gordley, *The Philosophical Origins of Modern Contract Law Doctrine* (Clarendon Press, 1991), pp.49–57; Holdsworth, Vol.viii, pp.42–45. In the 12th and 13th centuries, English law might also have developed similarly, although as the civil law on the continent came to be the study of the universities, it was rather the practising lawyers and judges who took and developed the English common law, and the direct influence of the Roman law reduced: Holdsworth, *Essays in Law and History*, see para.8-02 fn.4, pp.128–129 (citing the influence which civil and canon law had on Glanville and Bracton).
30 M. Hogg, *Promises and Contract Law* (Cambridge University Press, 2011), pp.79–83.
31 For the development into the modern civil codes of the European nation states see, e.g. Nicholas, see para.8-04 fn.28, pp.51–53; Stein, see para.8-04 fn.28, Ch.5; van Caenegem, see para.8-04 fn.28, Chs 4 and 5.
32 Some English legal historians see the doctrine of consideration as, at least in part, following from the civil and canon law doctrine of causa: see para.8-02 fn.5.
33 e.g. Italy, Spain and many Latin American countries.

itself has recently reformed its code to remove the requirement of "cause"[34]); and those which do not include such a requirement but focus more directly on the intention of the promisor to be bound to his promise, such as German law.[35] Even in the modern civil systems which have maintained the requirement of a "cause" for the legally-binding promise, the requirement has become controversial and often attenuated in its interpretation and application.[36] In general terms, one could say that there is much more of a focus on the promisor's intention, or the parties' intentions, to be bound as the basis of contractual enforcement of promises in the modern civil law, both in European jurisdictions and in the many other jurisdictions around the world which have taken one or more of the European codes as their model for their own civil codes.[37] In consequence, there is no inhibition in principle to allowing promises to be binding where there is nothing asked in return. An informal contract is not necessarily a bargain in the civil law systems, which widely recognise contracts of gift as well as contracts of exchange; the doctrine of consideration is a common law creature, and it has been limited to the common law jurisdictions.[38]

It should also be noted that in any attempts to produce general principles of the law of contract which can apply across the different traditions, whether internationally or just across the different European traditions, the different approaches of the systems to the principal justification for the enforcement of a promise (whether "consideration", "cause" or simply the parties' intentions) have to be resolved; and in recent proposals for possible harmonisation of contract law in Europe both consideration and cause have generally been rejected in favour of a model which focuses on the intentions of the parties.[39] This may also be relevant if we ever come to the point of making a root-and-branch review of contract law in England, where

---

34 The 1804 code, art.1108, set four conditions for the validity of a contract: consent, capacity, subject-matter and cause; since 1 October 2016, the new art.1128 sets only three: consent, capacity, and lawful and certain content. On the reform generally, see J. Cartwright and S. Whittaker (eds), *The Code Napoléon Rewritten: French Contract Law after the 2016 Reforms* (Hart Publishing, 2017).

35 For a general comparative discussion, covering English law as well as the French and German traditions, see H. Kötz, *European Contract Law*, 2nd edn (trans. G. Mertens and T. Weir, Oxford University Press, 2017), Ch.4. For sources (in translation) see H. Beale and others, *Cases, Materials and Text on Contract Law* (Ius Commune Casebook series), 2nd edn (Hart Publishing, 2010), pp.170–189 (French law before the 2016 reform, together with, Italian and Quebec law), 214–215 (German and Dutch law); and for a general comparative study, see J. Gordley (ed.), *The Enforceability of Promises in European Contract Law* (Cambridge University Press, 2001).

36 e.g. in French law, there was a debate over the 20th century as to whether the requirement of "cause" (*la cause*) should be retained: see, e.g. J. Rochfeld, "*A Future for la cause?*" and R. Sefton-Green, "*La cause or the Length of the French Judiciary's Foot*" in J. Cartwright, S. Vogenauer and S. Whittaker (eds), *Reforming the French Law of Obligations* (Hart Publishing, 2009), Chs 4 and 5; the debate culminated in its removal from the requirements of validity of contracts in the 2016 reform: see para.8-04 fn.34. The new civil code of Quebec of 1991, which came into force in 1994, retains the requirement that "it is ... of the essence of a contract that it have a cause" (art.1385), which is "the reason that determines each of the parties to enter into the contract" (art.1410). The new Dutch civil code of 1992, replacing the old code which had been based on the French civil code, removed the requirement of cause and adopted a German-style requirement of intention to be bound (arts 3:33, 6:213).

37 On reception of the European codes (and most particularly the French civil code) see K. Zweigert & H. Kötz, *An Introduction to Comparative Law*, 3rd edn (trans. T. Weir, Oxford University Press, 1998), Ch.8; M. Graziadei in M. Reimann and R. Zimmermann (eds), *The Oxford Handbook of Comparative Law* (Oxford University Press, 2006), pp.447–451.

38 See further para.8-05.

39 PECL, art.2:101(1); DCFR II.–4:101.

the question may be whether English law could sensibly abandon its requirement of consideration in favour of a different test, such as the parties' intentions.[40]

Consideration received in the common law outside England　Legal systems in 　**8-05**
the common law world—that is, those systems which have drawn their law from English law—have also adopted the doctrine of consideration. A contract, not contained in a deed, therefore requires consideration as a matter of principle in the law of such jurisdictions as Australia,[41] Canada (excluding Quebec),[42] India,[43] Ireland,[44] Malaysia,[45] New Zealand[46] and Singapore.[47] And consideration is a core element of a contract in the common-law jurisdictions in the United States.[48] However, as we shall see, there has been some re-thinking of the proper scope of consideration as a requirement of a legally-enforceable promise: some of these common law jurisdictions have allowed other doctrines to be introduced alongside consideration in order to allow promises to be enforceable in certain circumstances even though there is no consideration[49]; others have re-considered the scope of the doctrine of consideration itself, and there have been proposals for significant reform or even abolition of the doctrine.[50] The English judges sometimes appear more reluctant than their common law brethren around the world to re-think fundamental doctrines. However, the fact that other common law jurisdictions may be willing to reconsider the role and scope of consideration as the fundamental doctrine by which a simple promise may be legally binding, may in due course raise questions in the minds of the English judges too. Although this chapter and the following chapters are devoted principally to the scope and operation of the doctrine of consideration in English law, we shall also mention from time to time different approaches which appear to find favour in other common law jurisdictions.

II.　The Place of the Doctrine of Consideration in the Modern Law

Consideration as one element in the formation of a contract　Consideration is 　**8-06**
one of the elements which must be established in order to show a binding contract in English law. We have already seen that a contract is a legally enforceable *agreement*,[51] and that the agreement may either consist in the parties' common assent to

---

40　For criticism of the doctrine of consideration see para.8-40.
41　Seddon and Bigwood, Ch.4.
42　Fridman, Ch.3; Waddams, Ch.2, s.J.
43　Indian Contract Act 1872, ss.2(d), 10, 25.
44　R. Clark, *Contract Law in Ireland*, 8th edn (Dublin: Round Hall, Thomson Reuters, 2016), Ch.2.
45　Sinnadurai, Ch.3.
46　Burrows, Finn & Todd, Ch.4.
47　Phang and Goh, Ch.2.
48　Farnsworth, paras 2.2 to 2.4. Restatement of Contracts (2d) §§17 (consideration required for formation of contract if contract not formal nor within certain exceptions), 71 (to constitute consideration, performance or return promise must be bargained for; i.e. sought by the promisor in exchange for his promise and is given by the promisee in exchange for that promise), 79 (if requirement of consideration met, no additional requirement of benefit to promisor or detriment to promisee). Louisiana, with its civil law code, has no requirement of consideration, but an obligation requires a "lawful cause" (art.1966), which is "the reason why a party obligates himself" (art.1967).
49　In particular, the doctrine of promissory estoppel: see Ch.10, esp. paras 10-46 to 10-48.
50　See para.8-40.
51　See para.3-01.

a single written document,[52] or be formed during the parties' discussions through oral or written communications, typically when one party accepts an offer made by the other.[53] However, although the parties must be shown to have agreed on terms sufficient to form the contract,[54] it is not yet a legally enforceable agreement if the agreement does not also satisfy the requirement of sufficient consideration. It is the consideration which, in this sense, turns a mere agreement into a contract. Commonly, therefore it is said that the formation of a contract requires offer, acceptance and consideration.[55]

8-07 **Consideration gives focus to the defendant's promise** The requirement of consideration also changes the emphasis within a contract from the *parties' agreement* to the *defendant's promise*, and the reason why it should be legally enforceable. Rather than asking whether there is consideration for the agreement, we generally ask whether there is consideration for the promise which the claimant seeks to enforce. In most cases, this is only looking at the same thing—the "contract"—from two different angles: there must be an agreement between the parties as to the terms of the contract; but those terms can also be viewed as an exchange by which one party promises something in return for the other's promise or performance. The doctrine of consideration focuses on whether there was a sufficient "return" for the promise which the claimant seeks to enforce. If the contract is wholly executory—a promise of future performance in return for a promise of future performance[56]—the agreement will consist in each party making mutual promises which will also constitute at that moment sufficient consideration for the contract. The agreement, formed through offer and acceptance, will therefore typically contain the mutual undertakings which are themselves also the consideration: each party, by his own promise, provides consideration for the other's promise. In the case of a unilateral contract, such as a promise of a reward,[57] the acceptance (by performance, to earn the reward) will be at the same time the provision of (executed) consideration.[58] In all cases, therefore, there will be both an agreement and consideration, although in cases where the issue is whether there was sufficient consideration, the focus of the question is generally: did the claimant provide consideration for the defendant's promise? Or, in other words, what did the claimant promise, or do, which justifies his legal claim now to enforce the defendant's promise?

---

[52] See para.3-08.

[53] See paras 3-19, 3-25.

[54] The agreement is generally tested objectively: see paras 3-07, 3-08; and must be sufficiently complete and certain: see paras 3-13, 3-14.

[55] "an indivisible trinity, facets of one identical notion which is that of bargain": C.J. Hamson, "The Reform of Consideration" (1938) 54 L.Q.R. 233, 234 (criticised on historical grounds by Simpson (1975) 91 L.Q.R. 247, 260: "in reality consideration rubbed along alone for three hundred years before the trinity came into being"). It may be added that there is also a requirement of intention to be legally bound; for whether this is an additional element of the same significance as agreement (offer and acceptance) and consideration, or (at least in practice) a subsidiary test within English law, see paras 3-09 to 3-10.

[56] See para.8-12.

[57] See para.3-32.

[58] See para.8-13; Hamson, see para.8-06 fn.55 ("consideration may conveniently be explained as merely the acceptance viewed from the offeror's side" referring, however, to contract generally and not only to unilateral contracts).

Consideration has the effect of excluding gratuitous promises from contract: **8-08**
contract as bargain The requirement of consideration, provided by the claimant in order to enforce the defendant's obligations, or promises, within the contract,
demonstrates the essential nature of the contact as a bargain in English law. A person
can enforce another's promise—enforce the contract—because he has done
something, or at least promised to do something, in return for the promise which
he now seeks to enforce. The consideration he provides is an act or a promise in
return for the other party's promise; it is—in a broad sense—the price that he has
paid in order to earn the enforcement of the other's promise, at the latter's request.
We shall see the nuances of these various elements in the following section of this
chapter: consideration may be the "price" of the promise, but it need not be money
but can be any act or promise of benefit to the promisor (the defendant), and/or
detriment to the promisee (the claimant)—and the notion of "benefit" and "detriment" may be rather broadly interpreted.[59] It must be "in exchange for", or "in
return for" the defendant's promise, which means that what the claimant provides
by way of consideration must be at the promisor's request, at least implied.[60] But
the key point to notice from the outset is that the effect[61] of the doctrine of
consideration is that in principle it excludes from the scope of contract promises of
gifts, and other gratuitous undertakings where nothing is expressly or impliedly
requested in return, however seriously the promises and undertakings may have
been intended to be binding as a matter of law. The requirement of "consideration
for the defendant's promise" is not satisfied in the modern law just because the
defendant had a good reason for making the promise, whether a good moral, social
or economic reason, or a serious intention to be bound to fulfil the promise—it is
not, in other words, a version of a Roman or civilian doctrine of *causa*, which
focused on why the defendant's promise should be binding, from the defendant's
perspective. English law focuses on why the claimant should be entitled to enforce
the promise: what has the claimant done to earn it?[62]

Different reasons to recognise the legal enforceability of a promise Considera-   **8-09**
tion is not the only reason by which the law can justify the legal enforcement of

---

[59] See paras 8-23 to 8-35.
[60] See paras 8-15 to 8-17.
[61] This describes the modern law as it has now been developed. It does not necessarily assume that the
purpose of the historical development was to draw the line between gratuitous promises and bargains;
the history of the doctrine is complex: see para.8-02, esp. fn.5, and see Simpson, see para.8-06 fn.55,
at 263 ("the doctrine of consideration ... has never expressed the distinction between gratuitous and
non-gratuitous promises"). Note, too, that there need be no *real* bargain in the sense of a real
exchange of values, since the consideration need not be adequate and may even be nominal: see
para.8-25.
[62] See *Thomas v Thomas* (1842) 2 Q.B. 851 at 859, 114 E.R. 330 at 333–334 (Patteson J, noting that
"motive is not the same thing with consideration" because motive explains the promise from the
defendant's side, whereas consideration must move from the plaintiff); *Ashia Centur Ltd v Barker
Gillette LLP* [2011] EWHC 148 (QB); [2011] 4 Costs L.R. 576 at [20] (Tugendhat J: "A promise
does not become contractually binding simply because the making of the promise is potentially
advantageous to the promisor. The promise must do or refrain from doing something"). We shall
see that this aspect of the English doctrine was a significant contribution to the difficulty faced by
English law in admitting directly-enforceable third-party rights in contract: the third party has not
himself given anything for the defendant's promise, even if the promise was directed at conferring
a benefit on him, so the English courts saw no reason to allow the third party to bring a direct action:
he had not himself "earned" it: *Tweddle v Atkinson* (1861) 1 B. & S. 393, 121 E.R. 762; *Dunlop
Pneumatic Tyre Co Ltd v Selfridge & Co Ltd* [1915] A.C. 847, HL, see para.8-19.

promises; nor is it, indeed, the only reason by which English law in fact justifies their enforcement. We have already seen that a promise contained in a deed may be enforced by virtue of the formal instrument, without the claimant having to establish that he has given consideration: both gratuitous promises and bargained-for promises may therefore be enforceable where they are contained within a deed.[63] The deed focuses on the promisor's own expression of intention to be bound within the form of the deed as prescribed by law, a different perspective from the doctrine of consideration which focuses on the claimant's justification for enforcing the defendant's promise.[64] However, the doctrine of consideration looks at both sides: the reason that the claimant can be said to have earned the right to enforce the promise is by doing or promising something at the defendant's request; and the correlative is that the reason the defendant should have to perform his promise is because he has "received" the consideration he asked of the claimant[65] and so cannot deny that his promise is enforceable. Bargains are inherently bilateral,[66] and therefore the doctrine of consideration, in so far as it operates within the bargain theory of contract, can be seen from both parties' sides.

Yet another way of justifying the enforcement of promises is where the claimant has acted on the promise even though the defendant did not expressly or impliedly request him to do so. This is a claimant-sided justification: it might be limited in its operation so as to apply only where the defendant intended the claimant to act, or at least foresaw that he might do so. But it is a weaker justification to hold the defendant to his promise than where he requested the claimant to act. It does not enforce the defendant's promise as part of a bargain, but justifies its enforcement by reference to the claimant's *reliance* on the promise; and we shall see that there are circumstances in which English law gives force to a promise by reason of the claimant's reliance on it, through the doctrine of promissory estoppel.[67] However, the operation of promissory estoppel is quite narrowly limited in English law, although it has been developed much more extensively in certain other common law jurisdictions, and in particular the United States.[68] Questions remain to be answered about whether English law could also extend the operation of promissory estoppel so as to provide an alternative to the doctrine of consideration in the enforcement of promises; and such questions also raise significant broader questions about whether the legal bases for the enforcement of promises in English law should be reviewed and reformed, and even whether in such a reform the doctrine of consideration should itself be reformed or even replaced. These questions are considered briefly later[69]; first we must consider in some detail the operation of the doctrine of consideration.

---

63   See paras 7-01, 7-03, 7-18.
64   See para.8-07.
65   This does not mean that the defendant has necessarily himself obtained performance from the claimant directly. Consideration can be provided where the claimant provides a benefit to a third party, at the request of the defendant promisor: although the economic benefit may appear to accrue to the third party, it is sufficient to constitute consideration that the performance was at the defendant's request: he has obtained what he asked for, in return for his promise: see para.8-23.
66   Even a unilateral contract gives rise to a bargain, in the sense that it is because the claimant has chosen to perform, and has succeeded in doing whatever the claimant asked, that he is then justified in claiming the reward: see para.3-32 and para.8-13.
67   See Ch.10.
68   See paras 10-45 to 10-48.
69   See paras 8-40, 10-49 to 10-51.

Consideration in formation of the contract distinguished from "total failure of consideration" in performance   The doctrine of consideration discussed in this chapter is an element required for the formation of an informal contract in English law. During the performance of a contract there is sometimes said to be a "failure of consideration", but here "consideration" is used in the sense of *performance* of the contract after it has been formed, rather than the *promise of performance* (or, in the case of a unilateral contract, the performance set as the condition for acceptance of the offer[70]) which is an element assessed at the moment of formation. Where one party has wholly[71] failed to perform his side of the contract, whether his obligations were to deliver goods or to provide services, the other party may accept the breach and thereby discharge the contract, and may then have a claim to recover money which he has paid by way of his own performance.[72] The contract having been discharged, such a claim arises to reverse the defendant's enrichment, and is thus a claim for restitution on the ground of unjust enrichment, rather than a claim for a remedy for breach of contract.[73] However, the discharge of the contract for breach does not itself deny that the contract was properly formed, nor does it retrospectively annul the contract.[74] The notion of "total failure of consideration" following defective performance is therefore not part of the doctrine of consideration as a requirement for the formation of a contract.[75]

8-10

III.   PARTICULAR RULES WITHIN THE DOCTRINE OF CONSIDERATION

Elements of the doctrine of consideration in the formation of a contract   The doctrine of consideration, as it operates within the formation of a contract in English law, can be summarised in the following propositions: (1) the consideration, provided by the promisee (the claimant) in order to enforce the promise made by the promisor (the defendant) may be an act, or a promise, or forbearance by the promisee; (2) it must be provided by the promisee in return for the promise he seeks to enforce; (3) it must be provided by the promisee at the same time as the promisor's promise ("past consideration" is insufficient); (4) the act done or the promise made by the promisee as consideration must have some economic value: benefit to the promisor and/or detriment to the promisee; and (5) it may be at the same time an act or a promise which fulfils an existing duty to a third party, but generally not an existing duty owed to the promisor either under the general law or under an existing contract.

8-11

These propositions will be discussed in detail in the following paragraphs of this

---

[70]   See para.8-07 fn.58; para.8-13.

[71]   This is a restitutionary remedy, quite separate from a claim which may continue to be available under the contract for damages: *Stocznia Gdynia SA v Gearbulk Holdings Ltd* [2009] EWCA Civ 75; [2010] Q.B. 27 at [40]; and for the restitution of money paid English law requires the failure of consideration to be total, not merely partial, although this is criticised: Chitty, para.29-067; Treitel, para.22-004; Anson, p.623.

[72]   Chitty, para.29-061; Anson, pp.621–624.

[73]   Chitty, paras 29-061, 29-062; Treitel, para.22-001; Anson, p.620.

[74]   *Photo Production Ltd v Securicor Transport Ltd* [1980] A.C. 827, HL, at 844, 849–850.

[75]   See also, e.g. *Misa v Currie* (1876) 1 App. Cas. 554, HL, at 566 (Lord Hatherley: "at that time, as things then stood, there was a full consideration between Misa and Lizardi. The subsequent events which made that consideration fail cannot be taken into consideration in estimating their position at that time").

chapter. The doctrine of consideration as it applies to the variation of an existing contract will be discussed in Chapter 9.

(1) Consideration may be an Act, or a Promise, or Forbearance, by the Promisee

8-12 **"Executory" consideration: mutual promises are sufficient** The core of the doctrine of consideration is the exchange between the parties: the claimant's right to enforce the defendant's promise follows from the fact that he has done something at the defendant's request,[76] which the law recognises as being of some value to the defendant,[77] in return for the promise he seeks to enforce. However, from the outset it must be noted that what the claimant may do, by way of consideration in return for the defendant's promise, is simply to make a promise as requested by the defendant. The promise may take the form of a warranty of a fact or of a state of affairs, such as the guarantee given by the seller that a product has a particular quality, or complies with some particular description; such a "promise" is not a performance undertaking, but an assurance or undertaking of responsibility in relation to the facts stated.[78] The promise may, however, take the more usual form of undertaking to do (or to forbear from doing) something in the future[79]; in such a case the promise, being not yet fulfilled, is referred to as "executory"[80] consideration, and the contract which is formed through the exchange of mutual promises of future conduct is referred to as an executory contract. As long as what is promised to be done would, when done, be sufficient to constitute valid consideration,[81] and as long as there is nothing else in the language of the promise which prevents it from satisfying the requirements of valid consideration,[82] the promise is itself sufficient consideration and therefore, if the parties so intend, the contract is formed at the mo-

---

[76] See para.8-15.

[77] See para.8-23.

[78] e.g. a contractual guarantee of the truth of a representation made about the product being sold, which is therefore actionable as a breach of contract if it is not true, as well as giving rise to alternative remedies such as rescission or damages in tort for misrepresentation: Cartwright (Misrepresentation), Ch.8.

[79] cf. OED Online, March 2018, "promise, n.": "2. a. A declaration or assurance made to another person (usually with respect to the future), stating a commitment to give, do, or refrain from doing a specified thing or act, or guaranteeing that a specified thing will or will not happen".

[80] cf. OED Online, March 2018, "executory, adj. and n.": "3. Law. Of acts or dispositions: Designed to take or capable of taking full effect only at a future time. Opposed to *executed*". For the use of this terminology see, e.g. *Barker v Keete* (1678) 1 Freeman 249 at 250, 89 E.R. 179 at 180; *Payne v Wilson* (1827) 7 B. & C. 423 at 427, 108 E.R. 781 at 782; *Church v Imperial Gas Light and Coke Co* (1837) 6 Ad. & El. 846, 112 E.R. 324; *Independent Television Authority and Associated-Rediffusion Ltd v Inland Revenue Commissioners* [1959] 1 W.L.R. 259, CA, at 264; *Executive Jet Support Ltd v Serious Organised Crime Agency* [2012] EWHC 2737 (QB); [2013] 1 W.L.R. 1433 (construing "executed consideration" in Proceeds of Crime Act 2002 s.314(4)).

[81] e.g. the promise to do an act forbidden by law could not be valid consideration: *Dunton v Dunton* (1892) 18 V.L.R. 114, SC Victoria, at 119; and, if the thing promised would not be recognised by the law as having economic value (see para.8-23), the promise of it will not have value either.

[82] e.g. the promise to pay £10 *if the promisor should choose to do* so cannot be consideration because a promise which leaves performance entirely to the discretion of the promisor is insufficient, although the actual performance (the payment of £10) can be consideration: *Stabilad Ltd v Stephens & Carter (No.2)* [1999] 2 All E.R. (Comm.) 651, CA, at 660.

ment when the promises are exchanged[83] without having to wait for one or other party to perform his side or otherwise act on the promise.[84]

"Executed" consideration: the promisor may set the performance of an act as the consideration for his promise   The promisor may ask not for a promise in return, but for the performance of an act.[85] In such a case—a unilateral contract— the performance of the act (the consideration) may also be the acceptance of the offer which is contained in the promise.[86] In the case of an executory contract, when one party performs his side we can say that his consideration is now "executed" and the contract itself is "partly executed" since it is executed on one side but not yet the other. However, in the unilateral contract where the consideration is not the promise of performance but only the performance itself, at the moment that the contract comes into existence the consideration has already been executed, since the promisee never undertook to provide it, but by the act of providing it he thereby causes the promisor's promise to mature into a binding contractual obligation.[87]

8-13

Consideration may consist in either action or inaction (or a promise of either action or inaction); forbearance   The promisor may request the promisee to do something (or to promise to do something) as consideration for his promise, or he may request him *not* to do something, or to promise not to do something—to "forbear" to do something (or to promise to forbear). Forbearance may constitute consideration as much as a positive act, as long as it satisfies the general requirements for sufficiency of consideration. We shall see below that some requests for forbearance may raise questions about whether the forbearance by the promisee is of value to the promisor,[88] but there are many cases in which forbearance has been held to constitute good consideration, including the very common case of an agreement by both parties to forbear to take further legal proceedings and thereby to settle a dispute.[89]

8-14

---

[83] *Strangborough and Warner's Case* (1588) 4 Leo. 3, 74 E.R. 686.

[84] *Centrovincial Estates Plc v Merchant Investors Assurance Co Ltd* [1983] Com. L.R. 158, CA, at 159 (Slade LJ: "provided only that the offeree has given sufficient consideration for the offeror's promise, it is nothing to the point that the offeree may not have changed his position beyond giving the promise requested of him").

[85] Sometimes, however, where a promise is made on condition of the claimant doing or forbearing to do something it may be possible to imply a promise by the claimant so to do or to forbear: e.g. *Dunton v Dunton* (1892) 18 V.L.R. 114, SC Victoria, at 118 (express agreement to make payments to ex-wife, payments to cease if she "shall not conduct herself with sobriety, and in a respectable, orderly and virtuous manner", signed also by the wife, implied promise that she would so conduct herself).

[86] See para.3-32, for a general discussion of unilateral contracts and some of the difficulties of analysis which arise, including the fact that there may be an implied dispensation from the requirement to communicate acceptance if the performance itself constitutes acceptance.

[87] The analysis of a unilateral contract whereby a person provides consideration at the same time as accepting the offer is not limited to the well-known "reward" cases, but also forms the basis of certain commercial transactions, including cases where the offer is to enter into a bilateral (executory) contract with a person to whom the offer is addressed who chooses to perform the necessary act: see the cases cited at para.3-32 fn.193.

[88] See paras 8-29 to 8-31.

[89] See para.8-30.

(2)   The Consideration must be Provided by the Promisee in Return for the Promise He Seeks to Enforce

8-15 **The consideration "in return for" the promise is a promise, act or forbearance in exchange, at the promisor's request**   The doctrine of consideration gives to the common law contract the essential feature of a bargain between the parties.[90] The reason that the claimant can enforce the agreement—enforce the defendant's promise—is that he has promised, done, or forborne to do something in exchange for, or *in return for,* the defendant's promise: he has done what the defendant asked of him. It is not therefore sufficient that the defendant's promise caused the claimant to act in a way that he might otherwise not have done, if his so acting cannot be linked back to the promise by finding that the action was done for the defendant.[91] In a broad sense, the consideration is the price of the defendant's promise: but it is the defendant who sets the price; it is not for the promisee to decide to make a gratuitous promise binding by acting on it in a way that was not what the promisor requested.[92]

8-16 **The request may be express or implied**   The general approach to the formation of contracts is to assess the parties' intentions objectively, rather than purely subjectively.[93] Whether a promisor has requested something in return for his promise, and whether the promisee responds in return for the promisor's request, is therefore also to be judged objectively. The claimant need not be consciously aware of what consideration he is giving for the promise he accepts, as long as it appears to the claimant that the defendant made his promise in order to secure a particular form of conduct from the claimant in return, and the claimant in fact responds as intended by the defendant, or as he could reasonably understand the defendant to have intended.[94]

Not only is the promisor's request to be interpreted objectively; the request itself need not be express but may be implied. In many cases it is obvious on the facts that the promisor was making his promise for the purposes of securing a particular act or forbearance from the promisee in return.[95] However, there may sometimes

---

[90] See para.8-08.

[91] *Combe v Combe* [1951] 2 K.B. 215, CA, at 221, 223, 226–227 (wife's forbearance to apply to court for maintenance during divorce proceedings was not consideration for husband's promise to pay £100 a year because (inter alia) her forbearance was not requested by husband).

[92] *Lampleigh v Brathwait* (1615) Hob. 105 at 106, 80 E.R. 255 at 255 ("a meer voluntary curtesie will not have a consideration to uphold an assumpsit. But if that curtesie were moved by a suit or request of the party that gives the assumpsit, it will bind"; this case also raised an issue of past consideration: see para.8-20); *Commonwealth v Scituate Savings Bank* 137 Mass 301 (1884) at 302 (Holmes J: "It would cut up the doctrine of consideration by the roots, if a promisee could make a gratuitous promise binding by subsequently acting in reliance on it").

[93] For the objective test in the interpretation of offers and acceptances, see paras 3-02 to 3-08, esp. para.3-07.

[94] *Pitts v Jones* [2007] EWCA Civ 1301, [2008] Q.B. 706 at [18].

[95] e.g. *Crears v Hunter* (1887) 19 Q.B.D. 341, CA (promise of surety was obviously on the basis that the creditor would forbear to sue the principal debtor, although no express undertaking); *Alliance Bank Ltd v Broom* (1864) 2 Drew. & Sm. 289, 62 E.R. 631 (creditor's demand of security from debtor involved creditor giving some degree of forbearance to call in debt, although no express undertaking); cf. *Wigan v English and Scottish Law Life Assurance Association* [1909] 1 Ch. 291 at 298 (emphasising that in *Alliance Bank Ltd v Broom* and similar cases it was the forbearance that constituted the consideration: the mere existence of the debt is insufficient consideration for the later promise of security). See also *Banque Cantonale de Genève v Sanomi* [2016] EWHC 3353 (Comm)

be difficulties in determining whether the particular act or forbearance which the promisee claims as the consideration was (impliedly) requested by the promisor as the return for his promise, or whether he was really making the promise without any requirement of anything in return. This is a context where the courts may be able to make a purposive application of the test for an implied request: if the promisor appears seriously to intend to be bound by his promise, and the claimant has taken it as such and has acted on it in a way that might reasonably have been expected in the circumstances, it might not be difficult to say that the action was impliedly requested, so as to find consideration and avoid the defendant being able to resile from the promise.[96]

Implied request by the promisor and reliance by the promisee: boundaries   **8-17**
between contract, estoppel and unjust enrichment   The fact that the courts are able to find that the promisor impliedly requested the promisee to act on the promise, and that the promisee by so acting has provided consideration for the promise, tends to blur the distinction between contract and, on the one hand, promissory estoppel and, on the other hand, restitution for unjust enrichment.

Promissory estoppel requires the promisee to act on the promise in order to make it binding, although there is no requirement that the promisee's action be at the request of the promisor; merely that it be intended to be acted on, or that the promisor might reasonably have expected the promisee so to act on it.[97] *Combe v Combe*[98] stands as authority in the Court of Appeal that promissory estoppel does not generally give rise to new enforceable obligations: it is not a general substitute for consideration in the formation of contracts, but is limited to the modification of an existing contract.[99] If a court is therefore to find a new, binding promissory obligation (in the absence of a deed[100]) it must find consideration and therefore find that the promisee's promise, act or forbearance was at the request of the promisor. To do so, there may be an incentive to find an implied request in cases where the court

---

(promissory note: implied request for forbearance; note also the presumption that a party signing a bill of exchange or promissory note became a party for value: Bills of Exchange Act 1882 ss.30, 89). For the implied request in the case of a unilateral contract, see J.C. Smith, "Unilateral Contracts and Consideration" (1953) 69 L.Q.R. 99, in response to A.L. Goodhart, "Unilateral Contracts" (1951) 67 L.Q.R. 456.

[96] *Combe v Combe*, see para.8-15 fn.91, is itself an illustration of the difficulty of determining whether the promisee's act or (in that case) forbearance was impliedly requested by the promisor: CA held that it was not, but did not appear to give that issue much detailed attention and was not in any event apparently disposed to allow the wife to hold the husband to his promise (she was "better off than her husband": see Denning LJ at 222), so had no incentive to find an implied request. cf. however, A.L. Goodhart, see para.8-16 fn.95, at 458 ("if [the husband] was not making an offer to pay [the wife] an annual sum as long as she did not apply for maintenance, then it is difficult to see what other rational explanation can be given for the correspondence between [the parties'] solicitors"); J.C. Smith, see para.8-16 fn.95, at 106 ("the courts have in the past shown a much greater readiness to imply a request than did the Court of Appeal in this case, and it is submitted that the more liberal construction would be more in accordance with the actual intention of the parties"). See also *Shadwell v Shadwell* (1860) 9 C.B. N.S. 159, 142 E.R. 62 (promise by uncle to pay nephew on occasion of his marriage: valid consideration; Byles J dissented at 176–177, at 69, on basis that there was no request, express or implied, by the uncle that the nephew marry).

[97] See paras 10-23, 10-25.

[98] See para.8-15 fn.91.

[99] See paras 10-39, 10-40.

[100] See para.8-03; Ch.7 (esp. para.7-18).

seeks to hold the promisor to his promise.[101] If, however, the Supreme Court were to allow promissory estoppel to be the source of new obligations, the fact of the promisor's reliance could itself be sufficient without having to place it within the straitjacket of an implied request. We shall see this issue again in Chapter 10.[102]

The implied request as the basis of a finding of consideration is also linked to some of the older cases which explained liability designed to remedy an unjust enrichment by finding an "implied contract". Many of the rules which in the modern law are seen as belonging in the law restitution for unjust enrichment used to be seen under the heading of "quasi contract", resting on an implied contract between the parties which is now seen to be unreal, but which inevitably involved the courts finding, or implying, both a promise and a request that could constitute consideration for the promise in order to find a contract as the basis of the claim for money had and received.[103] Some cases where the courts have found an implied request in order to find a liability to pay for services received may therefore now need to be regarded with some caution, if a better explanation would be that the source of the liability is the duty to pay for the benefit received where the failure to pay would constitute an unjust enrichment, rather than an (implied) contract to pay.[104] There are, however, still cases which one can reasonably base on an implied contract,[105] showing that there is here something of an uncertain borderline between contract and unjust enrichment.

8-18 **A condition attached to a promise is not necessarily consideration for the promise** Sometimes the act done by the promisee which constitutes the consideration in a unilateral contract is referred to as his satisfying the "condition" set by the promisor in his offer.[106] It is important, however, to distinguish a promise which is conditional on an event happening (such as "I will pay you £1000 if you catch a cold this month"), and a promise which is conditional on the promisee doing or forbearing to do something (such as "I will pay you £1000 if you find my dog").

---

[101] See para.8-16.

[102] See paras 10-44 to 10-51. In the US, where promissory estoppel is already established as a source of obligations independently of a contract supported by consideration, there is less need to find consideration in order to render a promise binding: G.H. Treitel, "Consideration: A Critical Analysis of Professor Atiyah's Fundamental Restatement" (1976) 50 A.L.J. 439, 440. Denning LJ, who gave the leading judgment in *Combe v Combe* to restrict the operation of promissory estoppel, advocated extra-judicially a development of the doctrine of consideration so that "any act done on the faith of a promise should be regarded as sufficient consideration to make it binding": (1952) 15 M.L.R. 1, 9–10, although he was also a strong supporter of extending the scope of estoppel: see para.10-49.

[103] *Westdeutsche Landesbank Girozentrale v Islington LBC* [1996] A.C. 669, HL, at 710 (Lord Browne-Wilkinson: "The common law restitutionary claim is based not on implied contract but on unjust enrichment: in the circumstances the law imposes an obligation to repay rather than implying an entirely fictitious agreement to repay... In my judgment, your Lordships should now unequivocally and finally reject the concept that the claim for moneys had and received is based on an implied contract"); Goff & Jones, para.1-06.

[104] e.g. *Glasbrook Bros Ltd v Glamorgan CC* [1925] A.C. 270, HL, at 281–282 (Viscount Cave LC, quoting the trial judge: "when a colliery company or an individual requisitions police protection of a special character for a particular purpose, he must pay for it, and he must pay for it whether he makes a contract to pay or whether he does not—a promise to pay would be implied under those circumstances"); *Upton-on-Severn RDC v Powell* [1942] 1 All E.R. 220, CA (and see J.R. Spencer [1973] C.L.J. 104, 111–112).

[105] e.g. cases of liability arising during pre-contractual negotiations based on implied contract: see paras 2-24, 2-27.

[106] e.g. *Carlill v Carbolic Smoke Ball Co* [1893] 1 Q.B. 256, CA, at 262, 268, 274.

The former may be a conditional promise, but it is not a contract if the promisee does not also provide consideration—that is, act at the promisor's express or implied request to do something of value in exchange for the promise.[107]

Consideration is provided by the promisee: the problems of joint promisees   **8-19**
and third parties   The doctrine of consideration explains the enforceability of informal promises by reference to the promisee having earned the right to enforce the promise by having promised, acted or forborne to act in the way that the promisor requested. The corollary of this would be that a person named as beneficiary of an informal promise is not, in principle, entitled to enforce that promise unless he has provided consideration in return for that promise. This is commonly put in terms that the consideration "must move from the promisee", but the scope of this maxim is debated. It might mean that consideration must be given by the person who seeks to enforce the promise which was made to him (thus defining the party entitled to sue under the contract as not only a promisee but also a promisee who has personally given consideration). Or it might mean that consideration must be given by the (or, at least a) promisee, without at the same time limiting the right to sue to the promisee who personally provided the consideration (thus defining an enforceable contractual promise as one for which the promisee has given consideration, but allowing a promisee to count as a party entitled to sue under the contract even if he has not personally given consideration).[108] In most contracts this is a distinction without consequence, since the promisee generally provides the consideration, and it is the promisee who provided the consideration who seeks to enforce the promise. The analysis does, however, have consequences in two situations.

First, there is the case of a joint promisee where the consideration is provided not by him but only by his co-promisee. There is some debate about this situation. If consideration must be provided by the promisee as a condition of his right to sue to enforce the promise, then if a promise is made to A and B, with a request that A (but not B) act in return for that promise, in principle only A should be able to enforce it. B, although a promisee jointly with A, has not earned the right of enforcement because he has not been requested to do anything, and has not done anything, to enforce it. It has been suggested, however, that a more attractive view is that where the promise was made with A and B jointly, A and B should each be able to enforce it as long as one or other of them has provided consideration at the promisor's request.[109] This is not settled in the English cases, but has been indicated

---

[107] cf. the example given in *Shadwell v Shadwell*, see para.8-16 fn.96, at 69 by Byles J (dissenting in the case on the basis that there was no implied request on the facts): "Suppose a defendant to promise a plaintiff,—'I will give you £500 if you break your leg,'—would that detriment to the plaintiff, should it happen, be any consideration?", discussed by A.L. Goodhart, (1953) 69 L.Q.R. 99, 107. See also *Chappell & Co Ltd v Nestlé Co Ltd* [1960] A.C. 87, HL, at 109 (Lord Reid: acquiring and delivering chocolate bar wrappers was not merely a condition which qualified the person to buy a gramophone record but was part of the consideration because it was the doing of something of value to the seller, and required the buyer to incur a detriment—paying for the chocolate bars—which he might not otherwise have incurred).

[108] Anson, pp.103–104; Chitty, para.4-038; Treitel, para.3-023.

[109] *New Zealand Shipping Co Ltd v AM Satterthwaite & Co Ltd (The Eurymedon)* [1975] A.C. 154, PC, at 180 (Lord Simon, dissenting in the case, and in any event commenting on this point by way of obiter dictum: "Though this proposition rests only on dicta (see *McEvoy v Belfast Banking Co Ltd* [1935] A.C. 24, 36, 43, 52; and *Coulls v Bagot's Executor and Trustee Co Ltd* [1967] A.L.R. 385, 395, 400, 405), it seems to be an attractive proposition in respect of genuine joint promises. As Windeyer J said in his dissenting judgment in Coulls' case, speaking of 'a contract made with two

by the High Court of Australia,[110] and most commentators in England support it.[111] Whatever view one takes of that, however, it is important to realise that no issue arises where A provides consideration not only on his own behalf but also as B's agent in entering into the contract[112]; or where both A and B are requested by the promisor to make a promise in return, even if A is the one who performs the promise.[113] Given that a promise of performance is sufficient consideration,[114] A and B both provide consideration by undertaking joint or joint and several liability on their side of the contract, and this is not negated by the fact that it is A who in fact performs the contract and therefore discharges B's liability as well as his own.

Secondly, a third party, who is not even a direct promisee, is not entitled at common law to enforce the promise contained in the contract even if the promise provides expressly that he shall be entitled to do so; the contracting party, who was both promisee and provided the consideration, is the party with the right to bring any action.[115] This is the doctrine of privity of contract, developed in the nineteenth century as a consequence of the doctrine of consideration,[116] and maintained by the House of Lords as a fundamental doctrine of the common law of contract[117] until it was reformed by statute in 1999 to allow third parties in defined circumstances to have directly enforceable rights under contracts.[118]

---

or more persons jointly,' at p.405: 'The promise is made to them collectively. It must, of course, be supported by consideration, but that does not mean by considerations furnished by them separately. It means a consideration given on behalf of them all, and therefore moving from all of them'").

[110] *Coulls v Bagot's Executor and Trustee Co Ltd*, see para.8-19 fn.109.

[111] Chitty, para.4-043; Anson, p.104; Cheshire, Fifoot and Furmston, pp.109–110; Law Com. No.242, *Privity of Contract: Contracts for the Benefit of Third Parties* (1996, Cm.3329), para.6.9. Treitel, paras 13-034 to 13-036 says that it must necessarily apply in the case of joint promisees, and does not apply in the case of several promisees, but the area of doubt is the case of joint and several promisees. For cogent criticism and analysis of the issues, however, see B. Coote, "Consideration and the Joint Promise" [1978] C.L.J. 301.

[112] *McEvoy v Belfast Banking Co Ltd* [1935] A.C. 24, HL, at 43.

[113] Coote, see para.8-19 fn.111, at 305–306.

[114] See para.8-12.

[115] A problem with the promisee's action in such a case is whether he has an adequate remedy: unless he can obtain an order for specific performance of the promise in favour of the third party (as in *Beswick v Beswick* [1968] A.C. 58, HL) he may have no useful claim since in principle damages are only to cover his own loss and not that suffered by the third party: Chitty, para.18-051; Furmston, para.8.145; Treitel, para.14-023; Anson, pp.651–653.

[116] *Tweddle v Atkinson* (1861) 1 B. & S. 393 at 398, 121 E.R. 762 at 764 (Wightman J: "no stranger to the consideration can take advantage of a contract, although made for his benefit"; Crompton J: "the consideration must move from the party entitled to sue upon the contract. It would be a monstrous proposition to say that a person was a party to the contract for the purpose of suing upon it for his own advantage, and not a party to it for the purpose of being sued").

[117] *Dunlop Pneumatic Tyre Co Ltd v Selfridge & Co Ltd* [1915] A.C. 847, HL, at 853, 858, 862, 864; *Scruttons Ltd v Midland Silicones Ltd* [1962] A.C. 446, HL. It became subject to criticism, however: see, e.g. *Beswick v Beswick*, see para.8-19 fn.115, at 72 (Lord Reid); *Woodar Investment Development Ltd v Wimpey Construction UK Ltd* [1980] 1 W.L.R. 277 at 300–301 (Lord Scarman).

[118] Contracts (Rights of Third Parties) Act 1999; Chitty, paras 18-090 to 18-125; Furmston, Ch.6, s.A.III; Treitel, paras 14-090 to 14-122; Anson, pp.659–670; Cheshire, Fifoot and Furmston, pp.571–578. The Law Commission, proposing this reform, took the view that the doctrine of privity (which determines who can enforce a contract) was already separate from the doctrine of consideration (which determines the types of promises that can be enforced), and so the former could be reformed independently of the latter: Law Com. No.242, see para.8-19 fn.111, para.6.1.

(3)   The Consideration must be Provided by the Promisee at the Same Time as the Promisor's Promise: "Past Consideration" is Insufficient

Consideration "in return for" the promise implies a temporal link   The fact   **8-20**
that the consideration provided by the promisee must be "in return for" the promise,
at the promisor's request, carries the implication that it must be linked not only
causally with the promise but also temporally. If A gave B a book last week, asking for nothing in return, and today B promises to pay £20 citing as the reason for
his promise his gratitude for the book, the promise is not contractually binding
because B does not ask of A, nor receive, anything in return for it; the gift of the
book may have caused B to make his promise, but it was already complete before
the promise and cannot be the price of B's new, later promise.[119] Similarly, if A
entered into a contract with B last week to sell him a horse, and today A adds a warranty relating to the horse, there is no consideration for the later warranty which is
therefore not contractually binding: it is a purported variation of the contract by adding a new term, for which there is no consideration.[120] It was said by Lord Denman CJ in *Roscorla v Thomas*[121] that "the promise must be coextensive with the
consideration", and this is commonly put in terms that "past consideration" is not
sufficient consideration.[122] In other words, at the time when the promise, act or
forbearance which is alleged to constitute consideration for the promise was done,
it must have been done as the return for the promise. In the examples just given,
the book was not given in order to get the (later) promise of £20 in return; the
promise in the contract of sale of the horse to pay the price was made in return for
the promise to deliver the horse, not in order to get the (later) warranty relating to
it.[123]

The consideration may be given in return for a later promise   This strict rule,   **8-21**
requiring the consideration to be contemporaneous with the promise in return for
which the consideration is given, may sometimes appear to have exceptions
although (apart from a specific statutory exception[124]) they are not true exceptions
but depend on construction of the parties' acts and promises to discover the
consideration in accordance with the rule.

---

[119] See, e.g. *Re McArdle* [1951] Ch. 669, CA (equitable assignment which, according to the written
document, was "in consideration of your carrying out certain alterations and improvements to the
property" was not for valuable consideration because the works had in fact already been completed
and so the consideration was past consideration).

[120] *Roscorla v Thomas* (1842) 3 Q.B. 234, 114 E.R. 496. For the need to show consideration for the variation of a contract, and the consequential difficulties of unilateral variations, see below, Ch.9, esp.
paras 9-08, 9-10.

[121] See para.8-20 fn.120, at 237, at 498.

[122] e.g. *Roscorla v Thomas*, see para.8-20 fn.120, at 237, at 498 ("a consideration past and executed will
support no other promise than such as would be implied by law"); *Pao On v Lau Yiu Long* [1980]
A.C. 614, PC, at 630.

[123] See also *Wigan v English and Scottish Law Life Assurance Association* [1909] 1 Ch. 291 (mere existence of antecedent debt not consideration for later promise of security; fresh consideration, such as
a forbearance from suing to enforce the debt, is required); *Haigh v Brooks* (1839) 10 Ad. & El. 309,
113 E.R. 119, QB, affirmed (1840) 10 Ad. & El. 323, 113 E.R. 124, Ex.Ch. (guarantee of third-
party debt would not be binding if only in consideration of existing debt, but on facts the instrument was ambiguous and the evidence unclear).

[124] See para.8-22.

If an act is done expressly on the basis, as understood at that time by both parties, that the person for whom it is done will give or promise something in return, even though that is to be done later, there is no difficulty in finding that the earlier act and the promise which is made later to give effect to the understanding are sufficiently linked for the former to constitute sufficient consideration for the latter. There may not yet be a complete contract at the time of the earlier act because the promise to be made later is not yet sufficiently certain[125]; but when the promise is later made, it is directly linked to the earlier act which was already done in return for the promise, so as to constitute consideration for it and render it contractually binding.

If an earlier act can constitute valid consideration for a later promise where there is an express understanding of the parties to that effect, it is possible for the court to find consideration where there was an equivalent implied understanding. However, in order not to undermine the core requirements of consideration, where a past act is relied upon it is important to show not simply that the person performing the act did so on the basis that he intended it to be paid for later, but also that the other party at that time also so understood. The earlier act must satisfy the normal rules of consideration even though it antedates the promise for which it is to be seen as consideration: it must have been requested, expressly or impliedly by the (later) promisor,[126] and what was done must be sufficient to constitute consideration.[127] This was summed up by Lord Scarman in *Pao On v Lau Yiu Long*[128]:

---

[125] For the requirement of certainty, see paras 3-13 to 3-18. Such a case might sometimes be solved by saying that it was implied that the promise would be of a reasonable sum, or at the market rate, and so there was already a completed contract at the outset. If, however, there is no such contract, and if the party who requested the act to be done does not later make the promise to give rise to a contractual obligation, he may still be required to make payment on a non-contractual basis because he would otherwise be unjustly enriched by having received the benefit of the act as he requested it in circumstances where it was not intended to be gratuitous: see, para.2-27.

[126] See para.8-15; *Lampleigh v Brathwait* (1615) Hob. 105 at 106, 80 E.R. 255 at 255 ("a meer voluntary curtesie will not have a consideration to uphold an assumpsit. But if that curtesie were moved by a suit or request of the party that gives the assumpsit, it will bind, for the promise, though it follows, yet it is not naked, but couples it self with the suit before"); cf. *Hunt v Bate* (1567) 3 Dyer 272, 73 E.R. 605 at 606 (payment by claimant of money to bail defendant's servant not sufficient consideration for later promise by defendant to indemnify him, because payment was made not at defendant's request, but "of his own head"); *Eastwood v Kenyon* (1840) 11 Ad. & El. 438 at 451–452, 113 E.R. 482 at 487 (Lord Denman CJ: "the declaration really discloses nothing but a benefit voluntarily conferred by the plaintiff and received by the defendant, with an express promise by the defendant to pay money. If the subsequent assent of the defendant could have amounted to a ratihabitio, the declaration should have stated the money to have been expended at his request, and the ratification should have been relied on as matter of evidence; but this was obviously impossible ... In holding this declaration bad because it states no consideration but a past benefit not conferred at the request of the defendant, we conceive that we are justified by the old common law of England").

[127] e.g. it must have value (see para.8-23), and it must be legally enforceable and not unlawful. cf. *Kennedy v Broun* (1863) 13 C.B.N.S. 677 at 727, 740, 143 E.R. 268 at 287, 292 (promise to pay advocate, if made after the litigation, cannot be within the principle of *Lampleigh v Brathwait*, see para.8-21 fn.126, because the work that had been done by the advocate could not constitute consideration since law did not allow contract for payment of advocate's services).

[128] See para.8-21 fn.122, at 629 (and applied to hold that a promise for a fixed period not to dispose of shares in a public company, given at the request of the majority shareholders in order to avoid depressing the share price, and which was always intended by both parties to be compensated by a guarantee against a drop in the market price during the retention period, was good consideration for a guarantee to that effect given later by the majority shareholders).

"An act done before the giving of a promise to make a payment or to confer some other benefit can sometimes be consideration for the promise. The act must have been done at the promisors' request: the parties must have understood that the act was to be remunerated either by a payment or the conferment of some other benefit: and payment, or the conferment of a benefit, must have been legally enforceable had it been promised in advance."

The effect is that a court, wishing to hold a promise binding for which the promisee has already completed the act of forbearance claimed to be the consideration for the promise, can do so as long as it can bring the facts within this test.[129]

Exceptions to the rule that past consideration is not sufficient Old authorities and arguments to the effect that a pre-existing moral obligation could constitute sufficient consideration for a later promise which the promisor intended to fulfil that moral obligation, have long been rejected.[130] However, an exception developed by the common law[131] in certain circumstances to recognise a pre-existing debt or legal liability as consideration for the later promise was codified in the Bills of Exchange Act 1882. Under s.27:

    8-22

"(1) Valuable consideration for a bill may be constituted by—
    (a) Any consideration sufficient to support a simple contract;
    (b) An antecedent debt or liability. Such a debt or liability is deemed valuable consideration whether the bill is payable on demand or at a future time."

Therefore, although an existing debt owed by the promisor to the promisee is not in itself sufficient to support a simple promise to repay the debt, or to provide security for the debt,[132] this is varied to allow the existing debt[133] to constitute consideration for a bill of exchange such as a cheque,[134] and for a promissory note.[135]

---

[129] For the general reluctance of the courts to hold that there is no consideration for promise which the promisor seriously intended to be binding, see para.8-28. And in the context of past consideration, see *Re Casey's Patents* [1892] 1 Ch. 104, CA, at 115–116 (Bowen LJ: "Even if it were true, as some scientific students of law believe, that a past service cannot support a future promise, you must look at the document and see if the promise cannot receive a proper effect in some other way. Now, the fact of a past service raises an implication that at the time it was rendered it was to be paid for, and, if it was a service which was to be paid for, when you get in the subsequent document a promise to pay, that promise may be treated either as an admission which evidences or as a positive bargain which fixes the amount of that reasonable remuneration on the faith of which the service was originally rendered").

[130] See esp. *Eastwood v Kenyon*, see para.8-21 fn.126, at 450–451, at 486–487 (Lord Denman CJ, quoted at para.8-02 fn.21).

[131] *Oliver v Davis* [1949] 2 K.B. 727, CA, at 742 (Denning LJ, citing authority and commentary in *Smith's Leading Cases*, 13th edn (Sweet and Maxwell, 1929), pp.153–154, 635–636 (an edition of which he was one of the editors)).

[132] *Wigan v English and Scottish Law Life Assurance Association*, see para.8-20 fn.123. Other consideration is therefore required such as a variation in the terms of the debt or its repayment, or forbearance to enforce it: ibid., at 303; see para.8-16 fn.95.

[133] "Antecedent debt or liability" in s.27(1)(b) refers to that of the promisor or drawer of the bill: *Oliver v Davis*, see para.8-22 fn.131, at 735, 741–742 (the headnote is misleading).

[134] "Bill of exchange" is defined in s.3(1) as "an unconditional order in writing, addressed by one person to another, signed by the person giving it, requiring the person to whom it is addressed to pay on demand or at a fixed or determinable future time a sum certain in money to or to the order of a specified person, or to bearer".

[135] A promissory note ("an unconditional promise in writing made by one person to another signed by the maker, engaging to pay, on demand or at a fixed or determinable future time, a sum certain in

(4) The Act Done or the Promise Made by the Promisee Must Have Some Economic Value: Benefit to the Promisor and/or Detriment to the Promisee

8-23 **Consideration may be benefit to the promisor and/or detriment to the promisee** The core of the doctrine of consideration is the benefit which the promisor (the defendant) receives in return for his promise, or the detriment suffered by the promisee (the claimant) in return for the promise he seeks to enforce[136]:

> "The consideration, upon which an assumpsit shall be founded, must be for the benefit of the defendant, or to the trouble or prejudice of the plaintiff"

or in a much-quoted definition given by the Exchequer Chamber in 1875[137]:

> "A valuable consideration, in the sense of the law, may consist either in some right, interest, profit, or benefit accruing to the one party, or some forbearance, detriment, loss, or responsibility, given, suffered, or undertaken by the other."

These definitions refer to benefit *or* detriment. In practice, the consideration will commonly be *both* benefit to the promisor *and* detriment to the promisee, because the promisee promises, does or forbears to do something for the promisor at the promisor's request, in return for the promise[138]; what this costs the promisee is correspondingly to the benefit of the promisor. Given that a promise by the promisee is sufficient consideration as long as the thing promised could itself be consideration if performed,[139] we can see that the receipt by the defendant of the (binding) promise made to him by the claimant is recognised as a benefit to the defendant, and the making of that (binding) promise by the claimant is a detriment to the claimant.

There are, however, situations where it may seem difficult to identify any real benefit to the promisor, only detriment to the promisee (or vice versa). In such cases the courts may find consideration in the detriment alone, or the benefit alone, as the case may be.[140] For example, where the promisor asks the promisee to do, or to promise to do, something to his detriment which does not apparently benefit the

---

money, to, or to the order of, a specified person or to bearer": Bills of Exchange Act 1882 s.83(1)) is not a bill of exchange, but most provisions of the Act apply, with the necessary modifications, to promissory notes: s.89. See, e.g. *Savage v Uwechia* [1961] 1 W.L.R. 455, PC, at 458 (document referred to "value received" but there was no evidence what the consideration (if any) was: "if referring to a past consideration, [it] would be insufficient to support a contract for the sale of land although … it would be sufficient to support a promise to pay given in a promissory note [under Nigerian Bills of Exchange Ordinance]".

[136] Sir John Comyns, A. Hammond (ed.), *A Digest of the Laws of England*, 5th edn, (Butterworth, 1822), Action on the Case upon Assumpsit, B1; *Bolton v Madden* (1873) L.R. 9 Q.B. 55 at 56.

[137] *Currie v Misa* (1875) L.R. 10 Ex. 153 at 162 (Lush J, giving the judgment of the Court, and citing Com. Dig. Action on the Case, Assumpsit, B. 1–15); *Fleming v Bank of New Zealand* [1900] A.C. 577, PC, at 586 (Lord Lindley: "This definition has been constantly accepted as correct. Their Lordships so treat it"). See also *Miles v New Zealand Alford Estate Co* (1886) 32 Ch. D. 266, CA, at 289 (Bowen LJ, dissenting in the decision, and giving no attribution for his statement: "A valuable consideration may, of course, either consist of some right, interest, profit, or benefit which accrues to one party, or some forbearance, or detriment, or loss, or responsibility, which is given to or undertaken by the other").

[138] See para.8-15.

[139] See para.8-12.

[140] *Bolton v Madden*, see para.8-23 fn.136, at 57.

promisor directly, the doing of it, or the giving of the promise, can still be sufficient consideration—such as where the owner of a house gives a licence to another to occupy on the basis that the licensee will give up existing rent-controlled accommodation with the result that she has now lost the advantage of that other accommodation if her licence were to be terminated[141]; or where the promisor asks the promisee to do or promise something for a third party.[142] Another way of looking at such cases is that the mere fact that the promise or the act that the promisor requested has been made or done by the promisee is a benefit to the promisee: given that we do not inquire into the parties' motives,[143] and that we do not require any particular pecuniary value or equivalent in the consideration,[144] we can simply say that it is a benefit to receive what one asked for. However, if pressed to its apparently logical conclusion, that argument would allow the courts to hold that consideration is provided simply by the claimant's making a promise, or acting or forbearing to act, in accordance with the defendant's request without the promise, action or forbearance having any demonstrable value—which would seriously undermine the distinction between bare agreements and those supported by consideration.[145] Therefore, the courts generally look for some identifiable benefit to the promisor, capable of being valued, to count as consideration, even if the benefit is indirect rather than direct[146]; and where the benefit to the promisor is not apparent they focus on the promisee's detriment as the alternative. Similarly, where the promisee's acting, or giving a promise, in return is not apparently of any cost or detriment to him, the focus shifts to the benefit to the promisor, such as where the promisee is already bound to a third party to do what he does or promises to do. In such a case, even though it appears not to cost the promisee anything that he would not already have to incur, the promisor receives a benefit because he did not have a right to that performance himself.[147] We shall see that the most difficult—and controversial—situation is where the promisee claims that he has provided

---

[141] *Tanner v Tanner* [1975] 1 W.L.R. 1346, CA, at 1352 (Brightman J, finding consideration by inference and therefore holding that the licence was contractual rather than a bare licence and so gave the licensee greater protection against eviction). This appears to be an example of a unilateral contract, and in such cases the focus may often be on whether the claimant has done what the defendant asked (the performance, being both acceptance and consideration: see para.8-13) rather than on whether in fact the defendant has benefited from it: the fact that the defendant asked for it is enough to show that the performance is a benefit to him. See also *O'Sullivan v Management Agency and Music Ltd* [1985] Q.B. 428, CA, at 459 (Dunn LJ: "there is sufficient consideration if there is detriment to the promisee", citing Chitty, 25th edn (1983), Vol.I, paras 144 and 145; see now 32nd edn (2015), para.4-005).

[142] cf. *Dunlop Pneumatic Tyre Co Ltd v Selfridge & Co Ltd* [1915] A.C. 847, HL, at 853 (Lord Haldane LC: "if a person with whom a contract not under seal has been made is to be able to enforce it consideration must have been given by him to the promisor *or to some other person at the promisor's request*") and at 858 (Lord Atkinson: "The contract is as to them a nudum pactum, since no consideration moves from them to the respondents, *or to any other person or body at the respondents' request*" (emphasis added)).

[143] See para.8-24.

[144] See para.8-25.

[145] cf. *White v Bluett* (1853) 23 L.J. Ex. 36 (son's promise not to complain about father's distribution of property not consideration where son had no right to complain: see at 37 (Pollock CB: "By the argument a principle is pressed to an absurdity, as a bubble is blown until it bursts") and at 38 (Alderson B: "If this agreement were good, there could be no such thing as a *nudum pactum*")).

[146] *Chappell & Co Ltd v Nestlé Co Ltd* [1960] A.C. 87, HL, at 108 (Lord Reid: even if provision of chocolate wrappers was not of direct benefit, there may have been an indirect benefit by way of advertisement).

[147] See para.8-37.

consideration by promising or doing something to which the *promisor* was already entitled from him: in such a case it is not evident that the promisee's act or promise is either of detriment to him (he already had an obligation to do it) or of benefit to the promisor (he already had a right to it).[148]

8-24 **The consideration is judged by its value, not by the motive of the party who receives it** To determine whether the promisor receives from the promisee sufficient benefit to justify enforcement of his promise by the promisee depends upon whether he received in return a promise, act or forbearance which objectively has value, not upon what value the promisor in fact thought he was obtaining from it[149]; nor on his motives for asking for it or in making his own promise.[150] Therefore, where there was a promise by a man's executors to convey property to his widow for her life, expressed to be in consideration of the testator's desire to provide a home for his widow and on the basis that the widow would pay £1 yearly towards the ground rent and keep the premises in repair, the consideration in law for the promise was the payment of the ground rent and the repairs, not the testator's wishes.[151]

8-25 **The consideration must be of some value, but may be disproportionately small or even nominal: "consideration need not be adequate"** In determining whether an informal promise is binding by reason of the promisor having given consideration for it, the courts ask only whether there was consideration which had some value that the law can recognise by way of benefit to the promisor and/or detriment to the promisee; they do not engage with the question whether the value given is an adequate economic exchange for the promise for which it is provided as consideration—whether the consideration constitutes an appropriate benefit to the promisor or an appropriate detriment to the promisee. It is therefore generally said that there must be sufficient consideration (in the sense that there is consideration which the law can recognise—whether in money, goods, services or some other counter-performance[152]) but that the consideration "need not be adequate".

---

[148] See para.8-39.

[149] *Bainbridge v Firmstone* (1838) 8 Ad. & El. 743 at 744, 112 E.R. 1019 at 1020.

[150] *Thomas v Thomas* (1842) 2 Q.B. 851 at 859, 114 E.R. 330 at 333 (Patteson J: "Motive is not the same thing with consideration. Consideration means something which is of some value in the eye of the law, moving from the plaintiff: it may be some benefit to the plaintiff, or some detriment to the defendant; but at all events it must be moving from the plaintiff"); *Dunton v Dunton* (1892) 18 V.L.R. 114, SC Victoria, at 116 (Hood J, dissenting in the actual decision: "A man's motives cannot form any consideration for a contract. If this document is to be held binding upon the defendant it must be because there is some legal consideration moving from the plaintiff upon which the defendant's promise is founded"). See also *Hadley v Kemp* [1999] 2 E.M.L.R. 589 at 625. To consider the motives of the promisor in having made his promise would focus on why the defendant's promise should be binding from the defendant's perspective (along the lines of the civilian notion of *causa*), rather than what the claimant has provided (by way of consideration) to earn the right to enforce the promise: *Thomas v Thomas* at 859, at 333–334; see para.8-08.

[151] *Thomas v Thomas*, see para.8-24 fn.150.

[152] e.g. the supply of digital content: Consumer Rights Act 2015 s.33; or the provision of personal data or other data: cf. Proposal for a Directive on certain aspects concerning contracts for the supply of digital content, COM(2015) 634 final (9 December 2015) art.3. There must, however, be a net exchange: a promise to give £5 in return for a promise to give £50 is not without more good consideration because it is in substance just a promise of £45: cf. the cases on part-payment of an existing debt, see paras 9-17 to 9-22, and *Couldery v Bartrum* (1881) 19 Ch. D. 394, CA, at 399 (Jessel MR, quoted at para.9-21 fn.141).

In consequence even if, for example, the price paid under a contract of sale is very low, or so low as to be nominal rather than a real price at all,[153] it is still in the eyes of English law a contract of sale: the low or nominal price is the consideration,[154] even if objectively it is evident that there is no real sale, but a gift dressed up as a sale. Although the language of "bargain" is often used as shorthand to explain the doctrine of consideration,[155] this is misleading if it is thought to mean that there must in any sense be a real bargain between the parties.[156] As long as the transaction fits into the legal model of an informal contract where the promisee has promised, done or forborne to do something that can be recognised as an exchange for the promise he seeks to enforce, it is no concern of the courts to evaluate the exchange. A marked inequality of exchange may raise a question about whether the party who apparently agreed to the disadvantageous transaction did so through some misunderstanding or as a result of pressure.[157] But the unequal values that are exchanged do not in themselves invalidate a contract in English law: if that is what the parties have agreed, then the courts should give their agreement effect.

---

[153] "Nominal" consideration generally refers to a sum of money, or an object, which is promised as a token, rather than in any sense having a real value at all, and it may not even be paid over: see *Midland Bank Trust Co Ltd v Green* [1981] A.C. 513, HL, at 532 (Lord Wilberforce, discussing the use of the term in statutes dealing with real property rights: "'Nominal consideration' and a 'nominal sum' in the law appear to me, as terms of art, to refer to a sum or consideration which can be mentioned as consideration but is not necessarily paid. To equate 'nominal' with 'inadequate' or even 'grossly inadequate' would embark the law upon inquiries which I cannot think were contemplated by Parliament"). A common form of nominal consideration is a very small, token price such as £1 or even £5 in a transaction of very significant commercial value (cf. *Westminster City Council v Duke of Westminster* [1991] 4 All E.R. 136 at 146), or a small and apparently irrelevant thing such as a peppercorn (*Chappell & Co Ltd v Nestlé Co Ltd*, see para.8-23 fn.146, at 114 (Lord Somervell: "A peppercorn does not cease to be good consideration if it is established that the promisee does not like pepper and will throw away the corn") or "one red rose" (*Souglides v Tweedie* [2012] EWCA Civ 1546; [2013] Ch. 373 at [7]; the rose was in fact handed over: [16]). In *Midland Bank Trust Co Ltd v Green* at 532 Lord Wilberforce suggested that the price of £500 in return for the conveyance of a farm worth about £40,000, was not "nominal". A number of statutes refer to a "peppercorn rent" in relation to leases: e.g. LPA 1925 s.153(1)(b) ("merely a peppercorn rent or other rent having no money value"); Settled Land Act 1925 s.44(2) ("[a] peppercorn rent or a nominal or other rent less than the rent ultimately payable ..."); Leasehold Reform, Housing and Urban Development Act 1993 s.56(1) ("a new lease of the flat at a peppercorn rent for a term expiring 90 years after the term date of the existing lease").

[154] Sale of Goods Act 1979 s.2(1) requires the buyer to provide a money consideration, but sets no rule as to the value of the consideration.

[155] See para.8-08.

[156] cf. Simpson (1975) 91 L.Q.R. 247, 263 ("the doctrine of consideration ... has never expressed the distinction between gratuitous and non-gratuitous promises").

[157] The inequality may therefore in practice be evidence of a mistake, misrepresentation, or duress; and a significant inequality is of particular relevance in establishing an inference of undue influence (*Royal Bank of Scotland Plc v Etridge (No.2)* [2001] UKHL 44; [2002] 2 A.C. 773 at [14] (Lord Nicholls: "a transaction which calls for explanation"; see generally Chitty, paras 8-090 to 8-096; Treitel, para.10-020; Anson, pp.392–393) and within the definition of an "unconscionable bargain" (*Fry v Lane* (1888) 40 Ch. D. 312 at 333 (Kay J: "where a purchase is made from a poor and ignorant man at a considerable undervalue, the vendor having no independent advice, a Court of Equity will set aside the transaction"): Chitty, paras 8-134, 8-137; Treitel, para.10-45; Anson, p.401). There are also statutory controls regulating the value exchanged in the case of certain types of contracts, most commonly to prevent an excessively high price being charged to consumers: e.g. Consumer Credit Act 1974 ss.140A–140C, inserted by Consumer Credit Act 2006 ss.19–21. However, none of these doctrines or controls deny the existence of the contract; they only render the contract, supported by consideration, voidable or (in the case of statutory controls) give the courts other powers to intervene.

8-26 **Consideration may have a more particular meaning in other particular contexts** There are certain other contexts, beyond the application of the doctrine of consideration as a condition of existence of an informal contract, in which the law requires "consideration"; for example, the application of certain equitable principles or remedies are sometimes said to depend upon whether consideration has been given by the party seeking to invoke equity[158]; and the application of certain statutory rules depends upon whether a person has provided consideration.[159] In such cases, the courts will sometimes apply the same general approach as in the case of the formation of a contract, and allow any consideration which is sufficient within the contract rules even if it is only nominal.[160] But in the application of a statutory reference to "consideration" the words of the statute must be construed to determine whether consideration is to be more than just nominal, or may even

---

[158] It is sometimes said that an equitable assignment requires consideration, although this proposition is too broad, and the true rule is better seen as based on the proposition that equity will not assist a volunteer: if any step is necessary to *perfect* the assignment, the assistance of equity cannot be sought by a party who has not earned the right to it by having provided consideration: see Chitty, para.19-034; Furmston, para.6.278; Anson, pp.703–705. Similarly, the equitable remedy of specific performance will not be ordered in favour of a volunteer, with the result that a promise is not specifically enforceable if it is not supported by consideration, even if it is contained in an instrument executed as a deed: see para.7-18 fn.211. For the general principle that "equity will not assist a volunteer", see Hanbury and Martin, Ch.5. The equitable doctrine by which a bona fide purchaser of property (real or personal) takes free of prior equitable interests of which he has no notice also depends upon whether the purchase was for valuable consideration: e.g. *Bassett v Nosworthy* (1673) Cas. temp. Finch 102, 23 E.R. 55; *Thorndike v Hunt* (1859) 3 De G. & J. 563 at 570, 44 E.R. 1386 at 1388.

[159] e.g. statutes defining the tax consequences of transactions (such as Finance Act 1965 s.52(4)(b): charge on income deductible for corporate tax purposes had to be made "under a liability incurred for valuable and sufficient consideration"); or defining whether a prior transaction can be challenged by creditors in a case of insolvency (such as Insolvency Act 1986 ss.238(4), 339(3), 423(1): definition of transaction "at an undervalue"); and a number of statutes relating to real property where the protection of third-party rights depends on whether a property transaction was made for consideration, or where a person was a "purchaser" (defined by reference to having provided consideration) (such as LPA 1925 ss.84(7), 199(1), 205(1)(xxi)); Land Charges Act 1972 ss.4, 17(1); Land Registration Act 2002 ss.29(1), 30(1), 132(1); see generally *Midland Bank Trust Co Ltd v Green*, see para.8-25 fn.153, at 531 (Lord Wilberforce: "'Valuable consideration' requires no definition: it is an expression denoting an advantage conferred or detriment suffered. What each Act does is, for its own purposes, to exclude some things from this general expression")). Sale of Goods Act 1979 s.23 also gives protection to a "buyer" (in good faith and without notice of the fact that the seller's title is voidable) but only requires a buyer to have provided "money consideration" (s.2(1)), without requiring the value to be adequate, or of a fair equivalence. See also *Chappell & Co Ltd v Nestlé Co Ltd*, see para.8-23 fn.146, (records sold for 1s. 6d. plus three chocolate wrappers: there was clearly consideration in the payment of money, but the question (for the purposes of Copyright Act 1956) was whether the chocolate wrappers were included in the consideration).

[160] e.g. where equity insists on consideration to intervene to protect a party who (by virtue of having provided consideration) is not a mere volunteer (see para.8-26 fn.158) the courts generally apply the rules for what constitutes sufficient consideration in the formation of a contract: *Re McArdle* [1951] Ch. 669, CA (equitable assignment); *Bassett v Nosworthy*, see para.8-26 fn.158, at 104, at 56 (bona fide purchaser: "in purchases the question is not, whether the consideration be adequate, but whether 'tis valuable"). Some writers say that specific performance will not be granted of a contract supported by only nominal consideration: Treitel, para.21-046; Burrows (Remedies), p.495; Snell, para.17-19, but there are no clear cases in support, although there are obiter dicta: *Mountford v Scott* [1975] Ch. 258 at 261 (Brightman J; but cf. Russell LJ at 264) and writers do not always draw clear distinctions between inadequate consideration and nominal consideration. However, it seems more likely that the courts will order specific performance of a contract which has sufficient consideration (even if it is nominal) unless there is some other factor to justify its refusal: Chitty, para.27-038; Jones and Goodhart, pp.24–25; Anson, p.105-106; Hanbury and Martin, para.27-019.

have to be a fair value of exchange for what is done in return.[161] Such cases do not, however, concern us here, beyond noting that the courts will sometimes assume that the normal contractual interpretation of such phrases as "valuable consideration" or "good consideration", being terms of art within the law of contract, may be a good starting-point for interpreting similar phrases in other contexts, although this must yield not only to express contrary provision, but also to implied contrary interpretation.[162]

Allowing nominal consideration recognises as contracts transactions which in substance are gratuitous   It might seem curious that the English courts do not appear to be concerned with the underlying reality of the transaction: if there is a reluctance to give effect to informal gratuitous promises,[163] why do the courts turn a blind eye to the obvious fact that a promise supported by nominal consideration is in substance gratuitous? Two answers may be given.

8-27

First, there is no objection in principle to the enforcement of promises of gifts—after all, a gratuitous promise contained in a deed is enforceable by virtue of the formality of the deed.[164] The deed not only provides evidence of the promise, but also ensures that the promisor is aware of the significance of his promise and intends it to be binding: the *cautionary* aim of formality.[165] In a case of a sale at a nominal price, or of any other transaction in which one party provides only nominal consideration, we could similarly say that, although there is no "real" benefit to the promisor or "real" detriment to the promisee, the parties by agreeing on the nominal consideration must have chosen the form of a sale contract or of another bilateral contract in order to bring their transaction within the scope of the law, and in particular the party who makes the undertakings that are in substance gratuitous must have intended to be bound (assuming that there is no duress or other defect in the validity of the contract). Although consideration is not in law a formality

---

[161] e.g. *Ball v National and Grindlay's Bank Ltd* [1973] Ch. 127, CA, at 139 (in requiring "valuable *and sufficient* consideration" Finance Act 1965 s.52(4)(b), see para.8-26 fn.159, "sufficiency" connotes "an adequate quid pro quo of the liability incurred"); Insolvency Act 1986 s.238(4), 339(3), 423(1) (including within transaction "at undervalue" not only where the is no consideration but also where transaction by an individual was "in consideration of marriage or the formation of a civil partnership", or, by individuals and companies "a consideration the value of which, in money or money's worth, is significantly less than the value, in money or money's worth, of the consideration provided"; although the reference to "consideration" is itself understood in the same sense as in the formation of a contract: *Hill v Haines* [2007] EWCA Civ 1284; [2008] Ch. 412 at [30]). Statutes relating to real property vary in the circumstances in which they depart from the general common law definition of consideration in defining a "purchaser": LPA 1925 s.205(1)(xxi) includes marriage and formation of a civil partnership, but excludes nominal consideration in money; Land Registration Act 2002 s.132(1) defines "valuable consideration" as not including marriage consideration or nominal consideration in money); and Land Charges Act 1972 s.17(1) defines "purchaser" as one who take an interest in or charge on land "for valuable consideration" but in its operative provisions in s.4 generally simply refers to a purchaser but s.4(6) refers for one purpose to a purchaser "for money or money's worth" and for another purpose (and by cross-reference to Inheritance Tax Act 1984 s.272) excludes nominal consideration.

[162] *Ball v National and Grindlay's Bank Ltd*, see para.8-26 fn.161, at 139.

[163] See para.8-08.

[164] See para.7-18.

[165] See para.4-03. cf. *Foakes v Beer* (1884) 9 App. Cas. 605, HL, at 613 (Lord Selborne: "The distinction between the effect of a deed under seal, and that of an agreement by parol, or by writing not under seal, may seem arbitrary, but it is established in our law; nor is it really unreasonable or practically inconvenient that the law should require particular solemnities to give to a gratuitous contract the force of a binding obligation").

requirement, it can have a similar function to formality, particularly in protecting a party against being bound by an ill-considered gratuitous promise,[166] and to that extent Hobhouse J was correct to say that "[u]ltimately the question of consideration is a formality as is the use of a seal or the agreement to give a peppercorn".[167]

Secondly, although allowing nominal consideration may appear to be the courts' colluding in the evasion of a requirement for the formation of a contract on the bilateral exchange model, as long as their concern is only that the formality of a deed is being avoided—given that the same promise, if contained in a deed, would have been enforceable[168] —it is hardly a serious concern if a principal function of formality which is afforded by the use of the deed[169] is also afforded by the parties' deliberate use of nominal consideration in their (informal) agreement. The courts are not blind to the fact that the parties are dressing up a gift as a sale. But unless such a transaction is designed to have some improper effect, there is no reason to undo it. Some legal systems will look behind a contract of sale to check whether it is really a sale or a gift: for example, French law will not recognise a "disguised donation"[170] as a contract of sale, but this is on the basis that the parties who have set up their transaction as a contract of sale are probably seeking to avoid some consequence of gifts that does not apply to sales, or even to disguise an illicit transaction, and so the courts will re-characterise it as a contract of gift, rather than a contract of sale. To a French lawyer this is a question of finding the right characterisation of the contract, since a contract may be gratuitous or onerous[171]; and the characterisation of the contract as effecting a gratuitous transfer may have other consequences such as the imposition of tax, or being taken into account in the later distribution of the donor's assets on death.[172] To an English lawyer, there is no general category of "contracts of gift", so the courts do not have a concern to determine whether it is such a contract or is really a contract of sale[173]; and although

---

[166] See para.4-16.

[167] *Vantage Navigation Corp v Suhail and Saud Bahwan Building Materials LLC (The Alev)* [1989] 1 Lloyd's Rep. 138 at 147. See also O.W. Holmes, *The Common Law* (Boston: Little, Brown & Co, 1881), p.273 ("In one sense, everything is form which the law requires in order to make a promise binding over and above the mere expression of a promisor's will. Consideration is a form as much as a seal"); cf. L.L. Fuller, "Consideration and Form" (1941) 41 Colum. L.Rev. 799; C.G. Addison, *Treatise on the law of contracts*, 1st edn (W. Benning & Co, 1847), p.18 ("this rule [of consideration] has been wisely established by the law for the purpose of protecting weak and thoughtless persons from the consequences of rash, improvident, and inconsiderate engagements").

[168] See para.8-27 fn.164.

[169] The "cautionary" function: see para.8-27 fn.165.

[170] *Donation déguisée*; a *donation* is a gratuitous agreement to transfer property (movable or immovable).

[171] B. Nicholas, *The French Law of Contract*, 2nd edn (Clarendon Press, 1992), pp.44–45; c.civ. art.1107.

[172] Nicholas, see para.8-27 fn.171, pp.147–148, 195–196 (by using a *donation déguisée* the parties may seek not only to avoid the trouble of having their *donation* authenticated before a notary as required by c.civ. art.931, but also, by keeping it out of sight of the notary, to keep it out of sight of the tax authorities and so avoid tax on inter vivos gifts, or to avoid it being later taken into account in the compulsory distribution of the donor's assets to his family on death; or to hide the fact that it is an illicit payment). Since the reform of 2016 (see para.8-04 fn.34), c.civ. art.1169 provides that an onerous contract is a nullity where, at the moment of its formation, what is agreed in return for the benefit of the person undertaking an obligation is illusory or derisory.

[173] Indeed, the general approach of English law is not to attach such significance to the categorisation of types of contract as is common in civil law jurisdictions following their Roman law heritage: J. Cartwright, *Contract Law: An Introduction to the English Law of Contract for the Civil Lawyer*, 3rd edn (Hart Publishing, 2016), pp.57–63.

a gift may also have other consequences in law and, if hidden, must be revealed in order to ensure that the law is properly applied to it, English law does not use the law of contract and its categorisations to effect such a revelation but generally targets by distinct statutory provisions each type of transaction for which there is a policy concern where the transaction is gratuitous or for less than full consideration.[174]

The reluctance of the English courts to find that there is no valuable considera- 8-28
tion for a seriously intended promise   An informal promise made without consideration is not binding as a contract. However, the courts appear generally to be reluctant to find that a promise, made seriously with the intention that it should be legally binding, is unenforceable for the reason that the promisee has not provided consideration for it. Donaldson J said that "A defence of lack of consideration rarely has merit"[175] and the courts will sometimes look hard in order to discover[176] the consideration which justifies the enforcement of a promise. Some older cases can be explained as the courts' seeking to give effect to a promise through the law of contract for which a remedy in tort was not yet available. In particular, there were cases where the courts were willing to adopt rather artificial constructions of the facts in order to find that careless statements were contractually binding before remedies in tort for negligent misrepresentation were devised. In *De la Bere v Pearson Ltd*[177] the Court of Appeal held that newspaper proprietors, having advertised that the newspaper's city editor would answer readers' inquiries for financial advice, were liable in contract to a reader to whom the editor carelessly recommended a stockbroker who misappropriated the reader's investment. Vaughan Williams LJ found consideration on the basis that the defendants could insert the questions and answers in the newspaper if they chose to do so (even though the advice in the case was provided privately rather than through the pages of the newspaper), and "such publication might obviously have a tendency to increase the sale of the defendants' paper".[178] When the House of Lords later accepted that there could be a general tortious duty of care in making statements or giving advice to a person with whom the advisor has no contractual relationship,[179] Lord Devlin drew attention to *De la Bere v Pearson Ltd* as an example of the sort of case in which the courts had in the past found consideration in order to

---

[174]   e.g. values for any taxation imposed on capital transfers are set by separate rules: there is no general taxation on inter vivos gifts, but whether they are brought into account on death for the purposes of inheritance tax is governed by Inheritance Tax Act 1984, esp. ss.3 (definition of "transfer of value"), 10 (dispositions not intended to confer gratuitous benefit); transactions which were entered into by a deceased person for less than "full valuable consideration" less than six years before death with the intention of defeating an application for financial provision under Inheritance (Provision for Family and Dependants Act) 1975 may be reversed under s.10 of that Act; and there are statutory provisions to reverse certain transactions made at an undervalue for the purpose of putting assets beyond the reach of creditors: Insolvency Act 1986 ss.238, 339, 423 (see see para.8-26 fn.161).

[175]   *Thoresen Car Ferries Ltd v Weymouth Portland BC* [1977] 2 Lloyd's Rep. 614 at 619.

[176]   Treitel refers to the courts' "inventing" consideration, which he defines as "treating some act or forbearance as consideration quite irrespective of the question whether *the parties* have so regarded it": G.H. Treitel, "Consideration: A Critical Analysis of Professor Atiyah's Fundamental Restatement" (1976) 50 A.L.J. 439, 440; this follows a similar earlier discussion in F.M.B. Reynolds and G.H. Treitel, "Consideration for the Modification of Contracts" (1965) 7 Malaya L.Rev. 1, 2-3.

[177]   [1908] 1 K.B. 280, CA.

[178]   [1908] 1 K.B. 280, CA at 287.

[179]   *Hedley Byrne & Co Ltd v Heller & Partners Ltd* [1964] A.C. 465, HL.

bring the claim within the law of contract in order to provide a just result, but said that "today the result can and should be achieved by the application of the law of negligence and ... it is unnecessary and undesirable to construct an artificial consideration".[180]

Such cases cannot, however, be dismissed simply as old decisions which brought into the law of contract cases which really belonged in the law of tort. There is a broader trend of scepticism on the part of judges—not scepticism that goes so far as to seek to overturn the doctrine of consideration altogether in order to replace it with another test for the creation of contracts, such as the intention of the parties,[181] but scepticism which more openly seeks to find consideration where it will give effect to the intention of the promisor. We shall see this in cases involving the variation of contracts, where it may be argued that different considerations apply,[182] although the general approach goes wider than this. For example, Hobhouse J said[183]:

"Now that there is a properly developed doctrine of the avoidance of contracts on the grounds of economic duress, there is no warrant for the Court to fail to recognize the existence of some consideration even though it may be insignificant and even though there may have been no mutual bargain in any realistic use of that phrase."

This does not, however, mean that for every apparently seriously intended promise consideration must be found. There will be cases where the courts do not think that the promisee's claim deserves a generous interpretation of the facts in order to discover consideration.[184] But in any event they cannot ignore the requirement of consideration, and must be able to find something, however small, which they can hold to be of benefit to the promisor and/or detrimental to the promisee before they can judge that there is sufficient consideration to render the promise enforceable as a contract. In the following paragraphs we consider some examples of situations where the courts have, or have not, found sufficient consideration. First, we look at particular questions which arise in valuing the promisee's forbear-

---

[180] *Hedley Byrne & Co Ltd v Heller & Partners Ltd* [1964] A.C. 465, HL at 528.

[181] cf. however, see para.9-16.

[182] See paras 9-16, 9-24.

[183] *Vantage Navigation Corp v Suhail and Saud Bahwan Building Materials LLC (The Alev)*, see para.8-27 fn.167, at 147; and see *Kishenin v von Kalkstein-Bleach* [2014] EWHC 3416 (Ch) at [12] (initial rent-free period of lease; Deputy Judge Edward Murray: "it stands to reason that there was consideration for the lease. It is highly improbable that the claimant, himself an experienced businessman, would have agreed to the one year rent-free period unless there was 'something in it' for him"). See also, in the context of variation of a contract, *Williams v Roffey Bros & Nicholls (Contractors) Ltd* [1991] 1 Q.B. 1, CA (discussed at para.9-14) at 18 (Russell LJ: "whilst consideration remains a fundamental requirement before a contract not under seal can be enforced, the policy of the law in its search to do justice between the parties has developed considerably since the early 19th century when *Stilk v Myrick* (1809) 2 Camp. 317, 170 E.R. 1168 was decided by Lord Ellenborough CJ In the late 20th century I do not believe that the rigid approach to the concept of consideration to be found in *Stilk v Myrick* is either necessary or desirable. Consideration there must still be but, in my judgment, the courts nowadays should be more ready to find its existence so as to reflect the intention of the parties to the contract where the bargaining powers are not unequal and where the finding of consideration reflect the true intention of the parties") and at 21 (Purchas LJ). In the case of a bill of exchange, it is presumed that every party whose signature appears on the bill became a party for value: Bills of Exchange Act 1882 s.30(1).

[184] cf. *Combe v Combe* [1951] 2 K.B. 215, CA, where the Court did not appear to find the ex-wife's claim meritorious; see para.8-16 fn.96.

ance as consideration for the promise[185]; and cases where the alleged consideration is the promise of something which is impossible or illegal[186]; then we consider
a broader range of examples drawn from very different circumstances.[187]

The value of forbearance   Forbearance to take some particular action may   **8-29**
constitute good consideration, as long as it has value by way of benefit to the promisor, and/or detriment to the promisee. The fact that the defendant asked the claimant not to do something that he might otherwise have wished to do, and thereby to
restrict his freedom of action, is generally sufficient to persuade a court that the
forbearance in accordance with the request is valuable to the defendant.[188]
Moreover, given that the claimant by agreeing to restrict his freedom can be said
to have undertaken some detriment to himself, the normal requirements of
consideration can be satisfied. If, however, it is clear that the claimant would in any
event not have done the thing that he has promised not to do,[189] or could not do it,[190]
or was promising not to do something that he had no right to do,[191] he is not in fact
limiting his own action and the courts may hold that his promise to forbear is neither
of benefit to the defendant nor to the detriment of the claimant and is therefore not
sufficient consideration.

---

[185]   See paras 8-29 to 8-31.
[186]   See paras 8-32 to 8-33.
[187]   See paras 8-34 and 8-35.
[188]   *Hamer v Sidway* 27 N.E. 256 (1891), NYCA, at 257 (Parker J: "the promisee used tobacco, oc-
        casionally drank liquor, and had a legal right to do so. That right he abandoned for a period of years
        upon the strength of the promise ... We need not speculate on the effort which may have been
        required to give up the use of those stimulants. It is sufficient that he restricted his lawful freedom
        of action within certain prescribed limits upon the faith of his uncle's agreement, and now, having
        fully performed the conditions imposed, it is of no moment whether such performance actually
        proved a benefit to the promisor, and the court will not inquire into it; but, were it a proper subject
        of inquiry, we see nothing in this record that would permit a determination that the uncle was not
        benefited in a legal sense"). See also *Dunton v Dunton* (1892) 18 V.L.R. 114, SC Victoria, at 118,
        120 (ex-wife's promise to ex-husband to "conduct herself with sobriety, and in a respectable, orderly
        and virtuous manner" involved restriction on her liberty and was advantageous to her ex-husband
        for his benefit and that of their children).
[189]   *Arrale v Costain Civil Engineering Ltd* [1976] 1 Lloyd's Rep. 98, CA, at 106 (Geoffrey Lane LJ:
        "It is no consideration to refrain from a course of action which it was never intended to pursue",
        referring to *Cook v Wright* (1861) 1 B. & S. 559 at 569, 121 E.R. 822 at 826). See also *Miles v New
        Zealand Alford Estate Co* (1886) 32 Ch. D. 266, CA, at 286 (Cotton LJ: no consideration for
        compromise of claim under guarantee by party who had no intention to enforce it; although a state-
        ment by an individual having the right to sue would be sufficient to constitute consideration, a
        company must have formal decision of directors of shareholders' resolution to bring the claim before
        its non-enforcement can constitute consideration); see also Fry LJ at 300.
[190]   *Combe v Combe* [1951] 2 K.B. 215, CA, at 221, 226 (promise by wife during divorce proceedings
        not to apply to court for maintenance would not be binding on her so was worth nothing and could
        not be good consideration); cf. however, *Hill v Haines* [2007] EWCA Civ 1284; [2008] Ch. 412
        (compromise of statutory right to ancillary relief under Matrimonial Causes Act 1973 s.24 has value
        and so provides full consideration in money's worth for court's order for transfer of interest in
        matrimonial home, to prevent challenge as transaction at undervalue by transferor's trustee in
        bankruptcy under Insolvency Act 1986 s.339). For the general issue of whether a promise to do (or
        not to do) something which is impossible, or illegal or otherwise contrary to public policy, can
        constitute valid consideration, see paras 8-32, 8-33.
[191]   *White v Bluett* (1853) 23 L.J. Ex. 36 at 37 (promise by son not to complain about his father's distribu-
        tion of his property where father was entitled to make whatever distribution of his property he liked).

8-30 **Forbearance: the particular case of compromises** One context in which the parties may both[192] agree to refrain from taking a course of action, and thereby each by his own promise provides consideration for the other's promise of forbearance, is the contract of settlement or compromise, whether the agreement be to compromise a potential claim, or litigation or an arbitration[193] which has already been commenced; and whether the compromise relates to the whole claim or to particular aspects of it, such as an agreement not to raise a particular defence,[194] or not to seek a particular remedy, or is only as to the value of the claim.[195] The agreement may also be designed to clarify the precise scope of a previously ill-defined understanding between the parties and therefore to avoid disagreement and future dispute[196]; or it may be an agreement as to the facts, which can then be raised by way of estoppel against a party in subsequent litigation who seeks to assert the contrary.[197] We have already seen that the courts are reluctant to hold that an agreement, entered into between parties who seriously intend it to have legal effect, fails for lack of consideration.[198] Where the agreement is the compromise of a claim, this is reinforced by the courts' general disposition to favour compromises and to discourage unnecessary litigation or other disputes.[199]

If pursued to the end, each claim will generally result in success for one party

---

[192] For a multi-party compromise agreement between a debtor and a number of his creditors by which the creditors mutually agree to forbear from enforcing part of their debts, see *Good v Cheesman* (1831) 2 B. & Ad. 328, 109 E.R. 1165; see para.9-21.

[193] *Allied Marine Transport Ltd v Vale do Rio Doce Navegacao SA (The Leonidas D)* [1985] 1 W.L.R. 925, CA, at 933 (Robert Goff LJ: "The owners' abandonment of the reference, with all that this implies, including an abandonment of any right to obtain a declaratory award or to ask for an order for costs, would constitute good consideration for the abandonment of the charterers' claim as well as their abandonment of the reference"); *Huyton SA v Peter Cremer GmbH & Co* [1999] 1 Lloyd's Rep. 620 (compromise included agreement by one party to withdraw demand to arbitrate).

[194] *Binder v Alachouzos* [1972] 2 Q.B. 151, CA (agreement not to raise argument that credit agreement was unenforceable and illegal under Moneylenders Acts).

[195] *Truex v Toll* [2009] EWHC 396 (Ch); [2009] 1 W.L.R. 2121 at [30] (unliquidated debt may be converted into liquidated one as long as there is consideration, e.g. by a compromise agreement).

[196] *Anangel Atlas Compania Naviera SA v Ishikawajima-Harima Heavy Industries Co Ltd (No.2)* [1990] 2 Lloyd's Rep. 526 at 543–544.

[197] *Colchester BC v Smith* [1992] Ch. 421, CA (compromise acknowledging title of landowner and fact that occupation was not adverse possession: occupier estopped from going behind that agreement and asserting freehold title by adverse possession).

[198] See para.8-28.

[199] See, e.g. *Binder v Alachouzos*, see para.8-30 fn.194, at 158, 159–160; *Colchester BC v Smith*, see para.8-30 fn.197, at 435; *Brennan v Bolt Burdon* [2004] EWCA Civ 1017; [2005] Q.B. 303 at [22]. See also J. Beatson, *The Use and Abuse of Unjust Enrichment* (Clarendon Press, 1991), pp.100–103 (relationship between policy in favour of enforcing compromises, and rule against recovery of money paid under process of law). The court's duty to manage cases actively includes encouraging the parties to co-operate with each other in the conduct of the proceeding, encouraging them to use alternative dispute resolution and helping them to settle the whole or part of the case: CPR r.1.4(2)(a), (e), (f).

Other issues, which do not concern us here, may also arise in relation to the validity and scope of compromise agreements, such as the need to be sure that the parties have come to a genuine agreement without undue pressure by one party on the other; whether the terms of the agreement succeed in covering all the intended potential claims (see, e.g. *Bank of Credit and Commerce International SA v Ali* [2001] UKHL 8; [2002] 1 A.C. 251 on the difficulties of construing a general release of claims where the parties could not have realised that a particular head of claim might later exist); and whether a party who receives by the compromise a general release of all claims against him, but knows that the other party agrees the general release in ignorance of some particular subsisting claim that he could have brought, has a duty to disclose that claim (discussed obiter in *Bank of Credit and Commerce International SA v Ali* at [32] (Lord Nicholls), [69]–[70] (Lord Hoffmann)).

and failure for the other. It may therefore appear that the party who would have lost is not in fact giving up anything by agreeing the compromise. However, even in a very strong claim there is always at least the risk that the claim may not succeed, or may not succeed in full. No doubt the chances of success will be reflected in the price the parties agree in their compromise, although it does not matter if that chance is very small: for the agreement to constitute a valid contract of compromise it is sufficient that there is at least some risk of success and failure that is being bought off by the compromise agreement, given that as a general rule the courts do not concern themselves with the adequacy of the consideration.[200] The compromise also confers other benefits: even in the strongest claim not only is the risk of at least partial failure eliminated by the settlement, but also the costs of litigation,[201] and the general disruption which litigation causes,[202] and are avoided by both parties, and so each obtains some benefit from the agreement. The general approach was set out by Cockburn CJ[203]:

> "The authorities clearly establish that if an agreement is made to compromise a disputed claim, forbearance to sue in respect of that claim is a good consideration; and whether proceedings to enforce the disputed claim have or have not been instituted makes no difference. ... Every day a compromise is effected on the ground that the party making it has a chance of succeeding in it, and if he bonâ fide believes he has a fair chance of success, he has a reasonable ground for suing, and his forbearance to sue will constitute a good consideration. When such a person forbears to sue he gives up what he believes to be a right of action, and the other party gets an advantage, and, instead of being annoyed with an action, he escapes from the vexations incident to it."

Compromise of a demonstrably invalid claim   As long as the compromised dispute concerns a claim which, however strong, is at least arguable, each party gives consideration by agreeing not to pursue the dispute. There can be more difficulty in assessing the validity of the compromise of a claim which is clearly invalid, and which would fail *in limine* if the action were pursued. It is less obvious here that value is given by the party who would inevitably have lost, although the general policy in favour of upholding compromise agreements still points in favour of finding consideration for the agreement. The fact that the claim was wholly unfounded is not in itself an obstacle to the validity of the compromise as long as there was a genuine dispute between the parties, and the claim is made honestly by a party who does not know that it is unfounded.[204] Given that a

8-31

---

200   See para.8-25.
201   cf. however *Cook v Wright* (1861) 1 B. & S. 559 at 570, 121 E.R. 822 at 826–827 (where the claim was clearly bad and so would have failed *in limine* if it had not been compromised (see para.8-31) the "real consideration ... depends ... on the reality of the claim made and the bona fides of the compromise" rather than "the technical and almost illusory consideration arising from the extra costs of litigation"); *Wade v Simeon* (1846) 2 C.B. 548 at 564, 135 E.R. 1061 at 1067 (Tindal CJ: where no valid claim, "the defendant will recover costs, which must be assumed to be a full compensation for all the legal damage he may sustain", so no consideration; similarly Maule J at 566, at 1068).
202   *Pitt v PHH Asset Management Ltd* [1994] 1 W.L.R. 327, CA, at 332 (Peter Gibson LJ: consideration for lock-out agreement included forbearance from claiming injunction which could not have succeeded, but "that nuisance was something which the defendant was freed from by the plaintiff agreeing to the lock out agreement").
203   *Callisher v Bischoffsheim* (1870) L.R. 5 Q.B. 449 at 451–452.
204   *Callisher v Bischoffsheim* (1870) L.R. 5 Q.B. 449; *Miles v New Zealand Alford Estate Co*, see para.8-29 fn.189, at 283–284 (Cotton LJ), 298 (Fry LJ); See also Bowen LJ at 291 (although dissenting on the facts and therefore in the result): "the reality of the claim which is given up must be

unilateral mistake of fact or law is generally insufficient to render a contract void,[205] a mistake as to the validity of the claim made by the party who compromises a claim made against him is in itself insufficient to allow him to avoid the compromise agreement. A common (shared) mistake of fact or law may render a contract void, but only within narrow limits[206] and never where the parties have expressly or impliedly allocated in their contract the risk of the mistake[207]; in the case of a genuine compromise the essence of the contract is the settlement of the risk of outcome of the dispute, and this will often include the risk of what the court might find the facts or the applicable law to be.[208]

If, however, one party knows that the claim is invalid, a distinction must be drawn. Where it is the party against whom the claim is brought that knows that the claim is invalid, yet he submits to the compromise without advancing his defence of the claim, he is bound by the compromise. In some cases it may be clear that the fact that the defendant has submitted to the compromise has caused detriment to the claimant, such as where there was another person against whom a valid claim could have been brought but the defendant's agreement to the compromise has induced the claimant not to pursue, or even to seek to discover, alternative courses of action.[209] Even without such clear detriment to the claimant, however, the courts take a broad view of the facts in finding consideration where the defendant knows that the claim against him is invalid, on the basis that the defendant has at least obtained the benefit of avoiding being sued (even if the suit would have failed).[210]

---

measured, not by the state of the law as it is ultimately discovered to be, but by the state of the knowledge of the person who at the time has to judge and make the concession. Otherwise you would have to try the whole cause to know if the man had a right to compromise it, and with regard to questions of law it is obvious you could never safely compromise a question of law at all"); *LCP Holdings Ltd v Hombergh Holdings BV* [2012] EWHC 3643 (QB) at [47]–[49] (Judge Mackie QC, rejecting counsel's argument that it was necessary to hold a full trial to consider whether there were reasonable grounds for belief and to look into the state of mind of the parties: "one would expect a businessman (and many commercial lawyers) to have a good faith belief in a claim under the [agreement in the case]"). cf. J.N. Walker [1974] M.U.L.R. 537 at 539, discussing *Wigan v Edwards* (1973) 1 A.L.R. 497, HCA, and arguing that an unreasonable subjective belief in the validity of the claim should not be sufficient, otherwise "the stupid man obtains a benefit, whereas the intelligent man does not"; Beatson, see para.8-30 fn.199, at pp.102–103.

[205] *Smith v Hughes* (1871) L.R. 6 Q.B. 597 at 603, 606–607; *Statoil ASA v Louis Dreyfus Energy Services LP (The Harriette N)* [2008] EWHC 2257 (Comm); [2008] 2 Lloyd's Rep. 685 at [88]; Cartwright (Misrepresentation), para.15-10.

[206] Where the mistake is sufficiently serious to make performance of the contract impossible, or essentially different from that which both parties had contemplated: *Great Peace Shipping Ltd v Tsavliris Salvage (International) Ltd (The Great Peace)* [2002] EWCA Civ 1407; [2003] Q.B. 679 at [73], [76]; Cartwright (Misrepresentation), paras 15-19 to 15-28.

[207] Cartwright (Misrepresentation), paras 15-15 to 15-18.

[208] For a mistake of law which was based on an interpretation of case-law as it stood at the time of the contract, but was later changed by judicial decision, see *Brennan v Bolt Burdon*, para.8-30 fn.199; Cartwright (Misrepresentation), para.15-24; but for whether proof that a party entered into a contract having some doubt about the facts or a state of affairs can be held to have accepted the risk, see *Deutsche Morgan Grenfell Group Plc v Inland Revenue Commissioners* [2006] UKHL 49; [2007] 1 A.C. 558 at [27] (Lord Hoffmann); Cartwright (Misrepresentation), para.15-17.

[209] *Cook v Wright*, see para.8-30 fn.201.

[210] *Cook v Wright*, see para.8-30 fn.201, at 567, at 825 ("The defendant, according to his own evidence, never believed that he was liable in law, but signed the notes in order to avoid being sued"); at 569, at 826 ("The position of the parties must necessarily be altered in every case of compromise, so that, if the question is afterwards opened up, they cannot be replaced as they were before the compromise. The plaintiff may be in a less favourable position for renewing his litigation, he must be at an additional trouble and expence in again getting up his case, and he may no longer be able to produce

A claim which is known by the *claimant* not to be a valid claim cannot, however, form the basis of a valid compromise. Different reasons have been given for this, some relating to the fact that such a claim would be "fraudulent"[211] or not bona fide,[212] or contrary to public policy[213]; but it has also been said the claimant does not provide consideration by agreeing to give up a claim that has no value.[214]

Promise of act or forbearance which is impossible   Given that the claimant's   **8-32** promise, in order to constitute consideration to render the defendant's promise enforceable, must constitute a valuable benefit to the defendant or detriment to the claimant, one might expect that it would be an obstacle to finding the claimant's promise to be valuable consideration if it is shown that the performance of what he promised was in fact impossible. It will be a matter of construction whether the promise was really to do the impossible, and the courts may be reluctant so to hold if any other reasonable construction can be placed on the promise[215]; but it is not a bar to a promise being good consideration, that the claimant could not in fact perform the promise.[216]

A binding promise to do the impossible might seem a contradiction. Legal systems in the civil law tradition generally see substantive difficulties in holding such a promise to be legally binding and, not having a doctrine of consideration,[217] find other rules by which to address the issue.[218] For the civil lawyer the dif-

---

the evidence which would have proved it originally"). See also *Veitch v Sinclair* [1975] 1 N.Z.L.R. 264, SC Auckland (binding promise to pay for delivery up of document which promisee believed gave him binding option to purchase, but promisor knew or correctly believed was invalid, but payment was made to avoid trouble from promisee). cf. Beatson, see para.8-30 fn.199, at pp.100–106 (distinguishing the rules governing compromises from the rule against recovery of money paid under process of law).

211   *Callisher v Bischoffsheim*, see para.8-30 fn.203, at 452 (Cockburn CJ, obiter).
212   *Callisher v Bischoffsheim*, see para.8-30 fn.203, at 452 (Blackburn J, obiter).
213   *Wade v Simeon*, see para.8-30 fn.201, at 564, at 1067 (Tindal CJ: "It is almost contra bonos mores, and certainly contrary to all the principles of natural justice, that a man should institute proceedings against another, when he is conscious that he has no good cause of action").
214   *Wade v Simeon*, see para.8-30 fn.201, at 564, at 1067 (Tindal CJ: "Detrimental to the plaintiff it cannot be, if he has no cause of action: and beneficial to the defendant it cannot be" because any costs he incurs will be compensated); similarly Maule J at 566, at 1068. Tindal CJ also said that by admitting in the proceedings that he had no cause of action, the claimant "is estopped from saying that there was any valid consideration for the defendant's promise". In this case the claimant knew that he had no valid cause of action, but in saying that there was no consideration, the judges did not always distinguish between the fact that the claim was invalid, and the fact that the claimant knew about the invalidity. It has become clearer since this decision that the mere fact of invalidity of the claim is not sufficient: *Callisher v Bischoffsheim*, see para.8-30 fn.203. For the absence of consideration where the claimant has no intention to pursue the claim which he compromises, see *Miles v New Zealand Alford Estate Co*, see para.8-29 fn.189.
215   *Lord Clifford v Watts* (1870) L.R. 5 C.P. 577 at 585 (Willes J).
216   *Lord Clifford v Watts* (1870) L.R. 5 C.P. 577 at 588 (Brett J; this was not, however, put in terms so of the doctrine of consideration, but more broadly: "it is not competent to a defendant to say that there is no binding contract, merely because he has engaged to do something with is physically impossible").
217   See para.8-04.
218   e.g. in French law, a contractual obligation must have an *"objet"*—subject-matter which is possible and determined or capable of being determined: c.civ., arts 1163, with the consequence that "an impossible *objet* has no content and therefore a promise of an impossibility is null (*impossibilium nulla obligatio*)": Nicholas, see para.8-27 fn.171, p.116 (discussing the provisions of the civil Code (arts 1108, 1126–1130) before its reform in 2016: cf. para.8-04 fn.34); in German law a claim to performance is excluded by the fact that the performance of an obligation is objectively impossible

ficulty of acknowledging the binding promise to do the impossible follows from the nature of the duty to perform the obligation, which is generally also linked to the use of specific performance of the contract as a primary remedy: an obligation which cannot be performed cannot be enforced and so lacks an essential element of validity. English law, however, which sees the natural remedy for breach of a contractual obligation as the payment of damages,[219] has less difficulty of principle with the notion of the binding promise to do the impossible: a party who undertakes such an obligation takes on the risk of either being able to perform or, if performance is impossible (whether the impossibility flows from his own subjective circumstances, or from the fact that the promise is objectively impossible for anyone to perform), of paying damages to the other party for the loss which flows from his breach.[220] Impossibility of one party's performance, where *both* parties believed that it was in fact possible, may form the basis of a successful claim that the contract is void for common mistake but, as already noted, the doctrine of common mistake operates only in narrowly-defined circumstances.[221] Contracts where the subject-matter, unknown to both parties, has already perished, or for the transfer of property rights which both parties erroneously believe the transferor to have, or for performance which both parties erroneously believed to be possible as a matter of fact or law, have been held to be void not because the promise of (impossible) performance did not constitute consideration but because of the doctrine of common mistake.[222] However, even in the case of a common mistake, where the party whose performance is in fact impossible has expressly or impliedly taken the risk of its possibility, the contract is valid even though not capable of performance. There is therefore no impediment in the common law to a valid contract, for example, to transfer property which does not exist.[223]

8-33 **Promise of act or forbearance which is illegal or otherwise contrary to public policy** If the claimant promises to do or to forbear to do an act which is not impossible but is illegal, or is immoral or otherwise contrary to public policy according to the standards set by a specific statutory provision or by the common law, the courts have sometimes used the doctrine of consideration to explain why the result-

---

(i.e. impossible for the obligor and for any other person), and the other party can withdraw: BGB §§275(1), 326(5). In both legal systems a party who is responsible for the impossibility may still be liable for damages.

219 *Photo Production Ltd v Securicor Transport Ltd* [1980] A.C. 827, HL, at 848–849.
220 *Vehicle Control Services Ltd v Revenue and Customs Commissioners* [2013] EWCA Civ 186; [2013] S.T.C. 892 at [22] (Lewison LJ: "There is no legal impediment to my contracting to sell you Buckingham Palace. If (inevitably) I fail to honour my contract then I can be sued for damages"). If the non-performance constitutes a total failure of consideration which leads to the other party terminating the contract for breach, the obligation arises to repay money paid under the contract: see para.8-10.
221 *The Great Peace*, see para.8-31 fn.206, at [76]; see generally para.8-31.
222 For examples see generally Cartwright (Misrepresentation), para.15-26 and cases cited there.
223 *McRae v Commonwealth Disposals Commission* (1951) 84 C.L.R. 377, HCA; Cartwright (Misrepresentation), para.15-16. *McRae* may be an example of a case which, involving negligent misstatements about the existence of the subject matter, but being decided before the House of Lords in *Hedley Byrne & Co Ltd v Heller & Partners Ltd* (see para.8-28 fn.179) extended the law of tort to impose liability for careless misstatements, had to be brought within the law of contract: see para.8-28; however, it stands as good authority in the modern law of contract and was accepted in English law in *Associated Japanese Bank (International) Ltd v Crédit du Nord SA* [1989] 1 W.L.R. 255 at 268 and *The Great Peace*, see para.8-31 fn.206, at [77], [91].

ing contract is not valid.[224] However, in the modern law the more usual approach is to identify under a separate doctrine the basis on which the obligation of either party is illegal, immoral or otherwise contrary to public policy, rather than making the doctrine of consideration bear the burden of providing a remedy.[225] Indeed, it is preferable to use a general doctrine of illegality and public policy, since this not only focuses on the real issue but also allows the courts to draw distinctions between different forms of illegality in their legal effects for the contract. Consideration is a fundamental element in the formation of a valid contract: without consideration, there is no contract.[226] The consequences of promises which are illegal, immoral or otherwise contrary to public policy are, however, more nuanced: the contract may not be void, but only unenforceable for certain purposes, or have less than the full legal effect that a contract would otherwise have if not tainted by the illegality.[227]

Examples of sufficient consideration   Many illustrations could be given of sufficient consideration in the formation of a contract: in most bilateral agreements it is not difficult to identify the benefit which the promisee's promise, act or forbearance confers on the promisor, and/or the detriment which the promisee thereby suffers, and which therefore constitutes consideration for the promise. More interesting are the marginal cases: those in which it is less easy to identify in economic terms the benefit and/or the detriment, but where the courts (in England or in other common law jurisdictions) have held, or have at least said by way of obiter dictum, that there is sufficient consideration. Accordingly, it has been said that there was consideration in the following instances: **8-34**

(a)   the payment of a nominal sum of money, or the delivery or promise to deliver a chattel of nominal value such as a peppercorn, a rose, or a chocolate bar wrapper[228];

(b)   delivery of a chattel of lesser value than an outstanding debt of money tendered in full satisfaction of the debt, where so accepted by the creditor; similarly payment of a sum of money less than the full debt tendered in satisfaction of the whole earlier than the debt is due, or at a place different

---

[224]   e.g. *Featherston v Hutchinson* (1589) Cro. Eliz. 199, 78 E.R. 455 (promise to pay sheriff to release prisoner contrary to statute: the "consideration is not good"); *Harvy v Gibbons* (1674) 2 Lev. 161, 83 E.R. 499 ("the consideration being illegal, for the plaintiff cannot discharge a debt due to his master"); *Waite v Jones* (1835) 1 Bing. (N.C.) 656 at 662, 131 E.R. 1270 at 1272 (Tindal CJ: "if either part of the consideration be illegal, the whole falls to the ground; for a party cannot enforce a contract where the consideration is illegal, either in the whole or in part"); *Mallalieu v Hodgson* (1851) 16 Q.B. 689; 117 E.R. 1045 (composition between creditors including a fraudulent preference of one creditor: "the whole stipulation of a preference being a fraud on the part of the plaintiff towards other creditors, no part of it can be legally relied on by him as forming a material inducement for his deed. It could not form any part of a legal consideration": Erle J at 712, at 1053); *Combe v Combe* [1951] 2 K.B. 215, CA, at 221, 226 (promise not to apply to court for ancillary relief in divorce proceedings (if it had been requested and made) would purport to oust jurisdiction of court, so no consideration; see also para.8-29 fn.190). Where the claim that was purportedly compromised arose under a contract unenforceable as a gaming contract under Gaming Act 1845 s.18, it was said that the promise not to enforce an unenforceable obligation was no consideration: see, e.g. *Poteliakhoff v Teakle* [1938] 2 K.B. 816, CA; and cases at para.8-34 fnn.240 and 241; these cases are now changed since the Gaming Act 1845 has been repealed: Gambling Act 2005 s.334(1)(c).

[225]   See, e.g. Chitty, Ch.16; Treitel, Ch.11; Anson, Ch.11; R.A. Buckley, *Illegality and Public Policy*, 4th edn (Sweet & Maxwell, 2017).

[226]   See para.8-06.

[227]   See the works cited in see para.8-33 fn.225.

[228]   See generally para.8-25 and the cases cited there.

than required by the contract,[229] without the court's enquiring into the particular value attached by the creditor to the variation[230];

(c) a "certain amount of forbearance" by a creditor to sue for the debt as consideration for the debtor's promise to provide security, even though there was no promise by the creditor to abstain for any certain time from suing for the debt, and at any time after the promise the creditor might have insisted on payment and have brought an action[231];

(d) entering into an agreement in order to avoid the nuisance value of a claim that was threatened, or likely to be made, by the other party even if the claim would inevitably fail[232];

(e) the practical benefits received by a main contractor on a building project by the continued performance of an existing sub-contract by a sub-contractor, in return for the promise of additional payments to the sub-contractor, where breach of the sub-contract would cause delay in the performance of the main contract and give rise to penalty payments for the delay, or would involve the main contractor in trouble and expense engaging others to complete the sub-contract work[233];

(f) agreement by the tenant to a revised rent under a lease proposed by the landlord, even where the landlord's proposal was erroneously for a new rent below the current rent[234];

(g) co-operation given by minor shareholders in a company to the major shareholder in the sale of all shares to a third party in return for an undertaking by the major shareholder to guarantee payment by the third party, even

---

[229] *Pinnel's Case* (1602) 5 Co. Rep. 117a, 77 E.R. 237 ("the gift of a horse, hawk or robe, etc in satisfaction is good"; similarly payment of £5 at York can be good satisfaction of a debt of £10 payable at Westminster; but "payment of a lesser sum on the day in satisfaction of a greater, cannot be any satisfaction for the whole": see para.9-18). In that case, the part payment was good consideration because it was made early (£5 2s. 2d. paid on 1 October in satisfaction of debt of £8 10s. due on 11 November).

[230] *Pinnel's Case* (1602) 5 Co. Rep. 117a, 77 E.R. 237 at 117a, at 237 ("a horse, hawk or robe, etc might be more beneficial to the plaintiff than the money in respect of some circumstance, or otherwise the plaintiff would not have accepted it in satisfaction").

[231] *Alliance Bank Ltd v Broom* (1864) 2 Drew. & Sm. 289, 62 E.R. 631.

[232] *Pitt v PHH Asset Management Ltd* [1994] 1 W.L.R. 327, CA, at 332; *Veitch v Sinclair* [1975] 1 N.Z.L.R. 264, SC Auckland. In *Williams v Williams* [1957] 1 W.L.R. 148, CA, Denning LJ held at 151 that a wife provided consideration by her promise, in return for a weekly payment from her husband from whom she was separated, to support and maintain herself, indemnify her husband against her debts and not to pledge her husband's credit, on the basis that if they had not made the agreement the wife might otherwise have sought and received public assistance, or have pledged the husband's credit, and so the husband might have been summoned before the courts by the National Assistance Board or by tradesmen and (though he would have had a good defence) the husband thereby avoided the trouble, worry and expense of a defending himself. Hodson LJ at 153 and Morris LJ at 155 preferred not to rest their decision on this ground.

[233] *Williams v Roffey Bros & Nicholls (Contractors) Ltd* [1991] 1 Q.B. 1, CA. This is a controversial decision: see para.9-14.

[234] *Centrovincial Estates Plc v Merchant Investors Assurance Co Ltd* [1983] Com. L.R. 158, CA (the courts would not enquire into the adequacy of consideration (see para.8-25); and although their agreement to the new (lower) rent, which deprived them of the right to put forward any other figure, may be said to have little value to the tenants there was still some value: "if the [tenants] had refused to agree any figure at all, considerable inconvenience to the [landlords] might have resulted": it avoided further dispute and the cost of any possible referral to an independent valuer).

though the minor shareholders did not consciously realise that by co-operating they were subjecting themselves to a detriment[235];

(h)   the delivery up of a document which purported to be a guarantee, where the validity of the guarantee was doubtful (on the basis that it might have been given only for past consideration[236]) but the fact that this was arguable made its delivery up sufficient consideration[237];

(i)   agreeing an express choice of law clause in a contract, even though that same governing law might have been implied anyway[238];

(j)   an undertaking not to take steps to enforce an outstanding debt which would expose the debtor to detrimental social and business consequences of his default, e.g. by refraining from informing his customers of the default[239]; or by refraining from takings steps through a trade organisation to compel payment through social sanctions[240];

(k)   the chance of winning a prize, in exchange for the payment of cash for the ticket[241];

(l)   the exchange of cash for a token which can be used for a later transaction with the party who issued the token, such as a shop issuing a voucher which can be used at its face value, or a casino issuing chips for gambling[242];

(m)   the agreement to undertake further work in return for the payment of outstanding invoices for work already done[243];

(n)   the agreement by a pupil barrister to enter into the close, important and potentially very productive relationship with chambers which pupillage involves, and which thereby provides a pool of selected candidates who can be expected to compete with each other for recruitment as tenants, even though the pupil undertakes no obligation to do any work for his or her pupil

---

235 *Pitts v Jones* [2007] EWCA Civ 1301, [2008] Q.B. 706; see para.8-16 fn.94.

236 See para.8-20.

237 *Brooks v Haigh* (1840) 10 Ad. & El. 323 at 334, 113 E.R. 124 at 128, Ex.Ch., affirming (1839) 10 Ad. & El. 309 at 319–320, 113 E.R. 119 at 123, QB. The majority of the Exchequer Chamber also held that the mere delivery up of the paper on which the guarantee was written was sufficient consideration without reference to its contents. For the broader context of contracts of compromise, including cases where the compromised claim was demonstrably invalid, see paras 8-30 to 8-31.

238 *Anangel Atlas Compania Naviera SA v Ishikawajima-Harima Heavy Industries Co Ltd (No.2)* [1990] 2 Lloyd's Rep. 526 at 545.

239 *Hyams v Stuart King* [1908] 2 K.B. 696, CA, at 708.

240 *Hill v William Hill (Park Lane) Ltd* [1949] A.C. 530, HL, at 560. *Hyams v Stuart King*, see para.8-34 fn.239, was overruled by *Hill*, although not on the point of whether there was sufficient consideration, but in holding that the new contract was still one for the payment of a sum of money alleged to be won on a wager, and therefore not recoverable under Gaming Act 1845 s.18 (now repealed: Gambling Act 2005 s.334(1)(c)). If one party was subjected to illegitimate pressure into agreeing the compromise this does not go to the question of whether there was consideration (which is determined objectively) but to whether the compromise is voidable for duress: *Huyton SA v Peter Cremer GmbH & Co.* [1999] 1 Lloyd's Rep. 620 at 629–630.

241 cf. *Lipkin Gorman v Karpnale Ltd* [1989] 1 W.L.R. 1340 at 1370–1371 (Parker LJ); rejected by Lord Goff on appeal at [1991] 2 A.C. 548, HL, at 575 on the basis that under Gaming Act 1845 s.18, the right to the prize was unenforceable and so nothing was given in return; but this aspect of the argument has now been superseded by the repeal of the 1845 Act so that gambling contracts are now in law enforceable: see para.8-33 fn.224; and see Lord Goff at 577.

242 *Lipkin Gorman v Karpnale Ltd* [1991] 2 A.C. 548, HL, at 576 (Lord Goff; the objection to this analysis in the case of gambling chips, on the basis that the gambling contract was unenforceable under Gaming Act 1845 s.18, has now been superseded by the repeal of the 1845 Act: see para.8-33 fn.224).

243 *Truex v Toll* [2009] EWHC 396 (Ch); [2009] 1 W.L.R. 2121 at [32].

master which is not conducive to his or her own professional development[244];

(o) refraining from drinking liquor, using tobacco, swearing and playing cards or billiards for money until the age of 21 in return for payment of $5,000 by his uncle on his 21st birthday[245];

(p) the promise by an ex-wife to "conduct herself with sobriety, and in a respectable, orderly and virtuous manner" in return for payments from her ex-husband: she was thereby agreeing to surrender her liberty to conduct herself as she thought fit[246];

(q) the promise by a mother to ensure that her illegitimate child would be well looked after and happy, in return for a maintenance payment from the child's father[247];

(r) a man's entering into marriage in return for an undertaking by his new wife's father to transfer property to him,[248] or in return for a promise by his uncle to make an annual payment to him even though at the time of his uncle's promise he was already engaged to the woman.[249]

8-35 **Examples of no sufficient consideration** There are, however, cases which fall the other side of the line and where the courts have been unwilling to find a sufficient benefit to the promisor and/or detriment to the promisee to find sufficient consideration. Examples are:

(a) the promise by a son not to complain about his father's distribution of his property where the son had no right to complain because the father was entitled to make whatever distribution of his property he liked[250];

---

[244] *Edmonds v Lawson* [2000] Q.B. 501, CA, at [25] (taking a view of the process of pupillage in the round, and the relationship between chambers and the pupil; if simply viewed on the particular relationship between the pupil and the pupil master it would be impossible to find consideration).

[245] *Hamer v Sidway*, see para.8-29 fn.188, NYCA.

[246] *Dunton v Dunton* (1892) 18 V.L.R. 114, SC Victoria, at 119.

[247] *Ward v Byham* [1956] 1 W.L.R. 496, CA, at 498–499 (Morris LJ, on the basis that by this promise the mother undertook more than her existing legal duty in relation to the child; cf. para.8-38).

[248] *Hammersley v De Biel* (1845) 12 Cl. & F. 45 at 79–79, 8 E.R. 1312 at 1327 (this being "the principle of law, at least of equity". In equity marriage consideration was sufficient to allow a party to enforce a covenant even if he or she was a volunteer: Jones and Goodhart, p.25; and marriage consideration is used in an extended definition of consideration by some statutes: see para.8-26 fn.161); *Maunsell v White* (1854) 4 H.L. Cas. 1039, 10 E.R. 769 distinguished *Hammersley* on the facts (there was no sufficient promise to make the alleged settlement) but not the principle: see Lord Cranworth LC at 1055–1056, at 775–776 and Lord St Leonards at 1059–1060, at 777.

[249] *Shadwell v Shadwell* (1860) 9 C.B. N.S. 159, 142 E.R. 62. "Marriage consideration" has long been accepted as a category of consideration in support of family arrangements for support of the new couple (see, e.g. *Maunsell v White* (1854) 4 H.L. Cas. 1039 at 1055–1056, 10 E.R. 769 at 775–776 (although there was there no promise)); but see the explanation of the benefit/detriment by Erle CJ at 173–174, at 68: "a man's marriage with the woman of his choice is in one sense a boon, and in that sense the reverse of a loss; yet, as between the plaintiff and the party promising to supply an income to support the marriage, it may well be also a loss. The plaintiff may have made a most material change in his position, and induced the object of his affection to do the same, and may have incurred pecuniary liabilities resulting in embarrassments which would be in every sense a loss if the income which had been promised should be withheld"; and "The marriage primarily affects the parties thereto; but in a secondary degree it may be an object of interest to a near relative, and in that sense a benefit to him".

[250] *White v Bluett* (1853) 23 L.J. Ex. 36; see Pollock C.B. at 37: "If such a plea as this could be supported, the following would be a binding promise: A man might complain that another person used the public highway more than he ought to do, and that other might say, do not complain, and I will

[278]

(b)   part payment of a debt at the time and place when it is due,[251] in return for the creditor's undertaking to cancel the balance of the debt[252] unless, perhaps,[253] the creditor receives a practical benefit from receiving the part payment (such as where he has need of the funds or where he thereby avoids the risk of receiving less in the event of the debtor's insolvency);

(c)   a cheque drawn by the debtor in payment of a debt, since a cheque is only conditional payment of the sum which it represents.[254] Therefore, a cheque drawn for less than the full value of a debt, even if accepted by the creditor as full satisfaction, cannot discharge the debt since part payment of a debt which is already due is not in itself sufficient consideration for a promise to discharge the balance.[255] However, a cheque *drawn by a third party* can be sufficient consideration,[256] as can a composition between creditors, by which each creditor mutually agrees with the others and with the debtor to forbear from enforcing part of the debt owed to him.[257]

(d)   an antecedent debt, except in the case of a bill of exchange[258];

(e)   refraining from a course of action which it was never intended to pursue[259];

(f)   a promise which is in law unenforceable[260];

(g)   a promise by a religious house to "perform certain services in the nature of prayers for the benefit of the other party and his family".[261]

---

give you five pounds. It is ridiculous to suppose that such promises could be binding. ... the son's abstaining from doing what he had no right to do can be no consideration".

[251] cf. para.8-34 fn.229.

[252] *Pinnel's Case*, see para.8-34 fn.229; *Foakes v Beer* (1884) 9 App. Cas. 605, HL; *Collier v P & MJ Wright (Holdings) Ltd* [2007] EWCA Civ 1329; [2008] 1 W.L.R. 643 at [3], [6], [28], [44]; see paras 9-18, 9-19.

[253] For the conflict of authorities on whether a "practical benefit" (cf. *Williams v Roffey Bros & Nicholls (Contractors) Ltd*, see para.8-34 fn.233) can be sufficient consideration in this context, see *MWB Business Exchange Centres Ltd v Rock Advertising Ltd* [2016] EWCA Civ 553; [2017] Q.B. 604 at [37]–[49], [69]–[87] (and, on appeal, [2018] UKSC 24; [2018] 2 W.L.R. 1603 at [18]), and the discussion at paras 9-22, 9-23.

[254] *D&C Builders Ltd v Rees* [1966] 2 Q.B. 617, CA, at 623, 629, 632–633.

[255] See para.8-35 fn.252.

[256] *Hirachand Punamchand v Temple* [1911] 2 K.B. 330, CA: see para.9-21.

[257] *Good v Cheesman* (1831) 2 B. & Ad. 328, 109 E.R. 1165; see para.9-21.

[258] See para.8-22.

[259] *Arrale v Costain Civil Engineering Ltd* [1976] 1 Lloyd's Rep. 98, CA, at 106 (Geoffrey Lane LJ); see para.8-29 fn.189.

[260] The cases in which this has been applied involved contracts of gaming which at the time were unenforceable under Gaming Act 1845 s.18, although the 1845 Act has now been repealed: Gambling Act 2005 s.334(1)(c). See, e.g. *Poteliakhoff v Teakle*, see para.8-33 fn.224, and cases at para.8-34 fnn.239 to 242.

[261] *O'Neill v Murphy* [1936] N.I.L.R. 16, NICA, at 31 (Andrews LJ: "whilst expressly disclaiming any opinion which might be construed as in the slightest degree derogatory of the real value and efficacy of prayer, I can only say that no case cited to us or which I have found, can properly be relied upon as an authority for the proposition that a mere promise by one person to say prayers or to cause prayers to be said for another amounts in law to a good and valuable consideration for a contract not under seal. If such be the law it should be laid down by the highest judicial tribunal—the House of Lords"; Best LJ decided the case on other grounds and did not find it necessary to decide whether there was consideration).

(5)   Promise, or Performance, of an Existing Duty

8-36   **Is the claimant's promise, or performance, of an existing duty detrimental to the claimant, and/or of benefit to the defendant?**   We have seen that the doctrine of consideration is based around the notion that a claimant can enforce the defendant's promise because he has promised, done or forborne to do something, at the defendant's request, which benefits the defendant and/or is detrimental to the claimant.[262] A particular difficulty can arise where what the claimant promises or does is something he already has a duty to do: it does not appear to be a detriment to undertake a duty which one already owes, since it costs no more to fulfil it. However, the promise or performance by the claimant of an existing duty may still constitute a benefit to the defendant, at least in a case where the defendant does not already himself have a right to receive the performance of the claimant's existing duty. Accordingly, the fact that a duty is already owed by the claimant not to the defendant but to a *third party* is not an obstacle to the claimant's providing good consideration by promising it, or performing it, in a new contract with the defendant.[263] There are, however, difficulties where the claimant's duty is a *duty owed by law*, whether a general public duty or a more particularised statutory duty actionable by the defendant, and therefore one to which the defendant is already more or less directly entitled.[264] Where, however, the claimant's duty is already *owed by contract directly to the defendant*, the clearest argument can be made that the claimant's performance or promise of it is of no benefit to the defendant since it gives the defendant no more than that which he is already entitled to receive from the claimant.[265]

8-37   **Pre-existing contractual duty owed to third party is normally sufficient**   It may seem that a claimant who already owes by contract a duty to a third party to act or forbear to act in a particular manner does not incur any detriment in undertaking that same act or forbearance as the price of a new promise given by the defendant, since the cost to the claimant of performing the duty is not increased. However, if the new agreement between the claimant and defendant forms an executory contract,[266] the claimant by undertaking in favour of the defendant to perform the duty he already owes to a third party does suffer detriment by exposing himself to liability not only to the third party but also to the defendant if he does not perform that duty. This argument does not apply if the agreement is a unilateral contract where the performance by the claimant of the duty owed to the third party constitutes the (executed) consideration.[267] However, whether the contract is executory or executed, where the existing duty is owed by the claimant only to a third party and not to the defendant,[268] the defendant obtains a benefit by receiving the promise from the claimant, or his performance, and the fact that a third party also

---

[262] See para.8-23.

[263] See para.8-37.

[264] See para.8-38.

[265] See para.8-39.

[266] See para.8-12.

[267] See para.8-13.

[268] cf. *Hadley v Kemp* [1999] 2 E.M.L.R. 589 at 626 (claimants, three members of the band Spandau Ballet, did not provide consideration for promises made by defendant, another member of the band who composed most of their songs, by their undertaking to play in the band and contribute to success of the compositions, because they were already bound to do so in contracts which, although on their face were with a third party (the company through which the band operated), created mutual

has a right to that same performance is irrelevant as between the parties to the new contract. Since it is sufficient to show a benefit to the defendant resulting from the promise, act or forbearance given by the claimant as consideration at his request,[269] the benefit resulting to the defendant from the promise, or performance, of the pre-existing contractual duty owed by the claimant to a third party is sufficient consideration for the defendant's new promise. This was settled in *Scotson v Pegg*,[270] where the defendant agreed to unload a cargo of coal from the claimant's ship, in consideration of the claimant delivering the cargo. This was held to be a good contract, and it was irrelevant that the claimant had already entered into a contract with third parties to deliver the same cargo of coal in the same ship to the same place where the defendant agreed to unload the cargo. Martin B. said[271]:

> "the ordinary rule is, that any act done whereby the contracting party receives a benefit is a good consideration for a promise by him. Here the benefit is the delivery of the coals to the defendant ... Then is it any answer that the plaintiffs had entered into a prior contract with other persons to deliver the coals to their order upon the same terms, and that the defendant was a stranger to that contract? In my opinion it is not. We must deal with this case as if no prior contract had been entered into. Suppose the plaintiffs had no chance of getting their money from the other persons who might perhaps have become bankrupt. The defendant gets a benefit by the delivery of the coals to him, and it is immaterial that the plaintiffs had previously contracted with third parties to deliver to their order."

Pre-existing public law duty, or other duty created by the general law, is not normally sufficient   8-38   Where the claimant is already under a statutory or other legal obligation to do what he undertakes to the defendant to do in return for the defendant's promise, the courts will generally not accept that his undertaking constitutes good consideration.

The fact that the pre-existing duty is created by the general law has led the courts to explain their reasoning in two different ways. First, the rejection of contractual liability may be put in terms of public policy: although the defendant may receive the benefit of the promise or performance of the claimant's duty in return for which

---

obligations on the principle of *Clarke v Earl of Dunraven (The Satanita)* [1897] A.C. 59, HL (see para.3-21 fn.109) and so the defendant was already entitled to their performance.
[269] See para.8-23.
[270] (1861) 6 H. & N. 295, 158 E.R. 121. This case was approved by the Privy Council in terms which make clear that the promise of performance, as well as actual performance, of the duty owed to the third party can constitute good consideration: *New Zealand Shipping Co Ltd v AM Satterthwaite & Co Ltd (The Eurymedon)* [1975] A.C. 154 at 168 (Lord Wilberforce: "An agreement to do an act which the promisor is under an existing obligation to a third party to do, may quite well amount to valid consideration and does so in the present case: the promisee obtains the benefit of a direct obligation which he can enforce. This proposition is illustrated and supported by *Scotson v Pegg* which their Lordships consider to be good law"); *Pao On v Lau Yiu Long* [1980] A.C. 614, PC, at 632 (Lord Scarman: "Their Lordships do not doubt that a promise to perform, or the performance of, a pre-existing contractual obligation to a third party can be valid consideration"). Although the issue was not discussed in these terms, it also arose in *Shadwell v Shadwell*, see para.8-34 fn.249, since the nephew's engagement to his future wife constituted a contractually binding obligation (engagements to marry ceased to have effect as contracts only by virtue of Law Reform (Miscellaneous Provisions) Act 1970 s.1).
[271] (1861) 6 H. & N. 295, 158 E.R. 121 at 299-300, at 123. See also Wilde B. at 300–301, at 123 ("I accede to the proposition that if a person contracts with another to do a certain thing, he cannot make the performance of it a consideration for a new promise to the same individual. [See para.8-39.] But there is no authority for the proposition that where there has been a promise to one person to do a certain thing, it is not possible to make a valid promise to another to do the same thing").

he has made his own promise, nevertheless, at least where the duty is a public duty, it is contrary to public policy to allow the person to enter into a contract to make a profit from the performance of his duty beyond the payments which are allowed by law for its performance,[272] such as in the case of a police officer acting within his duty,[273] a sheriff executing a writ,[274] or a witness attending court.[275] Secondly, however, the rejection of contractual liability where the claimant alleges that he provided consideration by promising or performing a duty which already lay upon him by the general law may be put in the more general terms of absence of consideration: the promise or performance of a service which is required by law to be performed in favour of the defendant neither provides benefit to the defendant nor constitutes detriment to the claimant.[276]

Although it appears to be the older cases that focused on the public policy ground of rejection of the promise or performance of an existing legal duty as giving rise to a valid contract, this ground should not be forgotten. There has been some sign in the recent cases that the courts are reluctant to apply so strictly the rule that the promise or performance of an existing duty owed by the claimant cannot constitute good consideration, at least in a case where the promise or performance does in fact

---

[272] On the same principle, a payment of money to a public officer to obtain performance of a duty which he was required to provide without payment, is recoverable: *Morgan v Palmer* (1842) 2 B. & C. 729, 107 E.R. 554; Goff & Jones, paras 10-41 to 10-53 (discussing the line of cases where restitution is ordered of money paid following a demand made "*colore officii*").

[273] cf. *England v Davidson* (1840) 11 Ad. & El. 856; 113 E.R. 640 (police constable was entitled to claim reward by providing information leading to conviction of a felon; unless the services are clearly within the constable's duties the court "should not hold a contract to be against the policy of the law": Lord Denman CJ at 858, at 641); *Glasbrook Bros Ltd v Glamorgan CC* [1925] A.C. 270, HL, at 290 (Lord Shaw: "no charge can be exacted from a private citizen for the enforcement of a public duty ... it is against public policy that the performance of public duty shall be a matter of private purchase"; see also Viscount Cave LC at 281 and Viscount Finlay at 287).

[274] *Bilke v Havelock* (1813) 3 Camp. 374; 150 E.R. 1415 (claim for *implied* contract under which sheriff could be paid reasonable compensation in relation to executing writ failed. Lord Ellenborough said at 375, at 1416: "The law knows of no promise to pay the sheriff for executing the King's writ. Such an action as this never was heard of in Westminster Hall. It is the duty of the sheriff under a writ of fieri facias to seize the goods in his bailiwick belonging to the defendant. ... The office of sheriff would become a very lucrative one, if he could maintain an action for every ineffectual attempt by his officers to execute a writ"); *Wathen v Sandys* (1811) 2 Camp. 640; 170 E.R. 1279 (sheriff not entitled to charge candidates in election for charges incurred in execution of his office of sheriff).

[275] *Collins v Godefroy* (1831) 1 B. & Ad. 950, 109 E.R. 1040 (claim by attorney, subpoenaed as witness, for six guineas as compensation for loss of time failed on the basis that Perjury Act 1562 imposed the requirement to testify if subpoenaed and made limited provision for the witness's costs and charges to be covered: "on consideration of the Statute of Elizabeth [Perjury Act 1562], and of the cases which have been decided on this subject, we are all of opinion that a party cannot maintain an action for compensation for loss of time in attending a trial as a witness": Lord Tenterden CJ at 957, at 1042; but there was no acceptance of the alleged promise of payment anyway); cf. *Goulden v Wilson Barca* [2000] 1 W.L.R. 167, CA (Legal Aid in Criminal and Care Proceedings (General) Regulations 1989 (SI 1989/344) did not preclude solicitor representing a defendant in criminal proceedings under a legal aid order from entering into contract with proposed expert witness to pay personally his fees for attendance at court).

[276] *Collins v Godefroy*, see para.8-38 fn.275, at 956–957, at 1042 (Lord Tenterden CJ: "If it be a duty imposed by law upon a party regularly subpoenaed, to attend from time to time to give his evidence, then a promise to give him any remuneration for loss of time incurred in such attendance is a promise without consideration"); *Glasbrook Bros Ltd v Glamorgan CC*, see para.8-38 fn.273, at 300 (Lord Carson, dissenting; the majority found that the services provided went beyond those within the scope of the public duty and therefore there was consideration: see Viscount Cave at 285); *Thoresen Car Ferries Ltd v Weymouth Portland BC* [1977] 2 Lloyd's Rep. 614 at 619 (promise to pay council's charges for berthing vessel could not be consideration because there was a statutory obligation to pay the charges if the berth were used).

confer a benefit on the defendant. We shall see this in particular in the case of a pre-existing *contractual* duty,[277] but the developments there have also drawn on cases involving pre-existing general legal duties, such as the case of *Ward v Byham*[278] in which the promise by a mother to look after her illegitimate child was held to be good consideration for the promise by the child's father to make a weekly maintenance payment for the child's upkeep, even though at that time it was the mother (and not the father) who had the duty imposed by statute[279] to maintain the illegitimate child. Denning LJ said[280]:

"I approach the case ... on the footing that the mother, in looking after the child, is only doing what she is legally bound to do. Even so, I think that there was sufficient consideration to support the promise. I have always thought that a promise to perform an existing duty, or the performance of it, should be regarded as good consideration, because it is a benefit to the person to whom it is given. Take this very case. It is as much a benefit for the father to have the child looked after by the mother as by a neighbour. If he gets the benefit for which he stipulated, he ought to honour his promise; and he ought not to avoid it by saying that the mother was herself under a duty to maintain the child."

In so far as this appears to say that the mere promise or performance of the claimant's existing duty is a benefit to the defendant, it has not been accepted and, indeed, it would undermine the general rule requiring consideration in such cases[281]; but the idea contained in Denning LJ's statement that the performance of the existing duty would on the facts provide a benefit to the defendant has formed the basis of the idea that a "practical benefit" can be sufficient consideration. If the courts develop further this more relaxed approach to finding consideration in the promise or performance of an existing duty,[282] more reliance must be placed on the public policy arguments to determine which agreements, involving one party's promise to fulfil a duty imposed on him by the general law, should be allowed to have contractual force.[283]

However, if the claimant agrees to go beyond the performance of his legal duties, there is no obstacle to finding that by promising or providing the additional services he provides consideration for the defendant's promise, just as in any case in which a party promises or performs services to which the other party is not already entitled.[284]

---

[277] See para.8-39.

[278] [1956] 1 W.L.R. 496, CA.

[279] National Assistance Act 1948 s.42.

[280] [1956] 1 W.L.R. 496, at 498. See also Denning LJ's statement in *Williams v Williams* [1957] 1 W.L.R. 148, CA, at 151, quoted at para.8-38 fn.283.

[281] *North Ocean Shipping Co Ltd v Hyundai Construction Co Ltd* [1979] 1 Q.B. 705 at 713; *Williams v Roffey Bros & Nicholls (Contractors) Ltd* [1991] 1 Q.B. 1 at 11–13 (Glidewell LJ) and 20 (Purchas LJ).

[282] For the controversial development of the acceptance of "practical benefit" in *Williams v Roffey Bros & Nicholls (Contractors) Ltd* [1991] 1 Q.B. 1, see para.8-39 and generally paras 9-13 to 9-16.

[283] See also *Williams v Williams* [1957] 1 W.L.R. 148, CA, at 151 (Denning LJ: "a promise to perform an existing duty is, I think, sufficient consideration to support a promise, *so long as there is nothing in the transaction which is contrary to the public interest*" (emphasis added)).

[284] *England v Davidson*, see para.8-38 fn.273, at 858, at 641 (Lord Denman CJ: "there may be services which the constable is not bound to render, and which he may therefore make the ground of a contract"); *Wathen v Sandys*, see para.8-38 fn.274 (sheriff may charge for costs incurred at election candidates' request outside his duties as sheriff, such as erecting hustings and providing assessor and poll-clerks); *Glasbrook Bros Ltd v Glamorgan CC*, see para.8-38 fn.273 (police authority provided

8-39   **Pre-existing contractual duty owed to the other party is not normally sufficient**   The general rule is that[285]

> "If one person (A) makes a promise to another (B), and in return the other (B) promises that he will do something which he is already bound to A to do, B cannot rely on his own promise as the consideration which makes A's promise contractually binding."

The key point here is that B (the claimant) is already "bound to A" (the defendant) to do the thing which he promises to do; so the claimant's promising again the very same thing does not provide any benefit to the defendant. The clearest case[286] of such a direct and enforceable duty already owed by the claimant to the defendant is where they already have a contract containing the term which the claimant purports to re-use as consideration for the new contract. Moreover, the context in which such an issue can most easily arise is where there is an alleged variation of the initial contract involving the variation of only one party's obligations—such as the promise to increase the payment due under a contract for services where a party who has contracted to provide the services agrees in return only to continue to provide those same services. It has long been established that in such a case the promise to fulfil the existing contractual duty to provide the services cannot alone be consideration for the promise of the increased payment, since the claimant promises to do nothing beyond that which he has already undertaken.[287] However, more recently in *Williams v Roffey Bros & Nicholls (Contractors) Ltd*[288] the Court of Appeal was willing to consider whether, although the defendant receives in return for his promise of increased payment only a promise of the performance of services to which he is already in law entitled, the claimant's promise (or its performance) might in fact allow him to obtain some collateral advantage which can be recognised as sufficient consideration.[289] In this, the Court built on earlier cases such

---

protection services for a colliery during miners' strike, at request of colliery manager, which went beyond the scope of their public police protection duty); *Williams v Williams*, see para.8-38 fn.283 (husband's duty to maintain wife was suspended during period of wife's desertion and so for that period there could be a valid contract under which wife agreed to maintain herself in return for weekly payment from husband). In *Ward v Byham*, see para.8-38 fn.278, Denning LJ thought that the mother was only doing what she was legally bound to do, but Morris LJ at 498-499 interpreted the mother's promise (to "prove that [the child] will be well looked after and happy and also that she is allowed to decide for herself whether or not she wishes to come and live with [the mother]") went beyond the mother's statutory duty of maintenance of the child and so there was "ample consideration".

[285] *Hadley v Kemp*, see para.8-37 fn.268, at 625–626 (Park J).

[286] There is a close link, however, to cases where the duty is non-contractual, but is a particularised duty imposed by statute and capable of being employed by the defendant against the claimant: cf. *Williams v Williams*, see para.8-38 fn.283 (husband's duty to maintain his wife); *Ward v Byham*, see para.8-38 fn.278 (mother's duty to maintain illegitimate child).

[287] *Stilk v Myrick* (1809) 2 Camp. 317 at 319–20, 170 E.R. 1168 at 1169. For arguments about the basis of this decision in not only the doctrine of consideration but also public policy, see para.9-11.

[288] [1991] 1 Q.B. 1, CA.

[289] [1991] 1 Q.B. 1, CA at 16 (Glidewell LJ consideration where (inter alia) "as a result of giving his promise, [the party promising the additional payment] obtains in practice a benefit, or obviates a disbenefit"), at 19 (Russell LJ: "where ... a party undertakes to make a payment because by so doing it will gain an advantage arising out of the continuing relationship with the promisee the new bargain will not fail for want of consideration"), and at 21 (Purchas LJ: "the court is more ready in the presence of [the defence of economic duress] being available in the commercial context to look for mutual advantages which would amount to sufficient consideration to support the second agreement under which the extra money is paid").

as *Ward v Byham*[290] to develop an apparently more relaxed approach to finding consideration, under which it is sufficient if the defendant receives a "practical benefit" in return for his promise. *Williams v Roffey Bros & Nicholls (Contractors) Ltd* is still a controversial decision, but since it arose in the context of the variation of an existing contract, detailed discussion of the case, and of the general question of whether "practical benefit" to the defendant should be accepted as sufficient consideration, is deferred to Chapter 9.[291]

However, if the claimant by his promise or performance goes beyond his contractual obligations, there is no difficulty in finding consideration: he subjects himself to a detriment over and above his contractual duty, and he provides a benefit to the defendant additional to that to which he is already entitled.[292]

IV. CRITICISM OF THE DOCTRINE OF CONSIDERATION; PRACTICAL DIFFICULTIES AND SOLUTIONS

Academic and judicial criticism of the doctrine of consideration Within the law of contract, consideration is probably the most criticised doctrine. Amongst English academics and judges the doctrine of privity held that place until it was finally reformed by the Contracts (Rights of Third Parties) Act 1999.[293] The two doctrines—consideration and privity—are historically linked,[294] and the criticism of them has often taken a similar line: that the law fails to give effect to the intentions of the parties. In the case of privity, it was the fact that even if the parties by the terms of their validly-formed contract wished expressly to confer a directly enforceable benefit on a third party, they could not do so[295]; in the case of consideration it is that a person who makes a promise in circumstances in which he intends and reasonably expects it to be binding, in favour of another party who accepts the promise and reasonably believes it to be binding, cannot be bound to keep his promise if the promisee did not provide consideration for it. The Law Revision Committee in 1937 considered both doctrines and recommended radical reform of both[296]; although privity has now alone been reformed, this was because the Law Commission in the 1990s took the view that the doctrines were sufficiently distinct that the one could be reformed without the other.[297]

The Law Revision Committee had very strong objections to the doctrine of

8-40

---

[290] See para.8-38 fn.278; also *Williams v Williams*, see para.8-38 fn.283.

[291] See paras 9-14 to 9-16.

[292] e.g. *Pinnel's Case*, see para.8-34 fn.229 (paying part of a debt earlier than the date on which it falls due; similarly, it could be a benefit to the defendant to pay him on the due day, but at a place he may request different than that required by the contract); *Hartley v Ponsonby* (1857) 7 El. & Bl. 872, 119 E.R. 1471 (sailors no longer bound by their contracts to proceed with voyage on account of desertion by others, so promise to do so was good consideration for master's promise of additional payment); *Dunton v Dunton*, see para.8-34 fn.246 (wife's conjugal obligation to husband to conduct herself properly was released by the decree of divorce and so she could promise good conduct as good consideration in return for post-divorce maintenance payments).

[293] Implementing Law Com. No.242, *Privity of Contract: Contracts for the Benefit of Third Parties* (1996, Cm.3329).

[294] See para.8-19.

[295] *Tweddle v Atkinson* (1861) 1 B. & S. 393, 121 E.R. 762.

[296] Law Revision Committee, Sixth Interim Report, *Statute of Frauds and the Doctrine of Consideration*, Cmd.5449 (1937).

[297] Law Com. No.242, see para.8-40 fn.293, Pt VI; cf. para.6.17: "The recognition of [exceptions to the need for consideration], allied to academic criticisms of the requirement of consideration (in its classic sense of there needing to be a requested counter-performance or counter-promise), suggests that the doctrine of consideration may be a suitable topic for a future separate review by the Law

consideration[298]:

> "in very many cases the doctrine of consideration is a mere technicality, which is irreconcilable either with business expediency or common sense, and ... it frequently affords a man a loophole for escape from a promise which he had deliberately given with intent to create a binding obligation and in reliance on which the promisee may have acted."

The Committee did not go so far as to recommend its abolition, but made a series of recommendations designed to "prune away from the doctrine those aspects of it which can create hardship or cause unnecessary inconvenience."[299] We shall see one of their recommendations in Chapter 9, designed to deal with a difficulty caused by the doctrine of consideration in relation to the variation of a contract.[300] The others included two new general rules by way of alternatives to the doctrine of consideration: first, that an agreement should be enforceable if the promise or offer has been made in writing by the promisor or his agent and was intended to create a binding obligation,[301] and secondly that a promise which the promisor knows, or reasonably should know, will be relied on by the promisee should be enforceable if the promisee has altered his position to his detriment in reliance on the promise[302]; as well as more particular rules such as making firm offers binding without consideration,[303] and allowing the performance (or promise of performance) of an existing duty owed by law, or by a contract with the other party or a third party, to be deemed to be valuable consideration.[304]

There have been other critics of the doctrine of consideration, including a remarkable judicial exposition of the defects of the doctrine from the Court of Appeal in Singapore,[305] but also academic critics as well as supporters.[306] However, although we should note that there is still potential for a further systematic review of the

---

Commission. But for the present we see no practical difficulty in taking the limited step in this paper of recommending what may be regarded as a relaxation of the requirement of consideration to the limited extent necessary to give third parties rights to enforce valid contracts in accordance with the contracting parties' intentions".

[298] See para.8-40 fn.296, para.25.

[299] See para.8-40 fn.296, para.27.

[300] The rule in *Pinnel's Case*: see para.9-23.

[301] See para.8-40 fn.296, paras 29, 30, thus resurrecting the view of Lord Mansfield in *Pillans v Van Mierop* (1765) 3 Burr. 1663, 97 E.R. 1035; see para.8-02 fn.11.

[302] See para.8-40 fn.296, para.40, thus allowing what we now know as promissory estoppel to be relied on as a "sword": see para.10-38. The recommendations of the Law Reform Committee pre-dated the decision in *Central London Property Trust Ltd v High Trees House Ltd* [1947] K.B. 130, see para.10-16, and *Combe v Combe* [1951] 2 K.B. 215, CA, see para.10-39.

[303] See para.8-40 fn.296, para.38.

[304] See para.8-40 fn.296, para.36; cf. paras 8-36 to 8-39.

[305] *Gay Choon Ing v Loh Sze Ti Terence Peter* [2009] SGCA 3; [2009] 2 S.L.R.(R.) 332 at [92]–[118]. This is remarkable not only for its substance (considering the potential use of doctrines such as promissory estoppel, economic duress, undue influence and unconscionability in filling the gap that would be left by abolishing the doctrine of consideration), but also because it was a "coda on the doctrine of consideration" appended to the judgment of the court which had decided the case within the orthodox doctrine; and so it was avowedly obiter, more in the nature of an essay on need for reform and the possible forms which reform might take. The judgment of the court was delivered by Andrew Phang Boon Leong JA, who had also been a critic of the doctrine of consideration sitting in the High Court in *Sunny Metal & Engineering Pte Ltd v Ng Khim Ming Eric* [2006] SGHC 222; [2007] 1 S.L.R.(R.) 853 at [28]–[30] (again obiter). However, no formal change has been made to the law in Singapore, where consideration remains a standard requirement for the formation of a valid contract: *Gay Choon Ing v Loh Sze Ti Terence Peter* at [64]; *Brader Daniel John v Commerzbank AG* [2013] SGHC 284; [2014] 2 S.L.R. 81 at [69].

doctrine of consideration with a view to possible reform,[306] this is not the place to discuss it in detail. Rather, our focus should be the practical difficulties which flow from the doctrine in its current state, and the solutions that parties should seek to adopt in order to mitigate or avoid those difficulties.

Practical difficulties: uncertainty over the scope of consideration   The first   **8-41**
practical difficulty which arises from the doctrine of consideration is the uncertainty of the scope of its application. The core of the doctrine—the bilateral exchange of promises or performance—is straightforward: where there is a bargain between the parties, there is little difficulty in finding consideration provided by both parties.[308] The problem comes because in some cases the courts have extended the doctrine of consideration to allow a promise to be binding, but in other cases they have refused to take such a generously expansive view, therefore leaving uncertainty about how rigid or flexible the doctrine is in more difficult cases. We shall see a particularly good example of this problem in Chapter 9, where the courts at present take inconsistent views about whether the doctrine should be relaxed to allow the promise or performance of an existing contractual duty already owed to the other party to count as good consideration in the variation of a contract.[309] But difficulties are not limited to agreements to vary existing contracts, and there are cases where the courts have been willing to look hard in order to discover consideration even when there appears not to be any real basis for it under the orthodox doctrine.[310] In the context of finding the parties' agreement we saw that English law seeks to apply rules but sometimes their application can be very artificial: Lord Wilberforce, making this point, included a reference to the artificiality of the doctrine of consideration[311]:

"It is only the precise analysis of this complex of relations into the classical offer and ac-

---

306 See, e.g. the debate between P.S. Atiyah, "Consideration: a Restatement" reprinted in P.S. Atiyah, *Essays on Contract* (Clarendon Press, 1986) and G.H. Treitel, "Consideration: A Critical Analysis of Professor Atiyah's Fundamental Restatement" (1976) 50 A.L.J. 439; against: Lord Wright, "Ought the Doctrine of Consideration to be Abolished from the Common Law?" (1936) 49 Harv. L.R. 1225; in favour: C.J. Hamson, "The Reform of Consideration" (1938) 54 L.Q.R. 233; K.O. Shatwell, "The Doctrine of Consideration in the Modern Law" (1954) 1 Sydney L.Rev. 289; M. Chen-Wishart, "In Defence of Consideration" (2013) 13 O.U.C.L.J. 209.

307 Law Com. No.242, see para.8-40 fn.293, para.6.17, quoted at para.8-40 fn.297. Reform would have to be by legislation or by the Supreme Court, but the Supreme Court is reluctant to depart from its own well-established decisions, or even substantially to modify their effects, without a considered hearing before an enlarged panel (i.e. more than the regular panel of five Justices) in a case where the decision would be more than obiter dictum: cf. *MWB Business Exchange Centres Ltd v Rock Advertising Ltd* [2018] UKSC 24; [2018] 2 W.L.R. 1603 at [18] (Lord Sumption, declining to give guidance on the "difficult issue" of whether the decision in *Williams v Roffey Bros & Nicholls (Contractors) Ltd* [1991] 1 Q.B. 1, CA, and *Foakes v Beer* (1884) 9 App. Cas. 605, HL can stand together; cf. paras 9-17 to 9-23).

308 See paras 8-08, 8-12, 8-15.

309 See para.9-23, contrasting the relaxed view taken by the Court of Appeal in *Williams v Roffey Bros & Nicholls (Contractors) Ltd*, see para.8-40 fn.307, and *MWB Business Exchange Centres Ltd v Rock Advertising Ltd* [2016] EWCA Civ 553; [2017] Q.B. 604 with the narrower view taken in *Re Selectmove Ltd* [1995] 1 W.L.R. 474 and *Collier v P & MJ Wright (Holdings) Ltd* [2007] EWCA Civ 1329; [2008] 1 W.L.R. 643 under the authority of *Foakes v Beer* (1884) 9 App. Cas. 605, HL—uncertainty which has not been resolved by the Supreme Court in *MWB Business Exchange Centres Ltd v Rock Advertising Ltd*, see para.8-40 fn.307; see also paras 8-36 to 8-39.

310 See para.8-28.

311 *New Zealand Shipping Co Ltd v AM Satterthwaite & Co Ltd (The Eurymedon)* [1975] A.C. 154, PC, at 167, quoted also at para.3-20.

ceptance, with identifiable consideration, that seems to present difficulty, but this same difficulty exists in many situations of daily life, e.g., sales at auction; supermarket purchases; boarding an omnibus; purchasing a train ticket; tenders for the supply of goods; offers of rewards; acceptance by post; warranties of authority by agents; manufacturers' guarantees; gratuitous bailments; bankers' commercial credits. These are all examples which show that English law, having committed itself to a rather technical and schematic doctrine of contract, in application takes a practical approach, often at the cost of forcing the facts to fit uneasily into the marked slots of offer, acceptance and consideration."

The list given here by Lord Wilberforce includes cases where the difficulty is in finding the consideration. Sometimes it can be done—such as in the case of manufacturers' guarantees, where the courts can find that the guarantee is a contract with the purchaser, collateral to the contract of sale with the retailer, and that the consideration provided by the purchaser to the manufacturer is his entering into the contract of sale with the retailer.[312] Others are more difficult—the gratuitous bailment, where the bailee's duties to look after and restore the bailed chattel are duties imposed by law, although the courts have found some additional benefit and detriment in order to fit cases of bailment into the orthodox rules of consideration[313]; and bankers' irrevocable letters of credit, for which no satisfactory explanation can be found for the irrevocable nature of the bank's promise of credit even before the shipping documents are tendered, and which therefore seems to be a commercially expedient exception to the doctrine of consideration, given the international commercial significance of such obligations.[314]

8-42 **Failure of the law to reflect the parties' intentions and reasonable expectations?** One of the common criticisms of the doctrine of consideration, which reflects an underlying practical difficulty, is the fact that it does not adequately reflect the parties' intentions, and the promisee's reasonable expectations that the promise will be kept.[315] We have seen that the English law of contract seeks to give effect to the parties' (objective) agreement and intention to be bound, but that this is not the basis of a contractual obligation.[316] Systems outside the common law may focus their notion of contract on the parties' intentions,[317] but in the common law the doctrine of consideration adds an additional dimension: that the claimant's entitlement to enforce the defendant's promise depends on his having done something, in return for the promise, to earn the right to sue.[318] In a sense, then, it is unreasonable to criticise the doctrine of consideration for failing to give effect *simply* to the parties' intentions even where the promisee has not been asked to do anything in return for the promise he seeks to enforce, since that would be to change

[312] *Shanklin Pier Ltd v Detel Products Ltd* [1951] 2 K.B. 854; *Wells (Merstham) Ltd v Buckland Sand and Silica Ltd* [1965] 2 Q.B. 170; see also *Andrews v Hopkinson* [1957] 1 Q.B. 229 (contract with car dealer collateral to main contract with hire-purchase company).
[313] *Bainbridge v Firmstone* (1838) 8 Ad. & El. 743 at 744; 112 E.R. 1019 at 1020.
[314] For further analysis, see Treitel, para.3-159; Chitty, para.4-203; Anson, pp.120-122; Cheshire, Fifoot and Furmston, pp.80-81; M. Bridge (ed.), *Benjamin's Sale of Goods*, 10th edn (Sweet & Maxwell, 2017), para.23-073 (the letter of credit is an irrevocable unilateral offer, binding without acceptance or consideration; "This of course is incompatible with the principles of orthodox contract law, but documentary credits constitute a sui generis exception to such principles, based on internationally recognised mercantile usage").
[315] See, e.g. the criticisms of the Law Revision Committee, see para.8-40 fn.296, para.25.
[316] See paras 3-01, 3-04, 3-09.
[317] See para.8-04.
[318] See para.8-08.

fundamentally the legal basis of the promissory obligation. However, there is clearly a tension here, since the lawyers' bargain theory of contract may not match the expectations of lay persons who make promises and reasonably expect them to be binding. A good example is the problem of the firm offer, which is not in itself binding even if both the offeror and offeree intended it to be[319]: this can cause real difficulties for the parties negotiating a contract if one party needs to be able to take an offer, expressed to be open for a fixed period of time, as being irrevocable during that period and therefore capable of being safely acted on. Lord Wright put the criticism very strongly[320]:

> "most people naturally think of the firm option as really firm: there is expressly or by implication a promise to keep it open; not to do so would in ordinary understanding be a breach of faith, and the actual loss to the other party from the breach may be serious. Yet according to the common law, the absence of consideration prevents the offeree from having any claim; the offeror may snap his fingers at a serious bargain deliberately made. This, when stated to the man in the street, is likely to appear shocking. But such is the doctrine of consideration."

It should, however, be remembered that the courts are reluctant to find that there is no consideration in case where parties did in fact intend their agreement to be binding.[321] We have seen examples of the courts regarding consideration as an equivalent of a formality,[322] and loosening the application of the rules in order to find consideration in order to give effect to the intentions of the parties.[323] But as English law stands, evidence of the promisor's intention to be bound to his promise, and of the promisee's belief that the promise was seriously meant and will be binding, are not sufficient substitutes for the provision of consideration by the promisee at the promisor's request. The courts may sometimes be able to assist in finding consideration where the parties clearly intended the agreement to be binding, but the intention alone is insufficient in principle.

Well-advised parties can avoid the problems   The difficulties identified in the preceding paragraphs can be avoided by parties who are well advised. The principal problems stem from the lack of certainty over how far the courts will be prepared to go to find consideration in cases where it is not obviously a bargainembodying an exchange; and how far they will be able to do so in order to try to give effect to the parties' evidenced intention that their agreement will be binding. If the parties appreciate that these are the risks, then they can draft their contract in order to avoid them. In the case of an informal contract, the problems can be avoided by ensuring that it is clearly evidenced that there is consideration, within the orthodox doctrine, in return for the promise which might otherwise appear to be gratuitous—

8-43

---

[319] See paras 2-20, 3-30.
[320] Lord Wright, "Ought the Doctrine of Consideration to be Abolished from the Common Law?", see para.8-40 fn.306, at 1232–1233. Lord Wright chaired the Law Reform Committee which in 1937 proposed reform of consideration on a number of points, including making firm offers binding: see para.8-40 fn.303.
[321] See para.8-28.
[322] *Vantage Navigation Corp v Suhail and Saud Bahwan Building Materials LLC (The Alev)* [1989] 1 Lloyd's Rep. 138 at 147 (Hobhouse J, quoted at para.8-27).
[323] *Williams v Roffey Bros & Nicholls (Contractors) Ltd* [1991] 1 Q.B. 1, CA, at 18 (Russell LJ, quoted see para.8-28 fn.183). See also *Antons Trawling Co Ltd v Smith* [2003] 2 N.Z.L.R. 23, NZCA, at [93] (Baragwanath J: "The importance of consideration is as a valuable signal that the parties intend to be bound by their agreement, rather than an end in itself").

and even nominal consideration is sufficient for this purpose.[324] More secure still is the use of a deed to embody the agreement, since the deed will provide clear evidence of the promise, and no consideration need be provided because the deed is sufficient in itself to give binding force.[325] Where there is any risk of a transaction being held unenforceable for lack of consideration, therefore, it is advisable— and, indeed, common practice in commercial contracts—to execute it as a deed.

---

[324] See para.8-25.
[325] See para.7-18, although a gratuitous promise in a deed might not be specifically enforced: ibid. However, a deed has other advantages, including the longer limitation period: see para.7-19.

CHAPTER 9

CONSIDERATION IN THE VARIATION AND DISCHARGE OF A CONTRACT[1]

I.   VARIATION AND DISCHARGE OF A CONTRACT CONTRASTED WITH FORMATION

The formation rules apply also for variation (including novation) and for discharge by agreement   In this chapter we consider the case where the parties seek to vary or to discharge an existing contract. We have seen in the earlier chapters of this book that the creation of a contract requires the parties' agreement,[2] together with (if the agreement is not formalised in a deed[3]) consideration provided by each party in order to enforce the other's undertakings contained in that agreement.[4] In general terms, we can say that the variation or discharge of a contract, where it follows from the parties' agreement,[5] must comply with the same rules as those set for the formation of the contract: and therefore consideration must be provided by the party who wishes to enforce an agreement to vary or discharge their existing contract.[6] However, we shall see that something less than a contractual variation or

9-01

---

[1]   Chitty, paras 4-066 to 4-081, 4-117 to 4-129, 22-012 to 22-039; Furmston, paras 2.71 to 2.98; Treitel, paras 3-047 to 3-065, 3-100 to 3-110; Anson, pp.113–120; Cheshire, Fifoot and Furmston, pp.124–132; 142–147; Wilken and Ghaly, Ch.2; Sir G. Treitel, *Some Landmarks of Twentieth Century Contract Law* (Clarendon Press, 2002), pp.11–46; Burrows (Restatement) ss.8(5), (6), 12(1); Andrews, arts 122, 123.

[2]   See Ch.3.

[3]   See Ch.7, esp. para.7-18.

[4]   See Ch.8.

[5]   A contract may also be discharged without the parties' agreement: e.g. where it is terminated automatically by the occurrence of an event which frustrates the contract (Chitty, Ch.23; Treitel, Ch.19; Anson, Ch.14; Cheshire, Fifoot and Furmston, Ch.20), or where one party accepts a breach committed by the other which gives him the right to terminate (Chitty, Ch.24; Treitel, Ch.18; Anson, Ch.15; Cheshire, Fifoot and Furmston, pp.668–687). Such situations do not concern us here.

[6]   For certain limited categories of contract there are also additional requirements of formality either as a substantive condition for the creation of the contract: see Ch.5; or as evidence as a condition of its enforceability: see Ch.6. Where the formation of the contract required some additional formality, the *variation* of the contract must normally comply with the same formality requirement: see, e.g. see paras 5-40, (substantive formality); 6-20 (evidential formality), although a contract which the parties entered into by deed may be varied by an informal contract: see para.7-22. A contract to *rescind* or *discharge* a contract which was subject to the Statute of Frauds in its formation need not comply with the Statute where the agreement does not at the same time create new obligations within the scope of the Statute: *Morris v Baron & Co* [1918] A.C. 1, HL, applied to s.2 LP(MP)A 1989 by *Kilcarne Holdings Ltd v Targetfollow (Birmingham) Ltd* [2004] EWHC 2547 (Ch); [2005] 2 P. &

discharge of the contract can sometimes be given force by the law though doctrines such as waiver and estoppel.

(1)   The Nature of a Contractual Variation

9-02   **Variation as a contract superimposed on an existing contract**   The variation of a contract, as discussed in this chapter, is the contractual modification of one or more of the terms of an existing contract. The variation may be designed to favour only one of the parties (such as the increase or decrease of the price payable in a contract for the sale of goods or for the performance of services, without any corresponding increase or decrease of the seller's or supplier's obligations) or it may be a mutual variation in which both parties' obligations are varied (such as an increase in both the price to be paid and the goods to be sold or the services to be supplied). The variation may modify a party's primary obligations under the contract,[7] but may also cover other contractual terms, such as a choice of law clause[8] or any other clause which excludes or modifies the parties' primary obligations or otherwise regulates their contractual relationship. A contract creates legally enforceable obligations, whether those obligations are expressly defined by the parties or are implied; and each obligation imposes a duty on one party, with the correlative right in the other party. If those duties and rights are to be modified irrevocably by the agreement of the parties, that new agreement must itself have a sufficient force in law to override the contractually binding nature of the existing obligations. In principle, at common law this requires a new contract, superimposed on the existing contract.[9]

9-03   **The effect of the variation depends on the terms of the parties' new agreement**   The variation of a contract depends on what the parties agree in the terms of their variation. Given that the parties are in general[10] free to determine for themselves what primary obligations they will accept and any exclusion or modification of their obligations,[11] the parties are as free in agreeing a varied set of

---

C.R. 8; nor need a (non-contractual) forbearance or waiver of rights under a contract which was subject to the Statute of Frauds comply with the Statute: *Morris v Baron & Co* at 30–31; *Besseler Waechter Glover & Co v South Derwent Coal Co Ltd* [1938] 1 K.B. 408 at 416; see para.10-12 fn.70.

The parties may limit their own freedom to vary the contract by imposing requirements of form for a variation: *MWB Business Exchange Centres Ltd v Rock Advertising Ltd* [2018] UKSC 24; [2018] 2 W.L.R. 1603; see para.5-41.

[7]   For the language of "primary" obligations in this sense, see *Photo Production Ltd v Securicor Transport Ltd* [1980] A.C. 827, HL, at 848 (Lord Diplock).

[8]   *Mauritius Commercial Bank Ltd v Hestia Holdings Ltd* [2013] EWHC 1328 (Comm); [2013] 2 All E.R. (Comm) 898.

[9]   cf. *White v Blackmore* [1972] 2 Q.B. 651, CA, at 667 (Lord Denning MR: liability arising by contract can be excluded only by a contractually binding term). For the doctrines of waiver and estoppel by which the contractual obligations may be suspended or otherwise modified, see para.9-06. For the restricted circumstances in which the court may vary the terms of the parties' agreement scheduled to a Tomlin order, see *Community Care North East (a partnership) v Durham CC* [2010] EWHC 959 (QB); [2012] 1 W.L.R. 338; *Pannone LLP v Aardvark Digital Ltd* [2011] EWCA Civ 803, [2011] 1 W.L.R. 2275 at [27]; *Watson v Sadiq* [2013] EWCA Civ 882 at [50].

[10]   Subject, of course, to overriding rules of common law or statute such as those against contracts which are illegal or contrary to public policy: Chitty, Ch.16; Furmston, Ch.5; Treitel, Ch.11; Anson, Ch.11; and those restricting the effectiveness of certain exemption clauses or other unfair terms: Chitty, Ch.15; Furmston, Ch.3, ss.E, F; Treitel, Ch.7; Anson, Ch.6.

[11]   *Photo Production Ltd v Securicor Transport Ltd*, see para.9-02 fn.7 at 848, 850.

terms as they were in agreeing the initial contract. Variations of a contract may, however, take different forms designed to have the same final effect.[12] The variation may take the form of a second contract, supplementary to the initial contract, which records only the modifications. In such a case, the initial contract remains in force except in so far as it has been modified by the variation; the two contracts must now be read together, but whether only the initial contract, or also the variation, will be relied upon in any claim arising out of the contract will depend on the nature of the claim and which terms (unmodified or modified) are relevant to the claim or to any defences to the claim. The same effect of variation of the initial contract may, however, be achieved by what appears to be a quite different transaction: two interdependent agreements, by the first of which the parties agree to discharge all the existing obligations created by the initial contract on the basis that they are to replaced by the second agreement: a single, new contract which will become a freestanding contract no longer to be read in the context of the initial contract which has been superseded.[13] Whether the parties use the form of a supplementary variation of only particular terms, or a replacement of the old contract by a wholly new contract, depends on the circumstances and the parties' preferences. It may be thought to be clearer and more efficient to replace the initial contract with a new, freestanding document; and some forms of variation may require a complete new contract to replace the original in order to have full legal effect.[14] Where, however, there are relatively minor, self-contained changes, a supplementary agreement dealing with only those changes may be a more efficient way of effecting the variation, particularly if the drafting and execution of the variation is thereby made simpler.[15] For our purposes, however, it is to be noted that any variation of an obligation owed under an existing contract must satisfy the requirements for a contract, including (unless it is done by deed[16]) the requirement that the party seeking to enforce the variation provide consideration for it.

Discharge as a contractual variation   We have already seen[17] that one way of   **9-04**
effecting a variation of a contract is for the parties to create a wholly new contract
to replace their initial contract, which they agree at the same time to discharge. The
agreed discharge of some or all of the obligations contained in a contract is itself a
variation, whether or not the discharge of the existing obligations is to be fol-

---

[12] If the parties do not make the distinction expressly, it is a matter of interpretation of their agreement, which may sometimes not be an easy matter. Lord Dunedin suggested a test in *Morris v Baron & Co*, see para.9-02 fn.6, at 26: "The difference between variation and rescission is a real one, and is tested, to my thinking, by this: In the first case there are no such executory clauses in the second arrangement as would enable you to sue upon that alone if the first did not exist; in the second you could sue on the second arrangement alone, and the first contract is got rid of either by express words to that effect, or because, the second dealing with the same subject-matter as the first but in a different way, it is impossible that the two should be both performed".

[13] *Morris v Baron & Co*, see para.9-02 fn.6, at 26 (Lord Dunedin, adding that "When I say you could sue on the second alone, that does not exclude cases where the first is used for mere reference, in the same way as you may fix a price by a price list, but where the contractual force is to be found in the second by itself"); *Compagnie Noga D'Importation et D'Exportation SA v Abacha (No.2)* [2003] EWCA Civ 1100; [2003] 2 All E.R. (Comm) 915 at [57].

[14] e.g. novation where there is a change of parties: see para.9-05.

[15] e.g. where there are several parties to the contract, and the variation is to be of only the obligations owed between two of the parties who may be able to effect the variation without the involvement of the other party or parties.

[16] See para.9-26.

[17] See para.9-03.

lowed by the creation of new obligations. C has a right against D by virtue of their contractual obligation; for D to be released from the duty to perform that obligation requires C to have agreed to the release in a form which binds C as against D. Although there are other mechanisms of the common law and of equity by which a contractual duty might be suspended or released,[18] in principle at common law the discharge of existing contractual obligations requires a contractual variation[19] which (unless it is done by deed[20]) includes the requirement that D, as the party seeking to enforce the variation, provide consideration for it.

9-05   **Novation as a contractual variation**   One form of variation is the *novation* of an existing contract, a term which can be used to refer to a new contract between the same parties, but generally refers to a new contract under which a new party takes the place of one of the existing parties, and the retiring party is released—a variation of the existing contract by the substitution of one of the parties. Lord Selborne LC said in 1882[21]:

> "'novation' ... as I understand it means this—the term being derived from the Civil Law— that there being a contract in existence, some new contract is substituted for it, either between the same parties (for that might be) or between different parties; the consideration mutually being the discharge of the old contract. A common instance of it in partnership[22] cases is where upon the dissolution of a partnership the persons who are going to continue in business agree and undertake, as between themselves and the retiring partner, that they will assume and discharge the whole liabilities of the business, usually taking over the assets; and if in that case they give notice of that arrangement to a creditor, and ask for his accession to it, there becomes a contract between the creditor who accedes and the new firm, to the effect that he will accept their liability instead of the old liability, and on the other hand that they promise to pay him for that consideration."

The term "novation" as applied by the parties to their contract has no defining force: what the contract achieves will depend upon its terms. Therefore, the novation contract may involve the release ab initio of the retiring contracting party and the substitution of equivalent duties on the new party as if he had been a party from the beginning—the replacement of the initial contract by the new contract for all purposes in relation to past as well as future performance; or it may be so drafted as to involve a variation by substitution of the new party only in relation to future performance.[23] And the novation may generally be of the whole contract, so that all the obligations under the existing contract are discharged and substituted by the new contract between the new parties, but it is possible to discharge and replace only some of the obligations and therefore create by novation a contract involving a new party which supplements and varies the existing contract rather than replacing it.[24]

---

18   For waiver and estoppel, see para.9-06.
19   See para.9-02 fn.9.
20   See para.9-26.
21   *Scarf v Jardine* (1882) 7 App. Cas. 345, HL, at 351.
22   cf. Partnership Act 1890 s.17 (new partner is not thereby liable to existing creditors of the firm, and retiring partner does not thereby cease to be liable for existing partnership debts and obligations but may be discharged by agreement with new members and the creditors).
23   *Blyth & Blyth Ltd v Carillion Construction Ltd* (2001) 79 Con. L.R. 142 (OH) (in relation to rights which had already accrued under the partly-performed contract, tripartite "novation agreement" had effect only as assignment of rights, not discharge and replacement by new rights).
24   *Langston Group Corp v Cardiff City Football Club Ltd* [2008] EWHC 535 (Ch) (Briggs J at [42]: "it does not seem to me necessarily to follow that where a particular obligation is novated in that

For our purposes, however, it is important to note that a variation of a contract, even if it takes effect as a novation and substitution of a new party, must satisfy the requirements for the formation of a contract which (unless it is done by deed[25]) include the requirement that each party seeking to enforce the new obligations, or to claim that he has been released from obligations under the initial contract, provide consideration.

(2) Variation Contrasted with Waiver, Forbearance and Estoppel

A party to a contract may waive rights arising from it, or forbear or estop   **9-06**
himself from enforcing his rights   Even if a party to an existing contract does not by a contractual variation agree to modify or discharge the other party's duties (and therefore his own rights) arising under that contract, he may still restrict or exclude his ability to enforce those rights. The common law recognises the waiver of rights in a range of different circumstances in which the right is thereby relinquished, including the waiver either of the right to performance by the other party of a primary obligation under a contract, or of the right to pursue a remedy which has arisen by reason of the other party's breach of contract.[26] Similarly, a party may "forbear" to enforce his rights.[27] The doctrines of waiver and forbearance will be discussed further in Chapter 10[28]; but for present purposes it is sufficient to note that by the waiver of a contractual right—either the right to performance, or the right to enforce a remedy for breach—the party waiving the right loses the right without having received in return any consideration for its loss. However, the loss of the right may be only temporary and the party who waived the right may be able to give notice to the other party requiring him again to comply with the terms of the contract. Forbearance is also a temporary suspension of the contractual rights. Waiver is thus less fully effective than a contractually binding variation of the contract, although it is a very common occurrence in the context of the performance of commercial contracts.[29]

Similar in many respects to the doctrine of waiver, which was developed by the common law courts, is the doctrine of estoppel—and in particular the equitable doctrine of promissory estoppel, by which a party who represents that he will not enforce his strict rights under a contract may be estopped from so doing if the other party has acted upon the representation. The doctrine of estoppel will be discussed in detail in Chapter 10, including its relationship with the doctrines of waiver and

---

way by substitution of one obligor for another, the conclusion must be that a large and complex contract containing other obligations which are not so novated must be treated as having itself been terminated by novation and replaced by a wholly new contract. I put to Mr Driscoll the example of a contract between A and B containing ten distinct obligations owed by B to A. The substitution with A's consent of C for B as obligor in relation to one of those provisions, leaving the other nine unaffected as between A and B did not seem to me obviously a case of novation of the entire contract. Mr Driscoll submitted that it was, but he could offer no authority in point". How such a novation agreement is structured by the parties, and analysed by the court, may depend on the purpose for which the question needs to be answered: ibid., at [47]).

    For the different ways of effecting a variation see generally see para.9-03.

[25] See para.9-26.
[26] *Banning v Wright* [1972] 1 W.L.R. 972, HL, at 990 (Lord Simon of Glaisdale).
[27] A.J. Phipps, "Resurrecting the Doctrine of Common Law Forbearance" (2007) 123 L.Q.R. 286.
[28] See para.10-11.
[29] cf. Wilken and Ghaly, Chs 15 to 22, giving examples of waiver (as well as variation and estoppel) in a range of different kinds of commercial contracts.

forbearance[30]; but again it should be noted here that it is a mechanism by which the party making the representation can lose the right to enforce the contract without having received in return any consideration for the loss of the right. However, the loss of the right may only be temporary and the party who represented that he would not enforce it may be able to give notice to the other party requiring him again to comply with the terms of the contract.[31]

9-07 **Waiver and estoppel are negative and unilateral, whereas a contractual variation may be positive or negative, and unilateral or bilateral** In their very nature waiver and estoppel involve only one party giving up, at least temporarily, his rights under the contract—a unilateral modification of the enforceability of the contract, which is negative in the sense that it involves a reduction of the party's rights.[32] It is possible for a contractual variation to effect a similar unilateral reduction in the contractual rights, such as where a creditor remits part or whole of a debt; but given that the variation of a contract is simply a new contract superimposed on the old (whether to supplement it or to replace it),[33] it need not be negative but may also be positive, such as where the party receiving the performance of services agrees to increase the sum he contracted to pay for them; and it may be bilateral, such as where both parties agree to either decrease or to increase what they will perform under the contract and therefore what each will receive from the other (a reduction in payment in return for a reduction in services to be performed under the contract, or an increase in payment in return for an increase in the services). As we shall see, however, there can be difficulties in finding a contractual variation where the modification in the obligations to be performed is unilateral: the promise to remit a debt, unless it is effected by deed, requires some additional consideration in return, however small,[34] as does the promise to increase the price to be paid for services where the services are not themselves increased.[35]

II. THE REQUIREMENT OF CONSIDERATION FOR A CONTRACTUAL VARIATION

(1) The General Rule and its Application

9-08 **Consideration is required for the informal variation of a contract** Setting aside the case where the parties use a deed to effect the variation of their contract,[36] the variation—taking effect as a contract superimposed on the existing contract[37]—must be supported by consideration. In other words, each party who wishes to enforce the variation to the terms must show that he has given something in return[38]

---

[30] See para.10-11.
[31] For the question of whether promissory estoppel only suspends (revocably) the contractual right, or has the effect of irrevocably varying its enforceability, see paras 10-29 to 10-32.
[32] According to the traditional understanding of promissory estoppel in English law it is limited to promises not to enforce existing rights, and thus (like waiver) operates negatively (as a "shield"): see paras 10-19, 10-38. In some other common law systems estoppel can be used positively (as a "sword") to create new obligations: see paras 10-47, 10-48.
[33] See paras 9-02, 9-03.
[34] See para.9-17.
[35] See para.9-11.
[36] The use of a deed avoids with the need to provide consideration: see para.7-18 and para.9-26.
[37] See para.9-02.
[38] i.e. the consideration must be provided at the other party's express or implied request: see paras 8-15, 8-16 and at the same time as the promise that it is being used to enforce: para.8-20.

for the variation which constitutes a benefit to the other party and/or detriment to himself.[39]

The mutual variation or discharge of a contract inherently carries its own consideration It is sometimes said that where a contract contains obligations which remain outstanding on both sides, the parties' agreement to discharge the contract "generates its own consideration",[40] since each agrees to give up the right to enforce the other's obligations in return for the discharge of his own obligations. This is true regardless of the relative values of the parties' respective outstanding obligations, since the consideration for a contract need not be adequate[41] and so it is sufficient that each party has obligations of *some* value to give up, even if one party gives up much more than the other. The same argument holds in relation to a variation which does not discharge the whole contract but simply involves a reduction of both parties' obligations; each party obtains the benefit of a reduction of his own obligations in return for the detriment of a loss of the other party's obligations, regardless of the relative value that each party gives up. Similarly, a mutual agreement to increase the parties' obligations inherently carries its own consideration, since each obtains something more from the other in return for his own additional performance. In other words, in any agreement by which the obligations of both parties are varied *in the same direction*—both parties' obligations are increased, or both are decreased (in part or in whole)—the consideration is easily found in the mutual benefits and detriments which the agreement inevitably involves.

9-09

Unilateral variations require additional consideration If the modification of a contract agreed by the parties does not involve the increase or decrease of both parties' obligations, but is only a unilateral modification or discharge of the contract, the agreement will not inherently carry its own consideration, and additional consideration must be found in order to render the agreement to modify the contract binding as a contractual variation. This may arise in the case of the unilateral variation of a bilateral executory contract, where both parties have outstanding obligations under the contract but only one party's obligations are modified, whether by increase or decrease (such as the increase or decrease of the price in a contract for services without any corresponding change in the services to be provided); or where one party has an accrued right against the other which he agrees to vary or abandon. The latter right may arise outside the context of contract but be subject to contractual modification[42]; or where one party has fully performed his obligations under a contract, and thus has nothing to give up in return for his agreement to vary the other party's outstanding obligations (such as where the price is due for services that have already been fully performed, and the party who has received the services agrees to reduce the price or abandon the right to receive payment); or, more gener-

9-10

---

[39] See para.8-23.
[40] Chitty, para.4-078.
[41] See para.8-25.
[42] *Collin v Duke of Westminster* [1985] Q.B. 581, CA (alleged abandonment of tenant's statutory right to enfranchisement; see Oliver LJ at 595: "there is, in the law of contract, no room for a concept of unilateral abandonment", so either a representation giving rise to an estoppel (see Ch.10), or a contract for a mutual release, must be shown; and at 598: alleged abandonment was "entirely unilateral and unsupported by any consideration in the form of any inferential counter-promise or release on the part of [the landlords]").

ally, wherever the creditor agrees to the reduction or cancellation of an accrued debt. Although it appears to be clear as a matter of general principle that the contractual modification or discharge of an existing obligation requires consideration, and that (by contrast with a mutual variation) the unilateral variation will not inherently carry its own consideration, certain situations have arisen within the context of unilateral variations of existing contractual rights where the courts have had some difficulties in determining whether there is in fact consideration justifying the contractual enforcement of the variation. These "hard cases"—the unilateral variation of a bilateral executory contract, arising in particular from the decision of the Court of Appeal in *Williams v Roffey Bros & Nicholls (Contractors) Ltd*,[43] and the agreement to accept part-payment of a debt in satisfaction of the whole[44] —will be discussed in the following paragraphs of this section, and it will be seen that they even give rise to a fundamental question about whether the strict requirement of consideration for the variation of a contract should be maintained.[45]

(2) Hard Cases: I: Unilateral Variation of a Bilateral Executory Contract

9-11   **Consideration cannot in principle be found merely in the claimant's undertaking to perform his existing contractual duty** The agreement to vary a contract which involves a modification of only one party's obligations is not a *contractual variation* unless consideration is provided for it. If one party agrees to increase the price he will pay beyond that already provided for by the contract for services, for example, the other party must promise, do or forbear to do something in return for the promise of that increased price if he is to have the contractual right to enforce the new promise (i.e. to enforce the agreement as modified). Or if one party agrees to reduce the other party's duties owed under the contract, that other party must promise, do or forbear to do something in return for the promise that he will not have to fulfil his strict contractual duties if he is to have the contractual right to perform less than the original contract required of him. We have already seen that it is not sufficient for the claimant who seeks to enforce the defendant's promise to show that in return he agreed to continue to perform duties which he already owes by contract to the defendant.[46] The claimant undertook his existing contractual duties in return for the original obligations undertaken by the defendant at the moment of formation of the initial contract. He cannot re-use that same undertaking as consideration for a variation in the defendant's obligations: he provides nothing of benefit to the defendant that the defendant does not already have; and he undertakes no new detriment by promising something to the defendant that the defendant can already require of him.

This principle is well illustrated by the decision of Lord Ellenborough in *Stilk v Myrick*,[47] in which the facts were reported as follows[48]:

---

[43]   [1991] 1 Q.B. 1, CA; see paras 9-14 to 9-16.
[44]   See paras 9-18 to 9-22.
[45]   See para.9-24.
[46]   See para.8-39.
[47]   There are two reports, one by Campbell: *Stilk v Myrick* (1809) 2 Camp. 317, 170 E.R. 1168; the other by Espinasse: *Stilk v Meyrick* (1809) 6 Esp. 129, 170 E.R. 851. "Campbell's Reports have the better reputation": *North Ocean Shipping Co Ltd v Hyundai Construction Co Ltd* [1979] 1 Q.B. 705 at 712 (Mocatta J). Espinasse was counsel (with the Attorney-General) for the plaintiff in the case.
[48]   Taken from Campbell's report, see para.9-11 fn.47, at 317–318, at 1168–1169.

"By the ship's articles, executed before the commencement of the voyage, the plaintiff was to be paid at the rate of £5 a month; and the principal question in the cause was, whether he was entitled to a higher rate of wages?—In the course of the voyage two of the seamen deserted; and the captain having in vain attempted to supply their places at Cronstadt, there entered into an agreement with the rest of the crew, that they should have the wages of the two who had deserted equally divided among them, if he could not procure two other hands at Gottenburgh. This was found impossible; and the ship was worked back to London by the plaintiff and eight more of the original crew, with whom the agreement had been made at Cronstadt."

The argument on behalf of the defendant, the ship's captain, is reported as focusing not on whether the promise to pay the additional wages was supported by consideration, but whether it was void as contrary to public policy.[49] However, according to Campbell's report of the case, Lord Ellenborough rested his decision in favour of the defendant not on the ground of policy but on the absence of consideration: although the sailors, in taking on work which should have been done by the two members of the crew who had deserted, in fact provided services in addition to those that they had expected to perform, this additional work was already required of them by their contracts, so they gave nothing in return for the promise of the additional wages[50]:

"the agreement is void for want of consideration. There was no consideration for the ulterior pay promised to the mariners who remained with the ship. Before they sailed from London they had undertaken to do all that they could under all the emergencies of the voyage. They had sold all their services till the voyage should be completed. If they had been at liberty to quit the vessel at Cronstadt, the case would have been quite different; or if the captain had capriciously discharged the two men who were wanting, the others might not have been compellable to take the whole duty upon themselves, and their agreeing to do so might have been a sufficient consideration for the promise of an advance of wages. But the desertion of a part of the crew is to be considered an emergency of the voyage as much as their death; and those who remain are bound by the terms of their original contract to exert themselves to the utmost to bring the ship in safety to her destined port. Therefore, without looking to the policy of this agreement, I think it is void for want of consideration, and that the plaintiff can only recover at the rate of £5 a month."

The particular context of *Stilk* clearly raised an issue of public policy as well as the issue of what constitutes good consideration,[51] but it is the argument based on

---

49 "In West India voyages, crews are often thinned greatly by death and desertion; and if a promise of advanced wages were valid, exorbitant claims would be set up on all such occasions" (Garrow's argument, reported by Campbell, see para.9-11 fn.47, at 318, at 1169; similarly the Espinasse report, see para.9-11 fn.47, at 130, at 851). In both reports the only case said to be cited was *Harris v Watson* (1791) Peake 102, 170 E.R. 94 where a claim for additional wages was made by sailors not in port but during the voyage, and Lord Kenyon (at 103, at 94) based his decision on the argument of public policy: "If this action was to be supported, it would materially affect the navigation of this kingdom. It has been long since determined, that when the freight is lost, the wages are also lost. This rule was founded on a principle of policy, for if sailors were in all events to have their wages, and in times of danger entitled to insist on an extra charge on such a promise as this, they would in many cases suffer a ship to sink, unless the captain would pay any extravagant demand they might think proper to make".

50 Campbell's report, see para.9-11 fn.47, at 319, at 1169.

51 According to Campbell's report of *Stilk v Myrick*, see para.9-11 fn.47, at 319, at 1169, Lord Ellenborough also said: "I think *Harris v Watson* [see para.9-11 fn.49] was rightly decided; but I doubt whether the ground of public policy, upon which Lord Kenyon is stated to have proceeded, be the true principle on which the decision is to be supported". The Espinasse report, see para.9-11 fn.47,

consideration for which it has become accepted and the general rule is that the claimant does not provide sufficient consideration for the defendant's promise if he only promises in return an act or forbearance which he is already bound by contract to the defendant to do.[52]

9-12   **A promise, act or forbearance beyond the existing contractual duty can be sufficient consideration**   As Lord Ellenborough made clear in *Stilk v Myrick*,[53] the sailors would have had a good claim to the additional wages promised by the ship's captain if they had undertaken in return to perform tasks which were not within their existing contractual duties—such as if in the circumstances they had been at liberty to leave the vessel rather than being required to continue to sail it in the absence of the sailors who had deserted. This in fact happened in *Hartley v Ponsonby*,[54] where 17 members of a crew of 36 deserted while the ship was in port, and the master promised to pay additional wages to those who remained, including the claimant. The jury decided that the master made the agreement voluntarily, although he could not have obtained additional crew to make up the numbers at a reasonable price,[55] and that it was unreasonable for such a vessel to proceed on its voyage with a crew of only 19. His promise of additional wages was held to be binding, since the remaining sailors had been no longer bound by their contracts to proceed with the voyage and they therefore provided consideration by performing in the new circumstances the services they had agreed under the original contract. Lord Campbell CJ said[56]:

> "for the ship to go to sea with so few hands was dangerous to life. If so, it was not incumbent on the plaintiff to perform the work; and he was in the condition of a free man. There was therefore a consideration for the contract; and the captain made it without coercion. This is therefore a voluntary agreement upon sufficient consideration."

is less clear, never refers to consideration, and at 130, at 851 reports Lord Ellenborough as saying that "he recognised the principle of the case of *Harris v Watson* as founded on just and proper policy". For discussion of conflicting and uncertain points arising from the different reports (including whether the original contract was with the captain or with the shipowner), see F.M.B. Reynolds and G.H. Treitel, "Consideration for the Modification of Contracts" (1965) 7 Malaya L.Rev. 1, 4–6 (Reynolds and Treitel suggest that the underlying reason for the decision was policy and (at p.6) "it is a pity that *Stilk v Myrick*, or the report in Campbell, obscured the issue by introducing the idea of consideration"). In *Harris v Carter* (1854) 3 El. & Bl. 559 at 562, 118 E.R. 1251 at 1253 Lord Campbell CJ decided a similar case on the basis of the absence of consideration for the promise to pay additional wages to a sailor, but added that he could not agree with Lord Ellenborough in *Stilk v Myrick* in discarding the ground of public policy.

52   See, e.g. *Harrison v Dodd* (1914) 111 L.T. 47 (sailor did not give consideration for promise of overtime payment where his contract of employment already required him to give full service, following *Harris v Carter*, see para.9-11 fn.51, but referring only to consideration and not public policy); *Swain v West (Butchers) Ltd* [1936] 3 All E.R. 261, CA (general manager of company had contractual duty to do all in his power to promote interests of company, and so by promising to give evidence of managing director's dishonesty he did not give consideration for chairman's promise not to dismiss him); *Compagnie Noga D'Importation et D'Exportation SA v Abacha (No.2)* [2003] EWCA Civ 1100; [2003] 2 All E.R. (Comm) 915 at [44] (but the principle in *Stilk* did not apply there because the contract was rescinded and replaced, not varied: see para.9-03 and para.9-16 fnn.114, 115).

53   See para.9-11 fn.50.

54   (1857) 7 El. & Bl. 872, 119 E.R. 1471. See also *Yates v Hall* (1785) 1 T.R. 73, 99 E.R. 979 (promise by ship's captain to pay wages to sailor in return for his agreement to become hostage for the ship).

55   For the relevance of duress in such a case see para.9-15 fnn.86, 87.

56   (1857) 7 El. & Bl. 872 at 877, 119 E.R. 1471, at 877–878, at 1473.

It is always a question of construction of the existing contract whether what the claimant does or promises to do is within its strict requirements or is some additional service, however small, beyond that which he is already contractually required to perform. In this connection it should be remembered that the courts are generally reluctant to find that there is no valuable consideration for a seriously intended promise,[57] and so they may be well-disposed to find consideration in some small and rather technical addition to the claimant's own contractual duties.[58]

Furthermore, where what the claimant agrees to do in return for some additional benefit to be provided by the defendant is in fact no more than his existing contractual duty, but the claimant agrees it in circumstances where there is a genuine dispute between the parties about whether the claimant has a binding duty so to act, the agreement will be binding as a compromise. In such a case the consideration is not the promise to perform the pre-existing duty, but the promise to forbear to pursue the dispute about whether the claimant has such a duty.[59]

The performance by the claimant of his existing contractual duty may provide a "practical benefit" to the defendant   Although in most cases the consideration provided by the claimant constitutes both a benefit to the defendant and a detriment to the claimant, in principle it is sufficient for it to constitute either one or the other[60]; and therefore even if the claimant's promise, act or forbearance does not impose on him any new burden it may still constitute consideration if it is done at the defendant's request and confers a benefit on him. The difficulty, however, is in determining what constitutes a sufficient "benefit" in such a case. Although by agreeing to perform (or by in fact performing) a duty already owed to the defendant the claimant does not provide the defendant with anything to which he is not *in law* already entitled, it is not difficult to find situations in which there is a real benefit *in practice* for the defendant to receive that performance or even the assurance of it: in other words, although the promise or performance of an existing contractual duty may not constitute a *legal* benefit, it may constitute a *practical* benefit to the defendant.[61] Until relatively recently, the courts did not consider that such practical benefits, unaccompanied by some additional legal benefit, could constitute consideration,[62] although through some cases involving the promise to fulfil a duty imposed by law, rather than a pre-existing contractual duty, the courts

9-13

---

57 See para.8-28.
58 *Vantage Navigation Corp v Suhail and Saud Bahwan Building Materials LLC (The Alev)* [1989] 1 Lloyd's Rep. 138 at 147 (Hobhouse J: "there is no warrant for the Court to fail to recognise the existence of some consideration even though it may be insignificant and even though there may have been no mutual bargain in any realistic use of that phrase": plaintiffs' agreeing to appoint defendants as their gratuitous agents was consideration, although the agreement was voidable for duress).
59 See paras 8-30, 8-31. See, e.g. *Wigan v Edwards* (1973) 1 A.L.R. 497, HCA.
60 See para.8-23.
61 For discussion and criticism of the distinction between "legal benefit" and "factual benefit", see Reynolds and Treitel, para.9-11 n.51, noting at 15 that "it is always a factual detriment to give up one's tactical advantage in litigation, and if such a detriment were sufficient it would be possible to find consideration in virtually everything that could be called a renegotiation as opposed to a release".
62 See, e.g. *Foakes v Beer* (1884) 9 App. Cas. 605, HL, at 622 (Lord Blackburn, arguing that "all men of business, whether merchants or tradesmen, do every day recognise and act on the ground that prompt payment of a part of their demand may be more beneficial to them than it would be to insist on their rights and enforce payment of the whole"; but he did not press this and agreed with the rest of the House to affirm the established rule that part-payment of a debt cannot be consideration for the remission of the balance: see para.9-20).

have been inspired to develop the idea that a collateral, practical advantage which the defendant intended to obtain as a result of the claimant's promising to comply with his existing duty can be a sufficient benefit in return for the defendant's promise, and can therefore constitute consideration.[63] This development was taken up by the Court of Appeal in 1989 in the context of the promise to fulfil a pre-existing contractual duty in the—still controversial—case of *Williams v Roffey Bros & Nicholls (Contractors) Ltd.*[64]

9-14 **The decision in Williams v Roffey Bros & Nicholls (Contractors) Ltd** In this case the defendants (Roffey), main contractors for the refurbishment of 27 flats in a block of flats owned by a housing association, sub-contracted the carpentry work for the flats (first and second fix) and for the roof of the building to the claimant (Williams) for a total price of £20,000, the contract containing an implied term requiring interim payments at reasonable intervals, based on the amount of work done. Six months after Williams had begun the work, he had completed the work on the roof, the first fix to all 27 flats and the second fix to nine of the flats, and Roffey had made interim payments of £16,200. However, Williams was then in financial difficulty and Roffey became concerned that he would be unable to finish on time; and the time was critical because the main contract subjected Roffey to a penalty clause[65] with the housing association if the refurbishment was delayed. It was found by the trial judge that Williams' financial difficulty arose in part because the agreed price of £20,000 was too low to enable him to operate satisfactorily and at a profit (there was evidence that the reasonable price would have been £23,783) and in part because Williams had failed to supervise his workmen adequately.[66] Roffey promised to pay Williams an additional sum of £10,300, at the rate of £575 for each flat in which he completed his work, and in consequence Williams continued to work for a few more weeks until he had substantially (but not totally) completed the work on eight further flats, before ceasing work completely. Roffey had paid him only £1,500 more in that period. They had to engage other carpenters to finish the work, and as a result of the delay incurred one week's time penalty under their main contract with the housing association. The trial judge, affirmed by the Court of Appeal, ordered Roffey to make further payments which were due both under the original contract, and to fulfil the promise to pay

---

[63] See para.8-38; the key cases were *Ward v Byham* [1956] 1 W.L.R. 496, CA and *Williams v Williams* [1957] 1 W.L.R. 148, CA, in both of which Denning LJ sought to develop an even stronger rule, that the mere promise or performance of the claimant's existing duty, at the defendant's request, is a benefit to the defendant, although this has not been accepted, and some collateral practical benefit flowing from the performance of the existing duty on the facts of the case must be shown: see para.8-38; *Vantage Navigation Corp v Suhail and Saud Bahwan Building Materials LLC (The Alev)*, see para.9-12 fn.58, at 147; *North Ocean Shipping Co Ltd v Hyundai Construction Co Ltd* [1979] 1 Q.B. 705 at 713; *Williams v Roffey Bros & Nicholls (Contractors) Ltd* [1991] 1 Q.B. 1 at 11–13 (Glidewell LJ) and 20 (Purchas LJ).

[64] [1991] 1 Q.B. 1, CA; see para.9-14.

[65] No point appears to have been taken in the case about whether this was a true penalty clause (in which case it would not have been enforceable, thus undermining the argument that avoiding the operation of the clause could provide a practical benefit to Roffey: *Dunlop Pneumatic Tyre Co Ltd v New Garage and Motor Co Ltd* [1915] A.C. 79, HL; and now *Cavendish Square Holding BV v Makdessi* [2015] UKSC 67; [2016] A.C. 1172) or a liquidated damages clause. In building contracts, liquidated damages clauses are common: Chitty, para.37-121. Roffey did not take this point, and in argument admitted that they obtained the practical benefit of avoiding "the penalty for delay": [1991] 1 Q.B. 1 at 3.

[66] [1991] 1 Q.B. 1 at 6.

the additional £585 per completed flat, in respect of the work which Williams had in fact done.[67]

For our purposes, the key issue[68] before the Court of Appeal was whether Roffey's promise to pay the additional sum was binding, given that the promise made by Williams in return was only to continue to perform his existing obligations under the contract. Roffey's counsel accepted in argument that Roffey obtained benefits in return for their agreement to pay the additional sum:

"(i) to ensure that the plaintiff continued work and did not stop in breach of the subcontract; (ii) to avoid the penalty for delay; and (iii) to avoid the trouble and expense of engaging other people to complete the carpentry work"

but argued that these were only

"benefits of a practical nature; the defendants derived no benefit in law since the plaintiff was promising to do no more than he was already bound to do by his subcontract, i.e., continue with the carpentry work and complete it on time."[69]

In addition, Russell LJ noted that Roffey obtained the advantage of replacing what had hitherto been a haphazard method of payment by a more formalised scheme involving the payment of a specified sum on the completion of each flat.[70] The Court held unanimously that there was sufficient consideration, and although each of the judges made clear that the decision did not undermine the basic rule requiring consideration for the variation of a contract as illustrated by the earlier decision in *Stilk v Myrick*,[71] the way in which they expressed their reasons for finding consideration in the case was not identical.

Glidewell LJ relied heavily on the earlier cases in which it had been held that a claimant who undertakes to fulfil an obligation already owed by law to the defend-

---

67   The judge's calculation is set out by Glidewell LJ, [1991] 1 Q.B. 1 at 7; it included deductions for the fact that the works were substantially but not totally completed; and the judge also held that, because Roffey had refused to pay more than £1,500 in addition to the £16,200 interim payments, they were in breach of contract entitling Williams to cease work. Roffey's counter-claim for damages for breach of contract for Williams' ceasing work was therefore dismissed. For criticism of the judge's award in favour of Williams, which was calculated only to compensate him for the work in fact done, rather than the full expectation measure of loss flowing from Roffey's breach of contract, see M. Chen-Wishart in J. Beatson and D. Friedmann, *Good Faith and Fault in Contract Law* (Clarendon Press, 1995), p.123 at p.134.

68   The first issue considered by the Court was whether Williams had substantially completed the work on the eight further flats, so as to entitle him to any further payment; it held that he had, but the arguments about this do not concern us here.

69   [1991] 1 Q.B. 1 at 3, 10–11.

70   [1991] 1 Q.B. 1 at 19; see similarly Purchas LJ at 20. This item might more easily have been found to be consideration on orthodox principles of *legal* benefit, since the replacement of unclear terms by clear terms can be a legal benefit: *Anangel Atlas Compania Naviera SA v Ishikawajima-Harima Heavy Industries Co Ltd (No.2)* [1990] 2 Lloyd's Rep. 526 at 543–544; see para.8-30.

71   See para.9-11 fn.47; see Glidewell LJ in *Williams v Roffey* at 16 ("If it be objected that the propositions above contravene the principle in *Stilk v Myrick*, I answer that in my view they do not; they refine, and limit the application of that principle, but they leave the principle unscathed e.g. where B secures no benefit by his promise"); Russell LJ at 19 ("I do not base my judgment upon any reservation as to the correctness of the law long ago enunciated in *Stilk v Myrick*. A gratuitous promise, pure and simple, remains unenforceable unless given under seal") and Purchas LJ at 21 ("the rule in *Stilk v Myrick* remains valid as a matter of principle, namely that a contract not under seal must be supported by consideration").

ant,[72] or an obligation already owed by contract to a third party,[73] provides consideration for the defendant's promise where the defendant thereby obtains a practical benefit, and added that the recent development of the doctrine of economic duress "may provide another answer in law to the question of policy which has troubled the courts since before *Stilk v Myrick*,[74] and no doubt led at the date of that decision to a rigid adherence to the doctrine of consideration".[75] He developed a series of propositions, based heavily on the facts of the case itself, to express the present state of the law[76]:

"(i) if A has entered into a contract with B to do work for, or to supply goods or services to, B in return for payment by B; and (ii) at some stage before A has completely performed his obligations under the contract B has reason to doubt whether A will, or will be able to, complete his side of the bargain; and (iii) B thereupon promises A an additional payment in return for A's promise to perform his contractual obligations on time; and (iv) as a result of giving his promise, B obtains in practice a benefit, or obviates a disbenefit; and (v) B's promise is not given as a result of economic duress or fraud on the part of A[77]; then (vi) the benefit to B is capable of being consideration for B's promise, so that the promise will be legally binding."

Russell LJ also found that there was consideration because Roffey obtained advantages in return for their promise to pay the additional money, including the new payment arrangements,[78] but placed particular emphasis on the courts' willingness to find consideration to give effect to the intention of the parties where the variation was agreed without pressure[79]:

"whilst consideration remains a fundamental requirement before a contract not under seal can be enforced, the policy of the law in its search to do justice between the parties has developed considerably since the early 19th century when *Stilk v Myrick* was decided by Lord Ellenborough C.J. In the late 20th century I do not believe that the rigid approach to the concept of consideration to be found in *Stilk v Myrick* is either necessary or desirable. Consideration there must still be but, in my judgment, the courts nowadays should be more ready to find its existence so as to reflect the intention of the parties to the contract where the bargaining powers are not unequal and where the finding of consideration reflect the true intention of the parties. ...

True it was that the plaintiff did not undertake to do any work additional to that which he had originally undertaken to do but the terms upon which he was to carry out the work

---

[72] *Ward v Byham* and *Williams v Williams*, see para.9-13 fn.63, discussed by Glidewell LJ in [1991] 1 Q.B. 1 at 11–13, 15.
[73] *Pao On v Lau Yiu Long* [1980] A.C. 614, PC, discussed by Glidewell LJ in [1991] 1 Q.B. 1 at 14–15.
[74] [See para.9-11 fn.47; for the "question of policy" see para.9-11.]
[75] [1991] 1 Q.B. 1 at 13–14; and at 14–15 relying further in relation to duress on *Pao On v Lau Yiu Long*, see para.9-14 fn.73, at 634–635.
[76] [1991] 1 Q.B. 1 at 15–16. This passage from Glidewell LJ's judgment was quoted as the summary of the decision of the *Williams v Roffey* case by Kitchin LJ in *MWB Business Exchange Centres Ltd v Rock Advertising Ltd* [2016] EWCA Civ 553; [2017] Q.B. 604 at [42].
[77] [Proposition (iv) is problematic, since it uses the presence or absence of duress or fraud to determine whether there is consideration (and therefore whether the promise is contractually binding), whereas fraud and duress do not prevent a contract coming into existence but only make it voidable: *Dimskal Shipping Co SA v International Transport Workers Federation* [1992] 2 A.C. 152, HL, at 168. cf. also *Adam Opel GmbH v Mitras Automotive (UK) Ltd*, see para.9-15 fn.88.]
[78] [1991] 1 Q.B. 1 at 19.
[79] [1991] 1 Q.B. 1 at 18, 19.

were varied and, in my judgment, that variation was supported by consideration which a pragmatic approach to the true relationship between the parties readily demonstrates.

For my part I wish to make it plain that I do not base my judgment upon any reservation as to the correctness of the law long ago enunciated in *Stilk v Myrick*. A gratuitous promise, pure and simple, remains unenforceable unless given under seal. But where, as in this case, a party undertakes to make a payment because by so doing it will gain an advantage arising out of the continuing relationship with the promisee the new bargain will not fail for want of consideration."

Purchas LJ took a similar line to Russell LJ: he emphasised that, on the facts, the variation was beneficial to both sides, particularly in the new payment arrangements,[80] and that although there must be consideration for the variation of a contract, in the modern law the courts are more willing to find consideration in the absence of pressure[81]:

"The modern cases tend to depend more upon the defence of duress in a commercial context rather than lack of consideration for the second agreement. In the present case the question of duress does not arise. ... Nevertheless, the court is more ready in the presence of this defence being available in the commercial context to look for mutual advantages which would amount to sufficient consideration to support the second agreement under which the extra money is paid ...

As a result of the agreement the defendants secured their position commercially. There was, however, no obligation added to the contractual duties imposed upon the plaintiff under the original contract. Prima facie this would appear to be a classic *Stilk v Myrick* case. It was, however, open to the plaintiff to be in deliberate breach of the contract in order to 'cut his losses' commercially. In normal circumstances the suggestion that a contracting party can rely upon his own breach to establish consideration is distinctly unattractive. In many cases it obviously would be and if there was any element of duress brought upon the other contracting party under the modern development of this branch of the law the proposed breaker of the contract would not benefit. With some hesitation ... I consider that the modern approach to the question of consideration would be that where there were benefits derived by each party to a contract of variation even though one party did not suffer a detriment this would not be fatal to the establishing of sufficient consideration to support the agreement. If both parties benefit from an agreement it is not necessary that each also suffers a detriment."

Reception of the decision in Williams v Roffey   There are differences of detail and of emphasis in the judgments in the Court of Appeal in *Williams v Roffey*,[82] although some things are clear about the decision. All three judges emphasised that consideration is required for the variation of a contract[83]; *Stilk v Myrick* is still good law, but the application of the principle illustrated by that case should now be relaxed,[84] and the courts should be more willing to find consideration where the defendant, by asking the claimant to agree only to perform his existing obligations, intended thereby to obtain some other, practical benefit in addition to receiv-

9-15

---

[80] [1991] 1 Q.B. 1 at 20.
[81] [1991] 1 Q.B. 1 at 21, 23. At 23 Purchas LJ also agreed expressly with the reasons given by Glidewell LJ.
[82] See para.9-14.
[83] See para.9-14 fn.71. Russell LJ expressed interest in exploring whether the modification of the payment obligation in such a case could be effected through the doctrine of estoppel (see [1991] 1 Q.B. 1 at 17–18); Glidewell LJ at 13 was less forthcoming but found the argument "interesting"; for difficulties with this argument, however, see para.10-40.
[84] See para.9-14 fn.75, 79, 81.

ing the performance of the claimant's obligations.[85] The justification for this more relaxed approach is said to be to give effect to the intentions of the parties, and in particular to ensure that the variation of a contract should be enforceable where it has been freely agreed and not obtained by fraud or duress. Concerns in the older cases that a party could be unduly pressurised into agreeing a variation[86] can now be met by the argument that the courts have developed the law of duress to cover economic duress, and have recognised that the threat to break an existing contract can constitute illegitimate pressure sufficient to render the variation voidable.[87]

This may seem very attractive: the decision in *Williams v Roffey* appears to allow genuine re-negotiations of contracts to be enforced, even where the terms of the contract are varied only in favour of one of the parties, whilst using more nuanced doctrines to separate out those re-negotiations which have been unfairly obtained by fraud or duress.[88] However, the reaction of courts and academic commentators to the decision has not been wholeheartedly in support. In the English courts it has been applied in the context of a promise to perform an existing contractual duty not only in return for (as in *Williams v Roffey* itself) an increase in the contract price payable for services,[89] or the addition of some other new obligation to an existing contract,[90] but also in return for a reduction in the contract price,[91] and the release of existing claims,[92] although in two cases trial judges have followed *Williams v Roffey* only on the basis that, as a decision of the Court of Appeal, it is binding on them, rather than because they had any enthusiasm for it.[93] It

---

[85] See para.9-14 fn.76, 78, 80.

[86] This appears to underlie the "policy" concern of the old cases in which ships' captains might be pressurised into agreeing to increase the wages of sailors who threaten to mutiny: see para.9-11.

[87] See para.9-14 fnn.75, 79, 81. On the development of economic duress, see Chitty, paras 8-015 to 8-019; Treitel, paras 10-005 to 10-010; Anson, pp.378–379.

[88] *Adam Opel GmbH v Mitras Automotive (UK) Ltd* [2008] EWHC 3205 (QB); [2007] All E.R. (D) 272 (Dec) at [42] (David Donaldson QC: "The law of consideration is no longer to be used to protect a participant in such a variation. That role has passed to the law of economic duress, which provides a more refined control mechanism, and renders the contract voidable rather than void").

[89] *Adam Opel GmbH v Mitras Automotive (UK) Ltd*, see para.9-15 fn.88; *Attrill v Dresdner Kleinwort Ltd* [2012] EWHC 1189 (QB); [2012] I.R.L.R. 553 at [184]–[185] (promise of bonus pool for employees by investment bank in order to obtain benefit of stabilisation of workforce, to satisfy regulator and to incentivise staff; but there was consideration anyway in the employees' not exercising right to leave: at [186]–[188]; affirmed on appeal on basis that it was matter of fact for the trial judge: [2013] EWCA Civ 394; [2013] 3 All E.R. 607 at [95]). See also *Forde v Birmingham City Council* [2009] EWHC 12 (QB); [2009] 1 W.L.R. 2732 at [87].

[90] *Simon Container Machinery Ltd v Emba Machinery AB* [1998] 2 Lloyd's Rep 429 at 434–435 (addition of credit insurance to existing contract, where defendant had reason to think that claimant might otherwise seek to withdraw from existing contract and put at risk future orders). See also *Scomadi Ltd v RA Engineering Co Ltd* [2017] EWHC 2658 (IPEC); [2018] F.S.R. 14 at [57] (but there was also other consideration: at [58]).

[91] *Anangel Atlas Compania Naviera SA v Ishikawajima-Harima Heavy Industries Co Ltd (No.2)* [1990] 2 Lloyd's Rep. 526 at 544–545 (Hirst J, rejecting as a "narrow and artificial" a proposed distinction in the application of *Williams v Roffey* according to whether it is the claimant or the defendant who were providing the contractual services; defendant shipbuilders agreed to reduce price of vessel during slump in shipbuilding industry, in consideration of claimants' agreeing to take delivery in accordance with contract: this was a practical benefit to defendants because claimants were core customers, and their taking delivery would encourage other reluctant customers to follow suit).

[92] *Horwood v Land of Leather Ltd* [2010] EWHC 546 (Comm); [2010] 1 C.L.C. 423 at [41] (practical benefit for party agreeing to release claims in return for promise of payment of sum already due was in the increased confidence when (and even that) the sum would be paid; but there was anyway consideration without relying on the *Williams v Roffey* principle of practical benefit).

[93] *Adam Opel GmbH v Mitras Automotive (UK) Ltd*, see para.9-15 fn.88, at [41]–[42] (David

has also been distinguished as inapplicable to the case of a creditor's agreement to remit the balance of a debt in return for the debtor's payment of part of the debt, although this distinction was based on apparently conflicting authority in the House of Lords, rather than on any principled assessment of the merits of the decision in *Williams v Roffey* itself,[94] and most recently the Court of Appeal has accepted that "practical benefit" (in the sense developed by *Williams v Roffey*) can be good consideration for the variation or remission of a debt,[95] although the Supreme Court has left the question open.[96] In the courts in other Commonwealth jurisdictions, however, the reception of *Williams v Roffey* has generally been positive: for example, courts in Australia,[97] Canada,[98] New Zealand[99] and Singapore,[100] have ac-

---

Donaldson QC: "Though all three judges claimed to accept the rule in *Stilk v Myrick*, it is wholly unclear how the decision in *Williams v Roffey* can be reconciled with it. On analysis, the benefit or advantage lay in an act or promise wholly coincident with the plaintiff's existing contractual obligation. ... In terms of its result and the reasons advanced by the judges, however, *Williams v Roffey* would seem to permit any variation of a contract, even if the benefits and burdens of the variation move solely in one direction, and I am bound to apply the decision accordingly, whatever view I might take of its logical coherence"; *South Caribbean Trading Ltd v Trafigura Beheer BV* [2004] EWHC 2676 (Comm); [2005] 1 Lloyd's Rep. 128 at [108] (Colman J: "But for the fact that *Williams v Roffey Bros*. was a decision of the Court of Appeal, I would not have followed it. That decision is inconsistent with the long-standing rule that consideration, being the price of the promise sued upon, must move from the promisee" and criticising the reasoning of the three judges in *Williams v Roffey* (but holding at [109] that the variation was not binding because it resulted from a threat analogous to economic duress)).

94   *Re Selectmove Ltd* [1995] 1 W.L.R. 474, CA, at 481, applying *Foakes v Beer* (1884) 9 App. Cas. 605, HL; followed in *Collier v P & MJ Wright (Holdings) Ltd* [2007] EWCA Civ 1329; [2008] 1 W.L.R. 643 at [3]; *Corbern v Whatmusic Holdings Ltd* [2003] EWHC 2134 (Ch) at [6]; *Doussopoulos v Erste Bank Der Oesterreichischen Sparkassen AG* unreported 7 November 2000 (Mr Registrar Baister) at [6].

95   *MWB Business Exchange Centres Ltd v Rock Advertising Ltd*, see para.9-14 fn.76, at [49], [87].

96   *MWB Business Exchange Centres Ltd v Rock Advertising Ltd* [2018] UKSC 24; [2018] 2 W.L.R. 1603 at [18] (Lord Sumption, declining to give guidance on the "difficult issue" of whether the decision in *Williams v Roffey*, and *Foakes v Beer*, see para.9-15 fn.94, can stand together). For this significant and difficult conflict of authorities, see further paras 9-22, 9-23.

97   e.g. *Ajax Cooke Pty Ltd v Nugent* (1993) 5 V.I.R. 551, SC Victoria (variation in employment contract to include redundancy package was supported by consideration; but Phillips J noted with apparent approval that *Williams v Roffey* has made operation of the rule in *Stilk v Myrick* less rigorous); *Musumeci v Winadell Pty Ltd* (1994) 34 N.S.W.L.R. 723, SC New South Wales at 741–747 (Santow J, reviewing arguments for following *Williams v Roffey* in Australia, expanding at 747 the statement of Glidewell LJ, see para.9-14 fn.76, and applying it to the case of a promise to reduce rent under a lease in order to obtain practical benefit of retaining lessee as viable tenant); *Tinyow v Lee* [2006] NSWCA 80 at [61] (but holding that there was in any event consideration without reliance on the "practical benefit" test); *Dome Resources NL v Silver* [2008] NSWCA 322 at [61]–[67], but noting at [68] that "It is not necessary for present purposes to consider whether the concept of 'practical benefit' involves any departure from established principles relating to consideration". For further discussion and reference to other dicta and decisions, see M. Giancaspro, "Practical Benefit: an English Anomaly or a Growing Force in Contract Law?" (2013) 30 J.C.L. 12; and see generally Seddon and Bigwood, para.4.35.

98   *Greater Fredericton Airport Authority Inc v NAV Canada* (2008) 290 D.L.R. (4th) 405 (New Brunswick CA) at [25]–[32]. See generally Fridman, pp.98–104; Waddams, paras 133–140.

99   *Attorney General for England and Wales v R.* [2002] 2 N.Z.L.R. 91, NZCA, at 109; *Antons Trawling Co Ltd v Smith* [2003] 2 N.Z.L.R. 23, NZCA, at [93] ("The importance of consideration is as a valuable signal that the parties intend to be bound by their agreement, rather than an end in itself"). See generally Burrows, Finn and Todd, para.4.5.3.

100   *Sea-Land Service Inc v Cheong Fook Chee Vincent* [1994] SGCA 103; [1994] 3 S.L.R.(R.) 250 (but no practical benefit on facts); *Teo Seng Kee Bob v Arianecorp Ltd* [2008] SGHC 81; [2008] 3 S.L.R.(R.) 1114 at [89] ("the modern law on consideration has evolved and moved away from [the]

cepted and applied it, and have even sometimes taken it as a potential springboard for significant development of the doctrine of consideration, both in relation to the rules governing the part-payment of a debt,[101] and even in arguing for the removal of the requirement of consideration for the variation of a contract.[102]

9-16   **Criticism of the decision in Williams v Roffey; scope of the decision**   Critics emphasise that the notion of "practical benefit" is uncertain and unpredictable in when and where the courts may be able and willing to find it[103]; or that it will undermine the doctrine of consideration by allowing the courts in virtually every case where there is an agreed unilateral variation to find that there was some collateral benefit in fact received by the party who agreed to increase his obligations under the contract[104]; or that the effect of the decision in *Williams v Roffey* is to change the core notion of "benefit" within the doctrine of consideration, "with the consequential distortion, dilution and muddying of what we mean by contractual liability".[105] The controversial scope of the decision appears, however, to be quite narrow, in that it applies only where the claimant seeks to argue that what he has provided by way of consideration for the defendant's promise is to perform, at the defendant's request, only what he was already contractually obligated to the defendant to do.[106] This means that the parties are already in a binding contractual relationship, and the most common situation in which such an appeal to "practical benefit" will be made is in a case, such as *Williams v Roffey* itself, where the agreement is to vary the terms of that pre-existing contract in only the claimant's favour. The decision in *Williams v Roffey* does not undermine the core notion that a gratuitous promise is not in itself binding simply because the promisor intended to be bound by it, but retains the principle that a claimant can sue on a promise because he has promised, done, or forborne to do something at the defendant's request in return for

---

old position [of *Stilk v Myrick*]. The modern approach (albeit much criticised by academics) is encapsulated in the judgment of Glidewell LJ in *Williams v Roffey* [see para.9-14 fn.76]"). See also the dicta of Andrew Phang Boon Leong J.A. in *Sunny Metal & Engineering Pte Ltd v Ng Khim Ming Eric* [2006] SGHC 222; [2007] 1 S.L.R.(R.) 853 at [29]–[30] and *Gay Choon Ing v Loh Sze Ti Terence Peter* [2009] SGCA 3; [2009] 2 S.L.R.(R.) 332 at [70], [111]–[113] (developing arguments for reform).

[101] See paras 9-17 to 9-22; see esp. dicta in *Sunny Metal & Engineering Pte Ltd v Ng Khim Ming Eric*, see para.9-15 fn.100, and *Gay Choon Ing v Loh Sze Ti Terence Peter*, see para.9-15 fn.100.

[102] See esp. *Antons Trawling Co Ltd v Smith*, see para.9-15 fn.99; *Greater Fredericton Airport Authority Inc v NAV Canada*, see para.9-15 fn.98, at [31].

[103] See Reynolds and Treitel, see para.9-11 fn.51, p.14 (writing before the development of the law made by *Williams v Roffey*): "the court will tend to stress the factual benefit or detriment when it thinks that the agreement should be upheld, and the lack of legal benefit or detriment when it thinks that it should not". cf. *Horwood v Land of Leather Ltd* see para.9-15 fn.92, at [41] (Teare J: "Although counsel for the Claimants contended that this could not properly be regarded as a practical benefit the court should be slow to say that that which a business man says is a benefit is not; see *Williams v Roffey Bros* at p.21E–H per Purchas LJ").

[104] *Adam Opel GmbH v Mitras Automotive (UK) Ltd*, see para.9-15 fn.88, at [42] (David Donaldson QC: "*Williams v Roffey* would seem to permit any variation of a contract, even if the benefits and burdens of the variation move solely in one direction ... The law of consideration is no longer to be used to protect a participant in such a variation"). B. Coote, "Consideration and Benefit in Fact and in Law" (1990) 3 J.C.L. 23; M. Chen-Wishart, "Consideration: Practical Benefit and the Emperor's New Clothes" in J. Beatson and D. Friedmann (eds), *Good Faith and Fault in Contract Law* (Clarendon Press, 1995), p.123.

[105] Chen-Wishart, see para.9-16 fn.104, at p.124.

[106] See also para.8-39.

the defendant's promise.[107] In a case such as *Williams v Roffey*, what the defendant asked the claimant to do is to give a reassurance that he will in fact perform his existing obligations, and the defendant thinks it appropriate to offer in return the promise which the claimant now seeks to enforce. The element within the traditional requirements of consideration that is apparently undermined by the decision in *Williams v Roffey* is the rule that what the claimant provides to the defendant must be something of benefit to the defendant and/or detrimental to the claimant[108]; and the reason that this appears not to be fulfilled in a case of unilateral variation of the kind in *Stilk v Myrick*[109] and *Williams v Roffey* is that the performance for the defendant of what the defendant is already contractually entitled to receive from the claimant cannot give him anything more that the defendant already has, nor cost the claimant any more than he already owes. But *Williams v Roffey* allows the court to take a broader view of "benefit" to the defendant, so that as long as the defendant chooses to accept from the claimant a promise to do what he is (in law) already required to do as the price for his own new promise, and provided that the court can see that there was some collateral benefit thereby accruing to the defendant, it is sufficient to make the promise binding. The justification for the claimant's right to enforce the defendant's obligation remains that he has done what the defendant asked of him, and the defendant has thereby benefited in the way in which he sought to do.[110]

The context of contractual re-negotiations gives a particular context to this discussion. As long as the court has other mechanisms to deal with re-negotiations which are pressurised, or induced by fraud, then there is a general interest in allowing the parties' agreement to have force. It is not as strong as the policy in favour of compromises of disputed claims,[111] but there is a not-too-distant analogy in the courts' willingness to ensure that the contract does not break down where the parties choose freely to re-write their bargain. If there is some form of benefit accruing to both sides, even if it is only some collateral benefit enjoyed by the defendant in the form of the weakened version of "practical" benefit recognised by the Court of Appeal in *Williams v Roffey*, the courts are able to give effect to what is still, in reality, a bargain between the contracting parties.

There is a further significance in the fact that the context of *Williams v Roffey* is the variation of an existing contract. The parties have agreed their exchange in the initial formation of the contract, where the balance between the parties' obligations was fixed. The traditional view is that if that balance is to be adjusted, it requires a new contract, with consideration provided by each party as the price of his being able to enforce the varied terms.[112] But as long as some obligations under the contract remain unperformed by both parties, they could equally well achieve their object by an agreed discharge of the existing contract, and its replacement by a new contract which reflects the new, agreed balance.[113] If on the facts the court were able to find that this two-stage process was what the parties had agreed, there

---

[107] See para.8-08.
[108] See para.8-23.
[109] See para.9-11.
[110] See paras 8-07, 8-08, 8-15, 8-23.
[111] See para.8-30.
[112] See para.9-02.
[113] See para.9-03.

would be no difficulty in giving it force,[114] and the fact that the parties could not have achieved by a single step what they can achieve in two steps would not be a sufficient reason to refuse to recognise the transactions which they have effected.[115] Given that the courts appear to be well-disposed to ensuring that a genuine re-negotiation of the contract is enforceable, it could lead them to consider imputing to the parties the intention to effect their variation by the discharge of the old contract and its replacement by the new, even if the facts were not able to sustain it. This fiction has not been adopted by the English courts,[116] which have preferred to keep as close as possible to the traditional application of the doctrine of consideration, finding "benefit" even if it is apparently a significant relaxation of the rule as it had been understood until the decision in *Williams v Roffey*. A better approach might be simply to go to the heart of the matter: to accept that there is an interest in enforcing genuine re-negotiations of contracts, even variations which are in substance unilateral, and remove the requirement of consideration for a variation.[117]

(3) Hard Cases: II: Part-payment of a Debt

9-17   **Contractual reduction or discharge of a debt requires consideration or a deed**   Particular difficulties have arisen in practice in relation to the enforceability of a creditor's agreement to reduce or discharge the debtor's obligation to pay a debt. The debt constitutes a personal obligation on the part of the debtor to pay a sum of money to the creditor.[118] If that obligation is to be varied or discharged by the creditor's agreement, in principle such an agreement must take the form either of a contract supported by consideration provided by the debtor to the creditor, or of a deed executed by the creditor. Sometimes it is said that the debt will be reduced or extinguished by an "accord and satisfaction" between the parties, although this cannot be taken to indicate that the parties' agreement ("accord") to

---

[114] This is what the Referee appears to have done in *Watkins & Son v Carrig* (1941) 91 N.H. 459, 21 A.2d 591, SC New Hampshire. There was a rescission (discharge) and new contract by way of variation in *Compagnie Noga D'Importation et D'Exportation SA v Abacha (No.2)* [2003] EWCA Civ 1100; [2003] 2 All E.R. (Comm) 915.

[115] *Watkins & Son v Carrig*, see para.9-16 fn.114, at [2] (Allen CJ: "With full recognition of the legal worthlessness of a bare promise and of performance of a subsisting duty as void consideration, a result accomplished by proper means is not necessarily bad because it would be bad if the means were improper or were not employed. ... The result being reasonable, the means taken to reach it may be examined to determine their propriety"); *Compagnie Noga D'Importation et D'Exportation SA v Abacha (No.2)*, see para.9-16 fn.114, at [60] (Tuckey LJ: single document which effected variation by the two steps of rescission and a new contract should not be read as an (ineffective) single transaction: "that is not appealing to the substance of the transaction ... but creating a fiction which the parties have expressly avowed").

[116] The application of *Watkins & Son v Carrig*, see para.9-16 fn.114, was rejected on the facts by Mocatta J in *North Ocean Shipping Co Ltd v Hyundai Construction Co Ltd*, see para.9-13 fn.63, at 714, and by Purchas LJ in *Williams v Roffey Bros & Nicholls (Contractors) Ltd* [1991] 1 Q.B. 1 at 20.

[117] See para.9-24.

[118] It may arise from contract, such as the price payable under a contract of sale, or in other circumstances, such as a judgment debt, or the beneficiary's right to be paid a legacy by the personal representatives of the deceased; and it is a *chose in action* and therefore has potential proprietary characteristics, as well as being a contractual (personal) right: F.H. Lawson and B. Rudden, *Law of Property*, 3rd edn (Clarendon Press, 2002), pp.29–30. However, in this chapter we use as the core illustration the typical case of a debt arising as a contractual obligation owed by the claimant to the defendant, where the defendant agrees to reduce or discharge the sum due.

reduce or extinguish the debt will be effective simply by reason of the fact that the debtor fulfils his part by paying the agreed part of the sum due.[119] The mere informal agreement of the creditor to give up all or part of the debt is a unilateral, gratuitous undertaking and therefore not contractually binding. We shall see in Chapter 10 that there are circumstances where such an agreement may be given some force through doctrines of waiver and estoppel.[120] In this section, however, we consider the circumstances in which there is a contractual reduction or discharge of the debt.

The rule in Pinnel's Case   For the debtor to provide consideration to the creditor for the reduction or discharge of the debt he must promise, do or forbear to do something, at the request of the creditor, which constitutes a benefit to the creditor and/or detriment to the debtor.[121] Given that the court does not concern itself with the adequacy of consideration,[122] it does not matter how valuable the benefit may be to the creditor or how costly to the debtor. But it is no benefit to the creditor if the debtor gives him nothing more than his existing legal entitlement, and so it is not sufficient for the debtor to promise to pay, or in fact to pay, part of the debt in return for the creditor's agreement to reduce or discharge of the balance, since the creditor is already entitled to the part which the debtor promises to pay or in fact pays.[123] This is generally known as the rule in *Pinnel's Case*, after the decision of the Common Pleas in 1602 in which Coke reports the decision of the Court as follows[124]: **9-18**

> "it was resolved by the whole Court, that payment of a lesser sum on the day in satisfaction of a greater, cannot be any satisfaction for the whole, because it appears to the Judges that by no possibility, a lesser sum can be a satisfaction to the plaintiff for a greater sum: but the gift of a horse, hawk, or robe, &c. in satisfaction is good. For it shall be intended that a horse, hawk, or robe, &c. might be more beneficial to the plaintiff than the money, in respect of some circumstance, or otherwise the plaintiff would not have accepted of it in satisfaction. But when the whole sum is due, by no intendment the acceptance of parcel can be a satisfaction to the plaintiff: but in the case at Bar it was resolved, that the pay-

---

[119] *D&C Builders Ltd v Rees* [1966] 2 Q.B. 617, CA, at 632 (Winn LJ: "it is an essential element of a valid accord and satisfaction that the agreement which constitutes the accord should itself be binding in law, and I do not think that any such agreement can be so binding unless it is either made under seal or supported by consideration. Satisfaction, viz., performance, of an agreement of accord, does not provide retroactive validity to the accord, but depends for its effect upon the legal validity of the accord as a binding contract at the time when it is made"); see also Lord Denning MR at 622–623; Danckwerts LJ at 626. In the case, the issue was not only whether there was consideration (satisfaction) but also whether there was true accord (since the debtor put pressure on the creditor to accept less than the full sum due). cf., however, *Arrale v Costain Civil Engineering Ltd* [1976] 1 Lloyd's Rep. 98, CA, at 102 where Lord Denning MR appeared to use the term "accord and satisfaction" to cover the case where there may not be consideration for an agreed variation or discharge of an obligation.

[120] See paras 10-34 to 10-37.

[121] See para.8-23.

[122] See para.8-25.

[123] Payment by the debtor's personal cheque is equated to payment in cash: the creditor receives no greater benefit from the cheque than from the same amount of cash: *D&C Builders Ltd v Rees* [1966] 2 Q.B. 617, CA, at 623, 626, 629, rejecting the earlier contrary decision in *Goddard & Son v O'Brien* (1882) 9 Q.B.D. 37.

[124] (1602) 5 Co. Rep. 117a at 117a–117b, 77 E.R. 237 at 237–238. Coke repeated the point in Co. Litt. 212(b) commenting on Littleton who at section 344 gave the example of a mortgagee who accepts "a horse, or a cup of silver, or a ring of gold, or any such other thing in full satisfaction of the money … though the horse or the other thing be not of the twentieth part of the value of the sum of money".

ment and acceptance of parcel before the day in satisfaction of the whole, would be a good satisfaction in regard of circumstance of time; for peradventure parcel of it before the day would be more beneficial to him than the whole at the day, and the value of the satisfaction is not material: so if I am bound in £20 to pay you £10 at Westminster and you request me to pay you £5 at the day at York, and you will accept it in full satisfaction of the whole £10 it is a good satisfaction for the whole: for the expences to pay it at York, is sufficient satisfaction."

The case was determined on the basis of a point of pleading[125] but the principle as it would apply to the facts is clear. In the case, the defendant (the debtor) owed £8 10s. which was due on 11 November 1600; but on 1 October at the claimant's request he paid £5 2s. 2d., in full satisfaction of the whole. Although the payment was of a smaller sum than the debt, it was paid early, and this provided to the claimant a benefit which therefore constituted good consideration. If the agreement had been merely to pay less than the full sum *on the due date*, and *without anything more* being given by the defendant in return for the claimant's agreement to discharge the balance of the debt, there would have been no valid consideration and therefore the debt would have remained enforceable.

9-19   **Acceptance of Pinnel's Case in Foakes v Beer**   The rule in *Pinnel's Case* received the rather grudging formal acceptance of the House of Lords in *Foakes v Beer*.[126] That case was rather unusual: the balance of the debt which was said to have been discharged by part-payment was the obligation to pay statutory interest due on a judgment debt where the creditor agreed to accept payment of the principal debt by instalments, and the debtor then paid the principal debt in full in accordance with that agreement. There was disagreement in the House of Lords about whether, on its proper construction, the creditor's agreement to accept payment by instalments also included a promise not to claim the interest due on each instalment until its payment[127]; but all four members of the House agreed that, even if the agreement should be so construed, it would not be binding because of the rule in *Pinnel's Case*. The reasoning was clear: although the resolution of the Common Pleas, reported by Coke,[128] was not necessary for the decision in *Pinnel's Case* (since the debtor in fact provided consideration by reason of his early payment),[129] and the principle which it expressed had not been applied directly in later cases, it had been consistently assumed by the courts to be correct.[130] The House of Lords was not bound by any authority to apply the rule in *Pinnel's Case*; and they thought that it was a regrettable rule which might be better not followed.[131] However, the fact that it had been accepted for nearly three centuries was a sufficient reason for

---

[125] The defendant failed to plead that he had *paid* the sum in full satisfaction, only that the claimant had *accepted* it in full satisfaction, the tender of payment being determined by the payor rather than the payee: see (1602) 5 Co. Rep. 117a, at 117b, 77 E.R. 237 at 238.
[126] (1884) 9 App. Cas. 605, HL.
[127] Lord Selborne ((1884) 9 App. Cas. 605, at 610) and Lord Blackburn (at 614–615) construed the agreement as agreeing to not to sue for interest; Lord Watson (at 623) and Lord FitzGerald (at 624–627) construed it as only an agreement to allow payment by instalments, and not remitting the interest.
[128] See para.9-18 fn.124.
[129] See para.9-19 fn.126, at 617 (Lord Blackburn), 628 (Lord FitzGerald).
[130] See para.9-19 fn.126, at 612 (Lord Selborne), 617–622 (Lord Blackburn, reviewing the cases in detail), 628–629 (Lord FitzGerald).
[131] See further below.

the House not to disturb it.[132] This is an illustration of the reluctance of the English courts to change well-established principles of the common law,[133] but the decision in *Foakes v Beer* goes further than this: the House of Lords not only refused to depart from the long-accepted obiter dictum set out in *Pinnel's Case* but applied it for the first time directly in the case and so gave it the imprimatur of the binding authority of the House. A decision of the House of Lords could at that time be changed only by statute,[134] so the decision in *Foakes v Beer* set the rule in *Pinnel's Case* firmly as a principle of contract law, within the doctrine of consideration.

Doubts in Foakes v Beer about the merits of the rule in Pinnel's Case   The   **9-20**
decision in *Foakes v Beer*[135] may seem all the more surprising because in the House of Lords there was a marked general disapproval of the rule in *Pinnel's Case*. There was no suggestion that the general doctrine of consideration was wrong, or should be changed either in general or in relation to the variation of contracts. But there was a clear concern about the strict operation of the doctrine in the context of the rule that part-payment of a debt cannot be satisfaction for the whole debt. Lord Selborne said[136]:

"The distinction between the effect of a deed under seal, and that of an agreement by parol, or by writing not under seal, may seem arbitrary, but it is established in our law; nor is it really unreasonable or practically inconvenient that the law should require particular solemnities to give to a gratuitous contract the force of a binding obligation. If the question be (as, in the actual state of the law, I think it is), whether consideration is, or is not, given in a case of this kind, by the debtor who pays down part of the debt presently due from him, for a promise by the creditor to relinquish, after certain further payments on account, the residue of the debt, I cannot say that I think consideration is given, in the sense in which I have always understood that word as used in our law. It might be (and indeed I think it would be) an improvement in our law, if a release or acquittance of the whole debt, on payment of any sum which the creditor might be content to receive by way of accord and satisfaction (though less than the whole), were held to be, generally, binding, though not under seal; nor should I be unwilling to see equal force given to a prospective agreement, like the present, in writing though not under seal; but I think it impossible, without refinements which practically alter the sense of the word, to treat such a release or acquittance as supported by any new consideration proceeding from the debtor."

Lord Blackburn put it in the strongest terms—and, indeed, he said that he had hoped to persuade the House not to follow *Pinnel's Case*, but in the end he did not

---

[132] See para.9-19 fn.126, at 612 (Lord Selborne), 623–624 (Lord Watson), 629–630 (Lord FitzGerald).
[133] The American courts have not been so reluctant, at least on this point: see *Frye v Hubbell* (1907) 74 N.H. 358, 68 A. 325, SC New Hampshire at 330 (Parsons CJ: "The rule [in *Pinnel's Case*] is not a statute, or even a rule of property. Its validity depends upon its consonance with reason. While the almost universal acceptance of it may commend it to the court with almost irresistible force, still it is open for examination as to whether it was originally sound and whether the weight of the authority upholding it is not diminished or totally overthrown by the exceptions with which the rule cannot logically stand"); see further para.9-23 fn.192.
[134] i.e. until the House took the power in 1966 to depart from its own previous decisions: Practice Statement (Judicial Precedent) [1966] 1 W.L.R. 1234. The first opportunity for Parliament to deal with this came in 1937 when the Law Revision Committee proposed statutory reform of the doctrine of consideration, including the rule in Pinnel's Case: Law Revision Committee, Sixth Interim Report, *Statute of Frauds and the Doctrine of Consideration* Cmd.5449 (1937) at [33]–[35]; this was not, however, taken forward: see para.9-23.
[135] See para.9-19.
[136] See para.9-19 fn.126, at 613.

press this and acquiesced in the decision[137]:

"What principally weighs with me in thinking that Lord Coke made a mistake of fact is my conviction that all men of business, whether merchants or tradesmen, do every day recognise and act on the ground that prompt payment of a part of their demand may be more beneficial to them than it would be to insist on their rights and enforce payment of the whole. Even where the debtor is perfectly solvent, and sure to pay at last, this often is so. Where the credit of the debtor is doubtful it must be more so."

Foakes v Beer has been applied in a number of cases in the lower courts.[138] However, as we shall see in the following paragraphs, the courts have sometimes found solutions which appear to circumvent the strict rule in *Pinnel's Case*; and there has been further criticism of the rule. The Supreme Court has even expressed the view that the decision in *Foakes v Beer* "is probably ripe for re-examination" but declined to conduct such a re-examination, saying that—if it might lead to the Court departing from its earlier decision, or its effect being substantially modified— the re-examination should be before an enlarged panel of the Court, and in a case where the decision would form the ratio rather than merely obiter dictum.[139]

9-21   **Apparent and actual exceptions to the requirement of consideration for discharge of the balance of a debt**   Some cases where the courts appear to find a way round the strictness of the rule in *Pinnel's Case* are not exceptions as such, but involve the application of orthodox rules in order to find consideration for the agreement to discharge the balance of the debt. The parties to such a variation of a debt, if well advised,[140] will bring their agreement within the general rules for the formation of a contract by expressing the discharge of the balance of the debt to be in return not merely for the agreement to pay, or the actual payment, of part, but also for some other thing, however small. It cannot be in return for another sum of money, since the agreement to discharge £100 in return for payment of £1 is simply a gratuitous agreement to discharge £99 and the courts cannot ignore the obvious set-off of the two sums of money.[141] But, following the general principle that they

---

137   See para.9-19 fn.126, at 622; a similar point was made by counsel for the appellant at 607 ("It is every day practice for tradesmen to take less in satisfaction of a larger sum, and give discount, where there is neither custom nor right to take credit"). At 630 Lord FitzGerald agreed with Lord Blackburn "that it would have been wiser and better if the resolution in *Pinnel's Case* had never been come to." Lord Watson at 623–624 did not discuss this in detail, but agreed generally with Lord Selborne and Lord FitzGerald.

138   e.g. *Vanbergen v St Edmunds Properties Ltd* [1933] 2 K.B. 223, CA, at 234–235, 237; *D&C Builders Ltd v Rees* [1966] 2 Q.B. 617, CA, at 623, 626–627, 632; *Re Selectmove Ltd* [1995] 1 W.L.R. 474, CA, at 480–481; *Corbern v Whatmusic Holdings Ltd* [2003] EWHC 2134 (Ch) at [6]; *Collier v P & MJ Wright (Holdings) Ltd* [2007] EWCA Civ 1329; [2008] 1 W.L.R. 643 at [6].

139   *MWB Business Exchange Centres Ltd v Rock Advertising Ltd*, see para.9-15 fn.96, at [18] (Lord Sumption, with whom Lady Hale, Lord Wilson and Lord Lloyd-Jones agreed; Lord Briggs agreed on this point at [20]).

140   The simpler solution may be to use a deed: see para.9-26, although again this will normally be done only by parties who have legal advice to the effect that the agreement to discharge the balance of the debt is not in law enforceable in the absence of consideration or a deed.

141   cf. *Couldery v Bartrum* (1881) 19 Ch. D. 394, CA, at 399 (Jessel MR: "According to English Common Law a creditor might accept anything in satisfaction of his debt except a less amount of money. He might take a horse, or a canary, or a tomtit if he chose, and that was accord and satisfaction; but, by a most extraordinary peculiarity of the English Common Law, he could not take 19s. 6d. in the pound; that was *nudum pactum*"). Similarly, the courts do not see that the debtor's cheque for £300 gives the creditor any more benefit than £300 in cash, and therefore such a cheque cannot constitute

will not investigate the adequacy of consideration,[142] the courts will turn a blind eye to the value of whatever is promised in return, even in a case where the consideration is nominal and there is no real expectation that it will ever actually be paid over.[143] The statement of the principle in *Pinnel's Case* itself gave as the possible solution the substitution of something of small value for the discharged part of the debt,[144] and in *Foakes v Beer*[145] Lord Blackburn emphasised that this may be used successfully as a fiction.

Similarly, a debt may be validly discharged by part-payment within the orthodox rules for consideration where there is dispute about the value of the debt, even if the dispute is settled on the basis that the debtor will pay less than the sum claimed as due by the creditor and it is later shown that the creditor's claim was justified, and so the agreement was to give up the claim to the balance of the debt. The fact that the parties have entered into a genuine compromise of the claim renders it binding.[146]

A further basis to avoid the strict rule in *Pinnel's Case*, whilst still keeping within established contract doctrine, is if the extension of consideration to include "practical benefit", made by the Court of Appeal in *Williams v Roffey Bros & Nicholls (Contractors) Ltd*,[147] is accepted as applying in the context of part-payment of a debt. This is considered below.[148]

In other cases, however, the courts have not strained to find that there is consideration in the form of additional benefit to the creditor or additional detriment to the debtor in return for the payment of part of the debt, or to bring the agreement within some other established rule within the doctrine of consideration, but have admitted that an exception to the general rule must be made in order to give force to parties' transactions—especially commercial transactions.[149] Where the agreement to reduce the debt is made by the debtor with a group of his creditors, the fact that the creditors have mutually agreed to reduce the debtor's obligations if he pays part renders the agreement (and therefore the discharge of the balance of the debts) enforceable by the debtor himself as against each of the creditors.

---

consideration: *D&C Builders Ltd v Rees*, see para.9-20 fn.138.

142 See para.8-25.

143 For "nominal" consideration, see para.8-25 fn.153.

144 See para.9-18 fn.124, (the horse, hawk, or robe); similarly Co. Litt. 212(b) "though the horse or the other thing be not of the twentieth part of the value of the sum of money".

145 See para.9-18 fn.126, at 618, discussing the practice of pleading in cases involving part-payment of a debt, and referring to "a sham plea—that a chattel was given and accepted in satisfaction of the debt. The recognised forms were giving and accepting in satisfaction a beaver hat: *Young v Rudd* (1700) 5 Mod. 86, 87b E.R. 535, or a pipe of wine (3 Chit. Plead. 7th edn 92). All this is now antiquated. But whilst it continued to be the practice, the pleas founded on the first part of the resolution in *Pinnel's Case* were very common, and that law was perfectly trite. No one for a moment supposed that a beaver hat was really given and accepted; but every one knew that the law was that if it was really given and accepted it was a good satisfaction".

146 But the payment only of a sum admitted to be due cannot be consideration for the discharge of a disputed balance of a claim: *Ferguson v Davies* [1997] 1 All E.R. 315, CA. For compromises generally, see paras 8-30 to 8-31.

147 [1991] 1 Q.B. 1, CA; see para.9–14.

148 See para.9–22.

149 In *Collier v P & MJ Wright (Holdings) Ltd* [2007] EWCA Civ 1329; [2008] 1 W.L.R. 643 CA declined, however, to create a new exception for the case of creditor's agreement with joint debtor to accept payment from him alone of his proportionate share in return for creditor's promise not to sue for balance of debt, but such a case may be covered by the doctrine of promissory estoppel: see para.9-23 fn.197.

Sometimes this has been put in terms that the creditors' mutual agreement to forbear to enforce the balance of their debts supplied the consideration for the discharge of the balance[150]; or that each of the creditors, having bound himself to the others to forego part of his debt, could not be permitted to obtain an unfair advantage as against the other creditors by suing the debtor for the foregone part.[151] However, the simpler view is that the debtor, though a party to the agreement with the creditors, does not in reality provide consideration for the discharge of his debts[152] and that the agreed composition by the creditors forms an exception to the general rule in *Pinnel's Case*—an exception which is necessary to give effect to a sensible (and very common) commercial arrangement.[153] Where the creditors approve a debtor's proposal for a voluntary arrangement under the Part VIII of the Insolvency Act 1986, all the creditors are similarly bound by statute.[154]

Another established exception to the rule in *Pinnel's Case* is where the creditor accepts payment of part of the debt from a third party in satisfaction of the whole. As in the case of a binding composition amongst creditors, the debtor does not himself provide consideration for the discharge of his debt—and, indeed, in the case of a third-party payment he may not even be party to the agreement between the creditor and the third party. But it is well established that the payment by the third party, accepted by the creditor on that basis, can have the effect of discharging the debt. The courts have had some difficulty in agreeing on a common explanation for this.[155] It has been said that it would be fraud on the third party to accept his payment but then to continue to pursue the debtor, but also that it is part of the well-known rules of mercantile law as to payment.[156]

---

[150] *Good v Cheesman* (1831) 2 B. & Ad. 328, 109 E.R. 1165; *Couldery v Bartrum*, see para.9-21 fn.141, at 400 (Jessel MR).

[151] *Wood v Roberts* (1818) 2 Stark. 417, 171 E.R. 691; *Mallalieu v Hodgson* (1851) 16 Q.B. 689, 117 E.R. 1045; *Cook v Lister* (1863) 13 C.B. N.S. 543 at 595, 143 E.R. 215 at 235 (Willes J: "otherwise fraud would be committed against the rest of the creditors"); *Couldery v Bartrum*, see para.9-21 fn.141, at 400 (Jessel MR).

[152] *Fitch v Sutton* (1804) 5 East 230, 102 E.R. 1058. Corbin (1963), para.190 (and revised edn, 1995, para.7.18) suggests that the debtor provides consideration by giving up the opportunity to treat his creditors unequally. The composition amongst creditors could be seen as a problem arising from the doctrine of privity of contract: P. Birks and J. Beatson, "Unrequested Payment of Another's Debt" (1976) 92 L.Q.R. 188, 193–199; and since the enactment of the Contracts (Rights of Third Parties) Act 1999, the debtor might be able to argue that he can enforce the creditors' agreement as a third party; but such an analysis is not necessary, since the enforceability of the creditors' agreement without the debtor providing consideration is already an established exception.

[153] *West Yorkshire Darracq Agency Ltd v Coleridge* [1911] 2 K.B. 326; *Couldery v Bartrum*, see para.9-21 fn.141, at 399–400 (Jessel MR: "there came a class of arrangements between creditors and debtors, by which a debtor who was unable to pay in full offered a composition of something less in the pound. Well, it was felt to be a very absurd thing that the creditors could not bind themselves to take less than the amount of their debts. There might be friends of the debtor who would come forward and pay something towards the debts; or it might be that the debtor was in such a position that, if the creditors took less than their debts, he would have something over for himself and would exert himself to pay the dividend; whereas, if the creditors did not, they would get nothing or less than nothing, if they incurred costs in endeavouring to get payment").

[154] Insolvency Act 1986 s.260(2), as amended by Small Business, Enterprise and Employment Act 2015 Sch.9(2) para.67.

[155] The transaction between the third party and the creditor, if adopted by the debtor, may constitute a disposition which discharges the debt: Birks and Beatson, see para.9-21 fn.152, at 193, 195–199. However, for discussion of the general problem of when and how a third party can discharge a debt see Goff & Jones, *The Law of Restitution*, 7th edn (Sweet & Maxwell, 2007) para.1-018.

[156] *Cook v Lister*, see para.9-21 fn.151, at 594–595, at 235 (Willes J, giving the same reason for the

**The relevance of Williams v Roffey in relation to the discharge of the balance   9-22
of a debt**   We might expect the courts to reconsider the rule in *Pinnel's Case*—or
at least the circumstances in which it applies—in light of the decision in *Williams
v Roffey Bros & Nicholls (Contractors) Ltd*.[157] The performance by the claimant of
the contractual duty which he already owes to the defendant cannot normally
constitute consideration for the defendant's promise,[158] but where the performance
of such a pre-existing duty provides a collateral "practical benefit" to the defendant the courts have been willing to find consideration[159]; and this was applied in
particular by the Court of Appeal in *Williams v Roffey* to allow the defendant's
promise to increase the price payable under a carpentry sub-contract to be enforced
where the claimant's undertaking in return was only to continue to perform his
existing obligations under the sub-contract, but in consequence of that undertaking the defendant obtained certain "practical benefits" such as avoiding a penalty
for late completion under their main contract, and avoiding the trouble and expense
of finding a new carpentry sub-contractor.[160] This broader approach to the requirement that consideration provided by the claimant constitute a "benefit" to the
defendant was based on a desire of the courts to give effect to variations of a
contract which are freely[161] agreed by the parties, even where the variation in the
obligations is only unilateral.[162] This can be translated without apparent difficulty
to the case of part-payment of a debt where the creditor, although agreeing to
discharge the balance of the debt in return for part-payment, does so without fraud
or duress on the part of the debtor, and with a view to obtaining some collateral
benefit in consequence. The creditor may in practice obtain a benefit only from
actual payment of part of the debt, and not merely from the debtor's repetition of
his promise to pay the undischarged part.[163] But where the debtor in fact pays part

---

enforceability of a composition with multiple creditors); *Hirachand Punamchand v Temple* [1911]
2 K.B. 330, CA, at 337–338 (Vaughan Williams LJ, preferring, however, the analysis that the receipt
by the creditor created a trust in favour of the third party), 339 (Fletcher Moulton LJ, preferring
however, the view that the transaction between the third party and the creditor had the (dispositive)
effect of rendering the debt extinct); 342 (Farwell LJ).

[157] [1991] 1 Q.B. 1, CA; see para.9-14.
[158] See para.8-39.
[159] See para.9-13.
[160] See para.9-14.
[161] The development of the law of economic duress during the late 20th century was said in *Williams v
Roffey* to allow the courts to take a more relaxed approach to the requirement of "benefit"; and in
any case the better tools for determining whether a variation is enforceable are the doctrines such
as fraud and duress which will allow a party who has not fully or freely agreed to the variation to
avoid it: [1991] 1 Q.B. 1, CA, at 13–14, 18, 21; and see generally para.9-14.
[162] See para.9-16.
[163] In the context of part-payment of a debt, the Law Revision Committee recommended reform that
would allow the promise, as well as performance, of an existing duty to be good consideration, but
that the failure to perform should cause the original obligation to revive: see para.9-23 fn.188. In
MWB Business Exchange Centres Ltd v Rock Advertising Ltd, see para.9-14 fn.76, at [49] Kitchin
LJ held that the variation of the contract by the promise to comply with a revised payment schedule
was binding on MWB (applying the "practical benefit" analysis of *Williams v Roffey*), and "would
remain binding for so long as Rock continued to make payments in accordance with the revised payment schedule". Arden LJ favoured an alternative analysis under which the variation agreement took
effect as a collateral unilateral contract, binding on MWB once the first payment had been made,
adopting the analysis in M. Chen-Wishart, "Reforming Consideration: No Greener Pastures" in S.
Degeling, J. Edelman and J. Goudkamp (eds), *Contract in Commercial Law* (Sydney, Thomson
Reuters Professional Australia, 2016) and M. Chen-Wishart, "A Bird in the Hand: Consideration and
Contract Modifications" in A. Burrows and E. Peel, *Contract Formation and Parties* (Oxford

of the debt in return for the discharge of the balance, the creditor has the advantage of having the cash in hand, rather than having to enforce the debt—which is even more clearly a benefit if there is a risk that the debtor might be unable to pay by the time the legal process to enforce the debt has taken its course. This is not only "benefit" in a very real, practical sense, but appears to be recognised as such commercially by the fact that creditors do agree to discount debts in order to secure their payment[164]; and was even set out by Lord Blackburn in *Foakes v Beer*[165] as a compelling reason for departing from the strict rule in *Pinnel's Case*.However, we have seen that the House of Lords was not prepared to depart from the long-accepted principle that part-payment of a debt cannot be consideration for the release of the balance of the debt, and Lord Blackburn did not press his arguments based on the practical benefits to the creditor.[166]

The more recent acceptance of a broader principle of "practical benefit" in *Williams v Roffey* might seem to bring Lord Blackburn's arguments back to the fore, and to re-open the question whether, although in principle part-payment of a debt may not be consideration for the remission of the balance on the basis that it does not benefit the creditor to receive something to which he is already entitled, at least where on the facts the creditor agrees to accept part-payment with a view to obtaining some collateral practical benefit this could suffice to render the promised discharge of the balance binding. Such an approach would not even conflict with the rule in *Pinnel's Case*, nor require any reconsideration of the decision of the House of Lords in *Foakes v Beer*, since it would simply be an application of the (modern, developed) doctrine of consideration[167]: just as the decision in *Williams v Roffey* has accepted a shift in the notion of "benefit" within the modern doctrine of consideration in light of other developments in contract law since the time when the earlier cases took a stricter view,[168] so that same line of argument can explain why the narrower approach taken in the older cases to the finding of "benefit" to the creditor who accepts part payment of the debt should be similarly developed.

It might be objected that there is a difference in principle between a case such as *Williams v Roffey* (a contract for the performance of services) and the case of part-payment of a debt,[169] or that there is a difference in principle between a promise to pay more than the contractual sum due (*Williams v Roffey*) and the promise to pay less (the rule in *Pinnel's Case*).[170] These are distinctions which the courts can raise in order to seek to justify their maintaining different rules in the two differ-

---

University Press, 2010), p.89. This approach was not adopted by Kitchin LJ or McCombe LJ (see at [49], [67]).

164 For debt factoring as an illustration of receivable financing, see E. McKendrick, *Goode on Commercial Law*, 5th edn (Penguin, 2016), paras 29.23 to 29.25.

165 (1884) 9 App. Cas. 605, HL, at 622 "all men of business, whether merchants or tradesmen, do every day recognise and act on the ground that prompt payment of a part of their demand may be more beneficial to them than it would be to insist on their rights and enforce payment of the whole. Even where the debtor is perfectly solvent, and sure to pay at last, this often is so. Where the credit of the debtor is doubtful it must be more so".

166 See para.9-20.

167 *MWB Business Exchange Centres Ltd v Rock Advertising Ltd*, see para.9-14 fn.76, at [85] (Arden LJ).

168 e.g. *Stilk v Myrick*, see para.9-11 fn.47; and see generally para.9–14.

169 e.g. *Re Selectmove Ltd* [1995] 1 W.L.R. 474, CA, at 480–481; *Collier v P & MJ Wright (Holdings) Ltd*, see para.9-21 fn.149, at [3]; cf. the explanation of *Re Selectmove Ltd* given in *MWB Business Exchange Centres Ltd v Rock Advertising Ltd*, see para.9-14 fn.76, at [83]–[85] (Arden LJ).

170 J. O'Sullivan, "In Defence of Foakes v Beer" [1996] C.L.J. 219.

ent situations, but it cannot be denied that there is a fundamental inconsistency in the courts' willingness to consider collateral "practical benefit" as sufficient consideration in the two different situations. Although the most recent considered decision on this point in the Court of Appeal has accepted that the "practical benefit" analysis of *Williams v Roffey* can be applied to part-payment of a debt where the facts of the case so allow,[171] the Supreme Court in that same case has left the matter expressly undecided, in a passage which does not make clear whether the development of the law made by *Williams v Roffey* is in itself acceptable, whether it should be applied in the case of part-payment of a debt, or even whether the decision in *Foakes v Beer* needs to be overruled or modified[172]:

> "The issue is a difficult one. The only consideration which MWB can be said to have been given for accepting a less advantageous schedule of payments was (i) the prospect that the payments were more likely to be made if they were loaded onto the back end of the contract term, and (ii) the fact that MWB would be less likely to have the premises left vacant on its hands while it sought a new licensee. These were both expectations of practical value, but neither was a contractual entitlement. In *Williams v Roffey Bros & Nicholls (Contractors) Ltd*,[173] the Court of Appeal held that an expectation of commercial advantage was good consideration. The problem about this was that practical expectation of benefit was the very thing which the House of Lords held not to be adequate consideration in *Foakes v Beer*: see in particular p.622 per Lord Blackburn.[174] There are arguable points of distinction, although the arguments are somewhat forced. A differently constituted Court of Appeal made these points in *Re Selectmove Ltd*,[175] and declined to follow *Williams v Roffey*. The reality is that any decision on this point is likely to involve a re-examination of the decision in *Foakes v Beer*. It is probably ripe for re-examination. But if it is to be overruled or its effect substantially modified, it should be before an enlarged panel of the court and in a case where the decision would be more than obiter dictum."

(4) Uncertainties in the Present Law, and the Need for Reform

Williams v Roffey, and its conflict with Foakes v Beer We have seen in the preceding sections of this chapter that the decision in *Williams v Roffey Brothers & Nicholls (Contractors) Ltd*[176] has given rise to uncertainties which call for clarification. As a decision of the Court of Appeal, *Williams v Roffey* can be authoritatively clarified (and accepted, or overruled) only by a decision of the Supreme Court, or by statute. 9-23

The first uncertainty is the general acceptance of the Court of Appeal in *Williams v Roffey* of "practical benefit" as sufficient consideration, where that benefit

---

[171] *MWB Business Exchange Centres Ltd v Rock Advertising Ltd*, see para.9-14 fn.76 (agreement to reschedule payments due under licence agreement to occupy office space for minimum 12-month term, including deferment of accumulated arrears: trial judge held as matter of fact that there was "an element of possible commercial benefit to [MWB] in retaining an existing tenant, even if a questionable payer, in the hope of perhaps recovering its arrears rather than getting rid of them, probably saying goodbye to the arrears and allowing the property to stand empty for some time at further loss to themselves").

[172] *MWB Business Exchange Centres Ltd v Rock Advertising Ltd*, see para.9-15 fn.96, at [18] (Lord Sumption).

[173] See para.9-22 fn.157.

[174] See para.9-22 fn.165.

[175] See para.9-22 fn.169.

[176] [1991] 1 Q.B. 1, CA.

consists in only some collateral advantage which the defendant sought to obtain as a result of requesting the claimant to continue to perform contractual duties which he owed already to the defendant. We have seen that this has been controversial in the lower courts in England,[177] although recently it has been received positively in the Court of Appeal,[178] and in other common law jurisdictions,[179] but the Supreme Court has avoided making any substantive comment on the decision.[180] Although it has a real merit in allowing the courts to enforce genuinely agreed contract renegotiations, even where the substantive variation of the terms of the contract appears to be unilateral, there is a tension with the general principles of contract formation which base the binding force of promises, and agreements, on the bilateral exchange of values between the parties.[181]

The second uncertainty flows from the apparent conflict of authority between *Williams v Roffey* and the earlier decision of the House of Lords in *Foakes v Beer*.[182] The factual context of those two cases is different and therefore at least in a narrow sense distinguishable, allowing the lower courts to follow each separately— *Williams v Roffey* as the authority for a unilateral variation in a contract involving the increase[183] in contractual duties such as payment (and allowing "practical benefits" obtained by the defendant to constitute sufficient consideration for his promise to vary); *Foakes v Beer* as the authority for a unilateral reduction or discharge of a debt (the rule in *Pinnel's Case*[184]—refusing to allow the "practical benefits" obtained by the creditor to constitute sufficient consideration for his promise to reduce or discharge the balance of the debt). But this is a very unsatisfactory position where there is in reality an underlying conflict as to the scope that should be given to the "practical benefit" principle.[185] At present, in England, the Court of Appeal has responded with mixed messages: some courts have resisted opening up this question, and have rested their decisions in cases of part-payment of a debt on the fact that *Foakes v Beer* is the higher authority[186]; but most recently the court has accepted that the "practical benefit" analysis that was developed in *Williams v Roffey* can, where the facts support it, provide a basis for deciding that there is consideration for the creditor's promise to accept part-payment of the debt in satisfaction of the whole.[187]

The need to address this issue is not new. In 1937 the Law Revision Committee in England mounted a vigorous criticism of the rule in *Pinnel's Case*, and proposed that legislation be passed to give effect to the "powerful argument" for its abolition set out by Lord Blackburn in *Foakes v Beer*[188]:

---

[177] See para.9-15 fn.93.
[178] *MWB Business Exchange Centres Ltd v Rock Advertising Ltd*, see para.9-22 fn.171.
[179] See para.9-15 fnn.97 to 100.
[180] *MWB Business Exchange Centres Ltd v Rock Advertising Ltd*, see para.9-22 fn.172.
[181] See para.9-16.
[182] (1884) 9 App. Cas. 605, HL.
[183] *Williams v Roffey* has not, however, been restricted in its application to promises to increase the payment under a contract for services: *Anangel Atlas Compania Naviera SA v Ishikawajima-Harima Heavy Industries Co Ltd (No.2)*, see para.9-15 fn.91 (reduction of price).
[184] (1602) 5 Co. Rep. 117a, 77 E.R. 237; see para.9-18.
[185] See para.9-22.
[186] See para.9-22 fn.169.
[187] *MWB Business Exchange Centres Ltd v Rock Advertising Ltd*, see para.9-22.
[188] Law Revision Committee, Sixth Interim Report, *Statute of Frauds and the Doctrine of Consideration* Cmd.5449 (1937), para.35.

"This legislation would have the additional value of removing the logical difficulty involved in finding a consideration for the creditors' promises in a composition with creditors when not under seal.[189] It would be possible to enact only that actual payment of the lesser sum should discharge the obligation to pay the greater, but we consider that it is more logical and more convenient to recommend that the greater obligation can be discharged either by a promise to pay a lesser sum or by actual payment of it, but that if the new agreement is not performed then the original obligation shall revive."

No steps were taken, however, to act on that recommendation, and the impetus for reform was lost.[190] The case for reform is no less strong today; and, as we have seen, the development of the "practical benefit" analysis in *Williams v Roffey* provides further support for allowing the part-payment of a debt to be good consideration for the discharge of the balance where the parties so agree. Some other common law jurisdictions have indicated a willingness to re-think the case of part-payment of a debt, either in light of the development in *Williams v Roffey*,[191] or on more general grounds of principle similar to those set out by Lord Blackburn in *Foakes v Beer*.[192] But the stricter approach to the doctrine of precedent, as well as a reluctance to depart from well-established rules within the common law,[193] acts as a restraint on the development of the law in the English courts. Only the Supreme Court can resolve the apparent conflict between the cases, but in 2018 the Supreme Court missed the opportunity to give guidance on this for the present.[194] A definitive resolution of this "difficult issue"[195] is surely called for,

---

[189] [See para.9-21.]

[190] For a discussion of the possible reasons that reform was not pursued, see J. Beatson, "Reforming the Law of Contracts for the Benefit of Third Parties – A Second Bite at the Cherry" (1992) 45(2) C.L.P. 1, 10–15 (the priorities of the war of 1939, of course; but also other circumstances such as the retirement on ill-health grounds in 1938 of Lord Hailsham LC, who had actively supported the proposals). The Law Commission revived the proposal for the reform of the doctrine of privity of contract, which was also made in the Law Revision Committee's Report in 1937, and made a new proposal for reform in 1996: Law Com. No.242, *Privity of Contact: Contracts for the Benefit of Third Parties*, which was substantially enacted in the Contracts (Rights of Third Parties) Act 1999. However, the Law Commission in its 1996 report did not make any proposal to reform the doctrine of consideration, either generally or even in relation to the third-party rule: Law Com. No.242, Pt VI.

[191] See, in Singapore, dicta in *Sunny Metal & Engineering Pte Ltd v Ng Khim Ming Eric* [2006] SGHC 222; [2007] 1 S.L.R.(R.) 853 at [29]–[30] and *Gay Choon Ing v Loh Sze Ti Terence Peter* [2009] SGCA 3; [2009] 2 S.L.R.(R.) 332 at [70], [111]–[113]. In Australia: *Musumeci v Winadell Pty Ltd*, see para.9-15 fn.97, SC New South Wales at 741–747 (Santow J has "thrown out a challenge to the rule in *Pinnel's Case*": Seddon and Bigwood, para.4.38).

[192] See para.9-22 fn.165: see *Frye v Hubbell* (1907) 74 N.H. 358, 68 A. 325, SC New Hampshire at 329, 334; *Kramas v Beattie* (1966) 221 A.2d 236, SC New Hampshire at 237 (Kenison CJ: "A half a century ago New Hampshire by judicial decision, quietly and unheralded, modernized a portion of the law of consideration by lopping off one of the historical errors of the common law. It repudiated *Pinnel's Case*"). *Pinnel's Case* has also been rejected by the courts in Minnesota, and other state legislatures have limited its operation: Farnsworth, para.4.25. In some provinces in Canada the part-payment rule has been reversed by statute in relation to part-performance of obligations more generally: Fridman, pp.118–119; Waddams, para.140 (e.g. in Ontario: Mercantile Law Amendment Act, R.S.O. 1990, s.16: "Part performance of an obligation either before or after a breach thereof when expressly accepted by the creditor in satisfaction or rendered in pursuance of an agreement for that purpose, though without any new consideration, shall be held to extinguish the obligation"). In Malaysia, Contracts Act 1950 s.64 reverses the rule in *Pinnel's Case*: Sinnadurai, para.3.46.

[193] See para.9-19 fnn.132, 133.

[194] *MWB Business Exchange Centres Ltd v Rock Advertising Ltd*, see para.9-22 fn.172.

[195] *MWB Business Exchange Centres Ltd v Rock Advertising Ltd*, see para.9-22 fn.172, at [18] (Lord

to settle the law in such a way as to bring the law on part-payment of a debt in line with commercial expectation and practice. However, given the Court's reluctance to re-examine it except in a case which will raise the issue by way of ratio,[196] we may have to wait a very long time for another opportunity to arise. Statutory reform may therefore be necessary.

In relation to the rule in *Pinnel's Case*, the pressure for reform may, however, have been reduced by the development of other doctrines which may now give force to the promise not to enforce all or part of a debt, and in particular the doctrine of promissory estoppel. We shall see this doctrine in detail in Chapter 10, but we can note here that it allows the courts in certain circumstances to enforce promises even though they lack consideration because of the operation of the rule in *Pinnel's Case*.[197]

9-24   **Should consideration be required for an agreed variation of a contract?**   A fundamental question is whether it is right to continue to require consideration for the variation of a contract. Some legal systems in the common law world have taken the view that, once the parties have formed their contract according to the normal rules for formation (agreement, supported by consideration) the variation of that contract should depend only on the parties' agreement without an additional requirement of new consideration,[198] and therefore an agreed unilateral variation of the terms would in principle be as effective as a bilateral variation. We have already seen that, in the case of a contract where both parties still have outstanding obligations, if the parties agree to discharge the existing contract and replace it with a new contract in which only one of the parties' obligations is different from those which

---

Sumption).

[196] *MWB Business Exchange Centres Ltd v Rock Advertising Ltd*, see para.9-22 fn.172.

[197] cf. *Central London Property Trust Ltd v High Trees House Ltd* [1947] K.B. 130 at 135 (Denning J: "The logical consequence, no doubt is that a promise to accept a smaller sum in discharge of a larger sum, if acted upon, is binding notwithstanding the absence of consideration"); *D&C Builders Ltd v Rees* [1966] 2 Q.B. 617, CA, at 623–625 (Lord Denning MR). See also *Collier v P & MJ Wright (Holdings) Ltd* [2007] EWCA Civ 1329; [2008] 1 W.L.R. 643 at [2]–[6], [23]–[28], [42] (Arden LJ: creditor's agreement with joint debtor to accept payment from him alone of his proportionate share in return for creditor's promise not to sue for balance of debt was not supported by consideration, and no new exception to the rule in *Pinnel's Case* should be carved out; but "the brilliant obiter dictum of Denning J in the *High Trees* case … to a significant degree … achieves in practical terms the recommendation of the Law Revision Committee" (Sixth Interim Report, *Statute of Frauds and the Doctrine of Consideration*, Cmd.5449 (1937), which proposed reform of the rule in *Pinnel's Case*). However, Longmore LJ at [48] was more cautious in the conclusions he drew from the *High Trees* case; and see also *MWB Business Exchange Centres Ltd v Rock Advertising Ltd* [2016] EWCA Civ 553; [2017] Q.B. 604 at [61] (Kitchen LJ). For further discussion see para.10–37).

[198] e.g. UCC §2-209 (agreement modifying contract for sale of goods needs no consideration to be binding, but signed contract may impose requirement of signature for variation, and any requirements of Statute of Frauds must always be complied with); similarly UCC §2A-208 (agreement modifying contract for lease of goods). See also *Rosas v Toca* 2018 BCCA 191 (CA British Columbia) at [4] (Bauman CJ): "The time has come to reform the doctrine of consideration as it applies in [the] context [of variations of existing contracts], and modify the pre-existing duty rule, as so many commentators and several courts have suggested. When parties to a contract agree to vary its terms, the variation should be enforceable without fresh consideration, absent duress, unconscionability, or other public policy concerns, which would render an otherwise valid term unenforceable. A variation supported by valid consideration may continue to be enforceable for that reason, but a lack of fresh consideration will no longer be determinative. In this way the legitimate expectations of the parties can be protected. To do otherwise would be to let the doctrine of consideration work an injustice."

have been discharged, the variation will be binding: the agreement to discharge the old contract is binding, each party providing consideration by giving up its rights under the old contract against the other; and the new contract is binding by virtue of the new agreed exchange—the fact that the same result would be obtained by a unilateral variation of the old contract is not an obstacle, since the new contract does not depend on the old.[199] The English courts have not, however, developed this as a solution for unilateral variations in cases where the parties have not explicitly taken the two steps (discharge and new contract) to effect the variation.[200] It could be argued it would be better to assimilate the variation of a contract to its discharge and replacement by a new contract, and allow variations of executory contracts to be binding without insisting on the strict requirement of new, additional consideration for the variation. The parties are already in a binding legal relationship, and any concerns which the requirement of consideration might be thought to address[201] have already been met in its formation. As long as the parties freely agree to the variation[202] there may be less concern to regulate the re-balancing of the contract to the new agreed terms. We should not assume that the rules set by the law for the creation or acquisition of rights must always be the same as the rules set for the variation or loss of those same rights.

III. PRACTICAL ISSUES RELATING TO CONTRACTUAL VARIATIONS

Drafting issues in contractual variations   Where an existing contract is to be varied, it is important to be clear in the drafting of the variation both as to the structure of the variation which is being adopted, and as to the terms which will result from the variation.[203]   **9-25**

We have seen that a variation may take the form of either a supplementary contract which will have to be read with the (continuing) original contract, or a wholly new contract which supersedes the original contract.[204] There may be practical reasons for preferring one or other structure,[205] but it should be noted that the variation of the original contract (or of any term in the original contract) which was subject to statutory formality requirements is likely to have to comply with the same formality.[206] This can be a trap, particularly in a case where there is only a supplementary variation contract, if the draftsman does not check all the terms which are thereby affected and which might require some special formality.

If the variation takes effect as a novation involving a change of parties, care has to be taken to ensure that rights and duties of the obligations which are being released are fully and effectively replaced by the new obligations.[207] It is particularly

---

[199] See para.9-16.

[200] See para.9-16 fn.116.

[201] e.g. giving a good reason not only for the defendant to be bound by his promise but also for the claimant to have "earned" the right to enforce it by doing something at the defendant's request: see para.8-08; and acting as a substitute for formality in protecting the promisor's intention and against his being bound by an ill-considered gratuitous promise: see paras 8-27, 8-28.

[202] For this, the doctrines of fraud and duress are the better tools: see para.9-22 fn.161.

[203] For requirements of form for variation of a contract, see paras 5–40 to 5–41 (substantive formality requirements), 6–20 (evidential formality requirements), 7–22 (variation of deeds).

[204] See para.9-03.

[205] See para.9–03.

[206] See para.9-01 fn.6.

[207] See para.9-05

important to pay attention to matters which are outstanding at the moment of the novation, such as claims by or against the party leaving the contract, including those which are to survive the novation rather than being extinguished and transferred into the new contract.[208]

It may not be obvious that the consent of any person outside the parties to the variation is required, but sometimes consents must be obtained, such as where there are multiple parties to the original agreement but a variation is being made by only two of the parties but in a way which cannot take effect without the other parties' consent. Similarly, where a term in the original contract has created rights in a third party who has communicated to the promisor his assent to the term, or has relied on the term and the promisor is aware that he has relied or could reasonably be expected to have foreseen that he would rely, the contract cannot be rescinded or varied by the contracting parties in such a way as to extinguish or alter the third party's right without his consent[209]: an attempted variation against the third party in such circumstances will therefore fail to achieve its object and the third-party rights under the original (unvaried) contract will still be enforceable by the third party.

9-26   **Use of a deed for contractual variations**   A contractual variation, whether it takes the form of a supplementary agreement or a wholly new replacement contract, must satisfy the normal rules for the creation of a contract. In many cases it will be clear that consideration is provided by both parties for the variation, at least in a case where the variation is mutual in the sense that both parties' obligations are varied in the same direction.[210] However, we have seen that there are many cases in which the variation is in substance unilateral; and although the courts have sometimes been willing to look into the transaction in order to find consideration to make it enforceable where that was clearly the genuine intention of the parties[211] there are situations in which the courts have declined do so.[212] However, a solution can easily be found, either in ensuring that some consideration, even nominal, is requested by the party submitting to the variation and provided by the party benefiting from it; or in embodying the variation in a deed. The latter course is generally to be advised, since a deed avoids all questions about the existence of consideration,[213] and the drafting of the deed will focus the parties' minds on producing a clear set of terms by way of variation.

---

[208] cf. the effect of the "novation agreement" in *Blyth & Blyth Ltd v Carillion Construction Ltd*, see para.9-05 fn.23.

[209] Contract (Rights of Third Parties) Act 1999 s.2(1).

[210] See para.9-09.

[211] e.g. *Williams v Roffey Bros & Nicholls (Contractors) Ltd* [1991] 1 Q.B. 1, CA, see para.9-14.

[212] e.g. the rule in *Pinnel's Case*, see para.9-22.

[213] See para.7-18. A deed also has other advantages, including the longer limitation period: see para.7-19.

PART IV PROMISSORY ESTOPPEL

CHAPTER 10

THE ROLE OF PROMISSORY ESTOPPEL IN THE MODIFICATION OF A CONTRACT[1]

I.   The Doctrine of Estoppel

Promissory estoppel must be understood in the broader context of estoppel as a whole   The doctrine of promissory estoppel is peculiar to common law systems and, as we shall see,[2] even within the common law systems there is significant variation in the scope of operation of the doctrine. However, before we can consider promissory estoppel as it applies within English law, it is necessary to understand in general terms what is meant by "estoppel", and the range of situations it encompasses, whilst also noting other related doctrines which perform a similar function both in common law jurisdictions and outside the common law.   **10-01**

(1)   The Core Notion of Estoppel

The meaning of "estoppel"   The first challenge to understanding the notion of estoppel is the word itself. It is an archaic word with no current usage outside the technical legal context of the doctrine of estoppel,[3] but its core meaning is clear: a party who is "estopped" is stopped—barred or impeded—from doing something, or from taking some action which would otherwise be allowed by law; the "estoppel" is the legal bar or impediment in question. Lord Denning MR explained it in this way[4]:   **10-02**

---

[1] Chitty, paras 4–086 to 3–106, 4–130 to 4–138; Furmston, paras 2.100 to 2.135; Treitel, paras 3-066 to 3-099, 3-111 to 3-117; Anson, pp.122–136; Cheshire, Fifoot and Furmston, pp.132–142; Wilken and Ghaly, Ch.8; E. Cooke, *The Modern Law of Estoppel* (Oxford University Press, 2000); Spencer Bower (Estoppel), Ch.14; The Hon. Mr Justice K.R. Handley, *Estoppel by Conduct and Election*, 2nd edn (Sweet & Maxwell, 2016), Ch.13; Snell, Ch.12; Burrows (Restatement), s.12(2)-(6); Andrews, arts 4, 124.
[2] See paras 10-46 to 10-48.
[3] OED Online, March 2018, "estoppel, n.".
[4] *McIlkenny v Chief Constable of the West Midlands* [1980] Q.B. 283, CA, at 316–317; this case concerned the operation of estoppel *per rem judicatam*. See also B. Fauvarque-Cosson, *La Confiance Légitime et l'Estoppel* (Société de législation comparée, Paris, 2007), p.14, referring to the origin as the old French *étoupe*, and quoting the first French doctoral thesis on estoppel by J. Dargent, *Une théorie originale du droit anglais en matière de preuve: la doctrine de l'estoppel* (Imp. G.

"the word 'estoppel' only means stopped. You will find it explained by Coke in his *Commentaries on Littleton* (19th ed., 1832), vol. II, s. 667, 352a.[5] It was brought over by the Normans. They used the old French 'estoupail.' That meant a bung or cork by which you stopped something from coming out. It was in common use in our courts when they carried on all their proceedings in Norman-French. Littleton writes in the law-French of his day (15th century) using the words 'pur ceo que le baron est estoppe a dire,' meaning simply that the husband is *stopped* from saying something."

(2)   Varieties of Estoppel

10-03   **There are different forms of estoppel, with different rules**   A party may be "estopped" in various different contexts. In the seventeenth century, Coke identified three different forms of estoppel[6]; since then more have been recognised. Lord Denning painted a vivid picture[7]:

"there has been built up over the centuries in our law a big house with many rooms. It is the house called Estoppel. In Coke's time it was a small house with only three rooms, namely, estoppel by matter of record, by matter in writing, and by matter in pais. But by our time we have so many rooms that we are apt to get confused between them. Estoppel per rem judicatam, issue estoppel, estoppel by deed, estoppel by representation, estoppel by conduct, estoppel by acquiescence, estoppel by election or waiver, estoppel by negligence, promissory estoppel, proprietary estoppel, and goodness knows what else. These several rooms have this much in common: They are all under one roof. Someone is stopped from saying something or other, or doing something or other, or contesting something or other. But each room is used differently from the others. If you go into one room, you will find a notice saying, 'Estoppel is only a rule of evidence.' If you go into another room you will find a different notice, 'Estoppel can give rise to a cause of action.' Each room has its own separate notices. It is a mistake to suppose that what you find in one room, you will also find in the others."

This makes clear that not only are there many different forms of estoppel, but also their rules differ significantly. Commentators vary in their lists of forms of estoppel, and the groups into which they organise them,[8] but the forms of estoppel which

---

Frères, Tourcoing, 1943), p.232: "de même qu'on utilise le tampon d'étoupe pour obstruer une voie d'eau ... ainsi le plaideur emploie-t-il le moyen de l'*estoppel* au cours d'un procès judiciaire, comme il mettrait un bâillon aux lèvres de son adversaire, pour lui interdire péremptoirement d'alléguer telle prétention qui serait en contradiction flagrante avec certains faits" [just as you use a plug to stop up a water leak ... the litigant makes use of estoppel during the course of legal proceedings as if he were gagging his opponent to prevent his making any allegation which is clearly contrary to certain facts].

5   [Coke wrote: "it is called an estoppel or conclusion, because a man's own act or acceptance stoppeth or closeth up his mouth to alleage or plead the truth".]

6   Co. Litt. 352a: "it is to be observed that there be three kinds of estoppel, viz. by matter of record, by matter in writing, and by matter *in paijs*". Estoppel "by matter in writing" referred to what is now known as estoppel by deed (see para.10-04): all the examples of writing which Coke gave in this context were in fact of deeds; and estoppel "by matter *in paijs*" is what is sometimes still called "estoppel *in pais*" but is now generally known as estoppel by representation (see para.10-06). For the etymology of the word "pais" (an Anglo-Norman word of the same root as the modern French *pays*—country or region), and the use of the phrase "*in pais*", see OED Online, March 2018, "pais, n.": "*in pais*: in or within the country; relating to or designating actions, matters, etc., which are legally recognized despite not being formally recorded or performed".

7   *McIlkenny v Chief Constable of the West Midlands*, see para.10-02 fn.4, at 317.

8   See, e.g. Cooke, see para.10-01 fn.1; Halsbury 5th edn, Vol.47 (2014); Wilken and Ghaly, Chs 7 to 12; J. Cartwright, "*Protecting Legitimate Expectations and Estoppel: English Law*" in B. Fauvarque-Cosson (ed.), see para.10-02 fn.4, p.321 at pp.323–327 (also published at *http://www.ejcl.org/103/*

concern us in the context of the formation or variation of contracts are estoppel by deed, estoppel by convention, estoppel by representation, proprietary estoppel and promissory estoppel. There is also a question about whether these different forms of estoppel are all sufficiently distinct to have discrete rules or whether some of them, at least, should be grouped together so as to allow the rules traditionally applicable to one form of estoppel to inform the development of the rules of another.

Estoppel by deed[9] We have seen already that a statement in a deed may give rise **10-04** to an estoppel, on the basis that a deed is a solemn instrument intended by the party who executes it to be binding on him, and that such a party cannot be allowed to raise evidence to contradict any clear statement which he has made within the deed, whether in its recitals or in its operative parts.[10] Although this is a rule of evidence,[11] it has the indirect effect of changing the legal relationship, as against the party estopped, to that which reflects the deed. In practice, estoppel by deed overlaps significantly with the more general doctrines of estoppel by representation[12] and estoppel by convention,[13] and it has even been questioned whether it is useful to retain estoppel by deed as a separate category of estoppel, although the Privy Council has said that this may be going too far.[14] However, there is an advantage in that the mere statement in the deed estops the party who executes it with the intention of being bound by the statements, without the need to demonstrate reliance by the other party or a shared assumption between the parties[15]; and the deed has effect by way of estoppel in relation to the validity of the transaction which it embodies even where there is no express statement to found an estoppel by representation, such as where a party grants a lease without having himself the freehold estate out of which the lease can be granted, but he is estopped by his deed from denying that the relationship of landlord and tenant has been created.[16]

---

art103-6.pdf). There are specialist books on some areas: Spencer Bower (Estoppel) (reliance-based estoppel, but including estoppel by convention, estoppel by contract and estoppel by deed (Ch.8), proprietary estoppel (Ch.12) and promissory estoppel (Ch.14)); Handley, see para.10-01 fn.1 (estoppel by conduct, but including estoppel by deed (Ch.7), estoppel by convention (Ch.8), proprietary estoppel (Ch.11) and promissory estoppel (Ch.13)); The Hon. Mr Justice K.R. Handley, *Spencer Bower and Handley: Res Judicata* 4th edn (LexisNexis Butterworths, 2009); B. McFarlane, *The Law of Proprietary Estoppel* (Oxford University Press, 2014); A. Trukhtanov, *Contractual Estoppel* (Informa, 2017).

9 See generally Handley, see para.10-01 fn.1, Ch.7; Spencer Bower (Estoppel), paras 8.79 to 8.89.
10 See para.7-20.
11 *Greer v Kettle* [1938] A.C. 156, HL, at 171.
12 See para.10-06.
13 See para.10-05.
14 *Prime Sight Ltd v Lavarello* [2013] UKPC 22; [2014] A.C. 436 at [30]; cf Chitty, para.1-140; Wilken and Ghaly, paras 12.05 to 12.13 (who, however, raise arguments in favour of the distinction, including the greater potential for an estoppel by deed to bind third parties).
15 For the requirement of reliance in estoppel by representation, see para.10-06; and for the requirement of a common assumption of the parties in relation to the facts in an estoppel by convention, see para.10-05. The statement in *Prime Sight Ltd v Lavarello*, see para.10-04 fn.14, appears to be based on the assumption that a promise enforceable by deed is not necessarily a "contract", and that there may therefore be no "convention" for an estoppel by convention. cf. para 7–02 fn.29.
16 A "tenancy by estoppel", which binds also the tenant who takes the benefit of the supposed lease: Megarry and Wade, paras 17-125 to 17-127; *First National Bank Plc v Thompson* [1996] Ch. 231, CA, at 239 (Millett LJ, drawing the distinction between an estoppel by deed, and the "technical doctrine of estoppel": where the "the grant contained an express recital or other clear and unequivocal representation of the grantor's title, he was estopped from denying that he had the particular title which he had asserted").

10-05 **Estoppel by convention**[17] Where the parties to a transaction act on an assumed state of facts or law, each may be estopped in any subsequent litigation from denying that state of facts or law if it would be unjust to allow him to go back on their common assumption. The assumption must be either shared by them both, or made by one and acquiesced in by the other, but it must at least have been communicated between them,[18] although such communication may be effected when both parties conduct themselves towards each other on the basis of the assumption.[19] The estoppel is not designed to create new legal rights, or vary existing legal rights, but it can have that effect where the parties share (and act upon) a mistake as to the existence or scope of a contract and the mistaken effect (rather than the true legal effect) can be enforced.[20] It is not, however, limited to cases of "mistake", but also covers cases where parties have simply forgotten the true state of affairs.[21]

Estoppel by convention should be distinguished from *contractual estoppel*[22] where the parties by means of a binding contract agree that in any litigation between them certain facts shall not be open to challenge.[23] In that case, the estoppel takes effect by reason of a contract, and it is not necessary for a party who seeks to rely on the estoppel to show that he has relied on it or otherwise acted on it, or that it is unconscionable for the other party to resile from the conventional state of affairs that the parties have assumed.[24] In this chapter we are concerned with the

---

17 See generally Handley, see para.10-01 fn.1, Ch.8; Spencer Bower (Estoppel), paras 8.1 to 8.66.

18 *Republic of India v India Steamship Co Ltd (The Indian Grace) (No.2)* [1998] A.C. 878, HL, at 913 (Lord Steyn, relying on *K Lokumal & Sons (London) Ltd v Lotte Shipping Co Pte Ltd (The August Leonhardt)* [1985] 2 Lloyd's Rep. 28, CA, and *Norwegian American Cruises A/S v Paul Mundy Ltd (The Vistafjord)* [1988] 2 Lloyd's Rep. 343, CA); *Revenue and Customs Commissioners v Benchdollar Ltd* [2009] EWHC 1310 (Ch); [2010] 1 All E.R. 174 at [52].

19 *Blindley Heath Investments Ltd v Bass* [2015] EWCA Civ 1023; [2017] Ch. 389 at [75].

20 *Amalgamated Investment & Property Co Ltd v Texas Commerce International Bank Ltd* [1982] Q.B. 84 (guarantee given by plaintiff to defendant bank, to cover indebtedness to bank of one of plaintiff's subsidiaries, did not cover loan which had in fact been made not directly by the bank but through one of the bank's subsidiaries; but CA held that plaintiff was estopped from denying that the guarantee covered the loan (and that it was therefore liable to pay) on the basis that the parties acted together on assumption that the guarantee covered the loan and the bank allowed loan to remain outstanding when it could have called it in). cf. also *Pacol Ltd v Trade Lines Ltd (The Henrik Sif)* [1982] 1 Lloyd's Rep. 456, see para.10-41 fn.325, where the mistake was not as to the scope of the contract but as to who the parties to the contract were, in effect creating a liability through estoppel in a party who was not covered by the contract at all.

21 *Blindley Heath Investments Ltd v Bass*, see para.10-05 fn.19, at [79] ("The essence of the principle is that the parties have conducted themselves on a conventional basis which is, wittingly or unwittingly, different from the true basis. Whether the true state of things has been misappreciated, misremembered or forgotten should make no difference to whether the parties have in the event mutually adopted a common assumption").

22 Spencer Bower (Estoppel), paras 8.67 to 8.78; Trukhtanov, *Contractual Estoppel* (Informa, 2017).

23 *Prime Sight Ltd v Lavarello*, see para.10-04 fn.14, at [47] ("Parties are ordinarily free to contract on whatever terms they choose and the court's role is to enforce them. There are exceptions and qualifications, but these too are part of the general law of contract. ... In short, contractual estoppels are subject to the same limits as other contractual provisions, but there is nothing inherently contrary to public policy in parties agreeing to contract on the basis that certain facts are to be treated as established for the purposes of their transaction, although they know the facts to be otherwise"). See e.g. the operation of contractual estoppel in giving force to "no representation" and "non-reliance" clauses in a contract: *Peekay Intermark Ltd v Australia and New Zealand Banking Group Ltd* [2006] EWCA Civ 386; [2006] 2 Lloyd's Rep. 511 at [57], followed in *Springwell Navigation Corp v JP Morgan Chase Bank* [2010] EWCA Civ 1221; [2010] 2 C.L.C. 705 at [169]. For further references, see Cartwright (Misrepresentation), para.9-03, n.9.

24 *Springwell Navigation Corp v JP Morgan Chase Bank*, see para.10-05 fn.23, at [177]–[178]; and

circumstances where, short of a binding contract, parties can be bound to the creation or variation of obligations, and therefore we are not concerned with the scope or operation of contractual estoppel.

Estoppel by representation[25] A person who has made a representation of fact to **10-06** another, with the intention that the latter should act in reliance on it[26] and he does in fact rely on it, is estopped from asserting facts which contradict the representation.[27] The representation may be by words or by conduct, express or implied, and does not depend on whether the representor intended to convey a false impression or knew that his statement was false.[28] It has recently been held that it is possible for an estoppel by representation to be based on a representation of law,[29] although this may happen rarely in practice.[30] However, it certainly does not extend to statements of intention since if, as a general rule, a statement of intention were to become binding by reason of the other party's reliance on it—even where the representor intended such reliance—it would undermine the requirement that consideration be given to make a promise binding as a contract.[31]

The estoppel operates against the party who, having made the representation, seeks to raise facts which contradict it during the course of litigation between the parties. It is often described as a rule of evidence,[32] but some judges have resisted this label,[33] and although estoppel by representation is not designed to create new

---

see generally J. Braithwaite, "The Origins and Implications of Contractual Estoppel" (2016) 132 L.Q.R. 120.

[25] Otherwise known as "estoppel *in pais*": see para.10-03 fn.6. See generally Spencer Bower (Estoppel), Pt 1; Cartwright (Misrepresentation), paras 10-18 to 10-28.

[26] Or, if he did not so intend, he owed a duty to the other party to take care in his words or conduct from which the representation was inferred, and the negligence was a proximate or real cause of the representee being misled: this is often termed "estoppel by negligence": Spencer Bower (Estoppel), para.3.27; Cartwright (Misrepresentation), para.10-23.

[27] For the distinction between reliance on a representation to found an estoppel, and reliance on a (mis)representation to obtain remedies such as rescission of the contract or damages, see Cartwright (Misrepresentation), para.10-27.

[28] *Freeman v Cooke* (1848) 2 Exch. 654 at 663, 154 E.R. 652 at 656; *Cornish v Abington* (1859) 4 H. & N. 549, 157 E.R. 956.

[29] *Briggs v Gleeds* [2014] EWHC (Ch) 1178; [2015] Ch. 212 at [35]. The courts have traditionally insisted on a representation of fact, not law: e.g. *Territorial and Auxiliary Forces Association of the County of London v Nichols* [1949] 1 K.B. 35, CA, at 50; but in recent years the distinction between mistakes and misrepresentations of law, and mistakes and misrepresentations of fact, has been abandoned by the courts in relation to remedies in restitution and in contract: Cartwright (Misrepresentation), paras 3-34 to 3-37. It was in reliance on this development that Newey J decided in *Briggs v Gleeds* at [26]–[34] that estoppel by representation should similarly be developed: Spencer Bower (Estoppel) para.1.19.

[30] *Briggs v Gleeds*, see para.10-06 fn.26, at [35] (Newey J: "It will very often be the case that a statement about law will not be capable of giving rise to a relevant estoppel (because, say, it amounted to no more than an expression of opinion, the circumstances were such that the representee could not reasonably rely on it or allowing an estoppel would conflict with a statute), but I do not think there is an absolute rule to that effect any more").

[31] *Jorden v Money* (1854) 5 H.L.C. 185, HL, at 215–216, 10 E.R. 868 at 882 (cf. Lord St Leonards dissenting at 248, at 895); *Maddison v Alderson* (1883) 8 App. Cas. 467, HL, at 473. See further para.10-14.

[32] e.g. *Low v Bouverie* [1891] 3 Ch. 82, CA, at 105; *London Joint Stock Bank Ltd v Macmillan* [1918] A.C. 777, HL, at 818 (Viscount Haldane: "it is hardly a rule of what is called substantive law in the sense of declaring an immediate right or claim. It is rather a rule of evidence, capable not the less on that account of affecting gravely substantive rights").

[33] *Canada and Dominion Sugar Co Ltd v Canadian National (West Indies) Steamships Co Ltd* [1947]

legal rights or vary existing legal rights it can—as in cases of estoppel by deed and estoppel by convention[34]—have the effect of doing so, since the legal relationship between the parties is to be determined on the basis of the facts as set out in the representation. The party who made the representation is able in law to assert his rights and claim remedies as against the representee only in so far as they are consistent with the facts as he represented them.[35]

10-07   **Proprietary estoppel**[36]   Where one person (A) makes a representation or promise to another (B) to the effect that B has or shall have an interest in, or right over, A's property, intending B to act in reliance on the representation or promise and B does in fact rely on it, an equity arises by which A may be estopped from asserting his own rights to his property without giving effect to his representation or promise. This is proprietary estoppel, which is now well established as a mechanism by which property rights can be created informally.[37] It differs from the other forms of estoppel mentioned in the previous paragraphs of this chapter: it is narrower in the sense that it is limited to representations or promises relating to interests in property, and in particular land[38]; but it is broader than estoppel by representation since it applies not only to representations of the present (that the representee already has an interest in the representor's property) but also to representations, promises and assurances that he will have such an interest in the future. Indeed, it even applies where there is no positive representation or promise at all, but where A acquiesces in B's mistaken belief that B has, or will acquire, an interest in A's land and B acts in reliance upon that mistake without correction by A.[39] However, it is the substantive legal effect of proprietary estoppel, and the remedies which may be

---

A.C. 46, PC, at 56 (Lord Wright: "Estoppel is often described as a rule of evidence, as, indeed, it may be so described. But the whole concept is more correctly viewed as a substantive rule of law"); Cartwright (Misrepresentation), para.10-28.

[34]   See paras 10-04, 10-05.

[35]   *Low v Bouverie* [1891] 3 Ch. 82, CA, at 112; *Burkinshaw v Nicolls* (1878) 3 App. Cas. 1004, HL, 1026.

[36]   See generally Spencer Bower (Estoppel), Ch.12; MacFarlane, see para.10-03 fn.8; Cheshire and Burn, Ch.22; Megarry and Wade, Ch.16; Chitty, paras 4–139 to 4–185; Treitel, paras 3-118 to 3-152; and see para.5-28.

[37]   A legal estate or interest in land cannot be created or transferred without the formality of a deed (LPA 1925 s.52) and, in certain circumstances, completion of the disposition by registration (Land Registration Act 2002 s.27); proprietary estoppel is a mechanism by which an interest in the land can be created informally, in equity. For the significance of formality, and the avoidance of formality by the use of such equitable doctrines as constructive trust and proprietary estoppel, see, Ch.4, esp. paras 4-07, 4-13; and for the use of equitable doctrines in the case of a failure to comply with formalities for contracts relating to land, see paras 5-06, 5-26 to 5-29.

[38]   *Western Fish Products Ltd v Penwith DC* [1981] 2 All E.R. 204, CA, at 218; *Cobbe v Yeoman's Row Management Ltd* [2008] UKHL 55; [2009] 1 W.L.R. 1752 at [14]; *Thorner v Major* [2009] UKHL 18; [2009] 1 W.L.R. 776 at [2], [61]; *West End Commercial Ltd v London Trocadero (2015) LLP* [2017] EWHC 2175 (Ch); [2018] 1 P. & C.R. DG3 at [36] (Snowden J: "as Snell's Equity observes, given the authority of the decision in *Thorner v Major*, it is clear that only the Supreme Court or the legislature could remove the current proprietary limit to the operation of proprietary estoppel"). For cases not involving land, see *Tomlinson v Pickup* [2014] EWHC 4495 at [226]–[230] (shareholding in company); *Motivate Publishing FZ LLC v Hello Ltd* [2015] EWHC 1554 (Ch) (licence for intellectual property rights: but note interpretation and criticism in *West End Commercial Ltd v London Trocadero* (2015) LLP at [35]).

[39]   *Ramsden v Dyson* (1866) 1 H.L. 129; *Willmott v Barber* (1880) 15 Ch. D. 96 (see esp. the test set out by Fry J at 105–106). In *Taylors Fashions Ltd v Liverpool Victoria Trustees Co Ltd* [1982] Q.B. 133 at 151 Oliver J referred to "the *Ramsden v Dyson* principle—whether you call it proprietary estoppel, estoppel by acquiescence or estoppel by encouragement is really immaterial".

awarded, that make it very significantly different. It is certainly not simply a rule of evidence or procedure: whereas the other forms of estoppel may only *indirectly* have the effect of changing the parties' legal relationship by their being bound in any litigation on the basis of the estoppel, proprietary estoppel gives rise directly to an "equity" which is recognised as having proprietary characteristics[40]; and although the remedy awarded to satisfy the equity is within the (principled) discretion of the court,[41] it creates new rights in property which the representee may claim: it operates not only defensively (as a "shield") but also offensively (as a "sword").[42]

Promissory estoppel   Promissory estoppel is the subject of detailed discussion in this Chapter. But before we consider it in detail, it can be set very generally in the context of the other forms of estoppel discussed above. The clearest link is with proprietary estoppel: promissory estoppel, also, is not limited to statements or assumptions of present fact or law, but applies to representations or assurances about the future—promises. However, unlike proprietary estoppel, it applies not to interests in property but to promises more generally and so it finds its home in the books dealing with the law of contract, whereas proprietary estoppel belongs more naturally in the books dealing with land law.[43] Most significantly, in English law[44] promissory estoppel does not create new obligations that are directly enforceable by the representee: promissory estoppel does not create a new cause of action; it operates as a "shield" but not as a "sword".[45] Indeed, its operation is very narrowly limited to the modification of an existing obligation, where the representation is not to insist on the strict performance of the obligation owed by the representee to the representor, and the representee acts in reliance on the representation and thus renders it inequitable for the representor to enforce the obligation, at least without giving the representee further time.[46]

10-08

Unification of different forms of estoppel?   In England, there has been some discussion of the links between the different forms of estoppel, and whether differ-

10-09

---

[40] Land Registration Act 2002 s.116(a) (registered land); *ER Ives Investment Ltd v High* [1967] 2 Q.B. 379 (unregistered land).
[41] *Crabb v Arun DC* [1976] Ch. 179, 193; Cheshire and Burn, pp.916–919; Megarry and Wade, paras 16-020 to 16-027. The remedy does not necessarily enforce the representation directly: sometimes it will protect the representee's reliance rather than his expectation, especially where the representation did not promise a specific interest in the land, and where granting a remedy to protect the expectation would be disproportionate to the detriment suffered by the representee by his action in reliance on the representation: *Jennings v Rice* [2002] EWCA Civ 159; [2003] 1 P. & C.R. 8 at [21], [50]. See also *Davies v Davies* [2016] EWCA Civ 463; [2016] 2 P. & C.R. 10 at [41] (Lewison LJ: "What is not entirely clear from [*Jennings v Rice*] is what the court is to do with the expectation even if it is only a starting point. Mr Blohm suggested that there might be a sliding scale by which the clearer the expectation, the greater the detriment and the longer the passage of time during which the expectation was reasonably held, the greater would be the weight that should be given to the expectation. I agree that this is a useful working hypothesis").
[42] *Baird Textiles Holdings Ltd v Marks & Spencer Plc* [2001] EWCA Civ 274; [2002] 1 All E.R. (Comm) 737 at [52]; cf. para.10-08 fn.45.
[43] The contract books discuss proprietary estoppel in its relationship to promissory estoppel: e.g. Chitty, paras 4-139 to 4-185; Treitel, paras 3-118 to 3-152; the detail is however to be found in the land law books: e.g. Cheshire and Burn, Ch.22; Megarry and Wade, Ch.16.
[44] For different approaches elsewhere in the common law, see paras 10-09, 10-46 to 10-48.
[45] *Combe v Combe* [1951] 2 K.B. 215, CA; *Baird Textiles Holdings Ltd v Marks & Spencer Plc*, see para.10-07 fn.42; paras 10-38 to 10-39; 10-51.
[46] For whether promissory estoppel effects a permanent change in the obligation, or merely suspends it, see paras 10-29 to 10-32.

ences between some of them should be broken down—and in particular whether the rule that proprietary estoppel can create new interests in land, enforceable directly by the representee by virtue of his reliance on the representation,[47] should be translated to apply also to promissory estoppel and thus allow the reliance on a promise to render the promise binding and enforceable at the suit of the representee even in the absence of the elements which are normally required for the creation of a consensual obligation in English law: either consideration or a deed. This discussion is largely fuelled by developments elsewhere in the common law: as we shall see, in American law the courts have long accepted that the reliance on a promise may render it enforceable by the promisee in the absence of consideration[48]; and more recently the Australian courts have developed a similar principle.[49] The Australian development has proceeded on the basis of breaking down the distinctions between the different forms of estoppel, and in particular the distinctions between proprietary estoppel and promissory estoppel so as to allow promissory estoppel to create new obligations—to be used as a "sword". The English courts have so far resisted such a development, and it would take either legislation or a decision of the Supreme Court to achieve it.[50] We shall see the arguments which are made in this debate in Part V of this Chapter.

(3)   Other Related Doctrines, and Comparisons with Other Legal Systems

10-10   **Other related doctrines in the common law**   The doctrine of estoppel, and in particular promissory estoppel in so far as it can be used to modify an existing legally enforceable right, bears a marked similarity to certain other doctrines: waiver, forbearance and variation.[51] Although we are concerned in this chapter with

---

47   See para.10-07.

48   Restatement of Contracts (2d), para.90(1); see para.10-47.

49   See esp. *Waltons Stores (Interstate) Ltd v Maher* (1988) 164 C.L.R. 387, HCA; see para.10-48.

50   *Baird Textiles Holdings Ltd v Marks & Spencer Plc*, see para.10-07 fn.42, at [55], noting that CA is bound by the earlier decision in *Combe v Combe* [1951] 2 K.B. 215, CA. See further para.10-51. For a discussion of estoppel by representation, estoppel by convention, promissory estoppel and proprietary estoppel in Anglo-Australian law, arguing that "the way lies open for the development of a coherent and unified doctrine of estoppel moulded around the requirement of reasonable reliance", see E. Bant and M. Bryan, "Fact, Future and Fiction: Risk and Reasonable Reliance in Estoppel" (2015) 35 O.J.L.S. 427.

51   cf. also *Panchaud Freres SA v Etablissements General Grain Co* [1970] 1 Lloyd's Rep. 53, CA, where it was held that buyers could no longer challenge an incorrect date of shipment on a bill of lading: Lord Denning MR held at 57 that there was no waiver in the strict sense, because the buyers had not known of the breach which had entitled them to terminate for late shipment, but there was "estoppel by conduct", which applies where "a man has so conducted himself that it would be unfair or unjust to allow him to depart from a particular state of affairs which another has taken to be settled or correct"; Winn LJ at 59 thought that "what one has here is something perhaps in our law not yet wholly developed as a separate doctrine—which is more in the nature of a requirement of fair conduct—a criterion of what is fair conduct between the parties. There may be an inchoate doctrine stemming from the manifest convenience of consistency in pragmatic affairs, negativing any liberty to blow hot and cold in commercial conduct". See also *Syros Shipping Co SA v Elaghill Trading Co (The Proodos C)* [1980] 2 Lloyd's Rep. 390 at 392 (Lloyd J: "The principle established in *Panchaud Freres* has not yet been fully worked out by the Courts; in particular it is uncertain whether it is to be regarded as based on estoppel or whether it is a kind of waiver, and if so, what its limits are"); *BP Exploration v Hunt (No.2)* [1979] 1 W.L.R. 783 at 811 (Robert Goff J: "I do not read the *Panchaud* case as arising from the principle in *Hughes v Metropolitan Railway Co* [see para.10-15 fn.88] because the *Panchaud* case does not depend in any way upon the representee hav-

the doctrine of promissory estoppel, the potential overlap with the operation of these other doctrines will first be noted briefly here. Some difficulties can arise from the fact that the courts and writers are not always precise and systematic in their use of terminology and in the distinctions they draw between such doctrines as "waiver", "forbearance" and "estoppel", and different doctrines may be used in apparently similar cases without it being clear whether a technical distinction is being drawn. Some such examples may be a result of the historical development of the law. The modern development of the doctrine of promissory estoppel is generally traced to decisions which date from around the middle of the twentieth century,[52] and therefore it is not surprising that earlier cases, and even cases which were decided in the early years of the recognition of the modern doctrine, should have based their reasoning on other similar doctrines and that the authority of these earlier cases should continue alongside the developing doctrine of promissory estoppel. But even in the developed law there are deeper issues relating to the similarities and differences between these various different doctrines.

"Waiver" and "forbearance" The term "waiver" is used—unhelpfully[53] —in different senses. It can be synonymous with *election*, the doctrine by which a party faced with two logically inconsistent courses of action must choose, and once he has chosen it is too late to change his mind: by his unilateral act[54] (which may be   **10-11**

---

ing relied upon any representation by the buyer").

52 Beginning with the decision of Denning J in *Central London Property Trust Ltd v High Trees House Ltd* [1947] K.B. 130, see para.10-16, and gradually taken up in cases over the following years, although even in 1972 Lord Hailsham could say "the time may soon come when the whole sequence of cases based on promissory estoppel since the war, beginning with *Central London Property Trust Ltd v High Trees House Ltd*, may need to be reviewed and reduced to a coherent body of doctrine by the courts": *Woodhouse AC Israel Cocoa Ltd SA v Nigerian Produce Marketing Co Ltd* [1972] A.C. 741, HL, at 758.

53 *Ross T Smyth & Co Ltd v TD Bailey Son & Co* [1940] 3 All E.R. 60, HL, at 70 (Lord Wright: "The word 'waiver' is a vague term, used in many senses. It is always necessary to ascertain in what sense and with what restrictions it is used in any particular case. It is sometimes used in the sense of election as where a person decides between two mutually exclusive rights. Thus, in the old phrase, he claims in *assumpsit* and waives the tort. It is also used where a party expressly or impliedly gives up a right to enforce a condition or rely on a right to rescind a contract, or prevents performance, or announces that he will refuse performance, or loses an equitable right by *laches*. The use of so vague a term without further precision is to be deprecated"). The distinction between "waiver" and "variation" is also dependent on context: e.g. *Banning v Wright* [1972] 1 W.L.R. 972, HL, at 990 (Lord Simon of Glaisdale: "when the two words are used in a taxing statute, it is natural to suppose that the draftsman was trying to cover two different situations. If so, 'waiver of a term' would be apt to refer to the total relinquishment of the primary rights conferred by the term; 'variation of a term' the modification of the primary rights conferred by the term"); cf. at 980 (Lord Hailsham: "When a contract is broken the injured party in condoning the fault may be said either to waive the breach, or to waive the term in relation to the breach. What in each case he waives is the right to rely on the term for the purpose of enforcing his remedy to the breach. I cannot construe 'waiver' as only applicable to the total abandonment of any term in the lease both as regards ascertained and past breaches, and as regards unascertained or future breaches"). See also T. Dugdale and D. Yates, "Variation, Waiver and Estoppel—A Re-appraisal" (1976) 39 M.L.R. 680 at 681–682, listing six different meanings for the "troublesome term" of waiver in the law of contract.

54 Election does not require reliance by the other party. However, if there is in fact no election, the party whose conduct demonstrates (objectively) to the other party that he makes the election can be estopped by his conduct from denying that he has made the election if the other party relies on it: e.g. *Peyman v Lanjani* [1985] Ch. 457, CA, at 487–488, 495, 501 (alleged affirmation of the contract as bar to right to rescind contract for irremovable defect in assignor's title to lease: on the facts there was neither affirmation nor estoppel).

effected by words or by conduct) he has committed himself to one course, and "waived" the alternative.[55] But it can also be synonymous with *estoppel*, for example in the case where a party has a legal right but gives it up, in whole or in part, and temporarily or permanently.[56] In the context of contractual obligations, he may waive the right to claim a remedy for a breach which has been committed, or he may waive the right to performance of the obligations before they have been breached. This, we shall see, is the core context in which promissory estoppel operates. Sometimes waiver (in the sense of estoppel) is referred to as "forbearance", especially where the waiver of the right to the remedy or to performance of the obligations is only partial or temporary.

The common law developed the doctrines of waiver and forbearance by which a party could limit, suspend or relinquish his legal rights[57]; the development of the modern doctrine of promissory estoppel has its roots in cases in equity where the courts relied on the language of waiver or forbearance,[58] and it has therefore been come to be known sometimes as *equitable forbearance* or *equitable estoppel*.[59] However, in their underlying principles, there are differences in the operation of waiver, forbearance and estoppel.[60] The common law doctrine of forbearance relied on the parties' agreement to modify (temporarily) the performance of their

---

55 *Kammins Ballrooms Co Ltd v Zenith Investments (Torquay) Ltd* [1971] A.C. 850, HL, at 882–883; *China National Foreign Trade Transportation Corp v Evlogia Shipping Co SA of Panama (The Mihalios Xilas)* [1979] 1 W.L.R. 1018, HL, at 1024, 1034–1035; *Hain Steamship Co Ltd v Tate & Lyle Ltd* [1936] 2 All E.R. 597, HL, at 615 (party cannot approbate and reprobate); *Motor Oil Hellas (Corinth) Refineries SA v Shipping Corp of India (The Kanchenjunga)* [1990] 1 Lloyd's Rep. 391, HL, at 397–398.

56 *Kammins Ballrooms Co Ltd v Zenith Investments (Torquay) Ltd*, see para.10-11 fn.55, at 883; *Motor Oil Hellas (Corinth) Refineries SA v Shipping Corp of India (The Kanchenjunga)*, see para.10-11 fn.55, at 399; *Panoutsos v Raymond Hadley Corp of New York* [1917] 2 K.B. 473, CA (party waiving condition had to give other party time to comply with the condition before breach could be relied on to terminate the contract); *Société Italo-Belge pour le Commerce et l'Industrie SA v Palm and Vegetable Oils (Malaysia) Sdn Bdh (The Post Chaser)* [1982] 1 All E.R. 19 at 25 (Robert Goff J: "the second question in the case, viz. whether the buyers waived their right to reject the sellers' tender of documents. Both counsel for the buyers and counsel for the sellers were in agreement that the applicable principles were those of equitable estoppel"; and at 27 the Judge noted that the case was argued solely on the basis of equitable estoppel, and not election).

57 See A.J. Phipps, "Resurrecting the Doctrine of Common Law Forbearance" (2007) 123 L.Q.R. 286 for a valuable discussion of the common law doctrine of forbearance arguing that, although it has been "almost completely subsumed by the language and methodology of estoppel" (p.288), its neglect is unwarranted and it provides for the enforcement of promises to modify the "manner of performance" of contracts (although not the contract itself) through a doctrine which "is suspensory in nature and thereby revocable by either party upon the giving of reasonable notice, following which the contractual position, adjusted to take account of the delay in performance occasioned by the forbearance, will reassert itself" (p.313). For further discussion of the common law background see S.J. Stoljar, "The Modification of Contracts" (1957) 35 Can. Bar. Rev. 485.

58 *Hughes v Metropolitan Railway Co* (1877) 2 App. Cas. 439, HL, at 447.

59 *Soteriou v Ultrachem Ltd* [2004] EWHC 983 (QB); [2004] I.R.L.R. 870 at [120]; *Crosstown Music Co 1 LLC v Rive Droite Music Ltd* [2010] EWCA Civ 1222; [2012] Ch. 68 at [69], [110], [145], [146]; Chitty, para.4-086; Wilken and Ghaly, para.8.06.

60 For a wide-ranging discussion of the different concepts see *Commonwealth of Australia v Verwayen* (1990) 170 C.L.R. 394, HCA; e.g. Brennan J at 421, 423: "Election, estoppel and waiver are cognate concepts: each relates to the sterilization of a legal right otherwise than by contract ... These distinct doctrines serve different purposes: election ... ensures that there is no inconsistency in the enforcement of a person's rights; estoppel or equitable estoppel ensures that a party who acts in reliance on what another has represented or promised suffers to unjust detriment thereby; waiver recognizes the unilateral divestiture of certain rights).

contract—it was therefore bilateral rather than unilateral[61]; and it did not require a party seeking to invoke the forbearance to have relied on it, nor did it rest on any principle of unconscionability such as that which has become the foundation of the doctrine of promissory estoppel.[62] Waiver could allow the unilateral abandonment of a legal right without requiring the other party's reliance.[63] However, there are cases in the modern law where the courts have assimilated waiver with estoppel in requiring the waiver to be based on an unequivocal representation which has been relied upon by the representee,[64] and Lord Denning, in particular, was keen to draw the old cases of waiver and forbearance into his new doctrine of promissory estoppel[65]:

"If the defendant, as he did, led the plaintiffs to believe that he would not insist on the stipulation as to time, and that, if they carried out the work, he would accept it, and they did it, he could not afterwards set up the stipulation as to the time against them. Whether it be called waiver or forbearance on his part, or an agreed variation or substituted performance, does not matter. It is a kind of estoppel. By his conduct he evinced an intention to affect their legal relations. He made, in effect, a promise not to insist on his strict legal rights. That promise was intended to be acted on, and was in fact acted on. He cannot afterwards go back on it. I think not only that that follows from *Panoutsos v Raymond Hadley Corporation of New York*,[66] a decision of this court, but that it was also anticipated in *Bruner v Moore*.[67] It is a particular application of the principle which I endeavoured to state in *Central London Property Trust Ltd v High Trees House Ltd.*"[68]

To a large extent, the modern development of promissory estoppel has pushed aside the language of waiver and forbearance in cases where the doctrines in practice overlap, and has therefore allowed a simpler unified solution to the non-contractual unilateral modification of an existing contract.[69] In the following sec-

---

61 Phipps, "Resurrecting the Doctrine of Common Law Forbearance", see para.10-11 fn.57, 304—307; Stoljar, "The Modification of Contracts", see para.10-11 fn.57, 492, 527 (arguing that this was obscured when "waiver" was used in contrast with a contractual variation in avoiding the requirements of the Statute of Frauds: see para.10-12 fn.70).

62 Phipps, "Resurrecting the Doctrine of Common Law Forbearance", see para.10-11 fn.57, 311–312; Stoljar, "The Modification of Contracts", see para.10-11 fn.57, 490–492.

63 Brennan J in *Commonwealth of Australia v Verwayen*, see para.10-11 fn.60.

64 *Finagrain SA Geneva v P Kruse Hamburg* [1976] 2 Lloyd's Rep. 508, CA, at 534, 535; *Bremer Handelsgesellschaft mbH v Vanden Avenne-Izegem PVBA* [1977] 2 Lloyd's Rep. 327, CA, at 339–340; *Motor Oil Hellas (Corinth) Refineries SA v Shipping Corp of India (The Kanchenjunga)*, see para.10-11 fn.55, at 399; *Société Italo-Belge pour le Commerce et l'Industrie SA v Palm and Vegetable Oils (Malaysia) Sdn Bdh (The Post Chaser)*, see para.10-11 fn.56; *Liberty Insurance Pte Ltd v Argo Systems FZE* [2011] EWCA Civ 1572; [2012] 1 C.L.C. 81 at [39].

65 *Charles Rickards Ltd v Oppenhaim* [1950] 1 K.B. 616, CA, at 623. See also *WJ Alan & Co Ltd v El Nasr Export and Import Co* [1972] 2 Q.B. 189, CA, at 212–214 (Lord Denning MR, finding "waiver" by applying *Central London Property Trust Ltd v High Trees House Ltd*, see para.10-10 fn.52, and later cases decided under the doctrine of promissory estoppel), 218 (Megaw LJ: "In my view, if there were no variation, the buyers would still be entitled to succeed on the ground of waiver. The relevant principle is, in my opinion, that which was stated by Lord Cairns LC, in *Hughes v Metropolitan Railway Co* [see para.10-11 fn.58]").

66 See para.10-11 fn.56.

67 [1904] 1 Ch. 305, see para.10-15 fn.90.

68 See para.10-10 fn.52; para.10-16.

69 G.C. Cheshire and C.H.S. Fifoot, "Central London Property Trust Ltd v High Trees House Ltd" (1947) 63 L.Q.R. 283, 289–301, approving the development; cf. Phipps, "Resurrecting the Doctrine of Common Law Forbearance", see para.10-11 fn.57, criticising the loss of the common law doctrines.

tions in this chapter, in discussing the elements and operation of promissory estoppel we shall draw not only on cases which have applied the doctrine under that name, but also certain cases where the courts have applied the same principles under the other labels such as "waiver", although it is important to notice where the courts depart from the language of estoppel to be sure that they are not seeking to apply some other distinct principle.

10-12　**"Variation"**　The *variation* of a contract can be very clearly distinguished from promissory estoppel. We have seen that the variation of a contract, properly so called, is the *contractual* modification of one or more of the terms of an existing contract: that is, a new contract, superimposed on the existing contract, which therefore has force by virtue of the parties' agreement, supported by consideration (or a deed).[70]

10-13　**Civil law systems do not know "estoppel" but have functionally similar doctrines**　The doctrine of estoppel is not known under that name in civil law systems, although the circumstances in which estoppel is used in English law will often be replicated through other doctrines. Where a party has induced another to rely on his words or conduct, any legal system may wish to prevent him from reneging on what he has said, or to provide some form of remedy in favour of the party who has so relied. This may be done simply through the law of contract, given that the doctrine of consideration is not used outside the common law, and therefore in civil law systems a party may be more easily held contractually to his promise, whether it is to create a new obligation or to vary an existing obligation.[71] But the desire to prevent a party acting inconsistently with his words or conduct—to prevent him "blowing hot and cold"[72] —is well-known around the world and even without using the law of contract to render a promise binding, many systems will find some other doctrine or principle with similar effect.[73]

II.　PROMISSORY ESTOPPEL: DEVELOPMENT AND OUTLINE

10-14　**Before High Trees: estoppel by representation limited to statements of**

---

[70]　See para.9-02; and see generally Ch.9. The distinction between variation (as a contractual modification) and waiver or forbearance (as non-contractual modifications) appeared clearly in old cases in the context of contracts subject to the requirements of the Statute of Frauds (see para.6-05) since if there was no new contract the modification was not required to be evidenced in writing: e.g. *Besseler Waechter Glover & Co v South Derwent Coal Co Ltd* [1938] 1 K.B. 408; see para.6-20 fn.134.

[71]　See para.8-04.

[72]　cf. Winn LJ in *Panchaud Freres SA v Etablissements General Grain Co*, see para.10-10 fn.51; *Cave v Mills* (1862) 7 H. & N. 913 at 927–928, 158 E.R. 740 at 747 (Wilde B.: "the ... broad principle, that a man shall not be allowed to blow hot and cold—to affirm at one time and deny at another—making a claim on those whom he has deluded to their disadvantage, and founding that claim on the very matters of the delusion. Such a principle has its basis in common sense and common justice, and whether it is called 'estoppel' or by any other name, it is one which Courts of law have in modern times most usefully adopted").

[73]　For a detailed study, see B. Fauvarque-Cosson (ed.), *La Confiance Légitime et l'Estoppel*, see para.10-02 fn.4, with reports from 14 countries (common law, civil law and mixed systems), and discussing doctrines and principles such as legitimate expectations, *confiance légitime*, good faith, abuse of rights (*abus de droit*), unconscionability, *rechtsverwerking, venire contra factum proprium* and personal bar.

fact   The principal authority dating from the mid-nineteenth century which stood against the development of a doctrine of promissory estoppel was *Jorden v Money*,[74] where a majority of the House of Lords held that a representation of intention, or a promise, was insufficient to give rise to an estoppel. Estoppel by representation as applied in a court of equity,[75] as well as in a court of common law, could be based only on a representation of fact. The representation by a creditor to the debtor that she would not enforce the debt could therefore not have binding force unless it was contained in a contract[76]:

"I think that that doctrine does not apply to a case where the representation is not a representation of a fact, but a statement of something which the party intends or does not intend to do. In the former case it is a contract, in the latter it is not; what is here contended for, is this, that Mrs Jorden, then Miss Marnell, over and over again represented that she abandoned the debt. Clothe that in any words you please, it means no more than this, that she would never enforce the debt; she does not mean, in saying that she had abandoned it, to say that she had executed a release of the debt so as to preclude her legal right to sue.[77] All that she could mean, was that she positively promised that she never would enforce it. My opinion is, that if all the evidence had come up to the mark, which, for reasons I shall presently state, I do not think it did, that if upon the very eve of the marriage she had said, "William Money, I never will enforce the bond against you," that would not bring it within these cases. It might be, if all statutable requisites, so far as there are statutable requisites, had been complied with, that it would have been a very good contract whereby she might have bound herself not to enforce the payment. That, however, is not the way in which it is put here; in short, it could not have been, because it must have been a contract reduced into writing and signed; but that is not the way in which this case is put[78]; it is put entirely upon the ground of representation."

The decision in *Jorden v Money* was relied on by the House of Lords in 1873,

---

[74]   (1854) 5 H.L.C. 185, 10 E.R. 868.
[75]   The decision in *Jorden v Money* was an appeal in a case originally heard by the Master of the Rolls as a trial judge in the equity jurisdiction. In HL Lord Cranworth LC (see para.10-14 fn.74, at 213, at 881) referred to estoppel as "a doctrine not confined to cases in equity, but one that prevails at law also; and there are, in fact, more cases upon the subject at law than in equity", going on to discuss *Freeman v Cooke* (1848) 2 Exch. 654, 154 E.R. 652 and *Pickard v Sears* (1837) 6 Ad. & El. 469, 112 E.R. 179.
[76]   See para.10-14 fn.74, at 214–215, at 882 (Lord Cranworth LC); see also at 226–227, at 886 (Lord Brougham: "In all those cases, therefore, there was a misrepresentation of the facts. And the learned Master of the Rolls appears to consider that in this case there was a similar misrepresentation. In my opinion, there was a misrepresentation by Louisa Marnell of an intention as to her will, and a promise was made by her; but of misrepresentation of fact there was none. She simply stated what was her intention; she did not misrepresent her intention". Lord St. Leonards dissented, interpreting the representation as being that the debt had been abandoned, thus constituting a representation of fact (at 251, at 896), but also held that even if it were a representation of intention it would be binding (at 256, at 898).
[77]   [This would be an estoppel by representation of the fact that she had signed a deed which, when relied on by the representee, could have the (indirect) effect of preventing her suing to enforce the debt: see para.10-04.]
[78]   [cf. P.S. Atiyah, "Consideration: a Restatement", reprinted in P.S. Atiyah, *Essays on Contract* (Clarendon Press, 1986), p.179 at pp.233–240, arguing that the decision was motivated by a desire not to allow evasion of the Statute of Frauds and that the case is evidence that in the 19th century the courts were prepared (but for the operation of the Statute in a case where it applied) to allow reliance on a promise, even if not requested, to constitute good consideration, and therefore "there is not, and never was, any need for promissory estoppel" (at p.238); persuasively criticised by G.H. Treitel, "Consideration: A Critical Analysis of Professor Atiyah's Fundamental Restatement" (1976) 50 A.L.J. 439, 447–449.]

holding that a representation that bills of exchange would be paid could not form the basis of an estoppel because the representation was of intention, not of fact. Lord Selborne put the point forcefully[79]:

> "I apprehend that nothing can be more certain than this, that the doctrine of equitable estoppel by representation is a wholly different thing from contract, or promise, or equitable assignment, or anything of that sort. The foundation of that doctrine, which is a very important one, and certainly not one likely to be departed from, is this, that if a man dealing with another for value makes statements to him as to existing facts, which being stated would affect the contract, and without reliance upon which, or without the statement of which, the party would not enter into the contract, and which being otherwise than as they were stated, would leave the situation after the contract different from what it would have been if the representations had not been made; then the person making those representations shall, so far as the powers of a Court of Equity extend, be treated as if the representations were true, and shall be compelled to make them good. But those must be representations concerning existing facts."

10-15   **Before High Trees: waiver and forbearance in equity**   Although the House of Lords in *Jorden v Money* rejected the application of the doctrine of estoppel to representations of intention, or promises,[80] we shall see that the development of promissory estoppel in the twentieth century relied principally on another, later decision of the House of Lords from the nineteenth century: *Hughes v Metropolitan Railway Co.*[81] In this case, another appeal in the exercise of the equity jurisdiction,[82] the House of Lords refused to allow a landlord to enforce the forfeiture of a lease for the tenants' breach of a covenant in failing to repair the premises within the time set by the lease after service of a notice by the landlords, where the tenants had been led to believe that the notice requiring the repairs to be done was suspended during a period during which the parties were in negotiation for a possible surrender of the lease.[83] No mention was made of "estoppel": rather, the language used was of "waiver" of the requirement to complete the repairs within the required time[84]; or of the landlord having by conduct induced the tenants to believe that the strict terms of the lease would not be enforced as regards the time limit for the repairs[85]; or of the parties' agreed conduct having led the tenants to believe that the time limit was suspended.[86] The House of Lords did not consider

---

[79] *Citizens' Bank of Louisiana v First National Bank of New Orleans* (1873) L.R. 6 H.L. 352 at 360.

[80] See para.10-14.

[81] (1877) 2 App. Cas. 439, HL.

[82] cf. para.10-14 fn.75.

[83] The action which gave rise to the appeal was by the tenant, seeking to stay on equitable grounds the execution of a writ of ejectment which the landlords had successfully obtained in an earlier action.

[84] See para.10-15 fn.81, at 447 (Lord Cairns LC), 450 (Lord Selborne).

[85] See para.10-15 fn.81, at 448–449 (Lord O'Hagan), 453 (Lord Blackburn). This sounds like estoppel, but there was no discussion of the tenants' reliance: the concept and language of estoppel seem not to have been in their Lordships' minds in deciding the case, although the closest was perhaps Lord O'Hagan, who at 448–449 said: "if they acted, or failed to act, through a mistake induced by the conduct of the Plaintiff: if they were misled by it into the belief that his strict legal right was abandoned or suspended for the time, he cannot be allowed to take advantage of the forfeiture which was so accomplished".

[86] See para.10-15 fn.81, at 448 (Lord Cairns: quoted at para.10-15 fn.88). Indeed, this fits the facts more closely. The landlord issued the notice on 22 October 1874 requiring the repairs to be done within six months, i.e. by 22 April 1875; it was the tenants who then raised the possibility of surrender of the lease and said that they would defer beginning the repairs until they heard back from the landlords, and this led to some discussion over the price for the surrender until the negotiations broke

whether there might be any contradiction with earlier cases such as *Jorden v Money*[87] —indeed, they cited no case for their general approach, which they all regarded as an obvious principle of equity. Lord Cairns' statement, commonly cited in later cases, was[88]:

> "it is the first principle upon which all Courts of Equity proceed, that if parties who have entered into definite and distinct terms involving certain legal results—certain penalties or legal forfeiture—afterwards by their own act or with their own consent enter upon a course of negotiation which has the effect of leading one of the parties to suppose that the strict rights arising under the contract will not be enforced, or will be kept in suspense, or held in abeyance, the person who otherwise might have enforced those rights will not be allowed to enforce them where it would be inequitable having regard to the dealings which have thus taken place between the parties."

There was no suggestion that the landlord had deliberately taken advantage of the tenants in causing them to delay the repairs and therefore run the risk of forfeiture: it was enough that there had been an innocent suspension of the duty to comply with the time limit set by the notice for the completion of the repairs.[89] But the question inevitably arises whether this case could legitimately provide a springboard for a broader principle by which a party can vary the terms of a contract without consideration—and, indeed, what the case was authority for and how far it could be applied outside the context of its own facts.

The statement of principle quoted above from Lord Cairns' opinion was very closely tied to the facts of the case—including in its reference to cases where the "strict rights" which were to be suspended involved "certain penalties or legal forfeiture". However, it was made clear by the Court of Appeal in *Birmingham and District Land Co v London and North Western Railway Co* that the principle was not limited to cases of potential forfeiture, and it was re-stated by Bowen LJ in broader terms[90]:

> "if persons who have contractual rights against others induce by their conduct those against whom they have such rights to believe that such rights will either not be enforced or will be kept in suspense or abeyance for some particular time, those persons will not

---

down at the end of December, without the landlord at any time having expressly told the tenants that the notice was suspended. Lord Selborne also noted at 445 that it was in both parties' interests that the repair notice be suspended, if the negotiations might succeed. The repairs not having been done, the tenants proposed in April to proceed with the repairs but the landlord sought to forfeit in accordance with the original notice which set the deadline of 22 April. The House of Lords held that, in the circumstances, the landlord must give the tenants a reasonable time for the repairs to be done— which was measured as six months from the breakdown of the negotiations, i.e. until the end of June. The repairs had in fact already been completed by then, so the forfeiture was avoided.

87 It would be surprising if Lord Selborne, at least, thought that this could be a case of estoppel, given that in 1873 he had reaffirmed the application of *Jorden v Money* in limiting estoppel to statements of fact: *Citizens' Bank of Louisiana v First National Bank of New Orleans*, see para.10-14 fn.79; and in 1883 he again asserted the same point: *Maddison v Alderson* (1883) 8 App. Cas. 467, HL, at 473.

88 See para.10-15 fn.81, at 448; quoted as the applicable general principle by both Lindley LJ and Bowen LJ in *Birmingham and District Land Co v London and North Western Railway Co* (1888) 40 Ch. D. 268, CA, at 281 and 286.

89 HL rejected on the facts the suggestion of James LJ in CA that the landlord had "intentionally lulled [the tenants] to sleep, until it was too late to do the repairs": see at 443–444, 448, 453.

90 See para.10-15 fn.88, at 286. See also *Bruner v Moore* [1904] 1 Ch. 305 at 313, 315 (nothing in *Hughes* turned on the equitable doctrine of relief against forfeiture, nor was it necessary to find fraud: an innocent misrepresentation will raise the equity).

be allowed by a Court of Equity to enforce the rights until such time has elapsed, without at all events placing the parties in the same position as they were before."

Although the factual context of this decision was very close to that in *Hughes v Metropolitan Railway Co*, in that it also involved the suspension of a time limit for works to be done under the terms of an agreement, and therefore the suspension of the termination of the agreement in the event that the works were not done within the prescribed time,[91] this broader formulation of the general principle could later be applied outside that context to become the basis of the modern development of promissory estoppel.

10-16   **High Trees: the development of "promissory estoppel"**   In 1946 Denning J took up the *Hughes* and *Birmingham and District Land Co* cases[92] as the basis of his decision in *Central London Property Trust Ltd v High Trees House Ltd*,[93] which is now generally seen as the foundation of the modern doctrine of promissory estoppel in English law. Recognising the obstacle posed by the decision of the House of Lords in *Jorden v Money*[94] in requiring estoppel to be based on a representation of existing fact and not a representation as to the future, Denning J asserted that cases[95]

---

[91]   In this case, there was a building agreement—an agreement between a developer and a landowner, under which the developer would acquire leases of properties to be built on the land if (but only if) it had completed the properties by a specified date—but the landowner told the developer to suspend building operations during a period when there was uncertainty over a possible railway scheme affecting the land. The landowner sold the land to the defendant, subject to the existing agreement, and the defendant took possession of the land after the expiry of the period set by the agreement. The developer sought a declaration that the agreement was still subsisting and an injunction restraining the defendant from taking possession. It was held that the developer's right to continue to build was extended by the period during which the original landowner had told him to suspend work.

[92]   See para.10-15. The decisions did not appear to have significant impact at the time: e.g. the editions of S.M. Leake, *Principles of the Law of Contracts*, from 1892, 3rd edn (Stevens) to 1921, 7th edn (Stevens), made no mention of either.

[93]   [1947] K.B. 130.

[94]   See para.10-14 fn.74.

[95]   "The cases to which I particularly desire to refer are: *Fenner v Blake* [1900] 1 Q.B. 426, *Re Wickham* (1917) 34 T.L.R. 158, *Re William Porter & Co Ltd* [1937] 2 All E.R. 361 and *Buttery v Pickard* [1946] W.N. 25": [1947] K.B. 130 at 134. For his principal authorities, in addition to *Hughes v Metropolitan Railway Co* and *Birmingham and District Land Co v London and North Western Railway Co*, Denning J also relied on *Salisbury (Marquess) v Gilmore* [1942] 2 K.B. 38, CA, where MacKinnon LJ held at 51–52 that a landlord's statement to a tenant that he intended to demolish the property at the end of the lease, which induced the tenant not to undertake repairs required by the lease, gave rise to an estoppel: it was in substance a representation of fact that the house was "ripe for re-erection, it is doomed to demolition" and therefore was not inconsistent with *Jorden v Money*. Denning J had been counsel in *Salisbury (Marquess) v Gilmore* and his argument (reported at [1942] 2 K.B. 38, 42–43) presaged his later decision in *High Trees*:

"although this is not a strict case of estoppel (*Jorden v Money*), the equitable principle applies, which was laid down in *Birmingham & District Land Co. v London & North Western Ry Co*. That principle is that if a person with a contractual right against another induces that other to believe that it will not be enforced, he will not be allowed to enforce the right without at any rate putting that other party into the position he was in before. ... The only difficulty is created by *Jorden v Money*, where a distinction was made in a case where there was only a statement of intention. The doctrine there laid down does not apply here ... because *Hughes v Metropolitan Ry Co.*, which is also a decision of the House of Lords, applies here and shows that the plaintiffs had in effect waived the right to damages for breach of the covenant to leave in repair."

For further discussion of these cases, concluding that there was "a slim but sufficient catena of authority to warrant Denning J's generalisation" in *High Trees*, see G.C. Cheshire and C.H.S. Fifoot,

since *Jorden v Money* had demonstrated that in equity[96] a party making a promise which is "intended to be binding, intended to be acted on, and in fact acted on" could be restrained from acting inconsistently with it, even though there is no consideration for the promise[97]:

> "The courts have not gone so far as to give a cause of action in damages for the breach of such a promise, but they have refused to allow the party making it to act inconsistently with it. It is in that sense, and that sense only, that such a promise gives rise to an estoppel. The decisions are a natural result of the fusion of law and equity: for the cases of *Hughes v Metropolitan Ry Co.*,[98] *Birmingham and District Land Co. v London & North Western Ry. Co.*[99] and *Salisbury (Marquess) v. Gilmore*,[100] afford a sufficient basis for saying that a party would not be allowed in equity to go back on such a promise. In my opinion, the time has now come for the validity of such a promise to be recognized."

We shall see in the following paragraphs of this chapter how the principle set out by Denning J was accepted and refined. Here it is sufficient to note the—rather limited—scope of operation of the principle in the *High Trees* case itself. In 1937 the landlord company granted a lease of a block of flats in London to one of its subsidiary companies for 99 years at an annual rent of £2,500, with a view to the tenant granting occupation leases of the individual flats; but because of the intervention of the war, the demand for occupation leases was reduced, and the landlord agreed in writing that "the ground rent should be reduced as from the commencement of the lease to £1,250 per annum". The rent was paid at the lower rate; but towards the end of 1945 the landlord's receiver, appointed to protect the interests of the company's debenture holders, discovered that under the terms of the lease the rent was due at the rate of £2,500 a year and wrote to the tenant saying that the rent should in future be paid at the higher rate and claiming that arrears were due in respect of the rent having in fact been paid below the rate reserved by the lease. However, the action before Denning J was not in respect of the full amount of the arrears,[101] but only in respect of the sum due in the last two quarters of 1945—and by the beginning of this period, the market for occupation leases had recovered and the tenant had managed to let the flats fully. Denning J held that, on its proper construction, the landlord's promise "was that the ground rent should be reduced to £1,250 a year as a temporary expedient while the block of flats was not fully, or substantially fully let, owing to the conditions prevailing": and so the reduction of rent did not extend to the last two quarters of 1945.[102] The higher rent was therefore recoverable for the period for which it had been claimed, a decision of rather limited significance which turned on the construction of the scope of the landlord's

---

"Central London Property Trust Ltd v High Trees House Ltd" (1947) 63 L.Q.R. 283, 285–288.

[96] The argument that the "fusion of law and equity" allows a different scope of estoppel in equity, in distinction to the limited approach of *Jorden v Money*, is not convincing given that *Jorden* was itself an appeal within the equity jurisdiction of the House of Lords: see para.10-14 fn.75.

[97] [1947] K.B. 130, at 134–135.

[98] [The particular reference given by Denning J was to Lord Cairns' statement, quoted at para.10-15 fn.88.]

[99] [The particular reference given by Denning J was to Bowen LJ's statement, quoted at para.10-15 fn.90.]

[100] [See para.10-16 fn.95; and note in particular Denning KC's argument in that case.]

[101] Given that the tenant was the landlord's subsidiary company, these were "friendly proceedings to test the legal position in regard to the rate at which rent was payable": [1947] K.B. 130 at 131.

[102] See para.10-16 fn.93, at 135.

promise.[103] However, of much more significance is that, from the reasoning which Denning J employed in his judgment, it is clear that if the full arrears had also been claimed they would not have been allowed during the period when the promise was still operative. We shall see that this has significance not only in relation to the general application of the doctrine of estoppel in giving force to a promise, unsupported by consideration, not to insist on the strict performance of obligations due under a contract,[104] but also in relation in particular to the potential operation of the *High Trees* principle in giving force to an agreement to reduce or extinguish a debt.[105]

10-17 **Acceptance of the developments made in High Trees** From a short decision on a rather straightforward point of interpretation of a promise,[106] the decision of Denning J has become the foundation of the general principle of promissory estoppel in English law. It is important to note, however, that in Denning J's judgment there was no statement that can be applied as a general rule. He put the principle in terms of "a promise was made which was intended to create legal relations and which, to the knowledge of the person making the promise, was going to be acted on by the person to whom it was made and which was in fact so acted on".[107] But this is too broad, and does not define such things as the kinds of promise to which the doctrine applies, what it means to say that the promisee must have "acted" on it, whether the promise is permanently binding or may be revoked, and what remedy is available to enforce the promise. Moreover, it has to be remembered that *High Trees* was a decision at first instance, seeking to reconcile and apply earlier authorities, but in effect using the equitable doctrine of estoppel to which Denning J referred in order to circumvent the decision of the House of Lords in *Jorden v Money*[108] by allowing a representation of intention, or a promise, to form the basis of an estoppel. The cases which came after *High Trees* began to work out the implications of the doctrine, and decisions at the level of the Court of Appeal,[109] the House of Lords[110] and the Privy Council[111] accepted the general principle, but

---

[103] For debate as to whether the discussion of the principle of promissory estoppel in the judgment in *High Trees* was therefore obiter dictum, see the notes on the case at (1947) 63 L.Q.R. 278 (R.E.M.) and (1948) 64 L.Q.R. 28 (J.H.C.M.), reply by R.E.M. at 29.

[104] See paras 10-29 to 10-32.

[105] See paras 10-34 to 10-37.

[106] See para.10-16, esp. fn.103. The judgment in *High Trees* was unreserved and extempore, although it was on a point which Denning J had himself argued as counsel some years before: see para.10-16 fn.95.

[107] See para.10-16 fn.93, at 134.

[108] See para.10-14.

[109] The first significant decision was *Combe v Combe* [1951] 2 K.B. 215, CA; see para.10-39. cf. however, *Brikom Investments Ltd v Carr* [1979] Q.B. 467, CA, at 485, 490 (Roskill LJ: "I do not rest my decision on any question of promissory estoppel; and I do not think it necessary on the facts of this case to investigate the jurisprudential basis of that doctrine in order to arrive at what I conceive to be the right decision. It is necessary to do no more than to apply that which was said by the House of Lords and especially by Lord Cairns LC in *Hughes v Metropolitan Railway Co.* (1877) 2 App.Cas. 439. ... I do not think it is necessary in order to reach that result to resort to the somewhat uncertain doctrine of promissory estoppel" (but treating the case as one of contractual variation or waiver: see at 489).

[110] e.g. *Tool Metal Manufacturing Co Ltd v Tungsten Electric Co Ltd* [1955] 1 W.L.R. 761, HL; *Woodhouse AC Israel Cocoa Ltd SA v Nigerian Produce Marketing Co Ltd* [1972] A.C. 741, HL (but note Lord Hailsham at 758: "the time may soon come when the whole sequence of cases based on promissory estoppel since the war, beginning with *Central London Property Trust Ltd v High Trees*

explained it and refined its scope.[112] In 1964 the Privy Council in *Ajayi v RT Briscoe (Nigeria) Ltd*[113] acknowledged that the principle was a development that can be traced back to the judgment of Bowen LJ in *Birmingham and District Land Co v London and North Western Railway Co*,[114] and set out the elements in more detail[115]:

> "Their Lordships are of opinion that the principle of law as defined by Bowen LJ has been confirmed by the House of Lords in the case of *Tool Metal Manufacturing Co. Ltd v Tungsten Electric Co. Ltd*[116] where the authorities were reviewed and no encouragement was given to the view that the principle was capable of extension so as to create rights in the promisee for which he had given no consideration. The principle, which has been described as quasi[117] estoppel and perhaps more aptly as promissory estoppel, is that when one party to a contract in the absence of fresh consideration agrees not to enforce his rights an equity will be raised in favour of the other party. This equity is, however, subject to the qualifications (1) that the other party has altered his position, (2) that the promisor can resile from his promise on giving reasonable notice, which need not be a formal notice, giving the promisee a reasonable opportunity of resuming his position, (3) the promise only becomes final and irrevocable if the promisee cannot resume his position."

This provides a very helpful summary of the elements of the doctrine of promissory estoppel as well as highlighting some of the limitations on its scope of operation. In the following section we shall consider the elements of promissory estoppel in more detail.

III. THE ELEMENTS OF PROMISSORY ESTOPPEL IN ENGLISH LAW

Outline of the elements of promissory estoppel The doctrine of promissory estoppel, as it operates within the English[118] law of contract,[119] is concerned with   **10-18**

House Ltd, may need to be reviewed and reduced to a coherent body of doctrine by the courts").

[111] e.g. *Ajayi v RT Briscoe (Nigeria) Ltd*, see para.10-17 fn.115.

[112] For early commentary on and reception of the development, see Cheshire and Fifoot, "Central London Property Trust Ltd v High Trees House Ltd", see para.10-16 fn.95; J.F. Wilson, "Recent Developments in Estoppel" (1951) 67 L.Q.R. 330; A.T. Denning, "Recent Developments in the Doctrine of Consideration" (1952) 15 M.L.R. 1; J.F. Wilson, "A Reappraisal of Quasi-Estoppel" [1965] C.L.J. 93; for criticism, see F. Bennion, "Want of Consideration" (1953) 16 M.L.R. 441.

[113] [1964] 1 W.L.R. 1326.

[114] (1888) 40 Ch. D. 268, CA, at 286; see para.10-15.

[115] *Ajayi v RT Briscoe (Nigeria) Ltd* [1964] 1 W.L.R. 1326, PC, at 1330 (Lord Hodson giving the judgment of the Privy Council, which comprised Lord Morris of Borth-y-Gest, Lord Hodson and Lord Guest). It was applied as a correct statement of the law by Balcombe J in *Fontana NV v Mautner* [1980] 1 E.G.L.R. 68 at 71.

[116] See para.10-17 fn.110.

[117] For the language of "quasi-estoppel" see also Wilson, "Recent Developments in Estoppel" and "A Reappraisal of Quasi-Estoppel, see para.10-17 fn.112; and cf. *High Trees*, see para.10-16 fn.93, at 143 (Denning J: "they are not cases of estoppel in the strict sense. They are really promises"); B. McFarlane, "Understanding Equitable Estoppel: From Metaphors to Better Laws" (2013) 66 C.L.P. 267, 273, criticising the use of the term "estoppel": the name of the doctrine of promissory estoppel "verges on the oxymoronic. If a legal principle is to operate as a true estoppel, it cannot be based on a promise as to A's future conduct".

[118] For discussion of the scope of promissory estoppel in other common law jurisdictions, see paras 10-46 to 10-48.

[119] Promissory estoppel can also apply in relation to a representation not to enforce a right which does not arise by contract, such as a right arising by statute: *Durham Fancy Goods Ltd v Michael Jackson (Fancy Goods) Ltd* [1968] 2 Q.B. 839 (personal liability of company officer arising under CA 1948 s.108: "Lord Cairns [in *Hughes v Metropolitan Railway Co*, see para.10-15 fn.88] in his enunciation of the principle assumed a pre-existing contractual relationship between the parties, but this does

the situation where one party to an existing contract represents (or promises) to the other party that he will not insist on that other party fully performing his obligations under the contract, thereby providing a defence for the other party (the representee) if the representor later seeks to enforce the contract against him contrary to the representation he had made. Promissory estoppel therefore serves a function in the modification of a contract, but to understand the scope of operation of the doctrine we need to consider what representations or promises can support an estoppel; what state of mind is required of the representor in making his representation; what response is required of the representee by way of reliance on the representation in order to allow him to hold the representor to his representation; and whether the representor has irrevocably changed the contract in accordance with his representation, or can revoke his representation and require the representee to perform the contract strictly in accordance with its original terms (that is, whether the effect of promissory estoppel is only to suspend the contractual rights and duties, or to render their change permanent).

These issues will be discussed in detail in the following paragraphs of this section. Further questions about the limits of the role of promissory estoppel—whether it can be allowed to have the effect of discharging a debt, and whether there are any circumstances in which it can be used actively by the representee (rather than as a defence) or in order to create a new obligation—will be discussed in section IV of this chapter.

---

not seem to me to be essential, provided that there is a pre-existing legal relationship which could in certain circumstances give rise to liabilities and penalties": Donaldson J at 847), followed in *Augier v Secretary of State for the Environment* (1979) 38 P. & C.R. 219 at 227 (but this appears to be a case where the estoppel was used " as a sword": see para.10-41); or another personal right such as to occupy land without having an interest in the land: *Maharaj v Chand* [1986] A.C. 898, PC; or a right to some particular remedy such as rescission of a contract: *Goldsworthy v Brickell* [1987] Ch. 378, CA, at 410–411 (but the estoppel defence failed on the facts; and the defence of affirmation is more appropriate in such a case anyway); or the right to rely on a defence such as a limitation period: *Nippon Yusen Kaisha v Pacifica Navigacion SA (The Ion)* [1980] 2 Lloyd's Rep. 245 at 250; *Cooperative Wholesale Society Ltd v Chester de Street DC* (1997) 73 P. & C.R. 111 (Lands Tribunal) at 118. For other references to a "legal relationship" see *BP Exploration v Hunt (No.2)* [1979] 1 W.L.R. 783 at 810; *Nippon Yusen Kaisha v Pacifica Navigacion SA (The Ion)*, above, at 250, but this was then applied by Webster J in *Pacol Ltd v Trade Lines Ltd (The Henrik Sif)* [1982] 1 Lloyd's Rep. 456 at 466 to apply to a *putative* legal relationship, rather than an existing relationship: see para.10-41 fn.325. Where the obligation which is alleged to have been released or suspended by estoppel arises by statute, there will always be a question whether the policy of the statute would be subverted by the operation of an estoppel; and if the statute is one out of which the parties could not validly contract, it will generally not be possible for an estoppel to do what a contract cannot: *Evans v Amicus Healthcare Ltd* [2003] EWHC 2161 (Fam) at [279]–[297]; [2004] EWCA Civ 727 at [120], [2005] Fam. 1 (man's right under Human Fertilisation and Embryology Act 1990 to vary or withdraw consent to treatment and storage of embryos fertilised with his sperm in course of in vitro fertilisation could not be limited by any promissory estoppel arising from his representation that he would not withdraw consent); see also *Welch v Nagy* [1950] 1 K.B. 455, CA (estoppel by representation); *Keen v Holland* [1984] 1 W.L.R. 251, CA, at 261 (estoppel by convention), *Newport City Council v Charles* [2008] EWCA Civ 1541; [2009] 1 W.L.R. 1884 at [19], [30]. For the broader question of whether an estoppel can be allowed to circumvent a statutory formality requirement, see para.4-15.

(1)   Estoppel in the Modification of an Existing Contract

Promissory estoppel is limited to the modification of an existing contract, in the absence of fresh consideration   The doctrine of promissory estoppel is designed to give effect to promises not supported by consideration. If the obligation on which a party seeks to rely arises under the express or implied terms of a contract, he simply relies on the contract and there is no place for estoppel.[120]   **10-19**

According to the traditional understanding of the doctrine of promissory estoppel, the promise is not to enforce an existing legal relationship rather than to create a new legal relationship, and therefore the effect of the estoppel is to give some force to the modification of the existing relationship. This limitation of the scope of promissory estoppel will be considered further below.[121] But it means that, in the context of contractual obligations,[122] promissory estoppel fills a gap: it deals with the modification of an existing contract by means of a representation or promise which is not supported by consideration.[123] If there is consideration, it takes effect as a contractual variation.[124]

(2)   The Representation or Promise

The content of the representation: a negative promise   The representation which is given effect by the doctrine of promissory estoppel is in substance a negative promise: "one party to a contract … agrees *not to enforce his rights*".[125] In this, as we have seen, promissory estoppel has gone beyond the scope of the estoppel by representation which applies only to representations of (present) fact, and not to representations of future intention, or promises.[126] But it is important to remember   **10-20**

---

[120] *Secretary of State for Employment v Globe Elastic Thread Co Ltd* [1980] A.C. 506, HL, at 518 (Lord Wilberforce: "There was a contract with the employee that he would retain the benefit of his previous employment. To convert this into an estoppel is to turn the doctrine of promissory estoppel (the validity or scope of which I do not now examine) upside down. Even if an estoppel may give rise to a contractual obligation, it does not follow, and it would be a strange doctrine, that a contract gives rise to an estoppel"), overruling *Evenden v Guildford City Association Football Club Ltd* [1975] Q.B. 917, CA, where Lord Denning MR at 923–924 applied promissory estoppel to enforce a claim to a redundancy payment following the employer's representation relating to the employee's period of continuous employment; Browne LJ, by contrast, said at 926: "I agree with Lord Denning MR also that they are disabled on the basis of promissory estoppel; though it seems to me that, as there was a binding contract in this case, it is not necessary for the employee to rely on estoppel because he can rely on the contract").

[121] See paras 10-38.

[122] cf. para.10-18 fn.119.

[123] *Ajayi v RT Briscoe (Nigeria) Ltd*, see para.10-17 fn.115, at 1330, quoted at para.10-17: "when one party to a contract *in the absence of fresh consideration* agrees not to enforce his rights" (emphasis added).

[124] See paras 9-02, 10-12.

[125] *Ajayi v RT Briscoe (Nigeria) Ltd*, see para.10-17 fn.115, at 1330, quoted at para.10-17 (emphasis added). See also, e.g. *Hughes v Metropolitan Railway Co*, see para.10-15 fn.88 ("leading one of the parties to suppose that the strict rights arising under the contract will not be enforced, or will be kept in suspense, or held in abeyance,"); *BP Exploration v Hunt (No.2)*, see para.10-18 fn.119, at 810 (Robert Goff J: "a representation, express or implied, by one party that he will not enforce his strict rights against the other", summarising the elements which emerge from *Hughes v Metropolitan Railway Co*). The representation may be made by an agent, but only if the agent has authority (under the normal rules of agency) to make it: *Re Selectmove Ltd* [1995] 1 W.L.R. 474, CA, at 481.

[126] *Jorden v Money*, see para.10-14 fn.74; *High Trees*, see para.10-16 fn.93, at 143 (Denning J: "they are not cases of estoppel in the strict sense. They are really promises—promises intended to be bind-

that the promise is *not* to insist on the other party performing his full contractual duties—*not* to enforce one's full contractual rights. This limited context for the representation which gives rise to promissory estoppel explains the remedy which flows from it and the fact that, under this doctrine as it applies within English law, it cannot create new rights, but only vary existing contractual rights by reducing them, either temporarily or permanently.[127] This would not be a restriction if estoppel were to be allowed to create new rights—and thus to render enforceable a positive promise as much as a negative promise; but that would take the doctrine of estoppel outside its existing boundaries.[128]

10-21   **The representation may be express or implied**   The representation which gives rise to the promissory estoppel may be either express or implied.[129] One party to a contract may tell the other that he need not fully perform his contractual duties[130]; or one party's conduct,[131] or more broadly the dealings between the parties,[132] may communicate to the other party that he is being dispensed from the duty to perform. As with any remedies which the law provides for representations and promises, the question is whether the representation or promise has been sufficiently communicated to the party seeking the remedy, and this may be by words or by conduct.[133]

10-22   **The representation will be interpreted objectively, but must be clear and unequivocal**   For the purposes of promissory estoppel, as generally in the law of contract,[134] whether a representation has been made, and the meaning of the representation, are determined objectively: it does not depend on what the person

---

ing, intended to be acted on, and in fact acted on"); and generally paras 10-14, 10-16.

[127] See paras 10-38 to 10-40.

[128] See para.10-45.

[129] *BP Exploration v Hunt (No.2)*, see para.10-18 fn.119, at 810 (Robert Goff J: "a representation, *express or implied*, by one party that he will not enforce his strict rights against the other"; emphasis added).

[130] e.g. *Birmingham and District Land Co v London and North Western Railway Co*, see para.10-15 fnn.88, 91 (land owner told developer to suspend building operations because of the uncertainty over a possible railway scheme affecting the land).

[131] *Bremer Handelsgesellschaft mbH v Vanden Avenne-Izegem PVBA* [1978] 2 Lloyd's Rep. 109, HL, at 126 (Lord Salmon: "To make an unequivocal representation or waiver it is not necessary for the buyers to say, 'We hereby waive it'. It is quite enough if they behave or write in such a way that reasonable sellers would be led to believe that the buyers were waiving any defect there might be in the notice and were accepting it as effectively extending the date for delivery"); followed by Robert Goff J. in *Société Italo-Belge pour le Commerce et l'Industrie SA v Palm and Vegetable Oils (Malaysia) Sdn Bdh (The Post Chaser)* [1982] 1 All E.R. 19 at 25.

[132] e.g. *Hughes v Metropolitan Railway Co*, see para.10-15 fn.86; *Bruner v Moore*, see para.10-15 fn.90, at 315 (both parties treated period for exercise of option as not having ended). Where there is no express or implied representation of intention, but a shared (and communicated) assumption of fact or law in the parties' mutual dealings, the better analysis may be estoppel by convention: see para.10-05.

[133] cf. the "misrepresentation" by words or conduct in a claim for a remedy for pre-contractual misrepresentation: Cartwright (Misrepresentation), para.3-04.

[134] cf. paras 3-05 to 3-07 for the interpretation of the communications between the parties forming a contract. In that context there is a clear link to estoppel since in formulating the objective test for the formation of a contract in *Smith v Hughes* (1871) L.R. 6 Q.B. 597 at 607 (quoted at para.3-06) Blackburn J relied on *Freeman v Cooke* (1848) 2 Exch. 654 at 663, 154 E.R. 652 at 656—a case of estoppel by representation. A "misrepresentation" is similarly interpreted objectively for the purposes of remedies for pre-contractual misrepresentation: Cartwright (Misrepresentation), para.3-06.

making it intended to say, but how a reasonable person in the position of the representee would understand it[135] and how the representee did understand it.[136] However, there has been a significant emphasis in the cases that the representation, in order to form the basis of promissory estoppel, must be "clear and unequivocal". This follows from the decision of the House of Lords in *Woodhouse AC Israel Cocoa Ltd SA v Nigerian Produce Marketing Co Ltd*[137] where a contract for the sale of cocoa provided for payment in Nigerian pounds in Lagos, but by letter the sellers told the buyers that "payment can be made in sterling and in Lagos". The buyers claimed that this entitled them to make payment in Lagos on the basis of one pound sterling for one Nigerian pound (i.e. the nominal value of the price remained unchanged, but they were permitted to pay in the alternative currency). When the representation was made, the value of the two currencies was identical; but shortly afterwards sterling was devalued by 15 per cent against the Nigerian pound and so payment of the same nominal value in sterling became correspondingly more advantageous to the buyer. The House of Lords decided that the representation would not have been sufficiently clear and unequivocal to form the basis of a contractual variation of the price; and therefore it could not be sufficiently clear and unequivocal to form the basis of promissory estoppel: the nominal value in Nigerian pounds therefore remained the contract price, even if it were to be discharged in sterling (taking into account the rate of exchange between the two currencies). As Lord Hailsham put it[138]:

"it would really be an astonishing thing if, in the case of a genuine misunderstanding as to the meaning of an offer, the offeree could obtain by means of the doctrine of promissory estoppel something that he must fail to obtain under the conventional law of contract."

---

[135] *Bremer Handelsgesellschaft mbH v Vanden Avenne-Izegem PVBA*, see para.10-21 fn.131, at 126; *Bremer Handelsgesellschaft mbH v C Mackprang Jr* [1979] 1 Lloyd's Rep. 211, CA, at 225–226, 228, 230; *Société Italo-Belge pour le Commerce et l'Industrie SA v Palm and Vegetable Oils (Malaysia) Sdn Bdh (The Post Chaser)* [1982] 1 All E.R. 19 at 25; *Scandinavian Trading Tanker Co AB v Flota Petrolera Ecuatoriana (The Scaptrade)* [1983] Q.B. 529, CA, at 535; *Liberty Insurance Pte Ltd v Argo Systems FZE* [2011] EWCA Civ 1572; [2012] 1 C.L.C. 81 at [41] (Aikens LJ, apparently regarding this as a wholly objective test and ignoring the representee's understanding; but cf. para.10-22 fn.136).

[136] The representee's understanding is relevant because he must have relied on the representation: see para.10-25; but if he has a wider understanding of the representation than a reasonable person would have understood this does not prevent his reliance on it for the purposes of promissory estoppel as long as the reasonable interpretation is sufficient as a basis for the estoppel: *Fontana NV v Mautner* [1980] 1 E.G.L.R. 68 at 71 (but there was in fact no reliance and therefore the estoppel defence failed).

[137] [1972] A.C. 741, HL. For applications of this case see, e.g. *Finagrain SA Geneva v P Kruse Hamburg* [1976] 2 Lloyd's Rep. 508, CA, at 534 (burden of proof that representation was clear and unequivocal not discharged); *Allied Marine Transport Ltd v Vale do Rio Doce Navegacao SA* [1985] 1 W.L.R. 925, CA, at 941 ("silence and inaction are of their nature equivocal, for the simple reason that there can be more than one reason why the person concerned has been silent and inactive": Robert Goff LJ); *Azov Shipping Co Ltd v Baltic Shipping Co* [1999] 2 Lloyd's Rep. 159 at 173; *Baird Textiles Holdings Ltd v Marks & Spencer Plc* [2001] EWCA Civ 274; [2002] 1 All E.R. (Comm) 737 at [38], [84]; *Golstein v Bishop* [2013] EWHC 881 (Ch) at [97]–[98] (partner's statement that he would "take" only half his salary was ambiguous and the more natural meaning was that he would only draw half, not that he would give up the balance).

[138] [1972] A.C. 741, HL at 757; see also Lord Salmon at 770 ("No letter ... can assume the qualities of a chameleon. It cannot take on one meaning if you consider it as a possible contractual document and a contrary meaning if you consider it as a possible representation").

This requirement that the representation be "clear and unequivocal" ought not, however, to be interpreted as more stringent than in the formation of a contract[139]: putting promissory estoppel and contract on the same level is surely the sensible approach. The party relying[140] on a representation as a modification of his contractual obligations will have to show that it is certain[141] and clear in its meaning to the same standard as a similar contractual variation of the obligations.[142]

As in the formation of a contract,[143] silence and inaction do not normally communicate information sufficiently clearly, and so are not normally sufficient to form the basis of a representation for the purposes of promissory estoppel.[144] More than mere silence is therefore required, such as some other positive conduct which gives clear and unequivocal meaning to the inaction or silence.[145]

Sometimes a representation may not be entirely clear, although it is at least clear in part, or to some extent: for example, it might mean [A+B] or [A]; but it is clear that it means *at least* [A]. In such a case the normal approach to interpretation of contracts would allow the representation its effect as regards [A], but deny [B].[146] Such a situation might arise where one party to a contract clearly dispenses the other party from his obligation to perform a particular obligation, but does not make clear whether the dispensation is permanent or only temporary.[147] In such a case, even if promissory estoppel can have the effect of permanently varying the terms of the

---

139 cf. however, [1972] A.C. 741, HL at 762 (Lord Pearson: "It may be that the 'representation' or promise or assurance has to have *at least as much* precision as would be needed for a variation of the contract"; emphasis added; but this followed a more general statement which is consistent with the approach in contract: "In a case of this kind the alleged 'representation' or promise or assurance ought to be reasonably clear and definite both as to the terms of the contract which is being waived and as to the duration of the waiver").

140 The burden of proof that the representation is clear and unequivocal rests on the party seeking to rely on it: *Finagrain SA Geneva v P Kruse Hamburg*, see para.10-22 fn.137.

141 The requirement of certainty for promissory estoppel to the same standard as contract terms was assumed by CA in *Baird Textiles Holdings Ltd v Marks & Spencer Plc* [2001] EWCA Civ 274; [2002] 1 All E.R. (Comm) 737 at [38], [80], [91], although Mance LJ said at [85] that other forms of estoppel have different requirements, and that "a proprietary estoppel may arise from promises of an 'equivocal nature'". The context in which proprietary estoppel arises will vary, but includes a non-commercial context where the parties are not practised at explaining themselves in clear, technical terms: see para.4-13 fnn.98, 99. But this is not the point: as long as the representation on which the claim of proprietary estoppel is based is clear to the other party, that is sufficient. For a good example, see *Thorner v Major* [2009] UKHL 18; [2009] 1 W.L.R. 776, where the parties were "taciturn and undemonstrative men" (Lord Walker at [59]) and "[e]ven though clear and unequivocal statements played little or no part in communications between the two men, they were well able to understand one another" (Lord Rodger at [26]).

142 See also *Azov Shipping Co Ltd v Baltic Shipping Co*, see para.10-22 fn.137, at 173 (Colman J: "the objective construction of alleged representations is the same for the purposes of estoppel as for the constituents of a contract").

143 See para.3-39.

144 *Allied Marine Transport Ltd v Vale do Rio Doce Navegacao SA*, see para.10-22 fn.137, at 941.

145 *Société Italo-Belge pour le Commerce et l'Industrie SA v Palm and Vegetable Oils (Malaysia) Sdn Bdh (The Post Chaser)*, see para.10-21 fn.131, at 25; *Vitol SA v Esso Australia Ltd (The Wise)* [1989] 2 Lloyd's Rep. 451, CA, at 460.

146 cf. the *contra proferentem* rule, by which a party can rely on a clause he put forward, or a clause in his favour, only to the extent that it is not ambiguous: Lewison, para.7.08. cf. *Hiscox v Outhwaite (No.3)* [1991] 2 Lloyd's Rep. 524 at 534 (arbitrator found that representation had a clear limited meaning; issue was whether any *further* meaning was clear and unequivocal).

147 cf. *Collier v P & MJ Wright (Holdings) Ltd* [2007] EWCA Civ 1329; [2008] 1 W.L.R. 643 at [45] (Longmore LJ: scope of promise arguable; but this would then be determined at trial).

contract in accordance with the representation which has been relied on,[148] it cannot have effect greater than the scope of the representation[149]; and so the representation should surely be effective as to the temporary dispensation, but the representor would be able to revoke it and require the representee to resume the original contractual obligations.[150]

(3)   The Representor's State of Mind

The representor must have intended that the representee rely on the representation.   The requirement that the representee rely on the representation is considered below.[151] But it is sometimes said that, in order to allow the representee to raise the estoppel so as to preclude the representor from acting inconsistently with his representation, the representor must have intended the representee to rely on the representation,[152] or must at least have known that the representee would so rely.[153] This is consistent with other contexts in which a representation has legal consequences,[154] and in the context of promissory estoppel it makes good sense. Promissory estoppel is an exception to the requirement of consideration for the enforceability of a promise, and consideration requires the promisee to have promised, done or forborne to do something not merely in response to the promise but in return for the promise—at the promisor's request.[155] It would go too far to allow the representee to hold the representor to a representation merely by his unintended and unexpected unilateral act of reliance, but the

10-23

---

[148] See para.10-32.

[149] e.g. in *High Trees*, see para.10-16 the decision was based on the scope of the promise, i.e. during the war so long as the flats were not fully let, and there was no question of it operating beyond that.

[150] In *Troop v Gibson* [1986] 1 E.G.L.R. 1, CA, at 3 Sir John Arnold P left open a different question: whether, in a case of estoppel by representation "the requirement [that the representation be clear and unequivocal] is satisfied if there be more than one reasonable interpretation of the words used to make the representation, one of them being that relied upon by the party claiming the benefit of estoppel, or whether this must be the only reasonable interpretation". In the case of remedies for pre-contractual misrepresentation, if a similar issue arises and a statement, tested objectively, could equally well be understood in two senses, the representee must prove the meaning which he actually understood and relied on: it is not enough for him simply to claim that one of the meanings was actionable, or to leave it to the court to decide the "ordinary" meaning: *Smith v Chadwick* (1884) 9 App. Cas. 187, HL.

[151] See para.10-25.

[152] e.g. *Central London Property Trust Ltd v High Trees House Ltd* [1947] K.B. 130 at 134 (Denning J: "a promise was made which was intended to create legal relations and which, to the knowledge of the person making the promise, was going to be acted on by the person to whom it was made and which was in fact acted on", a formulation repeated by Lord Denning in later cases: e.g. *Robertson v Minister of Pensions* [1949] 1 K.B. 227 at 230; *Brikom Investments Ltd v Carr* [1979] Q.B. 467, CA, at 482; *Evenden v Guildford City Association Football Club Ltd*, see para.10-19 fn.120, at 924); *Goldsworthy v Brickell* [1987] Ch. 378, CA, at 411 (Nourse LJ: "the representation was made with the knowledge or intention that it would be acted upon by the defendant in the manner in which it was acted upon").

[153] In *James v Heim Gallery (London) Ltd* (1981) 41 P. & C.R. 269, CA, at 277–278, 280. If the representor knows that the representee will rely on the representation, or is likely to rely on it, he can still be said (obliquely, and objectively) to intend him to rely. The formulation of the test in other cases does not include the requirements of intention or knowledge: e.g. *Ajayi v RT Briscoe (Nigeria) Ltd*, see para.10-17 fn.115, at 1330, quoted at para.10-17.

[154] e.g. the remedies for pre-contractual misrepresentation generally require not merely reliance by the representee, but that the representor intended the representee to act on the representation: Cartwright (Misrepresentation), para.3-49.

[155] See para.8-15; para.10-39.

justification for binding the representor is clearly stronger where the reliance is what the representor intended. However, it does not appear to be a significant issue in practice since a party's intention is generally tested objectively,[156] and as long as it is shown that the representation was made with the objectively clear and unequivocal[157] meaning that the representee would be dispensed from strict performance with the terms of his contract, it would be unusual to find that the representor did not intend his representation to be acted on. The reported cases do not turn on the representor's intention, but on the meaning of the representation,[158] and on whether there was a sufficient act of reliance.[159]

10-24 **Promissory estoppel does not depend on bad faith on the part of the representor** It is irrelevant whether the representor acted in good or bad faith in making the representation, or in intending the representee to act on it.[160] The estoppel is designed to protect the representee not against the bad faith of the representor in having led him to rely on the representation, but against the inequity of allowing the representor to act inconsistently with his representation in the circumstances in which the representee finds himself in consequence of his having relied on it.[161]

(4) Reliance by the Representee

10-25 **The representee must have "relied on" the representation—"acted on it" or "altered his position"** A person is not estopped from acting inconsistently with his representation merely by reason of the fact that he has made it, but because the representee has relied on it. In estoppel by representation of fact[162] it is well established that the gist of the estoppel is the representee's *reliance* on the representation—he *acted on* the representation in the way in which the representor intended him to do.[163] This has been carried across to promissory estoppel, so that even if the representation or promise is sufficient to create an "equity" in the representee, it does so only once he has relied on, or acted on, the representation.[164] And in this sense "relied" or "acted" means that he has "altered his position"[165] —done something (or forborne to do something) in consequence of the representation.[166]

---

[156] See para.10-22 fn.134. The reliance on the representation may also be established objectively: see para.10-26.

[157] See para.10-22.

[158] See para.10-22.

[159] See para.10-25.

[160] *Hughes v Metropolitan Railway Co* (1877) 2 App. Cas. 439, HL, see para.10-15, at 443–444, 448, 453 (HL rejecting the suggestion of James LJ in CA that the landlord had "intentionally lulled [the tenants] to sleep, until it was too late to do the repairs", and noting that this was in any event irrelevant).

[161] See para.10-28.

[162] See para.10-06.

[163] *Freeman v Cooke* (1848) 2 Exch. 654 at 663, 154 E.R. 652 at 656; Spencer Bower (Estoppel), Ch.5.

[164] *Tool Metal Manufacturing Co Ltd v Tungsten Electric Co Ltd* [1955] 1 W.L.R. 761, HL, at 764 (Viscount Simonds: "the gist of the equity lies in the fact that one party has by his conduct led the other to alter his position").

[165] *Ajayi v RT Briscoe (Nigeria) Ltd*, see para.10-17 fn.115, at 1330, quoted at para.10-17 "an equity will be raised in favour of the other party. This equity is, however, subject to the qualifications (1) *that the other party has altered his position*" (emphasis added).

[166] e.g. *Société Italo-Belge pour le Commerce et l'Industrie SA v Palm and Vegetable Oils (Malaysia) Sdn Bdh (The Post Chaser)* [1982] 1 All E.R. 19 at 27 (presentation of shipping document). For

Proof of reliance If the representee cannot establish that he acted (or forbore to act) in reliance on the representation, he cannot hold the representor to his representation by means of the doctrine of promissory estoppel.[167] Proof of reliance requires not merely proof of some act or forbearance on the part of the representee, but also proof of a causal link between the representation and the act or forbearance. Sometimes it will be evident from the facts before the court whether the act or forbearance which the representee asserts in support of the estoppel defence was in fact a consequence of the representation on which he claims to rely. The burden lies on the representee to establish the elements of the estoppel, but where the representation was such that a person in the representee's position would reasonably be expected to act (or forbear to act) in the way in which the representee did act (or forbear), the court may infer the necessary reliance.[168]

10-26

The reliance need not be "detrimental" Sometimes the judges have used language suggesting that the reliance must be "detrimental" to the representee.[169] Lord Denning rejected this emphatically, and made clear that what was required was that the representee "act on" the representation, or "conduct his affairs" on the basis of the representation, or "alter his position" in response to the representation—but

10-27

---

examples of forbearance in reliance on a representation, see *Robertson v Minister of Pensions* [1949] 1 K.B. 227 at 231 (forbearance to get medical opinion relevant to disability claim); *Nippon Yusen Kaisha v Pacifica Navigacion SA (The Ion)* [1980] 2 Lloyd's Rep. 245 at 250 (omission to apply for extension of time in arbitration); *Golstein v Bishop* [2013] EWHC 881 (Ch) at [99] (no unequivocal representation; but if there had been, the representee's failure to take steps such as bringing partnership to an end (whether or not those steps would have been successful) would have been sufficient reliance).

167 e.g. *Ajayi v RT Briscoe (Nigeria) Ltd*, see para.10-17 fn.115, at 1331 (no evidence that hirer of lorries under hire-purchase agreement organised his business differently in reliance on representation that instalments could be withheld while lorries withdrawn from service); *Finagrain SA Geneva v P Kruse Hamburg* [1976] 2 Lloyd's Rep. 508, CA, at 535 (no unequivocal representation; but even if there had been, there was no evidence of any relevant conduct by way of reliance); *Allied Marine Transport Ltd v Vale do Rio Doce Navegacao SA* [1985] 1 W.L.R. 925, CA, at 941 (no unequivocal representation from the inaction of the other party to the arbitration; but even if there had been, there was no reliance because the representee's failure to take steps in the arbitration followed from a decision made at an early stage on practical grounds, not from any conduct or absence of conduct of the other party).

168 *Brikom Investments Ltd v Carr* [1979] Q.B. 467, CA, at 483 (Lord Denning MR: "Once it is shown that a representation was calculated to influence the judgment of a reasonable man, the presumption is that he was so influenced"), followed for proof of reliance for the purposes of proprietary estoppel in *Greasley v Cooke* [1980] 1 W.L.R. 1306, CA, at 1311 (Lord Denning MR). The same approach is used in relation to the proof of reliance on a misrepresentation for the purpose of remedies such as rescission and damages in the tort of deceit, and Lord Denning's statement echoes the language of the misrepresentation cases where it is clear that the "presumption" is only evidential, giving rise to an inference of fact that the representation was relied on: Cartwright (Misrepresentation), para.3-53. See also *Scandinavian Trading Tanker Co AB v Flota Petrolera Ecuatoriana (The Scaptrade)* [1983] Q.B. 529, CA, at 535 (Robert Goff LJ, citing no authority).

169 e.g. *WJ Alan & Co Ltd v El Nasr Export and Import Co* [1971] 1 Lloyd's Rep. 401 at 420 (Orr J: no estoppel because "there is no evidence of the respondents having acted to their detriment as a result of any representation by the claimants"); *Bremer Handelsgesellschaft mbH v Vanden Avenne-Izegem PVBA* [1978] 2 Lloyd's Rep. 109 at 127 (Lord Salmon: "the question then arises as to whether the sellers can rely on the waiver unless as a result of it they have acted to their detriment or whether it is sufficient if the sellers have conducted their affairs on the basis of the waiver ... I do not think that in this case it matters which of these two tests one applies because the sellers clearly acted on the basis of the waiver and also to their detriment in spending time and money"); *James v Heim Gallery (London) Ltd*, see para.10-23 fn.153, at 280 (Shaw LJ: no estoppel where parties not "led into any course of conduct which disadvantaged them").

that there was no requirement that the representee should suffer detriment in consequence[170]:

"A seller may, by his conduct, lead the buyer to believe that he is not insisting on the stipulated time for exercising an option.[171] A buyer may, by requesting delivery, lead the seller to believe that he is not insisting on the contractual time for delivery.[172] A seller may, by his conduct, lead the buyer to believe that he will not insist on a confirmed letter of credit,[173] but will accept an unconfirmed one instead.[174] A seller may accept a less sum for his goods than the contracted price, thus inducing him to believe that he will not enforce payment of the balance.[175] In none of these cases does the party who acts on the belief suffer any detriment. It is not a detriment, but a benefit to him, to have an extension of time or to pay less, or as the case may be. Nevertheless, he has conducted his affairs on the basis that he has that benefit and it would not be equitable now to deprive him of it.

The judge rejected this doctrine because, he said, 'there is no evidence of the buyers having acted to their detriment.' I know that it has been suggested in some quarters that there must be detriment. But I can find no support for it in the authorities cited by the judge. The nearest approach to it is the statement of Viscount Simonds in the *Tool Metal* case,[176] that the other must have been led 'to alter his position,' which was adopted by Lord Hodson in *Ajayi v. R. T. Briscoe (Nigeria) Ltd.*[177] But that only means that he must have been led to act differently from what he otherwise would have done. And if you study the cases in which the doctrine has been applied, you will see that all that is required is that the one should have '*acted* on the belief induced by the other party.' That is how Lord Cohen put it in the *Tool Metal* case,[178] and that is how I would put it myself."

This has been followed in later cases[179] and it is suggested that it is right, although

---

[170] *WJ Alan & Co Ltd v El Nasr Export and Import Co* [1972] 2 Q.B. 189, CA, at 213–214, rejecting the approach of the trial judge, Orr J, see para.10-27 fn.169. The other members of the court found that there was a contractual variation in this case; but Stephenson LJ at 221 also left open the question whether for waiver any alteration of position is sufficient, or whether it must be "an alteration to his detriment, or for the worse, in some sense". Lord Denning first made the point that detriment should not be required in an article in 1952, "Recent Developments in the Doctrine of Consideration" (1952) 15 M.L.R. 1, 5–6, although he there contemplated a possible distinction between a *promise* not to enforce strict legal rights (detriment not required; sufficient that the promisee acted on it) and a case where the representor by his *conduct* induced the other party to believe that his strict rights would not be enforced (action by the representee to his detriment may be necessary). This distinction has not been drawn in the decisions, and there seems to be no reason for it, given that a representation may generally be made by words or by conduct without formal distinction in relation to its effect in law: see para.10-21.

[171] *Bruner v Moore* [1904] 1 Ch. 305.

[172] *Charles Rickards Ltd v Oppenhaim* [1950] 1 K.B. 616, 621 [see para.10-31].

[173] *Plasticmoda Societa per Azioni v Davidsons (Manchester) Ltd* [1952] 1 Lloyd's Rep. 527.

[174] *Panoutsos v Raymond Hadley Corporation of New York* [1917] 2 K.B. 473; *Enrico Furst & Co v WE Fischer* [1960] 2 Lloyd's Rep. 340.

[175] *Central London Property Trust Ltd v High Trees House Ltd* [1947] K.B. 130 [see para.10-16] and *D&C Builders Ltd v Rees* [1966] 2 Q.B. 617, 624 [see para.10-36].

[176] [1955] 1 W.L.R. 761, 764 [see para.10-25 fn.164].

[177] [1964] 1 W.L.R. 1326, 1330 [see para.10-25 fn.165].

[178] [1955] 1 W.L.R. 761, 799.

[179] e.g. *Finagrain SA Geneva v P Kruse Hamburg* [1976] 2 Lloyd's Rep. 508, CA, at 535 (Megaw LJ); *Bremer Handelsgesellschaft mbH v Vanden Avenne-Izegem PVBA* [1977] 2 Lloyd's Rep. 133 at 165 (Mocatta J); *Brikom Investments Ltd v Carr*, see para.10-26 fn.168, at 482 (Lord Denning MR); *Fontana NV v Mautner* [1980] 1 E.G.L.R. 68 at 72 (Balcombe J, noting that in *Alan v El Nasr* Lord Denning "was considering the question of detriment at the wrong point in time": see para.10-27 fn.183; but also dismissing *Alan v El Nasr* and other cases which followed Lord Denning's statement as cases of waiver, where no reliance is required, rather than estoppel); *Société Italo-Belge pour le Commerce et l'Industrie SA v Palm and Vegetable Oils (Malaysia) Sdn Bdh (The Post Chaser)*,

it is not the whole picture. The point of promissory estoppel is that the representee is given an indulgence—he is told by the other contracting party that he need not comply fully with his contractual obligations. It is natural, as Lord Denning said in the passage quoted above, to see that what the representee does in response to this is a benefit to him, rather than a detriment. He is enabled to take action that he would not have been able to do had the indulgence not been granted. Two points, however, must be made.

First, the question is what "act", or "alteration of position" is required. If the representee takes some collateral action which he would not have been able to take without the representor having given him the indulgence in relation to his strict contractual obligations—such as rearranging his business affairs, or failing to take some other step which would have been necessary in order to be able to perform the contract but is no longer necessary in light of the representation,[180] it can clearly be said to be an action which constitutes an "alteration of his position" in reliance on the representation. There are a few cases where it is difficult to see that there has been any collateral action—just the continued performance of the reduced contractual obligations. The context in which this has occurred, but has been said to be sufficient to constitute the representee's "acting on" the promise, is in the part payment of a debt, where courts have apparently only looked to see that the representee has continued to pay the part which was not remitted by the representation which is said to be the basis of an estoppel.[181] In such a case it is difficult to see that there is any "alteration of position", and most recently the Court of Appeal has doubted whether simple part-payment of a debt (and its acceptance by the creditor) necessarily makes it inequitable for the creditor later to go back on the agreement and insist on payment of the balance.[182]

Secondly, even on the basis that what the representee must show is that he took some collateral action which constituted an "alteration of his position", and even though he will thereby in fact have benefited, there is still a place for the language of "detriment". But the question is not whether the representee *has suffered detriment* in reliance on the representation, but whether it *would be detrimental if he*

---

see para.10-25 fn.166, at 26-27 (Robert Goff J).

[180] See the examples given at para.10-25 fn.166 and para.10-26 fn.167.

[181] In *Central London Property Trust Ltd v High Trees House Ltd*, see para.10-23 fn.152, it seems to be assumed that merely continuing to pay the reduced rent under the lease was "acting" in reliance on the representation to reduce the rent: *Collier v P & MJ Wright (Holdings) Ltd* [2007] EWCA Civ 1329; [2008] 1 W.L.R. 643 at [39], [47]; and see Arden LJ at [42] (following agreed part-payment, "for [the creditor] to resile will of itself be inequitable"; cf. however, Longmore LJ at [46]–[48]; and para.10-36).

[182] *MWB Business Exchange Centres Ltd v Rock Advertising Ltd* [2016] EWCA Civ 553; [2017] Q.B. 604 at [61] (Kitchin LJ, focusing on the question whether it is inequitable for the representor to resile rather than whether the part-payment constitutes an alteration of position by the representee); see also Arden LJ at [92] (not seeing an inconsistency with her earlier approach in *Collier v Wright*, see para.10-27 fn.181). For a different approach to facts similar to the *High Trees* case, see *Je Maintiendrai Pty Ltd v Quaglia* (1980) 26 S.A.S.R. 101, SC South Australia, at 115 (White J: tenant would have had other choices open if landlord had not agreed to reduce rent, such as finding an assignee, or even abandoning the premises altogether—thus identifying the reliance as forbearance rather than simply the act of paying the balance). Using the language of "detrimental reliance", King CJ found at 106-107 that the evidence of detriment was sparse, but did not disturb findings of trial judge that the build-up of the unpaid balance would make it detrimental to be faced with a lump-sum liability; Cox J could not find detrimental reliance and dissented. For discussion of whether promissory estoppel should be allowed to effect the discharge of a debt, see para.10-37.

were required now to perform the contract[183]:

"the only question of considering whether [the representee] has altered his position, whether you say it as a matter to his detriment or whether you say because it would be inequitable to hold him to the original bargain, must be at the point of time at which the original representor says, "I didn't mean it, I want to go back to what I said'."

When the question is formulated properly in this way, it is clear that it is inextricably linked to the core question which arises in relation to estoppel: whether, and why, it is "inequitable" for the representor to go back on his promise.

10-28   **The equity arising from the reliance on the representation**   The "equity"[184] in favour of the representee is raised when he acts on the representation, as he was intended or at least expected by the representor to do,[185] by altering his position in the belief that the representee will keep his word, even though it is not embodied in a contract. The measure of the equity—the extent to which it is "inequitable" or "unconscionable" for the representor to go back on his representation is linked directly to the representee's alteration of position.[186] This in turn takes us to the

---

[183]   *Fontana NV v Mautner*, see para.10-27 fn.179, at 72 (Balcombe J). See also *Azov Shipping Co Ltd v Baltic Shipping Co.* [1999] 2 Lloyd's Rep. 159 at 174 (Colman J: "the underlying policy in giving effect to the estoppel is to prevent the unfairness to the representee which would arise if the representor were permitted to resile from his represented position as to the existing legal relationship between them"). There are similar remarks in relation to the notion of "detriment" in proprietary estoppel in *Gillett v Holt* [2001] Ch. 210, CA, at 232 (Robert Walker LJ: "The issue of detriment must be judged at the moment when the person who has given the assurance seeks to go back on it"); Lord Neuberger of Abbotsbury, "The Stuffing of Minerva's Owl? Taxonomy and Taxidermy in Equity" [2009] C.L.J. 537, 544–545 ("contract looks forward. Estoppel, on the other hand, looks back. It involves assessing the parties' rights as at the date they fall to be satisfied", relying also on *Walton v Walton* unreported 14 April 1994, CA, at [21]–[22] (Hoffmann LJ)).

[184]   *Ajayi v RT Briscoe (Nigeria) Ltd*, see para.10-17 fn.115, at 1330, quoted at para.10-17, "*an equity will be raised* in favour of the other party. This equity is, however, subject to the qualifications (1) that the other party has altered his position" (emphasis added). For the similar language of an "equity" being established in proprietary estoppel, see *Crabb v Arun DC* [1976] Ch. 179, CA, at 193 (Scarman LJ), although in that case the equity is a positive right which has proprietary characteristics: see para.10-07 fn.40. For the argument that the equitable defence of promissory estoppel can burden third parties such as assignees, see para.10-43.

[185]   See para.10-23.

[186]   e.g. *James v Heim Gallery (London) Ltd*, see para.10-23 fn.153, at 282–283 (Oliver LJ: "the party claiming the estoppel must have altered his position in such a way as to render it unfair or inequitable that the strict rights of the party should now be enforced between them"); *BP Exploration v Hunt (No.2)* [1979] 1 W.L.R. 783 at 811 (Robert Goff J.: "reliance by the representee (whether by action or by omission to act) on the representation, which renders it inequitable, in all the circumstances, for the representor to enforce his strict rights"); *Société Italo-Belge pour le Commerce et l'Industrie SA v Palm and Vegetable Oils (Malaysia) Sdn Bdh (The Post Chaser)*, see para.10-25 fn.166, at 27 (Robert Goff J: even if reliance is shown it may still not be inequitable for the representor to insist on his strict rights: it depends on the facts and whether the representee is prejudiced); *Scandinavian Trading Tanker Co AB v Flota Petrolera Ecuatoriana (The Scaptrade)* [1983] Q.B. 529, CA, at 535 (Robert Goff LJ: "since equitable estoppel is founded upon a representation, it can only be unconscionable for the representor (here the owners) to enforce his strict legal right if the conduct of the representee (here the charterers) has been so influenced by the representation as to call for the intervention of equity"). Similarly in relation to proprietary estoppel, see *Gillett v Holt*, see para.10-27 fn.183, at 232 (Robert Walker LJ). cf. *Hughes v Metropolitan Railway Co* (1877) 2 App. Cas. 439, HL, see para.10-15 fn.88, at 448 ("the person who otherwise might have enforced those rights will not be allowed to enforce them where it would be inequitable having regard to the dealings which have thus taken place between the parties").

question of whether the representor is free to revoke his representation and insist again on the full performance of the contract.

(5)   Is Promissory Estoppel Temporary or Permanent? Revocation of the Representation by the Representor

The representation may by its language be only temporary   Once it has been   **10-29** found that the representee relied on the representation in such a way as to render it inequitable for the representor to act inconsistently with it,[187] the question arises as to whether the change in the contractual obligations which has been effected by virtue of the representation is only temporary or may be permanent: that is, whether the representor can revoke his representation. However, it should first be noted that by its language the representation may only be temporary—the representor may only have given the representee a time-limited relief against having to perform the contractual obligations. In such a case, the relief comes to a natural end at the end of the period set by the representation, and the strict terms of the contract again become enforceable—not because the representor revokes his representation but because the representation never released the contractual obligations beyond the limited period. No notice is necessary to resume the original contractual position.[188] This, indeed, was the effect of the representation in the *High Trees* decision,[189] where Denning J construed the landlord's representation as being to reduce the rent only during the period while the block of flats was not fully, or substantially fully let, and so the reduction did not extend to the last two quarters of 1945, the period in respect of which the claim was brought.[190] If, however, the representation was not in terms limited, or if, though it was limited, the representor wishes to go back on his representation before the limit has expired, the more general question arises as to whether he can revoke his representation.[191]

---

[187]   See para.10-28.

[188]   *Tool Metal Manufacturing Co Ltd v Tungsten Electric Co Ltd* [1955] 1 W.L.R. 761, HL, at 785. cf., however, the curious statement of Denning J in *High Trees*, see para.10-29 fn.189, at 136: "If the case had been one of estoppel, it might be said that in any event the estoppel would cease when the conditions to which the representation applied came to an end, or it also might be said that it would only come to an end on notice. In either case it is only a way of ascertaining what is the scope of the representation".

[189]   *Central London Property Trust Ltd v High Trees House Ltd* [1947] K.B. 130, see para.10-16.

[190]   *Central London Property Trust Ltd v High Trees House Ltd* [1947] K.B. 130 at 135. A separate question, not raised by the claim but fundamental to the understanding of the doctrine of estoppel as Denning J set it out in *High Trees*, is whether the representation *could have been* revoked earlier; and whether, given that the representation was not in fact revoked before it expired by its terms, the rent not paid during the period when the promise was in force had been lost for ever: see para.10-35. Where, however, it is clear from the language of the representation that a debt is being only deferred any defence to its enforcement by way of promissory estoppel can only be during the period defined by the representation, and no more: *Ledingham v Bermejo Estancia Co Ltd* [1947] 1 All E.R. 749 at 751 (interest waived "until such time as the company is in the position to pay the interest": payment was merely postponed).

[191]   *Virulite LLC v Virulite Distribution Ltd* [2014] EWHC 366 (QB); [2015] 1 All E.R. (Comm) 204 at [125] (Stuart-Smith J: "*High Trees* would be a clearer factual example of the extinguishing effect of a representation if the landlord had given notice at a time when the war conditions still prevailed and had been held not to be entitled to recover the full ground rent until they ceased to prevail at some point in the future. It seems to me that there is scope for confusion in the use of the terms 'suspensory' and 'extinguishing' in this context").

10-30   **The representor can revoke his representation: normally, promissory estoppel is only temporary**   The starting-point in the doctrine of promissory estoppel is that the representation only suspends the representee's contractual obligations in accordance with the terms of the representation, and the representor may in principle revoke his representation and again insist on performance of the contract.[192] It was reflected in the list of the elements of promissory estoppel given by Lord Hodson in *Ajayi v RT Briscoe (Nigeria) Ltd*[193]:

> "the promisor can resile from his promise on giving reasonable notice, which need not be a formal notice, giving the promisee a reasonable opportunity of resuming his position".

This approach to promissory estoppel reflects the difference between a contractually binding promise and a representation given force by estoppel: if consideration is given for the promise, it is fully binding in accordance with its terms, and irrevocable by the promisor. A contractual variation of an existing contract is therefore binding and effects a permanent change in the original contract.[194] However, a mere representation, even though relied on by the representee, does not have the same force as a contract, and so cannot in itself effect a modification of an existing contract with the same force as a contractual variation.[195]

10-31   **The notice by which the representor may revoke his representation**   Lord Hodson's statement[196] not only makes clear that the representor may revoke his representation, but also points towards other key matters relating to the form of

---

[192] *Ajayi v RT Briscoe (Nigeria) Ltd*, see para.10-30 fn.193; *Collier v P & MJ Wright (Holdings) Ltd* [2007] EWCA Civ 1329; [2008] 1 W.L.R. 643 at [37]. Lord Cairns' classic statement in *Hughes v Metropolitan Railway Co* (1877) 2 App. Cas. 439, HL, see para.10-15 fn.86, at 448 ("strict rights under the contract *will not be enforced*, or will be kept in suspense, or held in abeyance": emphasis added) is ambiguous, but is generally taken to give effect only to temporary concessions: F.M.B. Reynolds and G.H. Treitel, "Consideration for the Modification of Contracts" (1965) 7 Malaya L.Rev. 1, 16 ("Unless this doctrine is given very limited operation, it will expel the notion of consideration from the field of renegotiations altogether"); J.F. Wilson, "Recent Developments in Estoppel" (1951) 67 L.Q.R. 330, 349–350 and "A Reappraisal of Quasi-Estoppel" [1965] C.L.J. 93, 106. Denning J in *High Trees*, see para.10-29 fn.189, at 134 thought that a promise "must be honoured", and did not apparently leave open the possibility of its revocation (strongly criticised by Reynolds and Treitel, "Consideration for the Modification of Contracts" at 17; and see para.10-35); and in *D&C Builders Ltd v Rees* [1966] 2 Q.B. 617, CA, at 624 (see para.10-36) Lord Denning MR said that the *Hughes* principle "may be applied, not only so as to suspend strict legal rights, but also so as to preclude the enforcement of them". In *Charles Rickards Ltd v Oppenhaim* [1950] 1 K.B. 616, CA, see para.10-31, at 623 Denning LJ, applying *High Trees*, said the promisor could not go back on a promise not to insist on a time limit for delivery, although he then admitted that the promisor could give "reasonable notice" to make time of the essence. This apparent contradiction may, however, reflect the idea that the dispensation from the *particular* breach in time for delivery, once waived, could not be reversed although there was still a duty to deliver and the (continuing) dispensation from the time obligation could be revoked on reasonable notice.

[193] [1964] 1 W.L.R. 1326, PC, at 1330, quoted at para.10-17.

[194] See Ch.9, esp. para.9-02.

[195] This explains further why the first question in relation to an alleged modification of a contract is whether there has been a contractual variation, supported by consideration; only if there was no variation does the question of estoppel arise: see para.10-19. cf. however, P.S. Atiyah, "Consideration and Estoppel: The Thawing of the Ice" (1975) 38 M.L.R. 65, 66 ("Whether the indulgence should be completely irrevocable or not should depend on construction rather than on the artificial distinction (if it is to survive at all) between a binding contractual variation, and a promise enforceable by way of promissory estoppel").

[196] See para.10-30 fn.193.

notice which the representor can effect the revocation. It must be "reasonable" notice; need not be formal notice; and its purpose is to give the representee "a reasonable opportunity of resuming his position".

What will constitute "reasonable" notice will depend on the facts. In *Hughes v Metropolitan Railway Co*,[197] where the tenant's obligation to undertake repairs within six months had been suspended during negotiations for a possible surrender of the lease, the House of Lords measured the reasonable time for the repairs to be done as six months from the breakdown of the negotiations. In *Charles Rickards Ltd v Oppenhaim*,[198] where a buyer of a custom-made car waived his right to terminate a contract by reason of the supplier's failure to complete and deliver the car in accordance with the condition as to time set by the contract, he was still entitled later to give reasonable notice to make time again of the essence: what was reasonable was to be measured at the date on which the notice was given, and could take into account the fact that the buyer had been pressing the supplier and the supplier had been promising that the car would be soon completed.[199] Moreover, there may be circumstances in which no period of notice is required to revoke the representation, and the representor can insist on compliance with the original contractual terms immediately.[200]

We have seen that the representation which dispensed the representee from strict compliance with the contract might be implied, rather than express[201]; it is therefore not surprising to find that the notice by which the dispensation is withdrawn need not only not be "formal notice"[202] —it need not take any particular form, or specify the withdrawal of the dispensation in any particular way[203] —but may even be implied: the question is simply whether the fact of the withdrawal is communicated to the representee sufficiently clearly.[204]

---

197 See para.10-30 fn.193, at 447, 452, 454. Similarly, in *Birmingham and District Land Co v London and North Western Railway Co* (1888) 40 Ch. D. 268, CA, see para.10-15 fn.91, the developer's right to continue to build under a fixed-term building agreement was extended by the period during which the owner had told him to suspend work.

198 See para.10-30 fn.193, discussed in terms of waiver (see para.10-11), although at 623 Denning LJ treated this as indistinguishable from promissory estoppel and applied the decision in *High Trees*, see para.10-29 fn.189.

199 See para.10-30 fn.193, at 624-625 (Denning LJ, approving the trial judge's decision that four weeks' notice was reasonable, given that the supplier's manager had the said the previous day that it would be ready in two weeks).

200 i.e. a notice must be given to inform the representee that the indulgence is at an end, but no *period of notice* is required: *Tool Metal Manufacturing Co Ltd v Tungsten Electric Co Ltd*, see para.10-29 fn.188, at 799 (Lord Cohen: concession which could be terminated by simply intimating to the other party that the concession was withdrawn); *Re Selectmove Ltd* [1995] 1 W.L.R. 474, CA, at 481 (not inequitable to demand payment of arrears where representee failed to honour promise to make current payment); *Société Italo-Belge pour le Commerce et l'Industrie SA v Palm and Vegetable Oils (Malaysia) Sdn Bdh (The Post Chaser)* [1982] 1 All E.R. 19 at 27 (sellers relied on buyers' implied representation that they would accept non-conforming shipping documents, but were not prejudiced during very short period of two days before buyers sought to enforce legal right to reject documents).

201 See para.10-21.

202 Lord Hodson in *Ajayi v RT Briscoe (Nigeria) Ltd*, see para.10-30 fn.193.

203 *Tool Metal Manufacturing Co Ltd v Tungsten Electric Co Ltd*, see para.10-29 fn.188, at 785 (Lord Tucker: "No authority has been cited which binds your Lordships to hold that in all such cases the notice must take any particular form or specify a date for the termination of the suspensory period. This is not surprising having regard to the infinite variety of circumstances which may give rise to this principle which was stated in broad terms and must now be regarded as of general application").

204 *Tool Metal Manufacturing Co Ltd v Tungsten Electric Co Ltd*, see para.10-29 fn.188, at 785 (counterclaim in action, asserting rights which had earlier been suspended by estoppel, was a clear

The purpose of the notice, according to Lord Hodson, is to give the representee "a reasonable opportunity of resuming his position".[205] There is a natural logic here: the reason that the representation is binding is that the representee, as intended or expected by the representor,[206] has relied on the representation by some act or forbearance which he would not otherwise have done; he has "altered his position".[207] Given that the representation is not irrevocably binding simply by virtue of the reliance, but is in principle revocable,[208] the revocation should be designed to allow the representee to undo that which he did by way of reliance on the representation. It is his reliance on the representation that makes it inequitable for the representor to go back on his promise; but if the representee is given a reasonable opportunity to undo that reliance—to "resume his position" to that which he had before he "altered his position"—it will then cease to be inequitable for the representor to insist on the performance of the contract strictly according to its terms.

10-32   **The representation may become irrevocable: exceptionally, promissory estoppel may be permanent**   The requirement that the representor give the representee a "reasonable opportunity of resuming his position"[209] as the condition of revocation of the representation also points to the circumstances in which the representation may be irrevocable. As Lord Hodson put it[210]: "the promise only becomes final and irrevocable if the promisee cannot resume his position." In other words, the circumstance in which the estoppel becomes permanent, and the modification of the contract becomes irrevocably binding, is where it is no longer reasonable to expect the representee to reverse whatever he did (or forbore to do) by way of reliance on the representation: it becomes permanently inequitable to insist on performance of the contract strictly according to its terms. However, there appear to be very few cases in which this has in fact happened.[211] One situation in which it is said that the effect of promissory estoppel can be to vary permanently the contractual obligation is where the representation is as to the remission of the whole or part of a debt. This, however, raises other difficulties and will be discussed separately below.[212]

---

intimation of reversal by representor of previous attitude and intention to enforce compliance).

[205] Lord Hodson in *Ajayi v RT Briscoe (Nigeria) Ltd*, see para.10-30 fn.193.

[206] See para.10-23.

[207] See para.10-27.

[208] See para.10-30.

[209] See para.10-31.

[210] *Ajayi v RT Briscoe (Nigeria) Ltd* [1964] 1 W.L.R. 1326, PC, at 1330, quoted at para.10-17.

[211] *Nippon Yusen Kaisha v Pacifica Navigacion SA (The Ion)* [1980] 2 Lloyd's Rep. 245 at 251 (Mocatta J: "a promissory estoppel to the effect that a party will not take a time bar point that has already accrued in his favour at the time of his representation is not susceptible to lifting by notice enabling the promisor to raise afresh at a much later date the time bar in his favour"); *Je Maintiendrai Pty Ltd v Quaglia* (1980) 26 S.A.S.R. 101 (SC South Australia by majority holding arrears of debt irrevocably discharged by promissory estoppel on basis of debtor's reliance). cf. J.F. Wilson, "A Reappraisal of Quasi-Estoppel" [1965] C.L.J. 93, 106 ("it is a curious fact that the courts have never yet had to consider the application of this principle to a case involving a promise permanently to waive contractual rights. All the major decisions from the *Hughes* case [see para.10-29 fn.192] down to the recent Privy Council case [*Ajayi v RT Briscoe (Nigeria) Ltd*, see para.10-32 fn.210] have involved temporary concessions").

[212] See paras 10-36 to 10-37.

(6) Pleading the Estoppel Defence

Duty to plead the estoppel defence and the facts relied on to establish it The
representee will typically raise the estoppel as a defence[213]: if sued by the representor under the terms of the contract, he argues that the representor is estopped, in
whole or in part, from bringing the claim because he is thereby acting inconsistently with his representation.[214] He therefore has the burden of establishing the
defence, and in order to discharge it he must plead the defence, together with all
the facts which are necessary to establish the various elements of the defence as set
out in the above paragraphs within this section: the representation, the way in which
he acted on the representation by changing his position, and why it is now
inequitable for the representor to seek to resile from his representation.[215] In a
number of cases parties who sought to rely on promissory estoppel to defend a claim
under the contract have failed (either at trial or on appeal) because they did not
plead the necessary elements at trial.[216] Because the scope of operation of the
promissory estoppel defence depends on findings of fact it may be inappropriate to
strike out a defence which will depend on the facts as the trial judge finds them.[217]

10-33

IV. The Limits of the Role of Promissory Estoppel in English Law

(1) Discharge of a Debt

Discharge of a debt without full payment: the rule in Pinnel's Case One question which arises in relation to the scope of operation of the doctrine of promissory estoppel is whether it can be used to effect the discharge of a debt without the
debt being paid in full. A creditor's representation to the debtor that he will *defer*
payment of a debt would not be an unusual example of the operation of promissory estoppel if the debtor acts on the representation by altering his position, since
the estoppel would provide a defence for the debtor against the creditor if he
brought a claim inconsistently with his representation without giving whatever
notice is necessary in the circumstances to enable the debtor to resume his position[218]; and even if the debtor may have to pay the debt once the effect of the estop-

10-34

---

[213] CPR Pt 15.

[214] i.e. the estoppel acts as a "shield" to the representor's claim: see further para.10-38.

[215] Under CPR r.16.5(2)(b) the defendant who denies an allegation and intends to put forward a different version of events from that given by the claimant, must state his own version in his defence.

[216] *Ajayi v RT Briscoe (Nigeria) Ltd* [1964] 1 W.L.R. 1326, PC, at 1330–1331 (defendant failed to plead
defence expressly so argument at trial did not address it and relevant facts not investigated);
Finagrain SA Geneva v P Kruse Hamburg [1976] 2 Lloyd's Rep. 508, CA, at 535, 542 (representee
had failed to secure necessary findings of fact of reliance); *Bremer Handelsgesellschaft mbH v
Vanden Avenne-Izegem PVBA* [1977] 2 Lloyd's Rep. 327, CA, at 340 (no evidence and findings of
fact at trial to establish reliance; reversed [1978] 2 Lloyd's Rep. 109, HL); *Goldsworthy v Brickell*
[1987] Ch. 378, CA, at 411 (no properly pleaded defence of promissory estoppel, and in consequence
the evidence at trial did not establish clear and unequivocal representation, or reliance); *Paragon
Mortgages Ltd v McEwan-Peters* [2011] EWHC 2491 (Comm) at [33]–[34] (witness evidence of
the alleged representation was unsatisfactory and lacking in any degree of particularity); cf. *Tool
Metal Manufacturing Co Ltd v Tungsten Electric Co Ltd* [1955] 1 W.L.R. 761, HL, at 781–784 (Lord
Tucker criticising lower courts for deciding earlier action on basis of inadequate pleadings).

[217] *Mears Ltd v Shoreline Housing Partnership Ltd* [2013] EWCA Civ 639; [2013] C.P. Rep. 39 at [24]
(estoppel by convention and estoppel by representation).

[218] The bringing of an action might itself constitute the notice that the period of suspension is over: *Tool
Metal Manufacturing Co Ltd v Tungsten Electric Co Ltd*, see para.10-33 fn.216.

pel is ended, the debtor would still have a defence in relation to the delay in payment in accordance with the strict terms of the contract. However, where the representation is not merely that the debt is suspended but that it is discharged, the operation of promissory estoppel—if it applies in such a case—will be an example of the permanent modification of the contract. We have already seen that permanent modification is possible in a case where it is no longer reasonable to expect the representee to reverse whatever he did (or forbore to do) by way of reliance on the representation.[219]

If promissory estoppel can achieve such a result, it appears that it will run contrary to the rule in *Pinnel's Case*,[220] which provides that "payment of a lesser sum on the day in satisfaction of a greater, cannot be any satisfaction for the whole", a rule which was accepted by the House of Lords in 1884 in *Foakes v Beer*.[221] However, the basis of the decision of the House of Lords was the doctrine of consideration. A simple discharge of a debt cannot be effected without consideration or a deed.[222] And even where the debtor in fact pays part of the debt in return for the creditor's promise not to enforce the balance, that payment of part cannot in itself be consideration for the creditor's promise to give up the balance because the creditor receives no benefit (he is already entitled to the part which the debtor pays) and the debtor undertakes no detriment (he is only discharging, and only in part, what he already owes),[223] although the operation of the doctrine of consideration in this context has recently been the subject of debate, in particular in cases where the creditor might be said on the facts to have obtained a "practical benefit" by reason of receiving at least payment of part of the debt.[224] The argument that promissory estoppel can irrevocably effect the discharge of a debt, or even of the balance of a debt where part is paid by the debtor, therefore focuses our attention on the relationship between consideration and estoppel—whether promissory estoppel can give binding force to the variation of a contract in the absence of consideration.

10-35   **The decision in High Trees in relation to part-payment of a debt**   The *High Trees* case,[225] which was the foundation of the modern doctrine of promissory estoppel in English law,[226] involved a question of the enforceability of a promise not to enforce a money obligation—the rent due under the terms of a lease. The claim made by the landlord's receiver was only for the full rent due under the lease after the promise had already run its course, but Denning J made clear that the arrears of rent which had not been collected during the course of the war, when the promise not to claim the full rent was operative, would not have succeeded. One way of looking at this is that the rent due under the lease accrued each quarter, and the landlord accepted part payment in satisfaction of the whole of that quarter's rent.[227]

---

[219] See para.10-32.
[220] (1602) 5 Co. Rep. 117a, 77 E.R. 237; see para.9-18.
[221] (1884) 9 App. Cas. 605, HL; see para.9-19.
[222] See para.9-17.
[223] See paras 9-18 to 9-19; for the requirement of benefit and/or detriment, see para.8-23. On the rule in *Pinnel's Case*, and its relationship to promissory estoppel, see further para.10-37.
[224] See paras 9-22, 9-23.
[225] *Central London Property Trust Ltd v High Trees House Ltd* [1947] K.B. 130. The facts are set out at para.10-16.
[226] See para.10-16.
[227] A different analysis would be that the effect of the promise was to reduce the level of rent due dur-

This is how Denning J appears to have viewed the case, and he recognised that it had the effect of circumventing the rule in *Pinnel's Case*[228]:

> "The logical consequence, no doubt is that a promise to accept a smaller sum in discharge of a larger sum, if acted upon, is binding notwithstanding the absence of consideration: and if the fusion of law and equity leads to this result, so much the better. That aspect was not considered in *Foakes v Beer*.[229] At this time of day however, when law and equity have been joined together for over seventy years, principles must be reconsidered in the light of their combined effect. It is to be noticed that in the Sixth Interim Report of the Law Revision Committee,[230] pars. 35, 40, it is recommended that such a promise as that to which I have referred, should be enforceable in law even though no consideration for it has been given by the promisee. It seems to me that, to the extent I have mentioned that result has now been achieved by the decisions of the courts."

However, this was not necessary for the decision in the case, and it went beyond the scope of the authorities on which Denning J relied to justify his development of the doctrine of promissory estoppel. But in making his point, and faced with the decision of the House of Lords in *Foakes v Beer*, he used the arguments that estoppel was not considered in that case, and that "law and equity have been joined", to use an equitable doctrine (estoppel) to circumvent a common law doctrine (consideration). Also apparently in his favour was the fact that he rested his development of promissory estoppel on, inter alia, the decision of the House of Lords in *Hughes v Metropolitan Railway Co*,[231] which was decided seven years before *Foakes v Beer*. However, Denning J's use of these arguments was only superficially convincing. *Hughes v Metropolitan Railway* was, as we have seen,[232] a limited decision where the House of Lords did not appear to think that they were creating, or applying, a broad doctrine of estoppel of the kind for which *High Trees* has now become the founding authority. It did not involve the permanent variation of a contract, only the suspension of a time-limit for works to be done; nor did it involve a debt or any other form of money obligation. There was therefore no conflict with the rule in *Pinnel's Case*; but if the members of the House of Lords in *Hughes'* case thought that they were creating, or applying, a doctrine of equity which could challenge the rule in *Pinnel's Case* it is curious that they did not call upon it when, seven years later, they were uncomfortable in applying *Pinnel's Case* in *Foakes v Beer* and, indeed, they appeared to be looking for reasons not to apply

---

ing the period when the promise was operative, and therefore only the lower rent accrued, and was paid. This would involve a less direct conflict with the rule in *Pinnel's Case*, and would limit the operation of the principle in *High Trees* to cases where the money obligation which is irrevocably varied is a continuing obligation under which particular obligations will accrue from time to time after the promise to accept less than the full amount has already been made: it would not necessarily apply to a simple promise to give up all or part of an already-accrued debt: cf. F.M.B. Reynolds and G.H. Treitel, "Consideration for the Modification of Contracts" (1965) 7 Malaya L.Rev. 1, 17 (arguing that if High Trees is authority for the "dubious" proposition that the landlord could not claim the arrears, it "should be confined to ... waiver of debts accruing periodically by instalments. It need not be extended to simple promises not to enforce debts or parts of debts").

[228] See para.10-35 fn.225, at 135.
[229] See para.10-34 fn.221.
[230] [Law Revision Committee, Sixth Interim Report, *Statute of Frauds and the Doctrine of Consideration* Cmd.5449 (1937); see para.10-37.]
[231] (1877) 2 App. Cas. 439, HL, relied on by Denning J in *High Trees*, see para.10-35 fn.225, at 134.
[232] See para.10-15.

it.[233] In *Foakes v Beer* the House of Lords did not apply an equitable doctrine of estoppel because it did not exist—or, rather, at most it existed at that stage only in an embryonic form, not yet fully developed but in any event only dealing with the temporary suspension of contractual rights. It should be remembered that in *Jorden v Money*[234] the House of Lords had refused to allow estoppel to extend to a representation of intention or a promise—on the facts of the case, a promise not to enforce a debt—and that the authority of *Jorden v Money* was clearly still accepted by the House of Lords in other decisions around the time of *Foakes v Beer*.[235] The step which Denning J sought to take in *High Trees*[236] was not only to develop promissory estoppel into a principled doctrine, but also to allow it to give effect permanently to promises which were not supported by consideration but have been acted upon; and even to extend this to promises to discharge debts. How successful Denning J was in this last point—allowing promissory estoppel to effect the discharge of a debt, and therefore to circumvent the rule in *Pinnel's Case*—depends on how far it has been accepted since the decision in *High Trees*.

10-36 **Cases after High Trees which indicate that promissory estoppel may be able to discharge a debt**   There are some authorities which have accepted that the doctrine of promissory estoppel developed in *High Trees* can go beyond the narrow decision in the *High Trees* case itself, although it is still not clear in what circumstances a simple representation not to enforce an accrued debt, if relied on by the debtor, can be given irrevocable force in discharging the debt and thereby circumvent the rule in *Pinnel's Case*.

We have seen that in *High Trees* the question of whether the landlord's right to the arrears of rent due under the terms of the lease had been irrevocably extinguished was not part of the decision, since no claim was made for the arrears.[237] However, that step was taken by way of ratio in an Australian case in 1980[238] and

---

[233] In particular, Lord Blackburn was on the verge of dissenting in *Foakes v Beer*; and Lord Selborne was also critical of the rule in *Pinnel's Case*: see para.9-20. Both sat in the House of Lords in *Hughes v Metropolitan Railway Co*, as well as in *Maddison v Alderson* (1883) 8 App. Cas. 467, HL, in which Lord Selborne at 473 reaffirmed the requirement from *Jorden v Money* that the representation for the purposes of estoppel be one of fact: see para.10-15 fn.87; J.F. Wilson, "Recent Developments in Estoppel" (1951) 67 L.Q.R. 330, 349–350.

[234] (1854) 5 H.L.C. 185, 10 E.R. 868; see para.10-14.

[235] See para.10-15 fn.87 and para.10-35 fn.233.

[236] See also para.10-16.

[237] See para.10-16.

[238] *Je Maintiendrai Pty Ltd v Quaglia* (1980) 26 S.A.S.R. 101, SC South Australia, where a landlord agreed the tenant's request to reduce the monthly rent for an indefinite period, but after 18 months claimed the arrears. In this case there was no decision about whether the promise was irrevocable for the future, i.e. the point on which the decision in *High Trees* rested (see King CJ at 106), but the focus was on whether the promise to reduce the rent was binding during the period when the landlord accepted the reduced rent in place of the full rent reserved by the lease. The decision (by a majority) was in favour of the tenant, but turned on whether there was sufficient reliance by the tenant to give the tenant a defence by way of promissory estoppel to the landlord's claim for the arrears: see para.10-27 fn.182. King CJ noted at the beginning of his judgment that the application of estoppel would have the effect of circumventing the decision in *Foakes v Beer*, see para.10-34 fn.221: "The appellant's promise to reduce the rent has no contractual force because it was made without consideration. The acceptance of a sum which is less than that legally due is not binding and does not extinguish liability for the balance unless there is fresh consideration: *Foakes v Beer*. The evidence does not disclose fresh consideration. The respondents' case therefore rests upon an estoppel to which the facts are alleged to give rise".

in a case at first instance in England in 1986.[239] These are all cases involving a failure to collect periodic payments during a period when a continuing obligation to pay was reduced.[240] There is no clear authority in favour of the use of estoppel to discharge all or part of a debt which has already accrued when the creditor makes his promise the creditor. In *D&C Builders Ltd v Rees*[241] the Court of Appeal held that a creditor's acceptance of the debtors' cheque for less than the full price due for work already done, and materials already supplied, under a building contract did not bar it from claiming the balance of the debt.[242] However, the reasoning was not unanimous. Winn LJ focused on the fact that there was no consideration for the agreement to accept less than the full sum due,[243] and made no mention of how estoppel might be relevant. Danckwerts LJ took principally the same line as Winn LJ, applying *Pinnel's Case* and *Foakes v Beer* in holding that there was no consideration for the promise,[244] although he did also discuss the fact that was no true accord here because the debtors had "behaved badly. They knew of the [creditors'] financial difficulties and used their awkward situation to intimidate them".[245] He also said that the debtors' position was not altered to their detriment by reason of the receipt given by the creditors, and so there was no ground "for treating the payment as a satisfaction on equitable principles".[246] Lord Denning, however, ac-

---

[239] *JT Sydenham & Co Ltd v Enichem Elastomers Ltd* [1989] 1 E.G.L.R. 257, noted [1990] C.L.J. 13 (J. Cartwright) (error in rent review led to landlord accepting for a year a lower rent than was properly due; landlord estopped, on the authority of *High Trees*, from claiming arrears of underpayment after error discovered, although there was no detailed discussion nor any mention of the potential conflict with the rule in *Pinnel's Case*). cf. *Dorkins v Wright* [1983] C.L.Y. 1364, Southport County Court (landlord agreed to reduce rent: on authority of *High Trees*, "The reduced rent lasted for 12 weeks; thereafter, the full rent under the lease again became enforceable": not clear whether the claim was for the arrears, or only for the full rent after the period of suspension). In *Ledingham v Bermejo Estancia Co Ltd* [1947] 1 All E.R. 749 there was an agreement not to claim interest which had already accrued due on a debt, as well as not to claim interest for the future; but Atkinson J decided that, on construction, the promise was only to postpone payment of the interest until the debtor's financial position improved, and not to cancel it. It is sometimes said that the decision of the House of Lords in *Tool Metal Manufacturing Co Ltd v Tungsten Electric Co Ltd* [1955] 1 W.L.R. 761, HL is evidence that estoppel can discharge the unclaimed arrears of an accruing debt (see, e.g. *Collier v P & MJ Wright (Holdings) Ltd* [2007] EWCA Civ 1329; [2008] 1 W.L.R. 643 at [37] (Arden LJ)) but the only issue before HL was whether the delivery of the counterclaim constituted sufficient notice to terminate the suspension of the compensation payments, and no point could be taken about the decision in an earlier action which had held that the compensation payments could not be claimed during the period of waiver, although the correctness of the decision in the earlier action was not affirmed or was even doubted: see esp. at 783–784 (Lord Tucker).

[240] cf. para.10-35 fn.227.

[241] [1966] 2 Q.B. 617, CA.

[242] There was no dispute as to the work done, nor as to the price payable, and therefore the agreement to accept less than the full price was not supported by consideration on the basis of it being a compromise of a disputed claim: see para.8-30.

[243] There cannot be an "accord and satisfaction" for the discharge of the balance of a debt without either consideration provided by the debtor, or a deed: and payment of a cheque by the debtor is no different from cash: see para.10-36 fn.241 at 632–633; see also paras 8-35, fn.254; 9-17, fn.119; 9-18, fn.123; 9-21, fn.141.

[244] See para.10-36 fn.241, at 626.

[245] It is not clear whether Danckwerts LJ would have used this argument in relation to the enforceability of the agreement if there had been consideration—i.e. allowing the debtors to rely on a defence of duress in having agreed to remit the balance of the debt, although at the time of this case "economic duress" had not yet been developed (cf. para.9-15 fn.87)—or whether it is linked to the following paragraph discussing the possibility of "satisfaction on equitable principles": para.10-36 fn.246.

[246] See para.10-36 fn.241, at 627. Danckwerts LJ also began his judgment by agreeing generally with

cepted that there was no consideration for the agreement to remit the balance of the debt,[247] but then proceeded to discuss at length the potential application of promissory estoppel in such a case, and rested his decision on the fact that the intimidation by the debtors prevented their reliance on estoppel. In a passage which strongly echoed his own judgment in the *High Trees* case, Lord Denning made clear that promissory estoppel can have the effect in equity of barring the creditor from claiming the balance of the debt, and that this has the effect of circumventing the *Pinnel's Case* rule[248]:

> "This doctrine of the common law has come under heavy fire. It was ridiculed by Sir George Jessel in *Couldery v Bartram*.[249] It was said to be mistaken by Lord Blackburn in *Foakes v Beer*.[250] It was condemned by the Law Revision Committee (1945 Cmd. 5449), paras 20 and 21.[251] But a remedy has been found. The harshness of the common law has been relieved. Equity has stretched out a merciful hand to help the debtor. The courts have invoked the broad principle stated by Lord Cairns in *Hughes v Metropolitan Railway Co.*[252]
>
> > 'It is the first principle upon which all courts of equity proceed, that if parties, who have entered into definite and distinct terms involving certain legal results, afterwards by their own act or with their own consent enter upon a course of negotiation which has the effect of leading one of the parties to suppose that *the strict rights arising under the contract will not be enforced*, or will be kept in suspense, or held in abeyance, the person who otherwise might have enforced those rights *will not be allowed to enforce them when it would be inequitable having regard to the dealings which have taken place between the parties.*'
>
> It is worth noticing that the principle may be applied, not only so as to suspend strict legal rights, but also so as to preclude the enforcement of them.
>
> This principle has been applied to cases where a creditor agrees to accept a lesser sum in discharge of a greater. So much so that we can now say that, when a creditor and a debtor enter upon a course of negotiation, which leads the debtor to suppose that, on payment of the lesser sum, the creditor will not enforce payment of the balance, and on the faith thereof the debtor pays the lesser sum and the creditor accepts it as satisfaction: then the creditor will not be allowed to enforce payment of the balance when it would be inequitable to do so. This was well illustrated during the last war. Tenants went away to escape the bombs and left their houses unoccupied. The landlords accepted a reduced rent for the time they were empty. It was held that the landlords could not afterwards turn round and sue for the balance, see *Central London Property Trust Ltd v High Trees House Ltd*.[253] This caused at the time some eyebrows to be raised in high places. But they have been lowered since. The solution was so obviously just that no one could well gainsay it."

In this statement Lord Denning simply assumed that what he had said in *High Trees* had been accepted. He asserted that the "principle has been applied to cases

---

Lord Denning.

[247] See para.10-36 fn.241, at 623–624, also holding that the payment by cheque by the debtor is not consideration where the payment of the same sum in cash would not be.

[248] See para.10-36 fn.241, at 624–625; cf. the quotation from *High Trees*, see para.10-35.

[249] (1881) 19 Ch. D. 394, CA, at 399 [see para.9-21 fn.141].

[250] [See para.10-34 fn.221 at 622; see para.9-20.]

[251] [Law Revision Committee, Sixth Interim Report, *Statute of Frauds and the Doctrine of Consideration* Cmd.5449 (1937). The date (1945) given by Lord Denning is erroneous.]

[252] [See para.10-35 fn.231, at 448, see para.10-15.]

[253] [See para.10-35 fn.225. These were not the facts of *High Trees*, where the reduction in rent was granted not to the occupation tenants, but to the mesne tenant by the head landlord: see para.10-16.]

where a creditor agrees to accept a lesser sum in discharge of a greater", but cited no authority apart from the *High Trees* case itself and there was in fact no line of cases in which the doctrine of promissory estoppel had been used to effect the discharge of a debt or part of a debt. In the *D&C Builders* case Lord Denning agreed in the result with Danckwerts LJ[254] and Winn LJ[255] because, although he would otherwise have said that the agreement to accept part-payment of the debt had the effect under the equitable doctrine of promissory estoppel of discharging the balance of the debt, on the facts the debtors could not rely on the estoppel as a defence because of their misconduct[256]:

> "In applying this principle, however, we must note the qualification: The creditor is only barred from his legal rights when it would be *inequitable* for him to insist upon them. Where there has been a true *accord*, under which the creditor voluntarily agrees to accept a lesser sum in satisfaction, and the debtor acts upon that accord by paying the lesser sum and the creditor accepts it, then it is inequitable for the creditor afterwards to insist on the balance. But he is not bound unless there has been truly an accord between them."

More recently, the Court of Appeal has given some impetus to the argument that the effect of the decision in *High Trees* can be to circumvent the rule in *Pinnel's Case*. In *Collier v P & MJ Wright (Holdings) Ltd*[257] an action was brought by a creditor against a joint debtor who claimed in his defence that the creditor had agreed to release him from the balance of the debt in return for his payment of his proportionate share.[258] The question before the court was only whether the defences raised triable issues and so whether the action should proceed to trial; and the Court of Appeal decided that there was no arguable defence based on the doctrine of consideration, given that the rule in *Pinnel's Case* had the authority of the House of Lords in *Foakes v Beer*,[259] but there was an arguable defence of promissory estoppel. However, the approach taken by Arden LJ was more positive than that taken by Longmore LJ.[260] Arden LJ noted that the effect of promissory estoppel is usually only suspensory, but said that "if the effect of resiling is sufficiently inequitable, a debtor may be able to show that the right to recover the debt is not merely postponed but extinguished".[261] The question at trial would be what made it "inequitable" for the creditor to claim the balance of the debt; the mere fact that time had elapsed would not be sufficient, but, on the authority of Lord Denning's judgment in *D&C Builders Ltd v Rees*,[262] it can be sufficient to show a "true accord" on which the debtor has acted by paying the balance of the debt[263]:

---

[254] See para.10-36 fnn.244 to 246.

[255] See para.10-36 fn.243.

[256] See para.10-36 fn.241 at 625.

[257] [2007] EWCA Civ 1329; [2008] 1 W.L.R. 643.

[258] The debt (capital and accruing interest) was owed jointly by three partners; the defendant alleged that the creditor had agreed to sever the debt so that one third would be discharged by the defendant severally; the creditor would look to the other two partners for the two-thirds balance. However, the other two partners became insolvent and the creditor sought the full original debt against the defendant.

[259] See para.10-36 fn.257, at [3], [6], [23], [28], [44]; see paras 9-20 fn.138; 9-21 fn.149; 9-22 fn.169.

[260] Mummery LJ at [50] simply said that there was a real prospect of success on the promissory estoppel issue.

[261] See para.10-36 fn.257, at [37], relying on *High Trees* and on *Tool Metal Manufacturing Co Ltd v Tungsten Electric Co Ltd* [1955] 1 W.L.R. 761, HL; cf. however, para.10-36 fn.239.

[262] See para.10-36 fn.248.

[263] See para.10-36 fn.257, at [42].

"The facts of this case demonstrate that, if (1) a debtor offers to pay part only of the amount he owes; (2) the creditor voluntarily accepts that offer, and (3) in reliance on the creditor's acceptance the debtor pays that part of the amount he owes in full, the creditor will, by virtue of the doctrine of promissory estoppel, be bound to accept that sum in full and final satisfaction of the whole debt. For him to resile will of itself be inequitable. In addition, in these circumstances, the promissory estoppel has the effect of extinguishing the creditor's right to the balance of the debt. This part of our law originated in the brilliant obiter dictum of Denning J in the *High Trees* case. To a significant degree it achieves in practical terms the recommendation of the Law Revision Committee chaired by Lord Wright MR in 1937."

This is a far-reaching statement, which in substance adopts the approach proposed by Lord Denning, and appears to require only the payment of the part of the debt by the debtor in order to render binding under the doctrine of estoppel the creditor's promise to release the balance. There is no collateral action in reliance on the promise[264]; just the performance by the debtor of the contractual obligations which he already owes. Longmore LJ appears to have felt uneasy about this: in his judgment he looked for whether the debtor "has relied on [the promise] in any meaningful way"[265] although he went on to accept that "as Arden LJ points out, it seems that on the authority of *D. & C. Builders Ltd v Rees* it can be a sufficient reliance for the purpose of promissory estoppel if a lesser payment is made as agreed"[266]; and he was more cautious about whether the approach of Lord Denning had fully succeeded.[267]

Most recently in *MWB Business Exchange Centres Ltd v Rock Advertising Ltd*[268] the Court of Appeal has accepted that the doctrine of promissory estoppel might, in an appropriate case, have the effect of extinguishing the balance of a debt, but doubted whether simple part-payment (and its acceptance by the creditor) necessarily makes it inequitable for the creditor later to go back on the agreement and insist on payment of the balance. Kitchin LJ said[269]:

---

[264] cf. para.10-27.

[265] See para.10-36 fn.257, at [46].

[266] See para.10-36 fn.257, at [47], although he emphasised the need for an "accord", as well as [at [45]] a clear agreement and doubted whether there was a sufficiently clear accord in this case.

[267] See para.10-36 fn.257, at [48] ("If, as Arden LJ puts it, the 'brilliant obiter dictum' of Denning J in the *High Trees* case did indeed substantially achieve in practical terms the recommendation of the Law Revision Committee chaired by Lord Wright MR in 1937, it is perhaps all the more important that agreements which are said to forgo a creditor's rights on a permanent basis should not be too benevolently construed"). It should be noted, however, that until the last paragraphs of her judgment, Arden LJ set out an orthodox account of the requirement of reliance on a representation in order to give rise to estoppel: the debt is not extinguished unless the effect of the creditor's resiling from his promise is shown to be inequitable (at [37]), and the mere fact that time has elapsed is not enough (at [39]). But the crucial point for Arden LJ was that in *D&C Builders Ltd v Rees* [1966] 2 Q.B. 617, CA, Lord Denning had said that in the case of a debt a true accord which is acted on by the debtor in paying the balance, gave rise to the estoppel (at [39]), so that "for [the creditor] to resile will of itself be inequitable" (at [42]). Longmore LJ's more cautious and orthodox approach at [46] appears to be preferable, even if at [47] he was also prepared to accept the authority of in *D&C Builders Ltd v Rees*. In short, the only authority for this radical view is really that of Lord Denning.

[268] [2016] EWCA Civ 553; [2017] Q.B. 604. The decision of Supreme Court in this case ([2018] UKSC 24; [2018] 2 W.L.R. 1603) did not touch on the issue of promissory estoppel.

[269] At [61]. McCombe LJ at [67] agreed generally with the decision but made no comment on the discussion of promissory estoppel. Arden LJ at [92] agreed with Kitchin LJ's statement in relation to promissory estoppel, and said that she did not see any inconsistency with her earlier approach set out in paragraph 42 of her judgment in *Collier v Wright*, quoted at para.10-36 fn.263).

"Drawing the threads to together, it seems to me that all of these cases[270] are best understood as illustrations of the broad principle that if one party to a contract makes a promise to the other that his legal rights under the contract will not be enforced or will be suspended and the other party in some way relies on that promise, whether by altering his position or in any other way, then the party who might otherwise have enforced those rights will not be permitted to do so where it would be inequitable having regard to all of the circumstances. It may be the case that it would be inequitable to allow the promisor to go back upon his promise without giving reasonable notice, as in the *Tool Metal Manufacturing Co Ltd* case[271]; or it may be that it would be inequitable to allow the promisor to go back on his promise at all with the result that the right is extinguished. All will depend upon the circumstances. It follows that I do not for my part think that it can be said, consistently with the authorities, including, in particular, the decisions of the House of Lords in *Foakes v Beer*[272] and this court in *Re Selectmove Ltd*,[273] that in every case where a creditor agrees to accept payment of a debt by instalments, and the debtor acts upon that agreement by paying one of the instalments, and the creditor accepts that instalment, then it will necessarily be inequitable for the creditor later to go back upon the agreement and insist on payment of the balance. Again, all will depend upon the circumstances."

Should promissory estoppel be allowed to circumvent the rule in Pinnel's   10-37
Case?   We have seen that the House of Lords, even when it accepted and gave its own authority to the rule in *Pinnel's Case* in *Foakes v Beer*,[274] did not approve it: Lord Blackburn was the most explicit critic, noting that as a result of *Pinnel's Case* the court could not give effect to practical commercial arrangements under which creditors have good reason to agree a reduction in a debt with their debtors.[275] But the House felt that, given that the rule in *Pinnel's Case* had been accepted for so long in the common law, they should not disturb it. Once the rule had the authority of the House of Lords, only statute could reverse it,[276] and there was a proposal by the Law Revision Committee in 1937 to reform the law and give effect to the views set out by Lord Blackburn in *Foakes v Beer*.[277] However, this proposal was not taken forward,[278] and there has been no further proposal for legislative reform of the rule in *Pinnel's Case*, although it is still seen as a "difficult issue"[279] within the common law rules for the variation of a contract which the Supreme Court has

---

[270] The cases discussed by Kitchin LJ in this section include *Hughes v Metropolitan Railway Co*, see para.10-35 fn.231; *Central London Properties Trust Ltd v High Trees House Ltd*, see para.10-35 fn.225; *Tool Metal Manufacturing v Tungsten Electric Co Ltd*, see para.10-36 fn.261; *D & C Builders Ltd v Rees*, see para.10-36 fn.241, and *Collier v P & MJ Wright (Holdings) Ltd*, see para.10-36 fn.257.

[271] See para.10-36 fn.261.

[272] See para.10-37 fn.274.

[273] [1995] 1 W.L.R. 474.

[274] (1884) 9 App. Cas. 605, HL.

[275] (1884) 9 App. Cas. 605, HL at 622; see para.9-20.

[276] i.e. until the House took the power in 1966 to depart from its own previous decisions: Practice Statement (Judicial Precedent) [1966] 1 W.L.R. 1234.

[277] Law Revision Committee, Sixth Interim Report, *Statute of Frauds and the Doctrine of Consideration* Cmd.5449 (1937) at [35]; an extract from Lord Blackburn's opinion in *Foakes v Beer* was quoted by the Law Revision Committee at [34]. The proposal of the Law Revision Committee is set out at para.9-23.

[278] See para.9-23 fn.190.

[279] *MWB Business Exchange Centres Ltd v Rock Advertising Ltd* [2018] UKSC 24; [2018] 2 W.L.R. 1603 at [18].

not yet resolved.[280] Lord Denning said that the development of the doctrine of promissory estoppel, allowing a creditor to be estopped from claiming the balance of a debt which he has agreed to forego, has achieved without statutory intervention what the Law Reform Committee proposed[281]; and Arden LJ has said the same, with evident approval.[282] If promissory estoppel can indeed circumvent the rule in *Pinnel's Case* in the way Lord Denning described, it might be a very helpful development given the difficulty in achieving statutory reform—and, indeed, the case-law development would reduce or even remove the need for statutory intervention if it has taken the law in the direction in which, by general opinion, it ought to have been reformed.

However, the developed doctrine of promissory estoppel has not fully overcome the rule in *Pinnel's Case*.[283] Promissory estoppel can certainly give force to a representation or promise which is not supported by consideration, at least where the representation is not to enforce an existing contractual right. But the reason that the representor can be held to his representation under the doctrine of estoppel is not simply that a promise, once made, or even once made and accepted by the promisee, should be kept; rather, it is that the representee has acted in reliance on the representation. Although he has not provided consideration, at the representor's request, in order to justify his claim to enforce the promise,[284] the representee has earned the right to hold the representor to his representation by acting on it— altering his position in reliance on the representation—in a way intended or at least expected by the representor,[285] so that it would now be inequitable for the representor to resile from his representation.[286] Although in principle the representation which is enforceable under the doctrine of promissory estoppel (unlike a contractual promise) is revocable by the representor giving the representee a reasonable time in which to reverse his change of position or otherwise to enable him again to perform his strict contractual obligations,[287] the representation may become irrevocable where it becomes permanently inequitable for the representee to be required to perform in accordance with the contract, such as where his alteration of position in reliance on the representation is irreversible.[288] However, this must always be a matter of fact, assessed at the time when the representor seeks to enforce the strict terms of the contract. There appears to be no reason why estoppel cannot apply to a representation that a *debt* will not be enforced—and so to that extent the *High Trees* doctrine has superseded the decision in *Jorden v Money*[289] in

---

[280] See para.9-23.

[281] *Central London Property Trust Ltd v High Trees House Ltd* [1947] K.B. 130 at 135, quoted at para.10-35; *D&C Builders Ltd v Rees* [1966] 2 Q.B. 617, CA at 624, quoted at para.10-36.

[282] *Collier v P & MJ Wright (Holdings) Ltd* [2007] EWCA Civ 1329; [2008] 1 W.L.R. 643 at [42], quoted at para.10-36.

[283] cf. F.M.B. Reynolds and G.H. Treitel, "Consideration for the Modification of Contracts" (1965) 7 Malaya L.Rev. 1, noting the problems set out by Lord Blackburn in *Foakes v Beer* (at 1), that only statute could reverse it (at 9: note that the article was written before the Practice Statement, see para.10-37 fn.276) but not accepting that the *High Trees* principle has achieved it (at 17–18) and proposing as a more general solution the statutory abolition of the requirement of consideration in the case of renegotiation of a contract (at 21: see also para.9-24).

[284] See para.8-15.

[285] See para.10-23.

[286] See para.10-28.

[287] See paras 10-30 to 10-31.

[288] See para.10-32.

[289] (1854) 5 H.L.C. 185, 10 E.R. 868; see paras 10-14, 10-35.

which the House of Lords held that a promise not to enforce a debt cannot be given force by estoppel since the representation must be one of fact, not intention or promise. And a representation that a debt will not be enforced could become irrevocable where the general test for the irrevocability of the representation has been satisfied—i.e. the representee's alteration of position in reliance on the representation is irreversible, in the sense that it is now permanently inequitable to insist on payment of the debt. To this extent, it ought therefore to be possible for promissory estoppel to circumvent the rule in *Pinnel's Case* and hold the creditor permanently estopped from claiming a debt, as the most recent decisions discussing this issue in the Court of Appeal have assumed.[290] But before being satisfied that this is so, the court must examine the facts of the alleged alteration of position, and be satisfied that the representee has discharged the burden of proof of his defence, including the "inequity" in allowing the representor to revoke his representation in light of the representee's alteration of position.[291] It may well happen that the facts disclose a good reason to prevent the representor claiming the full contractual debt, such as if the debtor, having been led to believe that he would not have to pay the debt, has in consequence irrevocably incurred other liabilities, rendering it unreasonable to expect him to find additional funds in order to pay the creditor; or where the debtor has made some other arrangements in his business which make it more difficult to repay the debt, or has foregone other opportunities which would have allowed him to repay the debt.[292] Such alteration of position in reliance on the representation would be a collateral action on the part of the debtor, and thus within the concept of an alteration of position as the courts appear to require it for the purposes of estoppel.[293]

Provided that some other alteration of position by the debtor beyond the part-payment is required, and therefore the simple part-payment (and its acceptance by the creditor) does not necessarily make it inequitable for the creditor later to go back on the agreement and insist on payment of the balance,[294] the conflict with the rule in *Pinnel's Case* is limited. Indeed, if the approach taken by the Court of Appeal in *MWB Business Exchange Centres Ltd v Rock Advertising Ltd*[295] is followed, allowing the court more easily to find consideration for the creditor's promise to accept part-payment of a debt in satisfaction of the whole where, on the facts, the creditor thereby obtains a "practical benefit",[296] the need to rely on promissory estoppel to give force to the creditor's promise will be correspondingly reduced. The law might even be developed to dispense altogether with the need for consideration for the variation of a contract.[297] But either way forward would avoid the need

---

[290] *Collier v P & MJ Wright (Holdings) Ltd* [2007] EWCA Civ 1329; [2008] 1 W.L.R. 643; *MWB Business Exchange Centres Ltd v Rock Advertising Ltd* [2016] EWCA Civ 553; [2017] Q.B. 604; see para.10-36.
[291] The burden of the elements of the defence lie on the representee: see para.10-33.
[292] cf. the discussion of possible reliance by White J in *Je Maintiendrai Pty Ltd v Quaglia* (1980) 26 S.A.S.R. 101, SC South Australia, see para.10-27 fn.182 (tenant, in a case similar to *High Trees*, by relying on the promise to reduce the rent may have lost other choices which would have allowed him to find the funds or at least escape the continuing contractual liability to pay).
[293] See para.10-27.
[294] See *MWB Business Exchange Centres Ltd v Rock Advertising Ltd* [2016] EWCA Civ 553; [2017] Q.B. 604 at [61] (Kitchin LJ) quoted at para.10-36.
[295] See para.10-37 fn.294.
[296] See para.9-23.
[297] See para.9-24. If the concern is that the doctrine which provides for the binding force of the agreement to give up the balance of a debt should be sensitive to whether there was a *genuine* agreement

to extend promissory estoppel, a doctrine which provides a less secure modification of a contract: normally only temporary, sometimes permanent, but in any event depending on the fact-sensitive determination of whether it is "inequitable" to allow the representor to insist on strict contractual performance at the time when he seeks to go back on his representation.[298]

(2) Estoppel as "Shield" not "Sword"

10-38 **Promissory estoppel provides a defence, not an action** The doctrine of promissory estoppel, according to the description of its elements in the earlier paragraphs of this chapter,[299] provides the representee with a defence against the representor acting inconsistently with his representation or promise; it does not give the representee a positive action to sue on the promise. In *High Trees* Denning J said[300]:

> "the courts have not gone so far as to give a cause of action in damages for the breach of such a promise but they have refused to allow the party making it to act inconsistently with it."

This is sometimes put in terms that promissory estoppel can be used by the representee as a "shield" (to defend an action by the representor on the strict terms of the contract) but not as a "sword" (to found an action against the representor to hold him to his representation).[301] However, it is not a matter of whether the estop-

---

(a "true accord" as emphasised by Lord Denning in *D&C Builders Ltd v Rees*, see para.10-37 fn.281) the doctrine of economic duress, though it was not yet developed by the time of the decision in *D&C Builders* (see para.10-37 fn.245), can now be employed: see para.9-22 n.161.

[298] In *MWB Business Exchange Centres Ltd v Rock Advertising Ltd*, see para.10-37 fn.294, CA held that there was a contractual variation; but had there not been consideration for the variation, the doctrine of promissory estoppel would not have made the creditor's promise binding because it was not inequitable for it to resile: ibid. at [63].

[299] See esp. paras 10-11 (the link between promissory estoppel and waiver or forbearance); 10-20 (the representation is a negative promise: a promise *not to enforce* the contract); 10-28 (the equity is to resist the representor going back on his representation and enforcing the contract); 10-33 (pleading the estoppel defence).

[300] *Central London Property Trust Ltd v High Trees House Ltd* [1947] K.B. 130 at 134; see para.10-16.

[301] The use of the legal language of "swords" and "shields" does not begin with the law of estoppel: e.g. *Zouch v Parsons* (1765) 1 Wm Bl. 575 at 577, 96 E.R. 332 at 333 (Lord Mansfield CJ: "the privilege of infants is a shield, and not a sword. It shall protect them from fraud and oppression, but shall not be turned into an offensive weapon to assist fraud and oppression"); *Heath v Crealock* (1874) L.R. 10 Ch. App. 22 at 28–29 (Counsel's argument: "The Defendants do not merely plead that they are purchasers for valuable consideration, but they want a conveyance of the legal estate from Stephens. They want the deeds not only as a shield but as a sword"). It seems to have been brought into the language of promissory estoppel by the argument of counsel for the husband in *Combe v Combe* (see para.10-39 fn.310), and is used regularly thereafter: e.g. *Evenden v Guildford City Association Football Club Ltd* [1974] I.C.R. 554 at 558 (Sir John Donaldson: "It is well settled that estoppels, whether promissory or otherwise, are 'shields and not swords or spears,' to use a familiar expression"); *Argy Trading Development Co Ltd v Lapid Developments Ltd* [1977] 1 W.L.R. 444 at 457 (Croom-Johnson J); *Syros Shipping Co SA v Elaghill Trading Co (The Proodos C)* [1980] 2 Lloyd's Rep. 390, see para.10-40; and especially when comparing the operation of proprietary estoppel which is said may be relied on as a "sword": *Pascoe v Turner* [1979] 1 W.L.R. 431, CA, at 436; *Hearn v Younger* [2005] Pens L.R. 49 at [120]–[122] (Etherton J). The use of the language of "swords" and "shields" in relation to estoppel has also been criticised or nuanced: e.g. *Amalgamated Investment & Property Co Ltd v Texas Commerce International Bank Ltd* [1982] Q.B. 84 at 105 (Goff J), 131 (Brandon LJ); *Azov Shipping Co Ltd v Baltic Shipping Co* [1999] 2 Lloyd's Rep. 159 at 175 (Colman J); *Baird Textiles Holdings Ltd v Marks & Spencer Plc* [2001] EWCA Civ

pel argument can be raised by a claimant or the defendant in an action,[302] but whether the representation, unsupported by consideration and not contained in a deed, can create a new right in the representee by virtue of his reliance on it, so that he can assert against the representor the benefit of a new obligation enforceable at law which would not have existed but for the representation on which he has relied. In the following paragraphs of this section we shall see that it is clearly established at the level of the Court of Appeal that promissory estoppel cannot, in principle, be used to create such new rights. If it were allowed to do so, this would provide a new method by which consensual promissory obligations could be created in English law, alongside but independent of the methods long established by the common law: consideration and a deed.[303] However, the fact that, as the authorities presently stand, the English courts have not yet taken that step does not preclude the possibility that the Supreme Court might do so. We shall consider some hints in the existing case-law which point towards such a development, but the broader question of whether there should be a reform of the doctrine of promissory estoppel so as to allow it to create new obligations will be discussed further in Part V of this chapter, where the different approaches taken to this matter in other common law jurisdictions, especially the United States and Australia, are also reviewed.

The decision in Combe v Combe In *Combe v Combe*,[304] at a very early stage in **10-39** the modern development of promissory estoppel following the *High Trees* decision,[305] the Court of Appeal was presented with an argument that the representee could sue to enforce a new obligation arising by reason of her reliance on the representation, even if it was not supported by consideration and was not embodied in a deed. During negotiations between a husband and wife after the decree nisi of their divorce had been pronounced, the husband promised to pay the wife £100 a year by way of maintenance. The wife claimed that, in consequence, she forbore to apply to the court for an order for maintenance, and that her forbearance rendered the husband's promise binding when, more than six years later, she sued her (ex-) husband to enforce the promise he had made. The wife's forbearance could not constitute consideration to make the promise binding, since the husband had not

---

274; [2002] 1 All E.R. (Comm) 737 at [52] (Judge LJ: the "misleading aphorism").

[302] Indeed, in both *Hughes v Metropolitan Railway Co* (1877) 2 App. Cas. 439, HL, and *Birmingham and District Land Co v London and North Western Railway Co* (1888) 40 Ch. D. 268, CA, the waiver/estoppel point was raised by the claimants in the action in response to arguments made by their defendants in seeking to enforce the strict terms of the contract against them: see para.10-15 fnn.83, 91. See also *Combe v Combe*, see para.10-39 fn.304, at 219 (Denning LJ: "Sometimes it is a plaintiff who is not allowed to insist on his strict legal rights. Thus, a creditor is not allowed to enforce a debt which he has deliberately agreed to waive, if the debtor has carried on business or in some other way changed his position in reliance on the waiver. ... On other occasions it is a defendant who is not allowed to insist on his strict legal rights. His conduct may be such as to debar him from relying on some condition, denying some allegation, or taking some other point in answer to the claim") and see also para.10-39 fn.311; *Amalgamated Investment & Property Co Ltd v Texas Commerce International Bank Ltd*, see para.10-38 fn.301, at 131-132 (Brandon LJ: "while a party cannot in terms found a cause of action on an estoppel, he may, as a result of being able to rely on an estoppel, succeed on a cause of action on which, without being able to rely on that estoppel, he would necessarily have failed": estoppel by convention); see also F.M.B. Reynolds and G.H. Treitel, "Consideration for the Modification of Contracts" (1965) 7 Malaya L.Rev. 1, 18.

[303] See Ch.8 (consideration); para.7-18 (deed as alternative to consideration).

[304] [1951] 2 K.B. 215, CA.

[305] See para.10-38 fn.300.

requested it.[306] But, applying the doctrine of promissory estoppel, the trial judge held that the promise was enforceable because it was an unequivocal acceptance of liability intended to be binding, intended to be acted on and in fact acted on, and therefore the wife could claim six years' arrears of payments.[307] The appeal against this decision forced the Court of Appeal to review the embryonic *High Trees* doctrine, and they took the opportunity to set limits on it. The trial judge's decision was reversed and the wife failed in her claim to enforce the husband's promise.

Given that the *High Trees* case was his own decision, it is perhaps not surprising that Denning LJ, though not the presiding judge in the court in *Combe v Combe*, was invited to give the first judgment; and he began his discussion by making a very clear statement about the limited scope of the doctrine of promissory estoppel[308]:

"Much as I am inclined to favour the principle stated in the *High Trees* case, it is important that it should not be stretched too far, lest it should be endangered. That principle does not create new causes of action where none existed before. It only prevents a party from insisting upon his strict legal rights, when it would be unjust to allow him to enforce them, having regard to the dealings which have taken place between the parties."

Similarly, Asquith LJ emphasised that the decision in *High Trees* did not undermine the doctrine of consideration[309]:

"It is unnecessary to express any view as to the correctness of [*High Trees*], though I certainly must not be taken to be questioning it; and I would remark, in passing, that it seems to me a complete misconception to suppose that it struck at the roots of the doctrine of consideration. But assuming, without deciding, that it is good law, I do not think, however, that it helps the plaintiff at all. What that case decides is that when a promise is given which (1.) is intended to create legal relations, (2.) is intended to be acted upon by the promisee, and (3.) is in fact so acted upon, the promisor cannot bring an action against the promisee which involves the repudiation of his promise or is inconsistent with it. It does not, as I read it, decide that a promisee can sue on the promise."

Both of these statements appear to say that the promisee can use estoppel only as a defence,[310] although they did go on to make clear that it is not simply available to a defendant in an action: if a claim is brought by the representee which is defended in such a way that ignores a representation made by the defendant on which the claimant had relied, the claimant may be able to raise the estoppel to prevent the defendant using the defence that he might otherwise have had.[311] Den-

---

[306] See para.8-15 fn.91; *Combe v Combe*, see para.10-39 fn.304, at 217, 221, 223, 226-227.

[307] [1950] 2 All E.R. 1115; see para.10-39 fn.304, at 217 (Byrne J, relying on statements by Denning J in three cases: *High Trees*, see para.10-38 fn.300, *Bob Guiness Ltd v Salomonsen* [1948] 2 K.B. 42 and *Robertson v Minister of Pensions* [1949] 1 K.B. 227). The limit to six years' arrears is stated only in the report of the CA decision (see para.10-39 fn.304, at 217; and in the statement of facts given by Denning LJ at [1951] 1 All E.R. 767 at 769), where it is said that earlier payments were barred by the Limitation Act 1939, presumably on the basis that the action was founded on simple contract (s.2(1)(a); see now Limitation Act 1980 s.5). This serves to emphasise that the effect of the estoppel, as found by Byrne J, was to create an obligation with the same force as a contractual obligation but without the normal requirements for the formation of a contact.

[308] See para.10-39 fn.304, at 219.

[309] See para.10-39 fn.304, at 225.

[310] See also Birkett LJ, para.10-39 fn.304, at 224, noting that Counsel for the husband had used the "very vivid" description of the doctrine "as a shield and not as a sword".

[311] Denning LJ, para.10-39 fn.304, at 219–220; Asquith LJ at 225–226. Birkett LJ at 225 gave as an example if the wife were now to bring (after more than six years) an application to the court for a

ning LJ set out the principle in very general terms[312]:

"The principle, as I understand it, is that, where one party has, by his words or conduct, made to the other a promise or assurance which was intended to affect the legal relations between them and to be acted on accordingly, then, once the other party has taken him at his word and acted on it, the one who gave the promise or assurance cannot afterwards be allowed to revert to the previous legal relations as if no such promise or assurance had been made by him, but he must accept their legal relations subject to the qualification which he himself has so introduced, even though it is not supported in point of law by any consideration but only by his word.

Seeing that the principle never stands alone as giving a cause of action in itself, it can never do away with the necessity of consideration when that is an essential part of the cause of action. The doctrine of consideration is too firmly fixed to be overthrown by a side-wind. Its ill-effects have been largely mitigated of late, but it still remains a cardinal necessity of the formation of a contract, though not of its modification or discharge."

The closing words of this statement put the operation of the doctrine of promissory estoppel firmly within the context of the modification or discharge of an existing contract, rather than in the formation of contract. Since the promise made by the husband to the wife would, if enforceable, have created a new obligation binding the husband to make the annual payment of £100 to the wife, where no obligation of that nature already existed, it is not the context in which estoppel could operate. Consideration or a deed are necessary for the creation of consensual promissory obligations in English law.[313]

Promissory estoppel is limited to the modification of an existing contract by reducing or discharging obligations, not by increasing them One point must be clarified in relation to the statement of Denning LJ in *Combe v Combe* quoted above.[314] He said that consideration "still remains a cardinal necessity of the formation of a contract, though not of its modification or discharge". The first part of this is clear: promissory estoppel cannot be employed as a substitute for consideration in the *formation* of a contract.[315] But the second part allows estoppel, in the absence of consideration, to have the effect of *modifying or discharging* a contract. The   **10-40**

---

maintenance order, she might be met by the argument that she had delayed too long; but to answer that argument she could use the husband's earlier promise to pay on which she had relied.

[312] See para.10-39 fn.304, at 220.

[313] This raises the relationship between the policy of protecting the doctrine of consideration and the policy of protecting the representee who relies on a representation which is unsupported by consideration: *Azov Shipping Co Ltd v Baltic Shipping Co* [1999] 2 Lloyd's Rep. 159 at 175; see para.10-45. *Combe v Combe* has been followed in many cases, cited as the general proposition for the rule that promissory estoppel cannot create a cause of action: e.g. *Beesly v Hallwood Estates Ltd* [1960] 1 W.L.R. 549, 560–561; *Argy Trading Development Co Ltd v Lapid Developments Ltd*, see para.10-38 fn.301, at 457 (Croom-Johnson J: plaintiffs claimed that defendants were estopped from alleging that there was no consideration for agreement to take over insurance of premises: "if there was no contract such as the plaintiffs sue on because it turns out that there was no consideration, then to estop Lapid from raising that in their defence would only be to try by a side wind to make the promise give rise to the cause of action. This the plaintiffs cannot do"); *Syros Shipping Co SA v Elaghill Trading Co (The Proodos C)*, see para.10-38 fn.301, at 391–392; *Hiscox v Outhwaite (No.3)* [1991] 2 Lloyd's Rep. 524 at 535; *Baird Textiles Holdings Ltd v Marks & Spencer Plc* [2001] EWCA Civ 274; [2002] 1 All E.R. (Comm) 737 at [34]–[35], [38], [87], [91].

[314] See para.10-39 fn.312.

[315] For further discussion of whether promissory estoppel *ought* to be able to have this effect, see paras 10-44 to 10-51.

question is: what sort of modification of a contract does this mean? If it is the modification of existing contractual obligations by their reduction—by the representor being estopped from enforcing his strict contractual rights by reason of the representee's reliance on his representation—then whether this is a temporary or permanent modification it is within the scope of the orthodox doctrine of promissory estoppel, as it has been established in the cases following *High Trees* and *Combe v Combe*.[316] But we have seen that a contractual obligation may also be modified by being increased; and so the question is whether the decision in *Combe v Combe* leaves open the possibility of promissory estoppel being used to give effect to a representation that the obligations owed by the representor in favour of the representee will be increased.

It should be evident that the answer is no. If the promise to pay the £100 a year in *Combe v Combe* cannot be enforced by means of estoppel, since to do so would be to allow the estoppel to be used "as a sword" in the sense that it would create a new right to claim a sum of money which would not exist but for the representation which has been relied on, then a promise to increase an existing contractual debt of, say, £200 to £300 would have the very same effect. There is a contractual right to £200; the right to the additional £100 would be a new claim for which consideration (or a deed) is necessary in order to make it contractually binding.[317] The cases which have developed the *High Trees* doctrine have consistently made clear that estoppel cannot create new rights[318]; and in *Syros Shipping Co SA v Elaghill Trading Co (The Proodos C)* Lloyd J held that the agreement of consignees of cargo to pay to the ship owners an additional sum of $31,000 in order to secure the discharge of the cargo could not be given effect by promissory estoppel[319]:

> "It is unnecessary to go back to the cases decided in the last century; it is sufficient to start with *Central London Property Trust Ltd v High Trees House Ltd*, the case which marked a turning point in the modern law of equitable estoppel. In that case, Mr. Justice Denning (as he then was), made it clear that the principle cannot be used to create a new cause of action; in the time honoured phrase, it can be used as a shield, not as a sword. He used similar language as Lord Justice Denning in *Combe v Combe* …
>
> In the present case the owners could have had no claim for the $31,000 which they are seeking to recover from the respondents in these proceedings if it were not for the 'agreement' of Feb. 28, 1977. They have no independent cause of action: they are suing on the naked promise to pay the $31,000; they are using equitable estoppel as a sword and not as a shield; and that they cannot do."

---

[316] See esp. *Ajayi v RT Briscoe (Nigeria) Ltd* [1964] 1 W.L.R. 1326, PC, at 1330, quoted at para.10-17; and for the fact that the modification may be temporary (suspension of enforceability of the contractual rights) or permanent (extinctive of the contractual rights), see paras 10-30, 10-32. In the latter case, as Denning LJ says in *Combe v Combe*, see para.10-39 fn.312, estoppel may effect a "discharge" of the contractual obligations which are the subject of the representation.

[317] See Ch.9, esp. paras 9-02, 9-08.

[318] e.g. *Ajayi v RT Briscoe (Nigeria) Ltd*, see para.10-40 fn.316, at 1330 (Lord Hodson: "Their Lordships are of opinion that the principle of law as defined by Bowen LJ [in *Birmingham and District Land Co v London and North Western Railway Co* (1888) 40 Ch. D. 268, CA, see para.10-15] has been confirmed by the House of Lords in the case of *Tool Metal Manufacturing Co Ltd v Tungsten Electric Co Ltd* [1955] 1 W.L.R. 761, HL, where the authorities were reviewed and no encouragement was given to the view that the principle was capable of extension so as to create rights in the promisee for which he had given no consideration").

[319] [1980] 2 Lloyd's Rep. 390 at 391–392. The problem arose because the charterers became insolvent during the voyage.

This should be the answer to any claim to enforce by promissory estoppel a promise to pay, or a promise to increase payment already due under a contract (or equally to perform any other non-monetary obligation or to increase an already contracted non-monetary obligation). However, there was a statement by one of the judges in the Court of Appeal in *Williams v Roffey Bros & Nicholls (Contractors) Ltd*[320] to the effect that, if the court had not found consideration provided by the sub-contractor to the main contractor in order to give contractual force to the main contractor's promise to increase the payments due under the sub-contract, it would have been interesting to consider whether promissory estoppel could fill the gap.[321] This was not, however, pursued; and, indeed, given that the effect of the decision in *Williams v Roffey* was to make it easier to find consideration (in the form of a "practical benefit" obtained by the promisor) in return for the promise of a unilateral variation of a bilateral executory contract,[322] there seems to be correspondingly less need even to consider the possibility of expanding the scope of promissory estoppel to this context.

Hints in the cases that promissory estoppel can be used to create new obligations   In addition to the fact that the judges in the Court of Appeal in *Williams v Roffey*[323] did not reject out of hand the suggestion that promissory estoppel could be developed to cover the agreement to increase an existing contractual obligation, there are hints in a number of other cases that estoppel might be used to create new obligations. However, these are cases where the courts did not seek to take a positive step of expanding the scope of the doctrine, but claimed that they were simply operating within the scope of the existing principles and, indeed, in many cases the argument based on promissory estoppel was only obiter dictum, or was an alternative ground to another which is less controversial. For example, where the Official Receiver, acting as liquidator of a company, told an unpaid creditor who had contracted to sell land to the company that he would join in a conveyance of land to a third party in order to realise the asset, it was held that the Official Receiver would be estopped from denying that he must perform his promise to join in the transaction to give it legal effect.[324] Where the charterers of a vessel dealt with a

10-41

---

[320] [1991] 1 Q.B. 1, CA, discussed in detail at para.9-14.
[321] [1991] 1 Q.B. 1, CA at 17 (Russell LJ: "Speaking for myself—and I notice it is touched upon in the judgment of Glidewell LJ—I would have welcomed the development of argument, if it could have been properly raised in this court, on the basis that there was here an estoppel and that the defendants, in the circumstances prevailing, were precluded from raising the defence that their undertaking to pay the extra £10,300 was not binding"). Glidewell LJ at 13 said "It was suggested to us in argument that, since the development of the doctrine of promissory estoppel, it may well be possible for a person to whom a promise has been made, on which he has relied, to make an additional payment for services which he is in any event bound to render under an existing contract or by operation of law, to show that the promisor is estopped from claiming that there was no consideration for his promise. However, the application of the doctrine of promissory estoppel to facts such as those of the present case has not yet been fully developed: see e.g. the judgment of Lloyd J in *Syros Shipping Co SA v Elaghill Trading Co* [see para.10-40 fn.319], 392. Moreover, this point was not argued in the court below, nor was it more than adumbrated before us. Interesting though it is, no reliance can in my view be placed on this concept in the present case".
[322] See paras 9-15 to 9-16.
[323] See para.10-40 fn.321.
[324] *Re Wyvern Developments Ltd* [1974] 1 W.L.R. 1097 at 1104–1105 (Templeman J, rejecting the argument that this was contrary to *Combe v Combe*: "the situation is different and estoppel applies where the promisor knows and intends that the promisee will irretrievably alter his position in reliance on the promise. The Official Receiver put into circulation a promise, on the strength of which both [the

claim by the owner of goods carried on the vessel in respect of damage to the goods, although under the shipping documents the charterers were acting only on behalf of the owners of the vessel and so were the wrong party against which the claim should have been brought, the charterers were estopped from denying that the claim could be brought against them where their conduct had led the owner of the goods to lose their claim against the proper defendants.[325] And where an applicant for planning permission undertook to provide improved sight lines at the entrance to the land, which induced the Secretary of State to grant permission including the condition of the improved sight lines, the applicant could not object to the condition.[326]

There are, however, broader questions of whether promissory estoppel should be developed beyond its current limited traditional role, so as to allow it to create new obligations, and provide a cause of action for a promisee who has relied on a promise without providing consideration; and whether promissory estoppel should be seen not as a freestanding doctrine but as part of a wider, general principle of equitable estoppel which would include at least also proprietary estoppel but also perhaps other forms of estoppel. Such developments might follow the lead of certain

---

creditor] and [the intending purchaser of the land] altered their legal relationships. They did so by entering into a contract which bound them both. Once that was done, the Official Receiver was estopped from denying that he was entitled and bound to perform his promise". This was obiter, because Templeman J held that the Official Receiver had bound himself contractually to join in the conveyance: at 1104).

[325] *Pacol Ltd v Trade Lines Ltd (The Henrik Sif)* [1982] 1 Lloyd's Rep. 456. The claim against the true defendant, the owner of the vessel, became barred by lapse of time, although the charterers agreed with owner of the goods to extend time for the (non-existent) claim against them. Webster J held that the claim was good against the charterers on various different bases, including estoppel by convention (which appears to be a more orthodox decision: cf. *Amalgamated Investment & Property Co Ltd v Texas Commerce International Bank Ltd* [1982] Q.B. 84, CA: see para.10-05 fn.20). But in relation to the claim for promissory estoppel, he sought to deal with the argument that there must be a variation of a existing legal relationship by (in effect) saying that it was sufficient if the parties *thought* that there was a legal relationship which is then given effect by estoppel: at 466 ("In my view, whatever be the precise meaning of the expression 'legal relationship', it applies to the relationship between two parties engaged in an exchange of correspondence in which one of them intends the correspondence to have legal effect in circumstances in which the other knows of that first party's intention and makes requests or purports to grant extensions of time which could only be of relevance to the first party if the correspondence between them affected their mutual rights and obligations. ... Moreover, in my judgment, the representation on their behalf that [the charterers] were the proper party to be sued on the bills of lading, if in fact they were not a party to the bills of lading, constituted a representation that they would not enforce their strict rights against the other; they were saying, for practical purposes, 'We will not take against you a point of fact and law upon which we would otherwise be entitled to rely in this legal dispute between us'"). For doubt or criticism of the case in relation to the promissory estoppel claim, see *Baird Textiles Holdings Ltd v Marks & Spencer Plc* [2001] EWCA Civ 274; [2002] 1 All E.R. (Comm) 737 at [89] (Mance LJ: "Some of Webster J's reasoning, read literally, comes close to saying that any conventional conduct objectively intended to affect legal relations may estop the parties from denying that it has that legal effect", but the decision was right); *Parkin v Alba Proteins Ltd* [2013] EWHC 2036 (QB) at [77] (Holroyde J distinguishing *Pacol* as a case where there was a contractual relationship between the parties: it did not therefore apply to case where estoppel would have effect of creating cause of action against a party which did not have legal existence for much of the relevant period—company not yet incorporated).

[326] *Augier v Secretary of State for the Environment* (1979) 38 P. & C.R. 219 at 226 (Sir Douglas Frank QC: "the undertaking given by Halls was a promise intended to be acted on whatever their rights under planning law, and I think that the Secretary of State acted to his detriment in granting a planning permission that he would not have granted but for the undertaking"; and promissory estoppel is not limited to existing contracts, but there was a "sufficient legal relationship" with the Secretary of State: cf. para.10-18 fn.119).

other common law jurisdictions which have allowed promissory estoppel to give rise to a cause of action. These questions are considered in Part V of this chapter.

(3)   Promissory Estoppel and Third Parties

The representation normally binds only the representor and benefits only the   10-42
representee   The effect of promissory estoppel is to provide one party to a contract[327] with a defence against the other party who seeks to act inconsistently with his representation or promise that he will not require strict performance of the terms of the contract, even though there has been no variation of the terms of the contract supported by consideration or embodied in a deed. Since the effect of the estoppel is not to vary the contract itself, but only to preclude the representor from going back on his representation not to enforce the contract if it is inequitable to do so at the moment when he seeks to enforce the contract, it is natural to think that the representation should bind only the representor, and should benefit only the representee, as a purely personal concession. There will normally be no question of third parties being bound or benefited by the representation, since the contract gives rise to obligations—rights and duties personal to the parties to the contract— and so any modification of that relationship through the operation of the doctrine of promissory estoppel ought equally to be relevant only to those parties.

Where the contract which is modified by promissory estoppel can bind or   10-43
benefit a third party, the third party may take subject to the estop-
pel   Although a contract is normally personal to the parties, there are situations in which third parties may take the benefit of, or be subject to the burden of, an existing contract[328] to which they were not original parties, and the question arises whether in such cases the estoppel may have an effect beyond the original parties to the contract.

The benefit of a contract may in certain circumstances be transferred by assignment, but the assignee takes "subject to equities", that is, subject to defences arising out of the contract which would have been available against the assignor had he not assigned.[329] There appear to be no cases in which the courts have had to consider whether an assignee of a chose in action is bound by an equity arising by

---

[327] Or another relationship giving rise to personal rights and duties: see para.10-18 fn.119, although in the context of this book we focus on the core example of the modification of a contract.

[328] The situation considered in this paragraph involves an existing contact which subsequently benefits a third party (e.g. by assignment), not a contract which from the outset confers an enforceable benefit on a third party under the Contracts (Rights of Third Parties) Act 1999. In the latter case, the third party's rights are protected by s.2 of the 1999 Act where the contracting parties seek by agreement to rescind the contract or vary it in such a way as to extinguish or alter his entitlement, once the third party has communicated his assent to the term under which he has the right, or he has relied on the term and the promisor is aware that he has relied or can reasonably be expected to have foreseen that he would rely. Any modification of the contract by promissory estoppel by the contracting parties should therefore be subject to the limitations of s.2 in so far as the modification would affect the entitlement of the third party. If it is the third party with a right under the 1999 Act who makes a representation not to insist on his entitlement under the contract, on which the promisor alters his position in reliance, the normal principles of promissory estoppel should apply as between those two persons.

[329] Chitty, Ch.19, esp. para.19-071; Furmston, Ch.6, Pt C, esp. paras 6.336–6.337; Treitel, Ch.15, esp. paras 15-039 to 15-040; Anson, Ch.22, esp. pp.705-706; Cheshire, Fifoot and Furmston, Ch.16, esp. pp.640–642.

way of promissory estoppel, but since promissory estoppel operates as a defence—and, indeed, according to the language developed by the courts the alteration by the representee of his position in reliance on the representation gives rise to an "equity"[330] —an assignment by the representor of the contractual right which has been suspended or otherwise modified by his representation should give the assignee no better right against the representee (the other contracting party) than if the representor had retained the benefit of the contract and sued to enforce it.[331] The representee ought to be able to raise the same defence by way of estoppel against the assignee as he could have raised against the representor, but subject to the same limitations: and so if the representor could have given notice to terminate the suspension,[332] the assignee should have the same right.

However, the courts have considered whether an estoppel can bind the representor's successor in two cases which arose in a similar context: where the representation was by a landowner in relation to the scope of the contractual rights exercisable over his land. Given that a party who acquires title to land can be bound by third-party rights attaching to the land, if a purchaser of land is burdened by a third-party right which arises from a contract which has itself been subject to modification by promissory estoppel, the purchaser might in principle be affected by the estoppel. The first case is *Birmingham and District Land Co v London and North Western Railway Co*,[333] where the representation (not to enforce a time limit within a building agreement) was made by a previous landowner, Mr Boulton, but was held binding on his successor, the railway company which had purchased the land subject to the agreement. Cotton LJ said[334]:

"The railway company bought subject to such rights as the Plaintiff company may yet have, and we have to consider what those rights are. ... I quite agree that what passed did not make a new agreement, but in my opinion, what took place between Mr. Boulton's agent ... and the Plaintiffs would have prevented Mr. Boulton from bringing ejectment or taking possession of the land as soon as the terms of years limited by the agreements respectively came to an end, it raised an equity against him which would prevent his so doing."

In this case the Court of Appeal did not consider in detail the nature of the building agreement, although there are indications that it took effect not only as a contract but as a lease,[335] or at least as an agreement for lease which would have proprietary effect against the purchaser who took with notice of it.[336] As such, it may not be

---

[330] See para.10-28.

[331] cf. Spencer Bower (Estoppel), para.6.24 ("It is submitted that an assignee of the benefit of a contract is bound by any estoppel binding on his assignor as to his rights under the contract").

[332] See para.10-30.

[333] (1888) 40 Ch. D. 268, CA; see para.10-15 fn.91.

[334] (1888) 40 Ch. D. 268, CA, at 276. See also Lindley LJ at 282 (emphasis added): "There had not, it is true, been any agreement to enlarge the time, but there had been such conduct as to preclude the lessors *and the railway company claiming under them* from treating the agreements as at an end upon the expiration of the term of years mentioned in them"; and Bowen LJ at 285: "inasmuch as they took with notice of the title of the Plaintiffs as against Boulton, such paramount interest could only exist upon the ground that the title of the Plaintiff company under the agreements had come to an end".

[335] Cotton LJ, referred to the "term of years limited by the agreements"; Lindley LJ, referred to the landowner as "lessor": see (1888) 40 Ch. D. 268 at 276. However, at first instance the developers' counsel referred to their "licence to enter and build": (1887) 36 Ch. D. 650 at 653.

[336] The agreement entitled the developers to build and to be granted leases of the individual houses once

surprising that this is a context in which an equitable defence which would have been available against the original landowner would bind his successor.[337]

The second case also involved a lease. In *Brikom Investments Ltd v Carr*,[338] Lord Denning MR expressed—in terms that were rather too broad—the view that both the benefit and the burden of an estoppel could run with the contract into the hands of third parties. Lord Denning assumed that if a landlord had represented to his tenant that he would not enforce one of the covenants in the lease (the obligation to contribute to the costs of repairs undertaken by the landlord), and then assigned the reversion, the assignee would be bound by the original landlord's representation; and the tenant's assignee could similarly take the benefit[339]:

> "Suppose that the landlords here (before or after doing the repairs to the roof) had assigned their reversion to a purchaser: and then that purchaser sought to recover the contribution from the tenants—contrary to the promise made by the original landlords. Surely the assignee of the reversion would be bound by the promise made by the original landlords. It would be most unjust and unfair if he could go back on the promise. Equity would not allow him to do it.
>
> Now if the assignee of the reversion takes subject to the *burden* of the estoppel, so also the assignee of the tenant should take subject to the *benefit* of it. ... The burden and the benefit run down the line of assignor and assignee on each side."

This was not part of the decision in the case,[340] and it must be viewed cautiously in that it assumes that a representation by way of modification of the terms of the lease automatically passes with the lease, without considering whether the modification was intended to be merely personal to the original parties.[341] The waiver of a covenant by a landlord is normally only effective in relation to particular

---

they were completed. An agreement for lease gives rise to an equitable lease under the doctrine of *Walsh v Lonsdale* (1882) 21 Ch. D. 9; Cheshire and Burn, pp.215–217, 978–979; and when the *Birmingham and District Land Co* case was decided an equitable interest in the land would have been binding on a purchaser for value who took with notice of it (under the system of unregistered conveyancing, before the modern system of registration of land charges was introduced by LPA 1925); now the precise analysis would depend on whether the title to the land is registered or not: Cheshire and Burn, pp.83–91, 143–146.

[337] The purchaser is bound by the lease; but if the defence arising by promissory estoppel constitutes an "equity", then, in so far as it affects the proprietary rights arising from the lease, it can also bind the purchaser, both in unregistered land and in registered land: Cheshire and Burn, pp.904–906. For discussion of the circumstances in which an estoppel affecting a lease, or another interest in land, can affect third parties, see also Spencer Bower (Estoppel), paras 6.25 to 6.45.

[338] [1979] Q.B. 467, CA.

[339] [1979] Q.B. 467, CA at 484.

[340] The case does not fit the normal model of promissory estoppel, since the representation by the landlords was made *before* the lease was signed, and so there was a modification of a contract before it was entered into, rather than the modification of an existing contract; and the majority of the Court of Appeal held that the landlord's representation was effective as a contractual variation or waiver: see Roskill LJ at 489 and Cumming-Bruce LJ at 490. cf. *City and Westminster Properties (1934) Ltd v Mudd* [1959] Ch. 129 at 145–146 (Harman J: "the present case does not raise the controversial issue of the *Central London Property Trust Ltd v High Trees House Ltd* decision. This is not a case of a representation made after contractual relations existed between the parties to the effect that one party to the contract would not rely on his rights": promise by landlord before execution of lease gave rise to collateral contract).

[341] cf. also Roskill LJ at 486 ("With great respect, I would not go as far as Lord Denning MR in saying it is now the law that the benefits and burdens arising from a promise made in circumstances such as those presently found by the judge, to quote the phrase he used a few moments ago, 'run down both sides.' It seems to me that the problem is far more complex").

breaches[342]; and although the landlord and tenant can enter into a collateral contract to vary the terms of the lease as between themselves, such a variation of the lease is normally done in the form of a collateral contract rather than as a variation of the lease for the very reason that it should be personal to the particular landlord and tenant and not release assignees from the terms of the lease which will bind them.[343] It would be curious if a landlord's representation not to enforce a term in a lease, if acted on by the tenant in reliance, could effect a change in the terms of the lease which a (personal) informal contract between the same parties would not achieve. However, the general proposition which underlies Lord Denning's statement— that the assignee of a right takes subject to any limitations on that right which have been created by the assignor—does conform to the general rule governing the rights of an assignee of a chose in action.

V.   THE ROLE OF ESTOPPEL IN THE CREATION OF OBLIGATIONS

10-44   **The traditional scope of promissory estoppel in English law**   In the earlier sections of this chapter we have considered the role which promissory estoppel can play in modifying a contract, and we have seen that the traditional view adopted in the English cases is that estoppel may suspend a contracting party's duty to perform one or more of his obligations, either temporarily or (sometimes) permanently,[344] but it may not create a cause of action in the representee by giving him new rights either by the increase of obligations under an existing contract,[345] or by creating a new obligation.[346] But there have been developments in other common law jurisdictions which raise the question whether the scope of promissory estoppel should be so limited; and there have also been some suggestions by the judges in English cases that they might be open to developing English law in this area, particularly by breaking down some of the distinctions which have been established between different forms of estoppel.[347] In this final part of the book we look briefly at this question, which is relevant for not only for the scope of promissory estoppel in its modification of a contract, but also for its potential in providing an additional cause of action for parties negotiating a contract which has not been concluded.[348]

(1)   The Relationship Between Consideration and Estoppel

10-45   **The traditional approach in England: consideration or a deed are required for the creation of a consensual promissory obligation**   As we have seen, for the creation of consensual promissory obligations English law requires consideration to be provided by the promisee, or a deed to be executed in the promisee's favour by the promisor.[349] Similarly, a variation of the contract requires, in principle,

---

[342] Cheshire and Burn, pp.281–283.
[343] *Morgan v Griffith* (1871) L.R. 6 Ex. 70; *Erskine v Adeane* (1873) L.R. 8 Ch. App. 756; *City and Westminster Properties (1934) Ltd v Mudd*, see para.10-43 fn.340.
[344] See paras 10-30, 10-32.
[345] See para.10-40.
[346] See para.10-38.
[347] For the different forms of estoppel see paras 10-03 to 10-08.
[348] See Ch.2, esp. para.2-30.
[349] See Ch.8 (consideration); para.7-18 (deed as alternative to consideration).

consideration or a deed.[350] According to the traditional role accorded to promissory estoppel, it may be used in the informal modification of an existing contract by reducing (generally temporarily) the enforceability of rights arising under the contract where the party with the rights has represented to the other party that he will not insist on strict performance in accordance with the contract, and the representee has altered his position in reliance on the representation in such a way that makes it inequitable for the representor to go back on the representation, at least without giving the representee the opportunity to resume the position of being able to perform.[351] To the extent that promissory estoppel can effect the informal modification of a contract that would normally require consideration, it might appear to undermine the policy requiring consideration,[352] and the decision of the Court of Appeal in *Combe v Combe*,[353] to the effect that promissory estoppel should be limited to the modification of a contract and should not be allowed to create a cause of action to enforce a new obligation, was designed to draw a clear line between the doctrines of consideration and of promissory estoppel. The policies underlying the two doctrines are different[354]:

> "[The decision in *Combe v Combe*] gives effect to the countervailing policy consideration that in English law a bare promise cannot be sued upon without consideration moving from the promisee. In the field of estoppel the policy of protecting this principle displaces the policy of protecting the representee from the unfairness that would result from the promisor resiling from his position."

The doctrine of consideration is based on the policy that the promisee must have promised, done or forborne to do something, at the promisor's request, in order to earn the right to hold the promisor to his promise; and the promisor is bound because he has received what he asked for.[355] The policy underlying promissory estoppel, by contrast, focuses not on whether the promisor has requested or received anything, but on protecting the reliance by the promisee[356]:

> "the underlying policy in giving effect to the estoppel is to prevent the unfairness to the representee which would arise if the representor were permitted to resile from his represented position as to the existing legal relationship between them."

Other varied approaches within the common law   The approach taken to the   **10-46**
doctrines of consideration and of promissory estoppel elsewhere in the common law is not always the same as in England. We have seen that there has been dissatisfaction with the doctrine of consideration[357]; and one response to this dissatisfaction has been to accept the doctrine of promissory estoppel as at least a limited

---

[350] See Ch.9, esp., para.9-08.
[351] See para.10-18.
[352] cf. *Brikom Investments Ltd v Carr* [1979] Q.B. 467, CA, at 486 (Roskill LJ, "it would be wrong to extend the doctrine of promissory estoppel, whatever its precise limits at the present day, to the extent of abolishing in this backhanded way the doctrine of consideration": note that the facts of this case did not in any event fit the model analysis of promissory estoppel: see para.10-43 fn.340).
[353] See para.10-39.
[354] *Azov Shipping Co Ltd v Baltic Shipping Co* [1999] 2 Lloyd's Rep. 159 at 175 (Colman J; repeated in *Thornton Springer v NEM Insurance Co Ltd* [2000] 2 All E.R. 489 at 519).
[355] See para.8-08.
[356] *Azov Shipping Co Ltd v Baltic Shipping Co*, see para.10-45 fn.354, at 174 (Colman J).
[357] See para.8-40, 9-23.

counterbalance to the requirement of consideration.[358] In general, other Commonwealth systems have adopted estoppel in the same way as the English courts, and at least initially they did so with the limitation of *Combe v Combe*[359] so that, as in England, promissory estoppel is not an alternative general method by which a promise may become binding and give rise to a cause of action in favour of the promisee who relies on it.[360] However, in some jurisdictions the limitation of *Combe v Combe* has been challenged, and in particular in 1988 the Australian High Court took the positive step of rejecting *Combe v Combe* and admitting that in principle promissory estoppel should be able to give rise to a cause of action to allow the promisee to enforce a promise unsupported by consideration. In this, Australian law was joining a well-established principle of promissory estoppel in American law, although the reasoning behind the developments in the two jurisdictions was not identical. Since these two jurisdictions have made the most direct inroads into the restriction, still maintained in England, that promissory estoppel should not create a cause of action, we shall first discuss them before considering whether a similar development might be made in England.

(2)   Promissory Estoppel in Other Common Law Jurisdictions

10-47   **Promissory estoppel in American law**   The courts in the United States developed a general principle to protect a party who relies on a promise made by the other party which is not contractually binding. This was already reflected in the first edition of the *Restatement of the Law of Contracts* in 1932[361]:

> "A promise which the promisor should reasonably expect to induce action or forbearance of a definite and substantial character on the part of the promisee and which does induce such action of forbearance is binding if injustice can be avoided only by enforcement of the promise."

Although this did not yet reflect the law across the American States,[362] it was very influential in encouraging the acceptance of the general principle,[363] and the original

---

[358] See paras 10-19, 10-35 to 10-37.

[359] See para.10-45 fn.353.

[360] In 1965 Jackson could list case-law which had accepted promissory estoppel in Australia, New Zealand, Malaysia, Northern Ireland and South Africa, and noted that in most instances the principle had been accepted as limited by *Combe v Combe* although he found evidence in Australia and New Zealand of courts going beyond that limitation: D. Jackson, "Estoppel as a Sword" (1965) 81 L.Q.R. 223, 243–246. In the modern law, see Fridman, pp.120–135 (Canada); Burrows, Finn & Todd, para.4.6 (New Zealand); Phang and Goh, paras 267–291 (Singapore); Sinnadurai, Ch.15 (Malaysia). For Australia, see para.10-48.

[361] *Restatement of the Law of Contracts* (American Law Institute, St Paul, 1932), §90, under the heading "Promise Reasonably Inducing Definite and Substantial Action". The Institute did not attach any Comment to §90, just four Illustrations.

[362] The Restatements are not statutory texts, but are highly influential statements of the rules of law, generally deduced from the case-law but sometimes containing new ideas and new rules which then themselves influence the developing case-law: Farnsworth, para.1.8. The first version of §90 in 1936 was based on a limited range of authorities in the case-law, but it "was destined to become its most notable and influential rule": Farnsworth, para.2.19.

[363] e.g. *Hoffman v Red Owl Stores* (1965) 133 N.W.2d 267, Sup. Ct. Wisconsin, accepting it in Wisconsin law: see at [1] (Currie CJ: "many courts of other jurisdictions have seen fit over the years to adopt the principle of promissory estoppel, and the tendency in that direction continues. As Mr. Justice McFaddin, speaking on behalf of the Arkansas court, well stated, that the development of the law of promissory estoppel 'is an attempt by the courts to keep remedies abreast of increased moral

text was further developed in the light of its application in later cases and academic discussion. In 1981 a revised version was published in the Second Restatement of Contracts[364]:

"A promise which the promisor should reasonably expect to induce action or forbearance on the part of the promisee or a third person and which does induce such action or forbearance is binding if injustice can be avoided only by enforcement of the promise. The remedy granted for breach may be limited as justice requires."

There is therefore a history in the United States of protecting reliance on a promise. It has become known as "promissory estoppel",[365] although some writers prefer simply to refer to it as liability for reliance.[366] But it has become a general principle by which a person making a promise can be bound to it where he did not receive consideration in return, but the promisee has reasonably acted (or forborne to act) in reliance on the promise in such a way as the promisor ought reasonably to have foreseen.[367] Promissory estoppel is therefore, in American law, a general alternative to consideration as a method of creating a cause of action to enforce a promise.

The scope of the liability under promissory estoppel is not, however, identical to a contract supported by consideration.[368] Although the promise is said to be "binding" by virtue of the reliance, it does not necessarily attract the same remedy as a contract: given that "the remedy granted for breach may be limited as justice requires", the courts may award damages calculated to protect the value of the promisee's reliance on the promise,[369] but there is also evidence of the courts treating promissory estoppel actions as traditional breach of contract actions and awarding remedies calculated to protect the promisee's expectation.[370]

---

consciousness of honesty and fair representations in all business dealings'").

[364] Restatement (2d), §90(1), under the heading "Promise Reasonably Inducing Action or Forbearance". A new §90(2) was added in 1981, providing that a charitable subscription or marriage settlement is binding under §90(1) without proof that the promise induced action or forbearance: this reflects the fact that the American courts have traditionally favoured charitable subscriptions and marriage settlements: see Comment *f.* to §90.

[365] Restatement (2d) Contracts, §90, Comment a.; *Hoffman v Red Owl Stores*, see para.10-47 fn.363, at [1] (Currie CJ: "The Restatement avoids use of the term 'promissory estoppel,' and there has been criticism of it as an inaccurate term. See 1A Corbin, Contracts, p. 232, et seq., sec. 204. On the other hand, Williston advocated the use of this term or something equivalent. 1 Williston, Contracts (1st ed.), p. 308, sec. 139. Use of the word 'estoppel' to describe a doctrine upon which a party to a lawsuit may obtain affirmative relief offends the traditional concept that estoppel merely serves as a shield and cannot serve as a sword to create a cause of action. ... We have employed its use in this opinion not only because of its extensive use by other courts but also since a more accurate equivalent has not been devised").

[366] e.g. Corbin, see para.10-47 fn.365 (also in revised edn, 1996, para.8.7); Farnsworth, para.2.19 (noting at fn.21 that the first use of the term "promissory estoppel" has been attributed to Williston (cf. para.10-47 fn.365)).

[367] For general discussion, see Farnsworth, para.2.19; and the Comments and Reporter's Note to §90. The widespread use of promissory estoppel is evident from the case law: see, e.g. M.J. Jimenez, "The Many Faces of Promissory Estoppel: An Empirical Analysis Under the Restatement (Second) of Contracts" (2010) 57 U.C.L.A. Law Rev. 669, analysing more than 300 promissory estoppel cases decided between 1 January 1981, and 1 January 2008.

[368] cf. however, Restatement (2d) Contracts, §90, Comment *d.* ("A promise binding under this section is a contract ...").

[369] Farnsworth, para.2.19.

[370] Jimenez, "The Many Faces of Promissory Estoppel: An Empirical Analysis Under the Restatement (Second) of Contracts", see para.10-47 fn.367.

The acceptance of this general doctrine of promissory estoppel, under which reliance by the promisee can be sufficient to render the promise binding without providing consideration for the promise, has had two significant effects within the American law of contract. First, it reduces the need to "find" consideration in order to make promise enforceable, and therefore it allows the focus of the doctrine of consideration in American law to be more squarely on the bargain the parties intended.[371] Secondly, it allows the courts to award a remedy in the pre-contractual phase to protect the reliance of one party negotiating a contract which is not in due course entered into, but where the other party had led him to believe that the contract would be concluded and that it was reasonable to incur expenses accordingly. A good illustration is the case of *Hoffman v Red Owl Stores*[372] where Red Owl, through its agent, represented to Hoffman that for the price of $18,000 it would build and stock a grocery store which Hoffman and his wife would run as franchisee; at Red Owl's suggestion Hoffman bought an option to purchase the site of the proposed new store, and sold his existing businesses when Red Owl's agent told him that "everything is ready to go. Get your money together and we are set". However, Red Owl increased the price during the ensuing negotiations, which failed without final agreement on the terms of the franchise contract. Red Owl was held liable to compensate the Hoffmans under the doctrine of promissory estoppel. It was not necessary to show that the promise embraced all the essential details of the proposed transaction so as to be the equivalent of an offer that would result in a binding contract between the parties if the promisee were to accept it[373]; and on the facts the court held, in exercising its discretion, that injustice would result if the Hoffmans were not granted some relief because of the failure of Red Owl to keep their promises which induced the Hoffmans to act to their detriment.[374]

10-48   **Promissory estoppel in Australian law**   In Australia the High Court has also accepted that promissory estoppel may give rise to a cause of action in favour of the party who relies on a promise which is not supported by consideration. The case which took this step, like the *Red Owl Stores* case in Wisconsin,[375] was one in which there was a breakdown of pre-contractual negotiations where one party had led the other to incur expenses in the expectation that the contract would be concluded.[376] However, given that the starting-point in Australian law was the acceptance of the doctrine of promissory estoppel as it had been developed by the English courts,[377]

---

371 G.H. Treitel, "Consideration: A Critical Analysis of Professor Atiyah's Fundamental Restatement" (1976) 50 A.L.J. 439, 440 ("In the United States, the narrow definition of consideration is supplemented by a broad doctrine of promissory estoppel which can, in particular, give rise to new causes of action. In England this possibility is generally denied; but the narrow scope of the doctrine of promissory estoppel is counterbalanced by the adoption of a broad definition of consideration").

372 See para.10-47 fn.363.

373 See para.10-47 fn.363, at [3], [4], [5].

374 See para.10-47 fn.363, at [6]. The jury had awarded damages, the quantum of which were subject to detailed discussion on appeal; but at [13] Currie CJ said "Where damages are awarded in promissory estoppel instead of specifically enforcing the promisor's promise, they should be only such as in the opinion of the court are necessary to prevent injustice. Mechanical or rule of thumb approaches to the damage problem should be avoided".

375 See para.10-47 fn.363.

376 For the restrictive approach in English law to remedies for the breakdown of pre-contractual negotiations, see Ch.2.

377 See para.10-46 fn.360; *Legione v Hateley* (1983) 152 C.L.R. 406, HCA, at 434–435 (Mason J and Dean J: promissory estoppel should be accepted in Australia, but not necessary on the facts to decide

the reasoning in Australia is different from that in the American cases, since it was necessary to justify breaking with the tradition which has imposed on promissory estoppel the limitation that it cannot create a new cause of action—in other words, the departure from the approach taken by the Court of Appeal in *Combe v Combe*.[378] The Australian developments are therefore of particular interest for the English courts.

The most significant decision was *Waltons Stores (Interstate) Ltd v Maher*[379] where the parties were negotiating with a view to Waltons taking a lease of property owned by Maher. Maher proposed to demolish existing buildings on the site and erect a new building which would suit Waltons' purposes. Draft documents were prepared and Waltons' solicitor assured Maher's solicitor that amendments to the lease were agreed; Maher executed the final form of lease and sent it to Waltons' solicitors, and began the building works. Without executing the lease on their part, Waltons later had doubts about the transaction and told their solicitor to "go slow" with it, and even after they later discovered that Maher had begun the demolition Waltons and their solicitors said nothing. Eventually they told Mahers' solicitors that Waltons did not want to complete the transaction: by then the new building was about 40 per cent complete. The trial judge, upheld by the Court of Appeal, held that there was no contract, but that Waltons were estopped from denying that there was a contract on the basis of an estoppel by representation (that is, their silence had led Mahers to believe that there had been a completion of the lease). However, the majority in the High Court held that there was no representation that there had been completion, only that there would be completion—that is, a representation not of present fact but as to the future. But Waltons were still estopped from retreating from their implied promise to complete the contract: the estoppel gave rise to a cause of action to allow Maher to hold Waltons to their promise.

The reasoning of the judges varied. Mason CJ and Wilson J applied promissory estoppel, holding that it does not require a pre-existing relationship, and thus going beyond the restriction of *Combe v Combe*.[380] Brennan J, however, went even further and sought to unite promissory estoppel and proprietary estoppel into a single principle of "equitable estoppel", which is designed to protect a person who relies on an assumption or expectation where it would cause him detriment if the assumption or expectation is not fulfilled and therefore it would be unconscionable for the other party who induced him to adopt the assumption or expectation not to fulfil it.[381] Deane J and Gaudron J followed the trial judge's decision on the

---

whether it extends beyond cases where parties are in a pre-existing contractual relationship).

378 See para.10-39 fn.353.

379 (1988) 164 C.L.R. 387, HCA.

380 (1988) 164 C.L.R. 387, HCA, at 399–401. They noted the development of promissory estoppel in the United States (see para.10-47) but did not follow it directly: "The proposition stated in §90(1) of the Restatement seems on its face to reflect a closer connexion with the general law of contract than our doctrine of promissory estoppel, with its origins in the equitable concept of unconscionable conduct, might be thought to allow. This is because in the United States promissory estoppel has become an equivalent or substitute for consideration in contract formation, detriment being an element common to both doctrines" (at 402).

381 (1988) 164 C.L.R. 387, HCA at 420, 423, 426. See the general summary at 428–429: "to establish an equitable estoppel, it is necessary for a plaintiff to prove that (1) the plaintiff assumed that a particular legal relationship then existed between the plaintiff and the defendant or expected that a particular legal relationship would exist between them and, in the latter case, that the defendant would not be free to withdraw from the expected legal relationship; (2) the defendant has induced the plaintiff to adopt that assumption or expectation; (3) the plaintiff acts or abstains from acting in

basis that there was a representation of fact (and so an estoppel by representation)[382]; but both added comments in relation to the scope of estoppel where the representation is as to the future, Gaudron J taking a similar line to Brennan J in preferring to see a unified "equitable estoppel" rather than a separate doctrine of promissory estoppel[383]; and Deane J taking an even more radical view that the unified doctrine of estoppel was a unification of not merely the equitable estoppels (promissory and proprietary) but also the common law estoppel by representation.[384]

Statements in later decisions in Australia in both the High Court[385] and the Federal Court[386] lend broad support to the new approaches set out in *Waltons Stores*, but the development has not gone unchallenged. There has been a strongly critical response from the Court of Appeal of New South Wales in which Handley JA, in particular, has voiced criticism both extra-judicially[387] and from the bench[388] reasserting the traditional position that promissory estoppel is negative in substance, and (unlike proprietary estoppel) does not create new rights.

(3) The Potential for Development of the Role of Promissory Estoppel in English Law

10-49   **The different forms of estoppel: categorisation or de-categorisation?**   One of the reasons given in the High Court of Australia in *Waltons Stores (Interstate) Ltd v Maher*[389] for developing promissory estoppel to allow the representee to have a

---

reliance on the assumption or expectation; (4) the defendant knew or intended him to do so; (5) the plaintiff's action or inaction will occasion detriment if the assumption or expectation is not fulfilled; and (6) the defendant has failed to act to avoid that detriment whether by fulfilling the assumption or expectation or otherwise".

382   (1988) 164 C.L.R. 387, HCA at 443 (Deane J), 464 (Gaudron J).

383   (1988) 164 C.L.R. 387, HCA at 459–460.

384   (1988) 164 C.L.R. 387, HCA at 447–449, 451–452.

385   *Foran v Wight* (1989) 168 C.L.R. 385, HCA, at 412 (Mason CJ), 435–436 (Deane J), 457 (Gaudron J); cf. at 450 (Dawson J: "Of course, this Court has gone further in *Waltons Stores (Interstate) Ltd v Maher* in discerning a broader foundation for promissory estoppel and in giving it an application beyond the context of pre-existing contractual rights. For present purposes it is unnecessary to rely upon that case"); *Commonwealth of Australia v Verwayen* (1990) 170 C.L.R. 394, HCA, at 407–411 (Mason CJ), 422, 428–429 (Brennan J), 440 (Deane J).

386   *S&E Promotions Pty Ltd v Tobin Brothers Pty Ltd* (1994) 122 A.L.R. 637, FCA, at 652–656; *Mobil Oil Australia Ltd v Lyndel Nominees Pty Ltd* (1998) 81 F.C.R. 475, FCA, at 511–513.

387   Hon. Justice K.R. Handley, "The three High Court decisions on estoppel 1988–1990" (2006) 80 A.L.J. 724 (reviewing *Waltons Stores* (see para.10-48 fn.379), *Foran v Wight* (see para.10-48 fn.385) and *Commonwealth v Verwayen* (see para.10-48 fn.385), and concluding at 737 that "There is no more need for a single overarching doctrine for estoppel than there is for torts"; and "Promissory estoppel is a defensive equity which restrains the enforcement of positive rights by a person whose promise induces a detrimental change of position which makes such enforcement inequitable"); Handley, *Estoppel by Conduct and Election* (see para.10-01 fn.1), paras 13-037 to 13-045. The limitation that promissory estoppel operates only as a defence no longer remains in New Zealand: Burrows, Finn and Todd, para.4.6.3.

388   *Saleh v Romanous* [2010] NSWCA 274; (2010) 79 NSWLR 453 at [74] ("A promissory estoppel is a restraint on the enforcement of rights, and thus, unlike a proprietary estoppel, it must be negative in substance"); repeated in *DHJPM Pty Ltd v Blackthorn Resources Ltd* [2011] NSWCA 348; (2011) 83 NSWLR 728 at [93] (and see also Meagher JA, giving the leading judgment, at [47]; and at [43] distinguishing between common law and equitable estoppel and noting that the different species of equitable estoppel have different characteristics). In the Court of Appeal of Western Australia, see *Westpac Banking Corp v The Bell Group Ltd (No.3)* [2012] WASCA 157; (2012) 270 F.L.R. 1 at [1747]; and in the Victoria Court of Appeal, see *Harrison v Harrison* [2013] VSCA 170 at [138].

389   See para.10-48 fn.379.

positive claim against the representor to make good his representation[390] was that the categorisation of the different forms of estoppel should be broken down. It is well established that under the doctrine of proprietary estoppel the representee who has relied on the representation that he has, or would acquire, an interest in the representor's land may sue the representor to obtain a remedy.[391] And proprietary estoppel is based on protecting the *equity* which arises from the representee's reliance on the representation—which has been said to be based on a broad underlying principle of unconscionability.[392] So why should the same underlying principle not apply equally outside the context of land, or even of property altogether?[393] To the apparently close relationship between proprietary estoppel and promissory estoppel it can be added that other forms of estoppel, which are not designed directly to enforce promises or agreements or to create new legal rights, can have that effect where one or both parties are estopped from denying a representation or assumption of fact or law with the result that the legal relationship between the parties is given effect in law on the basis of that representation or assumption.[394]

In England the support for this argument has been mixed. Even where judges have made statements in support of the de-categorisation of the forms of estoppel those statements have sometimes been rather more nuanced than might at first appear, and the statements have in any event not been necessary for their decisions: the courts have certainly not yet taken the step which was taken by the Australian court in *Waltons Stores* in using the argument to justify an extension of promissory estoppel. One of the strongest judicial statements was made by Lord Denning MR in *Amalgamated Investment & Property Co Ltd v Texas Commerce International Bank Ltd*[395]:

> "The doctrine of estoppel is one of the most flexible and useful in the armoury of the law. But it has become overloaded with cases. That is why I have not gone through them all in this judgment. It has evolved during the last 150 years in a sequence of separate developments: proprietary estoppel, estoppel by representation of fact, estoppel by acquiescence, and promissory estoppel. At the same time it has been sought to be limited by a series of maxims: estoppel is only a rule of evidence, estoppel cannot give rise to a cause of action, estoppel cannot do away with the need for consideration, and so forth. All these can now be seen to merge into one general principle shorn of limitations. When the parties to a transaction proceed on the basis of an underlying assumption—either of

---

[390] See para.10-48.

[391] See para.10-07.

[392] *Taylors Fashions Ltd v Liverpool Victoria Trustees Co Ltd* [1982] Q.B. 133 at 150 (Oliver J, drawing on recent decisions and concluding "So here, once again, is the Court of Appeal asserting the broad test of whether in the circumstances the conduct complained of is unconscionable without the necessity of forcing those incumbrances into a Procrustean bed constructed from some unalterable criteria").

[393] In *Waltons Stores*, see para.10-48, the representation did in fact relate to land, but it was not a typical case which would be argued under the doctrine of proprietary estoppel, since the representation was not to *grant* an interest in the *representor's* land, but to *take* an interest in the *representee's* land.

[394] For this argument in relation to estoppel by deed, estoppel by convention and estoppel by representation, see paras 10-04 to 10-05. In *Waltons Stores*, see para.10-48, the judges took different views about the extent to which the different forms of estoppel should be taken together: some favoured uniting the "equitable estoppels"; Deane J would also include estoppel by representation.

[395] [1982] Q.B. 84, CA, at 122. cf. Lord Denning's rather different picture of estoppel as a "big house with many rooms ... It is a mistake to suppose that what you find in one room, you will also find in the others": *McIlkenny v Chief Constable of the West Midlands* [1980] Q.B. 283, CA, at 317, quoted at para.10-03.

fact or of law—whether due to misrepresentation or mistake makes no difference—on which they have conducted the dealings between them—neither of them will be allowed to go back on that assumption when it would be unfair or unjust to allow him to do so. If one of them does seek to go back on it, the courts will give the other such remedy as the equity of the case demands."

However, this was a case which fell within the established principles of estoppel by convention,[396] and all three members of the Court in fact took that category of estoppel as the basis of their decision. At first instance in the same case, Goff J had engaged in a wide-ranging discussion of different forms of equitable estoppel, which appeared to be drawing them into a single wider doctrine[397]; but he did then draw clear lines around some aspects of the different established categories which meant that he did not use the de-categorisation argument to argue that promissory estoppel should be allowed to create new obligations.[398] There have been other statements, both judicial[399] and in academic or extrajudicial writing,[400] in support of the de-categorisation of estoppels which would appear to propose, or at least have the effect of, allowing a representee to sue to create a new obligation. However, there have been clear and sometimes very strong statements against de-categorisation, principally on the basis that it would create uncertainty since the very point of the existing categorisation is to separate the requirements or effects of the different forms of estoppel where they for good reason differ.[401]

---

[396] See para.10-05 fn.20.

[397] [1982] Q.B. 84 at 103: "It is no doubt helpful to establish, in broad terms, the criteria which, in certain situations, must be fulfilled before an equitable estoppel can be established; but it cannot be right to restrict equitable estoppel to certain defined categories, and indeed some of the categories proposed are not easy to defend".

[398] [1982] Q.B. 84 at 105, 106: "a promissory estoppel derived from *Hughes v Metropolitan Railway Co* is concerned with a representation by a party that he will not enforce his strict legal rights; of its very nature such an estoppel cannot enable a party to enforce a cause of action. But in other cases an estoppel may do so, as, for example, in cases of estoppel by acquiescence. ... In law and in equity, generally speaking a promise is only enforceable as a contractual obligation if it is supported by consideration; and neither law nor equity will perfect an imperfect gift. Furthermore, even if a purely gratuitous promise is acted upon by the promisee, generally speaking such conduct will not of itself give rise to an estoppel against the promissor; such an estoppel would be inconsistent with the general principle that purely gratuitous promises will not be enforced: see *Combe v Combe*".

[399] e.g. *Crabb v Arun DC* [1976] Ch. 179, CA, at 193 (Scarman LJ: "I do not find helpful the distinction between promissory and proprietary estoppel. This distinction may indeed be valuable to those who have to teach or expound the law; but I do not think that, in solving the particular problem raised by a particular case, putting the law into categories is of the slightest assistance").

[400] M.P. Thompson, "From Representation to Expectation: Estoppel as a Cause of Action" [1983] C.L.J. 257, 274; M. Lunney, "Towards a Unified Estoppel—the Long and Winding Road" [1992] Conv. 239; Lord Neuberger of Abbotsbury, "The Stuffing of Minerva's Owl? Taxonomy and Taxidermy in Equity" [2009] C.L.J. 537, 547–548 ("At least in broad terms, may not estoppel now be seen to be a generic term for a claim by a claimant who has changed his position in the reasonable and foreseeable belief that a defendant's act, statement, silence or inaction has a particular consequence, so that it would now be unconscionable for the defendant to repudiate that consequence (wholly or to an extent) at least without giving the claimant some compensation?").

[401] e.g. Sir G Treitel, *Some Landmarks of Twentieth Century Contract Law* (Clarendon Press, 2002), p.40: "No doubt the view that [the various kinds of estoppel] 'merge into one general principle' may encourage cross-fertilization between them, but it can equally encourage cross-infection and even cross-sterilization", expressing concern about the certainty of a general principle of estoppel "shorn of limitations" [Lord Denning MR in *Amalgamated Investment & Property Co Ltd v Texas Commerce International Bank Ltd*, see para.10-49 fn.395] which "make[s] it impossible to tell, even *after* all the relevant events, what the legal consequences of action on reliance on the promise will be. You have to go to court to find out"); R. Halson, "The offensive limits of promissory estoppel" [1999]

The role of promissory estoppel in pre-contractual negotiations One **10-50** potentially significant impact of allowing promissory estoppel to create obligations would be to provide a new remedy where pre-contractual negotiations break down. Indeed, we have seen that it was in cases of failed negotiations that courts in the United States[402] and Australia[403] developed the doctrine of promissory estoppel in order to compensate the party who had incurred losses in reliance on the anticipated contract. There are advantages in such a development, but there must also be concerns that introducing a new remedy could change the balance of risk between parties negotiating a contract. We have seen in Chapter 2 that English law takes a very restrictive approach to liabilities in the pre-contractual phase and the starting-point is that each party bears his own risk of failure of the negotiations, and so any expenditure incurred in the hope or belief that the contract will eventually be concluded is normally at his own risk.[404] The development of promissory estoppel to create obligations would not necessarily change this, but the newly-expanded doctrine would have to be applied carefully if the existing risk allocation is not to be undermined. There are already situations where the courts can use the law of unjust enrichment to protect a party to failed negotiations who has acted in anticipation of the completed contract,[405] but the courts will not do so where it would undermine the parties' understanding that each is still free not to conclude the contract.[406] Similarly, it should be clear that a party could not appeal to the doctrine of promissory estoppel to obtain a remedy for his reliance on an anticipated contract where his action in reliance was still within his own sphere of risk.[407] An advantage, however, in allowing a claim based on promissory estoppel would be to provide a remedy for the party who reasonably acts in anticipation of the contract,

---

L.M.C.L.Q. 256; B. McFarlane, "Understanding Equitable Estoppel: From Metaphors to Better Laws" (2013) 66 C.L.P. 267; *Republic of India v India Steamship Co Ltd (The Indian Grace) (No.2)* [1998] A.C. 878, HL, at 914 (Lord Steyn: "The question was debated whether estoppel by convention and estoppel by acquiescence are but aspects of one overarching principle. I do not underestimate the importance in the continuing development of the law of the search for simplicity. I, also, accept that at a high level of abstraction such an overarching principle could be formulated. But Mr. Rokison, for the defendants, persuaded me that to restate the law in terms of an overarching principle might tend to blur the necessarily separate requirements, and distinct terrain of application, of the two kinds of estoppel"); *Baird Textiles Holdings Ltd v Marks & Spencer Plc* [2001] EWCA Civ 274; [2002] 1 All E.R. (Comm) 737 at [84] (Mance LJ: the doctrine of estoppel "may take different shapes to fit the context of different fields"). cf. in the context of proprietary estoppel, *Taylor v Dickens* [1998] 3 F.C.R. 455 at 471 (H.H. Judge Weeks: "In my judgment there is no equitable jurisdiction to hold a person to a promise simply because the court thinks it unfair, unconscionable or morally objectionable for him to go back on it. If there were such a jurisdiction, one might as well forget the law of contract and issue every civil judge with a portable palm tree. The days of justice varying with the size of the Lord Chancellor's foot would have returned").

402   *Hoffman v Red Owl Stores* (1965) 133 N.W.2d 267, Sup. Ct. Wisconsin, see para.10-47.

403   *Waltons Stores*, see para.10-48.

404   See para.2-07.

405   See paras 2-26, 2-27.

406   *Regalian Properties Plc v London Docklands Development Corp* [1995] 1 W.L.R. 212 at 231; see para.2-08; see also *Attorney General of Hong Kong v Humphreys Estate (Queen's Garden) Ltd* [1987] 1 A.C. 114, PC, at 124 (no estoppel preventing party from proceeding with transaction where negotiations were subject to contract: "at no time did HKL indicate expressly or by implication that they had surrendered their right to change their mind and to withdraw").

407   cf. the reluctance to allow commercial parties who know that transaction is not binding to reverse the risk allocation in negotiating a contract by using a claim based on proprietary estoppel: *Cobbe v Yeoman's Row Management Ltd* [2008] UKHL 55; [2009] 1 W.L.R. 1752 at [18], [91]; see para.5-28, esp. fn.196.

outside his sphere of negotiating risk, but in circumstances where he does not provide the other party with a benefit of any kind that could give rise to a claim based on unjust enrichment.[408]

10-51 **Combe v Combe remains the binding authority until change is made by the Supreme Court or by legislation** If the step were taken to allow promissory estoppel to create new obligations, it would be very significant in providing an alternative basis of promissory obligation, and a competing policy based on the principle of reliance[409]; and further questions would have to be answered—such as what remedy could be awarded to protect the representee,[410] and whether opening up promissory estoppel in the creation of obligations might have an impact on the existing doctrine of consideration by reducing the need to find consideration in cases that can be covered by estoppel.[411] At present, however, it is clear that promissory estoppel remains a separate category of estoppel with its own rules as set out earlier in this chapter; and that one of those rules—on the authority of *Combe v Combe*[412] —is that it cannot be used as a substitute for consideration in the formation of a new binding promissory obligation.

Combe v Combe was a decision of the Court of Appeal, and any change must be made either by the Supreme Court[413] or by legislation. Neither is in prospect.[414]

---

[408] cf. *Countrywide Communications Ltd v ICL Pathway Ltd* [2000] C.L.C. 324 at 350, quoted at para.2-28.

[409] See para. 10-45; esp. *Azov Shipping Co Ltd v Baltic Shipping Co* [1999] 2 Lloyd's Rep. 159 at 175, see para.10-45 fn.354. See *Baird Textiles Holdings Ltd v Marks & Spencer Plc*, para.10-51 fn.413, at [54] (Judge LJ: "In reality, BTH's possible success in this litigation would depend on establishing liability against M&S in equity when it would not otherwise be liable in contract, and would represent a dramatic, if not indeed a revolutionary, development of the legal principles governing the enforcement of private obligations").

[410] cf. the remedy in proprietary estoppel, which may enforce the representation directly, but may also sometimes compensate either the expectation or the reliance: see para.10-07 fn.41. For the remedy for promissory estoppel in US law, see para.10-47, fnn.365 to 370.

[411] This could avoid the need for the courts to imply a request by the representor that the representee act in reliance on his representation: the representee's (intended, reasonable) reliance would itself be sufficient: see para.8-17. See also Treitel, "Consideration: A Critical Analysis of Professor Atiyah's Fundamental Restatement", see para.10-47 fn.371.

[412] [1951] 2 K.B. 215, CA; see para.10-39.

[413] *Baird Textiles Holdings Ltd v Marks & Spencer Plc* [2001] EWCA Civ 274; [2002] 1 All E.R. (Comm) 737 at [38]–[39], [55], [91].

[414] Law Revision Committee, Sixth Interim Report, *Statute of Frauds and the Doctrine of Consideration*, Cmd.5449 (1937), para.40, recommended that a promise which the promisor knows, or reasonably should know, will be relied on by the promisee should be enforceable if the promisee has altered his position to his detriment in reliance on the promise; but this was not taken further (see para.9-23 fn.190). Review by the Supreme Court depends on a case which raises the issue by way of ratio being taken to that court by the parties. In *Baird Textiles Holdings Ltd v Marks & Spencer Plc*, see para.10-51 fn.413, CA did not allow a claim to proceed to trial where it would be contrary to the decision in *Combe v Combe*; Sir Andrew Morritt VC said at [39]: "Counsel for M&S was, at one stage, inclined to concede that if we considered that the House of Lords, after the facts had been found at a trial, might adopt the propositions formulated by Mason CJ, Wilson and Brennan JJ in the *Waltons Stores* case, then it might be said that there was a real prospect of succeeding on the estoppel issue so that judgment under CPR 24.2 should not be given at this stage. In reply he submitted that the possibility that the House of Lords might adopt those propositions was an inadequate reason for allowing a trial. I agree. If I am right in believing that English law, as it now stands, does not permit the enforcement of an estoppel in the form alleged in this case then it is the duty of this court to apply it, notwithstanding that it may be developed by the House of Lords, who are not bound by any of the cases relied on, in the future"; see also Judge LJ at [55].

INDEX